# BERTOLT BRECHT:
# CRITICAL AND PRIMARY SOURCES

## VOLUME II

# BERTOLT BRECHT:
## CRITICAL AND PRIMARY SOURCES

# THEORY

## VOLUME II

*Edited by David Barnett*

BLOOMSBURY ACADEMIC
LONDON · NEW YORK · OXFORD · NEW DELHI · SYDNEY

BLOOMSBURY ACADEMIC
Bloomsbury Publishing Plc
50 Bedford Square, London, WC1B 3DP, UK
1385 Broadway, New York, NY 10018, USA

BLOOMSBURY, BLOOMSBURY ACADEMIC and the Diana logo
are trademarks of Bloomsbury Publishing Plc

First published in Great Britain 2020

Introductions and editorial content copyright © David Barnett, 2020
English language translations copyright © Romy Fursland, 2020 (unless otherwise indicated)

David Barnett has asserted his right under the Copyright, Designs and
Patents Act, 1988, to be identified as the Editor of this work.

For legal purposes the Permissions Acknowledgements on pp. 361–2 constitute
an extension of this copyright page.

All rights reserved. No part of this publication may be reproduced or transmitted
in any form or by any means, electronic or mechanical, including photocopying,
recording, or any information storage or retrieval system, without prior permission
in writing from the publishers.

Bloomsbury Publishing Plc does not have any control over, or responsibility for,
any third-party websites referred to or in this book. All internet addresses given
in this book were correct at the time of going to press. The author and publisher
regret any inconvenience caused if addresses have changed or sites have ceased
to exist, but can accept no responsibility for any such changes.

A catalogue record for this book is available from the British Library.

A catalog record for this book is available from the Library of Congress.

ISBN: HB: 978-1-4742-9945-9
HB set: 978-1-4742-9949-7

Series: Critical and Primary Sources

Typeset by Deanta Global Publishing Services, Chennai, India
Printed and bound in Great Britain

To find out more about our authors and books visit www.bloomsbury.com and
sign up for our newsletters.

# CONTENTS

## VOLUME II
## THEORY

Note on the Text and Common Abbreviations     ix

Introduction     1

### Part One   Negotiating Terminology

**Epic**

1   *Episch*, or, the Third Person     9
      *Fredric Jameson*

**Dialectics**

2   Dialectics and the Brechtian Tradition: Some Thoughts on Politicized Performance     17
      *David Barnett*

***Verfremdung***

3   The *Verfremdung* of Certain Processes through a Mode of Representation Usually Reserved for Customs and Traditions     31
      *Bertolt Brecht*

4   A Critical Response to Heidi M. Silcox's 'What's Wrong with Alienation?'     32
      *Anthony Squiers*

***Gestus***

5   Getting to the Gist of Gestus     39
      *Meg Mumford*

***Fabel***

6   The *Fabel*     57
      *Bertolt Brecht*

7   Brecht, the '*Fable*', and the Teaching of Directing     58
      *Craig Kinzer*

### Historicization

8  Art as the Speaker of History 69
   Astrid Oesmann

9  How Do I Learn to Learn? 78
   Bertolt Brecht

### Naivety

10 From Distancing Alienation to Intuitive Naiveté: Bertolt Brecht's
   Establishment of a New Aesthetic Category 81
   Karl-Heinz Schoeps

## PART TWO  MAJOR THEORETICAL WRITINGS

### Notes on *The Threepenny Opera* and *Rise and Fall of the City of Mahagonny*

11 Epic Opera and Epic Theater 97
   John J. White

### The Messingkauf/Buying Brass

12 The Drama of Ideas 127
   Martin Puchner

### Me-ti

13 Introduction to *Me-ti: Book of Interventions
   in the Flow of Things* 137
   Antony Tatlow

### Theatre Work

14 Brecht's *Theatre Work*: A Foundational Work and its Marginalisation 149
   Detlev Schöttker

## PART THREE  BRECHT AND OTHER MEDIA

### Radio

15 Apparatus without Spectators?: On the Deconstruction of the Medium in
   Brecht's *Ocean Flight* 165
   Patrick Primavesi

### Film

16 Utilizing the 'Ideological Antiquity': Rethinking Brecht and Film Theory 179
   Angelos Koutsourakis

## Music

17  Brecht and Music: Theory and Practice  205
    Kim H. Kowalke

## Brecht in the Information Age

18  Bertolt Brecht and the Internet  221
    Dorothee Ostmeier

### PART FOUR  THE PLAY OF IDEAS

## The Bible

19  Brecht and the Bible: A Study of Religious Nihilism and Human Weakness in Brecht's Drama of Mortality and the City  243
    G. Ronald Murphy

## Shakespeare

20  Brecht as Great Shakespearean: A Lifelong Connection  255
    David Barnett

## Capitalism

21  Tracing the Crimes of Capitalism: From Mahagonny to Nazi Germany  269
    Astrid Oesmann

## The Natural Sciences

22  Brecht and Science – Science and Brecht?: A Dialectical View  281
    Katharina Brinkert

## Thought from the Far East

23  Brecht's Materialist Ethics between Confucianism and Mohism  291
    Markus Wessendorf

## Comedy/Humour

24  The Poetic Anthropology of Comedy in Brecht's *Buying Brass*  313
    Ralf Simon

25  On Humour  323
    Bertolt Brecht

## Tragedy

26  Brecht and Tragedy  327
    Sean Carney

**Gendered Performance/Feminism**

27  Brechtian Theory/Feminist Theory: Toward a Gestic Feminist Criticism    339
    *Elin Diamond*

**Postcolonial Brecht**

28  A Postcolonial Brecht?    355
    *Marc Silberman*

PERMISSIONS ACKNOWLEDGEMENTS    361
INDEX    363

# NOTE ON THE TEXT AND COMMON ABBREVIATIONS

Texts first published in English have been reproduced as they were first printed, with any extracts in German, or other languages, retained as per the originals.

| | |
|---|---|
| **BBA** | Bertolt-Brecht-Archive |
| **BE** | Berliner Ensemble |
| **BFA** | See GBA |
| **BH** | *Brecht Handbook*, 5 volumes |
| **BS** | Brecht Sourcebook |
| **BT** | Brecht on Theatre: The Development of an Aesthetic |
| **DDR** | See GDR |
| **GBA** | Brecht, *Grosse Berliner und Frankfurter Ausgabe*, 30 volumes and an index volume |
| **GDR** | German Democratic Republic |
| **GW** | Brecht, *Gesammelte Werke*, 20 volumes |
| **JOURNALS** | Bertolt Brecht Journals |
| **LETTERS** | Brecht, Letters |
| **SLK** | Brecht, Schriften zur Literatur und Kunst |
| **SZT** | Brecht, Schriften zum Theater |
| **TFF** | Brecht, Texte Für Filme |

# Introduction

The importance of the publication of *Brecht on Theatre*, edited and translated by John Willett in 1964, cannot be understated. Willett selected what he considered to be Bertolt Brecht's most significant writings on theatre, some of which had not even appeared in German at that time. He offered an Anglophone readership a range of insights into a very different approach to conceiving of and approaching a theatre that was not concerned with reproducing the surface of reality, the main concern of the naturalists spearheaded by Stanislavsky and developed by his many disciples. Willett's collection has been read by theatre students and theatre-makers the world over and continues to represent a standard work for those with no access to the German originals. The new edition of the book, originally published in 2014, which adds a great deal of material that emerged in the years following Willett's pioneering work and updates existing translations, is certain to maintain interest in Brecht's theoretical positions for years to come.

Brecht's writings, however, have not proven to be easy reading. He introduced a wide range of ideas and terms about representation and performance that challenged received wisdoms concerning the role of the actor and the director, modes of performance and the very function of the theatrical event itself. At the heart of Brecht's interest is how theatre can represent the world with a view to changing it. In order to answer such a question, Brecht believed that it was not enough simply to consider the one term, 'represent', while taking the other, 'the world', as some kind of given. I shall discuss these two terms separately, beginning with the last one first.

To approach an understanding of 'the world', one requires a notion of what 'reality' might imply and how it might function. There are, of course, many theories regarding these complex concepts. Brecht encountered Marxism in the mid-1920s and found its ideas regarding the nature of the world illuminating and dynamic. What inspired him perhaps the most was the dialectic, the mechanism that speculated on how change takes place over time. To put this in a nutshell, the dialectical world view proposes that all change is brought about by contradictions, and that when contradictions become too great, human beings address them, either consciously or unconsciously, and bring about a new situation. A central idea is that human beings themselves are subject to the dialectic of individual and society. This accounts for the great differences between the ideas and behaviours of, say, women in Canada and women in China today, or of women in Britain today and those a hundred years ago. That is, the dialectic undermines any sense that thought or action is fundamentally innate but introduces contexts into the argument, and those contexts are historical (where one is in time), geographical (where one is in space) and social (how one's society is organized and where one finds oneself in that organization). Reality, then, is a continual and dynamic process of change. There is little that is stable because reality is riven by contradiction, and so change is the only constant.

Such an insight is radical and potentially revolutionary. Other understandings of reality may assume that there *is* a norm, something found, for example, in the medieval period as the 'divine right of kings'. This doctrine stated that because one was born into a particular family, one had the innate right and abilities to rule over a whole kingdom, nation or empire by the simple virtue of one's birth. Later on, in the class-based societies of the industrialized world, membership of a particular social and/or racial group came with qualities that appear immutable. The working class was there to toil and did not deserve the leisure or the decision-making privileges the bourgeoisie enjoyed; white people, by dint of their enterprise and 'superiority', had the right to form colonies in Africa and Asia and subjugate the indigenous peoples to their forms of governance, behaviour and managing an economy.

The Marxist dialectic, on the other hand, sees the world as constructed, built by values and events that are not inevitable, even less so natural, but that rest on the specific interests of specific social groups. What is more, power, that appears to be the sole domain of the dominant groups, is, in fact, negotiated, however tacitly, between the rulers and the ruled. The philosopher Hegel argued, in a discussion of the master/slave relationship, that the master only attains such a status because the slave recognizes him or her as such. While this agreement largely remains 'understood' and unquestioned, history shows how sustained and/or often violent dissatisfaction with such arrangements has led to both fundamental and more reformist social change. Abolitions of slavery, monarchies and other forms of oppression reflect the often unspoken power of the underdog as much as equality legislation or action on gender pay gaps.

The dialectic is thus a political approach to reality because it understands power, that central quality of a political relationship, as malleable and subject to the pressures of both those who wield it and those who suffer from it. Brecht latched onto this radical understanding of reality and asked how the theatre could represent it.

This volume, which collects essays from eminent scholars and primary material from Brecht himself, approaches Brecht's thoughts on representing reality in a number of ways. The first section, 'Negotiating Terminology', takes on some of Brecht's central ideas concerning theatre in a bid to open them up to further scrutiny. Terms that sometimes remain enigmatic or slippery in Brecht's own writings are addressed clearly in the scholarly essays. For example, 'Epic theatre' is an accurate translation from the German, yet the adjective 'epic' has been misunderstood in English due to its associations with 'epic' films, suggesting a grand panorama. Brecht, however, was going back to Aristotle's *Poetics* in which the ancient philosopher divided literary genres into three: the dramatic (plays), the lyric (poems) and the epic (narrated fiction). Brecht was trying to combine the dramatic and the epic genres in a bid to oscillate between the two, offering the spectator the immediacy of live performance and the distance of narrative framing.

Elsewhere, '*Verfremdung*' has proved to be a difficult term to apprehend, not least because Willett translated it as 'alienation'. Such a negative term in English does little to serve Brecht's purposes for a noun that represents a process of its own in German: making the familiar strange. In the current edition of *Brecht on Theatre*, the German is, quite rightly, retained because there is no easy, one-to-one translation available in English. Elsewhere, *Gestus*, a word of Brecht's own invention in the theatre, is both a central feature of Brecht's theatre *and* a term that Brecht employs so inconsistently that readers have to be remarkably sensitive to Brecht's context if they are to understand its meaning. Other terms, such as the *Fabel*, historicization and naivety, all receive scholarly comment in this volume in a bid both to explain them in context and to elucidate their implications for the theatre. The short contributions from Brecht offer new perspectives on the terms in question.

The volume then proceeds with essays that address a selection of Brecht's major theoretical writings. Each essay aims to comment on these writings and tease out the specific contributions they make to Brecht's ever-evolving thoughts on reality and its representation in the theatre. It is also worth noting that the selection includes an edited introduction to the *Me-ti* and an essay on *Theatre Work*. The *Me-ti* is an unfinished collection of short musings on politics, power, ways of behaving, dialectics and Brecht's contemporary historical landscape, and this remarkable work was only translated into English in 2016. The extract on humour, that appears later in this volume, is a characteristic example of how Brecht takes a common idea, applies a dialectical analysis to it, and reaches a playful and surprising conclusion. *Theatre Work*, on the other hand, is largely unknown to an Anglophone readership, and is unlikely to be translated any time soon. It documents the first six productions of Brecht's theatre company, the Berliner Ensemble, is richly illustrated (a minefield for a publisher seeking permissions for photographic reproduction) and anchored in practical work undertaken in the years 1949–51. Its value, however, is the time that Brecht and his colleagues take to reflect on the work done. The table of contents, for example, groups the many short articles not as they appear in the text, but thematically. Headings, such as 'direction', 'on acting', 'music' or '[particular] scenes', take material from all over the book and invite readers to compare reflections on several different productions together. So, while *Theatre Work* itself may not be familiar to the reader with no knowledge of German, Detlev Schöttker's essay in this volume will at least present cogent reasons for appreciating its importance.

Brecht did not only think about the theatre but mused on representation in other media. The volume *Brecht on Film and Radio*, published in 2000, already provided many of Brecht's thoughts on the two major forms of media that emerged during his lifetime. The essays included in the section on 'Brecht and other Media' elucidate his ideas not only on film and radio but on the use of music, and on how his reflections on media institutions and artistic ownership might affect our approach to electronic communication today.

The volume continues with a survey of Brecht's interactions with ideas, both cultural and political. Brecht was a voracious reader: the Brecht Archive in Berlin compiled and published a full inventory of his library that contains over 4,200 entries.[1] He 'collaborated' with ideas in much the same way as he collaborated with human beings. His mind was open to multifarious impulses, and he was always keen to see how they could challenge, enrich or indeed confirm his own ways of thinking on a wide range of topics. Brecht was attracted to ideas like a magpie and was happy to appropriate anything he considered useful for his own ends. It is thus a little unfair when critics characterize his theatrical innovations, for example, as a mere reassembly of material culled from medieval morality plays, Shakespeare and English Restoration theatre. Brecht may well have taken features found elsewhere, but their repositioning in his own intellectual landscape changed their purpose and meaning. Indeed, to perceive Brecht's theatre as one that is solely constructed of devices ignores the dialectical basis from which all the devices were to be re-functioned.

The essays included in this section address a broad sweep of influences: from the source that keeps recurring in his work, the Bible, to the stage plays of Shakespeare and his responses to capitalism. Brecht was also fascinated by the Eastern tradition of thinking, something not only to be found in the locations of some of his plays or the themes of his poems but more significantly in the design and execution of the *Me-ti*.

---

[1] See Bertolt-Brecht-Archiv (ed.), *Die Bibliothek Bertolt Brechts. Ein kommentiertes Verzeichnis* (Frankfurt/Main: Suhrkamp, 2007).

The final sections of this volume consider Brecht on comedy and tragedy before concluding with two essays that consider how more contemporary ideas of feminism and post-colonialism can be applied to Brecht's prodigious output.

This volume moves from Brecht's ideas to their influence and legacy in the present day. As such, Brecht the thinker is revealed as a lively and enduring one. This may appear to be a somewhat anachronistic position, however: after all, Brecht was a theorist who based his ideas on Marxism and its reception of the dialectic. In the light of historical events, most notably the fall of the Berlin Wall, the collapse of communism, and the vice-like grip capitalism holds over the economies of the world, Brecht may appear thoroughly outdated and only worthy of *historical* study. This volume begs to differ.

Brecht the theoretician of dialectics in the theatre has much to offer the present. He invites theatre-makers and audiences alike *not* to accept reality as natural or inevitable but to understand the processes that brought it about. If reality is always being built and rebuilt, the theatre can offer counter-narratives to dominant ideologies purporting that 'there is no alternative' to the systems and structures that benefit the few at the expense of the many. The goal, as ever, is to change that which causes pain or suffering. And this is a realistic goal given the dialectic's insistence that any situation is the consequence of both sides' agreement, as set out in the discussion of the master/slave relationship. Brecht actively encourages the theatre to look behind the surface of reality in order to show the different configurations of power and the ways they affect and inform opinions, behaviours and actions. As such, he embodies an activist impulse that is alive with optimism, as he stated in the motto to his *The Threepenny Lawsuit*: 'Contradictions are our hope!'[2]

---

[2]Bertolt Brecht, *The Threepenny Lawsuit*, in Brecht, *Brecht on Film and Radio*, ed. Marc Silberman (London: Methuen, 2001), pp. 147–99, here p. 148.

# PART ONE
# NEGOTIATING TERMINOLOGY

# Epic

CHAPTER ONE

# *Episch*, or, the Third Person

FREDRIC JAMESON

But the insistence on the primacy of the 'narrative' over the 'dramatic' can take other forms as well, and have other consequences – can 'estrange' in different ways. We have observed the way in which, following Döblin, a narrative can be stretched out and sliced up like a sausage, its parts and incidents slowly becoming fully fledged scenes and episodes in their own right. The overlap of the words 'epic' and 'narrative' in German, in fact, also reminds us that something like this theory was already developed by Goethe and Schiller in their April 1797 correspondence about Greek epic, and later elaborated by Auerbach in *Mimesis*: namely, what the latter calls the 'hypotactic',[1] the tendency of the various scenes to be not only additive and segmentary, but also 'immediate to God', to use Ranke's expression – each one bathed in a full light which excludes perspectivism and displays what should be only a secondary or subsidiary episode in the unfolding of a larger plot or intrigue, as though it were interesting in itself and a complete object of contemplation and delectation in its own right, like a series of independent tableaux side by side. The replacement of Brechtian theatre in such a classical tradition also offers a useful estrangement, and lends an interesting ambiguity to his own modernities.

But the effect of narrative is rather different when it is the subject or the character, the protagonist, who is its object. Now the result is not so much to make the objective action, with all its episodes and incidents, susceptible of a divisibility and an analysis that casts a different light on them, so much as to bring an uncanny strangeness to the subjective moment of decision and action itself, the 'proairesis' of the protagonist, with its wavering motives and intentions, its psychological impulses as well, and even its unconscious drives. After all, Freud's 'talking cure' was itself just such a narrative, in which the patient's story gradually returned upon its protagonist to throw all the latter's notions of self into a new light: can I really have been the one who ... it certainly begins to sound as though I really wanted . ... The analyst himself then does the prompting and provides the hints; your feelings for Herr K. ... for Frau K. ... Habermas has argued that Freudian psychoanalysis fundamentally proposes a rewriting, a retelling, in a new way, of the subject's implicit life narrative:[2] so that finally what emerges is less some new conception of the Unconscious as such than, rather, the capacity of narrative to restructure our 'imaginary' representation

---

Fredric Jameson, '*Episch*, or, the Third Person', in Jameson, *Brecht and Method* (London: Verso, 1998), pp. 51–8 and notes pp. 85–8.

[1] Erich Auerbach, *Mimesis* (Princeton, NJ: Princeton University Press, 1953), pp. 11 ff.
[2] Jürgen Habermas, 'Self-Reflection as Science: Freud's Psychoanalytic Critique of Meaning', in *Knowledge of Human Interests* (Boston, MA: Beacon, 1971), pp. 214–45.

of that *actant* which is self, ego, first person, or whatever; to modify our inner distance from this 'identity'; to reshape and construct in new ways that 'I think which must accompany all my representations'.

But it is important to think of what is thereby modified in a relational rather than a substantive way: not a self-entity so much as very precisely the 'function' designated by narrative semiotics or narratology. Remembering that for Kant the 'self' was also a noumenon, a thing-in-itself inaccessible to conscious thought and its categories, one can no doubt here also imagine the metaphysical flights we discovered when the names were stripped from things and events, allowing some primal nameless flux to be glimpsed underneath. But perhaps the play of social masks in Brecht is no less fascinating and mysterious, particularly when it is registered in the narrative prose of, say, the *Three-Penny Novel*, in which a multiplicity of Macheath-protagonists passes bewilderingly across the stage.

These narrative conversions or displacements are closely related to another familiar Brechtian technique, that of quotation: thus it is recommended that the actor quote his speeches and transmit his lines and his character's utterances to us as though in italics or between quotation marks – a rather peculiar recommendation which is generally understood as part of Brecht's onslaught on 'empathy' and Stanislavskian emotion. So presumably there is a first-person and also a third-person emotion which can be represented on stage: in the first, the actor 'would drown the stage with tears/and cleave the general ear with horrid speech ...' thereby eliciting a sympathetic fellow-feeling in the public thus called upon to 'identify' with him and with his 'dream of passion' and finally, in the last instance, to feel 'pity and fear' at the prospect of a fate the spectator might also have confronted.

Yet this notion of 'identification' is one of the most problematic and unexamined concepts in the arsenal of sociological cliché; nor are the sociologists the only ones to construct elaborate theoretical models of 'sociability' and 'society', of 'intersubjectivity' and 'interpersonal relations'. There exists, no doubt, some impersonal instinct, a life-anxiety or what is improperly personalized and anthropomorphized by the term 'self' in the expression self-preservation, which is manifested in the mute terror of birds, for example, in the face of the spread-eagled remains of one of their species nailed upon a barn door; and embodied even more ambiguously by the crowding of humans, full of visceral fascination and pleasurable horror, in front of a human corpse. But this has little enough to do with the pseudo-psychological concept of 'identification', which can at best be imagined in the form of some Lacanian mirror-stage. And in that case, would the 'lack of identification' between such selves mean that the 'other' was somehow excluded from the category of the human altogether?

In fact, I think that Brecht's positions are better read not as a refusal of identification but, rather, as the consequences to be drawn from the fact that such a thing never existed in the first place. In that case, 'third-person acting', the quoting of a character's expressions of feeling and emotion, is the result of a radical absence of the self, or at least the coming to terms with a realization that what we call our 'self' is itself an object for consciousness, not our consciousness itself: it is a foreign body within an impersonal consciousness, which we try to manipulate in such a way as to lend some warmth and personalization to the matter. The simplest models of identification are therefore rendered meaningless by this situation, in which at best, in a Lacanian complexity, two self-objects would entertain a complex and mediated relationship with each other across the gaps of isolated consciousness as such.

Quotation, then, or third-person acting, is a way of outflanking this situation, with its evident impossibilities, and ratifying the 'imaginary' nature of the self by holding it at a distance on stage and allowing its ventriloquism to designate itself. Yet something must be quoted, some 'already existing' and recognizable (or at least nameable) gesture must make up the substance of the quote, just as the gesture of the actor quoting his lines should also be identifiable as a type of conduct (if only the historically recognizable and legitimated conduct of acting itself). Thus, I must feel that the now classic Straub/Huillet film *Nicht Versöhnt* (1965), which has long been admired as some first Brechtian form of cinema, is not always consonant with the spirit of Brechtian narrative. This shorthand or Xeroxed film version of Heinrich Böll's complex novel *Billiard um halb-zehn* (1958), in which, either as a voice-over or in long deadpan monologues, the original text is somehow attached to a series of filmic images, can certainly offer any number of examples of 'quotation'; yet our temptation is always to remotivate what is given to us as utterly toneless and unmotivated in the first place. Thus the mother's hallucinatory stream-of-consciousness about the inhumanity of the Nazi period is cleverly transferred on to a long rambling speech to her son during his weekly visit to her in the asylum; but the non-professional to whom the role (or, better still, only the speech itself, the words of the monologue) have been confided only too successfully fulfils what must have been the Straubs' direction of her – namely, simply to read through the sentences as fast as possible without any expression whatsoever: at best, then, the spectator is tempted to reinterpret this very tonelessness as a symptom of that mental disorder the novel wishes emphatically to deny she has.

On the other hand, it seems possible that the medium is itself at fault and at stake: the 'acting' has already been done and is now irremediable, forever registered on a film that can be played again and again without the slightest changes or modifications being possible. On stage, however, we are at the very present of time of the performance: it is no longer available when it goes into the past (however irremediable its already acted gestures, they can never be witnessed again, only remembered) – but for this one long moment of its present the actor's gesture can still be modified; any number of possibilities throng the present of the stage, which is surely invested by what Deleuze called 'virtuality' – something far richer than mere possibility, and a kind of thronging within a present in much the same spirit in which Heidegger reinterpreted Nietzsche's will to power as an Aristotelian *energeia*. Whatever film can do, it cannot give that sense of emergence and *praxis*.

Yet all these arguments no doubt also give aid and comfort to Brecht's critics, who always maintained that Brechtian distanciation was impossible in the first place, and that we inevitably identify with Mother Courage and her 'tragedy' in spite of ourselves. Yet this is perhaps still to reify the self and 'personality' of the spectator rather than to grasp the nature of the 'third-person' narrative distanciation proposed by sentences like:

> 'der Marketenderin Anna Fierling ... kommt ein Sohn abhanden ...' 'the travelling camp merchant Anna Fierling ... loses a son ...'.

Brecht's own technical recommendations are perhaps initially more useful than any merely interpretive analysis. So it is that he proposes three 'techniques' for his actors:

> drei Hilfsmittel, [die] bei einer Spielweise mit nicht restloser Verwandlung zu einer Verfremdung der Äusserungen und Handlungen der darzustellenden Person dienen:
>
> 1. Die Überführung in die dritte Person.
> 2. Die Überführung in die Vergangenheit.
> 3. Das Mitsprechen von Spielanweisungen und Kommentaren,
>
> (XXII, 644)

three aids which may help estrange the actions and remarks of the characters being portrayed:

1. Transposition into the third person.
2. Transposition into the past.
3. Speaking the stage directions out loud.

(Willett, 138)

But I imagine that the critics' objections would then bear on the difficulty of identifying these techniques during an actual performance. During rehearsals we can always stop to compare the alternatives, but how can we tell during the play itself whether Olivier is quoting Shylock, acting the role out with genuine feeling, or simply hamming it up?

Perhaps in this instance, however, the actor is more important than the spectator, and we ought to begin by thinking of this Brechtian 'method' as a kind of ethos; or at least a moral training of a specific type. Loyola's use of narratives is well known, and has been the object of renewed attention precisely at the moment in which the whole question of performance is itself under renewed scrutiny.[3] Meanwhile, I have already mentioned some of the other charismatic or cult-founding directors for whom acting itself becomes a symbolic ethical practice – of impoverishment, for example, as in Grotowski.

Brechtian quotation is, I believe, that as well, although it is an ethic directed towards very different flaws and weaknesses in the human constitution. But how this is meant to work can better be observed in another place: thus, in a famous essay, Sartre conveys the effect of John Dos Passos's style in a way that is remarkably consistent with these Brechtian hints and recommendations. It is a style as simple and neutral as Camus's in *L'Étranger*, but as peculiar at the same time: betraying the internal operation of a strange kind of mechanism which shuts off the empathy (or 'identification') that might otherwise be expected, and thereby manages to seem mannered and artificial through the very transparency of its plainness and its everyday colloquial ordinariness. In Camus's French, the operation of a tense we do not use in the same way (and which the French do not use in written narration) – the *passé composé* – allows the trick to be identified. This is not so easy to do with Dos Passos's English. Sartre manages, however, to tease out Dos Passos's mechanism: he is writing first-person narrative in the third person – that is to say, he is doing in his prose what Brecht recommended to his actors. One is tempted (following Bakhtin and Deleuze) to think of a kind of foreign language within the familiar one (yet a foreign language which has, in some Borgesian way, exactly the same words as ours, the same syntax and grammar, etc., etc.). But that – which is true of all modernism

---

[3]See Roland Barthes, *Sade, Fourier. Loyola* (Œuvres, vol. 11). it might *be* argued, however, that the *Spiritual Exercises* are, on the contrary, a Stanislavskian text *par excellence*, demanding the most thoroughgoing identification and 'restlos' loss of self; yet note how Barthes describes their structure:

> non seulement la matière ascétique est brisée, articulée à l'extrême, mais encore elle est exposée à travers un système discursif d'annotations, de notes ... dès qu'un objet paraît, intellectuel ou imaginaire, il est brisé, divisé, dénombré ... .(p. 1089)

This text may be a better one to scan for the last traces of a Brechtian impulse in Barthes's later work than the more famous 'Diderot, Brecht, Eisenstein', which follows it by a few years, and in which Barthes's unhappy consciousness about realism and representation (with which he identifies the formerly avant-garde figures of his title) is more embarrassingly clear.

(following Bakhtin) or all minoritarian speech (following Deleuze) – is rather different and specific here. Here Sartre's critical machinery rewrites one of the principal interwar narratological oppositions (deriving from Gide and Ramon Fernandez): that between the novel (with its open present and future) and the *récit* (as a closed and henceforth immutable past): Dos Passos thus translates a novelistic present into the terms of that past, that immutability, which he conveys by way of the language of journalism, like a news report: 'From our special envoy: "Charlie Chaplin declares that he has just killed off the Tramp." Now I get it: Dos Passos reports all the utterances of his characters in the style of the press conference. ... How simple and efficacious this technique: all he has to do is narrate a life in the style of American news coverage and life crystallizes into the social ... .'[4] It is clear that Sartre here goes one step further than Brecht in identifying the language of the third-person narrative rewriting of a given act in terms of what is alienated and socially or collectively inauthentic (the Heideggerian 'man' or 'anybody' is mentioned, and a kind of Flaubertian vision of the omnipresence of the cliché and the stereotype under capitalism is also evoked).

But more to the point in our present context is the way in which this enthusiastic Sartrean endorsement includes its own specific type of ethic, an ethic in which the old opposition between individual morality and collective norms is transcended: At this point let Simone de Beauvoir, in her memoirs, have the floor:

> We were immediately bowled over by the deliberately shocking effects that Dos Passos had contrived. Cruelly, he observed mankind both in terms of the comedy labeled 'freedom' which they play our inside themselves, and also as the mere helpless projections of their situation. Sartre and I frequently attempted to observe some third person, or more often ourselves, in this stereoscopic fashion. Though we might walk through life in cheerful self-assurance, we were not guilty of self-complacency; Dos Passos had furnished us with a new critical weapon, and we took full advantage of it. For instance, we sketched out our conversation at the Café Victor as Dos Passos might have handled it: 'The manager smiled in a satisfied way, and they both felt furious. Sartre drew at his pipe, and said that perhaps it was not enough merely to sympathize with the revolution. The Beaver pointed out that he had his own work to do. They ordered two large beers, and said how hard it was to sort out what you owed other people from what you owed yourself. Finally they declared that if they had been dock workers they would undoubtedly have joined the Communist Party, but in their present position all they could be expected to do was always to side with the proletariat.' Two *petits bourgeois* invoking their unwritten work as an excuse for avoiding political commitment: that was the truth, and indeed we had no intention of forgetting it.[5]

It is less clear to what degree Sartre and Beauvoir practised this 'method' in their own novels; at any rate, their emphasis on social class and on the development of a critical self-consciousness of class among bourgeois intellectuals contrasts usefully as a technique with the Brechtian emphasis on history. For in Brecht it is less a matter of consigning a given individual to a preexisting social class, with its specific ideological values and outlook, than of transcending the double standard of individual and collective events.

---

[4]Jean-Paul Sartre, *Situations* I (Paris: Gallimard, 1947): pp. 20–21, 22–23; see also the essay on Camus's *L'Étranger* in the same volume.
[5]Simone de Beauvoir, *The Prime of Life*, trans. P. Green (New York: World, 1962), pp. 113–14.

It is as though retelling individual events as though they were historical ones were not merely a satiric technique but also a new mode of self-knowledge. Thus, the quotation from *Me-ti* with which we began this Part, and in which Me-ti remarked on the absence of ethical precepts in the 'classics' (in other words, in Marx, Engels and Lenin), concludes as follows:

> Dabei allerdings fand er also sehr nützlich gepriesen den historischen Standpunkt. So empfahl er dem Einzelnen nach vielem Nachdenken, sich selber ebenso wie die Klassen und großen Menschengruppen historisch zu betrachten und sich historisch zu benehmen. Das Leben, gelebt als Stoff einer Lebensbeschreibung, gewinnt eine gewisse Wichtigkeit und kann Geschichte machen. Als der Feldherr Ju Seser seine Erinnerungen schrieb, schrieb er in der dritten Person von sich selber. Me-ti sagte: Man kann auch in der dritten Person leben.
>
> (XVIII, 188)

He also thought in this context that the historical viewpoint had been most usefully recommended. So it was that after much reflection he advised the individual to consider himself historically just like classes and large groups of people and to behave historically. Life, when lived as the material for a biography, takes on a certain gravity and can make history in its turn. When the warlord Ju Seser [Julius Caesar] wrote his memoirs, he wrote about himself in the third person. One can also live in the third person, Me-ti said.

# Dialectics

CHAPTER TWO

# Dialectics and the Brechtian Tradition: Some Thoughts on Politicized Performance

DAVID BARNETT

The international financial crash of 2007–8 has had a palpable effect on the way politics has been reconceived. Marxism is no longer (quite) the dirty word it had become in political discourse since the fall of the Berlin Wall and the implosion of the Soviet Bloc. The success of Syriza in Greece, Podemos in Spain and the surprise victory of Jeremy Corbyn as leader of the UK's Labour Party, in addition to the discussion around Thomas Piketty's *Capital in the Twenty-First Century* (2014), have at least returned a more visible, unashamedly left-wing politics to the public realm. Marxism's theoretical underpinning, the dialectic, has understandably received less public attention, yet it and its dynamics have been subject to renewed academic study in recent years. In terms of theatre, there has been a revival of interest in both concepts of realism, a much-maligned term in postmodern thought, and, by extension, the foundational figure of dialectical theatre, Bertolt Brecht. This article considers contemporary understandings of dialectics before concentrating on Brecht's reception and articulation of the term in theory and in performance, and how his ideas may inform contemporary theatre practice.

## DIALECTICS AND RADICAL POLITICS

The appeal of the dialectic to revolutionary politics is primarily its critique of what those in power and their agents present as reality. That is, typically, that reality is in some way inevitable and that it is beyond human control to effect substantial change. A dialectical worldview, on the other hand, understands reality as composed of entities that are always in opposition with each other. The Hegelian proposition of thesis and antithesis, whose relationship is defined by contradiction, robustly criticizes any sense of permanence in a given state of being. The tensions between opposing entities, be they people, conditions or ideas, suggest a fundamental instability in reality. When reality is unstable, it is subject to change and is mutable. Correspondingly, contradiction becomes a motor of change and its identification a potential source of momentum.

Yet because entities themselves are also products of dialectical interaction, they are always 'impure'. The idea of the 'thing in itself', cut off from human or social influence, becomes intensely problematic because dialectical processes pervade interactions. In the light of this, it is difficult to assert that any one person, for example, has any fixed qualities independent of his or her social and historical context. One may, for example, revile racists and oppose their views and sometimes murderous actions, but the rise of neo-Nazism is also a social phenomenon, born of dissatisfaction with the status quo. It is no surprise that neo-Nazis also organize events that offer a sense of community, however offensive this community's ideas and manifestations might be. Racists are thus not irredeemable; they are contradictory and only by viewing them in their complex, dialectical entirety can one start to confront them.

As Fredric Jameson has pointed out, dialectics has traditionally been understood as either a system or a method (2009: 3). He notes that both terms have been discredited over time for fairly obvious reasons: systems are too totalizing and methods can be too easily instrumentalized. He is also concerned about the third term of the dialectical mechanism – the synthesis of the thesis and antithesis. Drawing on Slavoj Žižek, he dismisses synthesis as 'that stupid old stereotype' and contends that there are 'no real syntheses in Hegel' (57). Instead, he prefers the term 'neutralization' as 'a kind of negative work on the negative itself' (32). In the light of these issues, he proposes the move from 'the' dialectic to 'a' dialectic: this 'dialectic proceeds by standing outside a specific thought … in order to show that the alleged conclusions in fact harbor the workings of unstable categorical opposition' (26). Here Jameson highlights both instability and the interpenetration of apparently discrete entities in each other.

Bernd Stegemann articulates the qualities of a dialectical relationship:

> There is an A and there is a B, and there is a relationship between the two. There is the idea (*Begriff*) about a thing (*Sache*), there is the thing and there is the difference between the idea and the thing. Only when the relationship between the idea and the thing is considered as a part of the idea itself can one talk of the dialectical work of the idea.
>
> (2013: 64)[1]

This perhaps complicated formulation abstracts important features of more concrete occurrences. Stegemann offers the example of a group of prisoners interred because they are considered violent and who are also hungry. The warder throws in a piece of bread that leads to further violence in the acquisition of the scarce resource. Stegemann notes that the violent reaction confirms the necessity of the prisoners' incarceration only to an undialectical mind. The relationship between a propensity for violence, the material situation itself and the intervention of a third party, the warder, mean that there is no single interpretation of the response to the action. By taking each factor in turn, one could reach a different conclusion as to why the prisoners behaved as they did. The discrepancy between the 'idea' and the 'thing' reveals an unstable landscape that is marked by a tension between what has happened and what is thought about it.

Stegemann's description neatly sidesteps three of the main criticisms levelled at dialectics. The first is that the term is little more than a synonym for 'roundedness'. John Fuegi accuses Brecht as theatre director of this by asserting that if a character were painted in a particularly

---

[1] All translations from the German are mine unless otherwise acknowledged.

positive light in one rehearsal, Brecht would search for more negative elements in the next (1987: 158). This flattened notion of dialectics fails to acknowledge the processes that lead to contradictions, the relationships that lead to the construction of contradictory unities. Instead it seeks to leave the good and the bad as discrete parts within a whole.

A second simplification of dialectical analysis is that it is in some way teleological, that successive generations of contradictions lead to an end point, an 'end of history' where all contradictions have been resolved. Such an impulse is most clearly found in Hegel, but also at some points in Marx, such as the '1844 Manuscripts'. Jameson cites *The Eighteenth Brumaire of Louis Bonaparte*, the account of the coup staged by Louis-Napoléon Bonaparte in 1851, as a riposte to this charge in the later Marx. He notes that 'what we observe is indeed the very opposite of this allegedly pious rehearsal for longed-for truths, of history written as wish-fulfillment and as the simple-minded interaction of a few abstractions' (Jameson 2009: 287). Marx defers to the twists and turns of reality rather than imposing an ends-focused meta-narrative that leads to socialist salvation. Again, Stegemann's example refutes the charge of inevitability: there is no knowing how the prisoners would have behaved had the warder provided food for all. The situation is contingent upon *all* its different elements.

The third charge is summed up in the French adage 'plus ça change, plus c'est la même chose' ('the more it changes, the more it's the same thing'). This offers a critique of the *appearance* of change and essentially embodies the conservative position that things will always ultimately stay the same. Again, Stegemann helps counter this meta-assertion by proposing that any 'thing' is itself polyvalent, so that it is impossible to impute the quality of permanence. Arguably, the only permanence is a repeated discursive assertion that nothing has changed.

However, one final major criticism of dialectical thought, that of relativism, requires further consideration. Even if one accepts Jameson's and Stegemann's articulations of dialectical processes, they still run the risk of offering up reality as something endlessly open to multiple interpretation, depending on one's point of view. Yet in another work, Stegemann makes an interesting distinction between two terms: 'Wirklichkeit [actuality]' and 'Realität [reality]' (Stegemann 2015: 77). Actuality is what really happens; reality is how people respond to actuality. For example, one could objectively say that two people had an argument. The disputants, however, might contend that they were both in the right, presenting two different realities. Stegemann's conceptual distinction acknowledges the existence of many realities – something that would be difficult to refute – yet he goes on to reserve a privileged position for a particular one. He notes that in socialist thought, perspective is defined by class and not by individuals, and it is from this collective standpoint that interpretations can be made that may then lead to social change.

This argumentation harnesses the power of dialectics for radical politics. The potential for action is predicated on identifying contradiction and exploiting the necessary instability it suggests. Contradictions can endure for as long as they are tolerated, of course, but they never disappear. Dialectics provides a philosophical rigour for political movements that seek to change fundamental aspects of their actuality. Marxism, through its analysis of class, attacks the individual perspective promoted by capitalism and derives its ontology from larger social formations. In changing the perception of reality, dialectics can also refashion consciousness by exchanging categories of thought that seek to inhibit change for ones that accept and encourage it.

Stegemann, who is, by trade, a dramaturg, paves the way with philosophical argument for a theatrical art form he unashamedly calls 'realistic'. This is also the term Brecht used to describe the bases for his own representational strategies.[2] This may surprise the reader, given that Brecht rejected the dominant theatrical definition of realism, that it should reproduce the surfaces of reality we encounter in everyday life. Brecht's ideas on realism and dialectics can shed light on the potentially liberating forms available to a politicized theatre.

## Brecht as Dialectical Theorist

Brecht offered a conceptual rather than an aesthetic definition of realism in 1938 in a series of points that I have enumerated for clarity:

> *Realistic* means: [1] revealing the causal complex of society/ [2] unmasking the ruling viewpoints of the rulers/ [3] writing from the standpoint of the class that has in readiness the broadest solutions for the most urgent difficulties besetting human society/ [4] emphasizing the factor of development/ [5] concretely and making it possible to abstract.
>
> (Brecht 2014c: 203)[3]

In the first instance, realism is active (1–4): it is no longer a reflection of a situation, but an interrogation of it. The aim is to reveal the processes that lie beneath the surface (1, 2 and 4) and to take up a perspective solely based on class (3). Realism, because it is predicated on the collective rather than the individual, also strives to take the particular and to make it general (5). The status of the individual, however, is a special one, inflected by the dialectic. In another essay, written about a year later, Brecht considered how an eviction from a flat might be represented. He notes that to the evictor, the evicted man is just a number, another part of a process carried out day in, day out. Brecht speculates about whether 'it could be that the evicted man is only to be represented in his anonymity, i.e. indeterminate, as one of the masses, personally lacking in characteristics, so: as Unemployed Man X. That, however, would be wrong' (Brecht 1993: 522). Instead, he proposes that this X is, of course, an individual, but that his representation hinges on his struggle to assert himself as such in the face of a dehumanizing process that views him as just another number. This realistic detail, which seeks out a contradiction and dramatizes it, locates individuals in social systems and consequently permits a representation that is at once specific and general. If one then asks, in response to point 5, 'who does the abstracting?', it is the spectator, acting on the provision of well-articulated dialectical material.

Brecht approaches the world dialectically, in both his understanding of realism and his draft for its practical application on stage. Yet, as has been shown above, dialectics is a contested topic, not least by leftist theorists themselves, and so it is sensible to understand how Brecht understood the term.

Brecht encountered Marxism in the mid-1920s and became fascinated by dialectics. His most sustained treatment of dialectics is to be found in *The Book of Twists and Turns* (*Buch der Wendungen*), which is sometimes also known as *Me-ti*.[4] The 'book' is actually

---

[2] See Giles 2012 for a discussion of Brecht's concept of realism in the context of the Marxist thought of his times.
[3] It is worth drawing the reader's attention to the revised and updated translations of Brecht now available in the different English volumes cited in the references section. The volumes also offer much material previously unavailable to readers of English.
[4] This important work is due to be published in English translation for the first time in 2017. As there is no current agreed title for the work, I have chosen mine from a translation made elsewhere (Müller 1980: 43).

a collection of often short sections, whose order Brecht never stipulated and which was never published in Brecht's lifetime. He began writing the sections in the mid-1930s and worked, as he often did, in phases, up until the final documented section, written in 1955. Brecht chose the figure of the invented Chinese philosopher Me-ti as an allusion to a real, yet little-known figure, Mo-Tse. As Antony Tatlow notes: 'for Mo-Tse the prime cause of social problems was contradictions in society; his teaching amounts to a systematic attempt to do away – once and for all – with these contradictions, to remove the cause of conflict' (1977: 415). There was thus a clear affinity between older social thought and more recent dialectical analysis, yet Tatlow emphasizes that Mo-Tse's philosophy 'helped [Brecht] realize and formulate his views', rather than informing them, something attributable to Hegel, Marx and Lenin (431).

For the most part, *The Book of Twists and Turns* is an allegorical commentary on contemporary and recent events in Europe. Historical figures often appear in hardly disguised form (Karl Marx is Ka-meh, although Stalin is Ni-en), and Germany becomes Chima. It is difficult, however, to call this chinoiserie: the book refracts its subject matter through a Chinese philosophical mode that resists superficial pastiche and allows Brecht to discuss topical matters at a distance. The form comprises of short, self-contained reflections, rather than lengthy, complex chapters. Brecht admired Chinese philosophers' focus on social context and 'the closest connection between knowledge and action' (354), something at variance with the Western penchant for epistemology and metaphysics. Günther Heeg reads the fragments and their rendition as pieces consciously written in exile: 'the appropriation of foreign material suggests in the first instance the acceptance of foreignness as a basic acceptance of one's own existence' (2011: 140). Such a starting point acknowledges a dialectical conception of human identity and development in that the individual is always informed and constructed by material and experiences that lie beyond it.

The Chinese form, which tends to move sententiously from the particular to the general, allowed Brecht more than simple stylistic flourishes. Expression is often suggestive and pithy, as in the following example: 'terror strengthens timidity and courage, two qualities that are very dangerous for dictators' (Brecht 1995:136). The reader is left to work on the contradictory apophthegm: it, like many others in *The Book*, provokes further thought and potentially action. As Rodney Livingstone explains: 'in the *Me-ti* ... manner, attitude and the ideas expressed are all ... tightly intertwined', that is, the discrete sections differ little in their style and are designed to incite active reading in the first instance (Livingstone 1998: 62).

Brecht devoted many sections of *The Book* to the subject of dialectics, which he renamed 'the Great Method'. The fragmentary mode of organizing the different sections, in which there are no direct through-lines, means that Brecht did not set out an argument, as in the Western philosophical tradition, but deployed a montage form in which the parts communicate with each other suggestively rather than logically. In the following discussion, then, it cannot be said that Brecht develops his thoughts on the Great Method systematically; I have taken material strewn throughout *The Book* and connected it according to my own line of enquiry.

Brecht offers an often aphoristic account of dialectics, a term only used once and alluded to once in *The Book* itself. Its origin is simply offered thus: 'the Great Method came about when human beings saw one thing and another' (Brecht 1995: 160). This straightforward starting point hides an important principle: human beings did not simply accept the differences between things in the world, but sought to account for them. This observation already suggests activity as a central component of dialectical practice, one to which I will return below.

There are two substantial sections that address the Great Method directly and it is worth quoting them at length for obvious reasons.

> The Great Method is best grasped when one considers it as a doctrine about mass-processes (*Massenvorgänge*). It never treats things individually, but rather sees them in a mass of both similar or related things and different things, and then proceeds to resolve them into masses themselves.
>
> (184)

The aversion to taking anything in isolation is made plain, and the proposition, found in another section, that 'relationships are decisive' (71), sets up the broad terms of this dialectic: the thing-in-itself is banished. Yet here, Brecht extends the scope from 'similar' to 'different things' in order to acknowledge its possibility for connection with objects that may only *appear* to be unrelated. Jameson notes that Brecht's treatment of quantities in this section exposes 'the "metaphysical" basis' of this way of approaching the world: 'it means that one of the central tasks of the dialectic will be a search for the most "minimal unity"' (Jameson 1998: 114). He continues: 'this, then, is a fundamental social materialism, as opposed to a physical kind' (115). Steve Giles examines the role of materialism in Brecht's thought and notes that Brecht suspected an all-embracing materialism as too mechanistic and deterministic (1998: 100). As a result, Brecht offers a careful formulation in his best-known theoretical work, the 'Short Organon for the Theatre' of 1949. Here dialectics is articulated as a 'materialist dialectic' (Brecht 2014b: 242) and not 'dialectical materialism', as John Willett first translated it (Brecht 1964: 193). That is, Brecht did not associate himself with a (sanctioned and codified) system, but preferred to deploy his dialectic without doctrinal limitation, ultimately prioritizing dialectics over materialism.

The other major description of the Great Method proposes that it is

> a practical doctrine of alliances and the dissolution of alliances, of the exploitation and the dependencies of change, of the initiation of change and the changing of the initiators, of the division and the establishment of unities, of the dependence of oppositions on each other, of the reconcilability of mutually exclusive oppositions. The Great Method makes it possible to recognize processes within things and to make use of them. It teaches the asking of questions that enable action.
>
> (Brecht 1995: 104)

The chiastic style signals the full reach of dialectics: processes are mutually interdependent so that nothing remains unchanged. Its transformative power, however, is not specified and, in this reading, is freed of any trace of facile determinism. There is nothing mechanical about the description and so the emphasis is firmly placed on process and activity. The freedom from dogma also suggests a pragmatism identified by Klaus-Detlef Müller in the treatment of the revolutionary leader disguised as 'Mi-en-leh': 'Lenin's strong point, and in this he proves himself to be a master in the "grand method", is the ability to adjust his behaviour according to the situation' (Müller 1980: 52). Brecht is thus able to circumvent Jameson's criticism of dialectics as method, discussed above, because his dialectic is liberated from a restrictive, ends-focused narrative and allowed to move unfettered through history.

Elsewhere, Brecht discusses dialectics' relationship to epistemology. Under the guise of Me-ti, he proposes that one should not fix what can be known too firmly, as has been the philosophers' wont, as 'they are not interested in the more or the less, but the all or nothing' (Brecht 1995: 56). Brecht's ambitions are more modest: dialectics is not concerned with determining what can and cannot be known, but prefers to linger on a perpetual renegotiation of the limits of knowledge. Using a characteristic reversal, he writes: 'it is the whole world that creates a picture, but the picture never encompasses the whole world' (60). Brecht contends that knowledge (or judgements, as he puts it) has to be based on experience, not idealist, metaphysical systems. Yet such judgements cannot take on a life of their own by being linked together: therein lies dogma. Knowledge, for Brecht, has to start with an observation of processes, and these are likely to change over time, and so knowledge, too, will never be stable.

The dialectics that emerges from *The Book of Twists and Turns* is not tethered by any doctrine other than its own workings, and these are couched in terms that are broad and expansive. In this reading, 'the' dialectic becomes Jameson's 'a' dialectic, a mechanism with both the ambit to analyze any social formation and the openness to reach the most remarkable of conclusions, unfettered by meta-narrative.

A link with activity also runs through the fragments on the Great Method and this evokes the Marxist definition of 'critique': the application of theory to provoke practice. The emphasis on activity differentiates between two types of change. Tatlow notes that Brecht found Taoism's identification of 'the flow of things' important for a dynamic conception of the world, but that he 'did not believe that social change occurred by itself' (Tatlow 1977: 457). Intervention is the key term and the process that brings it forth is articulated with pithy precision in *The Book of Twists and Turns*: 'thinking is something that follows difficulties and precedes action' (Brecht 1995: 62). This is what Klaus D. Wagner calls Brecht's 'dialectic of the deed' (2015: 239) in that it emerges from a concrete situation and, with the requisite hunger for change, moves to action.

Around 1931, Brecht underplayed the idea that nature itself was dialectical and ascribed that view to those who read dialectics 'from the perspective of progress' (Brecht 2003: 103). He continued that dialectical thought was rather a way of criticizing common ideas and to proceed against dominant ideologies. Here it would appear that Brecht favoured the idea of dialectics as a weapon for challenging the discourses peddled by the proponents of the status quo. Yet as Giles writes:

> on the one hand, [Brecht] construes dialectic as a mode of cognition that discloses transformative contradiction. ... On the other hand, he implies that the contradictory processes uncovered by dialectical thinking are themselves ontologically real and thus able to resist the closure imposed by cognitive patterns ...
>
> (1998: 96)

The question arises as to whether this ambiguity affects the application of dialectics in the theatre.

## Dialectics on the Brechtian Stage

After fifteen years away from Germany, Brecht was finally able to return to the theatre in 1948. He founded a company a year later together with his wife, Helene Weigel, in what was shortly to become the German Democratic Republic (GDR). The Berliner Ensemble (BE) allowed him to work through the ideas he had developed in exile. The fruits of his and his team's labours, as suggested by the nature of the dialectics Brecht explored in *The Book of Twists and Turns*, were never definitive. They involved the application of a theoretical construct to dramatic fiction, and the results were always open to further modification in the light of experience. Indeed, for Brecht a show's premiere did not mark the point at which work on a production stopped: the dossiers held in the BE's archive testify to long-term monitoring, assessment and re-rehearsal over the life of any one show. The application of dialectical thought to dramatic material did not guarantee its own results: dialectics, as noted above, are complex, and no one can interpret contradictions from a privileged position outside history or society. Brecht the pragmatist called the phrase 'the proof of the pudding is in the eating' an 'iron law' in 1953 (Brecht 2014a: 251). Here he asked whether dialectical analysis proved itself in realistic representation, but he found that he had to reformulate his terminology.

In a note made in the last year of his life, Brecht acknowledged that realism in the theatre was always provisional. Käthe Rülicke, a dramaturgical assistant at the BE, transcribed Brecht's sentiment: 'realism is what is *more* realistic, it doesn't exist otherwise' (Rülicke 1956: 10). This conclusion, made after seven years' work with the company, suggests that theatrical representation of dialectical processes will always only offer an approximation of the world outside. The task of the director and the actors is nonetheless 'to discover the typical (*das Übliche*), the schematic; that can't be reconstructed afterwards' (ibid.). So, the necessarily approximate representations still had to be crafted out of a special kind of observation – not of the individual, but of the individual's dialogue with the social situation – in order to generate the complexity required to go beyond superficial mimesis.

Documentation at the BE reveals sustained attempts to analyze situations rather than characters and to develop appropriate staging responses in rehearsal. In a note to his 1954 production of *The Caucasian Chalk Circle*, Brecht stated: 'people don't act out of one motive, but always out of several, that are sometimes contradictory' (Brecht in Bunge undated: 44). Actors could no longer look inwards, but had to acknowledge their insinuation in more than one social nexus. For example, in *Battle in Winter*, a play about the failed Nazi campaign to capture Moscow during World War II, a returning émigré Prince is described as wanting to use the Germans to regain his estates while the Germans are using him for propaganda value in the Soviet Union: 'everyone is using everyone else for their own purposes' (Anon. a n.d.a.: 2). The production was thus concerned with contradictory performance so that the figure of the Prince was not allowed either to be completely in control of his actions or to be completely subject to the will of his German masters. Both impulses had to be shown in order to represent the complex situation. In the same production, it was noted that the play's main character, Hörder, was rehearsed in two different ways. First, the actor approached the figure as an unpleasant person because he was a Nazi soldier. Then, the actor 'played a sympathetic young man who, however, speaks and acts like a Nazi. It becomes clear that a young person is being made into a Nazi' (Anon. b n.d.a.: 13). The emphasis on dialectical process over surface appearance exposed the dialectics of identity negotiation in the figure, banished character as a 'thing in itself' and revealed politically charged features of the 'world' of the play.

For all the dialectical verve of the theatre work, however, there were some not inconsiderable limitations that Brecht placed on the interpretive possibilities offered to the audience. Meg Mumford has drawn attention to a certain simplification in Brecht's practice and identifies 'something closed about the performed structure of opposition, as if the promise of offering up multiple options had been replaced by a presentation of "the" alternative, the "socially efficacious" way of behaving, the "better" social solution' (2000: 45). This was in part due to a more theoretically constrained understanding of dialectics on Brecht's part. Having read Mao's 'On Contradiction', he agreed with the author's division of contradictions into a 'main contradiction' at the top of a hierarchy and a series of 'sub-contradictions' beneath it.⁵ In orthodox Marxism, the 'main contradiction' is the one between labour and capital, yet in *Seventeen Contradictions and the End of Capitalism* David Harvey argues for a far more heterogeneous treatment of the contradictions that pervade society (2014). His work is firmly founded in the Marxist tradition, yet it acknowledges several significant sources of social, economic and political crisis that may all vie for dialectical treatment, often together. Brecht's penchant for economism, not signalled in *The Book of Twists and Turns*, can reduce a broader identification of contradiction in his theatre work and restrict the spectators' interpretive freedom.

As a result of theoretical constraint, the problem for Brecht's stagecraft was that it conflated two related, but distinct issues. The first was the dialectical interrogation of dramatic material, the second its presentation. To Brecht, the two were intimately linked: to be a dialectician was to be a Marxist, and this implied a certain optimism. Brecht's motto to *The Threepenny Lawsuit* was 'Contradictions are our hope!' (2001: 148), and this inflection coloured Brecht's theatre practice, too. He was making theatre in the first socialist nation on German soil and believed that he was living in the better Germany. His stagecraft set about dramatizing class conflict in a way that loaded his dialectics in the favour of the working class (rather than only interpreting dramatic material through its perspective), applying implicit value judgements to his representations. See, for example, Brecht's production of Erwin Strittmatter's *Katzgraben*, a play about agricultural reform in the eponymous farming village. In one note, Rülicke considers a scene involving a farmer and his wife who are not members of the rural proletariat, the peasantry: 'of course we show [these problems] in a partisan way (*parteiisch*), but we can't flippantly dismiss the problems as such or make them look silly' (Rülicke 1953: n.p.). The note acknowledges that the production team had already determined the meaning of the couple's difficulties: they would be tarred with the Party's ideological brush even if they were not to be overtly trivialized. The couple were certainly represented in terms of their social affiliation. As such, their actions connected personal experience and the demands of class. Yet the audience were invited to view the couple's problems as ones that were not as serious as those experienced by figures lower down the social scale. So, while it is clear that dialectics were in play, they were being loaded in favour of a particular interpretation and not being offered to spectators for their own judgement.

The adjective and adverb *parteiisch* (partisan, partial) was not a pejorative term to Marxists of the early twentieth century; indeed it was an important tenet of socialist realism. Brecht had Me-ti pronounce on the status of partial opinions in response to the question whether one can be simultaneously objective and partisan: 'if the party is objectively right, then there is no distinction between objective and partisan' (Brecht 1995: 127). While the line is couched in the conditional, it appears that the criteria can be met and, in the evidence of some of Brecht's theatre work in the GDR, were.

It should not be forgotten, however, that Brecht's rehearsal and production practice of the 1950s were radical and innovative. Despite the examples given above, it would be crass to call Brecht's work wholly doctrinaire or rigid.⁶ The introduction of dialectical stagecraft and its dramatization of contradictory class-based society were not only feted in the GDR, but won prizes at festivals in Paris and adulation in London. The criticisms

---

⁵Brecht explicitly used the term in his appendices to the 'Short Organon'.
⁶See Barnett 2011 for arguments that attest to Brecht's commitment to a more open application of dialectics.

above, made from a contemporary perspective, should in no way diminish Brecht's achievements in pioneering consciously dialectical practices in the theatre or lessen their potential for modification.

## DEVELOPMENTS IN THE BRECHTIAN TRADITION

The optimism and the faith in certain aspects of the Party line that can be discerned in Brecht's post-war productions with the BE became ever less sustainable after his death in 1956 and, later, the traumas state socialism both perpetrated and endured. The hope of a bright, harmonious future was not realized, and theatre-makers started to decouple dialectical forms from loaded presentational modes. Stegemann, who makes a sustained plea for realism in the Brechtian tradition on the contemporary stage, offers the following definition: 'in realistic art, society's contradictions and human beings are presented differently than reality permits by itself' (2015: 12). The dialectical imperative is clear and present; attendant value judgements are not. Such a theatre can defer interpretation on stage and instead invite the audience to judge the status of material in new presentational forms.

The response to dissatisfaction with orthodox Brechtianism was the development of post-Brechtian theatre from the 1970s onward. It was not that theatre-makers like Ruth Berghaus, Einar Schleef or Heiner Müller doubted the dialectical connections between individual, society and history, or Brecht's critique of surface naturalism. Rather, they were wary of the conclusions that could be reached, preferring to leave contradictions more provocatively open than Brecht, and this had an effect on the ways they staged dramas. This not only reflects the problem with implied value judgements, noted above, but also one concerning the epistemological landscape within which they were working. Directors in the GDR were struggling with contradictions between the promises of socialism and their own everyday experiences. Their colleagues in the West were confronting the instability engendered by post-Fordist economics and a media-saturated environment in which knowledge was becoming ever more commoditized. As time has gone on, and globalization has extended its reach, alienation in the Marxist and metaphorical senses has increased, and the development of ever more complex financial and social systems has not halted the hegemony of what is today known as the '1 per cent'.

Müller understood dialectics in the following, open terms: 'Marx didn't devise a system, on the contrary, he worked on negation, on a critique of the existing state of affairs. Consequently, he was open to new realities in principle' (2008: 432). Here Müller is not that far from expressing Adorno's argument in *Negative Dialectics* in which synthesis is eschewed and contradictions are left to accumulate. His politicized theatre marks an affinity with the Brecht of *The Book of Twists and Turns*. His greatest success, in terms of critical and audience response, was his production of Brecht's *The Resistible Rise of Arturo Ui* at the BE in 1995. Dialectical ideas ran through the central character's construction, for example: 'Ui doesn't have a personality of his own, he's actually a nobody who always has to be constructed by others' (Vestner 1995: n.p.). Yet the production should not be mistaken for a Brechtian imitation: the rehearsal notes betray the post-Brechtian impulse of articulating and accruing contradictions without seeking to resolve them. The effects of this understanding of dialectics were clear to see in the final production. Arturo Ui, Brecht's Chicago gangster and allegorical representation of Hitler, was not presented wholly negatively. In such an interpretation he would have remained an object of critical enquiry, studied by the audience from a distance. Müller did not discard a dialectical approach to staging Ui, but the figure was also played as seductive and appealing. The dialectical inversions meant that the spectators were never too close to the figure, yet he was also allowed to break frame and entice the audience, acknowledging Hitler's charisma and undeniable successes. It is the audience that have to reconcile their attraction to a repulsive figure, not the production.

Post-Brechtian theatre retains the impulses present in *The Book of Twists and Turns* and translates them into a theatre practice that is uncomfortable with closed forms of signification. Dialectics continue to demystify, or at least open up, the complexities of surface reality, but are presented to the spectators for their own judgement. Of course, there is no such thing as 'theory-free presentation' – dialectics is itself an interpretive enquiry into actuality – yet the material on stage is not packaged in a way that elicits a particular response from an audience. As such, Brecht's vision of a dialectic that is free to approach different realities is still, at heart, a politically hopeful instrument: it gives the lie to the mantra that 'there is no alternative' and proposes that change is always, somehow possible.

# REFERENCES

Anon. a (n.d.a) 'Notate *Winterschlacht*', Berlin, Berliner Ensemble Archive, file 18.
Anon. b (n.d.b) 'Zur *Winterschlacht*', Berlin, Bertolt Brecht Archive, file 940.
Barnett, David (2011) 'Undogmatic Marxism: Brecht as director at the Berliner Ensemble', in Laura Bradley and Karen Leeder (eds) *Brecht and the GDR: Politics, culture, posterity*, Rochester, NY: Camden House, pp. 25–43.
Brecht, Bertolt (1964) 'Short Organum for the theatre', in Bertolt Brecht, *Brecht on Theatre: The development of an aesthetic*, ed. John Willett, London: Methuen.
Brecht, Bertolt (1993) 'Spielen, was hinter den Vorgängen vorgeht', in Bertolt Brecht, *Schriften*, volume two, eds Werner Hecht, Jan Knopf, Werner Mittenzwei and Klaus-Detlef Müller, Berlin and Frankfurt: Aufbau and Suhrkamp, pp. 520–3.
Brecht, Bertolt (1995) *Buch der Wendungen*, in Bertolt Brecht, *Prosa*, volume three, eds Werner Hecht, Jan Knopf, Werner Mittenzwei and Klaus-Detlef Müller Berlin and Frankfurt: Aufbau and Suhrkamp, pp. 45–194.
Brecht, Bertolt (2001) *The Threepenny Lawsuit*, in Bertolt Brecht, *Brecht on Film and Radio*, ed. Marc Silberman, London: Methuen.
Brecht, Bertolt (2003) 'Dialectics', in Bertolt Brecht, *Brecht on Art and Politics*, eds Tom Kuhn and Steve Giles, London: Methuen, pp. 103–4.
Brecht, Bertolt (2014a) *Katzgraben Notes 1953*, in Bertolt Brecht, *Brecht on Performance: Messingkauf and Modelbooks*, eds Tom Kuhn, Steve Giles and Marc Silberman, London: Bloomsbury, pp. 251–75.
Brecht, Bertolt (2014b) 'Short Organon for the theatre', in Bertolt Brecht, *Brecht on Theatre*, 3rd edn, eds Marc Silberman, Steve Giles and Tom Kuhn, London: Bloomsbury, pp. 229–55.
Brecht, Bertolt (2014c) 'The popular and the realistic', in Bertolt Brecht, *Brecht on Theatre*, 3rd edn, eds Marc Silberman, Steve Giles and Tom Kuhn, London: Bloomsbury, pp. 200–6.
Bunge, Hans (undated) *Tagebuch einer Inszenierung: Bertolt Brecht führt Regie bei seinem Stück 'Der kaukasische Kreidekreis'*, Berlin, Bertolt Brecht Archive, file 945.
Fuegi, John (1987) *Bertolt Brecht: Chaos according to plan*, Cambridge: Cambridge University Press.
Giles, Steve (1998) *Bertolt Brecht and Critical Theory: Marxism, modernity and the 'Threepenny' Lawsuit*, 2nd, revised edn, Bern: Peter Lang.

Giles, Steve (2012) 'Realism after Modernism: Representation and modernity in Brecht, Lukács and Adorno', in Jerome Carroll, Steve Giles and Maike Oergel (eds) *Aesthetics and Modernity from Schiller to the Frankfurt School*, Oxford: Peter Lang, pp. 275–96.

Harvey, David (2014) *Seventeen Contradictions and the End of Capitalism*, London: Profile.

Heeg, Günther (2011) 'Brechts chinesische Wendungen: *Me-ti* und die Praxis kultureller Flexionen', *Brecht* Yearbook 36: 135–48.

Jameson, Fredric (1998) *Brecht and Method*, London: Verso.

Jameson, Fredric (2009) *Valences of the Dialectic*, London: Verso.

Livingstone, Rodney (1998) 'Brecht's *Me-ti*: A question of attitude', in German *Monitor* 41: 62–73.

Müller, Heiner (2008) 'Da trinke ich lieber Benzin zum Frühstück', in Heiner Müller, *Gespräche*, volume two, ed. Frank Hörnigk, Frankfurt/Main: Suhrkamp, pp. 431–45.

Müller, Klaus Detlef (1980), '*Me-ti*', in Betty Nance Weber and Hubert Heinen (eds) *Bertolt Brecht: Political theory and literary practice*, Manchester: Manchester University Press, pp. 43–59.

Mumford, Meg (2000) 'Brecht on acting for the 21st century: Interrogating and re-inscribing the fixed', *Communications from the International Brecht Society* 29(1 and 2): 44–9.

Pikkety, Thomas (2014) *Capital in the Twenty-First Century*, Cambridge, MA: Belknap.

Rülicke, Käthe (1953) [documentation of *Katzgraben* rehearsals], Berlin, Berliner Ensemble Archive, file 13.

Rülicke, Käthe (1956) 'Besprechung mit Brecht am 3. 1. 56 über die Notate der bisherigen Proben', Berlin, Bertolt Brecht Archiv, file 2071.

Stegemann, Bernd (2013) *Kritik des Theaters*, Berlin: Theater der Zeit.

Stegemann, Bernd (2015) *Lob des Realismus*, Berlin: Theater der Zeit

Tatlow, Antony (1977) *The Mask of Evil: Brecht's response to the poetry, theatre and thought of China and Japan. A comparative and critical evaluation*, Bern: Peter Lang.

Vestner, Margit (1995) '*Der Aufstieg des Arturo Ui*: 5. Bild–Stadthaus', Berlin, Berliner Ensemble Archive, file 182.

Wagner, Frank D. (2015) *Hegel und Brecht: Zur Dialektik der Freiheit*, Würzburg: Königshausen und Neumann.

# Verfremdung

# CHAPTER THREE

# The *Verfremdung* of Certain Processes through a Mode of Representation Usually Reserved for Customs and Traditions

BERTOLT BRECHT
TRANSLATED BY ROMY FURSLAND

A visit, the treatment of enemies, a lovers' tryst, business agreements etc. can be subjected to the V-effect by being represented in the same way one would usually represent customs and traditions.

A persecuted man's plea for shelter can be subjected to the V-effect by representing it like a famous scene from history which is widely known, even in its finer details; it can also be subjected to the V-effect by representing it as a custom that is common in this part of the world. Represented in this way, the unique and singular process, which would otherwise retain its unique and singular character through the emphasis of its own peculiar features, is subjected to the V-effect because the behaviour it involves is portrayed as a universal behaviour, one which has developed into a custom. Even just the question of whether it could ever become a custom, and if so in which aspects, subjects the process to the V-effect.

Practically speaking: one way of doing this is to examine an act for incidents that might interest a historian or a chronicler of customs, and to create a series of titles in the language of these researchers, then act out the scenes to illustrate these titles.

---

Brecht, 'Verfremdung bestimmter Vorgänge durch eine Darstellungsart, die sonst Sitten und Gebräuche erfahren würden', in Brecht, *Schriften*, vol. 2 (Berlin and Frankfurt/Main: Aufbau and Suhrkamp, 1993), p. 213.

# CHAPTER FOUR

# A Critical Response to Heidi M. Silcox's 'What's Wrong with Alienation?'

ANTHONY SQUIERS

In the April 2010 edition of *Philosophy and Literature*, an article appeared entitled 'What's Wrong with Alienation?' by Heidi M. Silcox. In this article, Silcox makes an analogy between great German Marxist playwright Bertolt Brecht's estrangement effects and the psychological phenomenon of imaginative resistance. Silcox attempts to debunk Brecht's theory that his theatrical and literary techniques could cause the audience to experience their present reality in radically new and meaningful ways. Specifically, she argues that since Brecht's dramaturgy rejects empathy, his work completely detaches the audience from the performance, leaving them unengaged and thus unable to form significant responses. According to Silcox, emotional engagement with artistic communications is necessary for lasting impressions to form and didactic intention to be successful. She finds emotional engagement lacking in Brecht's work and then presents empirical evidence that purports to substantiate her claim.

Most research on Brecht has come from literary and theatrical perspectives or language studies. This research, therefore, reflects the interests of those disciplines and primarily seeks to speak to the literatures in those respective fields. As a consequence, much of the scholarship on Brecht is formalistic and focuses primarily on the structure or form of the text.[1] Recent work, however, has attempted to bring the study of Brecht beyond formalistic approaches in an effort to expand the purview of Brechtian scholarship by exploring him primarily as a Marxist philosopher.[2] Silcox's work is important because it goes beyond formalism and attempts to engage Brecht's ideas from a new perspective.

---

Anthony Squiers, 'A Critical Response to Heidi M. Silcox's "What's Wrong with Alienation?"', *Philosophy and Literature*, 39: 1 (2015), pp. 243–7.

[1] Anthony Squiers and Norm Roessler, 'Rethinking Brecht', *Communications from the International Brecht Society* 40 (2011): 119; hereafter abbreviated *RB*.

[2] Wolfgang Fritz Haug, 'Rethinking Gramsci's Philosophy of Praxis from One Century to the Next', *Boundary 2* 26, no. 2 (1999): 101; Wolfgang Fritz Haug, 'From Marx to Gramsci, from Gramsci to Marx: Historical Materialism and the Philosophy of Praxis', *Rethinking Marxism* 13, no. 1 (2001): 69; Anthony Squiers, 'Mother Courage as Surrealistic Video Game at Western Michigan University', *Communications from the International Brecht Society* 38 (2009): 63; hereafter abbreviated *MC*; Anthony Squiers, 'Bertolt Brecht and the Ethics of

However, several fatal pathologies in her theoretical conceptualization and empirical data leave her conclusions largely invalid. For example, Silcox makes several false assumptions about Brecht's theory of estrangement. First, she assumes that Brecht's work is meant to completely negate emotional response. This is not the case. As Brecht himself says, his epic theater was not meant to completely eliminate emotional response. He states, 'Some people have read into [my theory] the notion that I come out "against emotion and in favor of the intellect". This of course is not the case. I don't see how thought and feeling can be kept apart.'[3] Brecht recognizes the importance of emotional response, saying that 'the epic principles guarantee a critical attitude on the part of the audience, but that attitude is highly emotional'.[4] Furthermore, this notion is found elsewhere in Brecht's writings[5] and is also recognized by many preeminent Brecht scholars.[6] What epic theater attempted to do was eliminate one particular emotional response: full empathy with the protagonist. This, Brecht believed, would allow the audience to have an emotional response based on a critical and rational assessment of what they had seen.[7]

Second, Silcox incorrectly assumes that Brecht's estrangement effects were designed to alienate the audience from the performance. In fact, Brecht wanted the audience to be engaged with the performance. He required attentiveness and personal, intellectual commitment to it. The estrangement Brecht desired was an internal estrangement from one's current *Weltanschauung* or worldview.[8] This misconception is likely a result of Silcox's failure to make a distinction between alienation (*Entfremdung*) and estrangement (*Verfremdung*). Brecht, of course, uses the term *Verfremdungseffekt* (estrangement effect). Bloch draws a precise and accurate definition of *Verfremdung*. According to Bloch, while *Verfremdung* and *Entfremdung* 'are bound together by the alien', the former is the idea of making the familiar strange – as Brecht does with his *Verfremdungseffekt*.[9] *Verfremdung* connotes a defamiliarized conceptualization, whereas *Entfremdung* only implies a distancing, as Feuerbach uses it, to indicate a moving away from one's true self; Marx uses the term to indicate the moving away of one's labor product from one's self. Brecht's use of *Verfremdung* and not *Entfremdung* indicates that the moving away or distancing he

---

Praxis', *Consciousness, Literature and the Arts* 12, no. 1 (2011); hereafter abbreviated *BBEP*; Anthony Squiers, 'Brecht's *The Wedding*', *Communications from the International Brecht Society* 40 (2011): 56; Anthony Squiers, 'Contradiction and Coriolanus: A Philosophical Analysis of Mao Tse Tung's Influence on Bertolt Brecht', *Philosophy and Literature* 37, no. 1 (2013): 239; *RB*; Anthony Squiers, *An Introduction to the Social and Political Philosophy of Bertolt Brecht: Revolution and Aesthetics* (Amsterdam: Rodopi, 2014); Astrid Oesmann, 'The Theatrical Destruction of Subjectivity and History: Brecht's *Trommeln in der Nacht*', *The German Quarterly* 70, no. 2 (1997): 136; Astrid Oesmann, *Staging History: Brecht's Social Concepts of Ideology* (Albany: State University of New York Press, 2005); Fredric Jameson, *Brecht and Method* (London: Verso, 2000).
[3]Bertolt Brecht and John Willett, *Letters* (New York: Routledge, 1990), p. 316; here after abbreviated *Letters*.
[4]Bertolt Brecht, Hugh Rorrison, and John Willett, *Bertolt Brecht Journals* (New York: Routledge, 1993), p. 135; hereafter abbreviated *Journals*.
[5]Bertolt Brecht and John Willett, *Brecht on Theatre: The Development of an Aesthetic* (New York: Hill and Wang, 1992), pp. 23, 88; hereafter abbreviated *BT*; Bertolt Brecht, *The Messingkauf Dialogues* (London: Methuen, 1965), pp. 15, 57, 102.
[6]Carol Martin and Henry Bial, *Brecht Sourcebook* (London: Routledge, 2000), p. 37; hereafter abbreviated *BS*; Jean Paul Sartre, *Sartre on Theater* (New York: Pantheon Books, 1976); hereafter abbreviated *ST*; Augusto Boal, *Theatre of the Oppressed* (New York: Theatre Communications Group, 1985).
[7]Louis Althusser, *For Marx* (New York: Pantheon Books, 1990); Walter Benjamin, *Understanding Brecht* (London: NLB, 1973); *Letters*; *Journals*; *ST*; *BBEP*.
[8]*BT*; Erika Munk, *Brecht* (New York: Bantam Books, 1972), p. 4; hereafter abbreviated *Brecht*; *BBEP*, *MC*.
[9]*Brecht*, p. 4.

sought through these effects was a distancing of familiar conceptualization, not, as Silcox implies, a distancing of the audience from the play's performance and its content.

Finally, Silcox assumes that the primary idea of Brecht's text in his epic theater was to bombard the audience with moralistic messages. This too is a false assumption. Instead, Brecht attempted to portray realistic events and wanted the audience to come to their own conclusions about the moral implications of the events portrayed.[10] Brecht never intended epic theater to instruct its audience in moral behavior. As Brecht himself says, 'Many people ... attacked the epic theatre, claiming it was too moralistic. Yet moral utterances were secondary in epic theatre. Its intention was less to moralize than to study [society].'[11]

In addition to these problems, there is also a pathology with the empirical evidence Silcox uses to support her thesis. Silcox uses survey data taken of audience members after what she deemed to be a performance of epic theater in 1969. The survey attempted to gauge what types of effects the play had on the audience. As Silcox states, the director employed the same techniques as Brecht himself used. However, she fails to realize that the particular estrangement effects employed in this performance (e.g., speaking directly to the audience, sudden shifts in action) would no longer have worked as estrangement effects because the audience would have become too accustomed to them. Instead of standing outside the expectations of that audience's worldview, these effects would have been immersed in it.

While once at the vanguard of dramaturgy, many of Brecht's estrangement effects have been so widely adopted – not only in theater but in cinema and television – they are now (as they were even at the time of the survey) rather commonplace. As noted Brazilian critic Roberto Schwarz states, 'It is easy to note the use advertising has made of the most sensational discoveries of avant-garde art, among them the resources of the Brechtian actor.'[12] In order to produce the desired effect, then, one would need to create new estrangement effects; one cannot recycle the old. This is readily recognizable to those with dramaturgy backgrounds.[13] Since Brecht's original estrangement effects (which no longer work as estrangement effects) were employed, one would not expect audiences to be affected in the way Brecht theorized.

Moreover, when effective estrangement effects are employed, preliminary empirical evidence indicates that they work as theorized.[14] According to the article, students were provided with a discussion-board prompt on an online learning format. The prompt contained an account of a well-known biblical scene, which was produced using various Brechtian estrangement effects that sought to obfuscate its origin. These effects were specifically designed to be applicable to that particular audience by taking into account the common-sense, taken-for-granted, everyday *Weltanschauung* of it. Empirical evidence provided by the written responses of the students demonstrated that the effects were successful in compelling them to consider familiar events from a completely different context. Specifically, they produced a situation where the standard deference and

---

[10]*BS*, p. 29; Roberto Schwarz, 'The Relevance of Brecht: High Points and Low', *Mediations* 23, no. 1 (2007); hereafter abbreviated *RB*; *BBEP*; *ST*; Roland Barthes, *Critical Essays* (Evanston: Northwestern University Press, 1972).
[11]*BS*, p. 29.
[12]*RB*, p. 42.
[13]*MC*.
[14]*RB*.

uncritical acceptance of the Bible account was missing in all the students, and critical, new ways of understanding the narrative emerged.

In sum, Silcox's impulse to rescue Brecht from the type of formalistic studies that have limited research on him is a welcome and important one. However, her theoretical misconceptions about Brecht's epic theater and limitations in her empirical data leave her conclusions highly suspect.

*Gestus*

# CHAPTER FIVE

# Getting to the Gist of Gestus

MEG MUMFORD

Q: How many Brechtians does it take to change a light bulb?
A: Your Gest is as good as mine. [Glenn D'Cruz. 1991][1]

Problematical, vague, elusive. These are the terms typically used by critics who attempt to address Brecht's Gestus concept. Simultaneously it is described as fundamental to his dramaturgy[2] and as playing a key role in his theatre aesthetic.[3] Given the much touted centrality of the concept, it is surprising how little scholarship has been devoted to a consideration of its obscurity. Kenneth Fowler's recent work on the problem of Gestus and musical meaning is the first to offer such an account.[4] Through a critical historical analysis of the approach to Gestus contained in Brecht's theoretical writings, Fowler throws light on several contradictions which he believes are both inherent in the concept and fundamental to Brecht's confusing presentation of the term. In particular, he draws attention to an ambivalence concerning the relation between private and social gesture which points to a larger conflict between a bourgeois individualist and a Marxist materialist approach to gesture.[5] Through concentrating on the opaque nature of Brecht's Gestus descriptions, Fowler not only sharpens the definition of the concept but reveals it as a site of ideological tension within Brecht's struggle to forge a Marxist theatre.

Continuing in Fowler's vein, this chapter extends in several ways the discussion of Gestus as the embodiment of tension within Brecht's theatre. Firstly, it broadens the discussion of the contradiction regarding individualised expressive gesture and social bearing to incorporate a closer examination of the etymology of the term and its historical development. This task is assisted by the timely arrival of a new edition of Brecht's writings, complete with historical commentary and more specific time references. I have replaced Fowler's emphasis on the appearance of the term in reference to music with a focus on acting theory. And Fowler's concentration on Brecht's terminological inconsistencies, a major key to tensions within the Gestus concept, is widened to include

---

Meg Mumford, 'Getting the Gist of Gestus', in *Showing the Gestus*, unpublished PhD thesis, pp. 1–22

[1] Glenn D'Cruz. 'Illuminating Gestus: Towards a Political Theatre'. *Antithesis*, vol. 4, no. 2 (1991). 61.
[2] Gerold Koller. *Der mitspielende Zuschauer: Theorie und Praxis im Schaffen Brechts* (Zürich: Artemis. 1979). p. 27.
[3] Hans Martin Ritter. *Das gestische Prinzip* (Cologne: Prometh. 1986), p. 7.
[4] K. Fowler, *Received Truths: Bertolt Brecht and the Problem of Gestus and Musical Meaning* (New York: AMS Press. 1991). pp. 27–55. Another recent publication which deals with the issue of opaqueness, if only briefly, is Helmut Heinze's *Brechts Ästhetik des Gestischen: Versuch einer Rekonstruktion* (Heidelberg: Carl Winter Universitätsverlag. 1992). pp. 118–24.
[5] Fowler, *op. cit.*, p. 29.

the problem of what happens to a confusing usage of terms put through the mincer of English translation. A second extension of the discussion, and a concern central to this thesis at large, is the presentation and examination of the way Brecht and his co-workers applied the term Gestus to performance practice, particularly at the Berliner Ensemble. Like most critics, Fowler bases his commentary on published writings but, with the exception of texts such as *Theaterarbeit*, the *Modellbücher* and the *Katzgraben* notes, very few of these contain information about how the term and concept was employed during rehearsal. Moreover, Fowler's emphasis is on musical composition as distinct from the work of directors and actors. Drawing upon archive rehearsal notes, this chapter addresses the neglected area of Gestus in historical theatre practice [see Appendix II] and its relation to Gestus in theory. Does the practice clarify the theory or reveal similar ambivalences and tensions?

After exploring the problematic nature of the Gestus concept, I conclude the chapter with a consideration of its centrality and uniqueness to Brecht's Marxist theatre. Not surprisingly this discussion involves traversing the terrain of yet another tension-riddled area, encompassing the issue of whether Gestus denotes simply a traditional deictic technical device central to all theatre which vividly physicalises human behaviour, or a novel aesthetic principle.

## GESTUS IN THEORY: THE PROBLEM OF DEFINITION

### 1.1 A Polyseme

At the basic level of etymology the term Gestus is a polyseme and as such contains within it the seeds of confusion. In German the term is regarded as synonymous with *Geste* ('gesture') and *Gestik* ('gesticulation'). 'Gesture' in turn is a complex site of contrasting denotations. On the one hand, 'gesture' is connected with the concept of expressing inner attitudes and feelings through physical movement,[6] so in one sense, the term lends itself to a psychological model of behaviour, carrying with it the association of a spontaneous and personal psychological expression. On the other hand 'gesture' is defined as a communicative instrument, a consciously employed and socially encoded expression of information, such as a nod or shake of the head. It has been suggested that the latter model is better suited to Brecht's behaviourist and Marxist inspired art.[7] The opaque nature of Brecht's Gestus descriptions derives not only from the blurring of Gestus with *Gestik* but from the way Brecht employs both the psychological and the communicative model of gesture.

There are two other denotations relevant to the issue of Brecht's confusing usage. These meanings stem from the Latin derivation of the term and, given Brecht's familiarity with the language and classical literature from his Gymnasium days,[8] it is likely Brecht

---

[6]Günter Drosdowski (ed.) et al., *Duden: Das große Wörterbuch der deutschen Sprache*, vol. 3 (Mannheim: Bibliographisches Institut, 1977), pp. 1021–23; Gerhard Wahrig (ed.) et al., *Brockhaus Wahrig: Deutsches Wörterbuch*, vol. 3 (Wiesbaden: Brockhaus, 1981), pp. 195–197.

[7]Heinze, *op. cit.*, pp. 33–34. Heinze posits a possible friction in Brecht's work between what he describes as an old-fashioned psychological tradition and an avant-garde behaviourist, pragmatic and sociological position, yet he does not pursue the issue further.

[8]See Klaus Völker, *Bertolt Brecht: Eine Biographie* (Reinbek bei Hamburg: Rowohlt, 1988), pp. 12–13, 15; Michael Morley, '"Suiting the Action to the Word": Some Observations on *Gestus* and *Gestische* Musik', in Kim

was aware of them. In Latin, Gestus can denote, firstly, 'bearing', 'carriage', 'posture' and 'attitude'[9] and this meaning is more in line with Brecht's Marxist desire to emphasise socio-economically determined comportments and relations. As John Willett notes, the closest equivalent English word is the now Obsolete term 'gest'.[10] The second relevant Latin meaning refers to the notion of gestures made by an actor or orator according to the rules of art and/or for giving effect to oratory. Brecht seems to draw upon this definition when employing Gestus to mean rhetorically effective gesture or language. So as an etymological investigation reveals, Gestus can denote three different, if interrelated, types or ways of categorising human activity: expressive gesture, communicative gesture and socially significant comportment, and rhetorical gesture. Leaving aside the reference to rhetorical effectiveness, which I will consider in more detail at the conclusion of this chapter, I turn to the potential tension between expressive personal gesture and socially meaningful gesture or bearing. This section is indebted to Fowler's ground-breaking analysis. However, rather than merely summarising his argument with its focus on Gestus and music, I intend to use Fowler's analysis as a tool to examine Brecht's approach to the gestural role of the actor.

## 1.2 Gesture to Gestus: Ideological Progression

Brecht's first recorded use of the term Gestus occurs in his November 1920 review of a performance of Strindberg's *There are Crimes and Crimes* where he praises an actor for bringing Gestus and word together in a strong rhythmical unity.[11] Here the term is used in the conventional sense as synonymous with *Gestik*. Its next appearance is in a piece which was written in the wake of Brecht's first intense interaction with Marxism. Dated approximately 1927, 'About a Modern Type of Actress' heralds a shift away from the notion of Gestus as simply expressive gesture towards the concept of ideologically significant bearing or stance. In this fragment Brecht attempts to delineate two types within the category of bourgeois actress in the late nineteenth century. He describes the first type as one who, victimised by the heavy blows of fate, 'lays everything out on the table' with regard to her plight within the repressive bourgeois domestic scene. Her function was to convince the audience that even in the haven of the bourgeois world there was something amiss. The second type expressed the desire of the bourgeois female to experience something and, as this could occur only at the cost of men in the sense that it would threaten business, this type tended to have a diabolical streak:

> Her Gestus was directly opposed in a simple manner to the Gestus of version one in that it was theatrically displayed rather than inwardly enclosed ...[12]

Here Brecht juxtaposes not only theatrically externalised with introspective gesture but the differing 'comportments', or bearing and attitude, which each gestural code helps

---

H. Kowalke (ed.). *A New Orpheus: Essays on Kurt Weill* (New Haven and London: Yale University Press, 1986), p. 186.
[9]Charlton T. Lewis and Charles Short, *A Latin Dictionary* (Oxford: Clarendon, 1879), p. 814; Gerhard Wahrig (ed.), *Cassell's New Latin-English, English-Latin Dictionary*. 3rd ed. (London: Cassell, 1964), p. 265.
[10]John Willett. 'Note', in Brecht. *BT*, p. 42; J.A. Simpson and E.S.C. Weiner, *The Oxford English Dictionary*, 2nd ed., vol. 6 (Oxford: Clarendon, 1989), p. 474.
[11]'Strindberg's "Rausch"', November 1920, *BFA*, vol. 21, p. 84.
[12]'Über einen Typus moderner Schauspielerin', c. 1927. *BFA*, vol. 21, p. 214.

to convey – the comportment of the plaintive domestic victim and of the 'diabolic' adventuress respectively.

According to the historical commentary in the recent edition of his works, Brecht first employs the term in connection with his new Marxist approach to acting in a fragment titled 'The Trill Turn' ['*Der Nachschlag*'] c.1930.[13] Here the shift away from an emphasis on private expression towards the gestural display of social relations is clearly demonstrated:

> In this way the characters are created through an understanding of how they behave towards others.
>
> This is very important, because what counts for humanity in every grouping is that the individual is judged according to what he shows of himself to the group or what he does for it, and that the individual only sees in another's face what he can produce in it. It is not enough simply to be. The character of a person is generated by their function.
>
> The method of acting designed for this purpose is more concerned with gesticulation than expression. Words too should be oriented around a Gestus.[14]

As 'The Trill Turn' fragment testifies, Gestus is central to Brecht's attempt to concretise the way an individual's behaviour reflects and is shaped through social relations.

The revised notion of Gestus is obviously an integral part of Brecht's early experimentations in the late twenties and early thirties with a Marxist theatre theory and practice. More precisely it is connected with the struggle to realise in performance the Marxist premise that social being determines consciousness, social existence in turn being determined in the first instance by the mode and relations of production. This connection is clarified in theoretical works from the mid thirties onwards. Repeatedly, Gestus is defined as entailing the presentation of 'socio-historically significant' or 'typical' behaviour and events. Brecht used the terms 'significant' or 'typical' in a quite specific way to denote those humans and events which are most decisive for the developmental processes of society, for socialism and the progress of humankind rather than to mean the most frequently occurring or strikingly visible and obvious.[15] Hence Ritter argues, the gestic presentation of the 'significant' and 'typical' involves then, the gestural foregrounding of how behaviour is related to specific social circumstances in a given historical period, whether this behaviour accords with or contradicts the prevailing 'laws', and the way it constitutes a decision made in the given conditions rather than a natural event.[16] In 'On the Use of Music in Epic Theatre' 1935, Gestus is presented as crucial to the revelation of the laws underpinning human interaction:

> The epic theatre is chiefly interested in the behaviour of people towards one another, *wherever it is socio-historically significant (typical)*. It works out scenes in which people behave in such a way that the social laws under which they are acting are made visible

---

[13]'Der Nachschlag', c. 1930, *BFA*, vol. 21. pp. 389–390.
[14]*ibid.*, p. 390.
[15]'Das Typische', c. 1951, *BFA*, vol. 23 (1993). p. 141; '[Notiz zum Typischen]', January 1956, *BFA*, vol. 23. p. 381.
[16]Ritter, *op. cit.*, p. 114.

.... This means, from the aesthetic point of view, that the Gestus of the actor becomes particularly important. For the arts it is about cultivating the Gestus.[17]

And as Brecht's comments from 1936–38 on the New York performance of *The Mother* testify, the gestic performance can be achieved only by those with an awareness of historical materialism:

> The way of speaking and the Gestus here have to be carefully selected and formed on a large scale. As the spectator's interest is directed solely towards the behaviour of the characters, the relevant Gestus must in each case be, purely aesthetically speaking, significant and typical. Above all, the director must have an historical outlook. The little scene where Vlassova gets her first lesson in economics, for example, is by no means just an incident in her own life; it is an historic event: under the immense pressure of misery the exploited begin to think.[18]

The underlying Marxist emphasis on socio-historical determination is lucidly expressed in the 'Short Description of a New Technique of Acting which Produces a Defamiliarisation Effect' c. 1940. Here Gestus is described as 'the facial [*mimische*] and gestural expression of the social relationships prevailing between people of a given period'.[19]

These later writings, and particularly those of the fifties, attempt to explain how the socially typical gesture can be highlighted in performance. As Fowler notes, Brecht insists on the careful attention to the social context of any action.[20] 'On Gestic Music' 1937, one of Brecht's fullest explications of the concept, testifies not only to his interest in context but to his insistence on the Marxist presentation of that context.

> The artist is not happy till he achieves 'the look of a hunted dog'. The man then becomes just 'Man'; his Gestus is stripped of any kind of social particularity, it is empty, not representing any undertaking or operation among men by this particular man. The 'look of a hunted dog' can become a social Gestus if it is shown that through particular machinations of people, the individual can be degraded to the level of a beast ...[21]

The social context is one in which the victimising forces are depicted as social and 'man made' rather than as the mysterious hand of fate. In later relevant writings, such as '[On Gestus]' 1940, the importance of the context surrounding a gestural complex is reiterated:

> A man praying to his God, according to this definition, only becomes a Gestus when it occurs with regard to others or in the case where relations between humans appear.
>
> (The King praying in *Hamlet*.)[22]

---

[17]'Über die Verwendung von Musik für ein episches Theater', 1935. *BFA*, vol. 22.1, pp. 157–158. See also Brecht. *BT*. p. 86.

[18]'Anmerkungen zur "Mutter"', 1938, *BFA*, vol. 24, p. 172. See also Brecht, *BT*, p. 83.

[19]'Kurze Beschreibung einer neuen Technik der Schauspielkunst, die einen Verfremdungseffekt hervorbringt', c. early 1940, *BFA*, vol. 22.2, p. 646. See also Brecht *BT*, p. 139. Willett translates *mimische* as 'mimetic'. This is presumably because *mimische* means 'with reference to *Mimik*', and while *Mimik* commonly denotes facial expressions, it can also signify corporeal expressions in general. However, if Brecht had wanted specifically to mean 'mimetic' he could have used the German word *mimetisch*. See Günter Drosdowski (ed.) et al. *Duden: Das große Wörterbuch der deutschen Sprache*, vol. 4 (1978), p. 1787; Gerhard Wahrig (ed.) et al., *Brockhaus Wahrig: Deutsches Wörterbuch*, vol. 4 (1982), p. 677.

[20]Fowler, *op. cit.*, pp. 33–34.

[21]'Über gestische Musik', July/August 1937, *BFA*. vol. 22.1, p. 330. See also Brecht, *BT*, p. 104.

[22]'[Über den Gestus]', early 1940. *BFA*. vol. 22.2, p. 617. See also Fowler's translation, *op. cit.*, p. 31.

Or in 'Gesticulation' c. 1951:

> The carrying out of a piece of work, for example, is not a Gestus if it does not contain a social relationship such as exploitation or co-operation[23]

One of the important implications of the stress on context is that a Gestus cannot be achieved through a single gesture from a lone actor but is dependent upon the relation between this gesture and the social context unfolded throughout the performance.[24]

### 1.3 Gestus to Social Gestus: Ideological Confusions?

The outline of the historical development of the term given so far appears to depict a smooth passage from expressive gesture to a concept of Gestus as socially significant bearing or comportment within a social context. That is, it depicts an ideological shift from a liberal bourgeois emphasis on personal and naturally given expression to a Marxist emphasis on the relation between behaviour and the socio-economic network of determining forces. Yet many of the statements presented above contain the seeds of confusion and contradiction. Firstly, there is the disorienting use of the phrase 'social Gestus'. Closely related to this issue is the distinction Brecht seems to make between gesture which is socially significant and gesture which, due to its purely personal nature and lack of social context, is not.[25] A second major confusion is the continual blurring of the terms Gestus, *Geste* and *Gestik*.

'On Gestic Music' contains the first clear elucidation of a distinction between Gestus and 'social Gestus':

> Not every Gestus is a social Gestus. The defensive attitude [*Abwehrhaltung*] towards a fly is not yet a social Gestus, though the defensive attitude towards a dog could become one, if, for example, it revealed the battle which an ill-clad person has to wage against watch dogs. The attempt to avoid falling on a slippery surface results in a social Gestus as soon as falling down means that someone 'loses face'; in other words, as soon as someone suffers from a loss of value.[26]

Here Gestus without the accompanying adjective 'social' continues to denote bearing or attitude but now takes on the character of an individual's expression, abstracted from its social context and therefore one which does *not* allow (Marxist) conclusions to be drawn about social causality.[27] On the one hand, the distinction Brecht is making between Gestus and 'social Gestus' can be interpreted as part of his attempt to distinguish Marxist theatre from other theatre which may present comportments and attitudes, but attempted in such a manner that the presentation has non-Marxist fatalist or individualist undertones. Brecht's comments on the 'look of the hunted dog' mentioned above would appear to vindicate this interpretation. Arguing along similar lines Helmut Heinze relates the 'social Gestus' issue to Max Weber's distinction between personal behaviour, such as religious contemplation, which is socially oriented and that which is not. Heinze attributes Brecht's lack of interest in *Haltungen* isolated from their social context ('empty Gestus') to Brecht's

---

[23]'Gestik', c. 1951, *BFA*. vol. 23. p. 188. See also Fowler's translation, *op. cit.*, p. 36.
[24]Fowler, *op. cit* ., p. 33
[25]*ibid.*, pp. 31, 33.
[26]'Über gestische Musik', p. 330. See also Fowler's translation, *op. cit.*, pp. 32–33 and Brecht, *BT*, p. 104.
[27]Fowler, *op. cit.*, p. 33.

sociological perspective with its focus on what occurs between people and the formation of the individual through social relations.[28]

On the other hand, Brecht's use of the phrase 'social Gestus' is also a symptom of an uncertainty which pervades Brecht's writings on Gestus about whether there is a realm of human experience which can be separated from the socially significant, one which incorporates both so-called 'private' and accidental gestures. As Fowler suggests, Brecht's claim that not all gests are social would seem to contradict the maxim that social being determines consciousness.[29] Several critics tackle the problem of the Gestus/social Gestus distinction made in 'On Gestic Music' by dismissing it as a transitory phenomenon, one which is abandoned in later works.[30] However, while the distinction between the two terms is not directly discussed again, the use of the phrase 'social Gestus' is by no means transitory, appearing in the 'Short Description of a New Technique of Acting which Produces a Defamiliarisation Effect' 1940 and, even as late as 1948, in 'A Short Organum for the Theatre'.[31] Admittedly, the phrase does not feature in the later writings, 'Gesticulation' and '[On Gestus]' 1951, where its meaning appears to be subsumed once again under the umbrella term Gestus.

Yet while the phrase has been dropped, the distinction is still ominously present, this time in the guise of a distinction between gestural activity and Gestus. In 'Gesticulation', for instance, Brecht explains that the carrying out of a piece of work (involving a gestural complex etc.) is not a Gestus when it contains no social relation like exploitation or co-operation. Not only does this comment show that an ambivalence concerning the socially significant nature of all human activity was maintained; it also directly contradicts Brecht's Marxist pronouncement in 'On Gestic Music' that a work Gestus is definitely a 'social Gestus' 'because all human activity directed towards the mastery of nature is a social undertaking, an undertaking between men'.[32]

Brecht's indecisiveness about whether Gestus incorporates so-called 'private' gestures, including some psychological expressions and physiological states and reflexes, permeates his theoretical explanations. In the 'Short Organum', while the phrase 'social Gestus' rears its head, there are signs of greater certainty that even 'private' gestures are socially significant:

> The realm of attitudes/comportments [*Haltungen*] adopted by the characters towards one another is what we call the gestic realm. Bodily disposition/attitudes, [*Körperhaltung*] tone of voice, and facial expression are all determined by a social 'Gestus': the characters curse, compliment, instruct one another, and so on. The attitudes [*Haltungen*] which people adopt towards one another include even those which would appear to be quite private, such as expressions of physical pain during illness, or of religious faith.[33]

---

[28]Heinze, *op. cit.*, pp. 138–139.
[29]Fowler, *op. cit.*
[30]Ritter, *op. cit.*, pp. 16–17. Barry Joseph Batorsky, '*Gestus*' *in the Theaters of Brecht and Beckett* (Michigan: University Microfilms International, 1990), p. 51; Hansjürgen Rosenbauer, *Brecht und der Behaviorismus* (Bad Homburg: Gehlen, 1970), p. 61.
[31]Brecht, 'Kurze Beschreibung einer neuen Technik der Schauspielkunst, die einen Verfremdungseffekt hervorbringt', p. 646; 'Kleines Organon für das Theater', summer 1948, *BFA*, vol. 23, p. 89.
[32]Brecht, 'Über gestische Musik'. p. 330.
[33]Brecht, 'Kleines Organon für das Theater'. p. 89. See also Fowler's translation, *op. cit.*, p. 35 and Brecht, *BT*, p. 198.

At an earlier date Brecht was less certain. According to 'On Gestic Music' a Gestus of pain, 'as long as it is kept so abstract and generalised that it does not rise above a purely animal category, is not yet a social Gestus'.[34] It would be easy to attribute this incongruity to the evolutionary process of Brecht's thinking, to regard the 'Short Organum' as the product of a more advanced stage in the development of a Marxist political aesthetic, a development which had involved moving away from a bourgeois individualist notion of the private life of the autonomous subject towards a concept of the dialectical interplay between the 'private' and the 'social'. Yet as Brecht's 1951 commentary on the man carrying out a piece of work suggests, uncertainty about the social significance of gestures continued into the fifties.

Not only the Gestus/social Gestus distinction but also Brecht's ambivalent treatment of illustrative and expressive gestures are symptomatic of an uncertainty about the boundaries of the socially significant. Throughout the entire span of his theoretical writings Brecht spends much time caught between dispelling expressive gestures from the concept of Gestus or blurring the two together. These opposing tendencies are both manifest in 'On the Use of Music in an Epic Theatre' 1935. After explaining that the arts must cultivate the Gestus and that this means paying attention to 'socially meaningful gesticulation, not illustrative or expressive gesticulation',[35] Brecht goes on to describe a number of musical Gestus in a manner which makes them appear indistinguishable from the very type of expressive gestures he has just dispelled from the realm of Gestus. For example, there are references to an 'heroic yet naturally cheerful' and a 'severe, yet delicate and rational Gestus'.[36] Years later in 'Gesticulation' 1951, Brecht appears quite comfortable defining Gestus as a complex including illustrative gestures 'such as those which describe the size of a cucumber or the curve of a racing car' and expressive gestures 'which demonstrate spiritual attitudes: contempt, tension, helplessness and so on'.[37] Yet while from a Marxist perspective a progressive step is made towards breaking down the bourgeois concept of a private life separate from the public, the problematical lack of a real distinction between Gestus and gesture is perpetuated. This is due to the fact that Brecht maintains that a Gestus may consist simply of a basic attitude [*Grundhaltung*] such as 'that of satisfaction or of waiting'. In what way these basic attitudes are distinguishable from expressive gestures which demonstrate contempt, tension, and helplessness remains unclear.[38]

Fowler's examination of the contradictory use of terminology in Brecht's Gestus definitions makes clear that, whilst there is a consistently 'red thread' in Brecht's discussion of the matter, the concept carries with it ambivalences regarding the relation between two categories, the first being physiological reflexes or activities and what Brecht classes as 'private' gestures – for example, accidental falling on ice, brushing a fly away, work activities, 'private' prayer and physical pain in illness – and the second category being contextualised social bearings. As Fowler points out, critics have tended to focus on the 'red thread' without exploring the reasons for a generally perceived conceptual 'obscurity' and 'opaqueness'.[39] Brecht's theories have been treated as an homogeneous

---

[34]Brecht, 'Über gestische Musik'. p. 330. See also Brecht, *BT*. p. 104.
[35]Brecht, 'Über die Verwendung von Musik für ein episches Theater'. p. 158. See also Brecht, *BT*. p. 36.
[36]Brecht, 'Über die Verwendung von Musik für ein episches Theater'. p. 162. See also Brecht, *BT*, p. 88.
[37]Brecht, 'Gestik'. p. 188. See also Fowler's translation, *op. cit.*, p. 36.
[38]*ibid.*
[39]Fowler, *op. cit.*, pp. 38–40.

whole rather than a bundle of fragments, of thoughts in progress. Thus Patrice Pavis, whilst aware that the term remains 'very vaguely and contradictorily defined', nevertheless proceeds to iron out contradictions:

> The distinction between an *individual* gesture and a *socially* encoded one is also quite irrelevant to *Gestus*. For Brecht, gesture is not the free and individual part of man in opposition to the collective domination of language and ideology .... He does not own it personally; it belongs and refers to a group, a class, a milieu.[40]

This of course is the direction in which Brecht's thinking was moving, at least as it is reflected in his theoretical writings, but the comment does not describe the stony path and recurrent ambivalences.

### 1.4 Mimik *to* Gestik: *Psyche to Customs*

Fowler's analysis is self-admittedly focused on definitions of Gestus and gestic music. However, when his approach is extended to writings on acting and the performer where the term Gestus is not necessarily accompanied with a definition, it reveals that terminological confusions are nowhere more pronounced than when Brecht deals with the living human actor. Moreover, it is here that Brecht's tendency to blur Gestus with *Geste* and *Gestik* not only comes to the fore but is revealed as crucial to his rejection of bourgeois theatre and its purported emphasis on facial movement at the expense of gesticulation.[41] In the following quotations from statements related to acting theory it is difficult to ascertain which of the three Gestus definitions – expressive gesture, contextualised social bearing and the rhetorical gestures of a performer – Brecht is utilising:

> In this way the artist separates facial expression (showing observation) from gesture (showing a cloud), but without detracting from the latter, since the body's attitude/ posture [*Haltung*] is reflected in the countenance and is wholly responsible for its expression. At one moment the expression is of well-managed restraint; at another, of utter triumph! The artist has been using his face as a blank sheet, to be inscribed by the Gestus [social bearing?] of the body.
>
> 'Defamiliarisation Effects in Chinese Acting' 1936[42]

> My face is made-up, cleansed of
> All exceptional features, made empty, to mirror
> The thoughts, henceforth changeable like
> Voice and Gestus [*Gestik* ?].
>
> 'Make-Up' c. 1937.[43]

---

[40]Patrice Pavis, 'On Brecht's Notion of *Gestus*', in Patrice Pavis, *Languages of the Stage: Essays in the Semiology of the Theatre* (New York: Performing Arts Journal Publications, 1982), p. 44.
[41]Ritter notes that when Brecht speaks of the importance of the Gestus of the actor he mentions the shift from a *mimische* principle to a gestic principle. As Ritter explains, this shift involves the rejection of a 'cultivation of psychological conflicts' and their direct expression through facial expression. See Ritter, *op. cit.*, p. 18.
[42]Brecht, 'Verfremdungseffekte in der chinesischen Schauspielkunst', 1936, *BFA*, vol. 22.1, p. 201. See also Brecht, *BT*, p. 92.
[43]Brecht, 'Schminke', c. 1937, *BFA*. vol. 14 (1993), p. 376.

A simple method for the actor of defamiliarising the Gestus [*Gestik* ?] is to separate it from facial expression. He only need put on a mask and follow his actions in the mirror. In this way he will easily arrive at a selection of gestures which are rich in themselves. It is precisely because the gestures are selected that a V-effect occurs....

*Style and Naturalness*

The naturalness of the gestures and intonations must not be lost during the process of selection. It is not a matter of stylisation. In the case of stylisation gesture and intonation 'mean something' (Fear, Pride, Pity, etc.). A Gestus [*Geste, Haltung*] that is brought about through such stylisation reduces the flux of reactions and actions of the characters to a series of rigid symbols.

'Bringing out the V-effect' c. 1938[44]

Training in the athletic arts (dancing, fencing, even wrestling) is certainly important for the actor, because he must be able to master his body. However, it is even more important that he learn to communicate the Gestus [*Gestik*, comportment?] to his entire body, which needs training in the sensual.

'Athletic Training' c. early 1940[45]

All the time I changed myself into an actor,
showing
Gestus [*Gestik* ?] and intonation of a character and you
Changed yourself into a writer. Neither I nor you
Stepped out of our role.

'Letter to the Actor Charles Laughton with Regard to the Work on the Play "Life of Galileo"' c. 1946[46]

During rehearsal you should avoid speaking loudly as one hears oneself so badly. Loudness also brings certainty with it, and, when rehearsing, one should, with honest uncertainty, search for the intonation in the search for the Gestus [*Geste* ?].

'[Advice for Actors]' c. 1951[47]

Common to all these examples is the emphasis on the gestural side so that Gestus at times appears synonymous with gesture, and not an obviously 'socially significant' gesture at that! – despite Brecht's comment in 'On Gestic Music' that 'one should not understand Gestus as gesticulation'.[48] In several of the cases, this emphasis is attributable to the fact that Gestus is listed alongside vocal means of expression as if it were just one of the actor's tools. Furthermore, given Brecht's description of Gestus in c. 1940 as 'a complex

---

[44]Brecht, 'Hervorbringen des V-Effekts', c. 1938, *BFA*, vol. 22.1, pp. 355–356. See also Flower's partial translation of this section. *op. cit.*, p. 34.
[45]Brecht, 'Die athletische Ausbildung', c. early 1940, *BFA*, vol. 22.2, p. 615. See also Fowler's translation. *op. cit.*, p. 37.
[46]Brecht, 'Noch zerfleischten sich unsere Völker' from 'Brief an den Schauspieler Charles Laughton, die Arbeit an dem Stück "Leben des Galilei" betreffend', c. 1946, *BFA*, vol. 15 (1993), p. 180.
[47]Brecht, '[Ratschläige für Schauspieler]', c. 1951, *BFA*, vol. 23, pp. 183–184. See also Fowler's translation, *op. cit.*, pp. 37–38.
[48]Brecht, 'Über gestische Musik', p. 329. See also Brecht, *BT*, p. 104.

of gestures, facial expressions, and, usually statements, which one or more persons direct at one or more persons',[49] it would seem that making a distinction between Gestus proper and verbal expression is unnecessary, unless of course, Gestus is being used here simply to mean gesticulation.

As some of the examples above also demonstrate, Brecht's emphasis on the gestural side of Gestus is linked to his move away from a pattern of movement which focuses on facial expression. He is interested in the image of the face as a blank sheet, to be inscribed upon by the Gestus of the body and as a made-up surface, cleansed of exceptional features. The associated rehearsal technique is the wearing of a facial mask in order better to concentrate on the selection and execution of non-facial gestures. The tendency to regard facial expression as secondary is connected to Brecht's concern that the face is given an overly central position in bourgeois theatre as a mirror of the individual psyche. This theory is captured in a fragment from *Der Messingkauf* dialogues:

> The art of facial expression [*Mimik*] was given a tremendous boost when playwrights constructed long, tranquil, soulful acts and you could get good opera-glasses from the manufacturers. Faces had a lot going on in them in those days; they became the mirror of the soul, which meant that they had to be held very still, so that gesticulation dried up. It was all a matter of feelings; the body was just a container for the soul. The facial expressions varied from night to night; you couldn't count on them; too many factors were involved. But gestures were even less organised; they mattered almost as little as in the case of orchestral musicians, who also execute all kinds of gestures as they play.[50]

An earlier piece on 'The Retention of Gestures Through the Generations' 1935 further testifies to Brecht's concern that facial expression is somehow associated with expression of a private rather than social origin:

> Only he who has the typical superficial formulations of Western actors in mind – who create their characters merely out of small nervous [facial] features [*Zügen*] that have little to say and are more or less of private origin, signifying nothing typical – will not be able to imagine that alterations to gestures can mean really fundamental innovations in the creation of a character.[51]

While Brecht may be referring simply to character traits or nervous features of any sort, the German word *Zug* selected as the signifier of the concept 'features' is associated with facial features. By claiming that the small nervous features of the Western actor are more or less of private origin, Brecht again suggests that there is a private realm of behaviour separate from the realm of the socio-economically significant.

Complementary to this association of facial expression with the expressions of the psyche is Brecht's linking of gesture with customs and manners. In his commentary on the singing of the songs in *The Threepenny Opera*, Brecht says that the epic performer does not

---

[49]Brecht, '[Über den Gestus]', p. 616.
[50]Brecht, 'B160', from 'Der Messingkauf', c. 1945, *BFA*, vol. 22.2, p. 821. See also Brecht, *The Messingkauf Dialogues*. trans. and ed. John Willett (London: Methuen, 1965), p. 28. Brecht's tendency to link facial expression/*Mimik* with psychologising can be traced back to his early commentary on the work of the comedian Karl Valentin. See Brecht, 'Karl Valentin', autumn 1922, *BFA*, vol. 21. p. 102. In this fragment he praises both Valentin and Charlie Chaplin for their almost total rejection of *Mimik* and cheap 'psychologisms'.
[51]Brecht, 'Die Beibehaltung der Gesten durch Verschiedene Generationen', April/May, 1935, *BFA*, vol. 22.1, pp. 128–129.

concentrate on the emotional content of the song so much as the presentation of gestures 'which are the habits and customs of the body'.[52] And in a footnote to the section on opera in the notes on *The Rise and Fall of the City of Mahagonny* 1930, the gestic is again connected with the presentation of customs: 'The eye which directs everything towards the gestic is the moral sense. That is, the delineation of customs [*Sittenschilderung*]'.[53] Habits and customs are the embodiment of routinised social behaviour derived from a particular social background. As such they are of course much more visible traces of socio-economic inscription than facial expressions of the soul.

Heinze has cautioned that, while Brecht often uses the terms Gestus and *Geste* interchangeably, they should be regarded as interwoven rather than synonymous. He describes Gestus as the content or meaning of a gesture and admits that this content is none other than a complex of social relations which come into being and are expressed through material gestures. Drawing on Brecht's statement that the same Gestus may be expressed by any number of words and/or physical movements, Heinze goes on to define Gestus as the immaterial conceptual pendant to the sensual gesture, as abstract knowledge about social relations.[54] Indeed the arrival at a *Grundgestus* ('fundamental/basic Gestus') for an entire scene or play, an aspect of Gestus which will be discussed in further detail later, does require a high degree of intellectual analysis and synthesis. However, the dichotomous division into immaterial and material, or intellectual and sensual, does not seem to capture adequately the way Brecht repeatedly interweaves the two. For instance, when Brecht refers to the Gestus of an actor or character he is referring both to physical comportment (the sensual signifier) and its social significance (the more abstract meaning). His description of gesture as socially coded also reflects the way he regards gesture as both sensual human movement or posture and expression of social relations. Perhaps a more fruitful way of distinguishing Gestus and *Geste* as they are applied in Brecht's theatre is to regard the former as an artistic and ideological selection and combination of the latter.

The presentation of the term Gestus as synonymous with *Geste* is symptomatic of Brecht's attempt to create an approach to acting and a body language which he believes better explicates the premise that social being determines consciousness. Therefore, tracing the interchangeability of Gestus, *Geste* and *Gestik* in his writings not only illuminates ideologically resonant uncertainties about the relation between 'private expressive' and 'social' gesture, as Fowler has suggested, but reveals the political importance to Brecht of emphasising the close relationship between Gestus and physical gesture.

### 1.5 *German to English: Mincing with Words*

While Brecht's usage of the term Gestus and related words *Geste* and *Gestik* may be a bad dream, English translations are often a sheer nightmare. Firstly, when Gestus is being used in accordance with its meaning(s) in Latin there is no English equivalent except perhaps for the archaic term 'gest'. And then there is the issue of whether Brecht is simply using the term instead of *Gestik*, in accordance with conventional usage in the German

---

[52] 'Anmerkungen zur "Dreigroschenoper"', 1930, *BFA*, vol. 24, p. 65. See also Brecht, *BT*, p. 45.
[53] Brecht, 'Anmerkungen zu Oper "Aufstieg und Fall der Stadt Mahagonny"', autumn 1930, *BFA*, vol. 24, p. 77. See also Brecht, *BT*. p. 36.
[54] Heinze, *op. cit.*, pp. 118–124.

language. In those cases where Brecht does seem to be using the term in a conventional sense, Fowler suggests that it may be misleading to use the term 'Gestus' or 'gest' in a translation.[55] However, to avoid falling into the trap of ironing out the inconsistencies of usage, I would suggest that the term always be translated as 'Gestus' and that, if necessary, further commentary be provided in parentheses as exemplified in this thesis.

Translations can be doubly obfuscating if they combine an insensitivity to the term's multiple uses with a neglect of its historical development. Willett's translation of a Gestus definition in 'On the Use of Music in an Epic Theatre' 1935 is a case in point:

> This means, from the aesthetic point of view, that the actors' social gest [*Gestus*] becomes particularly important. The arts have to begin paying attention to the gest [*Gestus*]. (Naturally this means socially significant gest [*Gestik*], not illustrative or expressive gest [*Gestik*].) The gestic principle takes over, as it were, from the principle of imitation.[56]

Willett collapses the two terms Gestus and *Gestik* together and thereby starts a process whereby Brecht's uncertainty about the distinction between the two is erased. At the same time Willett recognises that there is indeed a distinction being made here between the two terms and tries to rectify the situation by referring to the actor's Gestus as 'social', even though this adjective does not appear in the original German. And in doing so Willett creates yet another of those intriguing Gestus/social Gestus divisions. As well, according to the time references given in the new edition of Brecht's works, this introduction of the division would also be premature.

Understanding in the English-speaking realm is also hindered by difficulties encountered in translating other key terms either related to Gestus or to the discussion of *Gestik*. One term which invariably appears in any discussion of what the Gestus is intended to demonstrate is the word *Haltung* which Willett translates as 'attitude'. Several critics have exposed this translation as problematical. In an article on the centrality of *Haltung* to Brecht's thinking, Darko Suvin gives preference to the terms 'bearing' and 'stance'. As Suvin asserts, *Haltung* is in German

> (as most other Brechtian terms) a fruitful polysemy or pun meaning bearing, stance, attitude, posture, behavior, and also poise or self-control. I prefer the first two terms, which I think translate the two main elements of *dynamics* and of *full bodily involvement* better than Willett's usual translation of 'attitude', and I shall use here 'bearing' because of the pleasing pun in English to other meanings and homophones of this word .... Brecht was constantly preoccupied with *Haltung* as a union of a subject's body-orientation in spacetime and of that body's insertion into major societal 'flows of things'.[57]

Batorsky's thesis on the role of Gestus in the theatres of Brecht and Beckett focuses on a further shortcoming of the translation 'attitude' and gives preference to the term 'comportment' instead:

---

[55]Fowler, *op. cit.*, p. 43.
[56]Brecht, *BT*, p. 86.
[57]Darko Suvin, 'Brecht: Bearing. Pedagogy. Productivity'. *Gestos*, vol. 5, no. 10 (1990). 12.

> John Willett's more common translation, 'attitude', leaves the term too ambiguous on the level of social significance. 'Attitude' connotes too much a psychological disposition. 'Comportment' carries the sense of an external, social position-taking. It connotes a program, a social project, while 'attitude' has the sense of a personal idiosyncrasy. The programmatic sense is closer to the way Brecht uses the term *Haltung* when he describes the gest.[58]

However, it could be argued that the terms 'bearing', 'stance' and 'comportment' are themselves limited by a connotational emphasis on outward conduct. Can they be regarded as adequately embracing the idea of emotional expression which Brecht does include in his references to *Haltung* and Gestus:

> An excellent way of judging a piece of music with a text is to try out in which attitude [*Haltung*], with which Gestus the performer ought to deliver the individual sections: politely or angrily, modestly or contemptuously, approvingly or argumentatively, craftily or without calculation.[59]

In the above case the translation 'attitude' would seem a more appropriate choice since both *Haltung* and Gestus are being described as the expression of a mental and emotional response towards something. Willett's translation, with its emphasis on posture which implies a mental state, seems appropriate in those cases where Brecht incorporates emotionally expressive gesture in his definition of Gestus.

Yet as Suvin aptly points out, Brecht is a master of polysemy and therefore no single translation is likely to prove totally adequate. Perhaps the most fruitful approach is to draw attention to the problematical nature of the term by offering more than one translation in order to indicate that the concept embraces both attitude and full bodily expression of social bearing and position-taking. The problem that then arises is the blurring of the two terms *Haltung* and Gestus. Indeed, Brecht often presents the two as synonymous, one example being the 1951 article in which he equates Gestus with the fundamental or basic *Haltung* of a person 'like satisfaction or waiting'.[60] Perhaps the main distinction between these terms is that Gestus refers not only to human behaviour in general but to the artistic practice of selecting, defamiliarising and showing certain significant *Haltungen*.

A final translation issue which has some 'bearing' on Brecht's 'attitude' towards the gestural nature of Gestus, (nightmare intended!) concerns the translation of the term *Mimik*. In German the word can mean simply the totality of movements in the face that express emotions, thoughts and so on. It can also denote the change in expression of both facial movements and other gestures either as a form of self-expression or in the imitation of another's experience. In one German-English dictionary *Mimik* may be translated simply as 'facial expression' while in another it is presented as meaning 'mimicry' or 'miming'.[61] In his translations Willett frequently opts for 'mime', presumably intending it to be used in the sense of 'to mimic' or 'imitate'. The resultant versions can

---

[58]Batorsky, *op. cit.*, p. 50.
[59]Brecht, 'Über gestische Musik', p. 331. See also Brecht, *BT*, p. 105.
[60]Brecht, 'Gestik', p. 188.
[61]Compare Peter Terrell (ed.) et al., *Collins German-English, English-German Dictionary* (London: Collins, 1980), p. 459 with Harold T. Betteridge (ed.), *Cassell's German-English, English-German Dictionary* 12th ed. (London: Cassell 1978), p. 417 and Karl Wildhagen and Will Héraucourt, *Wildhagen German-English Dictionary*, vol. 2 (Wiesbaden and London: Brandstetter, Allen and Unwin, 1972), p. 886. For a definition of the German words

be problematical for two reasons. Firstly, in English 'mime' is commonly used to signify a special sort of mimic art typified by the omission of any sort of verbal communication. And if Brecht had intended this as the meaning, he would have used either the word *Mime* or *Pantomime*, as he does in 'Gesticulation' when he describes *Pantomime* as a form of art where everything is expressed without language and speech.[62] One problem with Willett's translation is that the English-speaking reader may apply the common usage of the term 'mime' and consequently mis-read Brecht's article. Secondly, Willett employs this translation when Brecht is trying to make a distinction between facial expression and gesticulation. The following two translations [cf. my translations footnoted 42 and 50 in the text above] exemplify this point:

> In this way the artist separates mime [*Mimik*] (showing observation) from gesture [*Gestik*] (showing a cloud), but without detracting from the latter, since the body's attitude [*Haltung*] is reflected in the face and is wholly responsible for its expression …. The artist has been using his countenance as a blank sheet, to be inscribed by the gest [*Gestus*] of the body.[63]
>
> Mime [*Mimik*] started suddenly flourishing when playwrights constructed long, tranquil, soulful acts and you could get good opera-glasses from the manufacturers. Faces had a lot going on in them in those days; they became the mirror of the soul, which meant that they had to be held very still, so that the art of gesture [*Gestik*] dried up. It was all a matter of feelings; the body was just a container for the soul. This miming [*Mimik*] varied from night to night; you couldn't count on it; too many factors were involved. But gestures were even less organised …[64]

The second of the two translations, in blurring the *Gestik/Mimik* distinction, suggests that the aspect of bourgeois theatre Brecht is criticising is the focus on mimic art, when, in fact, Brecht neither in theory nor practice rejected mimicry or imitation *per se* – they had of course to be supplemented by defamiliarising processes – but rather an emphasis on facial expression of the soul at the expense of total body, including gestural, mimicry of social behaviour. That Brecht associated the emphasis on facial expression with psychologising is suggested by the way later in the fragment he attributes the emphasis to 'the Russian school', meaning the Stanislavskian proponents of psychological realism.

Willett's translation of *mimische*, the adjectival form of the noun *Mimik*, is also on occasion similarly problematic. For example, in the translation of Brecht's 1935 article on the use of music in epic theatre, in which Brecht describes the '*gestische* principle' as taking over from the '*mimische* principle', Willett translates the latter phrase as 'the principle of imitation'. In doing so he represses the way, even during the early twenties, Brecht often used the term *mimische* specifically and idiosyncratically to denote not simply 'mimic' or 'imitation' but psychologising theatre and its orientation around facial expression.[65] The supplanting of the '*mimische* principle' by the '*gestische* principle' entails not simply a

---

*Mimik, mimische* and *mimetisch* see: Wahrig, *Brockhaus Wahrig: Deutsches Wörterbuch*, vol. 4, pp. 676–677; Drosdowski (ed.). *Duden: Das große Wörterbuch der deutschen Sprache*, vol. 4, pp. 789–790.
[62]For a definition of 'mime' see Simpson and Weiner, *The Oxford English Dictionary*, vol. 9, pp. 789–790. For Brecht's use of *Pantomime* see Brecht. 'Gestik', p. 187.
[63]Brecht, *BT*, p. 92. See *BFA*. vol. 22.1, p. 201 and footnote 42.
[64]Brecht, *The Messingkauf Dialogues*, p. 28. See 'B160', from 'Der Messingkauf', p. 821, and footnote 50.
[65]For examples of Brecht's usage see: 'Karl Valentin', p. 102; 'Hanns Eisler', *Schriften zum Theater*, vol. 6, (Frankfurt on Main: Suhrkamp, 1964), p. 232; 'Verfremdungseffekte in der chinesischen Schauspielkunst',

replacement of photographic imitation with critical defamiliarising forms of imitation, but a shift away from the bourgeois theatre's emphasis on the individual psyche towards the expression of social *Haltung*. In this instance the phrase '*mimische* principle' is perhaps better translated as the 'principle of psychologising and of naturalising imitation'.

The translation difficulties surrounding the key terms Gestus, *Gestik*, *Haltung* and *Mimik* illuminate further reasons for the obscurity of the concept, particularly for an English speaking public. Brecht's poetically multivalent use of language, and German-English translators' inadequate solutions to the problems such a language raises, have not only contributed to the elusiveness of the concept but made a study of historical development of associated ambiguities well nigh impossible.

---

p. 201; 'Antigonemodell 1948. Vorwort', BFA, vol. 25, p. 80. For an argument similar to my own, see Ritter, *op. cit.*, pp. 18, 128–129.

*Fabel*

# CHAPTER SIX

# The *Fabel*

BERTOLT BRECHT
TRANSLATED BY ROMY FURSLAND

The magic must first be debunked, and then of course recreated. It is just important to be aware – when the skeleton is revealed, for example that this is not all there is. The flesh and the organs have already been removed. But the skeleton on its own has no life. You end up with a sort of profane anatomy, a bone structure; but of course you are not finished yet.

When I critically analyse a work, I throw that work into crisis, I criticise it. This means it has to prove itself under the most difficult of conditions – it has to show whether it really is a work of art – and in response to the most unartistic of questions. And at the end of all this, it must still exist. There are many, many crises I can subject a work to. The work does not exist because of or for these crises: it simply exists. Crisis is not the purpose of the work.

I change a work fundamentally: in other words, I go to its foundations. But the foundations are not the point. I let the work appear before me in its different permutations partly because I want to get at the scope of it. Its scope is determined by its variability, i.e. the serving of many different interests which run counter to each other.

---

Brecht, '[Die Fabel]', in Brecht, *Schriften*, vol. 3 (Berlin and Frankfurt/Main: Aufbau and Suhrkamp, 1993), pp. 192–3.

# CHAPTER SEVEN

# Brecht, the *'Fable'*, and the Teaching of Directing

CRAIG KINZER

> 'Once in a generation the world discovers a new way of telling a story: this generation's pathfinder is Brecht.'[1]

In the study of stage directing the examples of great directors of the past can provide the student with a variety of directorial techniques and a sense of the cultural and historical context of past production practices. The value of this study, however, is not in its capacity to teach students to replicate those practices or to recreate specific production style. Rather, it can help students develop a personal process, adaptable to a variety of texts and production situations. In examining past masters, the guiding question must be: How can we adapt without merely imitating; learn a sensibility as well as technique; take the living, breathing process of an artist and mold it to our own needs? How can a student director best absorb the working style of a master, acquiring the strengths of a time-tested process, and maintaining the freedom to use those skills in the development of *a personal* directorial style?

Bertolt Brecht stands as perhaps the most significant director and dramatist in twentieth century theatre, 'whose plays and new techniques of staging and acting have provided a personal instrument attuned to the peculiar temper of our time'.[2] In addition to a body of dramatic literature clearly ranking among history's finest, Brecht's legacy includes productions which astounded audiences in his home base of East Berlin as well as London and Paris. Early critics lauded his productions of *Mother Courage* and *Galileo* as signifying a breakthrough in modern dramatic technique. Carl Weber remembers the impact of seeing the 1949 *Mother Courage* production:

> It was the first time I had ever seen people on the stage behave like real human beings; there was not a trace of 'acting' in that performance, though the technical brilliance and perfection of every moment was stunning. The economy of the set, of every prop used, was absolutely overwhelming to one who had seen until then only run-of-the-mill – and sometimes the best – German Theatre. And it was astonishing how the

---

Craig Kinzer, 'Brecht, the "Fable", and the Teaching of Directing', *Brecht Yearbook*, 16 (1991), pp. 24–37.

[1] Kenneth Tynan, *London Observer* (June 26, 1955).
[2] Helen Kritch Chinoy, *Directors on Directing* (New York: MacMillan, 1976), 68.

idea of the play was brought across, without pushing, without hammering into the audience.³

Surely these are laudable qualities every student of directing should strive to achieve in his/her work. But what processual elements in Brecht's work were the source of these strengths? And how best to teach them in the academic environment?

Brecht's position in the academic theater is problematic, marred by the over-abundance of the playwright's own critical theory which has colored our perception of his actual working process. Like the works of Stanislavski, much of what we know and try to teach about Brecht comes to us through his own admittedly polemical writings about the theater, translated into English selectively, sometimes not in chronological order, and without the context of the actual productions to illuminate them.

Brecht's theories are examined in the classroom in order to illustrate what we believe to be 'Brechtian' practice, but we often fail to view the body of critical writing left to us as reflective of an *evolutionary* process, as it were, steps along the road in the artist's development. Moreover, Brecht himself was the ultimate circumstantialist, capable of adjusting his process to suit the needs of his audience, his actors and the story he wanted to tell. This essential fact of Brecht the director has often been lost on students of his drama, relying as we do on the polemical writings of his early period (largely abandoned by Brecht in the Ensemble days at the end of his career). Even the much vaunted and equally misunderstood term *Verfremdungseffekt* (untranslatable and largely misleading to post-Absurdist theater students) was modified and then virtually ignored by Brecht himself during this late period.[4] The notion of an *epic theater*, developed as the paradigm of 'theater for the scientific age', was also abandoned by Brecht in favor of the term 'dialectic theater'.[5] Theory must, then, be approached with caution and, to be thorough and historically fair, in the context of the work itself.

Reconstructions of Brecht's production process are available. First-hand documentation of the actual productions can be found in the exhaustive *Modellbücher*, or model books, compiled by Brecht and his collaborators during the triumphant postwar period at the Berliner Ensemble and elsewhere. David Jones, John Fuegi, and Carl Weber have added immensely to our understanding of how Brecht worked in rehearsal.[6] In searching for a valuable processual key to Brecht's work, the 'fable' emerges as a key directorial device. The 'fable' informed all aspects of his theatrical style, affected work with designers, actors and dramaturgs, and acknowledged the composition and historical position of his audience.

## THE FABLE

According to Carl Weber, one of Brecht's assistants at the Berliner Ensemble in the 1950s, the '"Fable" was, of course, Brecht's preferred term designating a play's plot as it is

---

[3] Carl Weber, 'Brecht as Director', *TDR* 12/1 (1967), 101–102.
[4] John Fuegi, *Bertolt Brecht: Chaos, According to Plan* (New York: Cambridge University Press, 1987), 184.
[5] John Willett, *The Theatre of Bertolt Brecht* (London: Methuen, 1977), 185.
[6] See David Richard Jones, *Great Directors at Work* (Berkeley: University of California Press, 1986), as well as Fuegi and Weber.

retold on stage from a specific point of view, in a clearly defined gestus'.[7] As with many terms in Brecht's dramatic theories, 'gestus' is difficult to translate into English. It can be rendered variously as gist or gesture, attitude or point; 'one aspect of the relation between two people, studied singly, cut to essentials and physically or verbally expressed'.[8] Brecht defines the term as a distillation 'of overall attitudes ... convey-[ing] overall attitudes adopted by the speaker towards other men'.[9] In the context of the fable, jest indicates the central thrust or essence of the play, capturing the director's attitude towards the text. More than a simple plot summary, the fable is intended to reflect the essential action of a play as the director (or production itself) intends it to be perceived by the audience. It indicates not only what happens but a sense of how and why it happens. Out of the numerous possible readings or interpretations of a text one is decided upon and will guide the execution of the production. The fable is an attempt to both capture and reflect that reading in a compact and distilled form.

An example of a fable can be found in *A Short Organum for the Theatre*, Brecht's seminal statement about the art of the theater written shortly before embarking upon his triumphant leadership of the new Berliner Ensemble. He describes a possible production of *Hamlet*:

> It is an age of warriors. Hamlet's father, king of Denmark, slew the king of Norway in a successful war of spoliation. While the latter's son Fortinbras is arming for a fresh war the Danish King is likewise slain: by his own brother. The slain kings' brothers, now themselves kings, avert war by arranging that the Norwegian troops shall cross Danish soil to launch a predatory war against Poland. But at this point the young Hamlet is summoned by his warrior father's ghost to avenge the crime committed against him. After at first being reluctant to answer one bloody deed by another, and even preparing to go into exile, he meets young Fortinbras at the coast as he is marching with his troops to Poland. Overcome by this warrior-like example, he turns back, and in a piece of barbaric butchery slaughters his uncle, his mother and himself, leaving Denmark to the Norwegians.[10]

The salient features of a Brechtian fable are here. This short, seven-sentence paragraph highlights the essential moments of significant action *from this particular director's point of view*. Of the countless possibilities available for *Hamlet* and its central dramatic line, Brecht has developed a particular reading of the play and captures it in the fable.

One can imagine the details of production which would reflect the point of view the fable implies: a harsh and gray world, littered with the signs of the preparations for war and conquest; a somewhat effete and ineffectual Hamlet, bewildered by the inefficacy of his intellectual training; a surrounding cast of fit and brawny Danes, warlike, brutal and quick to action, contrasted with Hamlet's own vacillation and reserve. Moreover, the production this fable reflects grows out of a particular time and place, in this case, the aftermath of World War II. The fable describes a production which would address the audience's memories of their recent past and the failure of rational discourse to stop

---

[7] Carl Weber, 'The Actor and Brecht, or: The Truth is Concrete', in *Brecht: Performance*, eds. John Fuegi, et al., *The Brecht Yearbook*, Volume 13/1984 (Detroit: Wayne State University Press, 1987), 71.
[8] Willett, 173.
[9] Bertolt Brecht, 'On Gestic Music', in *Brecht on Theatre*, Tr. John Willett (New York: Hill and Wang, 1964), 104.
[10] Bertolt Brecht, 'A Short Organum for the Theatre', in *Brecht on Theatre*, 202.

the horrors of world war. In a further note to this fable, Brecht points to the central thrust and impact he wishes his *Hamlet* to have:

> These events show the young man, already somewhat stout, making the most ineffective use of the new approach to Reason which he has picked up at the university of Wittenberg. In the feudal business to which he returns it simply hampers him. Faced with irrational practices, his reason is utterly unpractical. He falls a tragic victim to the discrepancy between such reason and such action.[11]

The brevity and vividness of this fable is the source of its strength and usefulness to the director. A clear, crystallized vision of the intended production reflects the central architecture of the text, and on its structure the more specific detailed choices of all aspects of the performance can be built. How the fable was generated is at the heart of Brecht's process as a director.

The fable was not something which developed in a vacuum, or which sprang solely from the imagination of the director, but was the result of rigorous analysis of text and its implications for the intended audience in a dialectical process with dramaturgs, designers and actors. In those instances when Brecht himself was the dramatist, such discussions informed both the writing and directing process. If a section of dialogue or action was deemed inappropriate to the agreed-upon fable, the playwright was capable of altering his own text accordingly.[12] When the text was by another author, each scene and moment in the play was examined in detail, and choices made about their central action. These choices led to a 'mini-fable', or scene title, for each larger segment of the play's narrative line. The *Couragemodell*, the model book for *Mother Courage*, contains brief smaller fables for each scene, reflecting the two or three essential events of the scene. These mini-fables served as the building blocks of the fable for the play, just as the scenes themselves are the materials out of which the larger drama is constructed.

By giving Brecht a clear central architecture, the fable allowed him the freedom to experiment with options for the delivery of the fable's essential gest. It served as guidepost for the myriad choices made in the production process by designers, actors, composers, as well as the director. The Berliner Ensemble's production 'style', much replicated and studied, was in truth a result of Brecht and his designers choosing only those visual elements which were essential to communicating the fable's basic gest to the audience.[13] The choices of detail made by the actors were similarly guided by the fable's essential gest. Brecht was often quoted as telling an actor, '… you must play the fable', in the execution of a moment of stage life.[14]

The fable was a device whereby Brecht both developed and refined the point of view he wished his production of a play to take. The fable was the point of engagement in the dialectical process of examining a text, testing the choices made in conception and execution, and an inevitable movement towards clarity in production. Through the process of developing it, he and his production team discovered the dynamics of a text, as well as the complexities which the text contained. As a director, Brecht used the fable as a guidepost for the choices which articulated the moment-to-moment reality of the

---

[11] *Brecht on Theatre*, 202.
[12] Weber, 'Brecht as Director', 103.
[13] See John Willett, *Caspar Neher, Brecht's Designer* (London: Methuen, 1986).
[14] Weber, 'The Actor and Brecht', 70.

performed event. These moments are the experiential building blocks which lead the audience to a clear perception of the text and the production's point of view.

## USING THE FABLE IN THE TEACHING OF DIRECTING

Clarity of execution and a strong point of view are at the heart of a director's task and one of the most difficult things to teach students of directing. I have found that students are often reluctant to take a strong stance regarding a moment of stage life, let alone an entire play. And those students who are able to develop a clear perspective on a text *in toto* and execute it in all aspects of their work are even rarer. Students, particularly early in their training, are daunted by the complexities of most plays. The burden of responsibility for guiding the multiple skills and perspectives of their fellow artists in a production enterprise can lead to a kind of creative paralysis, resulting in uncommitted or imprecise execution and frustration for the audience, the production team and the young director.

The technique of developing a fable is a valuable tool in training directors, and for a number of years I have assigned it as a part of a basic directing course.[15] It engages them early in a dialectical process of examination and analysis of a dramatic text; aids them in making strong, clear statements about their point of view of the play, which affect all aspects of their direction; and provides them with an important foundation for making the myriad and often perplexing choices which confront them in design meetings, casting, and rehearsals.

After an initial reading of the play, students are asked to write a rough first fable, 10-15 lines capturing their impressions of the play's central action. In this class all students are assigned a single play on which their work for the term is based. This allows the student a chance to explore in depth the complexities of the text and forces him/her to view the choices in execution made for a particular scene in the context of an entire production. I have also found it helpful to assign texts which the individual student has neither read nor seen before; this aids the student in avoiding preconceptions about the play or production, and helps him/her maintain a perspective on the play approximating that of the first-time viewer.

For the most part, this early fable is a frustrating experience, as students attempt for the first time to grapple not only with the complexities of a text but also with the emerging sense of their responsibilities as directors. Their first fable is often crammed with all of the plot elements they can recall and does not reflect any hierarchy of importance for those events. Conversely, significant plot points are sometimes missed or misunderstood, and language used to describe events is vague or murky. Certain characters make no appearance in the fable whatsoever, while others emerge as dominant forces, central to key events in the play. Points of mystery or questions the play raises in the audience's mind are often answered in the fable long before they would be in performance.

These very shortcomings, however, are useful in pointing the student toward the central issues which must be addressed in order to produce the play and are the beginnings of the dialectical process of analysis and choice essential to the development of a strong point of view. Revising the fable forces the student to analyze the dynamics of the text in greater

---

[15] I am indebted to Carl Weber of Stanford University for introducing me to the concept and usefulness of the fable.

detail and complexity. The effort to capture the essence of the play becomes a process of 'breaking the text open'.

After the initial attempt at a fable the student is assigned the task of developing 'scene titles' or mini-fables for each scene in the play. In order to accomplish this, of course, students must make decisions as to what constitutes a 'scene' or major dramatic event. (As a rule of thumb, students are encouraged to break the play down into 15–20 scenes.) The process of making these choices familiarizes them with the rhythms and dominant structure of the text. Moreover, these scene units will become a structural part of the play's final fable, and therefore the task of defining scene units is integral to the director defining his/her point of view of the play.

Once the play has been broken down, each scene is examined and a title or 'mini-fable' developed. These mini-fables are an exercise in encapsulating the essential action or event of each scene, just as the fable does so for the entire play. Because action is the central focus at this stage, students are encouraged to use active verbs rather than the passive voice in the scene titles. For example, in the second scene of Hellman's *The Little Foxes*, the family engages in a discussion of the upcoming manufacturing deal they have just concluded with a northern businessman. A title which reads, 'The family celebrates their new-found fortune and makes plans to capture it', would be preferable to 'Plans for the deal with Mr. Marshal are discussed'.[16] The first instance begins to capture a sense of the activity and energy of the scene: people on the stage are described as doing something. In the second, the plans are the central focus and the characters are secondary. The scene title reads as weak and passive, and character – surely the central focus of drama – is diminished. Students often struggle with this idea, since in their early work on a play they tend to be more concerned with information than with the particulars of character. Emphasis en action and character at this point in their work aids students in developing a sense of the dynamics of life on the stage, which will help them immeasurably when dealing with actors in rehearsal.

Students also have difficulty at this stage with the emerging concept of 'point of view' as it is reflected in these directorial devices. It is important to emphasize that the point of view contained in the fable is less overt than implied. Phrasing of a scene title or sentence in a fable can connote rather than denote the point of view the director takes.

Choice of verbs can convey the tone of a scene. The subject of a scene title indicates who the director feels is the most important character at that particular moment. In a sense, the fable is an exercise in concise writing. Working within the limitations of the form, the director's writing must be clear and spare, the result of equally precise analysis and decision-making about the play.

At this point in the process, the two exercises are beginning to work in concert with one another. As the student finds appropriate titles for each scene, the fable will consequently be revised to accommodate it and the increased understanding of the play which his/her analysis has engendered. Conversely, finding an accurate scene title can be guided by a strong and concise fable. The student is working on the general and the specific levels simultaneously, each level of analysis playing off the other while leading the student to a greater understanding of the text and its driving energy.

---

[16]This and subsequent examples are drawn from students' work in my classes at Northwestern University (Evanston, Illinois).

Just as developing a fable forces the director to analyze smaller units of the play's action, so does assigning scene titles necessitate a detailed examination of even smaller building blocks of the play – the moment-to-moment action and interaction of the characters. This is often called a 'scene score' in which the director makes decisions about the subjective actions of the characters in each beat of the play. The director is in essence viewing each scene from the point of view of each character in it, defining their actions and constructing their own particular arc or through-line. Like the scene titles and fable, this process will result in greater understanding of the text as a whole and increasingly sophisticated and concise statements in the scene titles and fable.

This process of developing a point of view on a play, through scoring, scene titles and fables, forces the student directors to explore alternative readings for each scene. In Hellman's *The Little Foxes*, for example, Horace's death scene could be titled: a) Regina kills Horace; b) Horace fails to stop Regina's schemes; c) Horace attempts to put a stop to Regina's maneuvers, but using the only weapons she has left, she lashes out at him; his distress brings on a fatal heart attack. These are three clearly distinct directorial readings of a pivotal scene and would result in significantly different performances, among which the director must choose. That choice will be guided by the fable and scene titles which the director is developing.

This three-tiered series of exercises, involving detailed analysis and choice of viewpoint, is a way of involving the director in a dialectical relationship with the material. Each level of engagement with the text will inform and alter the others. A strong fable can clarify significant moments in a scene. A clear and dramatic reading of a scene, captured in a mini-fable, can help illuminate the overall view of the play, as reflected in the fable. A detailed understanding of the moment-to-moment interaction of characters which a scene score provides will lead to a more concise reading of the true thrust of the play. As the process continues, the director will find that not only greater understanding of the play emerges but also that he/she is developing and committing to a personal reading of the text. With thorough preparatory work, that point of view will emerge in performance.

## USE OF THE FABLE BY THE DIRECTOR

As Brecht often said about his own theories, 'the proof of the pudding is in the eating'.[17] The benefits of these tools for the director in production are numerous. Most importantly, through this process of careful analysis and commitment, the director has developed for him/herself a set of tools which can be invaluable guides in the many choices which a director is constantly called upon to make.

The fable is helpful in working with designers to generate the visual elements of a production. A fable for *The Little Foxes* which stresses the conflict between the 'Old South' and the 'New South' might lead the director and designers to decide upon a set which mirrors that conflict. The play could be set in an antebellum home inappropriately furnished with 'nouveau riche' artifacts or in a more modest contemporary home with opulent and ornate decor, clearly reflecting the inhabitants efforts to rise above their station. A fable for O'Casey's *Juno and the Paycock*, which ties the events in the Boyle family to the struggles in Ireland in 1920, would lead to a set which includes the world

---

[17]Quoted in Weber, 'Brecht as Director', 105.

outside their tenement. In *The Little Foxes*, if Regina is viewed as a woman struggling to be free from male domination, her clothing might emphasize her youth and energy, constrained by uncomfortable garment lines. If greed is her driving force, the clothes will be rich and luxurious.

The process through which a director arrives at the fable for a play is analogous to that used by many actors in developing a character. Terms such as super-objective, objective, beat and action find parallels in the devices discussed for the director. Moving from fable to scene titles to scene scoring, the director proceeds through increasing degrees of specificity and detail, much as the actor constructs the details of a performance around a spine, or central architecture of a character.

| ACTOR'S PROCESS | TEXT | DIRECTOR'S WORK |
|---|---|---|
| character super-objective (spine) | play | *fable* |
| objective | scene | *scene title* |
| action (moment) | beat | *score* |

This approach supports work with actors in constructing their performances because the director has had to both develop an understanding of the play from the subjective point of view of each character and commit to a larger framework within which those characters must be viewed by the audience. He/she is therefore able to find ways in which the fable can be enacted in the immediate circumstances of the characters *in action*. In the scene from *The Little Foxes* in which Horace is stricken with a fatal heart attack, Regina's role in inducing his seizure is crucial to an audience's understanding of her as a character and therefore to the thrust of the play. A fable for the play which stresses the element of greed and the lengths that people go to obtain wealth may lead to a scene in which Regina clearly makes up her mind to kill him after he reveals his intention to stifle her plans. In a reading of the play stressing a woman twisted by the constraints of a patriarchal society, no such conscious and therefore malevolent decision will be made. Rather, we will see a Regina fighting back with the only tools left to her. The moment when she realizes Horace is about to die will focus on her recognition of the power she has if she does nothing to aid him. Her discovery is that for the first time in her life she has power and freedom – not because she can kill him but by simply letting things take their course.

I have found the most important benefit of these exercises in the fact that the director must *make choices*. Detailed analysis and clear thinking are necessary in order to make those choices, and through that the director becomes intimately involved in the text and with his/her personal vision of it. Directors can tackle the complexities of a text because they have a clear view of the whole, developed in the fable. They are able work with much greater attention to detail with a strong sense of the framework of the play to guide their choices. The fable is in reality an exercise in concise writing, and as with the Japanese haiku, the demands of the form encourage clarity and precision.

These qualities were a hallmark of Brecht's work as a director and are important among his many significant legacies. I have found that having applied these elements of Brecht's work process to non-Brechtian material and having mastered them, the directing student who moves on to an in-depth study of Brecht's theater is much better equipped to deal with his plays and his theories. They see Brecht in a fuller context, both as theorist and practitioner, polemicist and artist, and are able to reconcile the two in a full sense of his contribution to the theater of our time. They are able to take Brecht at his word:

> If the critics could only look at my theatre as the audience does, with starting out by stressing my theories, they might well simply see theatre – a theatre, I hope, imbued with imagination, humour and meaning – and only when they began to analyse its effects would they be struck by certain innovations, which they could then find explained in my theoretical writings.[18]

---

[18]*Brecht on Theatre*, 248.

# Historicization

# CHAPTER EIGHT

# Art as the Speaker of History

ASTRID OESMANN

Despite their somewhat antagonistic intentions, Brecht, Benjamin, and Adorno form a network of authors that provides an extraordinary approach to history and modernism. In this network, Benjamin is the key mediator between Brecht's concept of forgetting and Adorno's constructions of remembrance. Adorno's aesthetic theory is a meditation on history and memory in the wake of Auschwitz; Brecht's theatrical concept of *Verfremdung* (estrangement) rests on the retrospective presentation of evanescent events; and Benjamin's practice of interpretation is designed to reveal the historicity of the artifacts with which it is concerned rather than revealing history itself.[1] Numerous differences notwithstanding, Brecht, Benjamin, and Adorno all share a retrospective approach to reality. Rejecting any 'realist' approach, they examine reality through a critical gesture that emerges from the tension between past and present.

What unites all three is a shared suspicion of the Enlightenment's philosophy of history, especially of its belief in progress. Marxism shares this belief through its concept of the inevitability of revolution. This rational telos affects the formation of the modern subject in that history becomes a pedagogical project in which the subject matures with historical progress.[2] By defining human virtue in terms of historical progress, an 'enlightened' philosophy of history writes its own history:

> Indem Geschichtsphilosophie die humanen Ideen als wirkende Mächte in die Geschichte selbst verlegte und diese mit deren Triumph endigen ließ, wurden sie der Arglosigkeit beraubt, die zu ihrem Inhalt gehört. ... So aber wird nicht bloß Geschichte unmittelbar in ihr Gegenteil verkehrt, sondern die Idee selbst, welche die Notwendigkeit, den logischen Gang des Geschehens brechen sollte, entstellt. Die Gefahr des Seitensprungs wird abgewandt. Die als Macht verkannte Ohnmacht wird durch solche Erhöhung noch einmal verleugnet, gleichsam der Erinnerung entzogen.

> [By attributing humane ideas as active powers to history, and presenting them as history's culmination, the philosophy of history stripped them of the naivety inherent in their content. ... But not only is history thereby turned into its direct opposite, but

---

Astrid Oesmann, 'Art as the Speaker of History', in Oesmann, *Staging History* (Albany NY: State University of New York, 2005), pp. 17–26 and notes pp. 207–10

[1] Rainer Nägele, 'Reading Benjamin', in *Benjamins Ground: New Readings of Walter Benjamin*, ed. Rainer Nägele (Detroit: Wayne State University Press, 1988), 17.
[2] About the philosophy of history and subject formation in drama, see Astrid Oesmann, '*Nathan der Weise*: Suffering Lessing's *Erziehung!*' *The Germanic Review* 74:2 (1999): 131–45.

the idea, which was supposed to break the necessity, the logical course of events, is itself distorted. The danger of the 'freak event' is averted. Impotence mistaken for power is denied a second time by such elevation, as if erased from memory.]³

Adorno insists that the Enlightenment writes history by viewing its own teleological projections through a retrospective lens. By transforming 'virtuous' ideas into irresistible historical forces, the past is made to appear backward and the future progressive. For Adorno, this entails a denial of history's contingency because any true genealogy of the present will fall victim to the privileging of expectation over the experience of the past. The Enlightenment's philosophy of history rests upon amnesia – an amnesia that Adorno thought equally implicated in the project of a progressive subjectivity and in the catastrophes of twentieth-century German history.

The split between Lukács on the one side, and Brecht, Benjamin, and Adorno on the other takes place along the lines of the philosophy of history, Lukács considers reversed perception to be a constitutive part of capitalism but remains committed to a teleological philosophy *of* history whose Marxist concept of revolution is rooted in Christianity. In contrast, Brecht, Benjamin, and Adorno, in different ways and to different degrees, consult history to reflect on the present. The *memoire involuntaire* (involuntary memory) that has become famous as the nucleus of Benjamin's approach to mass culture and revolution also plays a fundamental role in Adorno's approaches to art and history. While Brecht does not follow Benjamin in taking his cues from either Proust or Baudelaire, his dynamic of remembering and forgetting involves something similar to Benjamin's notion of 'chock' (shock) as the moment when one awakes to an unexpected reality.

According to Adorno's understanding of *memoire involuntaire* (involuntary memory), the subject can perceive true history, the history of the object, only in 'bewußtlose Geschichtsschreibung' (unconscious writing of history). Adorno's model for this is found in Proust, and this *Bewußtlosigkeit* (unconsciousness) ties art to reality: 'Proust, bei dem genaueste ›realistische‹ Beobachtung mit dem ästhetischen Formgesetz unwillkürlicher Erinnerung so innig sich verbindet, bietet das eindringlichste Beispiel der Einheit pragmatischer Treue und – nach Lukács'schen Kategorien – unrealistischer Verfahrensweise' ('Proust, in whose work the most precise "realistic" observation is so intimately connected with the formal aesthetic law of involuntary memory, provides the most striking example of the unity of pragmatic fidelity and – in terms of Lukács' categories – unrealistic method').⁴ Involuntary memory as a form of remembrance occurs independently of subjective intention, which makes it a truer approach to reality than immediate observation. This, of course, brings to mind Freud's insistence that repressed memories are truer than conscious ones. Adorno bases his concept of experience (*Erfahrung*) on *memoire involontaire* (involuntary memory) despite the fact that Proust applies the term only to memories of things that the subject never experienced. Both represent memory as the construction of something new that remains beyond the subject's control.

Adorno roots involuntary memory as 'bewußtlose Geschichtsschreibung' (unconscious writing of history) in the autonomous work of art, a work of art free from the intention of

---

[3] Horkheimer and Adorno, 'Dialektik der Aufklärung', 255. English translation from Horkheimer and Adorno, *Dialectic of Enlightenment*, 186.
[4] Adorno, 'Erpreßte Versöhnung', 258. English translation from Adorno, *'Extorted Reconciliation'*, 222.

the artist and the recipient. The finished artwork differs from that intended by the artist because 'intention' is pure thought, whereas art is thought materialized through labor and matter. In addition, autonomous works of art embody the contradiction between genealogy and appearance. Through the production process, the material can emancipate itself from subjective intention, thus rendering the completed work of art unpredictable and freeing it from the intention of the subject who produced it. Art highlights the separation between subject and object and challenges the subject's need for identification. By resisting identification, autonomous art challenges both subjective meaning and objective rationality because art stands neither for itself nor for something else. It disrupts the *Verblendungszusammenhang* (context of blindness) and opens the possibility both for experience and for historical cognition based on remembering. Experience requires a distinction between the 'identical self' and the subject: 'Die subjektive Erfahrung wider das Ich ist ein Moment der objektiven Wahrheit von Kunst' (The subjective experience [*Erfahrung*] directed against the I is an element of the objective truth of art).[5] This distinction allows the subject to experience its own negativity, and through this true experience, the subject perceives itself as 'objectiv vermittelt' (objectively mediated). This then allows the subject to recognize that the wholeness of the self can only be achieved by dominating the object:

> Ergriffen wird das Ich von dem unmetaphorischen, den ästhetischen Schein zerbrechenden Bewußtsein: das es nicht das letzte, selber scheinhaft sei. Das verwandelt die Kunst dem Subjekt in das, was sie an sich ist, den geschichtlichen Sprecher unterdrückter Natur, kritisch am Ende gegen das Ichprinzip, den inwendigen Agenten von Unterdrückung.
> 
> [The I is seized by the unmetaphorical, semblance-shattering consciousness: that it itself is not ultimate, but semblance. For the subject, this transforms art into what it is in-itself, the historical voice of repressed nature, ultimately critical of the principle of the I, that internal agent of repression.][6]

*Bewußtsein* (consciousness) is the awareness of object-related subjectivity, an awareness that invalidates the false image of the *Ich* (I) and permits the subject to perceive the artwork as the historical representation of nature. By communicating history, autonomous art allows nature to occur. Note that the destruction of the self is tied to the subject's experience of art's language, which works as the 'geschichtlicher Sprecher unterdrückter Natur' (historical voice of repressed nature). Through the destruction of the self, the subject can perceive language as historical and thus recognize that history refers to *das Lebendige* (the living; that which is alive).

Understanding the connection between *das Lebendige* (the living; that which is alive) and history requires criticism that permits the unfolding of the artwork's essential center, the truth content (*Wahrheitsgehalt*), and links it to historical cognition. 'Die geschichtliche Enfaltung der Werke durch Kritik und die philosophische ihres Wahrheitsgehalts stehen in Wechselwirkung' (The historical development of works through critique and the philosophical development of their truth content have a reciprocal relation).[7] Here Adorno

---

[5] Adorno, *Ästhetische Theorie*, 365. English translation from Adorno, *Aesthetic Theory*, 246.
[6] Adorno, *Ästhetische Theorie*, 364–65. English translation from Adorno, *Aesthetic Theory*, 246.
[7] Adorno, *Ästhetische Theorie*, 194, English translation from Adorno, *Aesthetic Theory*, 128.

reveals the connections between his aesthetics and his concept of history by implicating history in one of the most abstract concepts of his aesthetics – the *Wahrheitsgehalt* (truth content). Truth content cannot be determined; instead, it provides a point of reference and a locus for reflection. Reflection upon the truth content links art to philosophy and to what Adorno calls *begreifen* – an untranslatable verb whose meanings range from intellectual understanding or comprehension to more physical grasping, touching, and feeling – thus presupposing critique, the task that links art to history. While reflection preserves the unknowable, labor constructs the historical inversion.[8]

According to Brecht the main task of his theatre is to construct historical inversion that produces *begreifen* (to grasp; to comprehend), a concept closely related to Adorno's vision of comprehension through labor. For Brecht, *begreifen* (to grasp; to comprehend) becomes possible through *eingreifen*, which encompasses several English verbs such as the physical 'to interfere' and the social 'to engage'. Brecht writes, 'Wir können den andern nur begreifen, wenn wir in ihn eingreifen können. Auch uns selbst können wir nur begreifen, indem wir in uns eingreifen' (24:182) (We can only grasp others when we are able to engage in them. We can also only grasp ourselves while we engage in ourselves).[9] The result is not consistency, but rupture, a rupture that allows the emergence of unpredictable history in place of the Enlightenment's coherent historical narratives. Brecht inserts the pain of the past into the staging of the present in order to signify the way that historical trauma constitutes reality. For Brecht, experience is the awareness of violent rupture that destroys the consistency of the historical narrative.

According to Adorno, productive aesthetic theory must follow the rules of the work of art – rules that necessarily remain implicit – because the work of art stands against historical narrative as 'ihrer selbst unbewußte Geschichtsschreibung' (self-unconscious historiography of their epoch).[10] Aesthetics must construct a historical experience out of art. Here, the presence of the subject is essential because 'Kunstwerke lassen desto wahrhaftiger sich erfahren, je mehr ihre geschichtliche Substanz die des Erfahrenden ist' (Artworks may be all the more truly experienced the more their historical substance is that of the one who experiences it).[11] For Adorno, history is a substantive reality in the present that needs to be mediated through the subject's experience of the past. The artwork, as 'sedimentierte Geschichte' (sedimented history), produces historical snapshots for the subject; Adorno's critical work seeks to do the same by combining contradictory elements such as intellect and material. Works of art are material producers of historical images, and images are not merely self-existent facts; they must be manufactured by men. The subject, according to Adorno, can only perceive history through images that come from the subject's history: 'Auf jeder ästhetischen Stufe erneuert sich der Antagonismus zwischen der Unwirklichkeit der imago und der Wirklichkeit des erscheinenden geschichtlichen Gehalts' (At every aesthetic level the antagonism between the unreality of the *imago* and

---

[8]Hohendahl, in *Prismatic Thought*, also remarks on Adorno's distinct notion of Marxism – distinct, as Hohendahl points out, because Adorno replaces the concept of base and superstructure with the concept of nature and labor. Peter Uwe Hohendahl, *Prismatic Thought: Theodor W. Adorno* (Lincoln: University of Nebraska Press, 1995), 213.

[9]All parenthetical citations of Bertolt Brecht appear as (vol.: page) and refer to Bertolt Brecht, *Werke: Große kommentierte Berliner und Frankfurter Ausgabe*, ed. Werner Hecht, Jan Knopf, Werner Mittenzwei, and Klaus-Detlef Müller, 30 vols. (Frankfurt a.M.: Suhrkamp, 1989–2000).

[10]Adorno, *Ästhetische Theorie*, 271. English translation from Adorno, *Aesthetic Theory*, 182.

[11]Adorno, *Ästhetische Theorie*, 272. English translation from Adorno, *Aesthetic Theory*, 183.

the reality of the appearing historical content is renewed).[12] The contradiction between image and reality secures the artworks autonomy; thus, the historical narrative that emerges from the perception of art, while derivative of the subject, is out of its final control.

In *Negative Dialektik* (*Negative Dialectics*), Adorno insists that the images produced by art must be translated. Negative dialectics provide a reading that reveals 'jedes Bild als Schrift' (every image as writing). Thus, as Rolf Tiedemann points out, Adorno's *Bilder* (images) are not *Abbildungen* (facsimiles). Instead, the work of art functions as a kaleidoscope that produces ever-new constellations that break the domination of the subject: 'Das Schriftähnliche solcher Konstellation ist der Umschlag des subjektiv Gedachten und Zusammengebrachten in Objektivität vermöge der Sprache' (What resembles writing in such constellations is the conversion into objectivity, by way of language, of what has been subjectively thought and assembled).[13] Language, as constellation, can condense into a monad that allows the object to emerge. The object needs to open itself to 'einer monadologischen Insistenz' (a monadological insistence),[14] and it is because of its monadological insistence that the object reveals history in general. The monad reveals the object's nonidentity, and history expresses itself through this negative revelation: 'Solche immanente Allgemeinheit des Einzelnen aber ist objektiv als sedimentierte Geschichte. ... Der Konstellation gewahr werden, in der die Sache steht, heißt soviel wie diejenige entziffern, die es als Gewordenes in sich trägt' (But such an immanent generality of something individual is objective as sedimented history. ... Becoming aware of the constellation in which a thing stands is tantamount to deciphering the constellation which, having come to be, it bears within it).[15] The critical unfolding of language as constellation recognizes both the object and its history, a suppressed history that emerges for a moment through the subject's mediation. The subject's intention is to reflect on the object, but the object actually reflects upon the subject. The self becomes subject by thinking itself object, and the subject based on the object is the product of abstraction and alienation. As a result, the object's specific history reveals the history of the subject.

The history of the subject via the history of the object takes more concrete shape in poetry, where language can reach society:

> Die spezifische Paradoxie des lyrischen Gebildes, die in Objektivität umschlagende Subjektivität, ist gebunden an jenen Vorrang der Sprachgestalt in der Lyrik, von dem der Primat der Sprache in der Dichtung überhaupt, bis zur Form von Prosa herstammt. Denn die Sprache ist selber ein Doppeltes. Sie bildet durch ihre Konfigurationen den subjektiven Regungen gänzlich sich ein; ja wenig fehlt, und man könnte denken, sie zeitigte sie überhaupt erst. ... Die Selbstvergessenheit des Subjekts, das der Sprache als einem Objektiven sich anheimgibt, und die Unmittelbarkeit und Unwillkürlichkeit seines Ausdrucks sind dasselbe: so vermittelt die Sprache Lyrik und Gesellschaft im Innersten.

---

[12]Adorno, *Ästhetische Theorie*, 133. English translation from Adorno, *Aesthetic Theory*, 86.
[13]Theodor W. Adorno, *Negative Dialektik* (Frankfurt a. M.: Suhrkamp, 1966), 167–68. English translation from Theodor W. Adorno, *Negative Dialectics*, trans. E. B. Ashton (New York: The Seabury Press, 1973), 165.
[14]Adorno, *Negative Dialektik*, 165. English translation from Adorno, *Negative Dialectics*, 163.
[15]Adorno, *Negative Dialektik*, 165. English translation from Adorno, *Negative Dialectics*, 163.

[The paradox specific to the lyric work, a subjectivity that turns into objectivity, is tied to the priority of linguistic form in the lyric; it is that priority from which the primacy of language in literature in general (even in prose forms) is derived. For language is itself something double. Through its configurations it assimilates itself completely into subjective impulses; one would almost think it had produced them. ... The unselfconsciousness of the subject submitting itself to language as to something objective, and the immediacy and spontaneity of that subject's expression are one and the same: thus language mediates lyric poetry and society in their innermost core.][16]

For Adorno, poetry as autonomous art, with its reduced referentiality, brings literature as close as it can go to language as matter, as script, and thus to social relevance. Adorno and Brecht both see language as the essential mediator between poetry, society, and history. Brecht, like Adorno, develops concepts of microhistory through poetic inquiry, and he inserts history in his plays through his concept of *gestus*, a concept he explains most clearly in his essay 'Über reimlose Lyrik mit unregelmäßigen Rhythmen' (On Rhymeless Verse with Irregular Rhythms):

> Es handelte sich, wie man aus den Texten sehen kann, nicht nur um ein »Gegenden-Strom-Schwimmen« in formaler Hinsicht, einen Protest gegen die Glätte und Harmonie des konventionellen Verses, sondern immer doch schon um den Versuch, die Vorgänge zwischen den Menschen als widerspruchsvolle, kampfdurchtobte, gewalttätige zu zeigen.
>
> (22.1:359)

> [It was, as one can see from the texts, not only a matter of a 'swimming-against-the-current' in a formal sense, a protest against the smoothness and harmony of conventional verse, but always-already of the attempt to show the affairs between men as full of contradictions, conflict-ravaged, violent.]

Brecht may have developed the concept of 'gestisches Sprechen' (gestic speaking) primarily for his poetry, but he did so while constantly thinking about theatre. Accordingly, he describes his concept of *gestus* as 'die Sprache sollte ganz dem Gestus der sprechenden Person folgen' (22.1:359) (the language should entirely follow the *gestus* of the person speaking). Brechts struggle with the historical material for his play *Leben Eduards des Zweiten von England* (*The Life of Edward the Second of England*) led him to develop a language that signifies the complexities and contradictions inherent in historical events. 'Gestisches sprechen' (gestic speaking) poses difficulties for reading and writing because it moves them into the realm of labor. Brecht, moving his discussion back and forth between Marlowe and Shakespeare, gives an example:

Statt zu schreiben:

> Seit sie da Trommeln rührten überm Sumpf
>
> Und um mich Roß und Katapult versank
>
> Ist mir verrückt mein Kopf. ...

---

[16]Theodore W. Adorno, 'Rede über Lyrik und Gesellschaft', in *Noten zur Literatur* (Frankfurt a.M.: Suhrkamp, 1974), 56. English translation from Theodore W. Adorno, 'On Lyric Poetry and Society', in *Notes to Literature*, vol. 1, ed. Rolf Tiedemann, trans. Shierry Weber Nicholson (New York: Columbia University Press, 1991), 43.

schrieb ich:
> Seit diese Trommeln waren, der Sumpf, ersäufend
> Katapult und Pferde, ist wohl verrückt
> Meiner Mutter Sohn Kopf. Keuch nicht!

(22.1:358–59)

[Instead of writing:
> Since they there beat drums over the swamp
> And around me sank steed and catapult
> My head is mad to me. ...

I wrote:
> Since there were drums, the swamp, drowning
> Catapult and horses, is probably deranged
> My mother's son's head. Don't gasp!]

Note that the rewrite eliminates the grammatical 'I' and breaks with the past tense. It also adds another historical dimension – that of the mother – and complicates the meaning of 'verrückt' (deranged) by including the possibility of physical displacement. Finally, Brecht adds an imperative that transforms the stanza from monologue into dialogue. To the macrohistorical presentation of Edward's life, Brecht adds an array of microhistories that become significant in the moment of performance.

Adorno's surprisingly similar concept of natural history takes shape in his essay on Hölderlin entitled 'Parataxis' in which he analyzes a process that he calls 'parataktische Zerrüttung' (paratactical disorder) in terms that resemble the Brechtian *gestus*. 'Parataktische Zerrüttung' (paratactical disorder) rests upon a notion of *Fügsamkeit* (obedience, submission, docility); as in all autonomous poetry, the subject follows the language: 'Losgelassen, freigesetzt, erscheint sie nach dem Maß subjektiver Intention parataktisch zerrüttet' (Set free, language appears paratactically disordered when judged in terms of subjective intention)[17] The destruction of the hypotactical, and thus hierarchical, order of a sentence in order to equate all syntactical elements is familiar from Brecht's concept of 'gestische Sprache' (gestic language). The 'parataktische Zerrüttung' (paratactical disorder) happens despite the subject's intention to establish coherent meaning. In Hölderlin, language-as-object creates the subject – 'Das Subjekt wird es erst durch Sprache' (The subject becomes a subject only through language)[18] – a subject mediated through language-as-object rather than through individual-as-agent.

The destruction of traditional notions of subjectivity and history is essential to Hölderlin's work, but it is the way in which one can trace the formation and destruction of the traditionally unified subject through Hölderlin's stanzas that makes his poetry unique for

---

[17] Theodore W. Adorno, 'Parataxis', in *Noten zur Literatur* (Frankfurt a.M: Suhrkamp, 1981), 475. English translation from Theodore W. Adorno, 'Parataxis', in *Notes to Literature*, vol. 2, ed. Rolf Tiedemann, trans. Shierry Weber Nicholson (New York: Columbia University Press, 1992), 135.

[18] Adorno, 'Parataxis', in *Noten zur Literatur*, 477. English translation from Adorno, 'Parataxis', in *Notes to Literature*, 137.

Adorno: 'Hölderlin hat die Ideale, die man ihn lehrte, ... zur Maxime verinnerlicht. Danach mußte er erfahren, daß die Welt anders ist als die Normen, die sie ihm einpflanzte' (Hölderlin believed in the ideals he was taught; ... internalized them as maxims. Later he was forced to learn that the world is different from the norms that had been implanted in him).[19] The historical experience that one witnesses in Hölderlin's poetry is the experience of difference between the inferiority of the subject and the 'reality' of the outside world. Parataxis, as Adorno observes, creates 'Korrespondenzen' (correspondences) rather than consistency and allows one 'Zeiten durcheinander zu schütteln, Entlegenes und Unverbundenes zu verbinden' (to mix eras together, to connect things that are remote and unconnected).[20] Hölderlin's experience builds along *Fügsamkeit* (obedience; submission; docility) toward pedagogy, at first constituting a virtuous *Innerlichkeit* (inwardness) that faces destruction through his *Fügsamkeit* (obedience; submission; docility) toward language. His poetry thus consists of one of the great contradictions of modern subjectivity: the denial of genealogy for the sake of a consistent pedagogical project of self-formation. Hölderlin presents this process in reverse: the virtue of pedagogy is disguised as violence in the reality of the world.

*Fügsamkeit* (obedience; submission; docility) and confrontation also create the dialectic in Brechts theatre. In contrast to Adorno, however, Brecht draws these insights from the culture of mass society that Adorno seeks to overcome. Brecht's starting point for theatrical dialectics is the 'Zertrümmerung der Person' (shattering of the person), which he considers the historical destruction of bourgeois subjectivity 'aus ihrer Ausdehnung in ihre kleinste Größe, ... und eigentliche Unentbehrlichkeit im Ganzen' (21:320) (from its enlargement to its smallest size, ... and actual expendability within the whole). The effect, for Brecht, is liberating because it denies the subject its fictional control of history, a denial he seeks to replicate in his concept of epic theatre: '*Die epische Form*, als den Vorgängen folgend und sich den Kurven der Realität anpassend, die solche Kurven »macht«, indem sie sie *mitmacht*' (21:320) ( *The epic form*, in following the events and adapting itself to the curves of reality, 'makes' such curves by *participating in* them). Brecht's theatre articulates the moment in which the subject experiences *Fügsamkeit* (obedience; submission; docility) and confrontation, a moment marked by violence. Brecht's concept of *gestus* seeks to articulate this moment that, as he explains, 'ist wohl verrückt / meiner Mutter Sohn Kopf' (22.1:359) (is probably deranged / My mother's son's head). The moment we cease to be in agreement with ourselves, we become able to agree with the historical reality around us. For Brecht, *Einverständnis* (*consent*) is the entrance into the multiple facets of any historical reality, an entrance available only through a commitment to intersubjective activity. This can only occur through language in which the *Ich* (I) emerges as an answer because it is always-already someone else. The *Ich* (I) as someone else derives from *ges-tus as* Brecht's technique of signification. On Brecht's stage this allows the actor citing her or his role to stress the arbitratiness of this signification while simultaneously emphasizing the physical reality of the body on stage. Brecht uses repetition to signify *Vergänglichkeit* (transitoriness), but signification is always a negative form of representation. By rejecting representation, Brechtian *gestus* signifies what it is not.

---

[19] Adorno, 'Parataxis', in *Noten zur Literatur*, 475. English translation from Adorno, 'Parataxis', in *Notes to Literature*, 135.
[20] Adorno, 'Parataxis', in *Noten zur Literatur*, 479. English translation from Adorno, 'Parataxis', in *Notes to Literature*, 138.

The history that Brecht's theatre presents is thus unpredictable. Brecht's technique of insertion blocks the construction of a historical narrative, opting instead to signify the negative side of dramatic representation, and in this way Brecht fulfills Adorno's demand for the construction of historical experience. Adorno's 'Was aber wäre Kunst als Geschichtsschreibung, wenn sie das Gedächtnis des akkumulierten Leidens abschüttelte' (But then what would art be, as the writing of history, if it shook off the memory of accumulated suffering) is answered by Brecht with the destruction of memory in order to unfold the historical event.[21] Brecht's theatre lives within the confrontation between the theoretical model and the theatrical play; he does not attempt to translate one into the other, Adorno's mediating subject differs from Brecht's subject-in-performance, but it is precisely this difference that enables Brecht's theatre to open the stage for the aesthetic, social, and historical truth content so essential to Adorno's philosophy and to do so for a much broader range of people than Adorno could ever speak to.

---

[21] Adorno, *Ästhetische Theorie*, 387. English translation from Adorno, *Aesthetic Theory*, 261.

# CHAPTER NINE

# How Do I Learn to Learn?

BERTOLT BRECHT
TRANSLATED BY ROMY FURSLAND

Learning, an act of acquiring and at the same time discarding. An act of criticism. Doing just as well and doing better. Changing and at the same time retaining one's self. Example: the realistic novel of the previous century. We find there the multi-faceted universe, the great causal complexes, the development of connections etc., dialectics. But the non-productive person does not know how to separate these elements from other, dead, elements. He or she does not know how to make these achievements workable, does not know that they can be repurposed. Does not know how to turn them into a technique, or describe them as such.

My advice: take the entire narrative technique of Balzac and just change the point of view and the address. 'Just'.

Strike report for directors, strike report for workers. 'Depict the Commune the way Zola depicted the war!' Could he depict the Commune? No. And we do not depict war the way he did. For us, the image of a human being emerges in a different way, based on different specifications. Our readers do not 'know' a man by being told the things about him which Zola told us. Different traits characterise him. A different side of him makes him knowable. He has to be placed in different situations in order to reveal himself. Of course, we can learn: in just as many situations, in just as complicated ones. We can learn: adjectives to describe character traits are not enough. Character traits must be developed via plotlines, within a complex of reactions and actions. And mingled with other traits. In order to show 'bravery', the writer must supply situations that show the type of bravery, its 'trajectory', its limits, its causes etc. And the writer must not isolate this trait from other traits; it must not appear chemically pure, but must enter into all kinds of bonds with other traits, show development etc. If we listen to a soldier we end up with an odd and very un-classical definition of the term *bravery*. He will say: so-and-so was brave or not brave, for example … (followed by different behaviours that contradict each other). Certain situations in which you used to be able to (or had to) show bravery now no longer serve to depict bravery or a lack of bravery (modern assaults or patrols). Etc.

---

Brecht, 'Wie lerne ich das Lernen?', in Brecht, *Schriften*, vol. 2 (Berlin and Frankfurt/Main: Aufbau and Suhrkamp, 1993), pp. 487–8.

# Naivety

# CHAPTER TEN

# From Distancing Alienation to Intuitive Naiveté: Bertolt Brecht's Establishment of a New Aesthetic Category

KARL-HEINZ SCHOEPS

Bertolt Brecht has become a 'classic' author, yet especially in the United States his so-called 'epic theater' has enjoyed little popularity. No doubt, there are a number of reasons for this, among them Brecht's Leftist politics and the desire of American audiences to be entertained without being instructed. Furthermore, most directors started with Brecht's theories, using the plays only as vehicles to illustrate theoretical pronouncements. The resulting lifeless productions did little to endear Brechtian theater to either critics or audiences. To be sure, Brecht's theoretical writings from the 1930s and 1940s did contribute to the often heavy-handed theoretical approach to Brechtian theater. However, without reducing the importance of Brecht's theoretical pronouncements, it can be said that his theater came first, his theory second, especially after World War II; theory was 'Das b zum a'.[1] At one point, Brecht even went so far as to state flatly: 'Zu unserer Spielweise gibt es keinen theoretischen Zugang'.[2] Nor did Brecht ever take his own theoretical pronouncements too seriously. This was neatly illustrated when he visited Milan in February of 1956 to attend rehearsals and first performances of his *Threepenny Opera*, staged and directed by the famous Italian theater director Giorgio Strehler. With copies of Brecht's *Short Organum* clasped tightly in their hands, young people approached Brecht, addressing him as 'Meister'. Brecht replied through an interpreter: 'Sagen Sie ihnen, daß ich kein Meister bin'. The young people then proceeded to ask him questions like 'Hier im Organon schreiben Sie, daß das epische Theater ...' Brecht cut them off

---

Karl-Heinz Schoeps, 'From Distancing Alienation to Intuitive Naiveté: Bertolt Brecht's Establishment of a New Aesthetic Category', *Monatshefte*, 81: 2 (1989), pp. 186–98.

[1] Bertolt Brecht, *Gesammelte Werke in 20 Bänden* (Frankfurt, 1967) 17:944. In the text, this edition is quoted as GW, plus volume and page number.
[2] Manfred Wekwerth, *Schriften: Arbeit mit Brecht* (Berlin, 1973) 71.

and replied: 'Was ich im Organon ausführe, gilt nur bis zu einem bestimmten Punkt; ... Nehmen Sie es nicht zu wörtlich. Theater vollzieht sich auf der Bühne.'[3]

Upon his return to Berlin in 1948, after fifteen years of exile, he again had a theater at his disposal where he could experiment and stage his plays. Practical considerations now took precedent over theoretical writings. Brecht also realized that his theories were largely misunderstood, often blocking access to his plays, rather than facilitating it. His theories of alienation and epic theater were translated into a cool and distancing approach to the plays; the result was stilted and lifeless productions. While still in the United States, Brecht had read Max Gorelik's important and influential work on theater, *New Theatres for Old* (1940). In the chapter 'Theatre is a Tribunal', Gorelik somewhat optimistically envisions epic theater as 'a type of theater suited to industrial, scientific and technological America'.[4] He summarized his description of epic theater as follows: 'On the whole the Epic style under the auspices of Piscator and Brecht would seem to resemble a resourceful lecture-demonstration rather than stage production as we have known it. It is in fact freely admitted that there is no sharp dividing line between epic drama and a demonstration in a surgical or chemical auditorium'.[5] When Brecht read this he was shocked to see what his theories had done to his theater:

> Max Gorelik, der in seinem buch *New Theaters for Old* über das epische theater referiert hat, bringt mich mehr und mehr auf die theoretischen lücken: ich sehe seine mißverständnisse. ein eigentümlich puritanischer geruch steigt von der gorelikschen reproduktion auf, etwas laboratoriumhaftes. die ästhetische seite schrumpft zum formalismus zusammen. (das theater eines wissenshaftlichen zeitalters wird zum wissenschaftlichen theater.)[6]

To counter these negative effects Brecht attempted to establish a new approach to his theater and the new aesthetic category of 'naiveté' (*die ästhetische Kategorie des Naiven*). His premature death prevented Brecht from fully developing this category. It was nevertheless a significant shift in his approach to theater that still has not received the attention it deserves. I shall attempt to illustrate this category by using *Urfaust*, *The Days of the Commune*, and *The Visions of Simone Machard* as examples.

Brecht always had an ambiguous attitude toward the German classic poets Goethe and Schiller. He admired their status as national poets and also, in a dialectical fashion, many of their works. When Germany was partitioned after World War II, Weimar, the city of Goethe and Schiller, became part of East Germany, later the German Democratic Republic. The year 1949 provided the one-year-old socialist German republic with an excellent opportunity to counter West German claims to be the sole heir of German traditions by celebrating the 200th anniversary of Goethe's birth. At that time, the official policies of the GDR were still oriented toward a united Germany, and German classics

---

[3] *Theater der Zeit* 11 (1974):37.
[4] Mordecai Gorelik, *New Theatres for Old* (New York, 1940) 442.
[5] Gorelik, p. 427.
[6] Bertolt Brecht, *Arbeitsjournal 1942–1955* (Frankfurt, 1973) 718 (15 January 1945). As soon as it had appeared in 1940, Gorelik sent his book to Brecht, who referred to it several times in his *Arbeitsjournal* (4 March 1941, 16 April 1941, and 25 September 1943), always complaining about the 'Intellektualisierung' and the 'Maschinenkult' in the presentation of his theater.

like Schiller and Goethe could be used to support these policies.[7] Since the Fascists had abused these classics, a new approach had to be found. However, the narrow-minded cultural policies of the GDR at that time (rejection of modernism, experiments branded as 'formalism') hampered such a new approach. In September 1949, Brecht had attended a performance of Goethe's *Faust* in the Deutsches Theater. His reaction was mixed.[8] He agreed that it was necessary to revive the German classics, but he disagreed with the way it was done.

Brecht's *Urfaust* production must be seen as his contribution to the debate on how to adapt the classics to the contemporary world. In 1952, he began preparations for a production of *Urfaust*. At the same time, his friend Hanns Eisler was also working on a libretto for his opera *Johann Faustus*, and the two artists exchanged ideas about their respective experiments. Both Eisler and Brecht chose the pre-Goethean *Faust* in their attempts at going beyond the accepted *Faust* reception. In his essay 'Einschüchterung durch die Klassizität', Brecht complained that traditional productions of *Faust* tended to obscure 'die ursprüngliche Frische der klassischen Werke, ihr damalig Überraschendes, Neues, Produktives, das ein Hauptmerkmal dieser Werke ist' (GW 17:1275). His goal was to peel off layers of sterile traditions in order to rediscover the original freshness of these works: 'Wir müssen den ursprünglichen Ideengehalt des Werks herausbringen' (GW 17:1276).

Brecht chose *Urfaust* for a number of reasons. A group of young people, including Käthe Reichel (later a well-known Brechtian actress) and the director Egon Monk (later to achieve prominence), had invited Brecht to view their production of *Urfaust*. Brecht immediately recognized the importance of this play because he saw it as the point of departure for German theater: 'Ohne *Urfaust* gäbe es keinen Woyzeck, keine realistische Theaterkunst'.[9] He also felt that the fragmentary character of the work made it easier to counter the 'Einschüchterung durch die Klassizität' and allowed more room for experimentation. For Brecht, *Urfaust*, together with Kleist's *Robert Guiskard* and Büchner's *Woyzeck*, belonged to a special category of fragments, 'die nicht unvollkommen, sondern Meisterwerke sind, hingeworfen in einer wunderbaren Skizzenform' (GW 17:1280). In the *Urfaust* drama, Brecht discovered the vitality, the fun, and the proximity to real life which he envisioned for his theater:

> Diese Fabel, welch ein Wurf! Der Einfall allein, den hochaktuellen Stoff von der Kindesmörderin mit dem alten 'Puppenspiel vom Dr. Faustus' zu verknüpfen! Diese Sprache: der Hans-Sachs-Vers grobianischer Prägung, gepaart mit der neuen, humanistischen Prosa! Diese Gestalten! Sie waren Volksgestalten gewesen und wurden wieder Volksgestalten! Welche Grundidee: die Tragödie des Gretchens als eine Episode bei der Vermenschlichung und Höherentwicklung des Individuums Faust! (GW 17:1281)

According to Brecht, the *Urfaust-Goethe* was still under the influence of Shakespeare, who is famous for mixing seriousness and levity even in tragedies (GW 17:1279). Brecht wanted to reintroduce into classical plays the element of fun that had been buried under

---

[7]See Werner Mittenzwei, *Das Leben des Bertolt Brecht oder Der Umgang mit den Welträtseln* (Frankfurt, 1987) 2: 459.
[8]See Brecht's *Arbeitsjournal 1942–1955*, p. 909.
[9]Wekwerth, p. 99.

centuries of spurious stiffness and dignity. To bring about this desired 'irreverent' effect of freshness and fun, Brecht suggested a 'naive' approach to the play, unencumbered by tradition, 'damit der teufel, die magie und das ganze brimborium des alten puppenspiels *naiv* vorkommen können .... also erdgeist als quakendes hockendes vieh à la bosch und der teufel als volksteufel mit hörnern und klumpfuß'.[10] With this 'naive' approach Brecht hoped to shock stodgy critics: 'der urfaust läßt sich lustig an mit den jungen leuten. ein schönes realistisches gedicht! freilich, so naiv gemacht, mag es ärger verursachen. unsere publikumsschulmeister fühlen sich unterschätzt, wenn man ihnen erlaubt, sich zu amüsieren'.[11] Apparently, Brecht and his team even went so far in their enthusiasum that Brecht had to resort to a word of caution: 'besprechung mit cas, hill, ruth, monk über urfauststil. wir sind zu naiv vorgegangen, goethe ist nicht naiv, sondern hat den späten genuß am naiven. ... so muß doch wieder öl in das brunnenwasser gegossen werden'.[12]

During the rehearsals for *Urfaust*, Brecht demonstrated the necessity of 'naiveté' in the approach to a play. Manfred Wekwerth reports: 'Es ist merkwürdig: Brecht hatte die "Kunst des Vergessens" zu einer solchen Meisterschaft entwickelt, daß er den *Urfaust* ansah wie ein fremdes Stück und "Goethinger" – wie er Goethe in sein Bayrisch übersetzte – wie einen neuen Autor. Er lachte, staunte, fand die "Sache spannend"; und von da an versäumte er keine Probe. So begann eine der interessantesten und theatergeschichtlich wichtigsten Arbeiten von Brecht. Man könnte sie die Phase seiner neuen Klassikeraneignung nennen, die sich erheblich von der der zwanziger Jahre unterschied'.[13] This 'naive' attitude allowed Brecht to penetrate to the 'Grundgestus' of a scene or of the whole play. For example, '*Urfaust* ist die realistische Geschichte eines Zauberers'[14] not 'der "ewige Wahrheitssucher" ("faustisches Streben", Spengler), Arroganz und Illusion des Abendlandes'.[15] Equally 'naive' was Brecht's view of the Gretchen tragedy. He was not so much interested in the tragic ending but in the fact 'daß Faust "das Mädchen verlassen muß, wenn man das für einen Nachteil hält"'.[16] Time and again Brecht emphasized this 'naive' approach. ('Das gibt die naive Geschichte'; 'Wir brauchen einen ganz naiven Ton.')[17]

In 1956, Brecht and his students Benno Besson and Manfred Wekwerth prepared a production of *Die Tage der Commune* for the municipal theater in Karl-Marx-Stadt.[18] In early August, 1956, shortly before Brecht's death, Wekwerth and Besson visited him in his country home in Buckow in order to discuss a number of questions that had to be resolved before rehearsals could begin in mid-September.[19] Brecht asked his students to narrate the plot as 'naively' as possible, and he reacted with 'naive' questions like 'Stopp, nicht so schnell, ... das verstehe ich nicht. Wer wandelt da um?' (referring to the national guard's change from the defense of the nation against the Germans to the defense of

---

[10]*Arbeitsjournal 1942–1955*, p. 971 (2 February 1952; my emphasis).
[11]*Arbeitsjournal 1942–1955*, p. 974 (15 February 1952).
[12]*Arbeitsjournal 1942–1955*, p. 975 (18 February 1952). The names refer to Caspar Neher (Brecht's friend and stage designer), Hainer Hill (a stage designer), Ruth Berlau (Brecht's friend and collaborator), and Egon Monk (one of Brecht's students and a stage director).
[13]Wekwerth, p. 99.
[14]Ibid.
[15]Ibid., p. 101.
[16]Quoted from Mittenzwei, *Das Leben des Bertolt Brecht* 2: 463.
[17]Wekwerth, p. 100.
[18]The play opened in Karl-Marx-Stadt on November 17, 1956. Director: Benno Besson; sets: Caspar Neher; music: Hanns Eisler. See my *Bertolt Brecht* (New York, 1977) 386.
[19]See Wekwerth, p. 67.

their class interests against the bourgeoisie) or 'Was passiert da eigentlich?' Again Brecht demonstrated 'die Kunst des Vergessens' by regarding his own play as something he had never seen before.[20] When a scene did not work, he quickly changed it, and he was happiest when he had found a dialectic solution: 'Die dialektische Lösung ist immer die lebendigere, vielfältigere, *naivere*'[21] – for example, in the scene where the women carry the government-delivered bread in their arms when they stop government soldiers from taking away the cannons. In rehearsals, 'naive' was one of Brecht's favorite words.[22] In the discussions for the rehearsals to *Die Tage der Commune*, he began to develop the new aesthetic category of 'naiveté'. Brecht stated: 'Die *Commune* muß *naiv* gespielt werden'.[23] He also complained that it was so difficult to discuss his theory of theater with other people, even with friends, because everybody twisted the meaning of what he really said and that an x always came out as a u ('Daß aus einem X andauernd ein U werde').[24] Apparently, Brecht continued, the simpler his pronouncements, the greater the misunderstandings. He asked himself what might have led to these misunderstandings, and it occurred to him that in presenting his theory of theater he omitted half of it because he reasoned that people would naturally supply this aspect themselves: the role of naiveté ('die Rolle des Naiven'). According to Wekwerth, Brecht therefore introduced the aesthetic category of naiveté ('die ästhetische Kategorie des Naiven') to counteract the onesided impact of his theater of estrangement. 'Er war ernsthaft überrascht, daß man sein Theater Jahre hindurch unnaiv betrachtet hatte. ... Das Naive ist eine ästhetische Kategorie, die konkreteste'.[25] In his view, beauty in art without naiveté was impossible. When pressed by his students to illustrate his category of 'naiveté', he gave a few examples:

> Naiv ist die Darstellung der ganzen Bevölkerung von Rouen in *Jeanne d'Arc* durch eine kleine Gruppe von sieben Personen.
>
> Naiv ist der geänderte Verlauf der 3. Szene in der *Commune* [the scene where the soldiers try to steal the cannons].
>
> Naiv ist das Auftreten einer Figur, wenn man sagen kann: Gerade jetzt kommt die und die. Oder: Gerade jetzt passiert das und das.
>
> Die Darstellung historischer Vorgänge bei Brueghel ist naiv, zum Beispiel *Der Sturz des Ikarus*.
>
> Das Gegenteil naiver Darstellung ist der Naturalismus.[26]

---

[20]Ibid., pp. 68f.
[21]Ibid., p. 70 (my emphasis).
[22]This applied not only to *Die Tage der Commune* but to other plays in rehearsal as well, including the rehearsals for Brecht's *Galileo*, which began on 14 December 1955. In a detailed description of these rehearsals, John Fuegi reports that for Brecht the Humpty Dumpty nursery rhyme and a quote from the great Bavarian comedian Karl Valentin captured the essence of the play: 'Instead of "lofty" analysis of his text, Brecht stressed with the Humpty Dumpty and Valentin quotations the very down to earth and *naive* (in a non-pejorative sense) quality of his work. In this, of course, he was returning to a classical tenet of German aesthetics: the "naive" viewed as a positive characteristic of the very greatest literature: the work of Homer and Shakespeare, for example'. See John Fuegi, *Bertolt Brecht: Chaos, According to Plan* (Cambridge, 1987) 173 (my emphasis).
[23]Wekwerth, p. 72 (my emphasis).
[24]Ibid., p. 73.
[25]Ibid.
[26]Ibid.

Since in English the word *naiveté* has a negative connotation, it should perhaps be rendered as directness, intuitiveness, naturalness, freshness, and vitality – although for lack of a better term *naiveté* is kept in this paper. At the same time, however, the term *naive* in the Brechtian context does not imply absence of artistry. This new category was intended to allow critics and viewers the unencumbered enjoyment of Brechtian theater, without the constant interposition of epic or alienating glasses. Brecht wanted people to look at his theater again, without being burdened by any theories. They should approach his theater as children approach the world around them: with freshness, wonderment, astonishment.

Again according to Wekwerth, Brecht informed his students in early August of 1956 that when he had overcome his illness, he planned not to return to his theater on a regular basis but to leave more of the practical operations to his students, including Besson, Palitzsch, and Wekwerth. Instead, he proposed to work on new plays about Einstein, Hans Garbe (a GDR activist and worker-hero), and other topics. In addition, he intended to rework his theory of theater, basing it on this category of naiveté ('Kategorie des Naiven') rather than on the estrangement effect. He died before he could realize all these plans.

*The Visions of Simone Machard* is one of Brecht's most neglected plays. Most scholars set it apart from Brecht's other works and give it short shrift as minor and insignificant. In 1967, Frederick Ewen wrote about *Simone*. 'The Visions of Simone Machard is an unusual play for Brecht to have written. It has a unified and single plot, uninterrupted by "epic" elements. It also has something unprecedented in Brecht, "visionary" scenes, with an angel.'[27] Martin Esslin actually seemed to like the play: 'On the struggle of occupied France he and Feuchtwanger were planning a modern version of the story of Joan of Arc, which later crystallized into a novel by Feuchtwanger and Brecht's *Die Gesichte der Simone Machard* (*The Visions of Simone Machard*), one of his most tender plays, whose little resistance heroine has clumsily naive visions of herself as an anachronistic Joan of Arc.'[28] Claude Hill revealed his personal bias when he wrote in 1975: 'Most professional Brechtians are embarrassed by this play, which strikes them as sentimental and simplistic. To compound the offense, it is also neither Marxist nor epic' – although he concedes that 'in purely theatrical terms the play is undoubtedly moving and effective'.[29] James K. Lyon calls *Simone* 'one of Brecht's least distinguished, critically problematical plays. ... this play is highly un-Brechtian. Visions, especially visions with angels, do not lend themselves to easy dramatization in the twentieth century. Further, no epic elements or devices interrupt the straightforward plot'.[30]

Brecht himself apparently did not share these sentiments since he never dissociated himself from the play; he referred to it several times in his letters. On 25 July 1956, he indicated to his publisher Peter Suhrkamp that he was reasonably satisfied with it:

> Jetzt zur 'Simone', ich glaube, diese Darstellung ist im großen und ganzen wahrheitsgetreu. Kann also nicht schaden, höchstens dem, der die Wahrheit sagt. Nun, legt's zu dem übrigen! Wir können das kleine Stück ruhig drucken, denke ich.[31]

---

[27] Frederick Ewen, *Bertolt Brecht: His Life, His Art, and His Times* (New York, 1967) 399.
[28] Martin Esslin, *Brecht: The Man and His Work* (Garden City, 1961) 69, and *Brecht: A Choice of Evils* (London [and] New York, 4th rev. ed. 1984) 64.
[29] Claude Hill, *Bertolt Brecht* (New York, 1975) 97.
[30] James K. Lyon, *Bertolt Brecht in America* (Princeton, 1980) 104f.
[31] Bertolt Brecht, *Briefe*, ed. by Günter Glaeser (Frankfurt, 1981) 785, no. 879. This edition will be used in the following text.

Ten years earlier, in a letter to Elisabeth Hauptmann, Brecht had included Simone in a list of great characters from his plays (letter 520, dated Santa Monica, July/August 1946).

So far, only Jürgen Albers as well as Wilhelm Große and Jan Knopf, following in Albers' footsteps, have given serious attention to *The Visions of Simone Machard*.[32] Albers maintains: '*Simone Machard* [ist] nicht nur unter dem Gesichtspunkt der Geschichtsbehandlung eines der interessantesten Stücke Brechts. Das Verhältnis von nationalen und sozialen Konflikten anhand des Jeanne d'Arc-Stoffs zu behandeln, diesen Stoff durch Visionen zu verfremden und dadurch Gegenwart und Vergangenheit gleichzeitig auf die Bühne zu bringen: das ist ein Experiment, das mehr Beachtung verdient, als es bisher erhalten hat.'[33] He then proceeds to concentrate his interpretation on the main character and the significance of her dreams.

It is true, *Simone Machard* does not belong among Brecht's greatest plays. We should bear in mind that it was not performed during Brecht's lifetime, and that Brecht never had a chance to revise it. But as Albers has already pointed out, the play does contain epic elements, especially in the dream scenes blending past and present, in the almost incomprehensible dream language, and in the music ('verworrene Musik'). Even sentences like 'Nicht eine Kaffeetasse darf dem Feind in die Hände fallen, nicht ein Schinken, nicht eine Dose Sardinen' or 'Die Zivilbevölkerung hat sich als ein großes Übel für den Krieg herausgestellt. ... Entweder man schafft das Volk ab oder den Krieg; beides kann man nicht haben' certainly have an alienating effect.[34] The visionary scenes, in which an angel in the shape of Simone's seventeen-year-old brother André appears to her, are by no means so unprecedented as Ewen assumes. They are a vivid reminder of the dream scenes in *The Good Woman of Setzuan*, in which the gods appear to Wang, the water carrier, and Shen Te, the prostitute. Like Shen Te, the lowly girl Simone is singled out by the gods for a special mission; she is chosen to save France: 'Johanna, Tochter Frankreichs, es muß etwas geschehen' (1857). The similarity to *The Good Woman of Setzuan* goes further: Simone, too, invents a cousin. Saint Joan of the Stockyards, we recall, also had dreams and visions and heard voices; in one of her dreams, she even sees herself as a leader of the revolution.[35] Visions also play an important role in *Schweyk in the Second World War*. The most famous vision in Brecht's plays is probably Jenny's song of the ship with eight sails in *The Three Penny Opera*, in which she describes the coming revolution.[36]

Contrary to Hill's or Esslin's beliefs, the play *Simone Machard* is also clearly Marxist. It is a reworking of the main theme of Brecht's earlier play *The Roundheads and the Pointed Heads*, 'Rich birds flock together' (*Reich und Reich gesellt sich gern*), yet without any allusions to the race issue. Brecht had to rework this theme because in 1942, when he collaborated with his Jewish friend Lion Feuchtwanger who had barely escaped from the clutches of the Nazis, it was obvious to him that the racial issue was more than just a front or cover for the Nazis to hide class differences, as he had maintained in *The Round Heads*

---

[32] Jürgen Albers, '*Die Gesichte der Simone Machard*: Eine zarte Träumerei nach Motiven von Marx, Lenin, Schiller', *Brecht-Jahrbuch 1978* (Frankfurt, 1978) 66–86. Wilhelm Große, *Bearbeitungen des Johanna-Stoffes* (München, 1980) 91–112. Jan Knopf, *Brecht-Handbuch Theater* (Stuttgart, 1980) 237–242. In addition, there is also a forthcoming article by Herbert Knust, 'Brecht's Dream-Playing: Between Vision and Illusion', which deals extensively with Simone and her dreams.
[33] Albers, p. 85.
[34] Brecht, *Gesammelte Werke* 5: 1868 and 1846. The page numbers in the text refer to this volume.
[35] *GW* 2:734.
[36] *GW* 2:415ff.

*and the Pointed Heads*. The subtitle of this play, 'Rich birds flock together', is repeated several times by Georges, one of the employees of the hostelry in *Simone*, when both the French and German capitalists conclude their business deals and the German captain promises Madame Soupeau to keep 'the mob' at bay (1887). The main issue of the play is not the French vs. the Germans but rich people vs. poor people, regardless of nationality. The voice that Simone hears and that commands her actions comes from her brother André, a member of the Communist Party and simple French soldier at the front. For Brecht, André's role was of crucial importance. In unpublished *Simone* materials in the Brecht Archives, we find a note in Brecht's handwriting, heavily underlined: 'Ihr Bruder war der einzige'.[37] Mme Soupeau, who regards herself and her ilk as representatives of the true France, calls André 'a gutter Gabriel' (*Gossengabriel*; 1901), a rabble-rouser from below and instigator of class struggle.

*The Visions of Simone Machard* is demonstrably an integral part of the Brechtian canon, much more challenging and complex than previously assumed. Furthermore, it is directly linked to Brecht's reassessment of his theory of theater in the 1950s, when he preferred 'naiveté' to 'estrangement'; it is the practical application of Brecht's attempts at reevaluating his theory of theater and establishing a new aesthetic category. Although this reorientation does not represent a radical departure from his previous approach, it is a shift away from an overburdened theoretical approach to a more direct and practical view – a view Brecht had always regarded as most important in his career as playwright and director.

*The Visions of Simone Machard* was written in collaboration with Feuchtwanger in 1942–43, while Brecht was in exile in Santa Monica, California. In fact, Feuchtwanger supplied much of the plot, based on his experiences in a French internment camp, a brickyard in Les Milles near Aix-en-Provence. Brecht had read the German version of Feuchtwanger's narrative, *Unholdes Frankreich*, which was published in English in 1941 as *The Devil in France* (New York: Viking Press).[38] By all accounts (including Feuchtwanger's and Brecht's) this collaboration went very smoothly[39] – except when it came to the age of the main character Simone. As Feuchtwanger noted: 'Die einzige Frage, über die wir uns nicht einigen konnten, war das Alter der Heldin. Dem Brecht wurde Jeanne-Simone während der Arbeit immer jünger, mir immer älter'.[40] Indeed, in Brecht's *Arbeitsjournal*, Simone went from 13 years of age (2 December 1942) to 11 years of age (May 1955).

In 1955, Brecht began preparations for a production *of Simone*, and he asked Feuchtwanger for a copy of the manuscript. In August of 1955, Feuchtwanger sent him the latest version, and Brecht replied in a letter to his old friend: 'danke für brief und stücktext. er scheint in Ordnung bis auf die allerletzten sätze, die etwas schwach klingen'.[41] In 1956, there were some plans to produce *Simone* in the GDR and in Paris, with both productions jointly directed by Besson and Jean-Marie Serreau (Brecht letter of 3 May 1956). *Simone*, therefore, was very much on Brecht's mind throughout that

---

[37] BBA 1192/25.
[38] See Bertolt Brecht, *Arbeitsjournal 1938–1942* (Frankfurt, 1973) 341 (24 December 1941). In 1943, Feuchtwanger used the same materials for his novel *Simone*, published in Stockholm in 1944.
[39] Lion Feuchtwanger, 'Zur Entstehungsgeschichte des Stückes Simone', *NDL* 5 (1957), no. 6:56–58. Brecht, *Arbeitsjournal 1942–1955*, p. 559 (20 December 1942).
[40] *NDL* 5 (1957), no. 6:57.
[41] Ibid., p. 58.

year of 1956: that is to say, during the same time he discussed the introduction of the category of 'naiveté' with his friends and students. Wekwerth mentions this new category only in the context of *The Days of the Commune*, but it seems reasonable to extend it to include *The Visions of Simone Machard*, especially since there is also a close thematic connection between the two plays: 'In times of war the common interests of the haves on both sides supersede the interests of the have-nots; the apparent national unity covers class-antagonisms only for a short time'.[42]

Even from his hospital bed in the Charité in Berlin, Brecht insisted in a letter to Feuchtwanger, dated 3 May 1956, that the role of Simone must be played by an eleven-year-old child:

> Das wichtigste Für eine Aufführung der *Simone* ist, daß die Hauptrolle unter überhaupt keinen Umständen von einer jungen Schauspielerin gespielt werden kann (auch nicht von einer, die wie ein Kind aussieht), sondern nur von einer Elfjährigen, und zwar einer, die wie ein Kind aussieht.[43]

We have to ask ourselves why Brecht felt so strongly about Simone being a child of eleven. It is true, on 25 November 1942, Brecht wrote in his *Arbeitsjournal* (549) that he made Simone a child mainly because he could not explain her patriotism. In 1956, however, Brecht's insistence on Simone's age was closely related to his changing view of his theater from one of 'estrangement' to one of 'naiveté', and he now regarded his play *Simone Machard* as one of the first dramatic realizations of this newly envisioned aesthetic category. The *Simone* productions in the GDR and in Paris did not materialize. Instead, the first performance of *Simone* took place on 8 March 1957 in Frankfurt (West Germany). It was directed by Harry Buckwitz, who had indeed followed Brecht's advice and successfully engaged an eleven-year-old actress.

Brecht's first Joan of Arc play, *Saint Joan of the Stockyards*, already contained a rejection of Schiller's idealistic positions. His new aesthetic category of 'naiveté' implied another confrontation with Schiller, this time with Schiller's definition of 'naiveté' as described in the essay *Über naive und sentimentalische Dichtung* (1795). For Schiller, too, 'naiv' means 'natürlich, unbefangen, kindlich; lateinisch nativus = angeboren, französisch: naif'.[44] However, his 'naiveté' was intimately tied to a moral idea in the Kantian sense, and nothing could be further from Brecht's intention. In fact, Brecht's category of 'naiveté' was firmly rooted in the material world; it turned Schiller's definition upside down, so to speak. Yet Schiller's definition of artistic 'genius' can be extended to include Brecht: 'Die verwickeltsten Aufgaben muß das Genie mit anspruchsloser Simplizität (*Einfalt*) und Leichtigkeit lösen'.[45] Some of the writers Schiller mentions as examples for this kind of 'naive' approach can also be found in Brecht's line of artistic ancestors: Cervantes, Shakespeare, Fielding and Sterne. In this respect, Brecht is a 'naive' poet since he combines 'nature' with art.[46]

Schiller's definition of 'naiveté' can also be applied to the character Simone. For him, 'naive' meant to follow one's immediate and natural instincts without reflection. In this

---

[42]Klaus-Detlef Müller, ed., *Bertolt Brecht. Epoche-Werk-Wirkung* (München, 1985) 268 (my translation).
[43]Brief 868; cf. *Briefe*, p. 779.
[44]Friedrich Schiller, *Über naive und sentimentalische Dichtung* (Stuttgart, 1966) 3.
[45]Ibid., p. 18.
[46]Ibid., p. 19.

sense, Simone is 'naive' since she acts 'naturally'. She does not understand, for example, why her fellow employees at the hostelry and her employers, the Soupeaus, talk a lot about resistance but do little when France is in danger. When the Germans approach their town of Saint-Martin, everybody realizes that something ought to be done with Soupeau's gasoline supplies in order to keep them from falling into the hands of the enemy. But Soupeau does not really want to give them up – his words that not even a coffee cup must fall into German hands mean absolutely nothing – and the employees do not really care either. Only Simone naturally assumes that the time has come to act and tells Mme Soupeau: 'Madame, ich laufe mit Père Gustave und Georges hinüber in die Ziegelei. Wir zerstören die Benzinvorräte' (1876). She is stunned and does not understand when Mme Soupeau dismisses her, instead of giving her support and encouragement. Like Shen Te, Kattrin, or Grusche, Simone does instinctively what has to be done; her actions appear naive and simpleminded only in a corrupted world. The term 'naive' as applied to *Simone* by no means equals 'simple' or 'lacking artistic refinement'. As Herbert Knust pointed out: 'Simone's "naive" or even "naturalistic" dream visions were at the same time, objectively, sophisticated epic theater'.[47]

The significance of 'naiveté' is clearly demonstrated by the choice of characters such as Saint Joan, Kattrin, Grusche, Shen Te, and Simone. It has always been a problem for Brecht, and Brecht critics alike, to explain these characters in terms of epic theater, distancing, and estrangement. All of them represent genuine and natural goodness in an evil world which must be changed, and their fate arouses the spectators' empathy. Brecht's category of 'naiveté' allows direct access to them. They appear 'naive' only to a world that has lost direct access to their human qualities. The fact that Brecht used a Saint Joan figure in three of his plays (*Saint Joan of the Stockyards*, *The Visions of Simone Machard*, and *The Trial of Joan of Arc at Rouen 1431*) highlights the particular importance he attached to this character.

Brecht's work is characterized by a dialectic interplay of continuity and change. His definition of 'naiveté' (freshness, directness, childlike wonderment) is actually not so far removed from his earlier definitions of the estrangement effect, which he characterized as a process of replacing familiarity with astonishment and curiosity.[48] As Johannes Goldhahn has pointed out,[49] the importance of 'naiveté' in Brecht's aesthetics can be traced back to the 1920s when Brecht praised George Bernard Shaw for his apparent 'naiveté':

> Als Theaterschriftsteller scheint es ihm ebenso *naiv* wie uns Jungen, für das Theater zu schreiben, und er bezeugt keine Spur von Lust, sich zu stellen, als wisse er das nicht: Er macht ausgiebig Gebrauch von *dieser Naivität*.[50]

In Brecht's view, Shakespeare was another prime example of the kind of 'naiveté' he envisioned for his theater:

> Wenn wir die Stücke Shakespeares betrachten, ... so müssen wir zu dem Schluß kommen, daß es irgendwann ein Theater gegeben hat, das mit dem Leben in einem

---

[47]Knust, 'Brecht's Dream-Playing'.
[48]See, for example, Brecht's essay 'Über experimentelles Theater', In *GW* 15: 301.
[49]Johannes Goldhahn, 'Nachdenken über Naivität', In *Brecht 85: Zur Ästhetik Brechts*, ed. by Brecht-Zentrum der DDR (Berlin, 1986) 212–223, and the chapter 'Produktive Haltung vergnüglichen Lernens: Naivität', in his *Vergnügungen unseres Zeitalters* (Berlin, 1977) 135–172.
[50]*GW* 15: 98 (my emphasis).

ganz anderen Kontakt stand .... Das Shakespearische Theater, Angriffen anscheinend überhaupt nicht ausgesetzt und dadurch *in unberührter Naivität*, konnte bei seinem Publikum ohne weiteres voraussetzen, daß es sich keinerlei Gedanken über das Stück, wohl aber Gedanken über das Leben machen würde.[51]

Brecht found further examples of this kind of artistic 'naiveté' in Brueghel's paintings and the theatrical performances given by itinerant companies at local fairs (*Schaubudentheater*). Goldhahn summarizes: 'In der künstlerischen Tätigkeit Brechts ... wirkten Naives und Naivität also seit eh und je als maßgebende Größen'.[52] 'Naiveté' and estrangement are closely connected: Brecht used the estrangement effect to produce the attitude of 'naiveté' which permits a fresh look at life and society. As Goldhahn formulated it: 'Verfremdung produziert Naivität'.[53] Goldhahn also points out that this kind of 'naiveté' is not to be confused with simplemindedness: 'Solcherart Naivität meint differenziertes Beobachten des Verhaltens von Menschen'.[54] But in the ensuing debates over the technical aspects of Brechtian theater, the concept of estrangement obscured the concept of 'naiveté', relegating it to the background. In the 1950s, however, there was a definite change away from earlier positions and a renewed emphasis on the concept of 'naiveté'. The goal of Brechtian theater remained to instruct and to entertain, but Brecht wanted a different approach to his plays. There is clear evidence that he attempted a reorientation of his theory of theater and of his theatrical practice toward the end of his life. *The Visions of Simone Machard* plays a pivotal role in this reorientation; Simone is the incarnation of the principle and new aesthetic category of 'naiveté'.[55]

The prominent emphasis given to the terms 'naive' and 'naiveté' during the last phase of Brecht's life should not tempt us, however, to rename his theater; 'theater of naiveté' would be just as misleading a term as 'epic theater'. Besides, if it had to be labeled at all, Brecht preferred the term 'dialectic theater'. The key to his work, however, is not 'estrangement' (or 'alienation') but 'naiveté', especially in the realization of his plays on stage. Epic elements and alienation effects are only means to an end; they are means of a 'naive' theater to return to a theater that allows the unencumbered viewing of a performance and the pleasures of astonishment and discovery.

---

[51]*GW 15*: 118 (my emphasis).
[52]Goldhahn, 'Nachdenken über Naivität', p. 216.
[53]Ibid., p. 218.
[54]Ibid.
[55]See also Goldhahn in *Vergnügungen unseres Zeitalters*, p. 145: 'Naives und Naivität verwirklichen sich in *literarischen Figuren*'.

# PART TWO
## MAJOR THEORETICAL WRITINGS

# Notes on *The Threepenny Opera* and *Rise and Fall of the City of Mahagonny*

CHAPTER ELEVEN

# Epic Opera and Epic Theater

JOHN J. WHITE

## ON THE SOCIOLOGY OF OPERA

The title's modest formulation 'Anmerkungen zur Oper [...]'[1] hardly leads the reader to expect the kind of totalizing theory and macroscopic statements contained in some parts of the *Mahagonny* notes. The alternative titles – 'Zur Soziologie der Oper' and 'Das moderne Theater ist das epische Theater' – give a very different impression. The *Ur*-title, 'Zur Soziologie der Oper', was evidently consonant with the editorial policy of a journal the very name of which (*Musik und Gesellschaft*) proclaimed a broad interdisciplinary remit. It also reflected the first section's concern with the sociopolitical significance of contemporary opera and theater *as institutions*. In fact, the first section's primary task is to diagnose the predicament of opera as a paradigmatic 'late capitalist' cultural phenomenon and at the same time assess the specific function of intellectuals and artists in late capitalist Weimar Republic society. Any serious suggestion of a diffident young Brecht, cautious about engaging in macroscopic pronouncements and large-scale sociopolitical theorizing, is dispelled by such magisterial pronouncements as 'Die großen Apparate wie Oper, Schaubühne, Presse usw. setzen ihre Auffassung sozusagen inkognito durch' (*GBA*, 24:74). Or the verdict on intellectuals operating within such dehumanizing 'Apparate' as 'mitverdienend' and 'ökonomisch betrachtet [...] mitherrschende, gesellschaftlich betrachtet schon proletaroide – Kopfarbeiter' (*GBA*, 24:74). Or the claim that, 'in der Meinung, sie seien im Besitz eines Apparates, der in Wirklichkeit sie besitzt, verteidigen sie einen Apparat, über den sie keine Kontrolle mehr haben, der nicht mehr, wie sie noch glauben, Mittel für die Produzenten ist, sondern Mittel gegen die Produzenten wurde' (*GBA*, 24:75). Any putative rhetoric of self-effacement would seem to be little in evidence in these instances.[2]

The explanatory paradigm underlying Brecht's picture of theater's commodification and its misrepresentation by those involved in it derives from the assumption that the

---

John J. White, 'Epic Opera and Epic Theater: "Anmerkungun zur Oper *Aufstieg und Fall der Stadt Mahoganny*"', in White, *Bertolt Brecht's Dramatic Theory* (New York: Camden House, 2004), pp. 31–66.]

[1]'Schon der Titel besagt, dass es nicht um die Grundlegung einer Theorie handelt, sondern um Erläuterungen zur Oper' (Knopf 2000, 78).
[2]The material in this first, 'sociological' section of the *Mahagonny* notes was so important to Brecht that he took much of it across, almost verbatim, into 'Über die Verwendung von Musik fur ein episches Theater' (cf. *GBA*, 22:160–61). As has been pointed out (*BHB*, 4:50) this section carries the germs of Brecht's 'Tui'-critique in *Der Tuiroman* (*GBA*, 17:9–161), where Stravinsky and Schoenberg are dismissed as 'zwei große Musiktuis' (*GBA*, 17:159).

agencies whose attitudes the notes are examining are the victims of what Friedrich Engels referred to as 'falsches Bewußtsein' or the Brecht of *Der Messingkauf* would call 'die Unwissenheit'. The other paradigm informing the first section of the *Mahagonny* notes, that of theater *qua* 'Produktion' within a complex system of supply and demand, is presented in an equally apodictic manner. This is the case, for example, with the interconnected claims that 'Ihre Produktion [i.e. that of musicians, writers, and critics] gewinnt Lieferantencharakter' and that the result is 'allgemein der Usus, jedes Kunstwerk auf seine Eignung für den Apparat, niemals aber den Apparat auf seine Eignung für das Kunstwerk hin zu überprüfen' (*GBA*, 24:75). This is as totalizing in its ideological scope as one of the key works on which it depended for its methodology: Georg Lukács's *Geschichte und Klassenbewußtsein* (especially the section 'Das Problem der Verdinglichung': Lukács 1923, 170–209). No wonder Brecht, who had already declared that the state of affairs he was about to describe had 'ungeheure Folgen, die viel zu wenig beachtet werden' (*GBA*, 24:74–75), felt entitled to charge recent reformers of opera with timidity – timidity of political vision as well as in their compromises with artistic radicalism. (He later refers to 'Fortschritte, welche die Folge von nichts sind und nichts zur Folge haben, welche nicht aus neuen Bedürfnissen kommen, sondern nur mit neuen Reizen alte Bedürfnisse befriedigen, also eine rein konservierende Aufgabe haben' [*GBA*, 24:82].) As the final section of the *Mahagonny* notes makes clear, any such narrowly 'aesthetic' perspective is deemed to be politically myopic, whereas Brecht, in his newfound indebtedness to *Kultursoziologie*, sees himself as scientifically 'objective' and immune to 'Verdinglichung'.

One might well ask why a playwright who had but recently turned to opera[3] and had, even more recently, claimed to have discovered that Karl Marx was his ideal audience,[4] should place such emphasis on the *sociology* of opera. What were the specific connotations of 'sociology' for him at this time?

Crucial evidence is to be found in an open letter to a certain 'Herr X.', entitled 'Sollten wir nicht die Ästhetik liquidieren?' (*GBA* 21:202–4[5]). Published below Brecht's name in the *Berliner Börsen-Courier* of 2 June 1927, this represents part of what the paper billed as 'ein polemischer Briefwechsel über das gegenwärtige Drama', with Brecht now replying to the opening salvo of 12 May: Herr X.'s 'Brief an einen Dramatiker. Der Niedergang des Dramas'. Herr X.'s tactic of addressing an open letter about the parlous state of contemporary drama to a 'young' man who persisted in remaining a dramatist was designed to cause maximum personal provocation, given that the two correspondents knew each other's positions extremely well by that time. For as many of the *Börsen-Courier*'s readers would have known, Herr X. was none other than the Marxist sociologist Fritz Sternberg, his 'first mentor', as Brecht called him in a 1927 dedication copy of his play *Mann ist Mann* (A Man's a Man). Sternberg was later to participate in the milestone Cologne radio discussion of January 1929 ('[Neue Dramatik]', *GBA*, 21:270–77) which began

---

[3]Evidence has come to light (*GBA Registerband*, 757) of *Mahagonny*'s, completion before *Die Dreigroschenoper*.
[4]In [Der einzige Zuschauer für meine Stücke]', c. 1928, Brecht recalls that when he initially read *Das Kapital* he understood his own work for the first time: 'dieser Marx war der einzige Zuschauer für meine Stücke, den ich je gesehen hatte. Denn einen Mann mit solchen Interessen mußten gerade diese Stücke interessieren. Nicht wegen ihrer Intelligenz, sondern wegen der seinigen. Es war Anschauungsmaterial für ihn' (GBA, 21:256–57).
[5]Willett renders 'liquidieren' with 'abolish'. However, the presence of this business term in other configurations in Brecht's writing of the period, e.g. 'Die Liquidierung der Jungen Bühne' and 'Liquidierung darf kein Akt sein' (*GBA*, 21:290–93), suggests that contemporary theater's prospects are assessed very much with an eye to the hard economic facts of life in the late 1920s, even if the vocabulary of the Soviet purges is prefigured in such a metaphor.

with Ernst Hardt, *Intendant* of the Westdeutscher Rundfunk, posing the question 'Warum Soziologie?' which the orchestrated exchange has Sternberg, Herbert Ihering, and Brecht endeavoring in their various ways to answer. Many parts of the ensuing discussion offer little more than a reprise of Sternberg's and Brecht's earlier *Berliner Börsen-Courier* exchange, although this time the writing is less polemical and there is more constructive clarification of positions. As planned, Sternberg is allowed in the radio discussion to reiterate the substance of his original letter, with Brecht replying in kind, this time with conclusive support from Ihering. But there is one important difference between the two clashes of minds. Brecht now pegs what had previously been a rather abstract defense of the sociological value of his work on the best of all possible arguments: his *Mann ist Mann*. In similar vein, the *Mahagonny* notes answer Brecht's rhetorical question 'Sollten wir nicht die Ästhetik liquidieren?' – albeit somewhat belatedly, but all the more forcefully – by citing Exhibit A for the defense of Epic Theater: his and Weill's *Mahagonny*. He could just as well have cited *Mann ist Mann* and *Die Dreigroschenoper*, because the existence and social critical power of these works meant that liquidation would have to be rejected as an option, as far as Brecht was concerned. Such a context makes it clear why Brecht felt obliged first to question and then defend his own artistic legitimacy, as well as that of his theories intended to legitimize Epic Theater.

Even at the time of the *Börsen-Courier* exchange, Sternberg seemed intent on provoking someone who had regularly attended his Marxist seminars throughout 1927 and whose thinking had been strongly influenced by his own published work on the subject of the relationship between the cultural superstructure and its societal base. A draft note by Brecht, entitled 'Soziologische Betrachtungsweise' (c.1928), advocated submitting German theater's current predicament to examination from a sociological point of view (*GBA*, 21:233–34). 'Soziologische Betrachtungsweise' reads like a blueprint for the first section of the *Mahagonny* notes. Even as late as 1932, Brecht was still working on a piece entitled 'Der soziologische Raum des bürgerlichen Theaters' (*GBA*, 21:557–59)[6] where one can still discern much common ground with Sternberg, even if signs of a widening gulf are beginning to show.[7] The paths of Sternberg and Brecht may have started to diverge by the late 1920s, with the latter coming progressively under Karl Korsch's influence, but as has frequently been pointed out, Brecht the syncretist did not simply abandon sociological analysis in order to align his conception of 'eingreifendes Denken' with Korsch's call for 'geistige Aktion',[8] He still took what he needed from Sternberg's methodology and uncompromising diagnosis. Seen in the terms of Marx's eleventh

---

[6]The term 'soziologischer Raum' is borrowed from the title of chapter 6 of Sternberg's *Der Imperialismus* (1925): 'Der soziologische Raum der materialistischen Geschichtsauffassung'.

[7]Fritz Sternberg (1895–1963) 'Diese Differenz zwischen dem Wissenschaftler Sternberg und dem Künstler Brecht ist, weil sie die erste einer Reihe Begegnungen von Wissenschaft und Kunst war, von großer Bedeutung. Daß Brecht den Standpunkt der Produktion notfalls auch gegen den der wissenschaftlichen Analyse aufrechterhielt, war eine Grundentscheidung, der er Zeit seines Lebens treu blieb' (Voigts 1977, 96). The exchange, as strong echoes of it in the Cologne radio discussion suggest, retained its importance for both participants. Its significance for Brecht can be gauged from the fact that he allowed it to be republished in the *Schwäbische Thalia der Stuttgarter Dramaturgischen Blätter* 41 (1927), 325–28 and in the Hamburg journal *Der Freihafen* 3 (1928), 8–11.

[8]Karl Korsch (1886–1961). In the wake of 'Bertolt Brechts marxistischer Lehrer' (Rasch 1963), a body of conflicting opinion has grown up on Korsch's importance for Brecht: Brüggemann 1973a and 1973b (76–138); *alternative* 41 (1965); Voigts 1977 (118–22); Knopf 1974 (149–64); and Knopf 1980a (413–15). Although Knopf 1980a (44) differentiates between Korsch's 'geistige Aktion' (Korsch 1966, 135) and Brecht's 'eingreifendes Denken', this does not necessarily invalidate the former's importance for Brecht's dialectical concept of interventionist thinking.

'Feuerbach-Thesis', Sternberg offered tools for its *interpretation*, but since Brecht wanted to *change* society, he needed something more politically interventionist than his mentor's academic sociological approach provided.

The aspect of Sternberg's thinking relevant to the *Mahagonny* notes is its unmitigatedly pessimistic, mechanical determinist diagnosis of the decline of modern drama, a phenomenon interpreted as the 'barometer' of the climate of a whole period. Brecht remains suitably impressed by a sociological method that sought to evaluate literature, not by adopting narrow aesthetic criteria, but diagnostically with reference to the society that produced it, a society represented by institutions ('Apparate'), the presence and hold of which both Sternberg and Brecht associated with the marginalization and even 'Liquidierung' of the individual,[9] In Brecht's words, 'Der Soziologe weiß, daß es Situationen gibt, wo Verbesserungen nichts mehr helfen' (*GBA*, 21:203). He concedes that it may be sociology's 'einfache und radikale Funktion' to prove that 'dieses Drama keine Existenzberechtigung mehr hat' (*GBA*, 21:202). But he refuses to let the matter rest there – understandably, since in Sternberg's diagnosis 'dieses Drama' means *all* drama. In a move calculated to accentuate the incompatibility of their views (but evidently intended to persuade Brecht to abandon his position and return to the purely sociological fold), Sternberg had concluded his open letter with the specific charge already intimated in his title: namely, that Brecht himself, who is assumed for argument's sake to share Sternberg's diagnosis, is at the same time *part of the problem*. He is roundly criticized for failing to draw the obvious conclusion from their shared assessment of the moribund state of modern theater and for his unwillingness 'dieses Drama, das nichts *als eine Photographie des Gestern, ein historischer Überrest ist*, zu liquidieren' (*GBA*, 21:675). 'Liquidating' drama would, in the *ad hominem* sense intended, have entailed giving up writing plays, as well as all other cultural activity. Brecht was not prepared to accept what Sternberg presented as the next logical step and decamp from drama and aesthetics and pitch his tent on the territory of critical sociology proper. The contrast in the *Börsen-Courier* exchange is therefore between Sternberg the sociologist, laying claim to objective insights, and Brecht the dramatist, by and large agreeing with his diagnosis, but not with his publicly announced remedy.[10] Brecht in fact refuses to draw any conclusions that would have amounted to artistic suicide; more important, he refuses to accept that drama is unable to contribute to radical social change.

The positions expressed here by Sternberg and Brecht supply an important subtext to the *Mahagonny* notes. Brecht continues to align himself with Sternberg's bleak assessment, but when it comes to the challenge to abandon drama and liquidate aesthetics, he draws a line in the sand. In his open letter, Brecht bows dutifully in his mentor's direction with the claim that 'keine andere Wissenschaft als die Ihre besitzt genügend Freiheit des Denkens, jede andere ist allzusehr interessiert und beteiligt an der Verewigung des allgemeinen zivilatorisehen Niveaus unserer Epoche. [...] Der Soziologe ist unser Mann' (*GBA*, 21:202–4). Yet while such a sociological standpoint may be an adequate tool for an assessment of the situation, in Brecht's eyes drama still had not lost 'die Verpflichtung und die Möglichkeit, das Theater einem *anderen* Publikum zu erobern.

---

[9]Cf. Sternberg 1963 (63) and Sternberg 1925 (107).

[10]Ironically, Brecht's *Berliner Börsen-Courier* reply lectures Sternberg on ideas Brecht has only recently acquired from him. For example, the suggestion that the sociologist's 'Skala [der] Schätzungen liegt nicht zwischen "gut" and "schlecht", sondern zwischen "richtig" und "falsch". Er wird ein Drama, wenn es "falsch" ist, nicht loben, weil es "gut" (oder "schön") ist' (*GBA*, 21:203) is, for example, pure Sternberg.

Die neue Produktion, die mehr und mehr das große epische Theater heraufführt, das der soziologischen Situation entspricht, kann zunächst ihrem Inhalt wie ihrer Form nach nur von denjenigen verstanden werden, die diese Situation verstehen' (*GBA*, 21:204). Using a familiar intellectual ju-jitsu move (the metaphor is the playwright's own), Brecht informs his readers that Sternberg had been invited – whether by Brecht himself or by Ihering on behalf of the *Berliner Börsen-Courier is not* said – to present a diagnosis of drama's condition 'weil ich von der Soziologie erwartete, daß sie *das heutige Drama* liquidierte'.[11] But when Sternberg delivers what he has been asked to deliver, Brecht adopts an antagonistic counter-position. For Voigts,[12] the fundamental difference between the two is that between cultural analyst and practising artist (1977, 96). While he may well have put his finger on the problem,[13] Sternberg has failed to appreciate that Epic Theater has the panacea. This helps explain Brecht's assertion that the new work being produced 'wird die alte Ästhetik nicht befriedigen, sondern sie wird sie vernichten'. That is to say, Epic Theater will be unacceptable to bourgeois aesthetics, but it is bourgeois aesthetics itself that will go under in the resultant struggle. Prefigured here are also later ideological differences between the perspectives of East and West German commentators on this transitional phase of Brecht's development.[14]

Rebuilding, as well as demolition, is the task Brecht allots to his and Weill's opera and even to the accompanying notes. The word 'liquidation' does not appear in the new context, not even in the early sections where it might have offered a stepping-stone to Brecht's remarks about the state of contemporary opera. Nor is there any explicit reference to Sternberg's particular brand of cultural sociology. The rejection of the title 'Zur Soziologie der Oper' for the second (*Versuche*) version can be interpreted as evidence of a widening rift between the two men. Even in *Musik und Gesellschaft*, Brecht may have been using 'Soziologie' in his title to signal differences as well as common ground. Nevertheless, the approach adopted in the first part of the *Mahagonny* notes still bears traces of Sternberg's methodology, even if the work ostentatiously begins with the more

---

[11]The unfolding exchange is marred by a number of confusions of expression, for which Brecht is largely responsible. In his original letter, Sternberg advocated the liquidation of 'dieses [i.e. contemporary] Drama' (*GBA*, 21:675), yet although the title of Brecht's reply talks about liquidating 'die Ästhetik', the target changes to 'das heutige Drama' in the very first sentence. This is followed by an unhelpful proliferation of terms, all presumably intended to echo the noun 'die Ästhetik': 'der Ästhet', 'ästhetischer Reiz', 'der ästhetische Standpunkt', and 'die alte Ästhetik' (*GBA*, 21:202–4).

[12]Despite this altercation, in 1928 Brecht continued to collaborate with Sternberg and Erwin Piscator (1893–1966) on a project to rework Shakespeare's *Julius Caesar* from a modern sociological point of view ('Das Stück enthielt so vieles, was in eine neue soziologische Konzeption nicht hineinpaßte' [Sternberg 1963, 35]). The collaboration is documented in Claas 1977.

[13]Sternberg had the distinct attraction of applying the sociological approach to theater and hence giving Brecht the opportunity to suggest that his own theoretical writings were beginning to build on current scholarly ideas.

[14]From Hecht's GDR vantage-point, the disagreement is not so much that between a representative of a pessimistically determinist 'Soziologismus' *and a practicing writer* for whom Sternberg's thesis of the 'Liquidierung des Individuums' need not as a corollary require the liquidation of either all contemporary drama or aesthetics. Rather, it is evidence of Sternberg's and the early Brecht's failure to allow for the 'Wechselwirkung' between the subjective factor and social conditions: 'es war undialektisch, wenn hier eine Einflußnahme des Menschen auf den Stoff rundweg übersehen wurde' (Hecht 1972, 32). By the time of *Mahagonny*, Brecht is shown to have progressed to a dialectical materialist position. Although Korsch has been air-brushed out of the picture, Hecht nevertheless offers a valuable account of Brecht's development from the vulgar determinist phase *of Mann ist Mann* to the dialectical position on the relationship between the individual and conditions in the *Mahagonny* notes and in his comments on *Die Mutter*.

positive question of whether and how opera can be revitalized. Only in piecemeal fashion does the connection between the aesthetic question and the underlying sociopolitical conditions responsible for the current crisis in late capitalism emerge. On one occasion Brecht does, however, echo his earlier response to Sternberg's letter

> Es wird gesagt: dies oder das Werk sei gut; und es wird gemeint, aber nicht gesagt: gut für den Apparat. *Dieser Apparat aber ist durch die bestehende Gesellschaft bestimmt und nimmt nur auf, was ihn in dieser Gesellschaft hält.* Jede Neuerung, welche die gesellschaftliche Funktion des Apparates, nämlich Abendunterhaltung, nicht bedrohe, könnte diskutiert werden. Nicht diskutiert werden können solche Neuerungen, die auf seinen Funktionswechsel drängten, die den Apparat also anders in die Gesellschaft stellen, etwa ihn den Lehranstalten oder den großen Publikationsorganen anschließen wollten. *Die Gesellschaft nimmt durch den Apparat auf, was sie braucht, um sich selbst zu reproduzieren.* Durchgehen kann also auch nur eine 'Neuerung', welche zur Erneuerung, nicht aber Veränderung der bestehenden Gesellschaft führt – ob nun diese Gesellschaftsform gut oder schlecht ist.
>
> (GBA, 24:75, my emphasis)

Instead of endorsing Sternberg's sociological judgment that works produced under such conditions have forfeited their 'Existenzberechtigung', Brecht now puts the counter-case in decidedly interventionist terms: 'Der Fehler ist nur, daß die Apparate heute noch nicht die der Allgemeinheit sind, daß die Produktionsmittel nicht den Produzierenden gehören, und daß so die Arbeit Warencharakter bekommt und den allgemeinen Gesetzen einer Ware unterliegt' (*GBA*, 24:76). The 'Dynamitstelle' in this passage (to borrow a word from Ernst Bloch's *Dreigroschenoper* essay [Bloch 1960, 187]) is the phrase 'noch nicht'. In 1930, this marks the key difference between Sternberg's position and Brecht's confidence that change is imminent.

## 'OPER – ABER NEUERUNGEN!'

The first three sections of the *Mahagonny* notes are structured under a series of interlocking headings:

(1) '*Oper – aber Neuerungen!*': making the case for a radical reassessment of opera as a cultural institution on the basis of a recognition of its socioeconomic function within the capitalist system of the Weimar Republic

(2) '*Oper –* ': a critical exposition of the preponderantly 'culinary' nature of opera prior to *Mahagonny*, which is presented as a work exploring the status of opera as an affirmative form of escapist entertainment[15]

(3) ' *– aber Neurungen!*': a survey of the main forms of innovation in Epic Theater and their political and aesthetic rationale. The structural and ideological innovations described take up the claim in (1) that the only acceptable innovations are those 'Neuerungen' leading to a radical change ('Erneuerung') of society.

---

[15] As the section on the *Mahagonny* notes in the *Brecht Handbuch* demonstrates, Brecht's and Weill's diagnoses of the contemporary malaise in opera have been seen as by and large accurate (*BHB*, 4:52–53).

This triad of interrelated headings is obviously intended to foreground the historical dialectic that has given rise to epic forms of theater and opera. The initial, elliptically phrased heading '*Oper – aber Neuerungen!*' hinges on an apparent contradiction: 'yes, keep opera', it seems to be saying, 'it does not necessarily have to be "liquidated" as a socially irrelevant anachronism, but if there is to be a reprieve, and not just a stay of execution, a radical rethink is called for'. What began by looking like an unexpected concession on Brecht's part (in the rallying cry '*Oper –* ') is modified by what the following '*aber*' implies: i.e. that it can only be legitimate to retain opera if it is revolutionized. Just what innovations Brecht has in mind are only gradually revealed. In any case, to propose keeping something that can only be preserved after a radical change in character and function is a question-begging stance to adopt. The ensuing paragraph plays with the reader's expectations in further ways.

> Seit einiger Zeit ist man auf eine Erneuerung der Oper aus. Die Oper soll, ohne daß ihr kulinarischer Charakter geändert wird, inhaltlich *aktualisiert* und der Form nach *technifiziert* werden. Da die Oper ihrem Publikum gerade durch ihre Rückständigkeit teuer ist, müßte man auf den Zustrom neuer Schichten mit neuen Appetiten bedacht sein, und man ist es auch: man will *demokratisieren*, natürlich ohne daß der Charakter der Demokratie geändert wird, welcher darin besteht, daß dem 'Volk' neue Rechte, aber nicht die Möglichkeit, sie wahrzunehmen, gegeben werden. Letzten Endes ist es dem Kellner gleich, wem serviert wird, es muß nur serviert werden! Es werden also – von den Fortgeschrittensten – Neuerungen verlangt oder verteidigt, die zur Erneuerung der Oper führen sollen – eine prinzipielle Diskussion der Oper (ihrer Funktion!) wird nicht verlangt und würde wohl nicht verteidigt.
>
> (GBA, 24:74)

Partly because of the programmatic section-title, the reader is initially expected to assume that Brecht wishes to associate his and Weill's collaborative work with various modish attempts to update opera. As the first paragraph implies, the issue was very much in the air at the time. In October 1927, the *Blätter der Staatsoper* (Berlin) organized an opinion poll on the theme 'Wie denken Sie über die zeitgenössische Weiterentwicklung der Oper?' In February 1929, the *Berliner Börsen-Courier* had published 'Über die Erneuerung der Oper', a topic to which *Das Kunstblatt* also devoted an entire number that same year. In such a climate of profound self-questioning, it was inevitable that certain figures on the contemporary musical scene would be perceived as part of a concerted project of renewal.[16] These ultra avant-garde experimenters must, in the public perception, have represented the sort of cultural developments that formed the context for *Mahagonny*.[17] Indeed, the impersonal subject 'man' of Brecht's first sentence appears to include himself,

---

[16] These included Ernst Krenek with his topical *Zwingburg* (1925) and the jazz-inspired *Jonny spielt auf* (1926); Darius Milhaud and Egon Wellesz, whose *L' Enlèvement de l' Europe* had shared the Baden-Baden stage with Brecht-Weill's original *Mahagonny Songspiel* in 1927, a year that had also witnessed the premieres of George Antheil's *Flight* and Stravinsky's *Oedipus Rex*, as well as Ernst Toch's experimental *Die Prinzessin auf der Erbse* (after Hans Christian Andersen), also performed at the Baden-Baden music festival. Max Brand's *Maschinist Hopkins* (1929) and Paul Hindemith's *Neues vom Tage* date from the same year. In a later comment, Brecht records his judgment that 'Hindemith und Strawinsky [scheiterten] unvermeidlich am Opernapparat' (*GBA*, 22:160). For a fuller picture of the musical context, see *BHB*, 4:54–55.

[17] The references to 'Lokomotiven, Maschinenhallen, Aeroplane, Badezimmer usw.,' as well as to *Gebrauchsmusik* and the fact that 'die Besseren verneinen den Inhalt überhaupt und tragen ihn in lateinischer Sprache vor oder vielmehr weg' (*GBA*, 24:82), allude, respectively, to works by Krenek, Brand, Antheil, Hindemith, and Stravinsky.

Suhrkamp, and Weill in the project. What follows, however, disabuses us of any such assumption. At the time, the musical scene might well have been awash with modishly avant-garde works, its cultural organs and the feuilleton press buzzing with controversies and debates about the critical state of opera and theater, but for Brecht any such sense of progress remained illusory. The end of the essay's first paragraph is so formulated as to make Brecht seem like a lone voice in a deceptively avant-garde wilderness, isolated because of his call for a fundamental discussion of first principles. But even this is only part of the unfolding picture. As soon becomes clear, the only justifiable form of debate about opera is the currently unavailable one addressing the need for a fundamental 'Funktionswechsel'. The main thrust of the *Mahagonny* notes is summed up in two sentences: one in the first section and the other right at the end of the last one. The first declares that the means of production are *not yet* in the right hands (*GBA*, 24:76). In the German original, the other reads: 'Wirkliche Neuerungen greifen die Basis an' (*GBA*, 24:84), translated in Willett, presumably in an effort to attenuate the Marxist jargon, with a horticultural metaphor: 'Real innovations attack the roots' (*BT*, 41). Yet as Brecht puts it more explicitly elsewhere: 'Der Schrei nach einem neuen Theater ist der Schrei nach einer neuen Gesellschaftsordnung' (*GBA*, 21:238). Which is why he thought of *Die Maßnahme* as 'Theater der Zukunft' in more than the simple sense that it was technically radical Epic Theater. In democratizing the theater as an institution, that work also prefigured a new form of egalitarian society (see Steinweg 1972, 196). But an attack on the 'base' (as opposed to tinkering with the 'superstructure') would hardly be achieved via *discussion* alone, even if discussion of the correct political kind would serve to clarify the need for intervention on a revolutionary scale.

Clearly what we have here is hardly the argument of someone still strongly influenced by Sternberg's sociological approach. Brecht is now explicitly availing himself of a more dialectical interpretive model. Its gradual establishment is the principal purpose of the first part of the *Mahagonny* notes. If genuine innovations attack the base, then the representatives of the avant-garde associated with the fashionable experiments of the time must be seen as little more than part of a pseudo-radical cultural epiphenomenon. This accounts for the sarcasm of the first paragraph's reference, using the superlative, to the would-be *dernier-cri* avant-garde ('die Fortgeschrittensten'), which becomes a rhetorical refrain in the following paragraphs: 'Diese Bescheidenheit in den Forderungen der Fortgeschrittensten hat wirtschaftliche Gründe, die ihnen selbst teilweise unbekannt sind' (*GBA*, 24:74), 'die Fortgeschrittensten denken nicht daran, den Apparat zu ändern' (*GBA*, 24:75). Having dissociated himself from such an avant-garde as categorically as he is about to hive off Epic Theater from its dramatic predecessors and contemporary rivals, Brecht effectively prepares the ground for interventionist innovation: in the shape *of Mahagonny* itself as well as on the theoretical front. For the terms in which Brecht-Weill's opera is discussed at the end of the *Mahagonny* notes apply just as much to the function of the accompanying notes: 'es stellt eben das Kulinarische zur Diskussion, es greift die Gesellschaft an, die solche Opern benötigt; sozusagen sitzt es noch prächtig auf dem alten Ast, aber es sägt ihn wenigstens [...] ein wenig an' (*GBA*, 24:84).

The presentational technique used in the first section of the notes is all too familiar from Brecht's plays. First, we are tricked by a caption into a misguided assumption, only to be forced to abandon such a naive misreading in the light of textual counter-evidence. The third caption's afterthought '– *aber Neuerungen!*' (the mock-enthusiastic exclamation-mark no doubt there to alert us to the fact) is a trap. Innovation that fails to attack the base does little to countermand the present 'culinary' nature of the medium.

To help anchor the main argument, various terms of contrast are introduced. The word 'Neuerung' (coupled with the promise of social 'Erneuerung') leads on to a distinction between acceptable and mere palliative ('culinary') innovations, well reflected in the way Willett's translation plays 'innovation' off against mere 'rejuvenation' and 'renovation' (*BT*, 34, 41). Those who are deluded enough to think they possess the apparatus are in turn shown to be possessed *by it*. Whether a work is 'gut' or 'schlecht' is superseded by the question of whether the society that produced it is 'gut' or 'schlecht'. Even the automatic assumption that the artist's current dependence on the apparatus must be a bad thing is brought into question: 'An sich aber ist die Einschränkung der freien Erfindung des einzelnen ein fortschrittlicher Prozeß. Der einzelne wird mehr und mehr in große, die Welt verändernde Vorgänge einbezogen. Er kann nicht mehr sich lediglich "ausdrücken". Er wird angehalten und instand gesetzt, allgemeine Aufgaben zu lösen' (*GBA*, 24:76).

Culinary imagery plays a major role in the unfolding argument. The apparatus appropriates the 'Kopfarbeit' of artists (seen as 'Kopfarbeiter') in order to serve it up 'zur Speisung[18] ihrer Publikumsorganisationen'; hence, what is required is audiences 'mit neuen Appetiten' (*GBA*, 24:74), whereas the current apparatus merely puts on the table ('serviert') what artists have created to cater for undemanding palates (*GBA*, 24:75). In the case of the superficially avant-garde innovations Brecht treats with cynicism in both the first and last sections of the *Mahagonny* notes, we are assured that 'der Kulinarismus war gerettet!' (*GBA*, 24:83). But this is no more than polemical sarcasm, for the implication is that society itself has not been saved. The initial antithesis 'kulinarisch' / 'fortgeschritten' is now unmasked as a false dichotomy, for one of the argument's main tactics involves insinuating that even avant-garde artists can be culinary without being aware of the fact. It is essentially in the light of this extended metaphor's socioeconomic associations that we are expected to understand the repeated claims about the 'culinary' nature of most opera. If deployed in isolation, such an image would give rise to a series of banal associations concerning pleasure and consumer--values. Hence, while the metaphor might be unobjectionable, it would remain tired and lacking in subtlety. Audiences, would be the implication, have 'appetites' which operas (or plays) obligingly satisfy. This is the rather predictable way the subject of appetites is treated at the beginning of 'Sollten wir nicht die Ästhetik liquidieren?' (*GBA*, 21:203) and in section 3 of 'Kleines Privatissimum für meinen Freund Max Gorelik' (*GBA*, 23:37). Such an indiscriminate use amounts to little more than a modish variation on Marx's image of religion as 'das Opium des Volkes' (in *Zur Kritik der Hegelschen Rechtsphilosophie*).[19] However, at this stage of the argument, Brecht inserts – between the charge that opera has hitherto been culinary and the above passage on such opera as a gratification of unworthy appetites – the claim that opera was 'ein Genußmittel, lange bevor sie eine Ware war' (*GBA*, 24:76). As a consequence, the attack becomes less purely aesthetic (art as gratification) than sociopolitical (gratification as commodity).[20] This neat twist justifies the earlier focus on the attitude of waiter, not diner

---

[18]Willett's pejorative 'to make *fodder* for their public entertainment *machine*' (*BT*, 34, my emphasis) palpably misses Brecht's register. The German term 'Speisung' is distinctly refined and helps continue the all too vivid metaphor of the (working-class) waiter serving food to an affluent diner.
[19]E.g. the references to bourgeois culture's 'Rauschgifthandel' (*GBA*, 22:162 and 164) and in the Preface to *Kleines Organon* (*GBA*, 23:65), where theater is charged with having degenerated into a branch of the bourgeois narcotics industry.
[20]In Voigts's reading (1977), '[die] Differenzierung von "kulinarischem Genuß" und "Appetit" zeigt, wie wichtig für Brecht der Kampf gegen die Ersatz-Funktion des Theaters war. Während der "Appetit" allgemein mit der

(to the meal or to the restaurant) or on that of the chef (to the recipes). It also throws light on why Brecht later turned his attention to another middleman in the complicated chain of commercialized artistic supply and demand: the 'culinary critic'. In a radio discussion of 15 April 1928, Brecht dismisses this figure as 'der auf ästhetische Reize aller Art fliegende Genußmensch' (*GBA*, 21:232). The main target is Brecht's arch-enemy Alfred Kerr,[21] who, as Hecht has observed, is being patronizingly treated as a *type*, not that this prevents the polemic from being intensely personal. Kerr had in fact been one of the participants in the Cologne radio discussion, although he was allowed to play little more than the role of whipping boy. Yet the ease with which Brecht moves from the idea of culinary opera and culinary drama to the less predictable subject of the culinary critic reveals the extent to which he sees the latter, not as an independent arbiter, but very much as part of the cultural apparatus. '*Bloße Agenten der Theater*' had been Brecht's verdict on critics two years before the *Mahagonny* notes (*GBA*, 21:236). It is this part of the notes that is as indebted to the Lukács of *Geschichte und Klassenbewußtsein* as to Sternberg's influence.

The culinary metaphor of the waiter for whom it is all the same which customer he waits on, as long as he gets paid for performing his job, is satirically focused on the superficial, avant-garde innovators who come in for a further drubbing in the final section, not the more obvious targets – the purveyors of sentimental dramas, kitsch operettas or Wagnerian *Gesamtkunstwerke*, about whose irrelevance both Brecht and his readers are assumed to be in agreement. ('Saustück' had been his term of abuse for one such work in 1922.[22]) The further metaphorical linking of innovation with a process of democratization is to be understood as deliberately subversive, given that we are still in the world of what Brecht saw as the Weimar Republic's pseudo-liberties. For this reason, the notion of giving the people new rights, but no chance to exercise them, leaves opera on one side in order to launch an attack on the base. As all this shows, the first section's title is now less innocent than it was on an initial reading.

Despite Brecht's resorting in parts of the notes to the discourse of Marxist analysis (opera as 'Ware', attacking 'die Basis',[23] and the controlling of works' reception as a form of manipulative 'Bewußtseinsindustrie'), his most extended metaphor, that of

---

Aufstiegsphase des Kapitalismus assoziiert wird, ist der Kulinarismus Ergebnis des Niedergangs: "Hier wird längst nicht mehr produziert, hier wird lediglich verbraucht, genossen und verteidigt".' Hence: 'Der Genuß erscheint nur in seiner zum 'Kulinarismus' verzerrten bürgerlichen Form als Ware und als Erholung' (85, 160).

[21] Cf. 'Die dialektische Dramatik', an unsparing diatribe against the dyed-in-the-wool bourgeois culinary critic Alfred Kerr (*GBA*, 21:434–35 ) and Brecht's occasional pieces against Kerr in the same volume (323–25). In 'Gespräch über Klassiker' 'culinary thinking' is also discussed: 'Das Bürgertum mußte seine rein geistigen Bemühungen so ziemlich liquidieren in einer Zeit, wo die Lust am Denken eine direkte Gefährdung seiner wirtschaftlichen Interessen bedeuten konnte. Wo das Denken nicht ganz eingestellt wurde, wurde es immer kulinarischer. Man machte zwar Gebrauch von den Klassikern, aber nur mehr kulinarischen Gebrauch' (*GBA*, 21:310). Audiences of the bourgeois theater of entertainment receive a similar broadside: 'Die Zuschauer genießen den Menschenschmerz rein als Amüsement, sie haben eine rein kulinarische Auffassung' (*GBA*, 21:229).

[22] In Brecht's review of the Augsburg première of W. Meyer-Förster's *Alt-Heidelberg*, in *Der Volkswille*, 15 October 1920 (*GBA*, 21:77). As a result, he was banned from attending any performance of Albert Lortzing's *Zar und Zimmermann* for reviewing purposes.

[23] Like many of the points in the *Mahagonny* notes, this model (generally indebted to Marx's 'Der achtzehnte Brumaire des Louis Bonaparte' [Marx-Engels 1958–68, vol.8 (1960), 111–94], and Georg Lukács's *Geschichte und Klassenbewußtsein*) had already appeared in an earlier form that was not as well worked out. Brecht had referred to theater, literature and art as the 'ideologischer Überbau' as early as November 1927 ('[Schwierigkeiten des epischen Theaters]', *GBA*, 21:210). He also uses both 'Basis' and 'Unterbau' (sic) in '[Basis der Kunst]' c. 1930 (*GBA*, 21:375–76).

'Kulinarismus', is less obviously part of a recently acquired Marxist model. And it tends to work via a cumulative process of satirical reduction and thus becomes, in this respect, interventionist rather than merely analytical. A related point is made elsewhere in the notes, not through abstract theorizing but by reference to *Mahagonny* itself, an operatic work whose subject matter Brecht once summed up as being 'der Kulinarismus' (*GBA*, 22:159). The passage this time literally involves eating. Having reminded readers that *Mahagonny's* content is pleasure, the notes underline the political implications of this by considering the potential impact of one particular episode in the work:

> Es soll nicht geleugnet werden, daß dieser Inhalt [der Genuß] zunächst provokatorisch wirken muß. Wenn zum Beispiel im dreizehnten Abschnitt der Vielfraß sich zu Tode frißt, so tut er dies, weil Hunger herrscht. Obgleich wir nicht einmal andeuten, daß andere hungerten, während dieser fraß, war die Wirkung dennoch provozierend. Denn wenn nicht jeder am Fressen stirbt, der zu fressen hat, so gibt es doch viele, die am Hunger sterben, weil er am Fressen stirbt. Sein Genuß provoziert, weil er so vieles enthält. In ähnlichen Zusammenhängen wirkt heute Oper als Genußmittel überhaupt provokatorisch. Freilich nicht auf ihre paar Zuhörer. Im Provokatorischen sehen wir die Realität wiederhergestellt. 'Mahagonny' mag nicht sehr schmackhaft sein, es mag sogar (aus schlechtem Gewissen) seinen Ehrgeiz darein setzen, es nicht zu sein – es ist durch und durch kulinarisch. 'Mahagonny' ist nichts anderes als eine Oper.
>
> (*GBA*, 24:77–78)

Mahagonny, the 'Paradiesstadt' where appetites are satisfied, is often, as Knopf has complained, interpreted as a 'Spiegelbild der kapitalistischen Welt'.[24] Brecht is even reported to have told an American interviewer that *Mahagonny* was 'set in an imaginary Florida' (Schevill 1961, 103). But as Knopf points out, such sloppy associations fail to do justice to the fact that Mahagonny was founded as a reaction against capitalism and the great cities (Knopf 2000, 105). The lure of consumables (whisky, food, adventure, women) is the main reason why the 'Goldstadt' becomes a mecca for 'DIE UNZUFRIEDENEN ALLER KONTINENTE', as the caption to scene 4 puts it. Yet even at plot-level, such indulgence has its dark side, as the image of the man dying of over-consumption shows.

The main significance of this episode for the *Mahagonny* notes exceeds mere plot-function. Brecht's concern is primarily with the requisite audience-response, one that would eventually be called dialectical, although for the time being he prefers to talk of 'Provokation'. What is said has meta-textual significance. The man depicted indulging in an act of gross self-gratification is watched by people observing the spectacle from the auditorium and meant to recognize an analogy to their own behavior as spectators of a calculatedly 'culinary' performance. Consequently, as the commentary suggests, they are provoked into stepping out of their role as 'culinary' spectators when, and because, they find the episode disturbing. That is to say, when they have realized that others must starve so that he can indulge himself, just as they are indulging in escapist enjoyment while what *Die Dreigroschenoper* calls 'die im Dunkel' struggle to survive. As Brecht puts it in his most memorable formulation of the predicament in 'An die Nachgeborenen' (*GBA*, 12:85):

> Man sagt mir: iß und trink du! Sei froh, daß du hast!
> Aber wie kann ich essen und trinken, wenn

---

[24]The phrase was originally Klaus Völker's (Völker and Pullem 1985, 112).

> Ich es dem Hungernden entreiße, was ich esse, und
> Mein Glas Wasser einem Verdurstenden fehlt?

Rather than merely caricaturing capitalism, the city Mahagonny – like opera itself, or, more specifically, like the opera of that name – represents a surrogate world (a 'Gegengründung'), But much more even than the fictive town, *Mahagonny* at the same time forces people to reflect on their behavior both in and outside the theater: 'Selbst wenn man die Oper als solche (ihre Funktion!) zur Diskussion stellen wollte', the end of the first section of the notes declares, 'müßte man eine Oper machen' (*GBA*, 24:76). That is: an opera designed, by *displaying* pronounced 'culinary' features rather than *being* culinary, to engender discomfort and insight, not an uncritically escapist opera. Under such circumstances, audiences are forced to bring the real world into the picture, not exclude it as the notes claim most opera does. 'Im Provokatorischen sehen wir die Realität wiederhergestellt.'[25]

The words 'kulinarisch' and 'Kulinarismus' do not appear in the following section, although it hardly requires a great leap of the imagination to realize that what Brecht calls the 'Dramatische Form des Theaters' has boundless culinary potential. The reason for such a lack of terminological continuity (at the same time as the section titles engage in an ongoing dialogue with one another) is that the *Mahagonny notes* are structured according to the selfsame 'epic' principle of relative autonomy of parts that the third section will shortly elucidate. The sections looked at so far form part of a deliberately segmented structure, the first, largely on a Marxist sociology of opera, being followed by an aesthetically oriented analysis of the 'culinary' nature of the medium and thus its affirmative function, then intercut by what looks to all intents and purposes like an excursus on the relationship between Epic and Dramatic Theater. Brecht does admittedly provide an explicit rationale for this last thematic shift, even if it hardly helps distract our attention from the fact that the new section differs radically from the preceding argument. Opera, ' – *aber Neuerungen!*' announces, 'war auf den technischen Standard des modernen Theaters zu bringen' (*GBA*, 24:78). To give substance to this declaration, Brecht explains just what kind of technical standard is meant. But to do so by no means 'harmonizes' (in his pejorative sense) the relationship between the previous section and the material to come. On the contrary, the sudden shift of focus from opera to theater creates a disjunctive effect comparable to the one §74 of the *Kleines Organon* refers to as an act of 'gegenseitige Verfremdung'. From the point when the title of the notes became 'Das moderne Theater ist das epische Theater', the discussion of opera was estranged by being approached via theater, with theater itself being estranged by having been placed within a context stressing the extreme 'Kulinarismus' of opera. In embryonic form, we are exposed to the same processes of montage, reciprocal estrangement, and 'Episierung' that characterize Epic Theater. Indeed, the section titles in these notes function in much the same way as Brecht's prefaces to the individual scenes of works of Epic Theater. (Perhaps this is one reason why the reader is referred by a footnote to the section on '*Titel*

---

[25]Brüggemann 1973, 156–57, posits a relationship between montage and 'Verfremdung' in which the formal elements of montage ('Distanz, Unterbrechung, Umfunktionierung') obey a defamiliarizing principle according to which they transcend theater's autonomy and separation from everyday life. This feature is prefigured in Brecht's remarks about scene 13 of *Mahagonny*.

*und Tafeln*' in Brecht's notes to *Die Dreigroschenoper*.[26]) The section headings employed in the *Mahagonny* notes are not scholarly headings, with the task of structuring a complex argument. They primarily represent challenges to the reader; and in doing so they create space for critical reflection. The word 'Neuerungen' used in two of the early section titles is clearly inserted to be deconstructed, to make some of its connotations appear questionable, and thus prepare the ground for a substantially more radical interpretation of what might constitute genuine innovation. The combination of italics and exclamation mark in the first heading, the way the second and third play with isolated parts of the first, and the use of a reporting (epic) preterite in a sub-section title within the third section ('*Musik, Wort und Bild mußten mehr Selbständigkeit erhalten*'[27]), all involve a dialectical play with expectations (not least because of the political metaphor of autonomy). They keep us on our toes in a way that has more in common with the techniques of Epic Theater than with the scholarly conventions of the time.[28]

One reason for such a strategy was hinted at in my earlier reference to 'falsches Bewußtsein'. By this I mean that a recurrent Brechtian method of combating the ideological inertia that false consciousness induces entails the creation of critical distance through carefully planted 'epicizing' elements, some of which had already been identified in Brecht's notes to *Die Dreigroschenoper*. There are 'Titel' in both the operas *Mahagonny* and *Die Dreigroschenoper* and in the notes to them, although 'Tafeln' can hardly figure in a published work of theory. And in the *Mahagonny* notes as well as in many of Brecht's other theoretical works, techniques of framing can be seen as logical corollaries of his suggestion that 'auch in die Dramatik ist die Fußnote und das vergleichende Blättern einzuführen' (*GBA*, 24:59). Methods of distancing that work in the theater can be equally effective in theoretical texts. After all, Brecht never tired of repeating his claim that the kind of de-familiarization he sought to achieve onstage was a phenomenon common in other walks of everyday life (witness 'Die Straßenszene'[29]).

Immediately preceding his two-column table contrasting Dramatic and Epic Forms of Theater, Brecht inserts the most important footnote he ever wrote: 'Dieses Schema zeigt nicht absolute Gegensätze, sondern lediglich Akzenverschiebungen. So kann innerhalb eines Mitteilungsvorgangs das gefühlmäßig Suggestive oder das rein rationell Überredende bevorzugt werden' (*GBA*, 24:78). So anxious is Brecht to ensure that his readers realize that the table's task is to make visual not absolute antitheses but merely shifts in emphasis, that he rounds off the 'Schema' with another footnote using the same metaphor: 'Über die Gewichtsverschiebungen innerhalb der Darstellung siehe Versuch "Dialog über

---

[26]'Literarisierung des Theaters' was written before the *Mahagonny* notes, and appeared in the *Programmblätter der Volksbühne* for the Berlin premiere of *Die Dreigroschenoper* in September 1928. The *Mahagonny* notes were written almost two years later.

[27]In Willett, the sentence loses much of its epic quality by being transposed into the present tense: '*Words, music and setting must become more independent of one another*' (*BT*, 38). In the new edition (*GBA*, 24:79), the following sub-subtitle – '*a) Musik*' – is indented to align it with the above sentence, which, since they are both italicized and there is no line-space between them, makes them together form part of a further sub-segmentalization of the argument.

[28]Giles 1997 adopts a similarly Brechtian 'Gestus': individual "section headings [being] inspired by [Brecht's] conversations on Kafka with Walter Benjamin in 1931 and 1934" (33). Such headings as 'Vor dem Gesetz', 'Der Verschollene', 'Der Prozeß', 'Das Urteil', 'Eine alltägliche Verwirrung', 'Ein Bericht für eine Akademie', 'Beschreibung eines Kampfes', 'Zur Frage der Gesetze', and 'Gib's auf!' are related to stages of the *Dreigroschenprozeß*.

[29]'Die Straßenszene. *Grundmodell einer Szene des epischen Theaters* (1940)' (*GBA*, 22:370–81).

Schauspielkunst'" (*GBA*, 24:79),³⁰ And, when presenting a second table contrasting Dramatic and Epic Opera, he reiterates the image ('für die Musik ergab sich folgende Gewichtsverschiebung' [*GBA*, 24:79]). To appreciate the strategy employed, it is necessary to bear in mind that the *Mahagonny* notes are something of a rarity among Brecht's theoretical writings because of both the frequency with which they resort to footnotes and the function that most of the notes serve. *Der Messingkauf*, more than fifteen times longer, has only five footnotes, *Kleines Organon* only one. Without exception, these all serve the conventional function of indicating a source. But when a source is signalled in the *Mahagonny* notes, for example in the perhaps surprising reference in note 10 to Freud's *Das Unbehagen in der Kultur* (*GBA*, 24:83), the argument is taken off in a substantially new unexplored direction and the failure of that footnote to indicate whether we are being offered a quotation from, or a paraphrase of, Freud means that readers will have to go and find out for themselves. (Which is what the editors of the new edition had to do before they could report that Brecht was quoting in abbreviated form from the 1930 Vienna edition of the work [*GBA*, 24:481].) The *Mahagonny* notes were not only the first of Brecht's theoretical writings to make intelligent use of an epicizing footnote strategy, they were also one of the last.³¹

Using a footnote to forewarn readers not to expect the 'Schema' to offer a simple set of absolute antitheses would under some circumstances simply have been a prudent preemptive move on Brecht's part (which might have been the case, had not the footnote's caveat been so stubbornly ignored in the coming years). Yet although it contains an important rider, Brecht's note still appears to be disturbingly at odds with the rigorous contrast implied by the column-headings '*Dramatische Form des Theaters*' and '*Epische Form*'. As, has been suggested, 'zur Verkennung von [Brechts] intendierter Schwerpunktsverlagerung mag der beim Lesen entstehende optische Eindruck der schlagwortartigen Gegenüberstellung zweier Formen des Theaters beigetragen haben' (*BHB*, 4:51). Although it has the appearance of a late caveat added to subsequent reprintings to fend off certain forms of misinterpretation, it was in fact already there in the *Musik und Gesellschaft* version. So we are left with a conundrum: why does Brecht use misleading absolutizing presentational strategies, if, as he claims, he is only concerned with shifts of accent? An alternative formulation such as 'Die dramatische Tendenz im Theater' and 'Die epische Tendenz' or recourse to the term 'Element' might arguably have saved him a number of later difficulties. But this is to miss the point. The goal of such disjunction is primarily 'epic' distancing. To be told in a footnote what the scheme *does not* show is on a par with Brecht's term 'nicht-aristotelisches Theater'. Making readers work *ex negativo* towards insights demands the kind of 'productivity' that Brecht the dramatist expects of his theater audiences.³² And in a more modest way, so too does the footnote

---

³⁰Although this note is deleted in the Malik edition, presumably because the final 'Gefühl' / 'Ratio' contrast has been removed, it arguably refers to the entire table, not just to its final contrast. More intriguingly, it is also missing from Unseld's *Schriften zum Theater* (GW. vol. 17) and *Brecht on Theatre*, although these reinstate the final contrast.

³¹There are two major exceptions: the *Antigonemodell 1948* (where the notes are of a conventional scholarly kind) and some of Brecht's theoretical writings that appear not to have been written for immediate publication (e.g. 'Über neue Musik' [*GBA*, 21:402–1], 'Über den Erkenntnisvorgang' [*GBA*, 22:410–12], and 'Einige Gedanken zur Stanislawski-Konferenz' [*GBA*, 23:236–39].) Here the uncommon phenomenon of a writer adding footnotes to penned draft material can best be accounted for by assuming that they function primarily as *aides-mémoire*.

³²In *Kleines Organon* §23, Brecht speaks of 'ein Theater, das die Produktivität zur Hauptqulle der Unterhaltung macht' (*GBA*, 23:74). The kind of productivity he has in mind is explained in 'Die dialektische Dramatik'

appearing at the end of the 'Schema' that refers us to 'Dialog über Schauspielkunst'. We are being invited to engage in the sort of intertextual 'vergleichendes Blättern' invoked in the 'Literarisierung des Theaters' section of the notes to *Die Dreigroschenoper*. At issue in this case is not the need to keep emotion at bay (feelings hardly represent a danger to someone consulting a table of contrasts in some notes on (an) opera). Rather, the purpose is to encourage what the sentence following immediately on from the one about footnotes in 'Titel und Tafeln' refers to as 'komplexes Sehen' (*GBA*, 24:59). Complex seeing, even if it is not yet necessarily synonymous with a dialectical response, is far removed from unthinkingly approaching theatrical developments in terms of simple antitheses. Like Epic Theater itself, the theorizing of Epic Theater evidently required new techniques of discursive presentation to facilitate the right kind of response.

## SCHEMING BRECHT

Brecht's table contrasting Dramatic and Epic Theater has probably been reproduced more often than any of his other theoretical utterances. Reproduced, that is, but seldom subjected to detailed exegesis, the honorable exceptions being Hultberg 1962 and Hecht 1972. Brecht's 'Schema' (*GBA*, 24:78–79) is reproduced below, with numbers added to the pairs of contrasting points, for the convenience of operating with the same reference-system as Hultberg uses.

|      | *Dramatische Form des Theaters* | *Epische Form des Theaters* |
|------|---------------------------------|------------------------------|
| (1)  | handelnd | erzählend |
| (2)  | verwickelt den Zuschauer in eine Bühnenaktion | macht den Zuschauer zum Betrachter, aber |
| (3)  | verbraucht seine Aktivität | weckt seine Aktivität |
| (4)  | ermöglicht ihm Gefühle | erzwingt von ihm Entscheidungen |
| (5)  | Erlebnis | Weltbild |
| (6)  | Der Zuschauer wird in etwas hineinversetzt | er wird gegenübergesetzt |
| (7)  | Suggestion | Argument |
| (8)  | Die Empfindungen werden konserviert | bis zu Erkenntnissen getrieben |
| (9)  | Der Zuschauer steht mittendrin, miterlebt | Der Zuschauer steht gegenüber, studiert |
| (10) | Der Mensch als bekannt vorausgesetzt | Der Mensch ist Gegenstand der Untersuchung |
| (11) | Der unveränderliche Mensch | Der veränderliche und verändernde Mensch |
| (12) | Spannung auf den Ausgang | Spannung auf den Gang |
| (13) | Eine Szene für die andere | Jede Szene für sich |
| (14) | Wachstum | Montage |
| (15) | Geschehen linear | in Kurven |
| (16) | evolutionäre Zwangsläufigkeit | Sprünge |

---

(written in the same year as the *Mahagonny* notes): '[Der moderne Zuschauer] wünscht nicht, bevormundet und vergewaltigt zu werden, sondern er will einfach menschliches Material vorgeworfen bekommen, *um es selber zu ordnen*. [...] er ist nicht nur mehr Konsument, sondern er muß produzieren' (*GBA*, 21:440–41).

(17)   Der Mensch als Fixum              Der Mensch als Prozeß
(18)   Das Denken bestimmt das Sein      Das gesellschaftliche Sein bestimmt das
                                         Denken
(19)   Gefühl                            Ratio

Hultberg's commentary, the first of its kind, sets out to demonstrate that 'dieses Schema ist nicht sonderlich klar':

> Mehrere Punkte scheinen überflüssig zu sein. So ist es schwer, zu sehen, daß 17 mehr sagt, als schon unter 11 gesagt ist; 2, 6 und 9 könnten auch unter einem Punkt zusammengefaßt werden, während dafür 4 und 19 widersprechend zu sein scheinen. (Entscheidungen und Ratio, die das epische Theater im Gegensatz zu dem Gefühl des dramatischen Theaters kennzeichnen sollen, sind zwar nicht Gegensätze, aber jedenfalls in keiner Weise identisch). Ferner ist es auch nicht klar, inwieweit die einzelnen Punkte auseinander folgen, oder ob sie ganz unabhängig voneinander sind, so daß man von einigen von ihnen absehen könnte. Daß das Bild, das Brecht vom 'dramatischen Theater' zeichnet, [...] überaus irreführend ist, bedarf keines näheren Nachweises; interessanter ist die Verwirrung, die das Bild des epischen Theaters prägt. Der entscheidende Punkt ist wohl 18, der deutlich Brechts deterministische, vulgärmarxistische Haltung zeigt. Falls dieser Punkt absolut gesetzt wird, ist ein eigentlich didaktisches Theater ja unmöglich. In dem Falle hat der Zuschauer nur die Möglichkeit, die Welt zu studieren (9), eventuell zu gewissen Erkenntnissen zu gelangen (8), aber wirkliche Entscheidungen (4), eine echte Aktivität (3) kann im Theater nicht erreicht werden. Wenn das Bewußtsein des Menschen ausschließlich von den sozialen Verhältnissen geformt wird, so ist das Theater eine Belustigung ganz ohne Bedeutung wie z .B. Sportkämpfe, was Brecht bisher ja auch behauptet hat.
>
> (Hultberg 1962, 107)

Hultberg concludes: 'Das *Mahagonny-Schema* ist der Versuch eines Kompromisses zwischen der alten und der neueren Auffassung, zwischen dem Sporttheater und dem Schultheater, und es ist daher höchst mißlich, daß es meist in kürzeren Darstellungen benutzt wird, um zu zeigen, was Brecht eigentlich mit seinem Theater wollte' (ibid.). Because of the seriousness of the points raised here, I should like to examine them in detail.

First, there is the damaging assertion that certain items are superfluous: that 17 says little more than had already been said in 11 and that 2, 6 and 9 could have profitably been conflated. Brecht could well have sensed a certain lack of economy in the 1930 version, for when he revised it for inclusion in 'Vergnügungstheater oder Lehrtheater?' he removed some of the redundant elements that Hultberg was still complaining about some quarter of a century later.[33] Yet none of these changes takes account of the main problems Hultberg was to have with the 'Schema'. To explain why, we need to distinguish between a *vertical* reading of the material and a *horizontal* one.

---

[33] Hultberg cannot have known this since *GW*, vol. 15 omits the 'Schema', indicating the omission with ellipsis dots, and wrongly stating that they refer to 'das Schema, das Brecht in der ersten Ausgabe der *Versuche*, H. 2, 1930, in den "Anmerkungen zur Oper *Aufstieg und Fall der Stadt Mahagonny*" veröffentlichte' (Anmerkungen, 9*). The subsequent Statement is equally misleading: 'Da Brecht dieses Schema später in der Form für unzureichend hielt und für den zweiten Druck der Anmerkungen in der Malik-Ausgabe, 1938, redigierte und ergänzte, wurde der Text hier ausgelassen und auf das gültige Schema verwiesen' (ibid.).

In the case of at least one pair of contrasts, syntax clearly forces us to read from the left-hand column across to the directly opposite equivalent on the right-hand side; 'Die Empfindungen werden konserviert / bis zu Erkenntnissen getrieben'. In the second, less frequently quoted 'Schema' contrasting Dramatic and Epic *Opera* (*GBA*, 24:80), the same shared subject again results in a situation where the reader can only make sense of the points by reading horizontally across from individual items in the left-hand column to their adjacant equivalents:

| | |
|---|---|
| Musik illustrierend | Stellung nehmend |
| Musik die psychische Situation malend | das Verhalten gebend |
| | (*GBA*, 24:80) |

But even where our reading is not a matter of being carried across by the syntax, entry by entry, from the left-hand column to the right-hand one, the horizontal paradigm (as in 6, 10, and 13 in the first 'Schema') still tends to predominate:

| | |
|---|---|
| Der Zuschauer wird in etwas hineinversetzt | er wird gegenübergesetzt |
| Der Mensch als bekannt vorausgesetzt | Der Mensch ist Gegenstand der Untersuchung |
| Eine Szene für die andere | Jede Szene für sich |

Only once does a grammatical pointer invite the reader to drop directly down to the next entry *in the same column,* viz. at the end of 2, when the 'aber' identifies an apparent contradiction between the passivity of 'macht den Zuschauer zum Betrachter' and 'weckt seine Aktivität'. This pairing involves issues vital to an understanding of Brecht's conception of Epic Theater, hence the anomalous feature is best regarded as a pattern-breaking 'Verfremdungseffekt'.

Many of Hultberg's quibbles and objections remain explicable only when read as part of a *vertical* reading of the right-hand column, even though, from its two polarizing headings onwards, Brecht's actual 'Schema' invites us to engage with the material by traversing from a characteristic in the left-hand column to its equivalent on the right. (Even the footnote denying absolute antitheses is predicated on the same linear paradigm.) Only someone bent on a vertical reading would have a modicum of justification in claiming 'es [ist] schwer, zu sehen, daß 17 mehr sagt, als schon unter 11 gesagt ist'. True, 'Der unveränderliche Mensch' may on a cursory reading mean the same as 'Der Mensch als Fixum', but as so often with this table of paired terms, it is what the characteristic in the one column is being set against that obviates any crude exercise in tautology. Brecht obviously refuses to pair 'Der unveränderliche Mensch' with the predictable 'Der veränderliche Mensch'. Instead, he juxtaposes it with 'Der veränderliche und verändernde Mensch'. And since 'verändernd' has no object, it remains for the reader to decide whether this means capable of altering himself or herself possibly refers to 'das gesellschaftliche Sein' mentioned in 18. This contrast's field of meaning is therefore not slavishly duplicated in 17. In any case, the German word in the left-hand column ('Fixum') is in a register significantly more technical – more scientific, even – than the phrase 'fixed entity' offered in Willett's English translation. And that it has a technical quality is understandable, given that the new concept has the task of preparing for an ideological contrast between idealist and materialist conceptions of reality, one which certainly refers to the notion of changing social conditions and not just individual human beings, once the context is supplied by the Foreword to Marx's *Politische Ökonomie*.[34] Hultberg also worries about the fact that 'Entscheidungen' (4) and 'Ratio' (19), while being 'zwar nicht Gegensätze', are 'in keiner Weise identisch'. But this merely raises the question of just what relationship is assumed to be the operative one. The 'ermöglicht ihm Gefühle' and the single noun 'Gefühl' of the left-hand column may appear synonymous, if one does not look too closely, but as Hultberg notes, the relationship between a theater leading to 'Entscheidungen' and a theater of 'Ratio' is a more complex one.

As the points looked at so far suggest, there is more than one way to respond to the *Mahagonny* 'Schema'. It can be read as proof of Brecht's incompetence when it comes to presenting important material in diagrammatic form (the breast-beating in his letter to 'Genosse M.' might seem like an invitation to view it thus). An alternative would be to treat it as part of an argument deliberately constructed according to a less discursive principle.[35] Hultberg unwittingly hints at what that principle might be when he complains: 'es [ist] auch nicht klar, inwieweit die einzelnen Punkte auseinander folgen, oder ob sie ganz unabhängig voneinander sind, so daß man von einigen von ihnen absehen könnte' (Hultberg 1962, 107). Now this sounds very reminiscent of Point 13's contrast between the situation in the '*Dramatische Form des Theaters*' ('Eine Szene für die andere') and that in the '*Epische Form*' ('Jede Szene für sich'). One of the repercussions of Epic Theater's relative autonomy of parts is that some points could be either replaced or omitted, as in Willett's 1959 account, where only eight of the 'Schema''s nineteen points are offered, or in the case of the *Left Review*'s new note to its reprint of 'The German Drama: Pre-Hitler', where, again, only a small selection is offered. Compare this feature with two remarks Brecht made elsewhere about Epic Theater: 'Eine gewisse Austauschbarkeit der Vorkommnisse und Umstände muß dem Zuschauer das Montieren, Experimentieren und Abstrahieren gestatten' (*GBA*, 24:182); and in the specific case of *Die Maßnahme*, 'ganze Szenen können eingefügt werden' (*GBA*, 22:351). My working hypothesis in what follows is that Brecht's 'Schema' like the *Mahagonny* notes in their entirety, displays features best understood as 'epic'. It is time to leave Hultberg on one side and look at this feature of the way the 'Schema' is structured.

One salient characteristic is a visual rhythm whereby juxtaposed phrases of varying length are repeatedly punctuated in the two columns by single pairs of antithetical characteristics: 'handelnd' / 'erzählend', 'Erlebnis' / 'Weltbild', 'Suggestion' / 'Argument', 'Wachstum' / 'Montage'. These (usually nominal) pairings have tended to become the main bones of contention in the table's reception. Apart from the fact that they are not invariably absolute antitheses, their reception has shown that Brecht's various contrasts are not always as lucid or without need of clarification

---

[34] *GBA*, 24:479 cites Engels's – Friedrich Engels (1820–1895) – *Ludwig Feuerbach und der Ausgang der klassischen deutschen Philosophie* (Vienna-Berlin, 1927, 27–28) as source, no doubt because Brecht's 'Nachlassbibliothek' contains a copy. But Engels's discussion of the relationship between 'Denken' and 'Sein' is not being quoted; the Foreword to the *Politische Ökonomie* is. Brecht could, however, have just as well made the point using Marx's and Engels's *Die Deutsche Ideologie*.

[35] In her discussion of analogous examples of seeming inconsistency in the various parts of *Kleines Organon*, Ana Kugli reminds her readers that "Unstimmigkeiten sind von der Forschung selten als eigene Qualität gewürdigt, vielmehr als eindeutige Unzulänglichkeit [...] herausgestellt worden, ohne dass dabei die [Brechtsche] Methodik reflektiert worden wäre" (*BHB*, 4:321 ). On this phenomenon, see also Kobel 1992.

as their reduction to single nouns might imply. The terms in the right-hand column identifying characteristics of Brechtian Epic Theater have been especially susceptible to divergent readings and in some instances possess a more specific connotation than might at first appear to be the case. Some are also more elevated (or more technical) in register than the English equivalents usually offered for them. Thus, for example, the contrast between 'Suggestion' and 'Argument' (in 7) acquires a far more specific referential framework once one realizes that in German 'Suggestion' tends to occur in depth-psychological contexts. In 'Dialog über Schauspielkunst' (which a footnote advises readers to consult), Brecht criticizes conventional empathie acting. Thespians of the old school, he complains, achieve their effects: 'mit Zuhilfenahme der Suggestion. Sie versetzen sich selber und das Publikum in Trance. [...] Sie haben etwa den Abschied darzustellen. Was machen sie? Sie versetzen sich in Abschiedsstimmung. Sie wollen, daß das Publikum in Abschiedsstimmung gerät. Niemand sieht zuletzt, wenn die Séance glückt, mehr etwas, niemand lernt etwas kennen, im besten Fall erinnert sich jedermann, kurz: jedermann fühlt' (*GBA*, 21:280). The appearance here of the term 'Suggestion' in close proximity to the words 'Trance' and 'Séance' establishes a connection between identificatory acting and hypnotism. The *Mahagonny* notes go on to declare: 'alles, was Hypnotisierversuche darstellen soll, unwürdige Räusche erzeugen muß, benebelt, muß aufgegeben werden' (*GBA*, 24:79). In the revised version of the 'Schema' from 1935 'Suggestion' has been expanded to: 'Es wird mit Suggestion gearbeitet' (*GBA*, 22:109), yet it is unlikely that Brecht's readers, especially non-German ones, will perceive that this statement is intended to take up the earlier reference to 'Suggestion' in the 'Schema'. The metaphor of hypnosis has taken over from the culinary as the main weapon in Brecht's polemical arsenal by this stage of the argument, and this long before Brecht has encountered the classic embodiment of such an approach: in the American reception of the Stanislavsky-System.

Other nouns in the German original possess different nuances or are in a different register to their standard English translations. 'Montage' might seem to be the only technical loan-word in the 'Schema' accurately reflected by its English equivalent, yet even it proves to be a false friend. Its primary association in German is with mechanical engineering rather than the dizzy heights of Dada and Surrealism. In *Mann ist Mann*, Galy Gay's transformation into a human fighting-machine is expressed using this connotation: 'Hier wird heute abend ein Mensch wie ein Auto ummontiert' (*GBA*, 2:123), i.e. as if he were a piece of machinery which could be taken to pieces and re-functionalized, to become a 'Kampfmaschine'. Brecht reinforced the mechanical association in his notes to the play (*GBA*, 2:157); the idea is echoed in Hecht's account of the link between montage and alterability: 'Die Veränderungen wurden in der ersten Fassung des Schemas noch als "Montage"-Akte gesehen (in der Art, wie die Soldaten beispielsweise Galy Gay "ummontierten")' (Hecht 1972, 53). Brecht in due course went on to use the cognate verb 'einmontieren' to refer more specifically to a structural principle in Epic Theater. In 'Über experimentelles Theater' (1939), he establishes a parallel between the insertion of didactic elements into a work and the technique of montage: 'Die belehrenden Elemente in einer Piscator- oder einer "Dreigroschenoper"-Aufführung waren sozusagen *einmontiert*, sie ergaben sich nicht organisch aus dem Ganzen, sie standen in einem Gegensatz zum Ganzen' (*GBA*, 22:546). The *Mahagonny* table's juxtaposition of 'Wachstum' with 'Montage' is replicated in the above observation, although the material inserted is now specifically defined as didactic. (Elsewhere Brecht speaks of the music and song being montage components.) Brüggemann (see note 25) relates the montage principle to the insertion of elements *from the real world* into an epic structure. Despite these highly specific interpretations, it is also possible to read 'montage' as denoting, not the intercalating of some circumscribed category of material, but possessing an over-arching epic macro-structure. Indeed, the table's contrast between organic growth and montage would appear to indicate that it is primarily at such a level of generality that the term is meant to be understood. Immediate context in the 'Schema' offers further support for such an assumption, for the contrast in 14 is sandwiched between a series of attempts at summing up differences between Epic Theater and Dramatic Theater in unambiguously structural terms:

| Eine Szene für die andere | Jede Szene für sich |
| --- | --- |
| [14].................................................................. | |
| Geschehen linear | in Kurven |
| evolutionäre Zwangsläufigkeit | Sprünge |

It is particularly this part of the 'Schema' that invites the conclusion that Brecht's conception of Epic Theater is to some considerable extent a structural one, standing in a prestigious German cultural tradition of contrasting the epic and the dramatic.

Consider, for example, the following extracts from the correspondence between Goethe and Schiller in April 1797 and their similarity to Brecht's account of the differences between Epic and Dramatic Theater:

> daß sie [die poetische Fabel meines *Wallensteins*] ein stetiges Ganzes ist, daß alles durchgängig bestimmt ist (Schiller, 18 April),

> daß die Selbständigkeit seiner Teile einen Hauptcharakter des epischen Gedichtes ausmacht (Schiller, 21 April).

> daß man von einem guten [epischen] Gedicht den Ausgang wissen könne, ja wissen müsse, und daß eigentlich das *Wie* bloß das Interesse machen dürfe. Dadurch erhält die Neugierde gar keinen Anteil an einem solchen Werke und sein Zweck kann [...] in jedem Punkte seiner Bewegung liegen (Goethe, 22 April).

> [der tragische Dichter] steht unter der Kategorie der Kausalität, der Epiker unter der der Substantialität. (Schiller, 25 April).

> das epische Gedicht [soll] keine Einheit haben (Goethe, 28 April).[36]

---

[36]*Briefwechsel zwischen Goethe und Schiller in den Jahren 1794 bis 1805*. In fact, Brecht makes repeated references to the correspondence during 1948, the year of his work on both *Kleines Organon* and the *Antigonemodell*. A note in *GBA*, 25:512 states that in the period leading up to the *Antigone* production in Chur that year, Brecht had been led by Lukács's 1934 essay 'Der Briefwechsel zwischen Schiller und Goethe' to engage in a protracted study of the correspondence. However, the journal entry for 8 January 1948 (*GBA*, 27:263) to the effect that it is the first time that he has been struck by the way Goethe and Schiller handle their public implies that he had lived with the material for some considerable time before that. Similarly, the way the argument in 'Vergnügungstheater oder Lehrtheater?' moves rapidly from the examples cited by Goethe and Schiller to a consideration of developments in the nineteenth-century bourgeois novel suggests that he was already familiar with Lukács's essay within a year of its first appearance, though whether he had read the actual correspondence by then seems more doubtful. There is no evidence that he had read Goethe's and Schiller's 'Über epische und dramatische Dichtung', although Lukács emphasizes its importance.

Here is Brecht on the same subject in 'Vergügnungstheater oder Lehrtheater?':

> Der Unterschied zwischen der dramatischen und der epischen Form wurde schon nach Aristoteles in der verschiedenen Bauart erblickt, deren Gesetze in zwei verschiedenen Zweigen der Ästhetik behandelt wurden. Diese Bauart hing von der verschiedenen Art ab, in der die Werke dem Publikum angeboten wurden, einmal durch die Bühne, einmal durch das Buch [...]. Der bürgerliche Roman entwickelte im vorigen Jahrhundert ziemlich viel 'Dramatisches,' und man verstand darunter *die starke Zentralisation einer Fabel, ein Moment des Aufeinandergewiesenseins der einzelnen Teile*. Eine gewisse Leidenschaftlichkeit des Vortrags, ein Herausarbeiten des Aufeinanderprallens der Kräfte kennzeichnete das 'Dramatische.' Der deutsche Epiker Döblin gab ein vorzügliches Kennzeichen, als er sagte, Epik könne man im Gegensatz zu Dramatik sozusagen mit der Schere in einzelne Stücke schneiden, welche durchaus lebensfähig bleiben. [...] [Die] Umwelt war natürlich auch im bisherigen Drama gezeigt worden, jedoch nicht als selbständiges Element, sondern nur von der Mittelpunktsfigur des Dramas aus, [...] Im epischen Theater sollte sie selbständig in Erscheinung treten.
>
> (GBA, 22:107–8; my emphasis)[37]

The idea is taken up and again modified a few years later in *Der Messingkauf*:

> Bei der aristotelischen Stückkomposition und der dazugehörigen Spielweise [...] wird die Täuschung des Zuschauers über die Art und Weise, wie die Vorgänge auf der Bühne sich im wirklichen Leben abspielen und dort zustande kommen, dadurch gefördert, daß der Vortrag der Fabel ein absolutes Ganzes bildet. Die Details können nicht einzeln mit ihren korrespondierenden Teilen im wirklichen Leben konfrontiert werden. Man darf nichts 'aus dem Zusammenhang reißen,' um es etwa in den Zusammenhang der Wirklichkeit zu bringen. Das wird durch die verfremdende Spielweise abgestellt. *Die Fortführung der Fabel ist hier diskontinuierlich, das einheitliche Ganze besteht aus selbständigen Teilen*, die jeweils sofort mit den korrespondierenden Teilvorgängen in der Wirklichkeit konfrontiert werden können, ja müssen. Ständig zieht diese Spielweise alle Kraft aus dem Vergleich mit der Wirklichkeit, d.h. sie lenkt das Auge ständig auf die Kausalität der abgebildeten Vorgänge.
>
> (GBA, 22:701, my emphasis)

It is only at the point where the above observation shades into a consideration of epic montage's fragmentary referentiality that it departs radically from the contrasts Goethe and Schiller make. In doing so it picks up the traces of an idea that had already been present in the passage in the *Mahagonny* notes about the man gorging himself to death in scene 13.

One could sum up by concluding that in the 1930s one of the main characteristics of Brechtian Epic Theater was a particular discontinuous kind of (montage) structure and that his theorizing on the subject builds on ideas in Goethe's and Schiller's correspondence, even if the question of generic characteristics has now become politicized and more specifically related to twentieth-century concepts of 'montage' in both engineering

---

[37]'Bemerkungen zum Roman' (originally published in *Die Neue Rundschau*, March 1917), quoted here from Döblin 1963, 21. Brecht spares his more squeamish readers the fact that Döblin's metaphor concerns the cutting-up of a live 'Regenwurm'.

and the visual arts. But if, as some other parts of the table suggest, all Brecht means by 'Episches Theater' is a theater of critical distance, then another area of un-clarity still remains, for at times the table refers to means and at times to ends. Of course, there is no reason why it has to focus exclusively on just the one or the other. Indeed, such shifting between the two may be a further strategy intended to provoke the reader into a 'productive' engagement with the material.

It was not until the late 1940s that Brecht returned to his earlier points about epic characteristics, now providing an account of them with reference to the Goethe-Schiller correspondence. In a journal entry for 3 Januar 1948, he notes:

> *Schiller* sieht erstaunlich deutlich die Dialektik (widersprüchliche Verknüpfung) in dem Verhältnis *Epos – Drama*. Meine eigenen Hinweise, das epische Theater betreffend, sind oft mißverständlich, da sie kritisch oppositioneller Natur sind und sich voll gegen das Dramatische meiner Zeit richten, das künstlich undialektisch gehandhabt wird. In der Tat soll einfach das epische Element in die dramatische Dichtart wieder hingebracht werden, freilich widersprüchlich. Die Freiheit der Kalkulation muß eben 'in dem mitreißenden Strom' der Geschehnisse etabliert werden.
>
> (GBA, 27:260–61)

Surprisingly, this, like the reference to the Goethe-Schiller *Briefwechsel* in §50 *of Kleines Organon* (GBA, 23:84), shows total disregard for the structural issues touched on at the stage of the exchange that appears to have been so important to him in the early 1930s. Conceivably, Brecht was already moving towards his later stated position that a concern with epic *structure* was too formalist (GBA, 23:386) and that, as Lukács had shown, one needed to progress beyond an obsession with discontinuity and the relative autonomy of parts to a dialectical conception of the material's relationship to the world depicted. This will later be summed up in §67 of *Kleines Organon*, where the gaps between the individual components of an epic structure are said to allow the audience 'mit dem Urteil dazwischen [zu] kommen' (GBA, 23:92). The archetype of a 'non-epic' play as a monolithic whole to which all of its parts cumulatively contribute is based on an anachronistic image of structure-as-growth derived from botany and probably being used here for satirical effect.[38] Whether Brecht's unnamed target was the Wagnerian *Gesamtkunstwerk*,[39] Max Reinhardt's theater, or the 'well-made' drama of the late nineteenth century, none of these is predicated on the metaphor of structure-as-growth offered as the contrast to epic structure.

One further, related feature of the *Mahagonny* 'Schema' demands caution. When Brecht contrasts the '*Dramatische Form des Theaters*' with the '*Epische Form des Theaters*', the word 'Form' probably means no more than 'type' or 'embodiment'. The two headings do not necessarily imply that the contrasts are primarily between what in

---

[38]See Salm 1971 for a survey of the genesis and implications of this botanical metaphor. 'Man sollte sich hüten', Brecht wrote at the time of work on the *Katzgraben* production, 'in alten Bildern zu denken. Die Vorstellung von der Blüte ist einseitig. Den Wert, die Bestimmung der Kraft und der Größe darf man nicht an die idyllische Vorstellung des organischen Blühens fesseln' (GBA, 27:322–23).

[39]'Sein Angriff auf das Gesamtkunstwerk beruhte wahrscheinlich weniger auf genauer Kenntnis der programmatischen Schriften Rickard Wagners wie *Oper und Drama* von 1851 [...] als auf seiner Kenntnis des Theaters und der Aufführungspraxis. [...] In der kurzen tabellarischen Gegenüberstellung [...] kam Wagner zweifellos als Hauptrepräsentant der ersteren Form in Betracht' (BHB, 4:52).

other contexts would be referred to as 'tectonic' and 'atectonic' or 'closed' and 'open' forms of drama. The structural debate did not end with Brecht's theory of Epic Theater and it was often conducted in equally antithetical terms. Certain items in the 'Schema' are very close to what Volker Klotz has to say about the teleological 'Zielstrebigkeit' of the 'closed' – Aristotelian – form of drama or Emil Staiger's observations on the epic work's 'Funktionalisierung der Teile'.[40]

One element closely related to the issue of different kinds of structure, the initial contrast between the dramatic form of theater ('handelnd') and the epic form ('erzählend'), has itself proved open to a variety of readings. Although often translated into English by the nearest available nouns – cf. Willett's 'plot' and 'narrative' [*BT*, 37) – the German words are gerundival and would be more accurately rendered by some such formulation as 'consisting of action' and 'telling a story' (though this would go against the economy of the way the initial contrast is expressed). But it is not at the grammatical level that the principal difficulty lies. It may be self-evident that Dramatic Theater consists of a 'Handlung' made up of a plethora of actions and hence that it is logical to associate the theater of dramatic suspense with dramatic action. The gerundival form has been chosen to create such intertwined associations. While not commenting specifically on the *Mahagonny* notes, David Midgley's account of Brecht's innovations explains that Epic Theater chose 'to adopt an approach which was "epic" in the sense of *telling* audiences about the world in which they were living'.[41] Such an explanation remains at a high level of generality; that is to say, entire epic plays are assumed to consist of single stories or parables that communicate political truths about the nature of society or demonstrate kinds of behavior. From *Die Maßnahme* to *Der kaukasische Kreidekreis*, Brecht's approach could be thought of as being parabolically 'narrative' in this wide sense. But a work like *Die Maßnahme* also narrates in another, more specific respect, one that the Goethe-Schiller *Briefwechsel* identifies as a key difference between the epic and the dramatic: 'Daß der Epiker seine Begebenheit als vollkommen vergangen, der Tragiker die seinige als vollkommen gegenwärtig zu behandeln habe' (Schiller to Goethe, 26 December 1797). With this temporal distinction in mind, one can see that individual scenes or local elements in Brecht's works stand out as being particularly epic, in the sense of narrating something as *completely past*. This is sometimes the method of entire plays (*Die Maßnahme* or *Die Ausnahme und die Regel*) or merely parts of works (scenes 2–5 of *Der kaukasische Kreidekreis* or the point in scene 10 of *Die Mutter* where Pelagea Wlassowa learns how her son Pawel died). What is more, 'erzählend' is an epithet that could also be applied to many of the devices that Brecht was to treat as part of the 'Literarisierung' of theater: for example, the use of captions, choruses, prologues and epilogues, reports, resumés, predictions, action-replays, and analyses. In 'Vergnügungsthearer oder Lehrtheater?' the section '*Die Bühne begann zu erzählen*' (*GBA*, 22:108) illustrates just how many ways there are for non-verbal forms of 'Erzählen' to be achieved via stage props, décor, sound effects, and lighting. In some sense, all these relatively local devices are also part of a move from a drama of action to a theater based to some greater extent on 'narrating events'

---

[40] Klotz 1968, 33; Staiger 1968, 168. Fundamental objections to the uncritical way in which Staiger derives abstract qualitative nouns (e.g. 'das Epische') from genre-concepts such as 'Epik' have been made in Ellis and Mowatt 1965.

[41] Midgley 2000, 123. Midgley is paraphrasing two essays of February 1929 ('Letzte Etappe: Ödipus' and 'Dialog über Schauspielkunst', *GBA*, 21:278–82), pieces that prefigure a number of points in the *Mahagonny* notes.

as *completely past or*, in some instances, yet to happen. In many instances, 'erzählend' has one further, equally important association: that of narrating things *to an audience*. In Epic Theater, it is not only characters who tell *each other* stories: narrating figures like the *Sänger* of *Der kaukasische Kreidekreis* or Wang in *Der gute Mensch von Sezuan* narrate directly *to the audience*. More important, this narrative function is also fulfilled by 'Spruchbände', symbolic costumes, body language, and stylized gesture. Once again, the idea in the left-hand column of the 'Schema' is clearer than its counterpart. However, given that this particular contrast dates from 1930, it is unlikely that the description 'handelnd' refers to the importance of 'die Fabel' for Epic Theater. As we shall see in the chapter on *Kleines Organon*, the latter only gradually became central to Brecht's post-exile theorizing, as it was bound up with his interest in Stanislavsky's late work. '[Die Methode der "physischen Handlungen" am Berliner Ensemble]' of 1953 stresses: 'Brecht verlangt immer, daß der Schauspieler auf den ersten Proben hauptsächlich die Fabel, den Vorgang, die Beschäftigung zeigt [...]. Er bekämpft mit aller Kraft die üble Gewohnheit vieler Schauspieler, die Fabel des Stücks sozusagen nur als unbedeutende Voraussetzung ihrer Gefühlsakrobatik zu benutzen, wie der Turner den Barren benutzt, um seine Gewandtheit zu beweisen' (*GBA*, 23:229). The contrast here, between a psychological theater based on individual characters' – and actors' – emotions, and an Epic Theater where plot is of vital significance to a work's political statement, differs substantially from the 'handelnd' / 'erzählend' contrast that begins the *Mahagonny* 'Schema'.

Just as the individual components of an epic structure tend not to be of equal value, so certain points in the *Mahagonny* 'Schema' stand out as more important than their neighbors. For Hultberg, point 18 is assumed ('falls dieser Punkt absolut gesetzt wird' [?]) to put many of the other characteristics in question. The point's tacit reference to Marx's writings will, it is assumed, cancel out a number of other items that put the stress squarely on change. Vulgar determinism wins the day over 'eingreifendes Denken' in such a scenario. By contrast, Hecht, who has little patience with non-dialectical determinism, chooses to attribute paramount importance to point 11, where man is seen as both 'veränderlich' and 'verändernd'. These epithets become significant evidence in his account of Brecht's development towards a more mature Marxism, inasmuch as what Engels calls the 'Wechselwirkung' between the subjective and determining factors is allowed for: 'Tatsächlich befand sich Brecht, die Grenzen des Behaviorismus erkennend, auf dem Wege zu einer dialektischen Einschätzung des Bewußtseins' (Hecht 1972, 63). The fact that this contrast was only added to the 'Schema' in the *Versuche* 2 version would appear to strengthen Hecht's reading. For the reference to Marx is inserted at a time when the title 'Zur Soziologie der Oper', showing Sternberg's influence, has been abandoned. And in any case, according to recent work, the covert quotation from Marx is less vulgarly determinist than Hultberg would have his reader believe.[42] One of the clearest statements of his new position comes in the 1933 notes to *Die Mutter*, where it is claimed that the spectator's 'Aufgabe seinen Mitmenschen gegenüber besteht darin, unter die determinierenden Faktoren sich selbst einzuschalten. Bei dieser Aufgabe hat ihn die Dramatik zu unterstützen. Die determinierenden Faktoren, wie soziales Milieu, spezielle Ereignisse usw., sind also als veränderliche darzustellen' (*GBA*, 24:127). In Hultberg's account, this appears to be little more than a brief explanation to point 11, while for

---

[42] See Avineri 1968, 75–77, on the misreadings of this passage and for an account of what Marx really meant.

Hecht it signals a new stage in Brecht's development. Thus, selective stress on one element in the table can lead to diametrically opposite conclusions: either Brecht is well on his way to a dialectical conception of Epic Theater (Hecht) – though the notes themselves are viewed as propounding 'eine typische Übergangstheorie' (Hecht 1972,46) – or he is a sad case of recidivism, unable to shake off the vestiges of his 'behaviorist'/'vulgar determinist' past (Hultberg 1962). Since neither contentious element was removed from the 1935 and 1938 versions of the 'Schema', it would be comforting to assume that they were retained for a purpose. For once, Brecht cannot hide behind his usual let-out clause that the 'Schema' shows mere shifts of accent, not absolute antitheses, for it is difficult to see that such a defense applies to the totalizing formulations in 11 and 18.

It may help at this stage to note that Hultberg had himself also detected *contradictions* in the table and to recall how central the notion of 'Widerspruch' is to Brecht's conception of Epic Theater. The true Brecht, it might therefore be argued, is not to be located in either 11 or 18. Which one he stands closer to may be less important for the table's impact than the fact that it confronts the reader with a contradiction (though one no more contradictory than the suggestion that 'epic' is essentially a structural concept and that the main differences between Dramatic and Epic Theater are of an essentially ideological nature). The *Mahagonny* 'Schema' does more than delineate mere shifts of emphasis rather than absolute antitheses; in places it also engages in a thought-provoking 'gegenseitige Verfremdung' of internal antitheses in order to provoke a dialectical response in the reader,

Brecht's table is designed as an exposition of the characteristics of Epic Theater and Opera and the political rationale behind them. In such a context, 'epic' means 'not "Einfühlungstheater"' (an *end*, inasmuch as a theater of distance is the *goal*); although also it signifies, as some parts of the 'Schema' make clear, whatever means, structural or non-structural, have to be used to achieve it.

One further connotation of 'epic', that suggesting an Olympian distance and hence an audience response based on cool, detached observation, caused Brecht the most problems. For over a quarter of a century, he repeatedly found himself having to define – and refine – his position, legislating which kinds of emotion Epic Theater rejected and which were permissible. His change of ground and the refinements to the original theoretical stance are well documented and analysed (in Dickson 1978, 233–38). The general picture is less the one of a wilfully misunderstood Brecht painted in the Lidingö letter than that of someone whose manifesto rhetoric initially resulted in an overstated position that subsequently had to be redefined. Removing the 'Gefühl' / 'Ratio' contrast from the table of course failed to make the problem disappear. Hence, Brecht's various attempts at differentiation, not only between various forms of feeling, but also between 'Ratio' and intelligence, common sense, and what would now be thought of as a lateral thinker's perspective on a problem. But no amount of clarification seems to have helped. To claim, as Brecht did in the Lidingö letter, that there is much emotion in scientific discovery and in the joy of learning even risks blurring vital differences between an emotional response to the results of a process and the atmosphere of inquiry in which an experiment is conducted.[43] Even empathy will eventually be re-admitted to the domain of Epic Theater, provided it is framed in such a way as to make the emotional experience productive.

---

[43]"Brecht tried to deny the inconsistency by claiming that science was actually not something unemotional, in that it involved the excitement of discovery. However, the analogy is quite unconvincing, for although it is possible

One principal objection to Brecht's long-term dialogue with the critics of this final contrast does not stem from the fact that the two nouns might erroneously be taken for absolute opposites, but results from his habit of changing the terms of the discussion. Although claiming that he is concerned with '*Akzent*verschiebungen', what is actually shifted in subsequent debates is the terminology. To substitute 'Einfühlung' for 'Gefühl', and to do so without offering a similar corrective to the other term in the pairing, is hardly likely to guarantee greater understanding of the original table. And as we shall see in the next chapter when we turn to the theory of the middle and late thirties, Brecht's position is not always helped by an undifferentiating concept of aesthetic distance. Whereas total identification might appear to be an absolute, the detachment implied in such items as 'macht den Zuschauer zum Betrachter', 'er wird gegenübergesetzt', 'studiert', or the claim that he views something as 'Gegenstand der Untersuchung' is less fixed than its contrastive function might lead one to suppose.

'Vergnügungstheater oder Lehrtheater?' offers an embryonic model of the way the 'Gefühl' / 'Ratio' contrast might have been more profitably handled. It comes in Brecht's observation that, independent of the fact that there are two different forms of dramatic structure and audience response, one still finds '"das Dramatische" auch in epischen Werken und "das Epische" in dramatischen' (*GBA*, 22:107). If, instead of substituting or redefining his lead concepts, Brecht had elaborated a similar gradational model where examples of both the theater of emotion and the theater of reason had been dissected more rigorously in terms of their various constituent parts, some of the misconceptions caused by the pairing of 'Gefühl' and 'Ratio' might have been avoided.[44] Although the more one moves from terms of contrast and simplifying juxtapositions to notions of the amalgamation of both dramatic elements within one overall dominant generic set of characteristics, the less likely it becomes that such a refinement could find adequate expression in tabular form. Or that it would make a sufficient splash. (When Brecht uses a 'vielleicht' in '[Schwierigkeiten des epischen Theaters]' – 'Das Wesentliche am epischen Theater ist es vielleicht, daß es nicht so sehr an das Gefühl, sondern mehr an die Ratio des Zuschauers appelliert' (*GBA*, 21:210) – one can sense how easily differentiation might suggest dilution.) Ironically, the paragraph coming immediately after the table, a paragraph that might conceivably have performed the function of further clarifying it, does operate with the terms 'radikale *Trennung der Elemente*' and '*Schmelzprozeß*'. But it does so, not in order to apply them to the mixture of dramatic and epic elements in all drama or to widen the scope to include the lyrical component that is so important in many of Brecht's plays. Instead, the emphasis is solely on the increased autonomy of '*Musik, Wort und Bild*' in order to avoid creating the kind of '*Schmelzprozeß*' that for Brecht was epitomized by the Wagnerian *Gesamtkunstwerk*. Regrettably, the discussion

---

to be emotional *about* science, emotions have no place in the procedures of science, whereas the theatre, even as Brecht himself practised it, is intrinsically bound up with the emotions' (Speirs 1987, 45).

[44]Not long after 'Vergnügungstheater oder Lehrtheater?' Emil Staiger published his *Grundbegriffe der Poetik*, an attempt to dissect the ingredients of what he saw as the lyrical, the epic, and the dramatic. While conceding 'daß jede echte Dichtung an allen Gattungsideen in verschiedenen Graden und Weisen beteiligt ist' (Staiger 1968, 10), he in practice focuses in turn on all the three genres in isolation and fails to do justice to the amalgam posited. An impure methodology, combined with a desire to relate generic concepts to an anthropological concern with 'fundamentale Möglichkeiten des Daseins überhaupt' (Staiger 1968, 209), led to the work's dismissal as a 'blind alley' (Duroche 1967, 105). See also Zutshi 1981. The failure of *Grundbegriffe der Poetik* in this respect mirrors Brecht's own unwillingness to pursue the posited shifts in emphasis into fine detail.

hurries quickly on at this point from an explanation of Epic Theater to a consideration of Epic Opera, formulated in such a way as to do little more than prepare for the discussion of music in the next section. This does for once look more like an example of one section 'für die andere' than each section 'für sich'.

The other nominal pairing that has given rise to unclarity is the juxtaposition of 'Erlebnis' and 'Weltbild' in point 5. In *Versuche* 2, the kind of experience he was referring to had already been characterized at the beginning of the section in which the table occurs: '[kulinarische Oper] nähert sich selber jedem Gegenstand in genießerischer Haltung. Sie "erlebt", und sie dient als "Erlebnis"' (*GBA*, 24:76). This is not an easy formulation, but it could refer to the aestheticizing cult of experience and the savoring of precious 'Augenblicke' associated in the German-speaking world above all with the *fin-de-siècle* Viennese neo-Romanticism of Hugo von Hofmannsthal and his contemporaries. Opera's hedonism is essentially a matter of escapism, in other words; it is this association that the table refers back to, just as we shall find that *Der Messingkauf* describes forms of superficial realism as 'Naturalist' to imply their anachronism. When the table was revised in 1935 exile for insertion into a new context, the strength of such a reference risked becoming obscure. Hence, the allusion is removed. The deficit is not substantial, however, even on the right-hand side of the table. For arguably *both* forms of theater mediate 'Weltbilder' in the sense that any such worldview is either an embodiment of the assumption that 'das Denken bestimmt das Sein' or that 'das gesellschaftliche Sein bestimmt das Denken'. In any case, a point recently made by Knopf has a bearing on the terminology used here: 'Wichtig [...] ist zu betonen, dass [Brecht] nie von Weltanschauung spricht oder Weltanschauung meint – im Gegenteil: im *Buch der Wendungen* wendet er sich explizit dagegen ("Kein Weltbild machen"); (*GBA*, 18:60) [...]' (*BHB*, 4:269). 'Weltbild', in other words, appears to relate to Brecht's revised 'Abbild' theory and to his materialist aesthetic rather than to the kind of idealist conception implicit in the term 'Weltanschauung'. As all this demonstrates, Brecht not only expended considerable energy trying to put right the various misreadings of the 'Schema' in the 1930 *Mahagonny* notes; he at the same time adjusted the material to its new context and to his own changed and still changing dramaturgical position.

# The Messingkauf/Buying Brass

# CHAPTER TWELVE

# The Drama of Ideas

MARTIN PUCHNER

> In the epic theater ... the actor sides with the philosopher.
>
> – Walter Benjamin

Brecht is readily acknowledged as one of the most influential reformers of twentieth-century theater. The dramatic text, acting, set design, music – Brecht overhauled each and every aspect of the theater, leaving nothing untouched. What is acknowledged much less is that this effort was driven by a deeply rooted 'mistrust of the theater' that can be traced back to Plato.[1] Plato's influence is visible in a number of Brecht's most cherished beliefs. For example, he designed plays that were addressed to reason rather than to emotions; he wanted audiences to analyze rather than enjoy; and sometimes his plays seemed to preach to audiences, bombarding them with theoretical declarations and views. But even if there is something intellectual about Brecht's plays and theater productions, they nevertheless differ significantly from other examples of Platonic drama, although the theater of Shaw is sometimes recognized as an important precursor. Brecht's plays are dominated by action, not dialogue, and they use all the trappings and tricks of the theater. Few of his plays contain characters who present themselves as philosophers. One of the few commentators to have nevertheless recognized a connection between Brecht and Plato was Brecht's friend Walter Benjamin, whose essay on epic theater, written in the early 1930s, concludes with an intriguing speculation about a Platonic tradition of drama.[2] Benjamin notes the affinity between Brecht's antitragic protagonists and Plato's Socrates, and singles out the *Phaedo* as a dialogue located 'at the threshold of drama'. This Platonic tradition, Benjamin goes on to say, is defined by its persistent distancing from tragedy, indeed from all conventional drama. But Benjamin warns us that this tradition is a strange one, hard to locate, a 'badly marked street', although even this metaphor is then qualified when he adds that we are dealing not with a true street but with a secret path.[3]

---

Martin Puchner, 'The Drama of Ideas', in *The Drama of Ideas: Platonic Provocations in Theater and Philosophy* (New York and Oxford: Oxford University Press, 2010), pp. 106–12.

[1] Elinor Fuchs, 'Clown Shows: Anti-Theatricalist Theatricalism in Four Twentieth-Century Plays', in *Against Theatre: Creative Destructions on the Modernist Stage*, ed. Alan Ackerman and Martin Puchner (New York: Palgrave, 2006), 28.

[2] Among the very few commentators to have connected Brecht to Plato is William E. Gruber in '"Non-Aristotelian" Theater: Brecht's and Plato's Theories of Artistic Imitation', *Comparative Drama* 21, 3 (Fall 1986): 199–213. In *Stage Fright: Modernism, Anti-Theatricality and Drama* (Baltimore: Johns Hopkins University Press, 2002) I also developed a Platonist reading of Brecht.

[3] Walter Benjamin, *Versuche über Brecht*, ed. Rolf Tiedemann (Frankfurt am Main: Suhrkamp, 1971), 34.

The somewhat unfamiliar view of Brecht I will present here can be taken as an elaboration of this Platonic genealogy, or path, indicated by Benjamin.

Brecht's most direct connection to dramatic Platonism is Georg Kaiser, who explicitly called for a renewal of drama in the name of Plato. Brecht's debt to Kaiser is well documented, although the skewed view most theater historians have of Kaiser, which generally does not include his Platonic project, has distorted the nature of this influence as well. But it was Kaiser's interest in Socrates and Plato that intrigued Brecht, who not only knew and admired Kaiser's Socrates play, *Alcibiades Delivered,* but also rewrote it as a short story. In the course of doing so, Brecht turned to Plato's *Symposium* to research the account of Socrates in battle given there. The Socrates theme emerges in several other texts as well, for example, in one of his Herr Keuner stories, but also in the play that comes closest to the kind of argument-driven, cerebral play one might more readily associate with the Platonic drama, *The Life of Galileo Galilei,* which in turn was inspired by Galileo's own dialogues. More generally, Brecht admired Socrates' critical edge, his dialectical reasoning, and his willingness to stand up to the powers that be even as he was skeptical about Plato's antidemocratic views. Still, it must be said that an interest in Socrates is one thing and a tendency toward dramatic Platonism is another. How did Brecht, the man of the theater, become associated with philosophical drama in the tradition of Plato?

Brecht's dramatic Platonism came to the fore when he was cut off from the actual theater during his years of exile, first in Scandinavia and then in the United States, in the 1930s and 1940s. By 1933, when he left Germany, Brecht had already formulated and put into practice most of the tenets of what he called epic theater. He had become famous for his estrangement effect, the desire to distance the audience from the theater by means of interruption, episodic plots, and other techniques of defamiliarization. Only by disturbing the basic, underlying familiarity with what happens onstage, Brecht argued, could theater makers induce audiences to consider events presented onstage critically, analytically, and in a new light. This new theory had become a theatrical success across Germany, turning Brecht and his group of collaborators into the most important new voice in the theater.

Brecht and his collaborators had to leave all this behind when they fled shortly after Hitler's rise to power, finding themselves cut off from the theater that had made them famous. It was during the following fifteen years in exile that Brecht wrote his most central plays, including *Life of Galileo Galilei* (1937–39), *Mother Courage and Her Children* (1939), *The Good Person of Sezuan* (1940), and *The Caucasian Chalk Circle* (1943–45). At the same time, he also experimented with other literary genres, including the novel, in the *Three Penny Novel* (1934) and *The Affairs of Mr. Julius Caesar* (1949), in addition to poetry. The man of the theater had become a writer.

Brecht used his distance from the theater for another, large project that would occupy him for the rest of his life: a reflection on and revision of the main elements of his theory of the theater. This effort took the form of a series of dialogues, oddly entitled *Messingkauf* (The Purchase of Brass).[4] The dialogues are all about the theater, and more particularly about Brecht's theater. Brecht himself is not referred to by name but is simply called, in keeping with his main occupation in exile, 'the Playwright'. The central components of Brecht's epic theater, including styles of acting, dramaturgy, use of music and set design, dramatic texts, and the role of the audience, are discussed among the participants, who are

---

[4]Bertolt Brecht, 'Der Messingkauf', in *Gesammelte Werke* (Frankfurt am Main: Suhrkamp, 1967), 16:499–657.

all theater people, including actors, a dramaturge, and a stagehand. These wide-ranging conversations also consider the political function of the theater, as well as its relation to science, and the question of whether the theater, in order to become a truly modern art form, must adhere to the tenets of Brecht's epic theater. The *Messingkauf* dialogues echo Brecht's immodest claim that the modern theater is the (that is to say, his) epic theater.

Even as the *Messingkauf* dialogues articulate the key elements of the epic theater, they do so with a crucial difference. The main character of the dialogues, the one around whom they are organized, is someone seemingly unconnected to the theater: a philosopher. *Messingkauf* is a series of dialogues in which Brecht revisits his entire theory of epic theater from the perspective of the philosopher. These dialogues can be seen as an attempt to view epic theater through a philosophical lens or, rather, to translate epic theater into philosophical theater. This translation takes place both on the level of content – the theory of theater – and on the level of form: Brecht chose to articulate this philosophical version of the epic theater in the form of a philosophical dialogue.

In the course of *Messingkauf*, it becomes clear that the philosopher who dominates the dialogue is in fact quite ignorant of the theater. He does not often go to the theater, does not especially value it, and is unfamiliar with its basic vocabulary; the theater professionals even have to explain to him the convention of the fourth wall. At the same time, he asks fundamental questions about how theater works, and he likes to peek behind the stage. In the process, the philosopher develops quite fundamental objections to the theater, in particular to the project of imitation. The theater professionals quickly assent to Aristotle's claim that the theater is based on the art of imitation. But instead of condoning imitation, the philosopher desires to go to the 'things themselves', sounding just like Socrates in the *Republic*, with whom he also shares a scorn for actors.[5] He declares that he feels crowded, even 'tyrannized', by actors who do not leave him 'room to think'.[6] Finally, he strongly disagrees with the other Aristotelian demand, quoted to him by the dramaturge, that theatrical imitation should incite the emotions of the audience, in particular fear and pity.

The objections raised by the philosopher tilt the dialogue: more and more the conversation revolves around satisfying the philosopher, and what gets developed in the ensuing conversations is an alternative to the theater as practiced by the theater professionals. Step by step, the philosopher unfolds the framework for a new and different theater, a theater suited specifically to his own philosophical purposes. The theater the philosopher demands is one that would be fully up-to-date, in keeping with the developments of the time. This means that the new theater would have to be scientific, addressed to the purpose of knowing, not feeling. The scientific theme brings the philosopher to one of his key concepts: that the theater should function like a laboratory, serving the purposes of knowledge and analysis. The philosopher here reiterates several components of Brecht's well-known estrangement effect: the emphasis on analysis rather than on empathy, the rule that audiences must not be drawn into the action of the play (their cigars must not go out), and that they should observe the events represented onstage acutely, with scientific interest. They must not merely look at the stage [*sehen*] but probe it critically [*prüfendes schauen*].[7] The philosopher, in other words, demands a particular kind of reception:

---

[5] Ibid., 511.
[6] Ibid., 512.
[7] Ibid., 640.

science resides in the beholder. Scientific theater means a particular attitude toward the theater, the attitude a scientist brings to an experiment.

The main distinction used by the philosopher to illustrate this point is the distinction between a planetarium and a roller coaster. Riding a roller coaster means experiencing the ups and downs of the story viscerally directly, emotionally, through the senses. The planetarium, by contrast, creates insight into the constellations.[8] It may still be impressive, pleasing, a sensory experience, but it does not stand in the way of understanding and analysis, as is the case with the roller coaster. The philosopher could ride the roller coaster (i.e., the regular theater that incites the emotions directly) and try, against all odds, to wrest pieces of insight from it; but this would be an uphill struggle, unlikely to succeed. So while in principle the analytic, scientific, and philosophical attitude can be brought to any theater, some theaters will make such an attitude all but impossible, while others will encourage it.

The main target of the philosopher's critique, however, is not emotionally heart-wrenching theater in the melodramatic tradition, nor the behavior of star actors who manage to ensnare an audience. Rather, it is the type of theater that at first sight might seem to be similar in kind to the scientific theater imagined by the philosopher, namely, naturalism. Naturalist theater, after all, began with a scientific impulse, derived from Darwin and others (as Wilde knew and objected to). Social life was to be presented without embellishment, as if under the microscope of the naturalists. While the naturalist novel and drama created an outcry because it meant dragging unpleasant facts of life – syphilis, corruption, adultery, incest – into art, the justification for this was mostly scientific rather than aesthetic: it was art's contribution to the understanding of the world.

But even the most unflinching, naturalist representation of unvarnished life is not yet scientific. In the words of the philosopher, not only must nature be represented, but also its laws must be revealed; nature must be 'found out'.[9] Here, the naturalists had only the vaguest idea or bandied about pseudoscientific assumptions about inheritance and the shaping power of the environment on character. For this reason, the slice-of-life approach of naturalism, the ambition to render nature in all its complexity and texture, needed to be given up so that theater could become truly scientific and aspire to the condition of the laboratory. A laboratory is an artificial, controlled environment, not a fully rendered slice of life; in a laboratory, life situations are put together on a trial basis to see what kind of insight and what laws they might yield. Indeed, the insight that there are laws governing nature, and in particular the actions of humans, is itself the most important element of this new laboratory theater.

When it comes to detailing which kind of laws are supposed to be revealed by theatrical experiments, the philosopher has recourse to Marxism. In an important distinction, however, he cautions against using the theater as a mere illustration of Marxist theories or predictions.[10] Indeed, the philosopher recognizes that Marxism does not explain so much the behavior of individuals as that of masses, of large groups and classes – not something the theater is particularly good at. But the theater, when used experimentally, can aim at a kind of intermediary realm, one that demonstrates the interconnectedness of individuals. This is where the new theater can come in, showing, through careful

---

[8] Ibid., 541ff.
[9] The philosopher says that reality 'muß … durchschaut werden'. Ibid., 520.
[10] Ibid., 531.

selection of individuals and scenes, the hidden connections and dependencies of seemingly unconnected, far-flung agents. The dramaturge, who mediates between actors and the philosopher, bemoans the fact that it used to be the case that antagonists confronted one another in a single space, directly, scenically. But now a man in Chicago operates a machine that can kill twelve people in Ireland. The theater, he implies, must be changed in order for those connections, and the laws governing them, to become visible.[11]

The more the philosopher explains what he wants from the theater and how it might be changed, the more horrified the theater practitioners become. All their most cherished goals, including the accurate rendering of complex, psychological characters and the task of fascinating the audience, seem to have gone overboard. For this reason, they refuse to recognize as theater what the philosopher demands; instead they call it *thaeter*, inverting the letters *a* and *e*.[12] What is the status of this *thaeter*? First of all, it is driven by historical urgency, the struggle against fascism. From this perspective, the antitheatrical moment, the reduction and reorientation of theater, is a rebuke to fascism's full-blown theatricality, its exploitation of an emotional theater for political purposes. Hitler's political mass theater is based on emotion and identification; and political events such as the burning of the Reichstag, the crucial turning point of Hitler's increasing hold on power and the sidelining of democracy, can be seen as theater on a grand scale.[13] The philosopher acknowledges that his *thaeter* also presses theater into a political function, though in a different, critical manner. This politicization may not be an ideal, but it is a necessity. *Thaeter* is necessary right now; 'it is not for eternity', but only for 'dark times'.[14] Once fascism in all of its guises is over, once socialism has won, we can all enjoy riding the roller coaster again.

Even more important than the content of the *Messingkauf* dialogues is their form. As a series of dialogues about the theater, *Messingkauf* belongs to a tradition that extends from Plato to Diderot's *Paradoxe*, Goethe's prologue to *Faust*, and Edward Gordon Craig's dialogues on the theater, not to speak of Wilde's critical dialogues. More important, they themselves are a kind of drama. The dialogues are arranged into different evenings, and they have been staged in various ways more than one hundred times since their premiere at the Theater am Schiffbauerdamm on October 12, 1963.[15] Brecht carefully calculated this theatrical dimension: while talking about theater (and *thaeter*), the participants, including the philosopher, sit on the stage. During the course of the discussion, the stage set, left over from another, regular show, is being slowly dismantled until the participants find themselves on an empty stage. This process epitomizes the philosopher's own dismantling of the theater. Emptying the theater, presumably, is what must happen in order for a *thaeter* to take place. At the same time, it is important to realize that the dialogues do not abandon the theater. This is perhaps the best indication that *thaeter*, despite its radical critique of the real existing theater, is not the theater's negation. Even though the philosopher is not particularly knowledgeable about the theater, and perhaps does not

---

[11]Ibid., 526.
[12]First introduction of the term in ibid., 508; it is elaborated in 638ff.
[13]Ibid., 560.
[14]Ibid., 649.
[15]Information based on John J. White, *Brecht's Dramatic Theory* (Rochester, N.Y.: Camden House, 2004), 248. White is one of the few commentators on Brecht to include the *Messingkauf* dialogues in his discussion of Brecht's dramatic theory.

like it much, he does find himself, on this occasion, in the theater. He is interested in it, if only for its potential for philosophy.

This self-reflective dimension of the dialogues is not lost on the participants, and Brecht makes sure that it does not escape our attention, either. It is of course the philosopher who insists on this self-referential quality of the evening, claiming, 'We too have made art for the past four nights'.[16] To be sure, the *Messingkauf* dialogues are not the only form of *thaeter* the philosopher is calling for, but they are one possible example of it. They have not overwhelmed the audience with melodramatic stories; they have addressed reason, even when the discussion has become heated; and they have shown that the theater itself is not naturally given, but made and therefore changeable.

Brecht did not usually present himself as a thinker or philosopher. One of his more memorable lines is an advocacy of '*plumpes Denken*' (best translated as 'crude thinking'), a predilection for simplicity rather than for needless complexity.[17] This attitude is also what gives the *Messingkauf* dialogues their title: the philosopher is like someone who wants to buy a trombone, not in order to make music, but merely for its brass. Boiling things down to essentials is certainly one aspect of Brecht's dramatic practice. Yet the *Messingkauf* dialogues are not all brass. They play music, they are art – albeit of a different type. Their music is one reminiscent of Platonic theater – perhaps this is the music made by Socrates in prison, something along the lines of Nietzsche's music-making Socrates. They rethink theater from a philosophical perspective, and they put this perspective into practice, as Plato and those writing in his tradition have done.

What happens if we take the philosopher's *thaeter* as a lens though which to look at Brecht's entire oeuvre? There is a set of plays that seems to be halfway between Brecht's great stage plays and the pared-down form of the *Messingkauf* dialogues, namely, his *Lehrstücke* or 'teaching plays'. They perhaps come closest to exemplifying the *thaeter* the philosopher calls for. They, more so than Brecht's other plays, are addressed to reason, presenting simple, experimental situations in which a character has to make a single, moral choice. The question of how this choice is made reveals much about social structures, about motivation, about society at large. In a pair of these plays, *The Yea-Sayer* and *The Nay-Sayer*, Brecht even creates two versions of the outcome in a way that is reminiscent of a laboratory experiment: it does not matter to the observer what the outcome is as long as we can observe the process that led to it.

Claiming that the *Messingkauf* dialogues, and through them Brecht's outlook on drama, should be placed in the tradition of Plato may seem counterintuitive given Brecht's dedication to historical materialism. Indeed, the philosopher's plea for a scientific theater is motivated by his belief in historical materialism. But it should be remembered that Platonic theater is not based on a metaphysical theory of abstract forms, what philosophers have extracted from Plato's dialogues and called philosophical idealism. Rather, it mediates between abstraction and a full immersion in the thick of life, a tug-of-war in which abstractions (ideas) are used strategically to uproot materiality and turn it into so many thought experiments. Like Brecht's *thaeter*, Platonic theater depends on the theater, uses the theater, takes place in the theater, and yet it subjects the theater to a crucial inversion. *Thaeter* is a good word for the 'secret path' Walter Benjamin recognized, a path

---

[16]Brecht, *Messingkauf* 644.
[17]For an incisive commentary on 'crude thinking', see Fredric Jameson, *Brecht and Method* (London: Verso, 1998), 25ff.

starting with Plato and extending to Brecht. Like Platonic theater, *thaeter* insists on using the theater for the purpose of knowledge, for the purposes of the philosopher. Brecht here articulates what Benjamin had recognized, but many have ignored: that Brecht's theater, too, can be described as a theater for philosophers, a theater uprooted from itself and turned to a new purpose.

Throughout his career, Brecht described his epic theater, and *thaeter,* as being directed against Aristotle and, more important, against the invocation of Aristotle as a way of defending dramatic and theatrical orthodoxies. Aristotle theorizes tragic action as caused primarily by fate and only secondarily by the actions of the protagonists, whereas in *thaeter* events can be changed by humans; Aristotelianism insists on the unities of space, time, and action, whereas *thaeter* wants to show the distanced interconnections of individuals. Insofar as *thaeter* is a philosophical rearticulation of epic theater, it presents what Brecht never tired of calling a non-Aristotelian theory of drama. This negative description has often been applied to modern drama more generally. What textbook does not revert to Aristotle as a foil against which to examine modernism's discontinuous and episodic plots?

But Brecht's theater can be described not only negatively as non-Aristotelian but also positively as Platonic. Plato of course wrote before Aristotle, but he defined his own dialogue, his own *thaeter,* one might say, against the dominant genres of Greek theater, subsequently theorized by Aristotle. In this sense Plato developed a theory and a practice of drama that is both pre-Aristotelian and non-Aristotelian. Throughout its history, Platonic drama has continued to battle Aristotelianism, and it has been able to flourish precisely at moments when Aristotelian drama was on the defensive. Modern drama is such a moment, the coincidence of a demise of Aristotelianism and a rise of Platonism. To the extent that a large number of dramatists – Wilde and Shaw, Strindberg and Kaiser, Pirandello and Brecht – participate in Platonic drama, it is possible to reformulate Brecht's claim that modern theater is non-Aristotelian as a claim that it is Platonic.

*Me-ti*

CHAPTER THIRTEEN

# Introduction to *Me-ti*: Book of Interventions in the Flow of Things

ANTONY TATLOW

During his visit to Moscow in March 1935 Brecht wrote to his wife, Helene Weigel, that he had seen the 'really splendid' Chinese actor Mei Lanfang. In a postscript, he asked: 'Have you already picked up Me-Ti? Does it look good now?' His copy of this remarkable book, published in 1922 – the first full translation into any European language, by Alfred Forke, of an ancient Chinese text – was being rebound in Svendborg. Forke entitled it *Mê Ti – the philosophical works of the social moralist and his followers.*[1]

Even given Brecht's shrewd but sporadic responses to Chinese culture, this 638-page example of detailed forensic sinological scholarship, otherwise of interest only to specialists, was an unusual acquisition, and it had surprising consequences. The text is a unique combination of tersely formulated, often witty aphorisms on human behaviour, of advice offered in the course of conversations on how best to conduct human affairs, of systematic, critical descriptions of cultural values and related social dangers, and of

---

Antony Tatlow, 'Introduction', in *Bertolt Brecht's Me-ti: Book of Interventions in the Flow of Things* (London: Methuen Drama, 2016), pp. 1–39.

[1]*Mê Ti, des Sozialethikers und seiner Schüler philosophische Werke* zum ersten Mal vollständig übersetzt, mit ausführlicher Einleitung, erläuternden und textkritischen Erklärungen versehen von Professor Alfred Forke (Berlin: Kommissionsverlag der Vereinigung wissenschaftlicher Verleger, 1922) in the series *Mitteilungen des Seminars für orientalische Sprachen an der Friedrich-Wilhlems-Universität zu Berlin*.

Given the many systems of transliteration and different European orthographic conventions, the transcription of Chinese names, which may themselves vary, can prove confusing. In order to distinguish between Brecht's *Me-ti*, as text and fictional person or persona, and Forke's translation of the Chinese text, I refer to the latter and its 'author' as Mo Di, which is another version of the author's name. In his text, Forke also uses the common honorific for Chinese philosophical teachers, *Mê-tse*, meaning Master Mê (墨子, in the pinyin transcription, Mozi), which explains why Brecht refers to 'Master Me-ti' and to 'Master Ka-meh' for Karl Marx. Quotations are my own translations. The *Letters* are quoted, where possible, from the English edition, London: Methuen, 1990 (here, with slight emendations, pp. 201–2). Other Brecht quotations are either from the Methuen/Bloomsbury edition or else, if not available, my own translations from the thirty-volume *Berliner und Frankfurter Ausgabe* (BFA).

obscure, sometimes incomprehensible arguments over logical problems formulated over two millennia ago.

Brecht found it a stimulating treasure trove. This is not to say that his own *Me-ti* is an interpretative engagement with the Chinese work. Brecht's is primarily occupied with the unfolding European crises, with the political theory and practice of Communism in the Soviet Union, as well as with personal affairs. But he could not have shaped his own text without this stimulus, and there are passages in the Chinese work, some of which he noted but did not directly use, that seem to echo his own thoughts. To cite one example: 'Generosity does not exclude the self.' Elisabeth Hauptmann, his close collaborator over many years, told me he was reading this Chinese 'philosophical' work from 1929.

[…]

Responsive to Chinese ideas from the early 1920s, Brecht drew on images and formulations from the three main streams of thought that shaped Chinese culture: Daoism, Confucianism and Buddhism.[2] We do not need here to delve deeply into this or to explain how these schools of thought were interpreted according to historical needs or filtered through different Western readings; we merely need to point out two general aspects: the presence of a more pervasive sense of flow and transience than can be found in predominantly essentialist Western philosophy and religion, and in consequence what, especially from a Western perspective, may seem paradoxical, namely a different sense of the interconnectedness of all things, including social phenomena, evident in Mo Di, and which also distinguishes a Daoist from the Heraclitean concept of flow.

In September 1920, Brecht's diary records: 'swimming + Lao-tse'. Daoist metaphors appear in *In the Jungle of Cities* (1923) and, memorably, in his 1938 *Legend of the origin of the book Tao Te Ching*, which was included in the *Svendborg Poems*. The Daoist critique of Confucian virtues is integrated into *Mother Courage* and his *Me-ti* texts, where praise of egoism, common to Daoism and Mo Di, is also developed.

In his poem 'The Buddha's parable of the burning house' Buddha refuses to answer theoretical questions about the nature of nirvana, when what matters most is to get out of the burning house, an attitude that both accords with Buddhist social philosophy and is reflected in popular Buddhist stories.

Brecht quoted Confucian texts and hung the splendid classic portrait of the great educator, who also went into exile at the age of thirty-five, in his study, as a warning that even the best teaching, a skill to which he aspired, can be frustrated and lose its focus. He commented wryly on passages in the Confucian Analects. He planned a play, *The Life of Confucius*, but completed only the first scene, The Jar of Ginger, in which the boy Confucius attempts to teach two young friends the virtues of self-restraint when eating ginger. This delightful scene ends when the jar finally reaches him and there is no more ginger left in it. Brecht made sketches for later scenes, and envisaged a Confucius sharply different from the traditional view. Though initially well-meaning, his advice was followed by the rulers

---

[2] A short general account of Brecht's response to East Asia can be found in my article 'Brecht's East Asia: a conspectus', *Brecht in/and Asia, The Brecht Yearbook* 36 (2011): 353–68, and earlier in greater detail in Antony Tatlow, *The Mask of Evil: Brecht's response to the Poetry, Theatre and Thought of China and Japan. A Comparative and Critical Evaluation* (Berne: Peter Lang, 1977).

because it suited them, although it was 'wrong'. Significantly, he would have illustrated the temptations facing the intellectual: accommodation with power. Brecht asked himself, in a note among the archive papers, if this view was historically justified (BBA 191/11).[3]

On one page of the *Me-ti* typescripts (BBA 136/49) is written only and in capital letters 'Rectification of names', and in brackets underneath also the phonetically correct German transcription of the Chinese 'Dschong Ming'. This term, a succinct expression of Confucian ethics, reminded of the need to adhere to the correct understanding of the behaviour required of your social and familial position: let a prince be a prince, a father be a father, a son be a son, and so on down the social scale, thereby sustaining the necessary authority structure. Here in Brecht's *Me-ti*, however, what is at stake is a realignment of the meaning of concepts that organize social life.

Confucius, aka Kung, appears in *Me-ti*, and Brecht had found in Forke's Mo Di an extensive and often funny critique of Confucian formalism and trickle-down morality, as in this passage:

> Through his pompous appearance and affected manner Confucius ruins the world, with zither music, singing, bells and pantomime he tries to educate pupils. Countless rules how to go up and down the steps are supposed to express ceremony and regulations concerning the gliding walk to impress the crowd. The teaching of the Confucians cannot serve as a norm and their ponderings are of no advantage to the people. (Forke, 407)

In the vivid parables of Chinese philosophers Brecht found a welcome practical counterweight to the abstractions of Western, including Marxist, thinkers. Like many people, the empathetic left-eyed Shen Te turns into an unsympathetic right-handed Shui Ta, because the gods have failed her. The Confucian philosopher Mencius (Mengzi), whose writings in Richard Wilhelm's translation (*Mong Dsi. Die Lehrgespräche des Meisters Meng K'o*. Jena: Eugen Dietrichs Verlag, 1916) were in Brecht's library, argued the task of the ruler was to create the conditions that enabled people to be 'good'. That the individual and the common good should coincide is something Hegel also advocated, but he did not speak with the memorable clarity of the Chinese. The *Communist Manifesto* addressed this problem by asserting that in the form of association that would replace that of class in class society, the free development of each would be the condition for the free development of all. But that did not happen, and it is ironic how common memory reversed this sequence and assumed, together with actual policy, that 'all', defined by whoever determined it, should naturally take precedence over 'each'.

[...]

## MO DI

Many passages in Mo Di criticize contemporary social values and practices, for example:

> Master Mê-tse said: if someone wants to employ a noble person of our day to slaughter pigs and he does not know how to do this, he will refuse. But if someone confers on him the post of minister of state, he accepts, even if he is not able for it. Is that not nonsensical?
>
> (Forke, 555)

---

[3] An account of Brecht's views on Confucius and of this projected play can be found in Tatlow, *The Mask of Evil*, pp. 382–409.

> If the superiors are only engaged to govern the state and to function as leaders of the people, they may well say: 'If somebody deserves punishment, then we will punish them.' But if superiors and inferiors are not in agreement, those punished by the superiors will be praised by the common people. The common people live close together; whoever wins their admiration will not be hindered in his behaviour in spite of any punishment by his superiors.
>
> (Forke, 227)

Mo Di, whose traditional dates Forke assumes as 480–400 BCE, making him an exact contemporary of Socrates (469–399), also offers systematic argument untypical of Chinese philosophy. Brecht sought, above all, to employ a way of speaking about contemporary problems, rather than developing any specific content, though there are parallels here too, as with his observation about generosity and the self, cited above, which resonates in *Me-ti* with much the same implications as in the Chinese text. Another passage in Mo Di shows why this is so:

> Love of people does not exclude the self, for it is among those, who are loved, and since this is the case, love also extends to your own person. What is normally called egoism is love of people.
>
> (Forke, 507)

There are, of course, less useful views in Mo Di, such as a condemnation of music as an unnecessary extravagance, and the general preference, in spite of concern for the common people, for a form of social organization that Forke described as social aristocratism.

In China, Mo Di has been associated with both left and right politics. His advocacy of universal love was seen as analogous to Christian thinking, and Chinese Christians naturally took pleasure in the fact that he lived long before Christ. It was claimed in the 1940s that the nationalist New Life Movement in the 1930s, an anti-Communist YMCA-inspired attempt at moral rearmament associated with Chiang Kai Shek's Guomintang, was 'virtually a total adaptation of the philosophy of life preached by Mo Di' (A. Tseu: *The Moral Philosophy of Mo Tse*. Taipei: China Printing, 1965, p. 399). Another view, expressed by Guo Morou, held that he preserved social hierarchy and also asked people to love one another, thus requiring the majority to love the minority. His ideas were also said to represent the rising class of freemen opposed to the clan aristocracy.[4]

Forke divided the work into four sections: Systematics, Dialectics, Conversations and Techniques of Warfare. The systematic section, developed in sequences of three parallel chapters, discusses specific topics, such as Preferring the Able, Instituting Similarity (of thought), Unifying Love, Condemnation of Fatalism, Condemnation of Offensive Warfare. Brecht did not attempt to develop a systematic exposition of topics in *Me-ti*, as in these chapters, though one German edition sought to derive a comparably systematic structure for the whole of *Me-ti*.

Brecht was more attracted to the *Dialectics* and *Conversations* sections. In *Dialectics*, logical and ethical questions are approached in the form of aphorisms, while *Conversations*, judged the most authentic section by Forke, presents often lively, short conversational narratives with sometimes paradoxical refutations of topical views and common practices. The term 'dialectics' obviously interested Brecht, who copied

---

[4] For further discussion of Mo Di's work, see Tatlow, *The Mask of Evil*, pp. 410–39.

in his *Me-ti* papers both the correct phonetic transcription of the Chinese character ming, and even the ideogram itself,(BBA 133/01), which is usually taken to refer to the 'school of logic'. Forke uses it as a heading for passages that state logical problems and explanations by later Moists, some of which Brecht marked in his copy and which certainly gave food for thought, since analogous ideas are formulated in his own *Me-ti*.

Forke interpreted 'dialectics' in Mo Di as skill in argument rather than as insight into a systematic structure of developing relations. Though these dialectics are not Hegelian, let alone Marxist, there are, nevertheless, unexpected compatibilities, and Brecht noted some passages that do link the perception of opposites and draw surprising conclusions from these observations.

Mo Di argued, among other things, against the nepotism of feudal families and social inequalities, which then lead to war, which he also condemned. He held that a belief in fatalism benefitted superiors but damaged their inferiors and observed that, while their superiors profit from it, in warfare two peasant armies attack one other, thereby neglecting to work the land. He believed that the people should be unified by 'love', and that social antagonisms should be prevented, if necessary by imposing unification. Brecht's differentiation, also in his poetry, between two social groups, 'die Oberen' and 'die Unteren' – meaning, literally, the upper and the lower ones – probably comes from Forke's translation, which uses these words to make this basic distinction.

In Mo Di, there are also passages like the following intriguing list of differently conceived opposites:

> white and black, the middle and the sides, talking and acting, studying and reality, justice and injustice, difficult and comfortable ... lasting and disappearing

but this particular text begins with the following striking comparison:

> Equal and unequal are interconnected: if you eat in a rich house, you can recognize having and not having.

(Forke, 460)

Whatever the original writers, or their translator, may have thought of these enumerations, they certainly seem like a shorthand for a dialectical philosophy and to imply a programme for acting, rather than merely thinking, which, if not definitively read out of them, can certainly be read into them.

## *ME-TI*

Brecht wrote the *Me-ti* texts from 1934 to 1955, mostly between 1934 and 1937. Occasionalist in character, they deal with recurring topics, though these are not systematically structured. Indeed, one of the 'subtle' themes that runs through the texts is the inherent danger of believing in systems. When no longer challenged by experience, practice ceases to innovate. Then, as one text suggests, experience is replaced by pre-established 'judgements'. Such judgements are determined by ideological belief. Professional administrators construct bureaucracies of thought, whose primary interest lies in preserving their own position to the detriment of individual and innovative producers.

This fundamental attitude, while recognizing the need for flexibility, explains why Brecht was so frustrated by the behaviour of what he called the 'camarilla' of opponents in Moscow who, when later installed as the government of the German Democratic

Republic, were determined to mitigate as far as possible his influence on public life and, above all, to deny it any effect on policy. What was criticized from outside, especially by conservative political voices in the Federal Republic, as his unquestioning support for, even subservience to the Communist 'system', appeared very threatening to its official proponents. Ruth Berlau describes how these texts came about:

> Brecht's *Me-ti* stories are a collection of philosophical, political and ethical thoughts about problems of our day. Whenever he came across such a question, he wrote a little story. He occupied himself with them for quite a long time. I think he wanted to try out a literary form for representing the dialectical method. His model was Lenin's essay *On Climbing High Mountains*, which he also quoted in *Me-ti*. The Chinese practice of allegorical description really suited him. Everything was clothed in a Chinese kind of wisdom.
>
> (Berlau, 78)

If we set aside the cliché of 'Chinese wisdom', which often connotes the wisdom of avoiding difficulties by ignoring infelicities, and think instead of the equally 'Chinese' love of paradox and wit that captivated Oscar Wilde and had its effect in *The Soul of Man under Socialism*, then Brecht's *Me-ti* aphorisms and stories do indeed owe something, apart from the relatively few examples of actual Chinese cultural material, to a fundamentally probing and, in its own way, dialectical view of the flow of things. This found a particular expression in China due, there too of course, to its frustration by the controlling forces it sought to oppose.

The Brecht Archive (BBA) holds around 550 unnumbered pages of *Me-ti* material in seven folders, which include copies or sketches for completed passages. There is no plan, or table of contents, or definitive section heading followed by appropriate texts, except for one folder (BBA 130/01–18), which contains a small number of texts under the heading 'condemnation of ethics'. And there is no authorized sequence for the 360 or so pieces that have been printed in the three separately published German editions, or in the volume of the collected works (BFA 18/45–194) that appeared in 1995.

The archive contains seven folders (BBA 129–134 and 136), with dedicated material, none of which is paginated. Another folder contains just over twenty unnumbered pages with copies and sketches found among papers in nine other separate folders. Folder 136/01–88 consists of a fair copy typescript made by his collaborator Margarete Steffin, entitled *Buch der Wendungen*, of a selection of texts from the other six folders. They are preceded by an introduction, which asserts that the book derives from an English translation of the Chinese by Charles Stephen, and by an incomplete list of invented 'Chinese' [*sic*] names and their real-life equivalents (Mi-en-leh for Lenin, Ni-en for Stalin, Ka-osch for Korsch, Kin-jeh for Brecht, Lai-tu for Berlau, and so forth), and followed by some seventeen pages of copies, handwritten sketches and other jottings.

While Steffin's typescript is conventionally capitalized, the texts in folders 129–134 are written in Brecht's characteristic lower-case typescript. Folder 129/01–50 begins with a page across which is only written '*Me-ti*' in Brecht's handwriting. Folders 129–134 also contain copies of texts, some of which have been differently corrected, but the variations are minor handwritten additions or erasures of a word. Brecht made copies in this manner, but did not get round to collating them with their different alterations into one 'final' corrected and hence 'correct' version.

Various headings, and possible allusions to titles, are written on or across some pages: *Buch der Wendungen* (a verbal pun, since 'Wendung' means 'turn' of events, and, in 'Redewendung,' 'turn of phrase' or 'figure of speech'), which led to the commonly used but unsatisfactory (because it is too imprecise and finicky) English title, 'Book of twists and turns'; *Me-ti*; *Büchlein mit Verhaltenslehren* (Booklet with behavioural teachings); *Buch der Eigenschaften* (Book of qualities/attributes); *Lehrbuch des Verhaltens* (Manual on behaviour); *Buch vom Fluß der Dinge* (Book on the flow of things) – but there is no evidence of a preferred title.

Allusions have been made to a connection with the celebrated Chinese *Book of Changes* (I Ching or, in pinyin, Yijing), one of the five classic books, whose standard German translation is *Buch der Wandlungen* (Book of transformations). The BFA notes to *Me-ti*, for example, state that Brecht 'used' Richard Wilhelm's translation (BFA 18/493) without, however, saying how or where. That truly extraordinary Chinese text works through all sixty-four hexagrams constructed by the possible combinations of three undivided and three divided lines, the undivided symbolizing the sky and the divided symbolizing earth. The commentary encompasses Heaven and Earth, interpreting natural forces in accordance with the Chinese Imaginary. Proposing correlations between these natural or metaphysical forces and human events, the cryptic and suggestive poetic texts constitute ancient Chinese culture's prophetic almanac of universal relations. There is, however, absolutely no affinity between *Me-ti* and the *Book of Changes* except in an entirely abstract sense, since both are concerned with observing and understanding change, though that change is very differently conceived.

Nor is there any visual connection between Chinese ideograms and the few 'image signs', which the same editorial BFA notes to *Me-ti* presume to derive from those sixty-four hexagrams. At one stage Brecht thought of these 'signs' as furnishing a possible, but never realized, *Me-ti* chapter, but he finally placed them in *Conversations of Refugees*.[5]

There is, however, a stronger verbal analogy between Brecht's use in *Me-ti* of the terms 'Great Method' for dialectics and 'Great Order' for socialism or Communism (to be replaced, too late, by 'Great Production') and the title of one of Confucianism's revered four books, the instructional 'Great Learning' (Daxue), which had earlier suggested the Great Pedagogy of the didactic plays, as well as with the expression for an old social ideal, 'Great Togetherness' or 'Great Harmony' (Datong), which was subsequently transferred to the idea of Communism.

Not only was *Me-ti* never 'completed', but the individual texts were not definitively 'signed off' for positioning, and the manuscript collection is unstructured.

[...]

## THIS EDITION

There is no approved or 'authorized' sequence for the *Me-ti* texts and this new edition is differently structured from the earlier alternatives [...].

The challenge, or danger, in proposing an entirely different sequence to anything hitherto presented, no matter with what 'political' effect – for if none is subjectively intended, its consequences will be objectively present – is the possibility of inferring an argument different from, even out of sympathy with, the perspectives that originally shaped them. They may seem inimical or to have been overruled by the passage of time

---

[5]They are included and explained in his diaries on 1 February 1942: see Bertolt Brecht, *Journals 1934-1955* (London: Methuen, 1993), p. 196.

and subsequent events, by the development of what Brecht called 'experience' confronting 'judgements', which amounts to practice trumping ideology. [...]

While placing the Lai-tu texts at the end of the sequence, I have also taken the 'Chinese' passages toward the beginning, though not bundled together, but in the context of various unfolding themes. The purpose is not to overemphasize them or the extent to which Brecht was beholden to Mo Di, as some critics have done, because that tends to mystify and to detract from the impact of the whole collection, but rather to show from the start what is happening, why there are suggestive analogies, and where they have their place, but also their limits.

The intention is, as it were, to get this out of the way in order to concentrate on the real historical and contemporary substance of these writings, instead of scratching our head when another 'Chinese' allusion crops up, at best constituting a distraction, as we either ignore it or wonder what on earth it really means. While these allusions do broaden the reach of what is said and also have a necessary estranging effect, the figure of Brecht's 'Me-ti' – part persona, part super-ego, confirming and confronting what the more autobiographical Kin-jeh [one Brecht's 'Chinese' references to himself], in his various guises, says and does – is of course a device for engaging with, and keeping a certain distance from, the often overwhelming difficulties of the day and their always changing, ever-conflicted interface between theory and practice.

Some texts first printed in the BFA edition are included, though a couple whose meaning remains incoherent are left out. The archive folders contain two intriguing allusions, which Brecht regrettably did not pursue: a handwritten note, 'dialog me ti + nietze' and 'nietzsche und seine benutzer' ('Nietzsche and his users', BBA 132/24), as well as three small pictures of a grinning Stalin's head, creating the effect of caricature, which take us some steps beyond the then current cliché in England of our one-time ally, the pipe-smoking Uncle Joe, towards something more comical and hence sinister (BBA 133/63).

Translation always raises its own problems. There is a special one with these texts. Brecht estranges many concepts and institutions, thereby inviting us to reconsider what they stand for and what they conceal. What may at first seem odd in English, either poorly or simply mistranslated, depends on conveying a similar effect. Thus 'Umwälzung' (frequently used for revolution) becomes upheaval or overthrow, party becomes association, smithmasters stand for factory owners, ploughsmiths for factory workers and headworkers for intellectuals, or Great Method for dialectics, Great Disorder for Capitalism, house painter for Hitler, and so forth. Such Chinese names as can be attached to historical individuals are listed below.

[...]

The texts range in style, from anecdote to short narrative, commentary, aphorism, poetry, paraphrase, incorporating versions of other texts (Kipling, Lenin, Marx). They constitute a defensive or critical response to social and political issues of the day, which are nearly always in some degree estranged by the manner of their telling. They neither aspire, like the writings of Korsch, to theoretical, let alone systematic, explanation of events, nor do they seek to inform about such events in a journalistic sense. Rather, they step back towards the events behind the events, in order to question them and their human causes and motivation from a deeper or wider perspective in the hope of showing what their sheer pressure and immediacy frequently obscures. That is ultimately a philosophical pursuit of the kind that Brecht admired, which seeks to shape a practice by understanding what really guides it.

The aim is not to align these texts with a specific contention, whether intrinsic or attributed, for all that time and changing circumstances must affect any reading, but to allow the contradictions they explore to speak for themselves. Rather than explicitly divided into sections, the passages are loosely gathered around unfolding topics. Many address political tactics and policy, especially seeking to explain, through estranging descriptions, for example, how and why Lenin adjusted his practice in the light of specific circumstances, while not losing sight of his ultimate goal. Others step back from such practice and tactics to reflect on this ultimate goal and whether it was being furthered or hindered by policy and concepts of governance, questions basically addressing the relationship between the individual and the state. The problems Stalin had grotesquely exacerbated did not disappear after his death. They were perpetuated in a system that Brecht later described in his letter to Berlau as too 'formal, superficial, mechanical'.

Facing these difficulties, Brecht sought to open up what we might call desire lines to counter the frustrations, and worse, experienced by so many who had turned to Communism, because of deeply held desires, which were repressed in what has been called the social unconscious, as the repository of what is longed for but cannot be realized under prevailing social rules and practices, and reinforced by alarm at the extent of 'homogenization', which allows for nothing 'undefined, fruitful, uncontrollable' (*On the productivity of individuals*).[6]

An insistent, emotionally powerful under- and often enough counter-current flows through Brecht's writing, which is opposed to system and to theory that has hardened into ideology, especially when policed by a class of administrators, privileged within a social culture, running the risk of turning people into what he calls in one passage 'the servants of priests' (*Ka-meh* [Brecht's version of Karl Marx] *on realizing the Great Order*).

In *Me-ti*, this dislike often takes the form of an apparently provocative condemnation of virtues and of a seemingly contrary insistence on the need for egoism or self-love, for the self-help that, as Mo Di argued, did not damage, but assisted others. Such deviating desire lines invite individual productivity and creativity, appealing to experience rather than 'judgements' or 'opinions', to the wisdom of ordinary people, once referred to as the masses.

The crisis of Capitalism, of how humanity's affairs are organized, which provoked the response of Communism, has changed since Brecht experienced and faced it, but some of these changes have become even more threatening. Far from over, let alone solved, this crisis is probably only just beginning.

---

[6] It is well known that Brecht rejected Freudian ego-psychology but, intriguingly, he asked himself in 1938 whether he really wanted 'to do away with the space where the unconscious, half conscious, uncontrolled, ambiguous, multipurposed could play itself out' (BFA 22.1/468). The unanswered self-questioning clearly implies: No! Whether or not subjectively envisaged, the concept, social unconscious, undoubtedly has explanatory strength. I discuss this further in 'Brecht's East Asia: A Conspectus', *The Brecht Yearbook* 36, pp. 356f.

*Theatre Work*

CHAPTER FOURTEEN

# Brecht's *Theatre Work*: A Foundational Work and its Marginalisation

DETLEV SCHÖTTKER
TRANSLATED BY ROMY FURSLAND

In the 1970s, Brecht criticism went much further both in its scope and in its intensity than criticism of other authors. Everything was discussed, and seemingly no stone was left unturned. The debate has since come to a standstill because the social and political dimension of literature, which Brecht represented better than anyone else, is no longer central to new ideas in the field of cultural studies. The protagonists of Brecht scholarship and a few of their adherents are still publishing but nobody is challenging them, meaning that shortcomings are not being addressed. This is certainly true of a volume which appeared in 1952 entitled *Theaterarbeit* [*Theatre Work*]; nothing was written about it, probably because Brecht's name appeared only as part of an editorial team, and theoretical statements are not the main focus of the text.[1] In editions and handbooks it features only marginally or not at all; in the *Große kommentierte Berliner und Frankfurter Ausgabe*, even the texts taken from the volume are inadequately edited.[2] In the five-volume edition of the *Brecht-Handbuch* (2001–2003), the volume is not treated as an independent work, meaning that the failings of the edition have not been corrected.[3] Yet the *Theatre Work*, with its 400 large-format pages, elaborate typography and many images, is not only more representative than all Brecht's other publications, but also

---

Detlev Schöttker, 'Brechts *Theaterarbeit*: Ein Grundlagenwerk und seine Ausgrenzungen', *Weimarer Beiträge*, 53: 3 (2007), pp. 438–51.

[1] Berliner Ensemble/Helene Weigel (eds.), *Theaterarbeit. 6 Aufführungen des Berliner Ensembles*, ed. Ruth Berlau, Bertolt Brecht, Claus Hubalek, Peter Palitzsch, and Käthe Rülicke (Berlin and Frankfurt am Main, 1961 [originally Dresden, 1952]). Cited in the text as *Th* with page number.
[2] Bertolt Brecht, *Werke. Große kommentierte Berliner und Frankfurter Ausgabe*, ed. Werner Hecht, Jan Knopf, Werner Mittenzwei and Klaus-Detlef Müller, 30 volumes and one index volume (Berlin and Weimar and Frankfurt am Main, 1988–2000). Cited in the text and below as BFA with volume and page number. Theoretical texts from *Theatre Work* are located in Volume 23 (also see below).
[3] Jan Knopf (ed.), *Brecht-Handbuch*, 5 volumes (Stuttgart, 2001-2003). Brecht's authorship is a prerequisite for some authors, however: see among others Vol. 1, pp. 48, 452, 581 and Vol. 4, pp. 9, 169, 191, 319, 342f, 495. The volume is briefly mentioned but not discussed in detail in Anna Kugli, Michael Opitz (eds.), *Brecht-Lexikon* (Stuttgart, 2006), 242–244 (the account of the volume largely confines itself to notes on Brecht's directing work).

includes the only comprehensive portrayal of epic dramaturgy during his lifetime. By neglecting this volume, therefore, careless Brecht scholars have perpetuated the policy which the cultural institutions of the GDR have been pursuing for political reasons since the beginning of the 1950s: the marginalisation of a foundational work.

*Background: Brecht's Communist critics:* – Whenever Brecht wrote about theatrical questions, productions of his own or other people's works formed the basis of his reflections. His only texts with a more theoretical bent are *Buying Brass*, which Brecht worked on in the USA from 1939 onwards but which were not published during his lifetime, and the *Short Organon for the Theatre*, which he wrote in 1948 and published a year later in a special edition of *Sinn und Form*. Both are exceptions. In the first case, Brecht felt compelled to explain the philosophical and dramaturgical foundations of his theatre because Georg Lukács claimed that Brecht's plays could not be described as realistic. In the second case, he wanted to create a conceptual foundation for the performance of his plays in Berlin following his return from exile in the United States. In August 1948 he described the text in his *Journal* as a 'short summary of *Buying Brass*' (BFA 26: 231), but did not include it in *Theatre Work* and relegated it to the 'Appendices' which he worked on from 1954 onwards.

In *Theatre Work* Brecht summarised his experiences over the course of more than thirty years' work as a dramatist and director, and presented his dramaturgy in a systematic way. An initial summary appeared in the form of the 'Notes on the Opera *Rise and Fall of the City of Mahagonny*', which appeared in 1930 in the second volume of the *Versuche [Experiments]*. Here, Brecht famously differentiated the 'epic form' of drama from the 'dramatic form', since he wanted to turn theatre from a 'consumable' into a 'learning medium' (BFA 24: 74ff.) Characters' actions were to be presented in a narrative way, as socially influenced behaviours, and not embodied in a theatrically emotive way as intrinsic to those characters' natures. This, however, brought Brecht into conflict with Georg Lukács, and his works were permanently excluded from the canon of Socialist Realism as a result. What happened has been described many times, but the long-term consequences for Brecht's work have never yet been properly examined. This is particularly true of *Theatre Work*.

In an article entitled 'A Virtue out of a Necessity' which appeared in 1932 in *Linkskurve*, the organ of the Association of Proletarian Revolutionary Authors, Lukács used passages from Brecht's 'Notes' on *Mahagonny* to denounce the reportage technique in novels by Socialist authors. He directed the same criticism at Brecht's play *The Decision*, which he criticised for 'abstract preaching' at the expense of 'revolutionary conviction'.[4] For a long time, Brecht's work was repeatedly accused of being 'abstract' by Lukács and his supporters. After visiting Moscow in 1932, Brecht set out his position in a series of essays. His position was partly informed by the 'First All-Union Congress of Soviet Writers', which was held in Moscow in 1934 and led to a call for writers to commit to Socialist Realism.[5] For Lukács, the most important criterion of a new realism was

---

[4]Georg Lukács, 'Aus der Not eine Tugend' (1932), in Lukács, *Schriften zur Literatursoziologie*, selected and introduced by Peter Ludz, 5th edition (Neuwied, 1972), 146 and 152. See also in this context Helga Gallas, *Marxistische Literaturtheorie. Kontroversen im 'Bund proletarisch-revolutionärer Schriftsteller'* (Neuwied and Berlin, 1971).

[5]See Hans-Jürgen Schmidt, Godehard Schramm (eds.), *Sozialistische Realismuskonzeptionen. Dokumente zum 1. Allunionskongreß der Sowjetschriftsteller* (Frankfurt am Main, 1974).

not the representation of visible reality but the emphasizing of its underlying historical laws, which meant that the bourgeois realism of the 19th century was augmented in line with historical materialism. 'Great realism, therefore,' Lukács wrote in 1938 in his essay 'Realism in the Balance', 'portrays an aspect of reality which is not immediately evident but which is permanent, and objectively all the more important'.[6]

With this essay Lukács entered into the expressionism debate in the Moscow journal *Das Wort* and immediately sent it off in a new direction, one which also affected Brecht's work. If the debate had originally been about whether the representatives of the avant garde had failed in the fight against Fascism, criticism was now being levelled at their aesthetic processes, such as montage, reduction and typification – techniques which Brecht too was influenced by. Lukács condemned these techniques as 'abstractions' but wrote more positively about Brecht himself: in Lukács' view, the scene *The Spy* (from the *Fear and Misery of the Third Reich* series), which had previously been printed in *Das Wort*, showed that Brecht was 'already leading the charge against the inhumanity of Fascism in a way he has not done before, with a multifaceted, finely graduated realism'.[7]

Brecht explicitly distanced himself from this co-opting of his work, and from August 1939 onwards several rebuttals appear in his *Journal*, until he eventually declares: 'The realism debate is going to hamper production if it goes on like this' (BFA 26: 321). In fact it was only his work on literary texts that was hampered – because Lukács' criticism had actually led Brecht to start reflecting on the foundations of his dramaturgy. The result of these reflections was (in addition to *Buying Brass*) a series of contributions to the expressionism, or realism, debate. They were not made public at the time, however, because they were turned down by the editors of *Das Wort*, and only appeared posthumously in the *Collected Works* (1967). We cannot therefore speak of a public Brecht-Lukács debate. That is a phenomenon of the early 1970s, when the discipline of literary studies began to grapple with different conceptions of realism.[8]

According to the title page of *Das Wort*, Brecht – along with Lion Feuchtwanger and Willi Bredel – was supposedly a member of the 'editorial team', but he had no influence on the decisions that were made because, like Feuchtwanger and later Bredel, he did not live in Moscow. For this reason he distanced himself from the editorial team in a letter to Bredel in summer 1938: 'Unfortunately, collaborating on *Das Wort* is becoming more and more problematic. The journal increasingly seems to be moving in a peculiar direction whereby a small clique, seemingly led by Lukács and Hay, is setting up a very specific ideal of literary form and consequently rejecting anything that doesn't conform to this formal ideal borrowed from the bourgeois novelist of the previous century. [...] I only ever get sent material from *Das Wort* which has already been selected, and my objections are almost never taken into account. This can't go on much longer, I'm telling you.' (BGA 29: 106). Since Bredel had gone to Spain in April 1937 to fight with the International

---

[6]Georg Lukács, 'Es geht um den Realismus' [Realism in the Balance], in Hans-Jürgen Schmidt (ed.), *Die Expressionismusdebatte. Materialien zu einer marxistischen Realismuskonzeption* (Frankfurt am Main, 1972), 216.
[7]Ibid., 229f.
[8]See Detlev Schöttker, 'Politisierung eines Klassikers. Brecht-Forschung zwischen Widerspiegelungstheorie und Avantgardismus', in Silvio Vietta and Dirk Kemper (eds.), *Germanistik der siebziger Jahre. Zwischen Innovation und Ideologie* (Munich, 2000).

Brigades against Franco's troops, Fritz Erpenbeck, one of Lukács's supporters, had been made senior editor of the journal. Brecht's articles were often boycotted.[9]

This state of affairs proved to be permanent. In 1946, Erpenbeck became editor-in-chief of *Theater der Zeit*, the only theatre journal in the Soviet occupation zone and the GDR, and from 1951 onwards was also head of the Central Programming Committee at the Ministry of the People's Education, and head of the Department of Performing Arts. Until Brecht's death, Erpenbeck never commented favourably upon any Brecht production and never published any of Brecht's texts in the journal he edited.[10] Instead, he repeatedly emphasised the incompatibility of epic theatre and Socialist Realism. He was also involved in banning the opera *The Trial of Lucullus*, which Brecht had written with Paul Dessau and staged in 1951. On 12 March 1951 the Secretariat of the Central Committee of the SED decided to drop the opera from the repertoire, and the next day Erpenbeck chaired a discussion about a private rehearsal staged for cultural officials, who confirmed the decision. A few days later on 17 March 1951, at the fifth meeting of the Central Committee, the campaign 'Against Formalism in Art and Literature' was agreed upon. This campaign also targeted epic theatre, and was directly related to the *Lucullus* opera.[11]

*The volume: A handbook of epic theatre.* – Brecht's decision to publish an overview of his work was directly linked to this campaign.[12] Two weeks later, on 2 April 1951, a 'provisional contract' was agreed with Dresdner Verlag for a volume to be entitled 'Theatre Chronicle of the Berliner Ensemble'.[13] The publication date was set for October 1951. The 'provisional contract' was signed by Peter Palitzsch, Claus Hubalek, Käthe Rülicke and Helene Weigel on behalf of the Berliner Ensemble. Palitzsch, who had contacts at Dresdner Verlag through his work as a graphic artist, was tasked by Brecht with designing the volume. Brecht himself remained in the background. However, he not only organised every detail of the volume, as reports from the time tell us, but was also the author of most of the texts. The fact that he did not act as editor has nothing to do with the collective aspirations of the work; it was a tactical move designed to make it easier to get approval to print the volume and to facilitate its distribution.[14]

---

[9] See David Pike, *Deutsche Schriftsteller im sowjetischen Exil 1933-1945* (Frankfurt am Main, 1981), 272ff.

[10] It was not until shortly after Brecht's death that a short article appeared about the set designer Kurt Palm (Issue 5/1956) and several months later a scene from *The Days of the Commune* (Issue 11/1956).

[11] Brecht's production of his adaptation of Goethe's *Urfaust* was cancelled in April 1952 after nineteen performances in Potsdam and in March 1953 after five performances in Berlin. In this context, see also Manfred Jäger, '"Nicht traurig, aber ungünstig". Brecht und sein Theater im schwierigen Milieu der DDR' in Jäger, *Sozialliteraten. Funktion und Selbstverständnis der Schriftsteller in der DDR* (Düsseldorf, 1973); Werner Mittenzwei, *Der Realismus-Streit um Brecht. Grundriß der Brecht-Rezeption in der DDR 1945-1975* (Berlin and Weimar, 1978), 21ff.; Petra Stuber, *Spielräume und Grenzen. Studien zum DDR-Theater* (Berlin, 1998), 68ff.; Martina Langermann, 'Kanonisierungen in der DDR. Dargestellt am Beispiel "sozialistischer Realismus"', in Renate von Heydebrandt (ed.), *Kanon macht Kultur. Theoretische, historische und soziale Aspekte ästhetischer Kanonbildungen* (Stuttgart and Weimar, 1998).

[12] For a chronology see Werner Hecht, *Brecht Chronik 1898-1956* (Frankfurt am Main, 1997), 952ff.

[13] Bertolt Brecht Archive 2093/05. I am grateful to the archive's director, Erdmut Wizisla, for his advice and further information.

[14] Peter Palitzsch confirmed this in a telephone conversation I had with him on 17 December 2003 (he died on 18 December 2004). Benno Besson, who was also part of the Brecht circle, when asked by Thomas Irmer about Palitzsch's work, replied: 'Brecht relied on him in particular for the book *Theatre Work* and for the programmes.' ('Wie Walter Ulbricht den "Drachen" sah. Der Regisseur über die Arbeit mit Brecht [...]', in *Berliner Zeitung*, No. 131 from 7/8 June 2003, 'Magazine', 4f.) Palitzsch is not alone. Manfred Wekwerth, another of Brecht's director colleagues at the Berliner Ensemble, reminisced about the intensive work on *Theatre Work* in Ahrenshoop

The fact that this was necessary in the case of *Theatre Work* is illustrated by the events that followed. Even before its publication (in May 1952), the volume had already attracted the attention of the authorities. A resolution by the Department of Culture at the Central Committee of the SED on 2 February 1952 states: 'The Arts Section is tasked with producing a report for the Secretariat on the work of the formalist Brecht circle. The theatre almanac published by the Berliner Ensemble should be subjected to particular scrutiny. Permission is granted for the almanac to be published. No grants are to be paid by the cultural fund. Criticism of the almanac should be prepared.'[15] We do not know if Brecht was aware that the volume was under observation. At any rate, however, he did not give his adversaries much of an opportunity to attack him, and was thereby observing a principle of the 'Five Difficulties in Writing the Truth', according to which 'cunning is necessary' in order to disseminate one's ideas (BFA 22: 88).

Theory was replaced by the depiction of dramaturgy in words and pictures. The productions featured in the volume illustrate the diversity of epic theatrical forms. In addition to Brecht's own plays *Mr Puntila and his Man Matti*, *The Mother* and *Mother Courage and her Children*, three adaptations are included: Gorky's *Vassa Zheleznova*, Lenz's *The Tutor* and Hauptmann's *The Beaver Coat and Conflagration*. As well as excerpts from the plays, the volume features photographs of productions, images of placards and stage sets, literary analyses, selected reviews, historical explanations, accounts of the directing, notes on characters, descriptions of scenes and articles about actors, music, set design, costumes and masks. The contents page does not reflect the actual order of the articles but is organised by theme: plots, direction, acting, linguistic issues, descriptions of scenes, publicity, photography etc. This establishes the volume as a handbook.

The concept of *Verfremdung*, which Brecht had first set out in *Buying Brass* and returned to later in the *Short Organon*, is no longer a key concern here. It was supposed to create a link between the performance on stage and the mental processing of that performance by the audience, but it did not actually emerge from performance practice and has been made so much of by pedagogically overheated Brecht scholarship since the end of the 1960s that other aesthetic processes of epic theatre have been neglected. In *Theatre Work*, Brecht used new categories to which he returned over and over again in the following years when he wanted to supplement or renew his theory: model, turning point and simplicity.[16]

The reflections on these fundamental aesthetic concepts are interspersed, however, with texts designed to prove that epic theatre is anchored in literary tradition, since this was one of the key points on which Brecht was attacked by his adversaries and where Socialist Realism claimed to be carrying on the bourgeois legacy. For this reason Brecht not only included texts from authors who were his friends (like Paul Dessau,

---

(Manfred Wekwerth, *Erinnern ist Leben. Eine dramatische Autobiographie*, [Leipzig, 2000], 62ff.) And Ernst Schumacher, who was familiar with the Brecht circle from 1949 onwards, is clear that Brecht's collaborators were far too young and inexperienced to create a book like *Theatre Work* on their own (Ernst Schumacher, *Mein Brecht. Erinnerungen 1943 bis 1956* [Berlin, 2006], 203–208).

[15]Printed in Joachim Lucchesi (ed.), *Das Verhör in der Oper. Die Debatte um die Aufführung 'Das Verhör des Lukullus' von Bertolt Brecht und Paul Dessau* (Berlin, 1993), 278 (available in the Archive of Political Parties and Mass Organisations in the GDR Foundation, in the Federal Archives).

[16]These concepts, like other fundamental concepts of Brechtian dramaturgy (*Fabel*, *Gestus* etc.), are not included in Kugli/Opitz (eds.), *Brecht-Lexikon*. The explanation of the key term 'Modelbooks' is incorrect and not consistent with the statements in BFA: 25 ('Theatre models').

Berthold Viertel, Paul Rilla, Elisabeth Hauptmann, Hans Meyer, Herbert Ihering and Anna Seghers) but also texts by Lukács about Gorky, Gerhart Hauptmann and naturalism. The fact that articles by Erpenbeck also appear (on the subject of Angelika Hurwicz and Regine Lutz, two actors of the Berliner Ensemble) makes clear the tactical nature of the volume. The names of the authors do not appear on the contents page, however, so as to give the impression of a collective work. The main aim, though, was to conceal the fact that most of the articles had been written by Brecht. They are credited either with his full name or with the abbreviation 'b.' Some are unattributed, but were written at the very least with Brecht's involvement.[17] Other articles were written by Brecht specifically for the volume, or published there for the first time.[18]

Following its publication Brecht himself was involved in promoting the volume, which he did largely by contacting the representatives of cultural institutions. In May 1952 he writes in a letter to Hans Meyer, who had been Professor of Modern German Literature at the University of Leipzig since 1948: 'Couldn't you write something soon about *Theatre Work*? Such publications still go unsung here.' (BFA 30: 125f.) In July Brecht writes to Helmut Holtzhauer, who was head of the State Commission for the Arts: 'Something needs to be done to promote the book *Theatre Work*. The book was not written just for specialists' (ibid., 132). And in August he comments in a letter to Friedrich Wolf: 'We would be very grateful to you, by the way, if you could encourage the Volksbühne to do something about distributing *Theatre Work* to its members' (ibid., 136). In June 1952 Brecht took part in a discussion of the book on Berliner Rundfunk (a Berlin radio station), but after that there was no further response to the book's publication.[19]

*Additions: Stanislavsky debate and Modelbooks.* – Ultimately it was not *Theatre Work* but another handbook that was promoted by the cultural institutions. This book had appeared in 1947 with Aufbau Verlag under the title *The German Stanislavsky Book. A Handbook of Acting According to the Stanislavsky System*.[20] It owed its pedagogical status to more than just its title. For its author Ottofritz Gaillard and the writers of the preface and the appendix, Maxim Vallentin and Otto Lang, were the founders and directors of the German Theatre Institute, which they had set up in Weimar in 1947 and which in 1953 had become the Leipzig Theatre School. Brecht read the book in mid-September 1947, in exile in Los Angeles. In his *Journal*, he writes: 'Reading *The German Stanislavsky Book* (Ottofritz Gaillard, Vallentin). They're doing it in Weimar now.' (BFA 27: 246). After his return from exile he expressed his antipathy more clearly. In early January 1948 he writes in the *Journal*: 'What I find particularly off-putting about the *German Stanislavsky Book*

---

[17]See also Gerhard Seidel's comments, *Bibliographie Bertolt Brecht. Titelverzeichnis*, Vol. 1: *Deutschsprachige Veröffentlichungen aus den Jahren 1913-1972. Werke von Brecht: Sammlungen, Dramatik* (Berlin and Weimar, 1975), 114–122.

[18]Some articles are printed consecutively in BFA (BFA 23: 162-175), but do not have a collective title, so the fact that they all belong to *Theatre Work* is evident only from the commentary; other articles are scattered, so that the reader has to go looking for them in and amongst other texts. A compilation of all the texts published by Brecht in *Theatre Work* – as in Seidel: *Bibliographie Bertolt Brecht* – is lacking. Some of the articles with no named author are not included at all, even though Brecht's authorship or involvement cannot be ruled out.

[19]See Werner Hecht (ed.), *Brecht im Gespräch. Diskussionen. Dialoge. Interviews* (Frankfurt am Main, 1975), 107ff. – In 1952 a licensed edition appeared with the Dusseldorf-based Progress-Verlag (2000 copies were printed) and in 1961 a further edition was published by Berlin's Henschel Verlag and Frankfurt's Suhrkamp Verlag (see Seidel, *Bibliographie Bertolt Brecht*, 114ff.)

[20]Ottofritz Gaillard, *Das deutsche Stanislavski-Buch. Lehrbuch der Schauspielkunst nach dem Stanislavski-System*, with a preface by Maxim Vallentin and an appendix on amateur performance by Otto Lange (Berlin, 1947).

is the homely moralistic tone that can't even be interpreted as "the morality of craftsmen" because the craft of a charlatan does not have any real morality.' (Ibid., 261).

This was no ad hoc judgement. Since the mid-1930s Brecht had been engaging with Stanislavsky's writing and formulating his own theories on theatre by differentiating them from Stanislavsky's system, which had been promoted in Tsarist Russia as well as in the Soviet Union and which was disseminated by many students. The faithful reproduction of visible reality, the identification of actors with their characters and the identification of the spectators with the events on stage were the cornerstones of the theory: the concept thus overlaps with naturalist theatre.[21] Whenever Brecht spoke dismissively about 'naturalism', he was not talking about the movement in German literature but about Stanislavsky's system, as the 'Naturalism' chapter of *Buying Brass* shows (see BFA 22: 703ff). At the same time he was becoming aware of the need to describe his own theatre in a systematic way. 'I read Stanislavsky's *My Life in Art* with envy and unease,' he writes to Erwin Piscator in July 1936. 'The man got his system in order, with the result that people are now signing up as Stanislavsky students in Paris and New York. Does it have to be this way? We really are unworldly dreamers.' (BFA 28: 558).

In 1953 Brecht was again confronted with Stanislavsky's directorial methods, when the State Commission for the Arts staged a conference to raise awareness of the Russian director's approach. The conference was held in Berlin from 17–19 April and was organised by Erpenbeck, among others. Brecht, Helene Weigel and other members of the Berliner Ensemble attended. Helene Weigel spoke on their behalf, giving a speech written by Brecht. He was trying to avoid confrontation, and had Weigel explain that 'the Berliner Ensemble began studying the Stanislavsky method some time ago and has tested out elements of it in rehearsal'. For this reason, Brecht claimed, it was pointless to 'create an artificial divide between our way of working and the Stanislavsky method' (BFA 23: 234ff.) In the run-up to the conference Brecht had in fact written a number of texts in which he addressed the Russian director's methods.[22] But they were rejected. In these texts Brecht did not distance himself from Stanislavsky himself but from his students' publications.[23]

The contributions to and results of the Stanislavsky conference were published in four issues of *Theater der Zeit* under the title 'Our Stanislavsky Discussion' (Issues 5–8). They included Helene Weigel's speech. Several articles are openly critical of the Berliner Ensemble's work. One of these is a piece by Harald Hauser, published in the sixth issue under the title 'Abstraction'. Hauser refers to *A Contribution to the Critique of Political Economy*, in which Marx described his method as 'ascending from the abstract to the concrete'. Hauser appropriates this phrase in order to prove the contradiction between Brecht's dramaturgy and the Marxist method. 'It seems to me that many of the Berliner Ensemble's performances deliberately linger in the abstract, or come to a standstill halfway between the abstract and the road back to the particular. [...] In this

---

[21] See Joachim Fiebach, *Von Craig bis Brecht. Studien zu Künstlertheorien in der ersten Hälfte des 20. Jahrhunderts*, 3rd revised and extended edition (Berlin, 1975); Manfred Brauneck, *Theater im 20. Jahrhundert. Programmschriften. Stilperioden. Reformmodelle*, 9th updated edition (Reinbek, 2001).
[22] A sizeable group of these texts are printed consecutively in BFA under the title 'Stanislavksy Studies' (BFA 23: 226-239); several others are scattered amongst other texts and have to be identified using the commentary.
[23] See Detlev Schöttker, *Bertolt Brechts Ästhetik der Naïven* (Stuttgart, 1989), 196ff.

I see a genuine conflict with the Stanislavsky method – not a difference of degree, but a *fundamental* contradiction.'[24]

Erpenbeck reinforced Hauser's criticisms in an article which appeared in the same issue under the title 'A Brief Editorial Intervention in the Debate': 'Bertolt Brecht probably thinks he is "going beyond" Stanislavsky in moving from the concrete to the abstract, as his *Organon* proves. In fact, however, Brecht's work lacks [...] the third way, which is necessary in order for the process to become a dialectical one and which in Stanislavsky's work – especially during his last few years – is indicated again and again: from the abstract back to the concrete, from the general back to the specific'.[25] In an article entitled 'The *Short Organon* and Stanislavsky's System', Brecht tried to defend himself, but ended up resorting to anecdotal evidence: 'How could anyone possibly simplify the *Short Organon* so drastically as to claim that it calls for pale, distilled creatures on the stage, schematic intellectual constructs? When anyone can see that Puntila and Courage, as portrayed by the Berliner Ensemble, are flesh-and-blood human beings bursting with vitality?' (BFA 25: 581).[26]

Initially there was no theoretical counteroffensive. Instead Brecht tried, following the *Theatre Work*, to elaborate his own system. The basis for this was 'models' of productions, which were to be presented in so-called 'modelbooks'. Both terms are used for the first time in *Theatre Work* (Th: 296ff.) and illustrated using the examples of *Puntila*, *The Mother* and *Mother Courage* (Th: 227ff. and 285ff.) In 1948 Brecht had already published a book entitled *Antigone Model 1948* (based on the staging of an adaptation of Antigone at the municipal theatre in Chur), but the actual model concept was first developed for *Theatre Work*. In 1954 Brecht signed a contract with Henschel Verlag for a series of books to be called 'The 'Modelbooks of the Berliner Ensemble'. The documentation of the *Mother Courage* production which featured in *Theatre Work* (Th: 227–284) served as an example. Photographs taken during the performances were an integral part of the modelbooks, and great care was taken with them. In a text by Ruth Berlau which Brecht edited for *Theatre Work*, we are told: 'The ability to create models of a reasonably precise nature arose from the development of theatre photography.' (Th: 341).[27]

The publication of the *Modelbooks* was a slow process, however. Following the failure of a plan to publish a volume on *Mother Courage*, also with Dresdner Verlag, a revised version of *Antigone Model 1948* appeared in 1955 as the first volume of the *Modelbooks* (reprinted, like the texts mentioned below, in BFA 25). The revision was based on the representational principles of *Theatre Work*. The pamphlet *Constructing a Role: Laughton's Galileo*, which was supposed to appear as the second volume, was completed in 1956 but not delivered; it was published only in 1958, two years after Brecht's death, in an extended form under the title *Constructing a Role. Galileo. A Courage Model* followed in the same year, as the third volume. Aside from the revised *Antigone Model*,

---

[24]Harald Hauser, 'Abstraktion', in *Theater der Zeit*, 8(1953)6, p. 14 (emphasis in original).
[25]'Kleine redaktionelle Einmischung in die Debatte' [probably Fritz Erpenbeck], in *Theater der Zeit*, 8(1953)6, p. 15.
[26]Inexplicably, the text is printed in BFA – together with another Stanislavsky article – as an 'appendix' to the 'Katzengraben'-Notes (BFA 23: 582).
[27]In BFA this text is printed, along with three others on 'theatre photography' also written by Ruth Berlau and edited by Brecht, in the commentary on the *Courage Model* 1949 (BFA 25: 531-533), although in *Theatre Work* the texts come at the end of the 'Models' chapter (Th: 341-346), which is concluded by Brecht with one of his own texts (ibid., 346).

then, Brecht did not live to see any of the other Modelbooks printed, meaning that the models presented in the *Theatre Work* form the most important basis for the idea.

*Revisions: 'Dialectics in the theatre'.* – After the Stanislavsky conference, Erpenbeck continued to criticise epic theatre. In 1954 he published a statement of principles entitled 'Epic Theatre or Dramatic Art?' In it, he writes: 'Since 1945 I have stated and justified my point of view many times. Not only in connection with Bertolt Brecht's work [...] I reject epic theatre as a viable way forward for the future. [...] There is no epic drama, because drama – as nobody can deny – is about actions, not narration.'[28] In the same year Brecht, who was familiar with this article of Erpenbeck's, announced that he was revising his theory. In the 'Appendices' to some of the sections of the *Short Organon*, he writes that 'the term "epic theatre"' was now being 'abandoned' because it was 'too humble and vague for the theatre it is meant to describe' (BFA 23: 289ff.) Since the appendices clearly were not sufficient, Brecht tried several times to launch into a full-scale reorientation, but did not often get further than introductory phrases: 'We will now attempt to move from epic to dialectical theatre. We did not consider or intend the praxis or the whole concept of epic theatre to be undialectical, by any means; nor can dialectical theatre do without the epic element. However, we are planning to effect quite a major transformation.' (BFA 23: 299).

Brecht's intentions when it comes to revising his theory are fleshed out in a collection entitled *Dialectics in the Theatre*. It consists of new texts in which productions by the Berliner Ensemble are analysed using individual scenes as examples. The process is the same as in *Theatre Work* (confirming the latter's bridging function). The texts themselves deal with the question of how social contradictions which lead to historical changes are to be represented on stage: in other words, with the application of materialist dialectics (BFA 23: 386–413). Theoretical issues – with the exception of reflections on the use of Mao Zedong's essay 'On Contradiction' (BFA 23: 389) – are not discussed. Brecht published five texts from the collection in *Aufbau* magazine in 1955, under the title 'From Dialectics in the Theatre' (Issue 11/12).[29] The other sections did not appear until after his death, in the fifteenth volume of the *Versuche* (1957). The volume had, according to Elisabeth Hauptman, 'been put together with Brecht's help' before he died (Foreword). The lead text emphasises, more clearly than the introduction to *Dialectics in the Theatre* (BFA 23: 386), that Brecht wanted to redefine his theatre: 'We will attempt here to describe the application of materialist dialectics to the theatre. The term "epic theatre" seems increasingly in need of such an interpretation of its content.'[30]

In conversations where Brecht went into detail about the reorientation of his theory, two concepts take centre stage: turning point and simplicity. The first addresses the application of materialist dialectics, the second the literary basis of the model concept. Both are also found in *Theatre Work*. The term 'turning point' is used in the text *Phases of Directing*. It describes the points in the plot which drive forward the action: 'Condense the plot down to half a typewritten page. Then split the plot up into individual events and identify the turning points, i.e. the key events which carry the plot forward.' (*Th*: 256).

---

[28]Fritz Erpenbeck, 'Episches Theater oder Dramatik?', in *Theater der Zeit*, 9(1954)12, p. 18.
[29]Bertolt Brecht, 'Aus "Dialektik auf dem Theater"', in *Aufbau*, 11(1955)11/12, pp. 1019–1024. The publication is not included in BFA, so the month specifications, which are added to the year of origin in order to emphasise the nature of the work, are missing.
[30]Bertolt Brecht, *Versuche*, Issue 15 (1957), 78.

The model concept is directly related to this process: 'The modelbook makes it easier to divide up the plot, e.g. the precise classification of mobilising events.' (*Th*: 300). The text does not appear in the BFA.

The method of representation is explained in detail in a volume which Manfred Wekwerth published in 1956 on the occasion of the Berliner Ensemble's production of the Chinese play *Millet for the Eighth Army*.[31] In line with the dialectical approach, it specifies: 'We have to cut up the play into "playlets" and in each "playlet" we must identify the particular contradictions which drive the plot forward. [...] We refer to the points in the plot at which a transition occurs as turning points.' The volume is structured like the *Modelbooks* but is not classed as one of them, with the result that it has gone unnoticed. Brecht's contribution to the production and its portrayal is evident from the fact that he used a section from Wekwerth's book in his *Dialectics in the Theatre*, under the heading 'An Example of Scenic Innovation' (BFA 23: 410).[32]

The development of a turning point is also the subject of a report which Wekwerth published in 1957 in the second special Brecht edition of *Sinn und Form*, entitled 'Locating an Aesthetic Category'.[33] This was prompted by a rehearsal of *The Days of the Commune* in early August 1956, some eight days before Brecht's death. The plan for the rehearsal was to work on the third scene, which is about the causes of the Paris uprising of 1871.[34] In this context Brecht employed a category which he claimed characterised the neglected 'half' of his 'theory'; this category was 'the naïve'. It was met with astonishment by his colleagues, but the term does appear in *Theatre Work* in reference to Brecht's methodology, in the article 'On the Folk Play' which he wrote in 1940 after finishing *Puntila*. The text even appears at the beginning of the volume: 'Naturally, we can accept the need for a theatre which is naïve but not primitive, poetic, but not romantic, down-to-earth, but not bound up with day-to-day politics.' (*Th*: 13).

Brecht explains the concept outlined here using a particular scene [from *Mr Puntila and his Man Matti*] as an example: 'It is undoubtedly difficult, with a play that is written in prose and depicts "ordinary" people, to talk not about primitiveness but about artistic simplicity. The four women from Kurgela being driven away (in Scene 7) is not a primitive but a simple event, and it needs to be acted poetically, as does the entire scene (the drive to get the legal alcohol and the brides).' (*Th*: 16). This is by no means a marginal note. For the idea of poetic and down-to-earth simplicity had accompanied the theory of epic theatre since its beginnings. Walter Benjamin in particular highlighted it in the articles he wrote on Brecht's works between 1930 and 1939. Brecht's 'subject matter', he writes in 1932 following the premiere of *The Mother*, 'is a sociological experiment about the

---

[31] Loo Ding et.al., *Hirse für die achte. Ein chinesisches Volksstück*, German version for the Berliner Ensemble by Elisabeth Hauptmann and Manfred Wekwerth (Leipzig, 1956) (includes as an appendix: *Hirse für die achte. Bericht über die Inszenierung des Berliner Ensembles von Manfred Wekwerth*). Since the volume has no page numbers, they are not specified here.

[32] The text is also one of the sections of *Dialektik auf dem Theater* which Brecht published in *Aufbau* magazine in 1955 (see footnote 29). Here it is dated 'February 1953'.

[33] Manfred Wekwerth, 'Auffinden einer ästhetischen Kategorie', in *Sinn und Form*, 9(1957) 1–3: 2nd special Bertolt Brecht edition.

[34] An amendment Brecht made to the text of *The Days of the Commune* is here quoted verbatim (ibid, 263) but is not taken into account in the BFA (BFA 8: 531ff.), even though it is central to the scene. See Schöttker, *Bertolt Brechts Ästhetik der Naïven*, 103ff.

revolutionizing of the Mother. This is linked to a series of simplifications which are not of a rabble-rousing nature but a constructive one.'[35]

Benjamin is referring here to the principle of reduction which underpins the category of the naïve. The idea is rooted in the poetics of the French and German Enlightenment, as 'noble simplicity', but also plays a central role in modern theories of art and architecture.[36] The poetry of the Enlightenment was inspired not only by the art of the ancient world but also by the language of the Bible, which is associated with a genre Brecht used in all his plays: the parable. The fact that, when asked in a 1928 interview with the magazine *Die Dame* which book had made the 'greatest impression' on him, he answered: 'You'll laugh: the Bible', is therefore more than just an anecdote (BFA 21: 248).

In one of his last conversations (which was recorded by Ernst Schumacher and published in October 1956 in *Neue deutsche Literatur*), Brecht did in fact profess his belief in the parable in accordance with the principle of reduction, thereby mounting an unassailable defence against the reproaches of his opponents: 'The parable is much cleverer than all other forms. Lenin used the parable not as an idealist but as a materialist. The parable enabled him to untangle complicated ideas. For the dramatist the parable is a godsend because it remains concrete even in abstraction by making the essential conspicuous.'[37] In effect, the parable concretises theoretical positions or illustrates complex reality in the form of a poetic model. In the 'Models' featured in *Theatre Work*, Brecht explained this process. Now, over fifty years after Brecht's death, it is high time we addressed the fact that a volume as important as *Theatre Work* appears in the *Große kommentierte Berliner und Frankfurter Ausgabe* only in the form of scattered texts, and is not dealt with at all in the *Brecht-Handbuch* or the *Brecht-Lexikon*. This needs to be put right. Or, as Brecht put it: 'He who says "a" does not have to say "b". He can also recognise that "a" was wrong.' (BFA 3: 71).

---

[35] Walter Benjamin, *Versuche über Brecht*, edited and with an afterword by Rolf Tiedemann, 5th edition (Frankfurt am Main, 1978), 45. – See also Erdmut Wizisla, *Benjamin und Brecht: Die Geschichte einer Freundschaft* (Frankfurt am Main, 2004).
[36] See Detlev Schöttker, 'Reduktion und Innovation. Die Forderung nach Einfachheit in ästhetischen Debatten zwischen 1750 und 1995' in Gerhart von Graevenitz (ed.), *Konzepte der Moderne* (Stuttgart, 1999).
[37] Ernst Schumacher, 'Er wird bleiben', in Hubert Witt (ed.), *Erinnerungen an Brecht* (Leipzig, 1964), 336.

# PART THREE
# BRECHT AND OTHER MEDIA

# Radio

# CHAPTER FIFTEEN

# Apparatus without Spectators?: On the Deconstruction of the Medium in Brecht's *Ocean Flight*

PATRICK PRIMAVESI
TRANSLATED BY ROMY FURSLAND

The *Lehrstück Lindbergh's Flight/Ocean Flight* was, in a practical sense, a failure. Measured against Brecht's own criteria, at least, it could be seen as 'worthless', because aside from those involved in the premiere, hardly anybody learned anything from it. The intended linking of a critical reflection on pioneering acts in the technological age with a radical change in theatre and radio did not come to pass, at any rate. The plan had been to extend the flying machine as a utopian setting for heroic achievements into an experiment in media technology, into apparatus in the sense of a medial and at the same time collective space. This airspace evaded realisation, however, and the attempt to carry over the crash in *The Baden-Baden Lesson on Consent* into a dialectical work about the myth of technical progress remained ambiguous, lying somewhere in between barbaric sacrifice and an ode to the changing nature of apparatus. On this basis we will examine the relationship of the *Lehrstück* model to the 'apparatus' as a phantasmatic metaphor, including in relation to positions in contemporary theatre work. An immediate reason to re-examine the text and the praxis which it outlines was Robert Wilson's production of *Ocean Flight* in January 1998 at the Berliner Ensemble. It was the first attempt in a very long time to stage the play; previously it had only been tested on the radio as a media studies vehicle for children and, in 1992, as a film by Jean-François Jung for the European cultural channel ARTE. Perhaps, despite all their faults, it is practical efforts like these which give the play new impetus; at the very least, they show the importance of new experiments.

---

Patrick Primavesi, 'Apparat ohne Zuschauer? Zur Dekonstruktion des Mediums in Brecht's *Ozeanflug*', *Brecht Yearbook*, 24 (1999), pp. 80–95.

With a view to the publication of *Lindbergh's Flight* in the 1930 issue of *Versuche*, Walter Benjamin, in his text about epic theatre, spoke of a new spatial order which would result from insights into the loss of former metaphysical connections. 'What today's theatre is all about can be more precisely determined with regard to the stage than with regard to the drama. It is about the burial of the *orkestra*. [...] But as has been the case with many conditions, in this case too, the theatre business has attempted to conceal it instead of taking account of it.'[1] Benjamin's diagnosis of this 'condition' has lost hardly any of its validity, even if it focused on the type of theatre that was still commonplace at the time by combining the displaced secularisation of the stage with spatial imagery. On top of the long-buried *orkestra* of ancient theatre, there would therefore be no place for the illusionary space of bourgeois literary theatre – at most for a podium upon which the epic theatre and the *Lehrstück* would have to establish themselves. Heiner Müller adopted and refined this plan, although this time in relation to the extraordinary theatre of Robert Wilson: 'This stage is a play space for Kleist's marionette theatre, a dance floor for Brecht's epic dramaturgy. An art without exertion, a simple step paves the way.' At the end of this extremely condensed text we are also told of Wilson's theatre of *resurrection*: 'His reality is the unity of man and machine, the next step of evolution.'[2] The dance floor (the buried *orkestra*) which Wilson levelled out for Brecht's epic dramaturgy is, of course, still a podium, not some kind of new place of worship or just a ballet stage. But it is a place where both the body and language would have a new role to play in relation to traditional dramaturgies, in between muteness, stuttering and song. In Wilson's first theatre productions, speech impediments were acted out onstage, and since then the distortion and/or musicalization of language to articulate subtexts in contrast to communicative discourse has shaped his work, as has the perfecting of visual and lighting effects. Müller, whose text *The Hamletmachine* Wilson had staged in 1986, saw in this theatre a realisation of the old dream of the convergence of mankind and machine. The title of the quoted homage *Taube und Samurai* [*Dove and Samurai*] plays with this kind of utopian unity, with the wisdom of fairy tales, 'that the history of human beings cannot be separated from the history of animals (plants, minerals, machines) except at the cost of their own downfall'. Müller's text on Wilson deals with the material reproach of Brecht's *Lindbergh's Flight* and at the same time paves the way for *The Baden-Baden Lesson on Consent* and its 'unity' of man and machine which is starkly illuminated from all sides and which has been integral to science fiction as well as the evolution of mankind ever since humans have come into contact with other animals, plants and minerals. At the same time, the dove/samurai hybrid can be read as a formula to describe the composition of the pilot in the *Lehrstück*: feathers and heavy armour, bird of peace and machine of war, old and new technology. And who better to stage Brecht's radio *Lehrstück* but Wilson, who once dreamt of theatre as a parallel montage and the mutual enhancement of a radio play and a silent film? In his own performances every downfall has the character of a resurrection, and every advancement happens within a stasis and a silence that make the noise of the

---

[1] See Walter Benjamin, 'Was ist das epische Theater?' (1st edition), in *Walter Benjamin, Gesammelte Schriften* (Frankfurt am Main, 1980), 519. For a more detailed interpretation of this passage see Patrick Primavesi, *Kommentar, Übersetzung, Theater in Walter Benjamins frühen Schriften* (Frankfurt am Main, 1998), 358ff.
[2] 'Taube und Samurai' in Frank Hornigk (ed.), *Heiner Müller Material. Text und Kommentare* (Berlin, 1988), 50.

apparatus audible and compromise the audience's habits of perception.³ The following reflection on the text will lead to this staging technique, starting from the question of the utopian apparatus which it launches and brings crashing down, and from the question of the spectator who is left out of this action on the stage and who must be *absent*.

'Here's the apparatus, get in.' This is how Brecht's *Ocean Flight* begins, with an invitation from an undefined community to everybody else to repeat the pilot's flight: 'By jointly / singing the notes / and reading the text.'⁴ The apparatus is geared towards the process of a repetition and as such already indicates the threshold of a medium designed to enable virtual participation, which excludes the body but integrates the voice. Not only the aeroplane is meant here, but also the apparatus of the theatre, which has grafted itself parasitically onto the other apparatus of the radio. This manipulation, this oscillating between the machines, also characterises the texts of Brecht's so-called 'Radio Theory' – despite the suggestive title, these texts tend to be sporadic and related to specific occasions. They were inspired less by the medium of radio than by the state of the theatre, which Brecht felt could neither meet the requirements of the age nor do justice to the new plays the age had given rise to – here, of course, he was thinking of his own plays. Brecht's first text about the medium of radio (published in 1927 in a theatre journal) comes to the austere conclusion:

> Our stage plays are better off being reproduced by any other medium than that of the theatre. Even a film version would be more easily understood and more convincing. For this reason the radio – a technical invention which must create for itself a mass need and not subordinate itself to an old, worn-out need – represents a major and productive opportunity for our plays.
>
> (BFA 21.1: 189)

In 1928 Brecht went even further with this diagnosis, which was largely directed against the theatre of the time. The *gestus* of this escalation is also striking because he attributes to the radio what the traditional view, at least, would always have reserved for the theatre: *vividness*, and the ability to *inspire fear*. At least in the fact that radio can only be perceived audibly, it can offer something which had apparently been missing from the theatre for a long time: a *cultivated* event:

> The radio is terrifying living proof of how bad our present-day theatre is. If the theatre would do its duty, there would only be one person willing to forego at least half the pleasure of a play (which consists of seeing and the feeling of palpableness) in order to experience the other half (hearing) in a really cultivated way.
>
> (BFA 21.1: 263)

It is important to note that the pleasure of these forms of perception (hearing, seeing and the feeling of palpability) remained reliant on separation and a contrasting montage of elements in Brecht's later theatrical concepts, too. And the fascination of one-dimensional radio need not be cancelled out by an improved theatre – particularly if the needs linked

---

³On Wilson's stage aesthetic and its close relationship to Heiner Müller's work, see Hans-Thies Lehrmann, 'Robert Wilson, Szenograph' in *Parkett* 16 (1988), 30ff.
⁴Bertolt Brecht, *Werke. Große kommentierte Berliner und Frankfurter Ausgabe*, 30 volumes, ed. Werner Hecht, Jan Knopf, Werner Mittenzwei and Klaus-Detlef Müller (Berlin and Weimar: Aufbau; Frankfurt am Main: Suhrkamp, 1988-1999), Plays 3 (cited hereinafter as BFA with volume number and page number). Here BFA 3: 9.

to the medium are not yet fixed. The assumption that stage plays are already produced by the author, and from then on demand to be reproduced, already calls for the separation into text and scene which cannot be eliminated by a collective production process, nor by the necessary utopia of a collective reception. Even if Brecht, with this *clumsy* rhetoric, was mainly concerned with the practical question of how and where his plays could best be performed, the fact remains that the work on the medium of radio (which was still largely unaware of its potential) in the *Lehrstücke* led to a plan for a new kind of staging. Radio was not, for Brecht, simply a stopgap solution for a beautifully designed but placeless and utopian theatre model; the conception of this theatre model itself arose from the scenically demonstrated tension between the media and the apparatus.

The word 'apparatus', etymologically speaking, signifies equipment – in the technical sense a device which is made up of many parts. Thus the medial imperative 'Here's the apparatus, get in' calls for not only a plurality of listeners and spectators but also a plurality of apparatuses, in order to short-circuit the theatre, radio and living room or classroom. This, perhaps more than just the application of the pedagogic principles of functional music[5], is what gives the experiment with *Lindbergh's Flight* the character of a model. As a gesture, not only the ocean flight but also the transmission and perception of a socially significant event are to be made recognisable, repeatable and – to put it broadly, in line with Benjamin's allusion to Brecht's Keuner stories – *quotable*. The programmatic significance of this project is illustrated by the effort Brecht invested in putting it into practice. Brecht wanted, with this radio *Lehrstück*, to give theatre and radio a new form: both were to be put to the test and altered by the process of performance. Thus, on the stage of the Baden-Baden Chamber Music Festival, whose theme was 'radio art for the masses in the technological age', radio and listeners came face to face. The fact that Brecht viewed the text as an experiment, which was not complete and which was designed chiefly to aid a process of self-reflection on the part of the author and the performers, is shown by the circumstances of the premiere, featuring music by Kurt Weill and Paul Hindemith. The first performance under the musical direction of Hermann Scherchen took place on 27 July 1929 in the recording studio of the Baden-Baden Spa Rooms. It was recorded there and transmitted via loudspeaker into the other rooms. Since a dress rehearsal planned by Brecht had to be cancelled, he was unable to achieve his aim of scenically demonstrating a new use of the medium of radio until a second performance took place on the following day.[6] Brecht continually intervened in this scenic demonstration with his own comments, thus adapting his (initially written) proposals about the set design of the experiment. His ideas about the function of radio and music as an *exercise* (captioned 'Radio theory') were projected onto a big screen. One of the principles was as follows:

---

[5]In order to emphasise this aspect, Klaus-Dieter Krabiel even suggested that the *Lehrstücke* were 'not stage plays, but practical art in the form of vocal music for amateur musicians and amateur actors.' *Brechts Lehrstücke* (Stuttgart, 1993), 225. However, there is no mention of the *Lehrstück*'s potential to overturn and change traditional forms of theatre, particularly in the *scenic* convergence of theatre and radio which Brecht was aiming for.

[6]See also Norbert Schachtsiek-Freitag, 'Bertolt Brechts Lehrstück *Der Ozeanflug*' in *Text + Kritik*, Bertolt Brecht special edition 2, edited by Heinz Ludwig Arnold (Munich, 1973), 131ff.; the chapter on *Lindbergh's Flight* in Dieter Wöhrle, *Bertolt Brechts medienästhetische Versuche* (Cologne, 1988), 45ff.; and the account in Krabiel, *Brechts Lehrstücke* (p. 43ff.) which draws on sources relating to the history of music and which differs on many points from previous assumptions about the circumstances of the first performance.

> Doing is better than feeling; [the listeners] should read along with the music and hum the missing parts, or follow the music with their eyes in the book [the musical score] or sing it aloud in unison with other people. In this way the state supplies an incomplete music but the individual makes it complete.[7]

In front of this projection, on one side of the podium, a room was indicated in which a man was sitting at a table with the musical score, taking on the part of the pilot or the listener. On the other side was a small orchestra with a grand piano, as well as the chorus and three of the soloists. In the middle of the stage stood a loudspeaker, broadcasting sounds played from records. Thus all the voices labelled 'radio' in the text of the play had a visible source in the scenic demonstration area: the continents of America and Europe, the city of New York and a ship, as well as the forces to be overcome during the flight: the fog, the snowstorm and sleep, the water and the engine as well as 'a big crowd' of spectators. This demonstrated how the radio would deliver to listeners at home what they could not produce themselves. The interplay was supposed to show that the radio could be transformed from a distribution device into a communication device, and how the listener could be shaken out of an attitude of passive consumption. The same objective was at the root of the *Lehrstücke*: to do away with the traditional spectator in the theatre, to involve the audience in the performance and to turn those who would once have been the recipients of a performance into 'present' participants in an exercise.

The *Lehrstück*, therefore, did not come into being on the basis of a theoretical concept but as a reflection of a still unsatisfactory praxis (perhaps necessarily unsatisfactory). This process can be foreseen from the name of the play, which was initially called simply *Lindbergh*, then *Lindburgh's Flight* and then *The Flight of the Lindberghs*. Later, after Brecht learned of the famous pilot's collaboration with the Nazis, he changed the title again to *Ocean Flight* – Charles Lindbergh's name was 'blotted out'. But even during the scenic demonstration the day after the first performance, Brecht experimented with the possibility of the pilot's part being sung by a chorus: 'Only through collective singing of the "I" part can a little of the pedagogical effect be salvaged'.[8] In line with this correction, important changes were made to the text: the pilot's 'I' in the original version (published in the radio magazine *Uhu* in 1929) becomes 'we' in the text of the first *Versuche* issue in 1930. The issue of empathy is addressed, with the pilot's part becoming plural: the pilots. The play text also mentions the engine which must do its job just like the man. The pilot talks to his engine: 'It's not much further now. Now / We have to pull ourselves together / We two' (BFA 3: 20). In the end he also thinks about the seven engineers and workers who built the aeroplane: 'I'm not alone, there are / Eight of us flying this plane'. With this reminder of the collective nature of the achievement, Brecht was quoting almost word for word from the account written by Lindbergh, which was already available in Germany in 1927, entitled *We (We Two in an Aeroplane over the Atlantic)* – although Brecht made significant alterations. If Lindbergh praised the financial backers of his venture as 'progressive citizens of St. Louis', Brecht specifically mentions the workers in the factory, the Ryan Airline Company. Thus the reference to collective achievement merges with the idea of unity between man and machine which Lindbergh symbolised ahead of many

---

[7] Cited from Reiner Steinweg (ed.), *Brechts Modell der Lehrstücke* (Frankfurt am Main, 1976), 38.
[8] Ibid., 69.

other pilots, racing drivers and astronauts.⁹ In response to the frequent accusation that by changing the final sentence from 'the unachievable' to 'the not yet achieved' in the *Versuche* version, Brecht was glorifying the pilot's mastery of the technology, it is worth noting that the battle against the more primitive technology has adverse consequences for both the 'I' and the identification of the hero with his machine. Thus the Lindberghs sing that the flight is effectively a struggle against their own aeroplane: 'My aeroplane, weak and shaky / My apparatus with all its defects / Is better than its precursors, but / By flying / I am struggling against my aeroplane and / Against the primitive' (BFA 3: 16). The 'Ideology' section also attacks God as a key cipher of disorder and ignorance. This section acts as a break in the flight, reminding the audience of the framework of the *Lehrstück* and the pedagogical undertaking of the play. But the next section sees the pilot, who has realised the capricious nature of the plane's steering controls and engine and almost crashed into the sea, experience very primitive fear: 'My God! That / Nearly did for us!' And throughout the flight, we are then told, the press and the voice of America on the radio talk mainly about the *luck* the pilot will need in order to arrive safely. The media, where it does feature, also represents rather antiquated technology governed by a traditional ideology. Even the successful flight can appear to be an inadequate venture in every sense, undertaken by a naïve pilot in a poor piece of apparatus, in the service of a false ideology. With this demystification of the apparatus, the *Lehrstück* sets in motion a process of disintegration which mainly affects the function of the performers. The challenge, based on the assumption of the frailty of all the people, materials and media involved in the flight, leads to transmission resistance which highlights the breach between individual and collective. The result of the *Lehrstück* shifting its focus from the audience to the performers is that the actor as the traditional *medium* of the theatre is transformed, his or her acting subjected to a relentless process of deconstruction.

The basis of the pedagogical enterprise to which this 'radio *Lehrstück* for boys and girls' belongs is a scenic ritual whereby theatre is presented on the podium as a ceremonial process in an age of science and technology. Beyond any dependence on ritual, what happens on stage is still shaped by an examination of the power of the collective compared to the individual. The crowd out of which the pilot ascends and which he returns to is also concerned about death, which runs through the flight as a rite of passage. What Brecht shows again and again is the symbolic sacrifice of the individual. An important moment in this respect is the pilot's arrival – its significance as an unresolved 'remnant' of a dialectical economy has been pointed out by Rainer Nägele.¹⁰ 'Scene 16: Arrival of the pilot Charles Lindbergh at Le Bourget Airfield near Paris: *Sound of a large crowd (radio)*, then: *The Lindberghs* I am Lindbergh. Please carry me / To a dark shed, so that / Nobody sees my / Natural weakness' (BFA 3: 23). At the moment where, with this difficult landing, the whole flight proves a success, the pilot is to suddenly disappear. The 'natural weakness' could signify exhaustion and a sense of shame – a desire not to sully the image of the hero (whose fame has gone before him) with the sight of the pilot's

---

⁹See Bernd Böhmel's article 'Charles Augustus Lindbergh – Landplatz für Dämonen' in the programme for *Ocean Flight* (Berliner Ensemble, 1998), which traces Lindbergh's history as that of a more or less naïve pioneer of new structures, particularly weapons technology, from his first gun at six years old to the flying machine, the V-2 rocket and the atom bomb.
¹⁰Rainer Nägele, 'Brechts Theater der Grausamkeit: Lehrstücke und Stückwerke' in *Brechts Dramen. Neue Interpretationen*, ed. Walter Hinderer (Stuttgart, 1984), 309.

real body. A kind of punishment fantasy: the idea that the pilot, in completing his flight – which from an ideological point of view was also supposed to oust God from the skies – believes he has forfeited his own life. Or else the shadow of Nungesser, the other pilot who recently died flying the same route, has suddenly caught up with him, demanding his share of pioneering glory. Evidently this scene, which was probably also rewritten for the 1930 *Versuche* volume, is linked to the pilot's crash in *The Baden-Baden Lesson on Consent*, which puts the wrecked flight crew on trial – until the scene 'Ostracism', where the singer leaves the stage. The pinnacle of the pilot drama is when the Thinking Man reaches his smallest dimension, when the Crashed Airman is suddenly no-one. The ritual dismemberment performed therein does not affect the individual parts of the apparatus but the phantasmatic unity of man and machine. At the very moment where the wreckage of the plane is carried from one side of the stage to the other and thus removed by the Crashed Airman, he has lost his face. His sentence is that he has forfeited his post and his humanity and therefore must die. Following his futile protest, the Crashed Airman loses his voice, and this too is held against him:

> Man, speak to us, we await
> Your voice from the usual place. Speak!
> He does not speak. His voice
> Is gone. Do not be afraid, man, but
> you must go now. Go quickly!
>
> (BFA 3, p. 44)

The apparatus – and here we might think not least of the Party machine – has disposed of the weak link and wrested the damaged flying machine away from the Crashed Airman. Only after the apparatus has been moved from the listener's side to the radio side can it be re-incorporated into the process of advancement. Thus at the end of the *Baden-Baden Lesson on Consent*, the mechanics are pardoned and asked to build better aeroplanes, never to lose sight of the goal of both changing the world and changing themselves at the same time, and above all to march. Once the singer playing the Crashed Airman has left the stage, however, and the actor has given up his role, the symbolic location of the listener is questioned; trapped in a crypt[11] which even the riots among the audience at the first performance could not break open. The fact that Brecht, for his part, did not want to make do with the idea of amateur music and functional music advocated by Hindemith is shown by his vehement objection to the composer's preface to the first edition of the musical score:

> Even if we expected individuals to 'align themselves with something', or that certain formal congruencies of an intellectual nature might arise on a musical basis, such an artificial and shallow harmony would never be able, not even for a few minutes, to act as a counterbalance to the formation of collectives on the broadest and most vital basis, which tear the people of our era apart with quite a different force.[12]

---

[11] Jacques Derrida points out that the crypt as a man-made site represents the demarcation of an outdoor space within a building, a kind of interior ostracism (see 'Fors', preface to Nicolas Abraham/Maria Torok, *Kryptonomie* [Frankfurt am Main, 1979], 9f.) A similarly paradoxical spatiality is found in Brecht's conception of the *Lehrstück* space as an apparatus which not only contains and incorporates various other apparatuses but excludes and eliminates them within itself.

[12] Cited from Steinweg, *Brechts Modell der Lehrstücke*, 59f.

Brecht was definitely not in favour of a 'singalong' or 'playalong' theatre, which would, by artificially creating a harmonious community of actors, have downplayed the problems of the age. The theatre of the *Lehrstücke* finds its own form of cruelty when it gets to the point where it has exhausted its material, where both the spectator and the actor have reached their smallest dimensions – all that remains are the chorus and the rhythm of a long march through the apparatus which needs to be disrupted. Perhaps this is the exercise which Brecht wanted the value of this *Lehrstück* to be contingent on: 'The *Lindbergh Flight* has no value if people do not learn from it. It has no artistic value that would justify a performance which did not serve this learning purpose.'[13] As a 'learning resource', the play was supposed to be split into two parts: the exercise facilitated by the text and the interruption of that exercise, which in Brecht's view 'is best done by a machine'. As well as being about an apparatus that disrupts the exercise, this is also about carrying out an exercise to determine how such a disruption might be effected. There can be no spectators of the apparatus, however: only participants. The apparatus disrupts and destroys itself and whoever has boarded it – almost like the machine in Franz Kafka's story *In the Penal Colony*. A theatre, then, which consumes its own medium, spectators and actors alike. A note written by Brecht in exile in 1937 on the theory of the *Lehrstück* also points in this direction:

> The key thing about the *Lehrstück* is that people learn by acting in it, not by watching it. In principle the *Lehrstück* does not need any spectators, although they can of course be put to good use. The *Lehrstück* is based on the expectation that the person acting in it can be socially influenced by the experience of performing certain behaviours, adopting certain attitudes, giving certain speeches etc.[14]

The disruption by the apparatus is about socially influencing the performers of the play, who make the actions, attitudes and speeches within the *Lehrstück* their own and perform them in order to change the apparatus of the theatre/the State in their turn by disrupting it.[15] On the other hand, the inclusion of antisocial models should not be neglected: 'reproducing antisocial behaviours and attitudes (as brilliantly as possible) can also be instructive'. What is important is the *nature* of the reproduction – that the performers do not identify or empathise with their roles and thus imply that the audience should empathise too, but that they reproduce individual actions and attitudes analytically, so that even unique characters can be demonstrated: 'particularly unique or idiosyncratic characters do not feature in the *Lehrstück*, unless uniqueness and idiosyncrasy are themselves the learning problem'. Just as the *Lehrstück* is supposed to replace the 'spectacle', the learning and teaching performer must replace the actor, which is also the reason why the term 'learning play' [the term Brecht chose when translating the term into English] is far more apt than the misleading word '*Lehrstück*' (literally: 'teaching play').[16] The proviso that 'unique, idiosyncratic characters' can

---

[13] Ibid., 6: Notes on the 'Flight of the Lindberghs' (*Versuche*, 1930).
[14] Ibid., 164.
[15] See Judith Wilke, 'Fleischmühle, Fremdkörper: zum Verhältnis von "Literarisierung" und Störung des Theaters bei Brecht' in *I'm Still Here/Ich bin noch da, The Brecht Yearbook* 22, ed. Maarten van Dijk et al., (Waterloo, Canada, 1997), 375–387.
[16] See also Florian Vaßen's overview of recent *Lehrstück* scholarship: 'Bertolt Brechts "learning-play": Genesis und Geltung des Lehrstücks' in *Brecht Then and Now/Brecht damals und heute, The Brecht Yearbook* 20, ed. Marc Silberman et al. (Madison, 1995), 201ff.

themselves become the *learning problem* makes clear that the *Lehrstücke* are not by any means aiming to simply eliminate or efface the individual in favour of newly emerging collectives. The crucial element is the process by which the individual has to come to terms with his or her own downfall or death, but by protesting against it, in opposition to collective violence, asserts the position or at least the voice of the subject.[17] This stage is not heroic, however; it signifies the smallest dimension of the individual, the knowledge of failure or defeat. In this sense, a moment of not-yet-knowing is necessary for the performer: 'it is crucial to have an intellectual command of the entire play. It is not advisable, however, to finish teaching about the play before actually acting it.'[18] Thus the experience of learning remains tied to the process of acting itself, since adopting an attitude or reproducing an action always goes beyond what our reason can predict. This *beyond* is crucial, however: it signifies the engagement of the body with what is being performed. The *Lehrstücke* frequently address extreme physical experiences: exertion, hunger, pain, injury and death. Brecht's insistence on the acting out of emotionally affecting, painful situations makes clear the extent to which the audience – who are not technically necessary to the *Lehrstück* – can be made use of. It is in precisely this context that the *Lehrstück* is a *practical* success if the disruption of the exercise by the apparatus turns into a disruption of the apparatus by the exercise; if both processes inform and provoke each other. Thus Brecht ends his retrospective and yet necessarily provisional note 'On the Theory of the *Lehrstück*' with a reference to the first performance of *The Baden-Baden Lesson on Consent*:

> Tremendous variety is possible in the *Lehrstück*. During the production of *The Baden-Baden Lesson on Consent*, the playwright and the composer stood onstage and kept intervening. The playwright publicly told the clowns where to perform their act, and as the crowd – with great reluctance and unease – watched the film showing dead people, the playwright instructed the narrator to call out at the end: 'The depiction of death which was received with reluctance will be viewed for a second time' and the film was played again.[19]

Not only the audience's applause is to be *utilised* but also – to an even greater extent – its discontent, which Brecht exploited and demonstrated by replaying the film. The repetition of the film demonstrates the apparatus *as* disruption. By bringing a film featuring dead people into the theatre, Brecht is touching on a sore point which is usually concealed by the unspoken pact between the stage and the audience: an illusory repression of death by the congregation of the theatre. The film is shocking because it breaks through into this illusory world with images of real corpses. And it is in precisely this situation that the 'tremendous variety' of the *Lehrstück* can be seen through the possibility of reacting to experiences in the process of acting, taking the audience's unrest and aversion and working with it on stage as resistance.

The exercise would consist first and foremost of changing people's ways of seeing, as well as (most importantly) reconstructing the apparatus of perception. This purpose

---

[17] See Hans-Thies Lehmann and Helmut Lethen, 'Ein Vorschlag zur Güte (Zur doppelten Polarität des Lehrstücks)' in *Auf Anregung Bertolt Brechts: Lehrstücke mit Schülern, Arbeitern, Theaterleuten*, ed. Reiner Steinweg (Frankfurt am Main, 1978), 302ff.
[18] Cited from Steinweg, *Brechts Modell der Lehrstücke*, 164.
[19] Ibid., 165.

can be served not only by shock effects but also by moments in which an expected emotional situation, like the excitement of welcoming the successful pilot or grief at his plane crashing, fails to materialise and is turned into something else. With *Ocean Flight* especially, this would involve a praxis which would have to use completely different models of aesthetic formalisation to repeat and scenically transpose the ritual of flight, crash and ostracism. This reverse side of the radio *Lehrstück*, which ranges from the shade of Nungesser to the natural weakness of the pilot to the ostracism of the Crashed Airman in the *Baden-Baden Lesson on Consent*, has so far made little impression on the stage or other media. On the contrary, the medium itself is usually glorified by the unity of man and machine, so that the operation of the media apparatus shapes that of the flight apparatus according to its own ideal, and cuts out or downplays the disruption. This is particularly true of the film *Lindbergh's Flight/Ocean Flight* by Jean-Francois Jung (1992), who at least tried to make the media coverage of the flight itself, as projected by Brecht, into a theme. Overall, however, the radio *Lehrstück* takes on the character of a children's toy, an Augsburg Puppet Theatre with broadband, complemented by documentary material from the American national celebrations for the aviator Lindbergh. If, on the other hand, one wanted to take seriously the pedagogical value of this radio *Lehrstück* 'for boys and girls' (to quote the subheading in the *Versuche* version of 1930), then instead of a child-friendly performance by adults to a supposedly naïve audience, one would have to make 'boys and girls' themselves the performers. One attempt in this vein which is still worth listening to is Kurt Veth and Tilo Medek's 1969 radio production for Deutscher Demokratischer Rundfunk (the GDR state radio broadcaster). They did not use the original music but worked with simple sound effects; in particular, the voices of the children performing the play were used as rhythmical instruments which chorally enhanced the text and were transformed, in many different ways, into floating melodies. The intensity of this production surpasses that of the only surviving recording featuring the cast of the first production (the short version *Lindbergh's Flight. Radiophonic Cantata*, broadcast on Berlin Radio Hour in 1930). By contrast, the speech in the later radio production featuring 'boys and girls' was divided into parts and played with articulation in a way that condensed not only the idea of changing childhood dreams in the media age but also a semiotic and gestic quality which is inherent in Brecht's text.

Thirty years later at the Berliner Ensemble, a young boy stumbles across the dark stage with a Gameboy in his hand – one of those little gaming computers shaped like a flying saucer or a flat landmine which help you train your memory using sounds, colours and movement pulses. The player has to keep reproducing and extending the sequence of key inputs repeated by his machine until a sobering warning tone alerts him to the fact that he has made a mistake and will have to try again. In Wilson's production the combination of sounds produced by the boy's machine became increasingly autonomous until finally he set it down on a podium, brightly lit against the otherwise completely dark stage, and picked up a piece of rock as if it were something from another planet. As he took his last few steps, he trod very carefully so as not to disturb the machine as it hummed away to itself. As if it were possible to abandon or at least modify the control unit of man and machine, to replace the machine with another animal, a rock. In this respect too, the production was inspired by the vision of Müller, who had long wanted to see a Brecht production by Wilson at the Berliner Ensemble and had to some extent paved the way for it. This, the first production of *Ocean Flight* in a very long time, can be seen as an attempt to both reject *and* carry forward the radio *Lehrstück*, as well as continuing the deconstruction of the medium of the actor with an ironic distance from traditional forms of pedagogy.

The entire principle of media communication was called into question by a kind of entropy in which despair about absolute emptiness could suddenly give way to comedy and vice-versa, so that there was no certainty for the audience even in the negation of all ideology. This effect was actually achieved without recourse to certain methods characteristic of the *Lehrstück* – the *Ideology* section was omitted, and Weill and Hindemith's music was not used. Together with the other parts of the evening, Müllers *Landscape with Argonauts* and a montage of Dostoevsky's *Notes from a Dead House*, Brecht's text appeared as a journey into an infinitely dark and yet entertaining night. The performance skirted the wall of a cemetery, a reproduction of an early picture by Man Ray, which adorned the curtain and recurred in the set design which was often hard to make out in the darkness. The flight mainly took place in the acoustic space of the theatre, however: a landscape of voices. The highlight was Scene 5, the pilot's battle with the fog. Long before the actor Bernhard Minetti appeared onstage, his voice floated through the dark of the auditorium with a ghostly quality, his warnings to the pilot already overlaid by the latter's reply: 'What you have just said / Calls for reflection ... '. Following this rhythmically constructed dissolution of the dialogue with the foreign element, the darkness was acoustically shattered by the sound of breaking glass and there in a star-shaped pool of light lay the pilot (played by Stefan Kurt), as if he had suddenly been thrown onto the stage through a window. On this unexpectedly created dance floor, he sang the English translation of the scene. This lent the performance, which had so far been rather static, moving as if in slow motion, a strange lightness all of a sudden, fluctuating between irony and madness, surface and abyss: 'Like the hell, I will! What you have just said / Calls for reflection. / If you get denser, maybe I really shall / Turn back.'[20] The following scenes continued in this comic vein: the pilot appeared, almost like the overzealous shooter in Wilson's *The Black Rider* or the boyish crashed pilot in an episode from his short film *Mr Bojangles' Memory*, as a grotesquely comic clown: his apparatus was a table floating in the air, his feet turned a wheel with pedals, which squealed loudly. This was reminiscent of Brecht's and Dudow's film *Kuhle Wampe*, as well as the curious attempts by the first pioneers of flight to take to the air using pedal-powered contraptions shaped like birds' wings: dove and samurai. Using the floating table, new variants of the *training* that began with the Gameboy were demonstrated – and its effects made themselves felt in the struggle with the snowstorm and drowsiness. The pilot, lulled to sleep by a child's voice ('Sleep, Charlie / The bad night is over ... '), was simply hit over the head with a white rabbit hand puppet, operated by himself, until he woke up. Beside him, meanwhile, burned a little floating sphere, similar to the image of the space shuttle Challenger hurtling to earth which was used by Wilson in his *Hamletmachine*. The question of progress thus more or less resolved itself. The exercise consisted this time of the comic dissolution of the *Lehrstück* into a piece that played with the theatrical apparatus and the apparatus of perception through parallel, not necessarily related but mutually reinforcing events. There is no longer any heroic paradigm to be found in flying, or crashing, or in the 'medium' – the intersection of man and machine – in view of the mass-scale and almost self-evident reality of the monstrous; at most

---

[20]See the English translation by John Willett in: Brecht, *Collected Plays*, 3rd edition (London, 1997), 6.

there are theatrical sparks of gallows humour, walking the tightrope between aesthetic formalisation and a vicious, sarcastic slapstick comedy. What Wilson's production established, in the passage from Brecht's radio *Lehrstück* to Müller's Argonauts to Dostoevsky's devastating analysis of modern mankind, was the transformation of the lesson into the play of a theatre machine which puts the presence of both the actor and the audience in inverted commas.

# Film

# CHAPTER SIXTEEN

# Utilizing the 'Ideological Antiquity': Rethinking Brecht and Film Theory

ANGELOS KOUTSOURAKIS

And why are we fighting he asked.
Because we want the world
in which our literature too belongs,
to be freed from disfigurement.

Peter Weiss, *The Aesthetics of Resistance*

## INTRODUCTION

The title of Alexander Kluge's latest film is *Nachrichten aus der ideologischen Antike – Marx/Eisenstein/Das Kapital* (*News from ideological Antiquity: Marx/Eisenstein/Capital*, 2008). The film is an experimental project dedicated to the exploration of Eisenstein's ambitious plan to turn Marx's *Capital* into a film. Throughout the film, Kluge interviews philosophers, theater practitioners, poets and academics who attempt to identify the relevance of Eisenstein's project and of Marx's *Capital* to contemporary reality. There are also numerous references to the work of James Joyce, who wanted to see his novel *Ulysses* filmed by Eisenstein. In many respects, the film is a 'study in dialectical method' which offers schooling in image reading. What merits attention in Kluge's film is the title itself, *News from Ideological Antiquity*, and that during the course of the film's disintegrated narrative there is a feeling that the present has much to gain from the past; and here the past refers both to the cinematic past (the works of political modernist filmmakers) as well as to Marxist thinking.

At one point in the film, Kluge idiosyncratically says: 'but reincarnation (*Wiedergeburt*) can take place even if you do not believe in it. How many times was Marx pronounced dead? Yet he comes back and his work is still au courant' (Kluge *Nachrichten*). Kluge's investment in 'ideological antiquity' and his firm belief that changing historical circumstances require a re-reading of key figures from the past provide the starting point for this article which focuses on another important modernist figure referenced in Kluge's film, namely Bertolt Brecht. My intention is to re-examine Brecht's writings on film and clarify some misunderstandings with respect to his reception on the part of film theory.

## DIALECTICS AS FORM

It is a commonplace argument among film scholars that modernist and Brechtian formal experiments have been absorbed and co-opted by Hollywood as well as by the advertising industry. Early in the 1970s, one of the film theorists of the time advocating the employment of Brechtianism as a methodological framework for the study of film argued that television 'at a formal level it seems "extraordinarily Brechtian"' (Brewster cited in Mathers 96). Similarly, Thomas Elsaesser argues that the sophisticated manipulation of media technology has led to the 'devaluation of once radical techniques and stances, such as Brechtian "distanciation"' (139). This view of Brechtianism strictly as a set of stylistic devices has led to major misunderstandings. Indicative, for example, is Gerd Gemünden's point that certain Brechtian formal elements laid the groundwork for the advent of apolitical postmodern artistic practices (58). Slippery usages of Brecht's *Verfremdungseffekt* that reduce it to 'a tool for drawing attention to a given representation' (Grodal, *Moving Pictures* 215) have not been helpful in understanding the interrelationship between aesthetics and politics. It is evident that this tautological equation of Brecht with a set of formal elements has flattened and obfuscated his political philosophy and his insightful critique of film as medium. Murray Smith wonders how the 'critical spectator' advocated by Brecht can acquire political consciousness solely by means of 'an estranging text' (138)? This question provides a good starting point to show that for Brecht the politicization of form does not simply rely on the manipulation of a set of formal elements that are radical in themselves, but on the linkage[1] between modernist forms of narration and the dialectical method. In this context, Brecht's *Verfremdungseffekt* is not merely a formal gesture but a polemical one that aspires to combine representation and a metacritique of it in order to distort one's familiar perception of reality and lead her/him to new forms of understanding.

To clarify this let us briefly return to Kluge's abovementioned film. At one point, Kluge quotes a crucial part from Eisenstein's 'Notes for a film of Capital', in which he says: 'the ancient cinema was shooting one event from many points of view. The new one assembles one point of view from many events' (18). Here Eisenstein's reference to a single 'point of view' synopsizes the scope of his unfinished grand project, which was not a single-minded propagation of a 'political message', but the teaching of dialectics as a gesture of negation and as a nonconformist mode of thinking. In other words, the amassing of fragments retains the object's narrative openness and encourages the audience to make its own associations, but points simultaneously to a concrete methodology which intends to facilitate the viewers' hermeneutical activity. This idea of teaching a 'method of thinking' is a crucial aspect of Brecht's politicized aesthetic too.

---

[1] I would like to draw the reader's attention to two new translations which are important in rethinking Brecht beyond the Anglophone canonical reception of his work. *Brecht on Theatre*. 3rd edition. Ed. Tom Kuhn, Steve Giles, Marc Silberman. London, New York: Bloomsbury, 2014 and *Brecht on Performance: Messingkauf and Modelbooks*. Ed. Tom Kuhn, Steve Giles, Marc Silberman. London, New York: Bloomsbury, 2014.

Brecht wrote *Der Dreigroschenprozeß* (one of his major essays on film) in 1931, during the same period that he developed his theory for a pedagogical theater – the *Lehrstück*. The main pedagogical aim of the *Lehrstücke* was the teaching of dialectics as 'a principle' which would encourage thinking in contradictions (Steinweg 87). These plays abolished the distinctions between actors and audience and were experimental exercises in political and social behavior, aiming to motivate practical thinking. This modification of the theater apparatus had an impact on Brecht's radical understanding of film art as a process which should combine politicization of form with a critique of institutional structures. Dialectics was to be employed not only to criticize conventional forms, but to challenge the artistic apparatus, something to which I shall return later. In other words, the political implications of an object derive from its ability to reconcile experimental formal practices with the dialectical method. Illuminating here is Brecht's definition of dialectics:

> In Wirklichkeit ist die Dialektik eine Denkmethode oder vielmehr eine zusammenhängende Folge intelligibler Methoden, welche es gestattet, gewisse starre Vorstellungen aufzulösen und gegen herrschende Ideologien die Praxis geltend zu Machen.
>
> (*Werke* 21 519)
>
> [In reality, dialectics is a method of thinking or rather a sequence of comprehensible methods which makes it possible to use it so as to combat certain rigid beliefs and assert Praxis against ruling ideologies.][2]

In these terms, Brecht's outlining of the dialectic (aside from the differences in scope and the methodological ones) is congruent with Hegel's understanding of the dialectic 'as a negative movement' (124). But most importantly, this commitment to the dialectic as a concrete mode of 'practical thinking' coincides with Hegel's line of reasoning in the sense that Hegel also thought that philosophy on its own cannot make us understand the intricacies of the world (193). Thus, philosophy turns into anti-philosophy, something that was pushed further by Marx in *Capital*, where the theoretical elucidation of the movement of capital has practical ambitions and goes beyond the descriptive goals of past philosophical traditions. These expositions can assist us in understanding a crucial aspect of Brecht's aesthetic, which could be summarized as follows: Brecht's promotion of formal abstraction and his commitment to dialectics as a gesture of negation is dedicated to making representation anew, but at the same time this nexus between formal experimentation and dialectic is a form of 'anti-art', in the sense that it rejects the tendency to understand narrative as a cosmos in itself. One cannot dissociate the reality within the narrative from social processes outside of it, a point he sets forth in a quite combative tone in his *Dreigroschenprozeß* essay: 'Als ob man von Kunst etwas verstehen könnte ohne von der Wirklichkeit etwas zu verstehen' [as if somebody could understand something about art without understanding something about reality] (SLK I: 184). As I proceed to show below, this is a central topos of his critique of the film medium, since he

---

[2]Unless indicated otherwise translations of German texts are my own.
Abbreviations of Brechtian texts in the text:
  SLK: *Schriften zur Literatur und Kunst*.
  SZT: *Schriften zum Theater*.
  TFF: *Texte Für Filme*.

proposes that cinema's reliance on mechanical reproduction has the potential to capture social structures which challenge traditional concepts of art.

## *TECHNIFIZIERUNG* AND THE PRIMACY OF THE APPARATUS

Once the dialectical method has been defined, one can appreciate Brecht's enthusiasm for the film medium and his understanding of it as a progressive one that can downplay standard character-based dramaturgy in favor of narratives that explore and analyze broader social and political processes. Much ink has been spilled on Brecht's anti-Aristotelian dramaturgy, but in order to understand this – particularly in relation to cinema – one needs to relate it to a Marxist understanding of the individual, as well as to the modernist specificity of the cinematic medium. Brecht drew on Marx's understanding of the individual as 'the ensemble of the social relations' (Marx, Engels 4). For Marx, the individual is not an independent entity nor does it have 'intrinsic' transhistorical characteristics. As he points out, to understand individuals beyond idealistic concepts of 'human essence' one should not see them 'as they may appear on their own, bus as they actually are' (35). While the statement 'as they are', might sound tautological, Marx clarifies that the individual's existence cannot be dissociated from her/his social role. Put simply, the individual's place in productive processes shapes her/his social existence. Elsewhere, Marx employs the term 'character masks' (*Capital* 757) to show how individuals from different classes cannot perceive labour beyond their interests, while in his famous treatise on the alienation (*Entfremdung*) of the worker, he alludes to the idea of the mask when he explains that the process of production alienates workers and makes them feel at home when they do not perform their 'human function' (for Marx the human function is the social/productive one), but their reproductive ones which he names as 'animal functions' (Marx, *EW* 327). Hence, the workers have to put on a mask while performing their social role.

This idea of the mask does not necessarily imply that behind the mask there is an authentic identity. As Dietmar Dath says, 'the term mask is a cinematic one' and refers to individuals who are wearing a mask and are unaware of it. But given the Greek origin of the word and that 'for the Greeks the character is the mask', Marx's use of the term is a 'pleonasm'. Dath gives as an example the individual capitalist and suggests that in actuality the person is the mask, there is nothing behind it. 'Society as a whole is behind it. It is an empty abstraction' (cited in Kluge, *Nachrichten*). Consequently, no individual action can be comprehended outside a social context. Marx's critique of the appearances of social phenomena and of the empirical understanding of the individual relies on the premise that in the modern world massive industrialization disguises social, political, and economic processes taking place under the veneer of things.

Now that the Marxist understanding of the individual is unpacked, Brecht's anti-Aristotelian rhetoric as regards film narration can be elucidated. For Brecht, film art was a modern phenomenon per se and as such mediation is its principal premise. A central precondition for revolutionizing film narrative and liberating it from the banality of dramatic and literary arts was the thematization of the very issue of mediation. This idea centers on the argument that the bourgeois drama and literature of the time effaced the traces of their performativity by striving to absorb the audience in a closed diegetic world. Cinema thus should downplay its dramatic roots and underscore its technological character. How are we to understand this? Brecht thought that the instrumentality of the new medium had the potential to expose in a negative way the 'enchantment' (*Verzauberung*) of social relationships under capitalism. Consequently, cinema's role would be the exposition of 'social masks' firstly in the narrative world, secondly on the extra-diegetic one in the auditorium. Rather than following the standardized tradition of bourgeois drama which treated the audience as a homogenous body, the task of the new medium would be the division of the audience by exposing the different social interests that are masked by conformist forms of narration. Put simply, the task of the *Verfremdungseffekt* in the cinema is to make strange the 'enchantment' of social relationships and to lead to – to use a term from Miriam Bratu Hansen – 'the distortion' of the 'distorted' social relationships. This is a standard modernist trope and, as Hansen explains it, is founded on the premise that 'since the world is already distorted, reified, and alienated, the iteration of that distortion, as a kind of double negation, is closer to the truth than any attempt to transcend the state of affairs by traditional aesthetic means' (8).

Brecht suggests that this gesture of negativity can be effective provided that cinema takes advantage of its medium-specific elements. In the *Dreigroschenprozeß* essay he discusses how film has an impact on reception and how it can revolutionize even literary and dramatic reception since 'der Filmsehende liest Erzählungen anders' [the film viewer reads narratives differently] (SLK I: 178). The verb 'reads' is not accidental, since Brecht argued for a reading attitude during the film-viewing process. Later, Brecht uses a term which is also employed by Adorno to describe the specificity of modern art (see Hansen 212). Brecht says that cinema can eventually lead to the 'Technifizierung der literarischen Produktion' [the technification of literature production] (SLK I: 178). In other words, the advent of the new media will have its effect on other forms of artistic production, which can benefit from the cinematic 'technification' of art. The revolutionary aspect of film resided in its reliance on 'instruments', rather than on the author's individual intuition. In a sentence that sounds like a manifesto for modern literature Brecht suggests that literature has much to learn from cinema, since conformist literary practices turn out to reproduce nothing but the author's '*Weltanschauung*' [world view] (SLK I: 179).

On the contrary, cinema has the ability to draw attention to the process (implying social processes as well as processes of mediation) over the finished product, as long as 'die Person wird von außen gesehen' [the individual is seen from the outside] (SLK I: 180). Brecht does not naively attribute transhistorical radical characteristics to the film narrative. The phrase *von außen* is the precondition for a political representational strategy that valorizes social conditions and actions over the characters' psychology.[3] But why is the conventional Aristotelian narrative incompatible with the cinematic medium? One needs to go back to Aristotle's definition of dramatic art to understand Brecht's call for a narrative that draws attention to the apparatuses of its own production as well as to the social apparatuses outside the world of the narrative. According to Aristotle, tragedy is 'μίμησις πράξεως σπουδαίας [25] καὶ τέλος' [mimesis of an action which is serious and complete in itself (translation mine)] (1449b). The key word in his definition is the adjective 'τελείας' which derives from the word 'τέλος' [purpose, end]. This mimesis,

---

[3]Steve Giles' influential analysis seems to miss this point. Giles suggests that Brecht thought that unlike the novel, cinema is not 'anthropocentric'. In actual fact, Brecht says that cinema can show things 'von außen' but on the condition that it emphasizes mediation as a problem in itself. See Steve Giles *Bertolt Brecht and Critical Theory: Marxism, Modernity and the Threepenny Lawsuit*. Berne: Peter Lang, 1997, 79.

which is 'complete in itself', draws attention to the purposes served by the character's action within the narrative; but this sense of completion produces a unified narrative cosmos whose relationship to the extra-textual social reality is hazy. Furthermore, the word 'τέλος' is the root of the adjective 'teleological' and given the ancient Greeks' tendency to use art to propagate timeless and thus ahistorical values, one senses that there is an element of fixity in this definition, as if social reality could not have been otherwise.

Brecht's view of the film as a medium that can see things from the outside emphasizes the dialectical aspect of human/social relationships so as to show that nothing serves 'τέλος' (telos), since social relationships are not eternally invariable but are subject to change. As Fredric Jameson says, for Brecht the central conflict is 'between the static and the dynamic, between that which is perceived as changeless, eternal, having no history and that which is perceived as altering in time and as being essentially historical in character' (53). From this historicized point of view, the Aristotelian paradigm of creating emotions 'δι' ἐλέου καὶ φόβου' [through pity and fear] (1449b) is no longer operative in the capitalist reality. Whereas Aristotle's understanding of representation was rooted in tragic unavoidability and a changeless 'human nature and truth', capitalism highlights social structures and divisions that question uncomplicated notions of a unified human nature and universal concepts of truth. Aristotle thought that dramatic art[4] is more important than history, because it can communicate transhistorical values: 'ἡ μὲν γὰρ ποίησις μᾶλλον τὰ καθόλου, ἡ δ' ἱστορία τὰ καθ' ἕκαστον τέγει' [because poetry focuses on the universal, whereas history on the historical specifics] (1451 b). For it is here that we can clarify the discrepancy between the two different definitions of dramatic art, since Brecht argued for a historicized representation, rather than for one predicated upon universals. To achieve this, one should abandon the typical tropes of dramatic/literary art, which has its emphasis on 'great individuals', and as he says in his essays on Georg Lukács: 'Für uns entstehen die Individuen bei der Gestaltung des menschlichen Zusammenlebens' [for us the individuals develop from the arrangement of the processes of human interactions] (SLK II: 39). But why then is the conventional dramaturgy of individual pathos passé? Brecht's answer is that 'capitalism is radical' (cited in Benjamin, *Understanding Brecht* 33) since it revolutionizes production and social relations. As such, whereas dramatic representations were structured upon the actions of self-determined individuals, capitalism focuses on phenomena that take place on a mass level. On this account, cinema's *Technifizierung* of representation can debunk abstract concepts of 'human nature and eternal virtues and values'. In an oft-quoted section Brecht says:

> In Wirklichkeit braucht der Film äußere Handlung und nichts introspektiv Psychologisches. Und in dieser Tendenz wirkt der Kapitalismus, indem er bestimmte Bedürfnisse in Massenmaßstab heraustreibt, organisiert und automatisiert, schlechthin revolutionierend. Er vernichtet weite Strecken Ideologie, wenn er, sich nur auf die 'äußere' Handlung konzentrierend, alles in Prozesse auflösend, den Helden als Medium, den Menschen als Maß aller Dinge aufgebend, die introspektive Psychologie des bürgerlichen Romans zerschlägt. Das Vonaußensehen ist dem Film gemäß und macht ihn wichtig. Für den Film sind die Sätze nichtaristotelischer Dramatik (nicht auf Einfühlung, Mimesis, beruhender Dramatik) ohne weiteres annehmbar.
>
> (SLK I: 199)

---

[4]For Aristotle, the word 'ποίησις' (poetry) includes the dramatic and epic art.

[In reality, the film needs external action and not introspective psychology. This is capitalism's tendency, by driving out, organizing and mechanizing certain needs on a mass scale revolutionizing things as such. When film concentrates only on external action, it does away with great areas of ideology, dissolves everything into processes, does away with the hero as the medium, with mankind as the measure of all things and smashes the introspective psychology of the bourgeois novel. Viewing things from an external standpoint is appropriate to the cinema and makes it important. For cinema, the phrase non-Aristotelian drama (a type of drama not based on empathy and mimesis) is appropriate.]

As it is evident, Brecht sees cinema's political value in its ability to create a fragmented diegetic pattern. This penchant for fragmentation is not radical in itself; but it can produce radical effects providing that it gives the audience time to reflect on the portrayed social processes and on processes of mediation, since film viewing is a social activity per se, while the medium of cinematic representation is the product of industrial (and thus social) processes outside the world of the narrative cosmos. Julian Murphet puts forward an analogous argument and suggests that cinematic perception is 'industrial' (180). In this regard, the reception of the narrative takes place on a mass level not only because of the massive aspect of the film-viewing process, but also because the very representational medium is the product of mass processes. Murphet goes on to make a Brechtian point tout court and suggest that the dialectics of film form is contingent on the fact that 'film technique mimics the commodity form' (183).

Murphet's point is strikingly similar to Brecht's celebration of the commodity character of the medium in the subsection titled 'Der Film ist eine Ware' [Film is a Commodity]. In this section, Brecht's optimism with regards to the medium derives precisely from the fact that it is a commodity and points out that 'Die Tatsache, daß im Kapitalismus die Welt in der Form der Ausbeutung und der Korruption in eine Produktion verwandelt wird, ist nicht so wichtig wie eben die Tatsache dieser Verwandlung' [The fact that in capitalism the world is transformed into production in the form of exploitation and corruption is not as important as this transformation] (SLK I: 193 194). The reader might have already noticed the point of convergence between Brecht and Benjamin's essay 'The World of Art in the Age of its Technological Reproducibility'. Brecht's influence on Benjamin's essay has been acknowledged by Steve Giles and Marc Silberman; surprisingly though, the importance of the *Dreigroschenprozeß* essay has not been recognized by film theory, nor has the essay become an integral part of film course syllabuses like Benjamin's (Gilles 113; Silberman, *Brecht and the Media* 451).

Brecht suggests that film's status as a commodity brings to the fore its reliance on apparatuses and this aspect of the medium can debunk universal values and ideologies that intend to stabilize the current state of social affairs. Benjamin's analogous point is that the reproductive aspect of the film medium leads to a 'radical renunciation of eternal value' (Benjamin, *The Work of Art and Other Writings* 28). The categorical conclusion drawn by both is that film establishes a new relationship between the audience and the apparatus and this can lead to a productive manipulation of their alienation (in the Marxist sense of the word). Before developing this point let us first clarify the very idea of the apparatus. According to Brecht, traditional concepts of art equate art with 'das rein

Menschliche' (abstract concepts of pure humanity)[5] (SLK I: 254) and fail to bring to light issues of mediation. Steve Giles explains that what is crucial to Brecht's argument is that, 'all human activity involves apparatuses' (148) but he claims that this is quite vague with respect to art. The key to comprehending this term is to resort to its literal meaning. The etymology of the Latin word apparatus derives from the verb *apparare* which literally means prepare. In other words, the participle *apparatus* stands for something that has been 'prepared/set up' before our own encounter with it. Giorgio Agamben suggests that the term 'apparatus' epitomizes the negotiated relationship between social beings and the 'historical element'. According to Agamben, 'apparatus' stands for 'literally anything that has in some way the capacity to capture, orient, determine, intercept, model, control, or secure the gestures, behaviors, opinions, or discourses of living beings' (14). Art falls into the aforementioned category; thus, when Brecht challenges traditional bourgeois theories of art for their hostility towards the apparatus he calls for a more reflexive attitude towards collective processes that orientate the audiences' responses and attitudes. The crux of this syllogism is that these collective processes are flattened out in conformist representational strategies. Dramatic tensions are shown as if they are detached from the broader social apparatuses.

Therefore, Brecht suggests that the exposition of apparatuses is propaedeutic to the revolutionizing of representation. This point was endemic to film theory of the 1960s and 1970s in France and in the UK, respectively. Relying on an Althusserian reconciliation of Marxism with psychoanalysis, critics writing for the French journal *Cahiers du Cinéma* and the British journal *Screen* analyzed the ideological aspect of the medium. Particular emphasis was placed on processes of subject construction, but the problem with this reception of Brechtian ideas was their return to the 'imaginary subject' who lapses into a 'dream state' while watching films and the somehow totalizing approach to the effects of particular cinematic narratives. Evidently, Brecht's understanding of the social and historical function of the apparatus was misunderstood. Preference was given to discussions that understood film spectatorship as an oscillation between unconscious pleasures (linked with the spectators' loss of control during the viewing process) and the illusion of control given by their immersion into the cinematic narrative (see Comolli, Narborni; Baudry; Heath). In a way, one senses that some of the writings of the time seemed to affirm 'transhistorical' assertions regarding cinema and spectatorship, and as Jacques Aumont rightly observes, the theory of the apparatus suffered from 'lack of historical specificity' (241).

Contrary to this return to the ahistorical subject, Brecht's understanding of the primacy of the apparatus is grounded in cinema's dependence on collective processes that cannot be understood under the abstract rubric of the 'human.' To illuminate this, one should point out the fact that cinema like photography is predicated upon what James Lastra calls the 'secondariness' of the subject (271). Brecht does not lament this medium specific characteristic, but on the contrary, considers cinema's non-anthropocentric quality to be a progressive aspect of the medium. This is also stated ex negativo in his 1929 essay on photography, in which he criticizes photographs which efface their status as mechanically reproduced materials and serve the sole purpose of expressing the artistic virtuosity of the photographer. As he says, this is not enough 'besonders, wenn sie nur beweisen wollen, daß man das damit machen kann, was man auch mit dem Pinsel machen kann' [especially

---

[5]This is my free translation. The literal translation would be 'the purely human'.

if they want to show things that can be done with a brush] (SLK II: 334). The nub of Brecht's critique is that photography – and as an extension cinema which originates from it – is a different art form which can establish new forms of representation and reception.

From this perspective, Brecht's critique of the new media is founded upon what David Trotter formulates as 'film as medium before film as art' (4). Drawing on the early cinema experiments as well as on modernist literature's fascination with cinema, Trotter explains that in the first decades of the 20th century, film became a 'meta-technology' whose key theme was the limitations of 'human perception' (4). But the word 'human' here implies the abstract individual, whose 'perception' and 'artistic' agency is undermined thanks to the prevalence of technological mediation. Trotter's point is congruent with Brecht's prioritization of the technological aspect of the medium which echoes social processes outside the world of cinema. The prevalence of these processes is not in line with 'heroic' individual narratives. On reflection, this argument is also valid in the current age of the digital revolution. One needs to consider the role of social media which allegedly aim to create individual 'online identities', but whose methods of constructing 'individual identities' rely on sets of predetermined mass interactions. Ultimately, they end up becoming methods of 'de-individuation'.

To return to the film medium, in Brecht's view, the indubitably technological property of film art calls attention to art's dependence on technological developments, and as an extension, to the economic and productive forces. The camera is engaged in a process that records reality and produces a copy of it at the same time. This dual function collapses the distinction between the original and the copy. In this way, cinema's dependence on mechanical reproducibility could strengthen the audience's understanding of the visible – and here the term refers to the filmic visible and the social one – as something that can be constructed and not as unchangeable. Illuminating from this point of view, is Marc Silberman's point:

> The camera's operation of registering physical reality – objects and gestures rather than emotions and psychology – in other words its *Von-Aussen-Sehen* (seeing from the outside) becomes the cornerstone of an aesthetics of making visible *das Sichtbarmachen*. Finally, in the cinema the perception of the image undergoes a disintegration of visual perspective with the levelling of difference between the image and the original. Aura is no longer attached to the photographic or cinematic image as material value, but to the process, to the functioning of the reproduction.
>
> (*The Politics of Representation* 451)

Silberman's comments succinctly synopsize the fundamental tenet of Brecht's writings on the medium which hinges on the view of cinema as a means of externalizing processes and structures which are mystified. By implication, cinema challenges the understanding of art as a reflectionist process, and the medium's political efficiency is grounded in its ability to engage with the material reality, so as to point to structures that are not necessarily comprehended even by the filmmaker. The prerequisite for the radical employment of the medium is that the story is an epiphenomenon. What matters most is the ability to use the technological apparatus so as to engage with the social reality and point to social mechanisms beyond the narrative world. Again, the similarity with Benjamin's critique of the media is striking. Not only because Benjamin suggested that the photographic lens gives access to the 'optical unconscious of capitalism' (Benjamin, *The Work of Art and Other Writings* 278) but also because he was equally optimistic regarding the medium's ability to thematize the fact that social existence is mediated by a plethora of apparatuses. As he says, 'the function of film is to train human beings in the apperceptions and reactions needed to deal with a vast apparatus whose role in their lives is expanding almost daily' (26). For Benjamin as for Brecht, the optico-acoustic aspect of the medium and the dialectical method shall coalesce and overlap, since the political efficacy of cinema depends on its ability to use sounds and images not to subordinate everything into a homogeneous story, but to activate collective thought processes.

Wolfgang Gersch refers to this as 'das Verhältnis von Destruktion und neuer Funktionalität' [the relationship between destruction and new functionality] (84). A prime example of a film which achieves this goal is Thomas Heise's *Material* (2009). In line with Heiner Müller's (the eminent post-Brechtian playwright and theater practitioner) idea of representation as 'material', the film is an assembling of materials from different periods of German history and consists of footage from old, unused films by Heise, from Fritz Marquardt's preparation of his production of Heiner Müller's play *Germania Tod in Berlin*, from the mass demonstration on Alexanderplatz in 1989, from the newly formed parliament in the East, and from the contemporary postreunification epoch. Towards the end, we see images from a preview screening of Heise's film *Stau Jetzt geht's los* (1993) in Halle/Saale. The film elaborated on the growing increase of a neo-Nazi sub-culture in the former DDR and some of the young right-wingers who were filmed were invited to attend the preview. The screening is suddenly interrupted when a group of leftists attack the cinema. The ensuing battle between the leftists and the neo-Nazis is captured by Heise's cameraman and is symptomatic of the film's understanding of history as a farcical repetition and recycling of past unfinished conflicts.

*Material* assembles images from different historical periods which are also shot with different cameras. Instead of a coherent dramaturgical pattern, Heise prioritizes voices, images, and sounds that thematize the very historical apparatus and draw our attention to a set of unresolved historical contradictions. It is a polyphonic narrative which refutes the idea that the fall of the Wall brought German history to a close. On the contrary, the film intends to identify structures behind the facticity of historical events, as well as to reveal historical contradictions which have been suppressed. Heise was a member of the Berlin Ensemble[6] and worked for many years as a theater director staging many texts by Heiner Müller; in *Material* he follows the latter's suggestions for a collective dramaturgy which resists simulation. Müller once said that history 'is covered with flesh and skin, surface. The main impulse is to get through the surface in order to see the structure' (cited in Prager 68).

But how does Heise achieve this in a film that is classified as a documentary? One of the key strategies is a commitment to a Brechtian *Historisierung* that crisscrosses the past with the present without always notifying the audience of the changes in historical time. The aim of this formula is the accumulation of individual instances of history so as to uncover the intricacies of the historical apparatus. The film starts by capturing a group of children playing among the ruins in Halle/Saale on the 9th of November 1989, the day that the border between East and West Germany was opened. Immediately after this, we jump one year in time. The voice-over reads: 'Something is always left over. Remnants that do not work out. So images lie around waiting for history.' In the following fragment the time has changed. The date is October 14th, 1990, and Heise captures the battle between the young squatters of the Mainzer Straße buildings and the police. The

---

[6]The theater was originally established by Brecht and his wife Helene Weigel in 1949.

dialectical contrast between the first images of the children playing in a derelict landscape and the post-unification conflict between the youth and the state apparatus puts forward the film's core thrust that the German unification did not bring political conflict to an end. After the end of this sequence, Heise moves back into the past, and we now see Fritz Marquardt discussing his theater production with his collaborators. Heise's voice-over introduces the new sequence: 'What remains lays siege to your mind. It's my image. The rooms, the gestures, the rhythms of the language.' In the midst of an agitated discussion, we hear Marquardt's stage designer explaining that the performance shall take place in the auditorium, because the audience has been moved to the main stage. This prolonged registering of the rehearsal discussions seems at a first glance irrelevant, but by viewing the film as a whole, one can understand these discussions as part of a self-reflexive comment on the film's representational tactic.

For instance, the reference to the radical changing of the audience's position in the theater is somehow expanded later on, when Heise records the massive demonstrations on Alexanderplatz taking place on November 4th, 1989. Here, the protagonist in the 'theater of history' is the mass, and Heise's camera lingers on peoples' faces, expressions, and hostile reactions to the Party officials who are addressing the public. A series of images from post-wall Berlin follow only to move back to another massive demonstration on November 8th, 1989, outside the Politbüro. Various people get on the podium to address their fellow citizens and celebrate their right to speak. Heise's documentation of these protests is important, because it brings to light historical images which were never shown in the media. For example, the majority of the protesters emphasize the need to defend the idea of Socialism by turning the DDR into a more democratic state that will give people access to political participation. In the midst of a public debate during the protest the image fades out and some intertitles appear quoting the *Internationale*.

> Es rettet uns kein höh'res Wesen,
> Kein Gott, kein Kaiser noch Tribun
> Uns aus dem Elend zu erlösen
> können wir nur selber tun!
>
> Unser Blut sei nicht mehr der Raben,
> Nicht der mächt'gen Geier Fraß!
> Erst wenn wir sie vertrieben haben
> Dann scheint die Sonn' ohn' Unterlass!
>
> [No Higher Being can Save us
> No God, no Kaiser, no Tribune
> We can only save ourselves from the misery
>
> Our blood is no longer feeding the ravens or the mighty vultures
> Only when we have expelled them for good
> The sun will shine forever]

This narrative interruption is followed by an actual image of the protesters enthusiastically singing the *Internationale*. In the shot that immediately comes after this one, Heise informs us that the day is November 10th, 1989, but there is a sound and image conflict, since the images on the screen emanate from the historical present (2008). Heise summarizes the events that led to the opening of the Wall, but there are no images from the people's celebrations. The film refuses to reproduce media simulations that flattened and down-played the people's uprising. As the voice-over comments: 'It's Saturday. The last week was a lie.' One is asked to think of the historical contradiction, since the people's uprising was appropriated to promote antithetical interests. Commenting on this, Heise explained that 'Helmut Kohl was not my dream', (cited in INDEPENCIA) and one of the film's intentions was to contradict 'the generally remembered images of public television of the Fall of the Wall, which was called 'The Change' in German, and the annexation of East Germany by West Germany that was its goal' (cited in *Material* Filmmuseum Edition 2011).

*Material* is perhaps the most germane paradigm of a contemporary film which utilizes Brecht's idea of the primacy of the apparatus constructively. Stripped of dramatic linearity and dialogue, the film turns into a meta-commentary on the intricacy of representation and history, putting forward the conjecture that both cinematic representation and historical reality involve complex processes that negotiate the boundaries between the visible and the invisible. It inaugurates a different type of film narrative that could be labeled as *Bildmaterial* (image-material) which returns to the essentials of audiovisual representation, so as to resist the reproduction of teleological narratives that simplify politics and representation. Heise compares his *modus operandi* with the act of 'digging', which is dedicated to discovering what is behind images and words. As he says, 'Similar to the mole, the work of collecting those images required a certain nose for the worthwhile as well as practice, since a picture seldom makes it apparent what it depicts and a sound seldom tells us of the part we can't hear' (*Material*, DVD). Heiner Müller introduced this idea in the theater by pushing Brecht's dialectical dramaturgy to its limits to create synthetic fragments that could free the collective imagination and resist the media's representational 'imperialism'. Müller's overarching idea is that art 'is a blind practice' (cited in Fiebach 84). Similarly, Heise's method relies on the acknowledgement of the non-anthropocentric aspect of the medium and of the primacy of the optico-acoustic apparatus, with the purpose of identifying the suppressed 'optical/historical unconscious'. The film is also clear proof that Brecht's modernist desire to thematize mediation and defamiliarize our historical environment by exposing its inherent aporias can still be deployed to politicize representation.

## CLARIFICATIONS AND MISUNDERSTANDINGS: REALISM, SELF-REFLEXIVITY, MONTAGE, EMOTIONS

The aforementioned observations provide a useful background for clarifying some misapprehensions of Brecht's writings by contemporary film theory. As mentioned earlier, Brecht emphasized the haecceity of the film medium – its capacity to register aspects of social/historical reality which elude human consciousness. He thought that this automatic inscription of social reality should be combined with a modernist narration which draws on the crisis of experience in modernity and can lead to a realistic portrayal of historical reality. In Brecht's terms, realism stands for a broader political concept and not simply a dramaturgical one. Cinema here plays an important role thanks to its indexical nature. As he says in one of his film fragments: 'Die Möglichkeit des Films liegt in seiner Fähigkeit, Dokumente zu sammeln' [cinema's potential lies in its ability to collect documents] (SZT 2: 222). In this context, realism is not necessarily consistent with dramaturgical coherence. He elaborates this further in the *Dreigroschenprozeß* essay where he explains that cinema needs to resist the tradition of the *Wortdrama* (verbal drama) (SLK I: 230) and avoid a tautological combination of images and words. The medium's realism is the outcome of a practice that does not use images and words strictly at the service of dramatic lucidity. Brecht's argument is that film should take advantage of its medium specific elements, something which he expresses clearly in an essay titled 'Über Filmmusik'. There he states that cinema should free itself from the theatrical tradition, because 'Es ist in der Tat niederdrückend, wie viel schlechtes Theater er [Film] produziert' [it is really depressing in fact, how much bad theater it [cinema] produces] (SZT 288).

Realism, therefore, occupies an important role in his writings on cinema, something that was not understood by 1970s film theory, to which I shall return below. The precondition for producing realist film narratives is that cinema should do away with the conventional theatrical and literary practices and explore its very modernist quality that is predicated on the secondary role of the subject. In his film script *Die Beule: Ein Dreigroschenfilm* (his adaptation of the *Threepenny Opera*), he reflects on the role of the camera and says: 'der Apparat sucht sich sozusagen Motive, er ist ein Soziologe' [the apparatus searches, so to speak, for motives, it is a sociologist] (TFF II: 333). Marc Silberman aptly describes this camera as 'gestic' (Silberman, *Whose Revolution* 321) establishing a clear connection with Brecht's idea of the social *Gestus*, which aspires to deconstruct individual actions so as to reveal their social foundations. *Gestus*, thus, seeks to demonstrate a set of social attitudes (*Haltungen*) that cannot be expressed solely through dialogue. Pointing to the crisis of representation in modernity, Brecht's idea of the social *Gestus* is modeled in a representational paradigm that intends to show and de-individuate actions.

There is a constitutive intersection between this idea of the camera as a provocateur and realism. More precisely, realism is not grounded in the reproductive quality of the camera, but in its productive one, which derives from its ability to 'show' rather than tell (δειξις/deixis instead of the Aristotelian μίμησις/imitation), so as to encourage analytical responses and to call attention to the processes behind the events. Seen through this prism, Brecht's realism is founded on the coexistence of representation and its metacritique. The camera's active engagement with the material environment is not merely concerned with reflecting actions, but with understanding the social context behind them. From the prolegomena, one can see that Brecht's view of cinematic realism is not far from theories of realism centered on the indexicality of the medium. Siegfried Kracauer's and André Bazin's theories of realism were predicated on the medium's ability to reveal rather than reflect reality. Kracauer thought that film can capture contingent aspects of social reality and disclose 'hidden aspects of the world about us' (49) while Bazin celebrated the fact that film art does not depend on individual expression but on the photographic image which does not 'create eternity, as art does', but benefits from 'the absence of man' (Bazin, *What is Cinema* II: 13–14). The resonances with Brecht's and Benjamin's points on the primacy of the apparatus, which were mentioned in the previous section, are more than apparent. Furthermore, in his analysis of Rossellini's *Paisà* (1946), Bazin praises the film for portraying actions without separating them from their material reality (38) while in an article on Visconti's *La Terra Trema* (1948) he points out in a Brechtian fashion that the film 'resists the seductions of drama' (41). Similarly, in his discussion of another Neorealist film, De Sica's *Ladri di Biciclette* (1948) he extols the film's engagement with the historical reality of the time and suggests that history has taken over dramaturgy (50).

With these comments in mind, it is evident that there are many meeting points between Brecht's writings on the medium and cinematic theories of realism. It is also noteworthy that his critique of conventional forms of representation was concerned with revealing 'real social processes' that are obfuscated by conformist narrative forms. As he says, 'Der Realist in der Kunst ist auch ein Realist außer der Kunst' [the realist in art is also a realist outside of art] (SLK II: 125). This is congruent with Brecht's idea that realism produces 'das eingreifende Denken' [interventionist thinking] (cited in Steinweg 87). Again, realism relates intrinsically to the dialectical method and not to stereotypical dramatic forms which show dramatic conflicts that fail to capture the changeability of social and historical reality. Brecht's critique was mainly directed towards literary and theatrical traditions which had influenced cinema, and the core of his argument was that changing historical circumstances change our understanding of realism. This was not necessarily comprehended by film theory of the late 1960s and 1970s produced in France and the UK. Critics writing for *Cahiers du Cinéma*, *Cinéthique* and the *Screen* assumed an antirealist rhetoric implying that Brechtian cinema was diametrically opposed to cinematic theories of realism. A pertinent example is Jean-Louis Comolli's and Jean Narboni's criticism against cinematic indexicality on the basis that what 'the camera in fact registers is the vague, unformulated, untheorized, unthought-out world of the dominant ideology' (60). In the same way, Jean-Paul Fargier, Jean-Louis Baudry, Stephen Heath, and Colin MacCabe consciously applied Brecht as a theoretical apparatus for the study of film in conjunction with an approach which understood Brecht and antirealism as being synonymous (Fargier 140; Heath 38; MacCabe, 'Realism and the Cinema' 12). Typical in this respect was also Peter Wollen's discussion of Bazin's theory of cinema as the opposite of a Brechtian 'materialist cinema' (9).

Recently, one of the key proponents of this axiom, Colin MacCabe, has re-evaluated his previous critique of Bazinian realism, acknowledging that modernism (and here we can assume Brechtianism) is not necessarily opposed to realism, since modernism's breaking of orthodox forms of representation encapsulated a desire to deal with the real ('Bazin as Modernist' 70). Analogously, Brecht's penchant for films that minimize character-based dramaturgy and utilize an episodic form indicates a desire for realism – a fragmented narrative pattern that de-individuates actions and reveals their real social and historical significance. This episodic narrative serves the purpose of preventing the audience from reducing everything to dramatized stories dissociated from the social totality. The filmmaker should freeze the actions and give the viewer time to ponder the represented social relationships and the questions/contradictions introduced by the narrative. Thus, the object reflects on the processes it represents and the audience is given time to step out of the narrative and reflect.

This provides the opportunity to clarify two Brechtian terms that have given rise to confusion to many film scholars. I refer to Brecht's call for anti-illusionist self-reflexive narratives. Brecht suggested that works of art that do not reflect on the reality they represent produce illusionism, but his understanding of illusionism is much more intricate than what many film scholars assume. Certain critics consider Brecht's view of illusionism synonymous with the idea that people are duped to believe that they 'are in the presence of the actual referents of cinematic images' (Carroll, 'A Reply to Heath' 94). Actually, illusionism for Brecht emblematizes undialectical depictions of social reality. Any dramatic conflict that fails to communicate the dialectical contradictions of the represented actions produces illusionism. 'Meiner Meinung kann alles, was mit Konflikt, Zusammenstoss, Kampf zusammenhängt, ohne materialistische Dialektik keinesfalls behandelt werden' [My opinion is that anything related to conflict, collision and struggle, can by no means be dealt with without materialist dialectics] (SZT 7: 296). This comment can also clarify the process of self-reflexive anti-illusionism which has also been misinterpreted by film scholars. Dana Polan, for instance, suggests that Bugs Bunny's (the American cartoon) address to the audience is an example of Brechtian self-reflexivity (n. pag.). Roberto Schwarz surmises that in the current context of globalized consumerism, the Brechtian self-reflexive elements have ceased to defamiliarize the audience and are constantly used for the purposes of mass consumerism (n. pag.). Justin Wyatt implies that high concept Hollywood films, which prioritize excess over narrative unity, employ devices from the modernist art cinema of the past. Wyatt goes so far to equate formal elements manipulated by Jean-Luc Godard and the modernist European art cinema from the 1960s with contemporary blockbusters (61). These comments are part of a current scholarly tendency which assumes that modernism – and in Brecht's case political modernism – has been de-radicalized.

This diagnosis errs in many respects, and the reason for this lies in the fact that the Brechtian model is routinely assumed to be a set of formal devices dissociated from the dialectical method that I mentioned earlier. But for Brecht, both self-reflexivity and anti-illusionism were not simply motivated by the will to remind the audience that they are watching a film/theater production. They are practices that intend to draw attention to processes outside the world of the cinema. Alexander Kluge has illuminated this quite succinctly: 'forms of perception, contents of reality, penetrate the cinema which did not originate in the cinema but arise from the permanently changing re-production of society' (Kluge, *The Sharpest Ideology* 194). The task of a self-reflexive anti-illusionist film practice is to produce dialectical contradictions and make the audience question the 'naturalization' of a set of relationships that are social and historical. On this basis, formal anti-illusionism should not be understood as an exposition of virtuosity on the part of a filmmaker, but as a commitment to formal experimentation with the intention of producing a negation of the social and cultural dominant.

A careful comparison between two different objects can demonstrate quite clearly the differences in method and make us understand Brecht's idea of reflexivity beyond the limits of tautology. The first example is from the 1980s American TV series *Moonlighting* and the second one from Michael Haneke's film *Funny Games* (1997). In both objects, the characters break the fourth wall frequently, but the objectives and the effects are poles apart. In *Moonlighting*, the third episode from the third season starts with the main characters David (Bruce Willis) and Maddie (Cybill Shepherd) looking at the camera and introducing themselves to the audience. They start musing on the success of the season and David says 'I am getting famous. I want to make a video, a funky video'. Suddenly, a group of singing and dancing musicians appear while both characters in the background respond to their theatrics. In the scene that immediately comes after this one, David asks for the audience's and Maddie's feedback; the sequence culminates with Maddie singing and dancing, and the show's titles rolling.

Let us now compare this to Haneke's method. *Funny Games* tells the story of a wealthy family which is held hostage and tortured by two young men Peter (Frank Giering) and Paul (Arno Frisch). Haneke does not give any evidence regarding their motives and formulates an unconventional narrative that intentionally frustrates dramatic psychological clichés. In the course of the narrative, Peter and Paul break the fourth wall numerous times. In one of those moments, Paul asks the hostages to place a bet for their lives. He then faces the camera and says: 'What do you think? Do they have a chance of winning? You are on their side aren't you?' Later on, when Anna (Susanne Lothar) begs them to kill them instead of continuing their sadistic games, Peter responds: 'Don't forget our entertainment value. We would all be deprived of our pleasure.' At another point in the film, the couple begs them once again to kill them, and Paul replies that the film has not reached the length of a feature film. He looks directly at the camera and asks: 'Do you think it is enough? But you want a real plot with plausible plot development don't you?' It is evident that these comments are not just comments on the narrative, but on social issues beyond the story.

From this simple contrast, we can see the different effects that two seemingly similar formal devices produce. In *Moonlighting*, reflexivity is used in service of narrative consumption. The characters reflect on their own function as mythical characters, solely for the purposes of celebrating the very myth of entertainment. Their address to the audience facilitates the audience's immersion into the narrative without offering hints that can make them question the object's social function. It is analogous to the conservative reflexivity of Hollywood films, whose 'innovation' is, as Jane Feuer puts it, a form of 'conservation' (cited in Stam 91). Antithetically, in Haneke's case, self-reflexivity forces the spectators to reflect on the medium's social function and on their own function as social beings. By means of these self-reflexive comments, he de-eroticizes film violence and invites the audience to examine their complicity vis-à-vis social issues outside the diegetic cosmos. One can clearly see how fallacious the common-place idea that Hollywood and advertising have de-radicalized modernist and Brechtian practices is. Aware of the fact that his politicized aesthetic might be reduced to aestheticized trickeries, Brecht stated that: 'Man wird daraufhin untersuchen müssen, wie denn nun der V-Effekt einzusetzen ist, was, für welche Zwecke da verfremdet werden soll' [one shall investigate how the V-effect is employed and for which purposes defamiliarization should be applied] (SZT 7: 192).

Nonetheless, both friendly and critical scholars tended to ignore this fundamental stipulation. Symptomatic of this trend was the propensity of 1970s film theory to valorize certain formal elements as ends in themselves. From Jean-Paul Fargier's problematic idea that a film's reference to the process of its own making can lead automatically to a materialist knowledge of the laws of social reality, to Heath's and MacCabe's point that montage is the prerequisite for radical cinematography, 1970s Brechtian reception missed the connection between politics and aesthetics, since nowhere does Brecht mention that certain formal effects are transhistorically radical (Fargier 143; Heath 125; MacCabe, 'The Politics of Separation' 47). It is true that Brecht valorized a film practice which manipulates montage sequences, but in his writings montage is a much more complicated term that is very much interrelated with his idea of the social *Gestus*.[7] In other words, montage is identical with interruptive strategies that intend to reveal processes behind the dramatic appearances. Like Eisenstein, Brecht thought that the value of montage hinges on the 'context' and the 'concepts' (Eisenstein SW 139) that one wishes to produce. In short, montage is not *ipso facto* radical.[8]

The work of Theo Angelopoulos – who has openly acknowledged his Brechtian influences – is a good case in point that shows how one can produce 'montage effects' without resorting to montage sequences. In *The Travelling Players* (1975), Angelopoulos

---

[7] Roswitha Mueller has also acknowledged this. See 'Montage in Brecht', *Theatre Journal* 39.4 (1987): 473–486.
[8] Again, this refutes moot points in contemporary film theory that montage has been deradicalized. Certainly, many commercial films and advertisements employ montage sequences, but they have not de-radicalized the method in the Eisensteinian and Brechtian sense. The difference lies in the fact that contemporary films employ montage sequences to establish *narrative continuity* (a risk pointed out by Adorno, see Bratu Hansen, 221), while for Eisenstein and Brecht montage was a method of narrative disruption.

uses eighty shots throughout the film, but he generates gestic/interruptive effects by manipulating the actors' gestures, as well as via sound-image counterpoints. Historical transitions and political changes take place within long, uninterrupted shots. We are only informed about them either by the use of radio announcements, which alert us about the shifts in time; or literally by means of social *Gesten* which are produced by the camera's interaction with the performing bodies and which showcase the shifts in historical time. Through these historical transitions, Angelopoulos interrupts the diegesis and creates dialectical contrasts between the historical past and present.

Brecht was also aware of the potential to produce montage effects via acoustic or textual effects that could invite the audience to question photographic transparency. In his own script *Die Beule*, he deplores sound cinema's habit to avoid the use of intertitles and he explains that in his film the intertitles are 'der geistigen Schauplätze ganzer Abschnitte' [the mental scenes of entire sections] (TFF II: 329). The production of gestic effects by means of intertitles signals Brecht's acknowledgement of cinematic specificity and his understanding that film is not, as Robert Bresson stressed repeatedly, 'photographed theater' (Bresson 3). But it also pertains to his idea of montage as a constructive process that resists reducing images and sounds merely to dramatic plot. A conspicuous example of such a *Bild-Text* montage is his own collection of photo-epigrams titled *Kriegsfibel*. The book contains photographs from popular wartime magazines accompanied by epigrams added by Brecht. The added text produces montage/gestic effects in the sense that it disrupts orthodox ways of image reading and contradicts the magazines' printed titles. A typical example is an image which was published by *Life* magazine in 1943 showing the burned skull of a Japanese soldier over an American tank. The original caption published by *Life* described the picture and stated dithyrambically that 'fire destroyed the rest of the corpse'. Brecht added the following text:

O armer Yorick aus dem Dschungeltank!
Hier steckt dein Kopf auf einem Deichselstiel
Dein Feuertod war für die Domeibank.
Doch deine Eltern schulden ihr noch viel

(*Kriegsfibel* 45)

[O poor Yorick from the jungle tank!
This puts your head on a tiller handle
Your fiery death was for the Domei Bank
To whom your parents still owe a lot]

One can identify the use of the text as a dialectical counterpoint, whose function is productive rather than descriptive. In many respects, *Kriegsfibel* encapsulates the basic method that Brecht intended to apply to the cinema: images and texts should not necessarily coalesce, nor should the text/sound simply describe the visual material. They should rather activate the viewers' critical faculties and enable them to produce meaning beyond the confines of tautology.

In short, Brecht wanted to produce collisions that do not perpetuate the audience's passive status. This point will help us expose the weakness of cognitive film theory's critique of Brecht. Cognitive film theory has not only been critical towards Brecht, but it has also largely contributed to the misinterpretation of his theory and practice. Cognitivists argue that film studies should focus on the audience's conscious activities which help them follow a narrative and not on unconscious political processes that guide them to certain responses. One of the key theorists, David Bordwell (and indeed the less dogmatic one)[9] suggests that – contrary to critical theory's axioms – the spectator is not 'passive' during the film-viewing process, but 'active' since she/he is 'cued by the film' to 'execute a definable variable of operations' (29). But this point disregards the ways film viewing can be standardized. John David Rhodes has criticized this from an Adornian angle:

> Bordwell is surely right that film viewing is 'a complicated, even skilled activity' (33), but his terms coincide exactly with Adorno's account of film spectatorship as the 'prolongation of work': skilled activities are exactly what is demanded of workers on the factory floor. The very fact that Bordwell must go to such pains to make apparent the spectator's work is proof of the fact that this skilled labor is routinized. (63)

It is exactly this 'routinized' attitude towards the material that Brecht opposed. In his view, canonical representational strategies do not simply ensure the reproduction of commodities, but they simultaneously reproduce the institutionalized subject and object relations. Cognitivists do not accept this and they make an analogous methodological mistake like the film theory of the 1970s, which they oppose. They treat the audience as a homogeneous body.

Brecht, by contrast, thought that the audience is an heterogeneous body and the political implications of an object are premised on its ability to divide the audience for political purposes. But the cognitivist return 'to the universal individual' serves also political purposes, which are of course different in scope. The problem with cognitivist film theory and its celebration of 'post-theory' (film's theory's naïve declaration of 'the end of history')[10] is its complete disregard for historical questions. Certain cognitivists, like Torben Grodal, ignore issues of cinematic specificity or the role of modernity in the establishment of cinema and approach film as part of a broader history of narratives. For Grodal, the popularity of certain films/narratives over others, as well as spectatorial responses can be attributed to biological and brain processes. In his words, 'when a viewer chooses to watch a film, he thereby chooses to be cued into having constant fluctuations of heartbeat, perspiration, adrenalin-secretion, and so on' (Grodal, *Embodied Visions* 43). Correspondingly, he surmises that even emotional responses to visual narratives are less dependent on social structures and more on biological processes, while he proposes that throughout the film-viewing process, 'the brain searches its memory files, aided by feelings of familiarity or unfamiliarity' (61). Grodal's arguments are problematic because they treat the individual, the body, and the brain in transhistorical ways. Susan Buck-Morss' following point invalidates this argument:

> The brain is thus not an isolable anatomical body, but part of a system that passes through the person and her or his (culturally specific, historically transient) environment. As the source of stimuli and the arena for motor response, the external world must be included to complete the sensory circuit. (13)

---

[9]Let me also acknowledge that despite my reservation towards Bordwell's aforementioned point, his general commitment to formalism can be very useful in identifying the interrelationship between politics and film aesthetics. His work has been very influential on my thinking. I would refer the reader to Bordwell's fascinating book *On the History of Film Style*. Cambridge, Massachusetts, London: Harvard UP, 1997.

[10]The truth is that certain cognitivists coming from different critical traditions have opposed this idea of the 'post-theory'. See for example, Warren Buckland *The Cognitive Semiotics of Film*. Cambridge: Cambridge UP, 2004.

By referring to some central axioms of cognitive film theory, we may comprehend that their critique of Brecht has political resonances. Noël Carroll is one of the most significant examples. Carroll adopts a critical view not only of Brecht, but of any modernist critique of representation, conducting the methodological mistake mentioned earlier. Reflecting on Brecht's anti-illusionism, Carroll states that 'the thesis appears to claim that spectators confronted by representations of apples are deceived – like those famous Greek birds – into believing that there are luscious, edible apples before them' ('Conspiracy Theories of Representation' 399). My previous clarification of Brecht's idea of anti-illusionist reflexivity shows that Carroll's understanding of Brecht's theory is thoroughly misleading. Brecht's anti-illusionism hinges on offering clues that can make one think differently. As he says: 'Alles kommt darauf an, dass ein richtiges Denken gelehrt wird, ein Denken, das alle Dinge und Vorgänge nach ihrer vergänglichen und veränderbaren Seite fragt' [It is important that the right thinking is taught; a way of thinking that questions everything and every process in its mutability and transitoriness] (SLK I: 287). Thinking in oppositions is the key to unveiling the political insinuations behind ahistorical notions of truth.

Here lies the main reason for the cognitivist hostility to Brecht, given that cognitivism embraces the very ahistorical ideas that Brecht criticizes. Typical in this regard is the cognitivist view that 'cognitions' affect the audience's emotional responses. Drawing on the popular melodrama *Stella Dallas* (1937), Carroll offers a schematic description of the feelings communicated. Focusing on the main character's maternal sacrifice, Carroll suggests that the audience identifies with her because of her 'virtue'. 'Thus, we do not merely pity Stella Dallas. We admire her as well' ('Film, Emotion, and Genre' 226). This point constitutes a typical example of an unreflected emotion, because it takes at face value a set of processes beyond the narrative. However, Brecht thought that emotions and feelings involve processes behind their appearances. Brecht would be in agreement with Bazin's critique of films that 'proceed from the commonplace presupposition that a necessary and unambiguous causal relationship exists between feelings and their outward manifestations' (*What is Cinema* I: 62).

Brecht's approach to emotions was analytical, and he did not reject them tout court as another cognitivist, Murray Smith suggests. Smith suggests that for Brecht emotional responses lead the audience to 'mistake the representation for reality' (132). He argues that emotions produce critical effects that negate Brecht's idea that empathy makes the audience confuse representation for its referent. I have already refuted this oversimplified understanding of 'illusionism' above, but it is crucial to point out that Brecht argued that emotions and feelings are fundamental in politicizing representation. The difference lies in the fact that his approach to emotions was not tautological. How could one arouse the audience's political capacity without provoking emotional responses? This is clearly formulated in *Der Messingkauf*, where the philosopher states that the audience and the actors should be emotionally involved; it is solely empathy that should be abolished (see SZT 5: 119). Elsewhere, Brecht explains that political art should reveal 'die gesellschaftliche Rolle der Emotionen, welche diese heute zum Vorteil der Herrschenden spielen' [the social role of emotions which are nowadays employed for the benefit of rulers] (SZT 3: 30). But unlike cognitivists, Brecht argues that emotions are not universal and transhistorical; they should not be shown as static, but as dynamic, that is to say, motivated by particular social circumstances in particular social situations. In this context, different social groups do not have uniform emotional responses. Emotions are 'ein widerspruchsvolles Gemisch' [a contradictory blend] (SZT 7: 297), and this is the main argument in his critique of Aristotelian dramaturgy; it reduces complex contradictory processes, because 'Sie müßten in subjektive (im Helden verlagerte) umgewandelt warden' [they must be converted into subjective ones – located in the hero] (SZT 5: 294). While the cognitivists regard emotions as transhistorical and universal, Brecht deems them to be socially defined and not subjective expressions of self-determined individuals. Thus, the cognitivist critique of Brechtian theory is not based on 'scientific facts' but on political disparities.

## THE SPECTER OF BRECHT

> That thou, dead corse, again in complete steel
> Revisit'st thus the glimpses of the moon,
> Making night hideous; and we fools of nature,
> So horridly to shake our disposition
> With thoughts beyond the reaches of our souls?
> Say why is this? Wherefore? What should we do?
>
> Shakespeare *Hamlet*, I, 4

A few years after the fall of the Berlin Wall, Jacques Derrida published an inspired book which maintained that Marx's political and philosophical heritage is more germane than ever. Derrida's argument hinges on the idea that Marxism needs to be transformed and be ready to keep with its fundamental 'principle', which is 'a radical critique, namely a procedure ready to undertake its self-critique' (110). Rather than sharing the superficial idea that history is over, Derrida explained the currency of Marx in a historical period that strived to depoliticize our historical present. The specter of Marx plays a role similar to the ghost in Hamlet; it can give us access to concealed information and instigate action. In a passage worth quoting Derrida states:

> We feel ourselves observed, sometimes under surveillance by it even before any apparition. Especially – and this is the event, for the specter is of the event – it sees us during a visit. It (re)pays us a visit [Il nous rend visite]. Visit upon visit, since it returns to see us and since visitare, frequentative of visere (to see, examine, contemplate), translates well the recurrence or returning, the frequency of a visitation. (125–126)

In the context of the current economic crisis in Europe it is obvious that the end of history has proved to be wishful thinking. Capitalism faces one of its worst crises, and a 'visit' from the radical 'specters of the past' can help us politicize film theory and practice. These historical circumstances make Brecht relevant once again, but following Derrida, radical thought can benefit not by accepting authority figures dogmatically, but by conducting its own auto-critique. But before returning to Brecht we need to elucidate his theory so as to explain the benefit from this dialogue with the past. Film theory needs to rethink past arguments, and as James Naremore puts it, 'If we toss away an older theory like an old dress or like a used car, we lose an important part of a long conversation' (126).

A sceptic could interject that Brechtian cinema is a 'finished project' and Brecht's influence on contemporary cinema is minimal. A closer look at the work of some influential filmmakers, who deal with unfinished historical and political conflicts, as well as at the cinema of countries afflicted by the economic crisis, shows that this objection is flawed. Michael Haneke is a good case in point. Haneke's work has been enthusiastically received by contemporary film theory, but its Brechtian aspect has been persistently downplayed.

His films are paragons of the Brechtian idea of using form to politicize representation something that he has also admitted in two interviews with Alexander Kluge. Haneke states that the two basic principles of his work are 1) commitment to form and 2) respect for the audience (cited in Kluge, *News and Stories* 2008). Elsewhere, Haneke uses an utterly Brechtian language and describes his work as 'Dramaturgie für widersprüchliche Verhältnisse' [dramaturgy of contradictory situations] which points to important issues outside the picture (cited in Kluge, *News and Stories* 2009).

In Germany, filmmakers like Thomas Heise as well as the New Berlin School (e.g., Angela Schanelec and Thomas Arslan) prove that Brecht's legacy is still significant. Some of these filmmakers have been taught by the Brechtian film-essayist Harun Farocki and make films in dialogue with Brecht and the New German Cinema of the 1960s/70s. The Danish auteur Lars von Trier included conscious references to Brecht in *Dogville* (2003) and *Manderlay* (2005). Importantly, in Greece, a country heavily plagued by the economic crisis, films like *Fascism Inc.* (2014) – a film which explains the recent rise of neo-fascism in Europe with reference to Brecht's essay Fünf Schwierigkeiten beim Schreiben der Wahrheit – *Debtocracy* (2011) and *Catastroica* (2012) inaugurate a new agit-prop documentary tradition reminiscent of the Dziga Vertov group's experiments; of great note is that these films follow alternative ways of production, since they are funded by their audiences (European citizens, Greek and EU unions) and they are distributed for free. They are practical examples of Brecht's idea of film as 'das Werk eines Kollektivs' [film as the work of a collective] (SLK I: 201). Last, but not least, Theo Angelopoulos died while shooting a film which returned to his Brechtian roots and had references to *The Threepenny Opera*. During the shooting of the unfinished film, he commented that: 'I always wanted to do something with Brecht's *Threepenny Opera*. Our current situation makes this play relevant. One should not forget that Brecht wrote it in 1928, one year before the Great Depression' (cited in Georgakopoulou).

These examples are an indication of Brecht's continuing influence on film practice and signal that there remains scope for further illumination of what Brecht can contribute to film studies. In *Deutschlandbilder* (1984), a Brechtian documentary on Nazi propaganda films, which resembles Brecht's *Kriegsfibel* project in scope, Hartmut Bitomsky and Heiner Mühlenbrock point out that the general practice of Nazi cinema was tautology and 'every tautology contains a deception ... moments of curiosity are rare'. The question needs to be posed to the present: how many contemporary films rely on tautological reasoning? Broadly, do media give rise to new forms of collective imagination and emancipation or do they perfect strategies of hegemony and subjection? While there are no glib answers to these questions, Brecht's theory can provide a methodological apparatus that may help us pose them and think politics and representation in more complex ways, instead of treating political questions morally. His writings take on a novel relevance in light of the current economic crisis and can assist us to historicize film theory in a neo-liberal era, in which certain political issues and social interests are presented under the rubric of 'the natural'.

# WORKS CITED

Agamben, Giorgio. *What is an Apparatus and Other Essays*. Trans. David Kishik and Stefan Pedatella. Stanford, California: Stanford UP, 2009. Print.

Aristotle, Περί Ποιητικής. http://users.uoa.gr/~nektar/history/tributes/ancient_authors/Aristoteles/poetica.htm, 20 March 2013.

Aumont, Jacques. 'The Variable Eye, or the Mobilization of the Gaze.' *The Image in Dispute*: *Art and Cinema in the Age of Photography*. Ed. Dudley Andrew, trans. Charles O'Brien. Austin: Texas UP, 1997. 231–258. Print.

Baudry, Jean Louis. 'The Apparatus.' *Camera Obscura* 1.1 (1976): 104–126. Print.

Bazin, André. *What is Cinema?* I&II. Ed. and trans. Hugh Gray. Berkeley, Los Angeles, London: California UP, 1971. Print.

Benjamin, Walter. *Understanding Brecht*. Trans. Anna Bostock. London: Verso, 1998. Print.

———. *The Work of Art in its Technological Reproducibility and Other Writings on Media*. Trans. Edmund Jephcott, Rodney Livingstone, Howard Eiland. Cambridge, Massachusetts: Harvard UP, 2008. Print.

Brecht, Bertolt. *Werke 21: Große kommentierte Berliner und Frankfurter Ausgabe*. Frankfurt: Suhrkamp, 1997. Print.

———. *Schriften zur Literatur und Kunst* I&II. Berlin, Weimar: Aufbau, 1966. Print.

———. *Schriften zum Theater* 1–7. Frankfurt a.M.: Suhrkamp, 1964. Print.

———. *Texte Für Filme* I & II. Frankfurt a.M.: Suhrkamp, 1983. Print.

———. *Kriegsfibel*. Berlin: Eulenspiegel, 2008. Print.

*Brecht on Theatre*. 3rd edition. Ed. Tom Kuhn, Steve Giles, Marc Silberman. London, New York: Bloomsbury, 2014.

*Brecht on Performance: Messingkauf and Modelbooks*. Ed. Tom Kuhn, Steve Giles, Marc Silberman. London, New York: Bloomsbury, 2014.

Bordwell, David. *Narration in the Fiction Film*. Madison: Wisconsin UP, 1985. Print.

Bresson, *Notes on Cinematography*. Trans. Jonathan Griffin. New York: Urizen Books, 1977. Print.

Buck-Morss, Susan. 'Aesthetics and Anaesthetics: Walter Benjamin's Artwork Essay Recosidered.' October 62 (1992): 3–41. Print.

Buckland, Warren. 'A Close Encounter with Raiders of the Lost Ark.' *Contemporary Hollywood Cinema*. Ed. Steve Neale and Murray Smith. London: Routledge, 1998. 166–177. Print.

Carroll, Noël. 'A Reply to Heath'. October 27 (1983): 81–102.

———. 'Conspiracy Theories of Representation.' *Philosophy of the Social Sciences* 17 (1987): 395–412. Print.

———. 'Film, Emotion, and Genre', *Philosophy of Film and Motion Pictures: An Anthology*. Ed. Noël Carroll, Jinhee Choi. Oxford: Blackwell, 2006. 217–233. Print.

Comolli, Jean-Louis, Narboni, Jean. 'Cinema/Ideology/Criticism.' *Cahiers du Cinéma* 1 969–1972: *The Politics of Representation*. Ed. Nick Browne. London: Routledge, 1990. 58–67. Print.

Derrida, Jacques. *Specters of Marx: the State of the Debt, the Work of Mourning and the New International*. Trans. Peggy Kamuf. New York, London: Routledge, 1994. Print.

Eisenstein, Sergei. 'Notes for a Film of *Capital*.' Trans. Maciej Sliwowski, Jay Leyda, Annette Michelson October 2 (1976): 3–26. Print.

———. *Selected Works I 1922–1934*. Ed. and trans. Richard Taylor. London: BFI, 1988. Print.

Elsaesser, Thomas. 'Political Filmmaking after Brecht: Farocki, for Example.' *Harun Farocki: Working on the Sightlines*. Ed. Thomas Elsaesser. Amsterdam: Amsterdam UP. 133–156. Print.

Fargier, Jean Paul. 'Parenthesis or Indirect Route.' Trans. Susan Bennett. *Screen* 12.2 (1971): 131–144.

Fiebach, Joachim. 'Resisting Simulation: Heiner Müller's Paradoxical Approach to Theater and Audiovisual Media since the 1970s.' *New German Critique* 73 (1998): 81–94. Print.

Gemünden, Gerd. 'Re-Fusing Brecht: The Cultural Politics of Fassbinder's German Hollywood.' *New German Critique* 63 (1994): 54–75. Print.

Georgakopoulou, Vena. 'Ο Τεό κατεβάζει Μπρεχτ στο λιμάνι.' Ελευθεροτυπία http://www.enet.gr/?i=news.el.article&id=221379, 21 July 2014.

Gersch, Wolfgang. *Film Bei Brecht*. Munich: Hanser, 1975. Print.

Gilles, Steve. *Bertolt Brecht and Critical Theory*: Marxism, Modernity and the Threepenny Lawsuit. Berne: Peter Lang, 1997.

Grodal, Torben. *Moving Pictures*: A New Theory of Film, Genres, Feelings and Emotions. Oxford: Clarendon P, 1997. Print.

———. *Embodied Visions*: Evolution, Emotion, Culture and Film. Oxford: Oxford UP, 2009. Print.

Hansen, Miriam Bratu. *Cinema and Experience*: Siegfried Kracauer, Walter Benjamin and Theodor W. Adorno. Berkeley, LA, London: California UP, 2012. Print.

Heath, Stephen. 'Lessons from Brecht.' *Screen* 15.2 (1974): 103–128. Print.

Hegel, *Phenomenology of Spirit*. Trans. A.V. Miller. Oxford: Oxford UP, 1977. Print.

Jameson, Fredric. *The Prison House of Language*: A Critical account of Structuralism and Russian Formalism. Princeton, Chichester: Princeton UP, 1972. Print.

Kracauer, Siegfried. *Theory of Film*. Princeton: Princeton UP, 1997. Print.

Kluge, Alexander. 'The Sharpest Ideology: That Reality Appears to its Realistic Character.' *Alexander Kluge*: Raw Material for Imagination. Ed. Tara Forrest. Amsterdam: Amsterdam UP, 2012. 191–196. Print.

———. *News and Stories* – 'Ich geh nicht in den Keller lachen!' TV program 22 June 2008.

———. *News and Stories* – 'Die rechte Hand Gottes – Michael Haneke über seinen preisgekrönten Film Das weiße Band'. TV program 01 August 2009.

Lastra, James. 'From the Captured Moment to the Cinematic Image: A Transformation in Pictorial Order.' *The Image in Dispute*: Art and Cinema in the Age of Photography. Ed. Dudley Andrew. Austin: Texas UP, 1997. 263–292. Print.

MacCabe, Colin. 'Realism and the Cinema: Notes on Some Brechtian Theses.' *Screen* 15.2 (1974): 7–27. Print.

———. 'The Politics of Separation.' *Screen* 16.4 (1975): 46–61. Print.

———. 'Bazin as Modernist.' *Opening Bazin*: Postwar Film Theory and Its Afterlife. Ed. Dudley Andrew, Herve Joubert-Laurencin. New York: Oxford UP, 2011. 66–76. Print.

Martin, Adrian, Naremore, James. 'The Future of Academic Film Study.' *Movie Mutations*: The Changing Face of World Cinephilia. Ed. Jonathan Rosenbaum & Adrian Martin. London: British Film Institute, 2003. 119–132. Print.

Mathers, Pete. 'Brecht in Britain: From Theater to Television.' *Screen* 16.4 (1975): 81–100. Print.

*Material*. Dir. Thomas Heise. 2009. DVD. Edition Filmmuseum. 2011.

Marx, Carl, Engels, Friedrich. *Collected* Works 5. Trans. Clemens Dutt, W. Lough, C.P. Magill. New York: International Publishers, 1988. Print.

Marx, Carl. *Capital*, vol. 1. Trans. Ben Fowkes. London: Penguin, 1976. Print.

———. *Early Writings*. Trans. Rodney Livingstone. London: Penguin, 1975. Print.

Mueller, Roswitha. 'Montage in Brecht.' *Theatre Journal*, 39.4 (1987): 473–486. Print.

Murphet, Julian. *Multimedia Modernism*: Literature and the Anglo-American Avant-Garde. Cambridge: Cambridge UP, 2009. Print.

*Nachrichten aus der ideologischen Antike*: Marx – Eisenstein – Das Kapital. Dir. Alexander Kluge. 2008 DVD. Suhrkamp, 2008.

Polan, Dana B. 'Brecht and the Politics of Self-Reflexive Cinema.' *Jump Cut*, (1974), http://www.ejumpcut.org/archive/onlinessays/JC17folder/BrechtPolan.html, 12 March 2010.

Prager, Brad. 'The Death Metaphysics of Heiner Müller's the Task.' *New German Critique* 73 (1998): 67–80. Print.

Rhodes, John David. 'Belabored: Style as Work.' *Framework* 53 (2012): 47–64. Print.

Schwarz, Robert. 'The Relevance of Brecht: High Points and Low.' *Mediations: The Journal of the Marxist Literary Group* 23 (2007) http://www.mediationsjournal.org/articles/the-relevance-of-brecht#endref_11 12 April 2013.

Silberman, Marc. 'The Politics of Representation: Brecht and the Media.' *Theatre Journal* 39.4 (1987): 448–460. Print.

———. 'Whose Revolution? The Subject of *Kuhle Wampe* (1932).' *Weimar Cinema: An Essential Guide to Classic Films of the Era*. Ed. Noah Isenberg. New York, Chichester: Columbia UP, 2009. 311–330. Print.

Smith, Murray. 'The Logic and Legacy of Brechtianism.' *Post-Theory: Reconstructing Film Studies*. Ed. David Bordwell and Noël Carroll. Madison: Wisconsin UP, 1997. 130–148. Print.

Stam, Robert. *Reflexivity in Film and Literature: From Don Quixote to Jean-Luc Godard*. Ann Arbor: Columbia UP, 1992. Print.

Steinweg, Reiner. *Lehrstück und episches Theater: Brechts Theorie und die theaterpädagogische Praxis*. Frankfurt a.M.: Brandes & Apsel, 1995. Print.

Trotter, David. *Cinema and Modernism*. Oxford: Blackwell Publishing, 2007. Print.

Unknown. 'Material. Thomas Heise.' *Indepencia*. http://independencia.fr/FESTIVALS/FIDthomasheise1.html, 29 April 2013.

Wollen, Peter. 'Ontology and Materialism in Film.' *Screen* 17.1 (1976): 7–23. Print.

Wyatt, Justin. *High Concept: Movies and Marketing in* Hollywood. Austin: Texas UP, 1994. Print.

# Music

# CHAPTER SEVENTEEN

# Brecht and Music: Theory and Practice

KIM H. KOWALKE

Brecht asserted in a 1935 essay that it was music which 'made possible something which we had long since ceased to take for granted, namely the "poetic theatre"' (*BT*, pp. 84–90). Music provided him with a powerful mechanism to reclaim and refunction in 'epic drama' the presentational mode of address, long a standard convention in most forms of music-theatre but discarded by modern drama after the 'fourth wall' had been dismantled by naturalism and realism. Brecht's relationship to music, therefore, was as essential as it was complex. Although little interested in musical repertoire or issues extraneous to his efforts in the theatre, ironically Brecht first gained wide public recognition through the musical settings of his works: opera librettos, plays with music, a ballet, dramatic cantatas, an oratorio, musical films, even commercial jingles. By 1931, music critic Hans Mersmann could even proclaim: 'New Music in Germany has found its poet. This poet is Bertolt Brecht.'[1] Although Brecht thereafter showed little interest in serving the

---

Kim H. Kowalke, 'Brecht and Music: Theory and Practice', in Peter Thomson and Glendyr Sacks (eds.), *The Cambridge Companion to Brecht*, second edition (Cambridge: CUP, 2006), pp. 242–58.

The most comprehensive surveys of 'Brecht and Music' have appeared in the German language. Joachim Lucchesi and Ronald K. Shull's *Musik bei Brecht* (1988) comprises a long introductory overview of Brecht's involvement with music, his known writings about music, a catalogue of compositions dating from his lifetime, and a discography. Less reliable are Albrecht Dümling's 736-page critical survey, *Lasst euch nicht verführen: Brecht und die Musik* (Kindler: Munich, 1985) and Fritz Hennenberg's three-volume *Das grosse Brecht-Liederbuch* (Suhrkamp: Frankfurt, 1984). The multi-author collection *Brecht und seine Komponisten* (ed. A. Riethmüller: Laaber, 2000) includes essays on Brecht's collaborations with Orff, Hindemith, Wagner-Régeny, Dessau and Eisler. In English, the best brief overview remains John Willett's 'Brecht and the Musicians' in *Brecht in Context*. John T. Gilbert's *Bertolt Brecht's Striving for Reason, Even in Music* is a serviceable, though uncritical, chronicle of Brecht's engagement with music. More provocative is Kenneth Fowler's 65-page *Received Truths: Bertolt Brecht and the Problem of Gestus and Musical Meaning*.

Of Brecht's musical collaborators, Weill has received the broadest scholarly attention and most of that literature is in English. Excellent entry points for students are David Drew, *Kurt Weill: A Handbook*; David Farneth, ed., *Kurt Weill: A Life in Pictures and Documents* (Overlook: New York, 2000); Foster Hirsch, *Kurt Weill on Stage* (Knopf: New York, 2002). Stephen Hinton's *Cambridge Opera Handbook* is the definitive resource for *The Threepenny Opera*; the Kurt Weill Edition includes both the holograph score in facsimile and a critical edition of the original 1928 stage version (text and music), with expert scholarly commentary accompanying each volume. The Kurt Weill Foundation for Music publishes a free semi-annual newsletter, as well as source books for the major Brecht/Weill works. All of the Brecht/Weill collaborations have been published and recorded. Publication and recording of Eisler and Dessau are less complete, while much of the music composed for original

modernist agenda of 'New Music', only one of his nearly fifty completed dramatic works lacks music. Over 600 of his more than 1,500 poems refer to musical genres in title or structure; intended as songs, most were set as such during his lifetime. Subsequently, despite copyright disincentives, there have been well over a thousand additional settings, including many by major composers.

Music serves as a pillar so central to many of his theoretical constructs and as a parameter so determinant for the shape, diction and delivery of his texts that Brecht's legacy cannot be fully understood or properly assessed without reference to music. Confidence in his own musicality allowed him to influence settings of his texts, to criticise compositions by the less independent of his collaborators, and even offer them his own melodies, of which almost a hundred have survived. The remarkably small number of multiple settings of Brecht's poems during his lifetime attests to the authority commanded by those composed in direct collaboration with him. Today these songs are not infrequently still miscredited to Brecht rather than to the composers, with the attendant assumption that musicians who worked closely with him were transmitting Brecht's own readings of his poems.

Brecht's poetic impulses had first manifested themselves in 'songs to the guitar, [as he] sketched out verses at the same time as the music'[2] and primitively notated them with his own ecphonetic symbols. Like Wedekind's models, many of these early poems were intended to be sung either in private to a small group of friends or in informal public settings. Eyewitnesses to Brecht's mesmerising live performances – whether in theatre, cabaret or brothel – concur in their accounts of his magnetism (not to mention his entourage) of a magnitude that we now expect only of rock stars. The songs did not really exist as independent texts, *per se*, because the author's, composer's, performer's and protagonist's personae all coalesced into a single voice – Brecht's. Carl Zuckmayer described that voice as 'raw and trenchant, sometimes crude as a ballad singer's, with an unmistakable Augsburg accent, sometimes almost beautiful, soaring without any vibrato, each syllable, each semitone being quite clear and distinct'.[3] That description certainly fits the only commercially released shellac recordings of Brecht singing: the two ballads from *The Threepenny Opera* within his vocal capability, the 'Ballad of Mac the Knife' and its motivic retrograde, 'Das Lied von der Unzulänglichkeit menschlichen Strebens'. Definitely not beautiful, yet charismatic and unforgettable in effect, Brecht's razor-sharp performance from 1929 (re-released on compact disc, Mastersound DFCDI-110) slices the text's syntax to reveal new strata of sense, while the rattler-rolled r's roil the otherwise almost stoic surface of his nasal, coarse tone.

Prior to 1925 Brecht handled the music for all productions of his plays himself; each included several songs. Some were *contrafacta*, wherein one or more pre-existent melodies were stripped of their original lyrics to allow a new text to engage in provocative dialogue with the images associated with the too-familiar music, 'putting quotation marks, as it were, around a lot that was cheap, exaggerated, unreal'.[4] More numerous were strophic ballads with neutral accompaniments and primitive, recitative-like original melodies that

---

productions remains inaccessible. The friendliest introduction to Brecht/Eisler is Albrecht Betz, *Hanns Eisler: Political Musician*; Dessau awaits a reliable biography in English.

[1] Mersmann, 'Die neue Musik und ihre Texte', *Melos* 10 (May/June 1931), p. 171.
[2] Brecht, *Arbeitsjournal*, vol. 1, 3 August 1938.
[3] Quoted by Willett, in *Brecht in Context*, p. 152.
[4] *Ibid.*

insured textual pre-eminence. At their most successful they reified Brecht's goal: 'they must be cold, plastic, unflinching, and, like tough nutshells when they get caught in his dentures, knock out a few of the listener's teeth'.[5] Brecht's earliest critical champion Herbert Ihering wrote of *Drums in the Night* that one really felt 'the whip-driven rhythms of his sentences' only when Brecht sang and accompanied himself on the guitar. In response, audiences 'whistled, yelled, howled, and applauded'; they were anything but cool, rational, or 'distanced'.[6] Yet Brecht admitted that in these first plays 'music functioned in a fairly conventional way. There was usually some naturalistic pretext for each musical piece' (*BT*, p. 84).

After Brecht realised that what Hanns Eisler would later call his 'colossal musicality without technique' would be inadequate to address music's role in the non-Aristotelian, 'dialectic' drama he was beginning to envision, he regularly recruited or was recruited by professional composers, to whom he tried to harness his own musical intuitions and aspirations.[7] Unqualified to write both libretto and score (as the antipodal Richard Wagner had done), Brecht found himself in a double bind: on the one hand, music's importance within the epic model required collaboration with composers of stature; on the other, he was unwilling to serve merely as the librettist most of them were continually seeking. He feared they would insist on 'music having its own meaning' and resist his control over its composition and performance. Suspicious of all 'autonomous' music, particularly those attributes associated with the nineteenth-century tradition of *espressivo*, Brecht rejected the opulence of operatically trained voices and the narcotic sensuality of string-dominated orchestration:

> A single glance at the audiences who attend concerts is enough to show how impossible it is to make any political or philosophical use of music that produces such effects. We see entire rows of human beings transported into a peculiar state of intoxication, wholly passive, self-absorbed, and according to all appearances, doped. Their gapes and stares signal that these people are irresolutely, helplessly, at the mercy of unchecked emotional urges ... Such music has nothing but purely culinary ambitions left.
>
> (*BT*, p. 891)

Brecht distrusted musicians in general, he said, because they tended to view texts as 'series of words which are there to give them the opportunity to enjoy themselves'.[8] Because music tends to stimulate the listener so seductively and potently – as though without mediation, he feared that his poems, would become mere material for music and be embraced without critical reflection Consequently his own voice, no longer present as the performer's, would be appropriated by the composer's. He intuited that 'in most encounters between poetry and music, poetry can become the more powerful of the two only by the intentional acquiescence or the unintentional incompetence of the composer'.[9] To counteract this, Brecht eventually tried to posit a new paradigm. one which challenged

---

[5] Brecht, *Tagebuch*, 26 August 1920; quoted in *Musik bei Brecht*, ed. Lucchesi and Shull, p. 97.
[6] *Berlin Börsen-Courier*, 9 December 1923; quoted and translated by Fuegi, *Bertolt Brecht: Chaos, According to Plan*, p. 15.
[7] Eisler's comment was recorded by Hans Bunge, *Fragen Sie mehr über Brecht: Hanns Eisler im Gespräch* (Rogner and Bernhard: Munich, 1970), p. 210.
[8] Brecht, 'Texte für Musik', GW, xix, p. 406; reprinted in Lucchesi and Shull, *Musik bei Brecht*, pp. 150–1.
[9] Edward T. Cone, *The Composer's Voice* (University of California Press: Berkeley, 1974). p. 45.

what he feared was fundamental to the very nature of music. If it were to escape both its formalism and emotional entanglements, music would have to be turned inside out and become '*Misuk*', the term he invented in the 1950s for the radical refunctioning of both composition and performance that he required. Not even Hanns Eisler, who shared so many of Brecht's other values, however, could endorse so restricted a definition.

> Brecht's rejection of certain sorts of music was so extreme that he invented another variety of music-making, which he called '*Misuk*' ... For a musician it is difficult to describe *Misuk*. Above all it is not decadent and formalist, but extremely close to the people. It recalls, perhaps, the singing of working women in a back courtyard on Sunday afternoons.[10]

Ultimately the irreconcilable contradiction between Brecht's need for and suspicion of 'cultivated' music would limit its role within his post-1936 theatrical works and his wider impact on music theory and practice.

Although his younger brother Walter and, later, Elisabeth Hauptmann had already transcribed some of his early melodies, the first of Brecht's professional musical collaborators, Franz S. Bruinier (1905–28), not only re-notated, arranged and orchestrated a handful of Brecht's melodies (including 'Pirate Jenny' and the 'Barbara-Song') but also composed his own settings of several poems (including 'Surabaya Johnny'). Dead from tuberculosis at twenty-three, Brainier was followed briefly by Erwin Piscator's house composer, Edmund Meisel (1894–1930), who arranged the 'Man is Man Song' for the poet himself to sing in the Berlin Radio 1927 production that brought him to Kurt Weill's critical attention. When Weill (1900–50) and Brecht met shortly thereafter, they immediately explored the possibility of writing a full-scale opera, then collaborated on a half-dozen other large-scale projects during the four years of the rise and fall of plans and prospects for *Mahagonny*. They experimented with various recipes for hybrid genres of music-theatre in which the domination of music was not a given: the *Songspiel Mahagonny* (Baden-Baden, 1927), the plays-with-music *The Threepenny Opera* (Berlin, 1928) and *Happy End* (Berlin, 1929), the radio cantata *Der Lindberghflug* (Baden-Baden, 1929; first version jointly with Hindemith), the 'school opera' *He Who Said Yes* (Berlin, 1930), incidental music the Berlin production of *Man is Man* (1931). Independently, Weill also set assorted pre-existent poems as the cantatas *Vom Tod im Wald* (1927) and *Das Berliner Requiem* (1928). Despite unexpected public and critical Success, their always non-exclusive collaboration dissolved in 1931 – when common aesthetic and sociological tenets proved insufficient to overcome the centripetal force of their divergent views of the function of music in the theatre. They managed to collaborate only once in exile, for the symphonic ballet with songs, *The Seven Deadly Sins* (Paris, 1933) – Weill's orchestral masterpiece, which Brecht dismissed after its première under Balanchine as 'not very significant'.

Brecht's concurrent but brief association with Paul Hindemith (1895–63), the foremost German composer of the post-war generation, was more rancorous and less productive. Although Hindemith failed to complete all of the movements assigned to him for the joint version (with Weill) of *Der Lindberghflug*, he did finish the score for its sequel, the first of Brecht's learning plays with music. Commissioned for and premièred at the modern

---

[10]Eisler, 'Bertolt Brecht und die Musik', *Sinn und Form* (1957), pp. 439–41; trans. by Marjorie Meyer in *A Rebel in Music: Selected Writings*, ed. Manfred Grabs (International: New York, 1978), pp. 173–4.

music festival which Hindemirh co-directed, and scored for amateur soloists, chorus, orchestra and offstage brass band, this *Lehrstück* created a scandal in Baden-Baden. But it was not performed again for three decades; Brecht withdrew his text and retitled its literary revision, *The Baden-Baden Cantata of Acquiescence* to clarify its didactic content, which had, in his opinion, of acquiescence to clarify its didactic content, which had, in his opinion, been all but buried by Hindemith's emphasis on the joys of communal music making for its own sake. Their confrontation over the rejection of *The Measures Taken* for the 1930 New Music Festival precluded the possibility of further collaboration.

Only in 1930, after completing his Marxist studies and setting himself the task of extracting an economically determined aesthetic system from the conditions of the class struggle, did Brecht find his ideal musical colleague and friend in Hanns Eisler (1898–1962), who more than matched Brecht's new commitment to art for ideology's sake. Although Eisler had independently set several of Brecht's poems earlier, their full-scale partnership commenced with *The Measures Taken* (Berlin, 1930); it would span nearly three decades. During this period Brecht would formulate and reformulate his theories on the proper nature and function of music within the epic model in a series of prescriptions to which Eisler's music (for their collaborative dramatic works) conforms more closely than that of any other composer. Highly effective but strictly subordinate to the text, Eisler's incidental but substantial scores for *The Mother* (Berlin, 1932), and *Round Heads and Pointed Heads* (Copenhagen, 1936) served as paradigms of the delicate dialectical relationship between text and music required 'to fulfill the demans of an epic theatre' (*BT*, p. 89). Ironically, with the exception of the score for *Schweyk in the Second World War* (Warsaw, 1957; rev. 1959) which he completed after Brecht's death, none of Eisler's other incidental music for plays by Brecht – *Fear and Misery of the Third Reich* (1945), *Life of Galileo* (1947), *The Days of the Commune* (1950) – reached that standard of excellence. Perhaps recognising that the design of Brecht's mature plays constricted music's role, Eisler concentrated on film scores – including *Kuhle Wampe* (1931) and *Hangmen Also Die* (1942) – and free-standing songs, song cycles and cantatas based on Brecht's texts. In so doing, he extended the tradition of the German *Lied* in new directions – with an individual idiom that recaptured the technical advances he had perfected during his years of study with Arnold Schoenberg – to create a body of politically engaged songs of the highest standard.

During the fifteen years of exile when Brecht produced most of his finest plays, he rarely collaborated with composers to create musico-dramatic entities, as he had in the previous decade. Rather, music played a less formative role, as the dramatist maintained full control by calling in musicians only for certain numbers – after the script had been completed. Among these lesser figures were the Finnish composer/conductor Simon Parmet (1897–1969), Franz Lehar's musical executor Paul Burkhard (1911–77), and the Swiss composer Huldreich Georg Früh (1903–45). Post-war collaborations with Carl Orff (1895–1982) and Gottfried von Einem (1918–96) aborted prematurely, while that with Rudolf Wagner-Regeny (1903–69) yielded only two scores.

In the last decade of his life, however, Brecht's principal composer was Paul Dessau (1894–1979). Although Dessau had heard *Songspiel Mahagonny* in Baden-Baden in 1927 and had already composed songs for the Paris première of *Fear and Misery* (1938), he had no substantive contact with Brecht until 1942, when the composer was supporting himself as a labourer at a chicken farm in New Jersey. Brecht noted in his diary that Dessau was 'much less developed and set in his ways than Hanns Eisler', and in order to remain in close contact Brecht convinced him to move to Hollywood, and five years later, to East Berlin.[11] Indeed, Dessau described his contact with Brecht and his ideas as decisive; they immediately began work on three large-scale projects that were never finished, including a huge oratorio, the *Deutsches Miserere*. Beginning in 1946, Dessau wrote new incidental music for *Mother Courage and Her Children* and, a year later, *The Good Person of Szechwan*. After returning to Europe, he composed scores for productions of *The Exception and the Rule* (1948), *Mr Puntila and his Man Matti* (1949), *Man is Man* (1951), *The Caucasian Chalk Circle* (1954), as well as several cantatas and the opera *The Condemnation of Lucullus* (1949). Believing that opera is 'the most powerfully expressive genre with which to highlight artistically the social issues of our time', Dessau continued after Brecht's death to set his texts, including an operatic treatment of *Puntila* (1957–9). Maintaining a more deferential attitude toward Brecht than had Eisler, not to mention Weill, Dessau consistently provided what Brecht asked for. Today, however, after the dissolution of the GDR, Dessau has achieved little independent identity.[12] Theatres now routinely substitute newly composed music for his incidental scores, a practice almost inconceivable for Brecht's joint musico-dramatic ventures with Weill and Eisler.

No other composer achieved the *Mitarbeiter* (co-worker) status Brecht reserved for only Weill and Eisler, who not only supplied music but also contributed to the overall conception and actual text of their collaborative works. At the time each began working with Brecht, he had already rejected the aesthetic assumptions and hierarchies which modernism had inherited from romanticism and left largely unaltered. At approximately the same time, both composers ended studies with their formidable teachers – Weill with Ferruccio Busoni, Eisler with Arnold Schoenberg – and set off in new directions on their own, each seeking in his own way to transcend the self-preoccupation, subjectivity and ultimately isolation of the New Music and to forge new contacts with mass culture and mass audiences for a socially engaged musical art. In collaborations with Georg Kaiser (*Der Protagonist*, 1924–5) and Iwan Goll (Der *neue Orpheus*, 1925), Weill had decisively rejected both musical and literary expressionism and embraced popular idioms. Eisler's musical reorientation, evident in the *Zeitungsausschnitte*, op. 11 (1925–7), preceded his first discussions and collaboration with Brecht by at least four years; in 1926 he had shocked his teacher by declaring: 'I am bored by modern music, it is of no interest to me; much of it I even hate and despise.' Yet, as David Drew observed, 'neither the power nor the extraordinary durability of his collaboration with Brecht would have been attainable but for the self-awareness and the mastery he had first achieved within Schoenberg's orbit and then developed on the tangential path he took in 1927'.[13] By then Eisler was a committed Marxist in both theory and practice: as music critic for the communist *Die rote Fahne*, composer of militant workers' choruses and marching songs, and leader of the study group Dialectical Materialism in Music.

Whereas Weill's lifelong commitment to a renewal of the musical theatre rested on socialist sociological premises, Eisler's political agenda rendered any theatrical ambitions incidental. Yet aesthetically and technically they had more in common than just Brecht:

> For many years the parallactic view of Brecht's musical collaborators that tendered them figuratively and even functionally indistinguishable from Brecht himself was

---

[11]*Arbeitsjournal*, vol. 1, 6 November 1944.
[12]The most comprehensive (if ideologically distorted) consideration of Dessau's collaboration with Brecht is Fritz Hennenberg's *Dessau-Brecht: musikalische Arbeiten* (Henschel: Berlin, 1963).
[13]David Drew, 'Eisler and Austrian music', *Tempo*, 161/162 (June and September 1987), pp. 28–9.

supposed to justify the idea that resemblances between (for instance) the music of Weill and Eisler were simply attributable to the influence of Brecht. Today it is perhaps permissible to suggest that Weill was one of the means whereby Eisler temporarily freed himself from Vienna. Of all the composers who were to a greater or lesser extent struck by Weill's deeply paradoxical achievement he was the only one at that time who had both the technical equipment and the strength of mind and musical character to turn to his own advantage a wide range of possibilities ... The influence was mutual – there are traces of Eisler in Weill's music until as late as 1938.[14]

While Brecht considered Eisler's settings to be 'the tests of his poems, what productions were to his plays', he credited Weill with 'first providing what [he] had needed for the stage'.[15] The four years of his nearly continuous collaboration with Weill were transitional ones for Brecht; he concentrated on Marxist studies begun in 1926, published his first collection of poetry, and completed only those dramatic works in which music was essential rather than incidental. Creatively at a disadvantage in that he had no experience of working with a composer of stature, he found himself perilously close to performing the normal functions of a librettist.[16] Yet it was in these pieces of socially engaged music-theatre that the montage techniques which have become fixed in public consciousness as 'Brechtian' were developed and the dramaturgical foundations of 'epic' drama laid. The four cornerstones of that new theatre comprised an unsentimental, repertorial, *sachlich* mode of presentation; development of new didactic genres for production outside the state-subsidised system; adaptation of cinematic techniques; and radical separation of the elements. With the latter Brecht tried to avoid the detested muddle of the Wagnerian *Gesamtkunstwerk*, where the various constituents are fused and consequently degraded. He hoped to bypass altogether what he called 'the great struggle for supremacy between words, music, and production – which always brings up the question "which is the pretext for what?": is the music the pretext for the events on the stage, or are these the pretext for the music?' (BT, p. 37).

Weill recognised Brecht's dilemma and in 1929 confided to a friend his strategy for dealing with it:

> Music has more impact than words. Brecht knows it and he knows that I know. But we never talk about it. If it came out in the open, we couldn't work with each other any more. Brecht asks for complete submission. He doesn't get it from me, but he knows that I'm good and that I understand him artistically, so he pretends that I'm utterly under his spell. I don't have to do anything to create that impression. He does it all himself.[17]

---

[14]*Ibid.*, p. 28.
[15]Brecht's comment about Eisler is quoted in Willett, *Brecht in Context*, p. 162; his appraisal of Weill appears in the *Arbeitsjournal*, vol. 1, 7 October 1940. Other than the two 'cantatas', *Vom Tod im Wald* and *Das Berliner Requiem*, outside the theatre Weill composed only two songs with texts by Brecht. Eisler, in contrast, was a prolific composer of self-standing *Lieder*, many with texts by Brecht.
[16]*The New Grove's Dictionary of Music and Musicians*, s.v. 'Brecht, Bertolt', by David Drew.
[17]Felix Jackson, 'Portrait of a quiet man: Kurt Weill, his life and his times', unpublished biography (photocopy in Weill-Lenya Research Center, New York), p. 110.

Brecht indeed later claimed that he 'had whistled things for Weill bar by bar and above all performed them for him'.[18] This familiar account of Brecht's ventriloquism (and single-handed rescue of his 'dummy' from Schrekerian 'atonal psychological operas') has been obliquely substantiated by a frequently cited essay published under Lotte Lenya's name but written by her second husband, George Davis; 'Sometimes Brecht impressed on Kurt his own ideas for a song, picking out chords on his guitar. Kurt noted these ideas with his grave little smile and invariably said yes, he would try to work them in.' The original typescript includes another sentence suppressed in publication: 'Naturally they were forgotten at once'.[19] With two or three celebrated exceptions, Weill proved an unwilling mouthpiece for Brecht's melodies. He was as aggressive as the poet when it came to defending his territorial imperative; in a recently rediscovered interview from 1934, when the interviewer commented on the dominant role Brecht had played in their collaboration, Weill answered him sharply:

> It almost sounds as if you think Brecht wrote my music ... Brecht is one of modern Germany's greatest literary talents; but being a great poet doesn't necessarily mean he's also a good composer ... Brecht is a genius, but for the music in our joint works, I alone am responsible.[20]

Although Brecht and Weill always remained wary of one another and retained the formal mode of address, what permitted them to pursue common goals, while gradually realising that aesthetic and sociological premises were insufficiently shared, was the mediating concept of *Gestus*, a term introduced into print by Weill in December 1928.[21] Within the dramaturgy of a music-theatre which strove to illuminate social relationships between characters rather than internal psychological states, Weill and Brecht both conceived *Gestus* as a means of making manifest on stage the behaviour and attitudes of human beings toward one another.[22] They agreed that music was indispensable in communicating the fundamental *Gestus* of a theatrical situation. A new 'gestic' language, combining dramatic, lyric and epic modes of poetry, would require a 'gestic' music in which musical autonomy and expressivity would yield before dramatic and sociopolitical purposes. In their respective prescriptive essays, Weill and Brecht borrowed terminology and exchanged examples as each groped toward a working definition of both *Gestus* and *gestische Musik* based on his own reading of their evolving practice.

For Brecht, *Gestus* was but one of several strategies for 'epicisation' of interpretation, presentation and reception of his dramatic works. Although he progressively referred to *Gestus* in less behaviourist and more Marxist terms (characters' social relationships must

---

[18]*Arbeitsjournal* vol. 1. 16 October 1940.
[19]'That was a time!', *Theatre Arts* (May 1956); reprinted as 'August 28, 1928', in *The Threepenny Opera*, trans. Eric Bentley and Desmond Vesey (Grove Press: New York, 1964), p. ix. George Davis derived the essay from interviews with Lenya and Elisabeth Hauptmann; the transcripts of those interviews and the type script of the essay are now in the Weill-Lenya Research Center. The nature and extent of the few documented musical 'borrowings' by Weill. from Brecht are discussed by David Drew in *Kurt Weill*, pp. 201–5.
[20]Ole Winding, 'Kurt Weill i Exil', *Aften-Avisen* (Copenhagen), 21 June 1934; German trans, in Weill, *Musik und Theater: gesammelte Schriften*, ed. Jürgen Schebera and Stephen Hinton (Henschel: Berlin, 1990), pp. 314–17.
[21]'Der Musiker Weill', *Berliner Tageblatt*, 25 December 1928; reprinted in Weill, *Musik und Theater*, pp. 52–4.
[22]For specific insight into *gestische Musik*, see Michael Morley, 'Suiting the action to the word: some observations on *Gestus* and *gestische Musik*', in Kim H. Kowalke, ed., *A New Orpheus* (Yale University Press: New Haven, 1986), pp. 183–201.

be presented as determined by economic and political factors), initially it seems to have served primarily as a means to reserve space within the song for his own poetic voice/persona and to dictate readings of his texts by both composer and performer. He claimed 'to be thinking always of actual delivery', how his authorial voice would be mediated by the performer for the spectator.[23] Recognising that the 'text' of music-theatre is fully assembled and experienced only in performance, Brecht adhered to the 'inflexible rule that the proof of the pudding is in the eating'. By fixing the rhythm, stress, pitch, timbre, pauses, phrasing, dynamics, tempos and intonation of his poetry in a musical setting, Brecht hoped to make his works virtually performer-proof and ensure a 'drug-free' effect on their audiences. Because he realised that 'the effectiveness of this music depends largely on the way in which it is performed', it is not accidental that the concept of *Gestus* emerged only after he had stopped writing and publicly singing his own songs, when he himself could no longer entirely control the reading of his poems (*BT*, p. 88).

Although Weill's theoretical formulations were equally inconsistent and undeveloped, the practical significance of the concept was very different for him. He described *Gestus* almost exclusively as a technical tool of the composer, with historical precedents in the music of Bach, Mozart, Beethoven, Offenbach and Bizet. He assumed that *Gestus* would enable music to regain a privileged position in the overall structure of musical theatre works, 'right down to the execution of the smallest details'. *Gestus* could channel and focus music's communicative capacities and free it from its traditional parallelism to the text, as well as its descriptive and psychological functions, thereby granting wider melodic, formal and harmonic latitude. Gestic music could articulate that which the text does not make explicit and thereby provide a subtext ready-made for the performer. The resulting 'play' between the music and the lyric – particularly frustrating expectations and subverting conventions – could convey complicated layers of meaning and contradictory attitudes.

When Brecht wrote that 'Weill's music for [the opera *Mahagonny*] is not purely gestic', he called attention to the discrepancies in both theory and practice inherent to their respective gestic formulas (*BT*, p. 87). Fixing the *Gestus* and separating the ingredients according to various recipes had failed to settle the 'great struggle for supremacy' between text and music. Perhaps the unresolved dissonance between Weill's and Brecht's non-unison voices is best heard at the climactic clash over Ernst-Josef Aufricht's Berlin production of the full-length *Rise and Fall of the City of Mahagonny* at the Theater am Kurfürstendamm in December 1931. Although it had been cast largely with singing actors rather than the originally intended opera singers (necessitating certain cuts and simplifications to which Weill had reluctantly acquiesced) and accompanied by a reduced orchestra of less than forty players, during rehearsals Brecht bemoaned that 'all is washed out by the music'. In a scene worthy of *Capriccio*, he publicly denounced Weill as a 'phoney Richard Strauss'. Lawyers threatened to stop rehearsals, and in a last-ditch effort to salvage his production, Aufricht convinced Brecht to bow out. Leaving *Mahagonny* to Weill and designer Caspar Neher (who had already written the libretto for *Die Bürgschaft* with Weill), Brecht instead staged *The Mother*, his adaptation of Gorky's novel, in the theatre's basement, with his wife Helene Weigel, Ernst Busch, Theo Lingen and Margarete Steffin among the cast.

---

[23] Brecht, 'Über reimlose Lyrik mit unregelmässigen Rhythmen', *Das Wort* 3 (March 1939); reprinted in *GW*, xix, pp. 395–403.

The move downstairs was decisive, irreversible and symbolic of a much larger shift: Brecht left behind opera, the commercial theatre and Weill; thereafter Brecht would hail *The Mother* – with Eisler's nine songs, ballads and choruses – as the classic model for politically mature epic theatre:

> Far more deliberately than in any other play of the epic theatre, the music in *The Mother* was designed to induce in the spectator a critical approach. Eisler's music can by no means be called simple. Qua music it is relatively complicated, and I cannot think of any that is more serious. In a remarkable manner it makes possible a certain simplification of the toughest political problems.
>
> (BT, p. 88)

With what Ernst Bloch labelled the 'radical monotony' of his music, Eisler succeeded in refunctioning the *Song* – Weill and Brecht's concoction, combining aspects of the *Lied*, the American popular song and the opera aria, that first had taken the stage in a role central to epic dramaturgy in the *Songspiel Mahagonny* and then had achieved worldwide recognition in *The Threepenny Opera*. 'Lob des Lernens' (In Praise of Learning), 'Lob des Kommunismus' (In Praise of Communism), and 'Grabrede über einen Genossen' (Funeral Oration for a Comrade) were in no danger of being 'misunderstood', of embarrassing the playwright as had the *Schlager* (hit-tunes) of *The Threepenny Opera* – 'the light music of 1930', for which, T. W. Adorno claimed, the public had mistaken them. The concurrent productions of *Mahagonny* and *The Mother* evinced how far Weill and Brecht's paths had diverged; the critic of *Die rote Fahne* compared Eisler's score to Weill's:

> Here there's no monstrous orchestra as on the Kurfürstendamm for Weill's score for Brecht's *Mahagonny*; no intoxicating violins, bloated wind sonorities, flowing harmonies, but rather a very small ensemble of a couple of brass players, percussion, and piano. But here there is sharp, clear voice-leading, brittle march rhythms, proletarian songs that grip you tensely from the first to the last note. In the incidental music for *The Mother*, Eisler's ability to bind words, sentences, slogans into a unified structure of striking effect through music reveals itself anew in a transcendent way.[24]

Eisler himself suggested much later that Weill had never really understood Brecht's ideas: 'he saw only the innovative effects, not what was really going on'. The reverse, of course, was equally true. And with their popularity undiminished, the products of the Brecht–Weill collaboration continued to pose problems for Brecht long after their premières. His retrospective dissatisfaction with them is most vividly demonstrated by the fact that he either repudiated or unilaterally revised each of them, eventually republishing all but one in literary versions incompatible with Weill's music. In two cases Brecht paralleled these revisions with commentary reinterpreting or correcting, from his maturing Marxist perspective, the 'misunderstandings' engendered by the originals. In his and Peter Suhrkamp's lengthy notes to *Mahagonny* published in 1930, Brecht acknowledged that in the eating, the opera had turned out to be 'culinary through and through'. *Mahagonny* had demonstrated that opera could not be reformed; it must be demolished and replaced:

---

[24] Quoted in Albrecht Dümling, *Lasst euch nicht verführen: Brecht und die Musik* (Kindler: Munich, 1985), pp. 354–5.

The opera *Mahagonny* was written three years ago, in 1927 [*recte* 1927-30]. In subsequent works attempts were made to emphasise the didactic more and more at the expense of the culinary element. And so to develop the means of pleasure into an object of instruction, and to convert certain institutions from places of entertainment into organs of mass communication.

(*BT*, pp. 41–2)[25]

If Brecht's notes to *Mahagonny* set forth theoretically an aesthetic and political agenda for epic theatre that the opera itself had failed to address, much less accomplish, the notes to *The Threepenny Opera* were intended as a corrective to the performance practice that had accounted for its unexpected success, which Brecht (and his Marxist critics) now viewed as 'mistaken'. In an interview with himself dating from about 1933, Brecht answered the question, 'What, in your opinion, accounted for the success of *The Threepenny Opera*? I'm afraid it was everything that didn't matter to me: the romantic plot, the love story, the music.'[26] His revisions to the text and the new notes reflect what he would have liked the play to have been, in the light of the dire post-première changes in political and economic circumstances and his subsequent experiments with didactic modes of music-theatre, principally with Eisler. Informing subsequent readings of the play with tropes on the original seemed Brecht's best bet for bringing out a clear socio-political message absent or diffused in the text of the 'comic literary operetta' (then still being staged around the world), which *Die rote Fahne* had dismissed as an 'entertaining mishmash without a trace of modern social or political satire'.

Brecht's *Threepenny Opera* notes were intended to be corrective rather than descriptive in yet another sense: several sections are barely camouflaged attempts to reverse text–music relationships inherent in the original. If the text had lost round one in the struggle for supremacy, Brecht was not inclined to concede the bout. (In 1933 Weill informed his publisher that he would have to attend the New York première of *The Threepenny Opera* because 'Brecht wants to go, which means that the music would be pushed completely into the background'.)[27] Brecht would simply change strategies: the composer's need not be the last nor necessarily the decisive reading of a poetic text. An audience's reading will be based to a large degree on that of the director and performers, who give empirical voice to the personae of poet, composer and dramatic characters and modulate those with their own. Thus, in the section of *The Threepenny Opera* notes entitled 'About the singing of the songs', Brecht admonishes actors not 'to follow the melody blindly'. 'There's a way of speaking against the music which can be very effective just because of an obstinate matter-of-factness, independent of and incorruptible by the music and rhythm.' He also stipulates that 'the actor must not only sing but show a man singing' (*BT*, pp. 44–5).

In these three suggestive sentences Brecht set forth the underpinnings of what thereafter would be taken at face value to be the essence of authentic 'Brechtian' performance practice. By calling for uncultivated voices that have resisted training in classical technique

---

[25]For a comparison of Weill's and Brecht's comments on *Mahagonny*, see Stephen Hinton, 'The concept of Epic Opera: theoretical anomalies in the Brecht-Weill partnership', in *Festschrift Carl Dahlhaus* (Laaber: Laaber, 1988), pp. 285–94.
[26]See Kim H. Kowalke, 'Accounting for success: misunderstanding *Die Dreigroschenoper*', *The Opera Quarterly* 6 (Spring 1989), pp. 18–38; also Stephen Hinton, 'Misunderstanding *The Threepenny Opera*' in *Kurt Weill: The Threepenny Opera*, pp. 181–92.
[27]Weill to Universal Edition, 6 February 1933.

and by reminding his actors that they need not sing all the time, the aesthetic distraction of the 'voice-object' is minimised, and the scope of the performer's (and consequently also the composer's) voice restricted. Leaving the melody 'unsung' at crucial moments simultaneously muffles the composer's and mutes the character's virtual voice to allow the poetic persona to be heard without competition, clearly enunciating the text while the singing voice retreats. The composer is banished to the orchestral pit, but Brecht offers him compensation for loss of his voice. Invoking the *lyrisches Ich*, in German literary criticism a construct roughly analogous to 'persona', Brecht suggests that

> In the orchestra, no matter how small, lies your chance as a musician ... Your orchestra is your troupe, your gang, your constant. True, it has to supply supports for the aforementioned non-musicians; otherwise he [the actor] will collapse, bur every instrument that you can wrestle free from this duty is won for you, for the music, sir! ... Instruments don't speak per 'I' but rather per 'he' and 'she'. What forces you to share the feeling of the 'I' on stage? Where are your own feelings? You are entitled to adopt your own position to the song's theme. Even the support you give can serve other arguments![28]

Requiring that the actor 'not only sing but show a man singing' can be read as a parallel effort to ensure that the poetic persona also shares the stage with the protagonist. Brecht distances the performer from the performed and differentiates the presence of the character from that of the performer. With characteristic dialectics, Brecht requires the actor to depict her or his character's reality and yet stand outside it observing as an eyewitness: 'The singer becomes a reporter, whose private feelings must remain a private affair' (BT, p. 38).[29] The poet thereby forges an alliance with the performer, who then stands in for him as narrator and commentator, displacing the protagonist as author of the words being sung. Thus even a solo performance is a type of montage, a combination of mimetic immediacy and diegetic distancing, a composite of dissected realities. Although intended to seem 'naive' to an audience, it is anything but simple for the performers, who must demonstrate awareness of their own presence in the performance.

When used sparingly for narrative passages of speech-like declamation by singing actors consciously holding additional vocal resources in reserve, and not out of necessity, 'theory' proved itself effective in the practice of the *ad hoc* company of actors, operetta singers and cabaret artists who had gathered around Brecht: Peter Lorre, Oskar Homolka, Carola Neher, Helene Weigel, Ernst Busch, Kurt Gerron, Harald Paulsen, Theo Lingen, Kate Kühl, and, of course, Lotte Lenya. Most were indeed actors first, with razor-edged diction, but almost all of them could also really sing; the theatrical system required such versatility, and the customary training of actors had nurtured it. Paulsen, for example, took over Tauber's roles in Lehar, and Weill chose Ernst Busch for the *Heldentenor* role in Weill's *Der Silbersee*. Carola Neher and the young Lenya were both soprano songbirds with voices aptly described by Ernst Bloch's characterisation of Lenya's – 'sweet, high,

---

[28]*Arbeitsjournal*, vol. 1, 2 February 1941. In his notes to *Mahagonny*, Brecht had asserted that 'the orchestral apparatus needs to be cut down to thirty specialists or less'.
[29]Because often the performer is 'reporting' rather than experiencing first-hand, many of Brecht's songs may be sung interchangeably by various characters within a given play or even in different plays. Thus, at different times in the run of the original production of the *Threepenny Opera*, Polly and Lucy each sang the 'Barbara-Song', and in later years Lenya appropriated 'Pirate Jenny' for Jenny's role.

light, dangerous, cool, with the radiance of the crescent moon'. *The Threepenny Opera's* sensational popularity had propelled many members of that loose collective into the recording studio: the songs appeared on more than forty discs with twenty different labels. A large selection of these shellac recordings have now been re-released (Capriccio CD 10346 and 10347); that is as close as we can come to sampling the original pudding, a bit of *echt* Brechtian performance practice.

But in the wake of posthumous interpreters of Brecht ranging from the composers Cerha, Henze and Berio to singers as diverse as David Bowie, Robyn Archer, Dietrich Fischer-Dieskau, Dagmar Krause, Teresa Stratas, Tom Waits and Sting, 'Brechtian' has now come to mean something very different from what would have been recognised as such in performances of the Weimar period. A 'performance tradition' based on theory post-dating the works in question, with precepts from a later period of Brecht's career misapplied to Works from an earlier, is now routinely invoked as a standard for the entire Brecht canon and, because of his paradigmatic stature, beyond. Whereas 'Brechtian' originally denoted an unsentimental, 'cool', repertorial, *sachlich* presentation, closely allied to the matter-of-fact directness of popular singers and cabaret artists, it was nonetheless musically accurate. Now, however, by privileging *ex post facto* theory over the musical demands of the works themselves, a 'Brechtian' approach has been extended to repertoire, most notably to some of the Weill–Brecht pieces, which barely survive such treatment. The common practice of transposing songs down to actresses' speaking registers produces the now *de rigueur* Brechtian bark reminiscent of Brecht's widow Weigel. High notes are frequently replaced or rendered as *Sprechstimme*, musical subtleties ignored, the youthful vulnerability that once balanced textual toughness lost. Rearranging scores for smaller ensembles has eliminated much of the play among personas and inhibited the music's counterpoint to the lyric; the text may seem to win, but the song certainly loses.

The enforced orthodoxy of prevailing 'Brechtian' performance practice has diminished the poet as much as 'his' composers, for Brecht's inimitable voice is never truer, more telling or more powerful than when competing for cohabitation with worthy music sung by performers capable of meeting the particular challenges it presents. Only when the wide range of music associated with Brecht has been performed and recorded accurately will it be possible to 'prove the pudding', to test theory against practice and assess fairly the full impact of Brecht's contradictory musical impulses and ideas.

# Brecht in the Information Age

# CHAPTER EIGHTEEN

# Bertolt Brecht and the Internet

## DOROTHEE OSTMEIER

The advent of new technologies challenges the ethical, social and legal ideologies of society. At the beginning of the 21st century it is the World Wide Web with its infinite possibilities for the exchange of information which has called the commercial conventions of the capitalist society into question. Arguably the most visible challenge to date arose during the last year with the advent of software facilitating exchange of MP3 music files over the Internet without payment to copyright holders. The explosive popularity of the idea led in short order to a lawsuit filed by A&M Records in December 1999 'against Napster, Inc., an Internet start up'.[1] The suit, backed by the Recording Industry Association of America (RIAA) and joined by seventeen record companies, demanded that Napster cease operation. The RIAA's lawsuit provoked diverse discussions in court, in the popular press and on the Internet centering on conflicts between the profit-driven interests of the recording industry and the interests of its artists and customers who criticize the industry's criteria and business strategies for the production, distribution and marketing of music. While some object to the exchange of music without payment others focus their criticism on the industry. Popular artists Courtney Love and Prince,[2] for example, sharply disparage the music industry's bolstering of consumerism at the expense of the music lovers' demand for artistic productions. They complain that the marketing and packaging of their work as 'disposable entertainment' (Prince 1) undermines its artistic merit, especially when, for example, single songs are taken from their original albums in order to attract buyers to an otherwise 'poor selection of forgettable songs' (Prince 2).[3]

---

Dorothee Ostmeier, 'Bertolt Brecht and the Internet', in Maarten van Dijk et al. (eds.), *The Brecht Yearbook / Das Brecht-Jahrbuch*, 26 (2001), pp. 234–55.

[1] 'Full text of Judge Patel's Ruling.' n.d.: 2. http://news.cnet.com/News/Pages/Special/Napster/napster_patel.html
[2] Courtney Love. 'Courtney Love does the math.' http://www.salon.com/tech/feature/2000/06/14/love/print.html
Prince. '4 [sic]The Love Of Music. 2 Very Different Approaches.' http://www.npgonlineltd.com/
[3] At present, October 2000, the controversy has spread and also involves software companies, book publishers, radio and film industries which fear to lose business to software providers who pirate their services and offer them for free. Charles C. Mann reports that he accessed 'Pamela Anderson Video', computer software, French television shows, 'Yo Yo Ma's latest version of the Bach solo-cello suites', 'cheat files for a computer game named "Obsidian"', 'a plain text copy of *Riding the Bullet*', 'and a preliminary version of a DivX software kit for ripping and playing DVDs' ('The Heavenly Jukebox'. *The Atlantic Monthly*, September 2000, 58–59). On the other hand,

These criticisms echo Bertolt Brecht's 1930 fight against the then-fledgling film industry's controlling power when the Nero film company altered plot and substance of *Die Dreigroschenoper* without consulting him. Claiming that the company had ignored parts of the contract with him Brecht, the author, filed a lawsuit against the company on 30 September 1930, shortly after the film production had started on 19 September 1930.

As in the Napster case the conflicts between the interests of the industry and the avantgarde were based on issues of intellectual property, censorship,[4] and the relationship between artists, art and its patrons and audience. Brecht objected to the industry's focus on commercial success and its demotion of the audience to customers; Napster provided software which freed the customers from their dependence on the industry's music selections. I discuss Napster here as an avantgarde business which – founded by a college student – collected no revenues and charged its clientele no fees[5] before it started to collaborate with the German media giant Bertelsmann October 31, 2000.

This essay relates the controversies about the use of the Internet technology to debates of the late 1920s and early 1930s, especially to discussions centering on Bertolt Brecht's lawsuit against Nero Film Company. Brecht uses his report and commentary about the lawsuit in his essay *Der Dreigroschenprozeß* – written in spring and summer 1931 and published in January 1932 – as a means to reflect on the relation between the commercial and aesthetic aspects of film production. After examining the social activism of the 'Prozeß' I will zero in on Brecht's revision of the terms *Apparat*, *Kollektiv* and *Ware* and demonstrate how he associates their economic and social connotations with his aesthetic concerns. He rejects the bourgeois aspects of these terms and explores their innovative potential for reforming film production in the Weimar Republic. The social structures inherent in the use of film technology become the model for the production of anti-bourgeois art. This new definition offers criteria for the re-evaluation of avant-garde film and media theories of his time, and I will investigate how these criteria offer new perspectives on the current debates shaping the Internet.

Brecht studied Marx' *Das Kapital* in 1928, but this as well as the few other texts by Marx and Engels, which had been edited before 1933, did not present systematic ideas about the fundamental structures of proletarian art and film (Gallas 21-22). Thus it fell to the proletarian revolutionary authors – who were organized in the 'Bund proletarisch-revolutionärer Schrifteteller' (BPRS)[6] founded in 1928 – to evaluate and reform the established artistic genres and to explore their capacity to revolutionize

---

the physicians association support Napster because they are concerned about the lawsuit's restriction of the free flow of information.
[4]In the Napster case issues of censorship were indirectly raised by the industry's choice of the artists it marketed.
[5]"Full text of Judge Patel's Ruling', 4.
[6]The 'Bund proletarisch-revolutionärer Schriftsteller'(BPRS) had been founded in October 1928 to address questions about the relationship between modern art forms – inner monologues, epic theater, twelve tone music etc. – and class consciousness. Are these art forms expressions of class consciousness or of modern communication and reproduction techniques and the demands of their new audiences? (Helga Gallas, *Marxistische Literaturtheorie. Kontroversen im Bund proletarisch-revolutionärer Schriftsteller* (Frankfurt/ M.: Roter Stern, 1978), 96, 109–10). Helga Gallas points out that Bertolt Brecht, Walter Benjamin and Hanns Eisler as members of the BPRS represent unique positions in their approach to Marxist aesthetic theory. They were ignored or sharply attacked by G. Lukács, the most articulate representative of the BPRS and its journal *Die Linkskurve*, which represented the position of the RAPP (Gallas 96, 109–10). H. Gallas argues that the controversies between the revolutionary authors of the Weimar period, the proletarian as well as bourgeois authors, anticipated the controversies of the *Expressionismus Debatte*, which arose after 1933 between the exiles in the Moscow journal Das Wort (18–30).

bourgeois society. Between 1927 and 1932 Brecht extended his reformation of poetic and theatrical forms to include also radio theory and film. *Der Dreigroschenprozeß*[7] is Brecht's first far-reaching text about film which links social issues to film theory before he produced *Kuhle Wampe* between August 1931 and February 1932 together with Ernst Ottwald and Slatan Dudow.

Brecht lost the suit against Nero and chose not to appeal. Soon thereafter he reviewed the proceedings critically in *Der Dreigroschenprozeß*. The text is designed as a montage of legal documents, of newspaper articles, interpersed with Brecht's commentary: He describes first the proceedings of the actual lawsuit, then quotes in chronological order miscellaneous excerpts from newspaper articles which outline the issues raised by the suit, and finally he offers his own commentary reflecting on his experiences with the bourgeois legal system and its depiction in newspapers and journals. The montage of conflicting newspaper excerpts confronts the reader with a conglomeration of varying perspectives.[8] Then Brecht reveals to the reader that such conflicting statements all stem from the same ideological prejudices:[9]

> Die ideologische Schizophrenie des Kleinbürgers, der die Zeitungen schreibt, zeigt sich in dem Beisammensein verschiedener Vorstellungskreise ... Er hat mindestens zwei Vorstellungen zu einer Sache: Die eine bezieht er aus der großen bürgerlichen Idealität, welche das Individuum, die Gerechtigkeit, Freiheit und so weiter gegen die Wirklichkeit durchsetzen wird, die andere aus der Wirklichkeit selber. ...
>
> (182–83)

Undermining the independence of each newspaper and author, he treats all journalists alike as 'Kleinbürger', as representatives of bourgeois thought. The aggressiveness of Brecht's attack becomes apparent when he labels besides Dr. Frankfurter, Nero's lawyer, also Siegfried Kracauer – since 1921 an editor for the 'Feuilleton' of the renowned leftist *Frankfurter Zeitung* – members of the petite bourgeois class. Promoting an ivory-tower-aestheticism Dr. Frankfurter discourages collaboration between artists and film industry in order to protect their artistic work from commercialization. Kracauer, in contrast, encourages the industry to employ artists in order to refine film.[10] Both authors insert a

---

[7] Bertolt Brecht. 'Der Dreigroschenprozeß. Ein soziologisches Experiment.' *Gesammelte Werke in 20 Bänden*, ed. Suhrkamp Verlag in Zusammenarbeit mit Elisabeth Hauptmann, 18 (Frankfurt/M.: Suhrkamp, 1967): 139–209. (Page numbers of references to this essay are given parenthetically in the text; references to this edition are cited as GW, Gesammelte Werke).

[8] Brecht quotes from *Neue Zeit des Westens, Berliner Tageblatt, B.Z. am Mittag, Frankfurter Zeitung*, and from film journals *Der Film, Der Scheinwerfer*, et al.

[9] Brecht views the tension between the diverse opinions and the similarity of their underlying ideology as most humorous: 'Die Pressestimmen sind im großen und ganzen chronologisch geordnet, aber die Anordnung zieht ihren Humor daraus, daß die Auszüge aus verschiedenen Zeitungen so stehen, wie sie auch in einer einzigen hätten stehen können' (182).

[10] In a *Frankfurter Zeitung* article from 18 April 1931 (160), Siegfried Kracauer grants film producers the right to view art as service to the capitalist enterprise: 'Sie [die Produzenten] brauchten meinetwegen nichts von Kunst zu verstehen, aber sie müßten imstande sein, ihren Nutzwert einzukalkulieren' (160). As long as art refines the film ('veredeln,' 160) the film functions only as a technological device for the dissemination of bourgeois art. The apparatus is not seen as an independent and detached artistic medium. It is raped by art, Brecht says (161). Bourgeois art is so dogmatic and inflexible that it kills the inventive functions (Brecht/Benjamin) of new technology. Satirically Brecht equates the commercial interests of the movie theater owners with those of the 'Fueilletonisten' calling them 'Physiker and Metaphysiker' of 'Publikumsgeschmack'. Brecht often does not

typically bourgeois art-film dichotomy: art as an idealistic, film as a realistic project, which involves industrial production and marketing. Brecht claims: 'Selbst unsere Freunde von links fanden den Prozeß überflüssig' (183). Since they argue within the parameters of the pre-established ideological system Brecht labels these authors a 'Kollektiv' in furthering the proletarization of society:

> Hier ist ein Kollektiv an der Arbeit, das den Einzelteil an der Produktion unkenntlich macht. Wodurch wird es gebildet? Es wird durch den Klassenkampf gebildet. Durch die gemeinsame Arbeit des Proletarisierens und das gemeinsame Schicksal des Proletarisiertwerdens.
>
> (182)

Between 1929 and 1933 'collectivation' was central for the policies of the Soviet government which rigorously pursued the transformation of traditional agriculture. 'The peasantry were forced to give up their individual farms and join large collective farms (kolkhozy).'[11] While this was considered an innovative economic strategy at the time, Brecht ironically utilizes the term 'collective' to describe the bourgeois press' traditional system of argumentation. He refers to its reactionary double standard, the split between idealism ('bürgerliche Idealität') and realism ('Wirklichkeit'), present in Kracauer's and Frankfurter's views which sustain the capitalist economy of the bourgeois system.[12]

Brecht views the representatives of the Weimar judiciary as members of this reactionary collective. Winning or losing the lawsuit was not his main purpose. He filed the suit in order to provoke the legal and journalistic institutions into action and thereby to demonstrate their ideological bias:

> Man konnte ihn nicht von Anfang bis Ende mit dem Bestreben führen, ihn zu gewinnen, oder dem Bestreben, ihn zu verlieren – er hätte dann nichts ergeben. Man mußte sich ihm anvertrauen und lediglich darauf bauen, daß er in irgendeiner Weise etwas Klarheit über die Art und Weise, wie heute geistige Dinge sich materiell umsetzen, schaffen würde.
>
> (153)

Subjecting Weimar jurisdiction to his analysis and evaluation, Brecht's investigation demonstrates the limits of bourgeois concepts of art, film and commerce which underlie the rulings and do not reconcile artistic with commercial, intellectual with materialistic interests. Thus the title of the essay 'Prozeß' has three different meanings or at least connotations. First of all, it refers to the actual lawsuit, secondly to the public thought

---

identify the authors of the introductory quotes of his sub-chapters, he mostly refers to the journals in general. In regard to the *Frankfurter Zeitung* he only mentions Dr. Frankfurter, the lawyer of Nero, by name. But since the publishers of *Große kommentierte Berliner und Frankfurter Ausgabe* have identified the quote Brecht's criticism of the 'Feuilletonisten' seems to be indirectly addressed to Kracauer. Bertolt Brecht. *Schriften I. Große kommentierte Berliner und Frankfurter Ausgabe*. 21, ed. Werner Hecht, Jan Knopf, Werner Mittenzwei, Klaus Detlef Müller (Berlin, Weimar: Aufbau; Frankfurt/M.: Suhrkamp 1992), 783. (Quoted as GBA).

[11]'Collectivization'. Britannica.com. 1 December 2000. http://www.britannica.com

[12]Brecht dismisses the art-film dichotomy as typically bourgeois and develops an alternative approach: he introduces film as art and modern art as filmic arguing that art in the time of cinematography forfeits all conventional elitist and sublime connotations. Walter Benjamin explores this topic further in 1935 when he scrutinizes the rise of fascism as resulting from the discrepancy between technological advancement and the limits of bourgeois ideology in 'Das Kunstwerk im Zeitalter seiner technischen Reproduzierbarkeit'.

processes and debates stimulated by the suit, and thirdly to Brecht's critical examination of the ruling's underlying ideology. His investigation is not only a theoretical and analytical endeavor – as investigator himself Brecht plays an active role by challenging the constituents of the social fabric. Indeed, he actually disputes the legality of Nero's business strategies, the legal system which promotes them and the journalism which discusses them. His essay sets an example for cultural criticism in that it does not only represent only the theoretical endeavor of a single author and is not only content-oriented. As an 'experiment' it presents diverse social processes before analyzing their results. The subtitle of the treatise defines this 'Prozeß' as 'soziologisches Experiment'. The social reality – and not a theory – becomes the object of the investigation. For Brecht, cultural theory is cultural practice: The law suit 'schafft Klarheit'. He insists:

> es hat nämlich keinerlei Aussicht auf Erfolg, sich eine bestimmte 'Kultur' auszudenken, zu der man die Realität überreden will. Durch solche Deduktionen nimmt man sich nur die Möglichkeit, das Funktionieren der Realität zu begreifen und so herauszufinden, was an dem schon Vorgehenden revolutionäre und was reaktionäre Tendenzen sind. Das Experiment mobilisiert die Widersprüche dieser Art in den Dingen und Vorgängen und hält den Vorgang selbst während der Untersuchung in Gang.
>
> (208)

Contemplation of culture only abstracts from reality, applies its theories without being engaged in it. Brecht calls his sociological experiment an expression of a scientific method which analyzes and reviews generally unnoticed social processes.[13] Reflecting on the verb 'begreifen' he privileges its literal over its abstract connotations. 'Das Begreifen ... ist ein Griffe finden' (209). Definitions should make their substance 'handlich' (207) and render a 'Zugriff' and 'Handhabung des Stoffes' (207). As the conductor of the experiment Brecht is affected by its outcome. At each stage of the proceedings he has to modify his action. 'Begreifen' and 'Griffe finden' implies risk taking. This is especially visible when he first rejects a settlement fee offered by Nero's lawyer, arguing: 'Es handelt sich nicht um die materielle Seite' (145). Only after the ruling does he accept Nero's offer to cover the legal fees and to return the filming rights to him. The acceptance of the money does not undermine his goal to expose Weimar's reactionary legal system at this time.[14]

This avant-garde social activism was inspired by his encounter with the Russian poet, author and theoretician of art, Sergei Tretiakov whom Brecht's poem 'Ist das Volk unfehlbar?' calls 'Mein Lehrer'.[15] Walter Benjamin quotes Tretiakov as one of the most radical anti-bourgeois authors. In 'Der Autor als Produzent' (April 1934)(686) he writes:

---

[13]This social activism can function as an early very practical example for the critical 'Haltung' which Brecht demands later from the audience in his theater. In *Kleines Organon für das Theater* he writes: 'Welches ist die produktive Haltung gegenüber der Natur und der Gesellschaft, die wir Kinder eines wissenschaftlichen Zeitalters in unserem Theater vergnüglich einnehmen wollen? Die Haltung ist eine kritische' (GW 16, 671).

[14]Ludwig Marcuse accuses Brecht of covering up his financial interests in the lawsuit (see 'Kommentar' in GBA 21, 779). My approach does not speculate about Brecht's personal intentions, it analyzes his text *Der Dreigroschenprozeß* as a new innovative genre for his social criticism.

[15]Brecht knew Tretiakov at least by April 1930, but probably by 1929. Fritz Mierau argues that Brecht re-edited Tretiakov's play *Ich will ein Kind haben* in 1929 and that this was the only Soviet play which interested Brecht. (Fritz Mierau, 'Sergej Tret'jakov and Bertolt Brecht. Das Produktionsstück, *Ich will ein Kind haben*' (Russian title). *Zeitschrift für Slawistik* 20.2 (1975): 226–41, and F.M., *Erfindung und Korrektur. Tretjakows Ästhetik der Operativität* (Berlin: Akademie Verlag, 1972), 33, 278 Anm. 52. As author of the socialist revolution Tretiakov was

Als 1928 in der Epoche der totalen Kollektivierung der Landwirtschaft die Parole: 'Schriftsteller in die Kolchose!' ausgegeben wurde, fuhr Tretjakow nach der Kommune 'Kommunistischer Leuchtturm' und nahm dort ... folgende Arbeiten in Angriff: Einberufung von Massenmeetings; ... Inspektion von Lesesälen, Schaffung von Wandzeitungen und Leitung der Kolchos-Zeitung; Berichterstattung an die Moskauer Zeitungen. ...[16]

(686–87)

Tretiakov transferred his poetic competence to organizing the communal life of the kolkhos. The title 'Schriftsteller in die Kolchose!'[17] quotes the official Moscow formula which Tretiakov actually followed when he left Moscow in 1928.[18] In his lecture 'Der Schriftsteller und das sozialistische Dorf' presented in Berlin to the 'Gesellschaft der Freunde des Neuen Rußland' on January 21, 1931, Tretiakov describes his experiences as 'ständiger Mitarbeiter im Rat des Kolchos, Leiter der Bildungsarbeit' by outlining his concept of the 'operierenden Schriftsteller' and of 'faktographische Literatur'. He insists that – in order to change the social reality in the kolkhoz – new genres have to be explored and that the author must be de-professionalized:

Operative Beziehungen nenne ich die Teilnahme am Leben des Stoffes selbst. Grob gesagt: eine wichtige Sache auszudenken – ist belletristischer Novellismus; eine

---

invited for a lecture tour to Germany in December 1930 where he was already well known through performances of his piece *Brülle China* by the Meyerhold Theater in Moscow (Ingrid Belke, 'Siegfried Krakauer als Beobachter der jungen Sowjetunion'. In *Siegfried Krakauer. Neue Interpretationen* ed. Michael Kessler and Thomas Y. Levin (Tübingen: Stauffenburg 1990), 17–38. Brecht defended the performance in a fragmentary piece in April 1930 (GW 15:204–5) and introduced Tretiakov's presentation 'Der neue Typus des Schriftstellers' for the Berliner *Internationale Tribüne* in April 19, 1931 (Belke 30). The friendship between the two authors is evidenced by the exchange of letters and other texts. In 1976 F. Mierau published the letters Tretjakov sent to Brecht between 1933 and 1937. See F. Mierau, *Erfindung und Korrektur*, 258–72. Only three of Brecht's letters to Tretlakov have survived (GBA 28:357, 370, 398–99). In a letter of May 27, 1934 (Mierau 262), Tretiakov mentions the publication of his translations of Brecht's epic dramas, and in the same year he publishes his essay 'Bert Brecht' in *Internationales Theater*. (Sergei Tretiakov, 'Bert Brecht', in *Die Arbeit des Schriftstellers. Aufsätze, Reportagen, Porträts*, ed. Heiner Boehncke, tr. Karla Hielscher (Reinbek bei Hamburg: Rowohlt, 1972), 146–58). About the similarity between Brecht's and Tretiakov's avantgardistic social realism see Heiner Boehnke 'Nachwort', 199–200.

[16]Walter Benjamin, 'Der Autor als Produzent'. *Gesammelte Schriften* 2.2, ed. Rolf Tiedemann, Hermann Schweppenhäuser (Frankfurt/.M: Suhrkamp, 1980), 686, 687. Benjamin links Tretiakov's to Brecht's agenda utilizing the vocabulary of both authors. Besides Brecht he also refers to the work of Eisler (694), John Heartfield (693), and Aragon (700) and distinguishes these intellectuals of the radical left from more conservative ones, as for example, from Heinrich Mann, Döblin, Tucholsky, etc., who thematize the revolution but do not change the traditional bourgeois genres. Fritz Mierau explains: 'Benjamin reagierte damit auf den aktuellen deutschen Streit um die Rolle der Zeitung' and names Rudolf Borchart and Gottfried Benn as other opponents of Benjamin's agenda.(31)

[17]Sergei Tretjakov, '"Schriftsteller in die Kolchose!" *Die Arbeit des Schriftstellers. Aufsätze Reportagen Porträts*, 103–10.

[18]Belke, 31. Tretiakov's talks and essays about his experiences point out the discrepancy between the official instructions for his mission and the reality of his work. The conflicting instructions see the writer either as informant or as psychologizing realist. They either demand – 'Beobachtet vor allen Dingen, wie die Kolchose wirtschaften. Den Zügen des Alltagslebens schenkt keine Beachtung. Das Alltagsleben ist eine zweitrangige, abgeleitete Erscheinung' – or they ask, 'Von Wirtschaft habt ihr sowieso keinen Schimmer, Brüder von der Feder ... Schreibt von lebendigen Menschen", ihren Wünschen, Gedanken, Erlebnissen. Gebt ein Bild des Alltags' (Tretiakov, 103).

wichtige Sache zu finden - ist die Reportage; eine wichtige Sache aufzubauen – ist Operativismus. ... Der Arbeiter am Sozialismus, mit literarischem Können ausgerüstet – das ist der Ausgangspunkt der neuen Literatur. Der berufsmäßige Schriftsteller gliedert sich organisch in die Aufbauarbeit ein und lernt nicht nur die Kunst, das Leben zu konterfeien, sondern auch das Leben zu verändern.

('Der Schriftsteller und das sozialistische Dorf', 120–21)

With this turn against such classic realist authors as Tolstoi, Dostoyevski – strongly supported and canonized as 'schöne Literatur' by the 'Russische Assoziation proletarischer Arbeiter' (RAPP, 1928–1932),[19] Tretiakov does not distinguish between the fictional and biographical subject. Promoting the art of political and/or social intervention, 'utilitäre Produktionskunst' (Trommler 592), he initiated the realism of the socialist avant-garde artist who explores social processes by mingling with society and utilizing his art to innovate, provoke or challenge given conditions.[20] Aesthetization or thematization of social conflicts is not sufficient; art has to accentuate its pragmatic edge.

Where Tretiakov cultivates the everyday life in the Russian kolkhoz[21] Brecht revolutionizes German political art. As widely discussed in the scholarship of the last thirty years Brecht not only propagates revolutionary themes but also actively reinvents and rearranges the setting and functions of the bourgeois theater in order to engage the audience through epic devices into the theatrical process or to turn the audience into acting participants in the 'Lehrstück'.[22] H.L. Gruman reports that 'Brecht's 1930 Production of *Die Maßnahme* [...] used the audience as an active "Control Chorus".' This collaboration between actors, producer and audience carries on the tradition of the leftist collective theater movement in Weimar Germany (1928-1933) which was inspired by Soviet proletarianism and was further developed by the Piscator-Kollektiv founded in November 1929 after the Piscator Bühne closed.[23] All initiatives shared the

---

[19]See Heiner Boehncke, 'Nachwort', 193.
[20]Tretjakow, 'Woher und Wohin?' Quoted in Heiner Böhncke, 'Nachwort', 200.
[21]Walter Benjamin refers besides Sergei Tretjakov to Bertolt Brecht as an author whose work does not only present an ideology but also is actively involved in altering and challenging its institutional structures: 'Er [Brecht] hat als erster an den Intellektuellen die weittragende Forderung erhoben: den Produktionsapparat nicht zu beliefern, ohne ihn zugleich, nach Maßgabe des Möglichen, im Sinne des Sozialismus zu verändern' (Walter Benjamin, 'Der Autor als Produzent', 691). Benjamin as well as Tretiakov in his short sketch 'Bert Brecht' refer to Brecht's theater, especially to *Die Maßnahme*, as example, but never to the *Dreigroschenprozeß*.
[22]In 'Anmerkung [zu den Lehrstücken]' (first published in 1957) Brecht writes that the *Lehrstücke* were designed as 'Stücke, die für die *Darstellenden* lehrhaft sind. Sie benötigen so kein Publikum' (GW, 17:1035). See also Klaus Dieter Krabiel, *Brecht's Lehrstücke: Entstehung und Entwicklung eines Spieltyps* (Stuttgart and Weimar: Metzler, 1993). Also Reiner Steinweg ed., *Auf Anregung Bertolt Brechts: Lehrstücke mit Schülern, Arbeitern, Theaterleuten* (Frankfurt/M.: Suhrkamp, 1978), and *Das Lehrstück. Brechts Theorie einer politisch-ästhetischen Erziehung.* (Stuttgart: Metzler, 1972).
[23]Harris L. Grumann gives a short introduction to the tradition of the Weimar theater collectives in 'The Piscator-Kollektiv: Form and Content in the Political Theater'. See *Brecht: Performance. Brecht: Aufführung. The Brecht Yearbook* 13, 1984. 21–37, 22. In contradiction to Joel Schechter ('Beyond Brecht: New Authors, New Spectators.' *The Brecht Yearbook* 11 [1982]), who stresses Brecht's innovative contributions to audience-participation theater Gruman views Brecht merely as an important recorder of the Piscator-Kollektiv's experiments. Gruman 36, Footnote 24. See also the comprehensive and detailed documentation *Theater der Kollektive Proletarisch-revolutionäres Berufstheater in Deutschland 1928-1933 Stücke, Dokumente, Studien*, ed. Ludwig Hoffmann (Berlin: Henschelverlag, 1980). See also D. Ostmeier's short summary of the controversies about how Brecht's learning plays engage actors and audiences: Dorothee Ostmeier, 'The Rhetorics of Erasure:

common goal to subvert the bourgeois theater's aura of high culture. Brecht transposes this motivation into his actual theatrical experiments, his theater theory and his clearly directed and aggressive attack on the representatives of legal and public institutions in *Dreigroschenprozeß*.[24] The actual Dreigroschenprozeß uses legal means to stir up a public debate before the essay, 'Der Dreigroschenprozeß', analyzes the presentation of these discussions of the legal system's strategies and values in journals and newpapers. Here Brecht applies Tretiakov's approach to let the otherwise silent reality speak (Knopf 179) by uncovering the obliviousness of the cultural politics of conservative and leftist intellectuals.

His theoretical writings about theater – 'Anmerkungen zur Oper "Aufstieg und Fall der Stadt Mahagonny"'[25] – and film are linked by his insertion of economic and technological vocabulary in the discussion. Viewing opera, 'Schaubühne' and journalism as 'Produktionsapparate' Brecht reveals to their artists, writers, journalists that they are not, as they imagine, in control of the apparatus; rather, the economically motivated apparatus is in control of their work. They are unknowingly pushed in the role of suppliers and/or contractors:

> Ihre Produktion gewinnt Lieferantencharakter. Es entsteht ein Wertbegriff, der die Verwertung zur Grundlage hat. Und dies ergibt allgemein den Usus, jedes Kunstwerk auf seine Eignung für den Apparat, niemals aber den Apparat auf seine Eignung für das Kunstwerk hin zu überprüfen.
>
> (1005)

Subjecting art to their economic interests, cultural institutions commodify it, censor it, and control its market value. This is a vivid example of the proletarization of artists by capitalist ventures. We will see later that this argument is still used today by popular artists against their producers.

Brecht explores the potentials of the film genre by presenting film as an ideal alternative to the backward opera and by uncovering innovative connotations of the terms 'apparatus', 'collective' and 'commodity'. The social apparatus of the opera has a long-standing tradition of separation between composer and institution, since the institution uses the composer's work as a commodity.[26] As Brecht experienced with

---

Cloud and Moon in Brecht's Poetic and Political Texts of the Twenties and Early Thirties'. *German Studies Review* 23 (May 2000): 276.

[24]The theatrical and theoretical re-evaluation of the conventional opera paves the way for the attack on the representatives of legal and public institutions in 'Dreigroschenprozeß'. Brecht suggests that his opera *Aufstieg und Fall der Stadt Mahagonny* – composed in 1929 after *Die Dreigroschenoper* and before the actual law suit against Nero-Film AG – thematizes and satirizes its own genre, the irrational, culinary and pleasurable aspects emphasized by the musical setting of each opera. *Mahagonny* grotesquely demonstrates how pleasure as the essence of the opera turns into a commodity. 'Sie [die kulinarische Oper] war ein Genußmittel, lange bevor sie eine Ware war' (GW 17:1006). *Mahagonny* employs anti-aesthetic means to sabotage the conventional opera's aestheticism.

[25]Brecht published the 'Anmerkungen' in the second volume of his journal *Versuche* (1930) before *Der Dreigroschenprozeß* which appeared together with the filmscript *Die Beule* in the subsequent third volume Wolfgang Gersch describes Brecht's radically sharpened attack on the conditions of the bourgeois society in *Die Beule*. See Wolfgang Gersch, *Film bei Brecht* (München: Hanser, 1975), 48–58.

[26]As a counterexample Brecht refers to Richard Wagner's operas as a 'Gesamtkunstwerk' which serve reactionary purposes: they use modern technology to arrange the spectacle of the stage and reduce the ideological content to its pleasurable aspects. Brecht seems not to be familiar with or ignores alternative concepts of the

the sale of his film script this is also true for the cinema: producers buy filmscripts and assume all rights to manipulate them. The sale encompasses the intellectual property of the artist.[27]

Brecht's term 'neue Apparate' for film technology stresses his alteration of the concept 'Apparat' by distinguishing the inventive capacity of the camera from its reactionary use by the ignorant entertainment industry. Contrasting the 'Schöpfungen der Apparate' (159) with those of bourgeois art he subverts their closed ideological concepts of the omniscient and all-pervading author and the psychology of characters. He emphasizes that films, especially silent films, view persons from an external perspective. Characters are controlled by social acts, 'menschliche Handlungen' and 'gesellschaftliche Prozesse', and not by their individual psyche. Thus the concept of type replaces that of characters.[28] Film technology becomes the paradigm for Brecht's art criticism. Neither epic nor dramatic art is immune from the influence of film. Its construction of reality, of 'Künstliches', 'Gestelltes' (162), undermines the mimetism of the bourgois novel, drama and film. Twice Brecht attacks Thomas Mann's essay 'Über den Film'[29] and its promotion of 'lebenswahres und wirklichkeitsechtes szenisch-mimisches Erfindungsdetail' in film (169) and its exclusion of the apparatus from the definition of art and humanity (207). Appropriating Marx' definition of man as toolmaking animal (207)[30], Brecht inscribes mechanistic vocabulary in the definition of man and replaces the individual 'Erlebnis' by the 'Verdinglichung der menschlichen Beziehungen' (161). 'Die eigentliche Realität ist in die Funktionale gerutscht', Brecht argues (161).[31] The terms 'Verdinglichung', and 'Funktionale' link his views on film and his anti-aesthetic to his social and economic considerations. Freeing the term 'apparatus' from being vaguely used as a metaphor for the functions of bourgeois institutions ('Produktionsapparate') and from being loaded

---

'Gesamtkunstwerk' which promote collaboration of the artists and the arts as, for example, Wassily Kandinsky's approach. Of course, Kandinsky's abstract aestheticism does not address social or political concerns.

[27]Brecht argues that the genre of film should annihilate such a violation: 'Um mit den neuen Apparaten die Wirklichkeit zu fassen, müßte er [der Regisseur] Künstler sein, schlimmstenfalls Wirklichkeitsgenießer, aber keinesfalls Kunstgenießer, also stellt er, was einfacher ist, mit ihnen "Kunst" her, die bekannte, erprobte, die Ware. Er hat den Ruf eines geschmackvollen Arrangeurs, es heißt: er "versteht etwas von Kunst"! als ob man von Kunst etwas verstehen könnte, ohne von der Wirklichkeit etwas zu verstehen! Und hier fungiert als Wirklichkeit gleichzeitig mit dem Stoff der Apparat. Eine solche Situation schaffte den neuen Apparaten nicht die Möglichkeiten, die für sie an sich bestünden'. (161)

[28]The first part of *Kuhle Wampe* – independently produced by Brecht, Slatan Dudow and Hanns Eisler between summer and spring 1931/1932 – presents the suicide of an unemployed young man, portraying the economic disaster of the lower classes after the reduction of unemployment benefits for young people by Brüning. The success of this typification became obvious when a censor complained: 'Ihr Arbeitsloser ist kein richtiges Individuum, kein Mensch aus Fleisch und Blut ... Er ist ganz oberflächlich gezeichnet ... aber die Folgen sind politischer Natur und zwingen mich, Einspruch gegen die Zulassung Ihres Filmes zu erheben. Ihr Film hat die Tendenz, den Selbstmord als typisch hinzustellen ... als Schicksal einer ganzen Klasse' (Bertold Brecht. 'Kleiner Beitrag zum Realismus.' Bertolt Brecht, *Kuhle Wampe. Protokoll des Films und Materialien*, ed. W. Cersch, W. Hecht (Frankfurt/M: Suhrkamp 1969), 93–96).

[29]*Schünemann's Monatshefte*, August 1928 (quoted, in GBA 21:787).

[30]See reference in GBA 21:787.

[31]Brecht introduces the general difference between mimetic bourgeois art and anti-realist film art without detailing the technical aspects as, for example, Rudolf Arnheim does in 'Film als Kunst' (1932) or without distinguishing his concepts of film from the expressionist fantasies, abstract montages, or experimental films of the 1920s. He also does not outline a list of stereotypical film motifs which represent the daydreams of bourgeois ideology in Kracauer's articles for the *Frankfurter Allgemeine Zeitung* (March 11–19, 1927). See Kracauer's, *Das Ornament der Masse* (Frankfurt/M.: Suhrkamp 1977), 280.

with these institutions' ideological history, Brecht examines the social implications of the term: film technology sets social norms by demanding collaboration among its users.

> Tatsächlich sollte der Film nichts machen, was ein Kollektiv nicht machen kann ... Was für ein Kollektiv haben wir heute im Film? Das Kollektiv stellt sich zusammen aus dem Financier, den Verkäufern (Publikumsforschern), dem Regisseur, den Technikern und den Schreibern.
>
> (172)

Since the production of film is based on the close collaboration of artists and producers Brecht replaces the concepts of the author through the concept of the collective. The representatives of commercial interests are not privileged over the artists. In fact, the produced film should not indicate the contributions by single collaborators. 'Wer wünschte da nicht sofort, der Einzelanteil an der Produktion möchte unkenntlich sein?' By not insisting on individualistic or corporate financial interests the members of the film collective collaborate on a common mission to teach and to turn the audience into a collective itself. 'Tatsächlich kann ein Kollektiv nur Werke schaffen, welche aus "Publikum" Kollektive bilden können.'(173). The social requirements of the apparatus determine the strategies of production and therefore their product, the film as well as its effect on the audience.[32]

Brecht distinguishes two concepts of the collective contrasting progressive collectives which are fashioned by the social potentials of innovative technology, in this case film, with the reactionary collectives of journalists, and lawyers which are controlled by pre-given ideological values. Journalism and law sustain the bourgeois social order which the innovative film work overthrows. He discusses actual film techniques only indirectly by reference to photography. He privileges the daguerreotype over the light-sensitive cameras of his time in order to outline his ideas of innovative film techniques. 'Bei den alten lichtschwachen Apparaten kamen mehrere Ausdrücke auf die ziemlich lange belichtete Platte; so hatte man auf dem endlichen Bild einen universaleren und lebendigeren Ausdruck, auch etwas von Funktion dabei.' (174).

What promoters of light-sensitive cameras view as a disadvantage of daguerreotypes Brecht sees as their advantage: they do not imitate reality but make visible the functions of the apparatus. They become a model for his speculation about the possibilities of most modern cameras: 'Vielleicht gibt es eine Art zu photographieren, den neueren Apparaten möglich, die Gesichter zerlegt?' (174). These cameras construct new perceptions of reality and make its hidden and invisible aspects visible. As an example Brecht alludes to photographs of factories:

> Eine Photographie der Kruppwerke oder der AEG ergibt beinah nichts über diese Institute...Die Verdinglichung der menschlichen Beziehungen, also etwa die Fabrik, gibt die letzteren nicht mehr heraus. Es ist also tatsächlich 'etwas aufzubauen', etwas 'Künstliches', 'Gestelltes'. Es ist also ebenso tatsächlich Kunst nötig.
>
> (161–62)

---

[32]By privileging the collective over the individual, Brecht undermines the definition of the collective in capitalist production which attributes singular and unique works to individuals, and the common and ordinary work to mass production, that is, to say, to proletarian collectives.

Socially critical art examines and analyzes the appearance of reality, its 'Gesicht', its facade, and exposes its conditions. It deconstructs in order to construct. Brecht applies this logic also to the filming process. 'Die Filmtechnik, die nötig war, um aus dem Nichts ein Etwas zu machen, war gezwungen, vorher aus dem Etwas ein nichts zu machen.' (176). New technology defamiliarizes the ordinary and opens up new perspectives. Brecht strongly encourages producers to utilize those functions of the cameras which are least likely to produce an imitation of reality.[33]

The production of *Kuhle Wampe* serves as an example for Brecht's actualization of collective collaboration.[34] The film's visual montage of Anni Bönike's hallucinations exemplifies its capacity to construct realities hidden by mimetic realism. The retrospective record of the film taken by W. Gersch and W. Hecht lists twenty-eight shots which associate a wide array of images – sections of the sign of a gynecologist, advertisements for baby formula, cosmetics and other medicine, resignation notes, window displays of coffins, baby shoes etc. – for one and a quarter minutes. The montage literally displaces Anni's head. The script reads: 'Kindergesichter kreisen um sie. Ihr Kopf wird allmählich ausgeblendet. Es setzt eine Montage ein.'[35] The images from different social contexts indicate Anni's confusion after her boyfriend's disinterest in her pregnancy. While Anni loses control of her perception, the visual reality disintegrates into fragments. They constitute the visionary reality of the tensions, anxieties and hopes which mark Anni's uncertain state between mortality and fertility. These moments of total estrangement indicate also the beginning of her alienation and ensuing emancipation from the patriarchal social order. Thus the montage interrupts the rhythm of the *mise-en-scène*, highlighting the editor's presence and the silent reality hidden behind words and appearance.

Brecht's concept of the apparatus links technological to social advancement, and film production becomes the paradigm for his ideas for restructuring society. Around 1931 he writes:

> Der Kollektivist setzt nicht seinen Gruppenapparat gegen die Masse, sondern in die Masse hinein. Die Menschen wirken aufeinander. Die Masse besteht nur aus Agenten. Der Kollektivist sieht die Menschheit als einen Apparat, der erst teilweise organisiert ist.
>
> (Schriften 1.5:21, 518)

The bourgeois dualism between individual and the masses, idealism and reality is missing here and is replaced by the interaction between collectives and their agents. Brecht inverts the relation between 'individuum' and 'dividuum'. The individuum is defined by its external participation in several collectives; it is dividable and thus a dividuum, whereas

---

[33] In his thorough study, Wolfgang Gersch does not mention this alienating function of the camera. *Film bei Brecht* (München: Hanser 1975).
[34] Film critics in 1932 always refer to *Kuhle Wampe* as a 'Gemeinschaftsarbeit' of Bert Brecht, Ernst Ottwald, Hanns Eisler and S. Dudow (Gersch, Hecht 143, 153, 157), and Bernhard von Brentano uses most appropriately the term 'Kollektiv' when he writes: 'Fast ein Jahr lang arbeitete ein kleines Kollektiv miteinander, um neben der Industrie einen Film zu produzieren. Brecht, Dudow, Ottwald, Eisler unterstützt von den Schauspielern Thiele und Busch und einer Anzahl proletarischer Kultur- und Sportorganizatronen.' See *Bertolt Brecht. Kuhle Wampe. Protokoll des Films und Materialien*, ed. Wolfgang Gersch, Werner Hecht. (Frankfurt/M.: Suhrkamp, 1969) 162.
[35] Gersch, Hecht 40.

the collective cultivates more and more individual features.[36] Film art offers a means for this invention of the individuum: collectives produce their artistic work which gives these collectives their individual features.

In *Der Dreigroschenprozeß* Brecht goes a step further than in his learning play *Das Badener Lehrstück vom Einverständnis* (1929) which also links technological to social advancement. Having survived a crash, the aviators face their wrecked plane and invoke Lindbergh's transatlantic flight and fight for their physical survival. This fight turns into a reexamination of their ethical values and only those two aviators who adjust to the demands of a life as a collective, to the erasure of the individual's assertiveness, will be allowed to construct the plane's new motor. Their avaricious colleague – who bases his self-confidence on his individual accomplishments as aviator ignoring his collaborators[37] – is expelled: 'denn / Der uns brauchte und / Dessen wir bedurften: das / War er.' In this play the supervision of the 'Gelernte[r] Chor' precedes technological advancement. It is not the social requirement of the apparatus, in this case the motor of the plane, which demands restructuring of the group of engineers. In *Der Dreigroschenprozeß* a control such as the 'Gelernte[r] Chor' and its ideology is missing and replaced by Brecht's explication of the social and technical demands of film technology. Brecht is leaving behind his explicit insistence on ideology.[38] Instead technology becomes an instrument for social progress, for the formation of collectives.

How does Brecht deal with the commercial aspects of film production and with film as commodity? As he experienced with the sale of his manuscript to Nero, film companies automatically assume all rights to manipulate the manuscripts and can ignore any further contracts with the author. Brecht had originally asked to be actively involved in the production of the 'Dreigroschenfilm'. When he complained that Nero had not solicited his input the company tried to renegotiate this part of the contract. By losing the lawsuit against Nero Brecht found that the appropriation of intellectual property by strong financial and marketing interests is sanctioned by law (180). Manuscripts turn into commodities, and by losing all rights to their work authors are forced to leave their manuscript prey to every possible manipulation and distortion. In 1933 Brecht responds to the question 'Was, meinen Sie, macht den Erfolg der *Dreigroschenoper* aus?':

> Ich fürchte, all das, worauf es mir nicht ankam: die romantische Handlung, die Liebesgeschichte, das Musikalische. Als die 'Dreigroschenoper' Erfolg gehabt hatte, machte man einen Film daraus. Man nahm für den Film all das, was ich in dem Stück verspottet hatte, die Romantik, die Sentimentalität usw., und ließ den Spott weg. Da war der Erfolg noch größer.
>
> Und worauf wäre es Ihnen angekommen?

---

[36]In the end of 1929 he writes in his notebook: 'Was sollte über das Individuum auszusagen sein, solang wir vom Individuum aus das Massenhafte suchen. Wir werden einmal vom Massenhaften das Individuum suchen und somit aufbauen' (Bertolt Brecht. GBA 21, *Schriften* 1:359).
[37]This functions as the antithesis to the aviators in the preceding learning play *Der Ozeanflug* (1928/1929). The eight aviators speak of themselves in the first person singular as 'I' and upon their arrival in Paris they praise the 'Kameraden in den Ryan Werken von San Diego' who manufactured the motor. 'Aber meldet meinen Kameraden in den Ryanwerken von San Diego / Daß ihre Arbeit gut war.' Bertolt Brecht. GW 2, *Stücke* 2:584.
[38]About the weakened function of the 'Kontrollchor' in *Die Maßnahme* see Dorothee Ostmeier, 'The Rhetorics of Erasure: Cloud and Moon in Brecht's Poetic and Political Texts of the Twenties and Early Thirties', 282–83.

Auf die Gesellschaftskritik. Ich hatte zu zeigen versucht, daß die Ideenwelt und das Gefühlsleben der Straßenbanditen ungemein viel Aehnlichkeit mit der Ideenwelt und dem Gefühlsleben des soliden Bürgers haben.

(GBA 26, 299)[39]

This strategy of reversing the author's intentions, ironically contradicts the bourgeois ideals of the artist's intellectual property and personal freedom. The freedom of artistic production is corrupted as soon as the manuscript turns into a commodity for the film industry. Exposing this inconsistency which marks bourgeois culture Brecht demonstrates the logical necessity of redefining the term 'Ware'. He agrees that film – 'auch der künstlerischste' (167) – is a commodity, but instead of complaining about this fact he espouses his redefinition. Offering a shortcut through Marx's detailed analysis of the commodity he criticizes essayists who argue that art frees the film from falling into the status of a commodity:

Wer das meint, hat keine Ahnung von der ummodelnden Kraft des Warencharakters. Die Tatsache, daß im Kapitalismus die Welt *in der Form der Ausbeutung und der Korruption* in eine Produktion verwandelt wird, ist nicht so wichtig wie eben die Tatsache dieser *Verwandlung*.

(167)

The mobility of the commodity supercedes temporary economic systems, in this case the capitalist system. And since the process of commodification is not restricted to things but involves people as well, they lose their priviledged status; the commodity equalizes things and people. The exchange value is seen qualitatively and not in quantitative and materialistic terms. Its social implications are stressed:

Aber nur wer die Augen schließt vor der ungeheuerlichen Gewalt jenes revolutionären Prozesses, der alle Dinge dieser Welt in die Warenzirkulation reißt, ohne jede Ausnahme und ohne jede Verzögerung, kann annehmen, daß Kunstwerke irgendeiner Gattung sich hier ausschließen könnten, denn dertie-fere Sinn des Prozesses besteht ja darin, kein Ding ohne Beziehung zum andern zu lassen, sondern alle zu verknüpfen, wie er auch alle Menschen (in Form von Waren) allen Menschen ausliefert, es ist eben der Prozeß der Kommunikation schlechthin.

(168)

Brecht stresses the communal and collaborative aspects of the commodity exchange which undermine capitalist exploitation. He abstracts the social aspects of the commodity from its economic reality, suggesting that these social aspects should control the economic reality. Applied to film this reversal of emphasis challenges the profit-driven industry. The industry's financial preoccupation ignores the collaborative implications of its technology which equally subjects actors, bodies, body parts, props, and other objects to its filming and editing devices. Thus the film's production is the perfect means of establishing new alliances between things, people, film producers and audiences. Brecht introduces it as paradigm for a universal process of communication.[40]

---

[39]The commentary speculates that this text presents a fictional interview designed by Brecht in the second half of 1933 (GBA 26:595; GBA 22.2:883).
[40]Wolfgang Gersch undermines these far-reaching progressive functions of Brecht's definition of the commodity when he claims: 'Als Ware aktiv auf Bedürfnisse der Konsumenten reagierend, neue Zwecke schaffend, ist der

The concepts of the commodity and the collective overlap: as commodities people are subjected to each other, and as agents in collectives they actively affect each other. The two terms outline the passive and active attitudes which mark the social collaboration among members of collectives.

Brecht's arguments against the closed structure of the bourgeois apparatus, his concerns about intellectual property and especially his view about the communicative function of film technology anticipate a comment by Napster's CEO, Hank Barry in July 27, 2000 about the communicative functions of the Internet: 'Napster shows that the Internet is designed for file sharing'.[41] Barry refers to the eighteen months during which Napster users were able to log on to each others' hard drives in order to download music files *gratis*. This new technology allows users to form anonymous collectives which share common interests. They can access and copy popular and rare music and are not restricted by the choices offered by the record industry. This special software empowers the customers to put together their own music selections and to explore music otherwise unpublished. It also 'allows artists to communicate directly with their audiences', Courtney Love, the popular singer, argues.[42] The essay 'Courtney Love Does the Math' sharply disparages the record industry as ruthless financial and intellectual exploiters of their artists. As in Brecht's case the industry claims ownership of the artistic work, which involves nowadays not only ownership of copyrights but even the artists' name for a Web address.[43] Love concludes: 'Recording artists have essentially been giving their music away for free under the old system, so new technology that exposes our music to a larger audience can only be a good thing' (Love, 4). She encourages artists to leave the boring culture of the status quo by buying into new technology and selling music for less. Then artists might 'sell 100 million copies instead of just a million' (Love, 6) and more artists will have a chance to present and distribute their work successfully.

With the emancipation of customers and artists from their dependence on record companies Napster's software enforced a concept of the commodity which Brecht theoretically explored in the *Dreigroschenprozeß* as 'Prozeß der Kommunikation schlechthin'. (168). The commodity is freed from purely economic and arbitrary corporate interests.[44] Scott Rosenberg, *Salon*'s managing editor, distinguishes the phenomenon and idea 'Napster' from the company and argues that the idea of 'peer to peer' software will remain although individual companies might lose court battles.[45] Hank Barry claims in a interview of July 27, 2000 that 'there are over 21 million members of the Napster

---

Film für Brecht Beispiel einer funktionsbestimmten Kunst, wobei ihn in diesem Fall nur die Tatsache der Funktion, nicht aber deren soziale Sinngebung interessiert' Gersch 83.

[41]Cecile Barnes, 'Napster CEO fights for life of music' 7/27/2000. http://news.cnet.com/news/0-1014-201-23 66873-0.html

[42]'The present system keeps artists from finding an audience because it has too many artificial scarcities: limited radio promotion, limited bin space in stores and a limited number of spots on the record company roster. The digital world has no scarcities' (Love 6).

[43]'But the bill also created an exception that allows a company to take a person's name for a Web address if they create a work for hire' (Love, 3).

[44]Courtney Love lists the arbitrary 'factors that made a distributor decide to push a recording through the system' (7).

[45]Scott Rosenberg, 'Why the music industry has nothing to celebrate'. 27 July 2000. http://www.salon.com/tech/col/rose/2000/07/27/napster_shutdown/print.html

community who think one-to-one file sharing is legal'.[46] Alternate projects like Gnutella and Freenet which offer Napster-like MP3 file transfer capability without being linked to one central server will go underground. By creating 'a world of total connectivity' (Love, 9) internet technology gains the power to undermine corporate interests. The commodity enters a new phase. Web and Internet technology replaces the mediating and profiteering industry, and the commodity circulates without its intervention and creates collectives of people with the same interests. Courtney Love designs her utopia of a new economy:

> [I will] allow millions of people to get my music for nothing if they want and hopefully they'll be kind enough to leave a tip if they like it ... A new company that gives artists true equity in their work can take over the world, kick ass and make a lot of money. We're inspired by how people get paid in the new economy. Many visual artists and software and hardware designers have real ownership of their work.
>
> (7/8)

Love knows that the artists' and audience's criteria for the production and reception of the artistic product have to change. Artists have to become independent of being promoted to celebrity status[47] and the audience has to be liberated from being manipulated by advertising: 'people who've enjoyed the experience I've provided will be happy to shell out a little more money to cover my costs. Especially if they understand this context, and aren't being shoveled a load of shit about "uppity" artists' (8/9). Relationships are centered on the shared interest in the artistic work, and not based on the manipulations through promotion techniques.[48]

The Web's power to associate customers and artists with each other is one example how the technology of the 21st century realizes Brecht's utopian vision of overcoming the conventional concept of the commodity. In *Der Dreigroschenprozess* he argues:

> In diesem Sinne ist die Umschmelzung geistiger Werte in Waren (Kunstwerke, Verträge, Prozesse sind Waren) ein fortschrittlicher Prozeß, und man kann ihm nur zustimmen, vorausgesetzt, daß der Fortschritt als Fortschreiten gedacht wird, nicht als Fortgeschrittenheit, daß also auch die Phase der Ware als durch weiteres Fortschreiten überwindbar angesehen wird. Die kapitalistische Produktionsweise zertrümmert die bürgerliche Ideologie.
>
> (201/204)

Wrecking the commodity status of the commodity is Brecht's and Love's goal. Love is in the position to take the control in her own hands, to hire a 'Webmistress' (7) and to circulate her own music files. This empowers the artist to outline his/her criteria for companies of the new economy. Love advises: 'If you're going to start a company that deals with musicians, please do it because you love music' (13). Resisting being a service to the industry she switches the roles around: companies provide a service to the musician and the musician provides a service to the audience. The term 'service' should replace

---

[46]Cecily Barnes. 'Napster CEO fights for life of music firm.' 27. July 2000. http://news.cnet.com/news/0-1014-202-2366873-0.html

[47]'In a society of over 300 million people, only 30 new artists a year sell a million records. By any measure, that's a huge failure' (6).

[48]'Let us do our real jobs. And those of us addicted to celebrity because we have nothing else to give will fade away. And those of us addicted to celebrity because it was there well find a better, purer way to live ...' (7).

the term product. Thus she privileges the social function of the commodity over the economic function and she trusts that business based on social responsibility will outlive profit-oriented commerce.[49]

Her view mirrors Brecht's view although there is one major difference between both artists: Brecht stresses the educational function of art, whereas Love is committed to offering an enjoyable experience to her audience, 'Kunstgenuß', an attitude Brecht criticizes.[50] The philosophical intentions of both might be different, but their view of technology as a challenge to bourgeois business strategies is the same. In shifting Marx' focus on class struggles to his focus on the relation between capitalist business strategies and the social implications of technology, Brecht predicted that capitalism will become its own enemy, that it created technological means which undermine the systems on which it is based.[51] Brecht's approach to film technology is radicalized by Love's view of the democratizing functions of the Internet and their potential of creating new societal interactions.

During the composition of this article in Fall 2000 Napster's service changed. The New York Times reported November 1, 2000: 'Napster ... agreed yesterday to a plan to change course and charge a fee for its service, distributing part of the fee as royalties to record companies.'[52] Challenged by the high costs and the uncertainty of the lawsuit's outcome the company agreed to accept the financial assistance of Bertelsmann which in turn received an option to buy a stake in the company. Bertelsmann is one of the companies which sued Napster for copyright infringement. Thus the suit served the capitalist enterprise and Napster's business is in danger of turning again to the status quo: the company compromised the Napster idea ignoring the innovative social potentials of its own technology. With this reactionary move Napster acceded to industrial interest. It is not clear if and how the move compromises the company's original cutting-edge social impact. Will royalty fees again go to the record companies and the artists' needs and rights be ignored?[53] The renewed empowerment of the industry boosts its control over the production and distribution of music files. But file sharing programs without

---

[49]An editorial, 'King's Closure', in the *New York Times* on 1 December 2000 suggests that the suspension of Stephen King's online serial novel *The Plant* constitutes a failure of electronic publishing and thus could be seen as counter example to Courtney Love's Utopian vision of internet publishing. Stephen King's response does not support this claim. See http://www.stephenking.com

[50]'I'm doing good work, I believe that the people who enjoy it are going to want to come directly to me and get my music because it sounds better ... I'm providing an honest, real experience' (Love 8).

[51]'Die Wirklichkeit kommt dann an den Punkt, wo das einzige Hindernis für den Fortschritt des Kapitalismus der Kapitalismus ist' (204). Brecht here contrasts impersonal capitalist production with its ideology of personal intellectual property.

[52]Matt Richtel and David D. Kirkpatrick, 'Napster to charge Fee for Music Rights'. 1 Nov. 2000. http://www.nytimes.com/2000/11/01/technology/01MUSI.html

[53]While proofreading this article in October 2001 I checked again the news on the Napster Website. In order to comply with legal demands Napster is still working on developing a new technology. The company promises now that 'file sharing ... will be back' and that it reached a 'preliminary agreement with the National Music Publishers' Association (NMPA) which means that songwriters will get paid when their works are shared' (http://www.napster.com). This new business direction indicates that the controversial debates about the lawsuit against Napster have forced the NMPA at least to rethink and redesign their attitude towards the artists. It is not clear at this point 'whether Napster's millions of users will return to it when it reopens its doors in its new incarnation – as a for-pay service ...' and if it will regain its prominence as 'the largest widely accessible library of music ever assembled' (Scott Rosenberg, 'Revenge of the file sharing'. http://www.salon.com/tech/col/rose/2001/07/20/napster_diaspora/index.htm)

a central server, as for example Gnutella, Bearshare, LimeWire et al., have gained enormous popularity and will continue to operate, giving users the chance to boycott corporate business. Popular file sharing could slowly subvert the bourgeois order that is the basis for the continuance of the capitalist enterprise. It will at least split social attitudes and social consciousness; Internet file sharing promotes the communicative functions of the commodity as they were envisioned by Brecht and overcomes the commodity's profit margin.

PART FOUR

# THE PLAY OF IDEAS

# The Bible

# CHAPTER NINETEEN

# Brecht and the Bible: A Study of Religious Nihilism and Human Weakness in Brecht's Drama of Mortality and the City

G. RONALD MURPHY

'Sie werden lachen: die Bibel.'[1] This mysterious but well-known Brechtian utterance, so often taken as another example of his irony with its emphasis on *lachen*, is a statement that, more than any other, grants jocularly veiled access to the deepest and longest lasting literary influence in Brecht's lifetime of writing. Despite this clue as to what may well be the most significant level of Brecht's thought, few critics have undertaken any systematic exploration of his use (and abuse) of the Bible.[2] Most authors are content to acknowledge biblical influence in the realm of Brecht's language,[3] and only a few seriously point the way to what may be lying beyond phonology.

---

G. Ronald Murphy, 'Introduction: The Problem', in Murphy, *Brecht and the Bible: A Study of Religious Nihilism and Human Weakness in Brecht's Drama of Mortality and the City* (Chapel Hill: U of North Carolina P, 1980), pp. 3–12 and notes pp. 95–6.

[1] Brecht had been asked the question of what was 'der stärkste Eindruck' on his writing. The now famous answer was printed in the Berlin ladies' magazine *Die Dame* of 1 October 1928. Cf. Martin Esslin, *Brecht: The Man and His Work* (New York: Doubleday, Anchor Books, 1961), p. 106.

[2] Siegfried Mews concludes his extensive review essay devoted to studies of Brecht and world literature with the following remark: 'It is an indication of the areas still to be explored that so far, despite repeated references to the prominence of Biblical influences in Brecht's work, no comprehensive study is available on the subject.' Siegfried Mews, 'Bertolt Brecht and World Literature', *Papers on Language and Literature*, 13 (1977), 108.

[3] Martin Esslin's essay provides a typical example: 'Brecht's language also has a firm basis in the chief source of modern standard German. ... And in fact the vigorous, outspoken language of Luther's Bible pervades the writings of the atheist and blasphemer Brecht. He made masterly use of biblical construction: the juxtaposition of contrasted half-sentence, parallelisms, repetition, and inversion. Equally marked throughout Brecht's life was the influence of the street ballad. ...' Esslin, ibid.

The language of Brecht's drama is, I believe, the most important in the twentieth century, but the continual conflict in basic understanding and in critical interpretation of his works reveals that there is something enigmatic about the style, and content, of Brecht's works that results in controversy even among well-intentioned contemporary critics and perhaps causes his contemporaries to miss the level on which he is frequently speaking.

Bertolt Brecht was raised in a mixed Catholic-Protestant household. His father, Berthold Friedrich, was a Catholic from the Black Forest, and his mother, Sophie Brezing, was a Protestant. Eugen Berthold was confirmed in the biblical Lutheran tradition of his mother, something which may indicate either deep religious differences within the house, or weakness or generosity on the part of the father.[4] There is little information on this question, but one is more than justified in speculating that the presence of religious dualism in the Brecht family, far more than Hebbel's *Judith*,[5] gave Brecht the first incentive to write *Die Bibel* with its Catholic-Protestant conflict, in which the willingness of the 'weak' father to compromise principle for the sake of peace and life is defended, and the hard righteousness of the Bible-reading grandfather is opposed.[6] Another author, writing on the problem of Brecht's antagonism to the middle class, has also come to the conclusion that the Brecht household was extremely important, though in relation to a different question:

> Erinnerungen an das Elternhaus finden sich nirgendwo. Man kann es ablesen nur an den Protestreaktionen des jungen Brecht. Betrachtet man Photos von Brechts Vater, eines biederen und tüchtigen Direktors einer Papierfabrik, oder Bilder des kleinen Berthold Eugen, eines pfiffigen Bürschchens mit runden lebendigen Augen, in sauberem Matrosenkragen, so kann man sich des Gedankens nicht erwehren, daß Brechts fanatischer Haß auf die Bourgeoisie in diesem Elternhaus seine bestimmte Ursache haben müsse.[7]

One might not be going too far in speculating that the mere existence of a perhaps subtle Catholic-Protestant dialectic at home between the father's and the mother's families may not only have given the inspiration and the point of view for the religious conflict of *Die Bibel* and of *Mutter Courage*, but also may have first conditioned the mind of the young Brecht to dialectic and relativistic thinking in general – and given it the oscillating restlessness that would always seek truth but never seem to be content with any single-minded, absolute system of truths.

The Bible itself, written as a collection of religious truths, but unwittingly the object of 'religious' conflict, was Brecht's earliest source for dramatic material. This is true

---

[4]Recent study indicates that the latter view is the more probable. W. Frisch and K. W. Obermeier cite the following on Brecht's father in *Brecht in Augsburg: Erinnerungen, Texte, Fotos; eine Dokumentation* (Frankfurt/M: Suhrkamp, 1976), p. 22: 'Er war ein nüchterner, liberal eingestellter Mann. Kam das Gespräch einmal auf religiöse Fragen, dann sei er ernst geworden und habe gesagt: "Das kann jeder halten, wie er's will".'

[5]Cf. Reinhold Grimm, 'Brecht's Beginnings' in *Brecht*, ed. Erika Munk (New York: Bantam, 1972), p. 26 (first published in *The Drama Review*, 12, [Fall, 1967]).

[6]Ronald Gray did not know of the existence of *Die Bibel* at the time of his book, but even without this evidence, he attaches the same importance to Brecht's mixed religious background as does the present author. Cf. Ronald Gray, *Bertolt Brecht* (New York: Grove, 1961), pp. 2–3.

[7]Marianne Kesting, *Bertolt Brecht in Selbstzeugnissen und Bilddokumenten* (Hamburg: Rowohlt, 1959), pp. 12–13.

not only for *Die Bibel*, but for other early plays as well, most of which we do not now have. Brecht read the Bible continually as a constant source from which to draw dialectic conflict:

> In seinen Erinnerungen an Brechts Augsburger Zeit im Jahre 1919 hat H. O. Münsterer [in *Panorama*, Munich, August 1959, pp. 7-8] von zwei nahezu fertigen Dramen aus jener Zeit berichtet: 'Das eine dieser Dramen führt anfangs den Titel *David oder der Beauftragte Gottes*, der später in *Absalom und Bathseba* abgewandelt wurde.' Der Stoff ist aus der Bibel entnommen, die Brecht bekanntlich immer wieder las und deren Stil von ihm in manchen Arbeiten nachgebildet wird. David ist bei aller aus der Heiligen Schrift ersichtlichen Immoralität der Mann Gottes. Die Eingangsszene zeigt Absalom im Burghof, den Soldaten der Leibwache zuhörend, die sich über die Schliche des alternden Königs recht anrüchige Histörchen erzählen. Da erscheint oben auf der Mauer David, eine riesige Silhouette. 'Ich will Abrechnung halten mit meinem Sohne Absalom!' Beklemmende Stille, Vorhang, eine Exposition also, wie sie Brecht in seinen Meisterjahren nicht wirkungsvoller hätte geben können.[8]

Biblical material can be seen not only in the early plays, but thinly disguised throughout the later plays as well, for example, the Abraham and Lot story (Genesis 18:20–19:29) in *Der gute Mensch von Sezuan*, and in Solomon's decision (1 Kings 3:13–28) in *Der kaukasische Kreidekreis*.

In using the Bible in this way, Brecht is far from doing something out of the ordinary, but rather conforming to a common and one of the oldest tendencies of German men of letters. For instance, Brecht's more conservative contemporaries, Thomas Mann (the *Joseph* novels) and Hermann Hesse (*Siddhartha, Demian*) also made extensive hermeneutic use of the Bible, although both possess a cooler, more distanced literary relationship to it than does Brecht. Nietzsche's superman competes with the Scriptures in an agonistic trial of superiority. Goethe's *Faust* is, in many respects, from the angelic choirs and the Dies Irae, from the 'Christ ist erstanden' to the 'Her zu mir', unthinkable without the biblical tradition. Schiller's Karl and Franz Moor play out their roles in a version of the Prodigal Son that rivals the original in intensity if not in brevity. Lessing's Three-Rings theme is a protest against religious wars and intolerance and is remarkably akin in general thrust to *Die Bibel* and *Mutter Courage*. Less veiled is the religious tradition in the Baroque and in Reformation literature where Luther's Bible became the work that formed modern literary German. But when one goes back to *Parzifal* and medieval German, one finds oneself in a much older, almost patristic, tradition of the use of the Bible. Here the hero is not so much the focus of moral struggle or the victim of social circumstance, but, as in *Oedipus*, he is guilty of not realizing who and where he is, of not realizing that he is at the very table of God when he is there. Brecht, it seems to me, in his use of the Crucifixion and Death, is thematically quite close to this older point of view of Sophocles and Wolfram.

In any case, there is a long German literary tradition, only briefly sketched here, of writers using the Bible, overtly and covertly, in such a way that the sacred and the profane are closely mixed. The proportions and the purpose of the mixture are always different, according to the style and intent of the author. Brecht's particular way of using the Bible is the fundamental question this book seeks to answer.

---

[8]Hans Mayer, *Bertolt Brecht und die Tradition* (Pfullingen: Neske, 1961), p. 50.

When King Edward is about to be betrayed to his enemies in *Leben Eduards des Zweiten von England* because of his homosexual affair with Gaveston, the audience is suddenly met with a strange sequence of events. The betrayer, Baldock, is trying to think of how to hand the king over to his pursuers. He says to Mortimer, the king's enemy: 'Die Bibel lehrt uns, wie's zu halten ist. / Wenn Eure Leute kommen mit Handfesseln und / mit Riemen, will ich zu ihm sagen: Lieber Herr / beruhigt Euch, da habt Ihr ein Handtuch. Und dem / ich dann das Handtuch reiche, der ist es.'[9]

When Baldock comes to the king's hiding place, he is invited to share the king's supper: 'Trink unser Wasser mit uns, iß unser / Salz und Brot' (GW, I, 251). The tired King Edward declares that 'alles ist eitel' (GW, I, 252), and then lays his head on the Abbot's lap. A noise is suddenly heard and, though Spencer says it is just the wind and snow, Baldock says, 'Ich dachte, es sei ein Hahnenschrei' (GW, I, 253). Spencer alludes then to sleepiness as promising no good, when suddenly soldiers appear and ask the question: 'Wer unter euch ist der König?' (GW, I, 254).

After Spencer's denial that there is a king present, the drama reads: 'Baldock *geht auf Eduard zu*: Nehmt dieses Tuch, ich bitt Euch, lieber Herr. / Ihr habt Schweiß auf Eurer Stirn' (GW, I, 254). The king is then seized but: '*Eduard im Abgehen, zwischen Bewaffneten, sieht Baldock an. Baldock weint*' (GW, I, 254).

The entire situation of the Last Supper, the Agony in the Garden and the Arrest has been reset, and brings about a deliberate confusion of the audience's feelings toward the king, whom the audience has been allowed to keep in less-than-polite disrespect up until this point. Why does Brecht use the Bible in this way? Is he satirizing the Bible or even more deeply mocking Eduard's delusions? Why does the audience react subconsciously to the transformed version of the Passion with sympathy and not with rejection?

Brecht scholars do not enter into this discussion frequently, perhaps put off too quickly from a study of his use of the Bible because of their prior knowledge of the author as 'the atheist and blasphemer Brecht'. As perceptive a theological literary critic as Paul Konrad Kurz, S. J. can only write in a general way of *Mutter Courage*: 'Eine der Vergänglichkeit zugeordnete Tiefenschicht Brechts – aus der schon Baal und eine große Anzahl der frühen Gedichte lebten – wird sichtbar, Elementares, das sich wehrt im Streit mit der Umwelt, im Streit mit dem Sterben, … eine innerweltlich unwiderlegbar anti-Salomonische Desillusionierung.'[10] He even notes in his section on Brecht as *Der Unbequeme*: 'Von frühen Jahren an begleitete Brecht das Bewußtsein des Sterbenmüssens. Seine Baal-und-Villon-Lyrik enthält als stets anwesende Partner zwei unheimliche Gestalten: Gott und Tod.'[11] Despite this rather accurate analysis, Kurz fails to specify the literary patterns or images in which God is always present as a partner of death.

Reinhold Grimm must be given the credit for first giving proper emphasis to the role of the Bible in Brecht's works and assembling long lists of examples to prove his point. In the chapter in which he discusses Brecht's theory and practice of citation he writes:

> Die meisten Belege freilich stammen aus der Bibel: 'Nun, mein Sohn, herein mit dir zu deinem Feldhauptmann and setz dich zu meiner Rechten.' 'Ich kenne den Elephanten

---

[9]Bertolt Brecht, *Gesammelte Werke in 20 Bänden* (Frankfurt/M: Suhrkamp, 1967), I, 249. Hereafter abbreviated as GW followed by volume (Roman numeral) and page (Arabic numeral).
[10]Paul Konrad Kurz, *Über moderne Literatur* (Frankfurt/M: Josef Knecht, 1969), Vol. II, p. 54. Trans. Sr. Mary Frances McCarthy as *On Modern German Literature* (University, Alabama: University of Alabama Press, 1971).
[11]Ibid., p. 84.

nicht.' 'An den Wassern des Michigansees/Sitzen wir und weinen' ... Schließlich neigt das parodistische Element dazu, sich zu verabsolutieren: 'Als die Herren ächzend und mit Mienen, als unterschrieben sie das Todesurteil für ihre liebsten Anverwandten, ihre Namen auf das Papier gesetzt hatten, gingen sie schnell auseinander, ein jeglicher in seine Stadt.'[12]

Grimm's theory is that Brecht's use of the Bible is a device of *Verfremdung*, an attempt to revive a cliché by the shock of seeing it either 'slightly' altered or in an entirely different situation from its original context. This is done, he believes, most frequently in parody of the original meaning (as is certainly true in the examples he cites above). He also notes a more serious Brechtian use of the Bible:

> Man darf hier nichts verharmlosen. Wenn die Soldaten im pestverseuchten Florenz die Gasse, wo Galilei wohnt, absperren – eine notwendige, aber für die Betroffenen unmenschliche Maßnahme – bemerkt der Forscher bitter: 'Sie hauen uns ab wie den kranken Ast eines Feigenbaumes, der keine Frucht mehr bringen kann.' Unter solchen Umständen zitiert, richtet sich das Bibelwort gegen sich selber.[13]

Although Grimm does not like the seriousness of such an attack on the New Testament, he does seem to indicate that it is almost an attack from *inside* the Bible, a kind of internal conflict within the Bible suddenly exposed. Brecht stings the reader by exposing the occasional incidents of apparent or real indifference or cruelty in the Book that is read, in his view, far too mindlessly by its cultural and religious followers. Thus in addition to the type of use to which biblical allusion is put in the Eduard-Baldock scene, where it is used to elicit sympathy for the king's situation, we see Brecht also has a second style of usage. Brecht occasionally sets up serious conflicts between different parts of the Bible, including parts of the New Testament against parts of the Old Testament. This second use of the Bible, then, puts the Bible into a dialectic relationship with itself; but is this poetic delight in blasphemous dialectic, or an attempt to 'wake up the class'?

In referring to the incident in the *Dreigroschenoper* where Macheath looks at Brown, and Brown 'weeps bitterly' (GW, I, 446), Grimm gives his theory as to Brecht's underlying purpose in so using the Bible – blasphemy:

> Das biblische Muster verfremdet den Vorgang im Stück; zugleich aber bedeutet die Wahl dieses Musters eine extreme und durchaus mit beabsichtigte Blasphemie: die Spannungen zwischen den beiden Bereichen wirken dialektisch, ... So sehr Brecht als Dichter aus der Sprache der (Luther-) Bibel gelernt hat, seine Haltung zu ihrer Botschaft ist kompromißlos ablehnend.[14]

Here, I believe, Grimm may have been misled both by the randomness of the examples he selected from Brecht and by a too univocal concept of the Bible as 'a' book, having one single undifferentiated message.[15] Although Brecht does indeed use parts of the Bible many times in the parodistic and blasphemous – and often humorous – way Grimm

---

[12] Reinhold Grimm, *Bertolt Brecht: Die Struktur seines Werkes* (Nürnberg: Hans Carl, 1962), pp. 44–45.
[13] Ibid.
[14] Grimm, *Brecht: Die Struktur seines Werkes*, p. 45.
[15] Grimm later modified his opinion on Brecht's use of the Bible and referred, much more accurately I believe, to Brecht's 'lebenslange und höchst komplexe Abhängigkeit von der Bibel' in Reinhold Grimm, *Bertolt Brecht und die Weltliteratur* (Nürnberg: Hans Carl, 1961), p. 5.

demonstrated, there are other parts of the Bible whose message Brecht uncompromisingly accepts. It is my conviction that his negative attitude to the messages of Genesis and the Resurrection accounts, for example, is not at all the same as his attitude to other books of the Old Testament such as Ecclesiastes, or to the Crucifixion accounts of the New Testament whose message he is only too ready to accept, and to use. The fact that Brecht is able to accept certain parts of the Bible based on their specific content has also been noted by Barbara Woods. Commenting on such passages as Brecht's use of 'you shall not bind the mouth of the ox that is threshing the grain', she says: 'For the tendency of the critics is to concede that Brecht is indebted to Biblical style, but to assume that his avowed atheism leads him to reject all Biblical teachings. ... After all, the Bible contains a good deal of material not strictly theological, such as practical and moral precepts; and Brecht finds little cause to dispute such Biblical sayings.'[16] This, at least, is the burden of my own contentions concerning Brecht's use of the Bible, though I would go beyond the practical and moral precepts of the Bible.

Thomas O. Brandt holds a similar opinion to that of the earlier Grimm, except that he holds the purpose of Brecht's use to be provocation rather than blasphemy, and protest against rather than denial of too-easily-held faith: 'Den bequemen, traditionellen, unerworbenen Glauben zu zerstören, daran lag ihm.'[17]

The only full-length studies of this entire question, however, are a dissertation by Gary Neil Garner[18] and Hans Pabst's *Brecht und die Religion*.[19] Unfortunately, though, Garner does not undertake the exhaustive internal analysis of the plays that the resolution of this question demands, but instead begins and ends with an a priori philosophical approach that tends to deduce Brecht the poet from nineteenth-century German philosophy. Pabst's book is a much more thorough and satisfactory work though it also suffers from seeing Brecht from a too sociologically restricted perspective. Not too surprisingly, Garner and Pabst come to the conventional conclusion that Brecht is a kind of unoriginal nineteenth-century Marxist-humanist using drama and the Bible as a means of propaganda. That there is some truth in such a view, no one will deny, but it does little to explain such figures as Kattrin, Baal, Paul Ackermann, and Grusche. The poetic problem itself of the nagging persistence of certain specific parts of the Bible in many of Brecht's plays remains.

The poetic and stylistic problem of the almost fixed recurrence of certain phrases and events of biblical 'drama' and their almost constant association with the protagonist(s) and his fate, results in the often-observed, but supposedly prohibited, audience sympathy with Brecht's heroes and heroines. Henry Hatfield has expressed this paradox quite clearly:

> A whole battery of devices aims at 'distancing' the spectator. Characters step out of their roles, wear masks, or comment on the action. ... Slogans are projected onto a screen or written placards; some witty, some, in the didactic works, almost insultingly simplistic, which again serves to alienate the audience. ...

---

[16] Barbara Allen Woods, 'A Man of Two Minds', *The German Quarterly*, 42 (1969), 46.
[17] Thomas O. Brandt, 'Brecht und die Bibel' *PMLA*, 79 (1964), 176.
[18] Gary Neil Garner, 'Bertolt Brecht's Use of the Bible and Christianity in Representative Dramatic Works'. Diss., Louisiana State University, 1969. Available from University Microfilms, Ann Arbor, Michigan.
[19] Hans Pabst, *Brecht und die Religion* (Graz: Styria, 1977).

Precisely the best of Brecht's dramas, however, often conflict with these theories. The fortitude of Mother Courage, the goodness of the Chinese prostitute Shen Te, and above all the devotion of Grusche (in *Kreidekreis*) evoke our sympathy, quite in a traditional sense.[20]

This traditional sympathy can not be explained in terms of pure *Verfremdungstheorie*. Can the biblical context of each of these dramatic actions be a covert means of transcending the estrangement without destroying it?

Hans Mayer, remarkably enough in view of his sometime Marxist background, is the person most responsible for advancing the question of the importance of the Bible for Brecht beyond the status first given to it by Reinhold Grimm. Referring again to the use of Peter's denial of Christ, he comments: 'Natürlich steht in alledem viel mehr als eine bloße, durch Zitat fixierte Anspielung. Mit Recht sieht Reinhold Grimm in den meisten Bibelzitaten eine Anwendung des Verfremdungsprinzips, ein dialektisches Reizverhältnis zwischen Ursprung und Aktualisierung des Bibelworts.'[21] He is led to go further by the text of a cantata written by Brecht in 1949 for the composer Gottfried von Einem, in an attempt to determine Brecht's standpunkt. Mayer cites the cantata text below and then comments:

'Schaut's, jetzt hat er ihn durchstochen!
Schaut's, der starke Folterknecht!
Schaut's, er hat die Wahrheit g'sprochen!
G'schieht ihm recht! G'schieht ihm recht!'

Das ist nicht der Standpunkt des Evangelisten, wie in der Matthäus-Passion, es ist auch kein mitteilender Kommentar. Die Passion wird von außen gesehen, von der Menge her, die in schauriger Bewunderung für den Folterknecht, auch ein bißchen verächtliches Mitleid für das Opfer aufbringt.[22]

Mayer has perceived the location of the point of view of the writer of the cantata as being within the Gospel scene, but shockingly (and estrangedly) enough, among the distracted crowd who, too easily fascinated by the powerfulness of the guard, do not realize what is happening. He then modifies his agreement with Reinhold Grimm's earlier thesis on Brecht's use of the Bible: 'Blasphemie, Anspielung, Verfremdung. Trotzdem ist da noch mehr.'[23]

It is my purpose to get at this 'noch mehr'. This is a somewhat delicate task, since Brecht's usages of the Bible may be 'Rufe aus der Tiefe, aber nicht empor zu irgendeinem "O Herr".'[24]

This, of course, brings us to the serious problem of Brecht's atheism, and the question of how an atheist could possibly make sincere use of any part of the Bible. Brecht's atheism, in his earlier years at least, is partially a denial, as he put it, of the God of romanticism and of war: 'Gott, das war das hohe C der Romantik. Der Abendhimmel über

---

[20] Henry Hatfield, *Modern German Literature, The Major Figures in Context* (London: Edward Arnold, 1966), p. 136.
[21] Mayer, *Brecht und die Tradition*, p. 50.
[22] Ibid., pp. 51–52.
[23] Ibid.
[24] Ibid.

dem Schlachtfeld, die Gemeinsamkeit der Leichen, ferne Militärmärsche, der Alkohol der Geschichte ... die Zuflucht der Sterbenden und der Mörder' (GW, XX, 4).

Brecht's primeval, pre-Marxist concern about the God of those who die, not just because of an enemy's stroke, but because of an enemy even more primitive and more sovereignly indifferent, such as cancer, remains: 'Der Mann, der am Krebs verendete, suchte mit allen Mitteln die Poesie dieses peinlichen Geschehnisses auf die Zunge zu kriegen, er malte sich Bilder vom Leid der Erde, die ihn ausspie, vom Schmerz der Hinterbleibenden oder der grandiosen und ihn ergreifenden Ironie ihrer Gleichgültigkeit und vom Dunkel, das ihn aufnahm' (GW, XX, 4–5). The point of view Brecht takes here is that of the dying man, that of Baal at the end, with the great question of the darkness ahead for the dying. Brecht views 'God' as a desperate attempt of the dying to save themselves. After describing how all men, each according to his intelligence, have made ever more clever attempts to deceive themselves into believing that there is a God who saves from the darkness, Brecht, who is only too intimately involved in this question, concluded that all human efforts to invent a God are doomed to failure: 'Als die wimmelnde Masse der Wesen auf dem fliegenden Stern sich kennengelernt und ihre unbegreifliche Verlassenheit empfunden hatte, hatte sie schwitzend Gott erfunden, den niemand sah, also daß keiner sagen konnte, es gäbe ihn nicht, er habe ihn nicht gesehen' (GW, XX, 5).

Brecht sees religion as man's terrified response, almost the response of a trapped animal, to his feeling of being totally abandoned in the universe that gave him birth (*Verlassenheit* will occur prominently in the plays we shall study) and to his uncontrollable fear of the oncoming darkness of death. These two feelings, and the concomitant problem of 'being good' in such a world, are the key to Brecht's nonsatiric use of the Bible. The parts of the Bible that Brecht uses empathetically are those in which these two feelings, the feeling of being abandoned and the fear of death, as well as the problem of 'being good', are most poignantly expressed. The other books of the Bible are either satirized, handled humorously, or ignored.

In the plays studied, Brecht's use of the Old Testament is heavily restricted to the Wisdom literature and Prophetic literature. Among the Wisdom writings Brecht leans most heavily on Ecclesiastes, Job, and the Psalms. These books are most congenial to Brecht since they too, like most of the Old Testament, operate under the assumption that there is no real afterlife (no *Jenseits*) for man, and have a dominating awareness of death and abandonment, unrelieved by their belief in God and His immortality.

In Prophetic literature, especially Isaiah, the problem of being good among men and of exposing the phenomenon of religion's ignoring of social injustice while paying careful attention to the performance of ritual, is the whole burden of the message. Here also there is no real belief in things being 'fixed up' after death for the poor and the oppressed, 'the widow, the orphan, the resident alien', and so the religious man must help them now, since – as Brecht would say – '[Wir] können einem toten Mann nicht helfen' (GW, II, 564).

Although Brecht may parody almost any well-known verse or verses from the New Testament, especially moral ones, for achieving humor or satire, he also makes empathetic use of the New Testament. But his use is almost totally restricted to the events of the Passion and Death accounts, especially St. Matthew's Passion. The Resurrection accounts are never used.

Thus we return to Mayer's original observation, 'Blasphemie, Anspielung, Verfremdung. Trotzdem ist da noch mehr.' This 'noch mehr' I have found to be primarily located in a line of plays which begins with *Die Bibel* and culminates in *Mutter Courage*. The plays in this line are characterized by the use of some variation of the 'city' or 'besieged city' motif, there is no 'happy end', and the hero or heroine is ultimately confronted with abandonment and death in a way that is evocative of the Crucifixion.

By contrast, Brecht's use of the Bible, in other plays with apparent religious themes, such as *Leben des Galilei*, in which there is no serious confrontation with death, rarely go beyond the realm of argumentation and dialectics and seldom exceed the extent that one finds even in *Baal*. The same is true for plays occupied with socio-moral questions rather than the life-death question, such as *Der gute Mensch von Sezuan* and *Der kaukasische Kreidekreis*. Concerning these plays, I am in general agreement with Grimm's modified analysis of Brecht's use of the Bible. Only in his tragedies of abandonment and death does Brecht, it seems, go beyond the level of 'blasphemy, allusion, and alienation' that Grimm believes to be typical of Brecht's general use of the Bible.

In order to show that there is a fundamental affinity of thought between Brecht and certain authors and parts of the Bible on the question of death and human goodness, an affinity that did not change in the course of time, I have tried to trace the persistence of these patterns over long periods of Brecht's life. For this reason I have selected four plays for detailed analysis that are widely separated chronologically (the reader can easily extrapolate to others). Except for *Die Bibel*, the plays are approximately ten years apart. Since each play deals with some tragic aspect of 'the city', both change and persistence of attitude on the part of Brecht can be easily seen. The four plays are *Die Bibel* (1914), 'the city besieged'; *Baal* (1918), from the early jubilantly nihilist period because it so clearly revels in death's long siege of life; *Mahagonny* (1927–29), from his period of transition to communism; and *Mutter Courage* (1938–39), from his later, mature period.

The backbone of each chapter is an 'outline commentary', which I hope will be a convenient help for the reader, and which I hope will help even the more skeptical not to laugh except perhaps in recognition. 'Sie werden lachen: die Bibel.'[25]

---

[25] In April 1977, the author received a letter from the *Brecht-Archiv* in Berlin, informing him that, in response to his request that a search be made for a possible copy of the Bible in Brecht's library, a small, well-marked, pocket edition had been found. On the flyleaf was written: *bertolt brecht 1926*, in his own handwriting. The present author's analysis of the marked scriptural passages, which substantially corroborate the present work, can be found in: 'Brecht's Pocket Bible', *The German Quarterly*, 50 (1977), 474–84.

# Shakespeare

# CHAPTER TWENTY

# Brecht as Great Shakespearean: A Lifelong Connection

DAVID BARNETT

## FORMAL CONFLUENCES: BRECHT RE-READS SHAKESPEARE

Brecht approached Shakespeare from a variety of positions and tended towards making generalizing comments which left the relationship to more specific points of reference somewhat opaque. If one cannot locate a point of departure for Brecht, one theme dominates, that of Shakespeare's utility to the contemporary playwright and theorist, and its evolution shows both how problematic and productive it was to Brecht, and how it opened up other lines of inquiry along the way.

He mentions Shakespeare in passing in 1925[1] as a 'long dead dramatist' whose 'material' nonetheless could breathe new life into a moribund theatrical system.[2] The key word in this early piece is 'material'. Wilhelm Hortmann proposes a Brechtian definition of material as 'the re-workable substance of a play' and this lies at the heart of Brecht's relationship to Shakespeare.[3] Brecht was keen to exploit whatever could be reused or, as he preferred to call it, re-functioned, 'umfunktioniert'. In Shakespeare Brecht valued the richness and the openness of his texts. In January 1929, he defined the dramatic in the plays as being 'wildly eventful, passionate, contradictory, dynamic'.[4] The connection between such expansiveness and its utility for a contemporary audience had been made two years earlier in a speech Brecht wrote as an introduction to his adaptation of *Macbeth* for the radio:

---

David Barnett, 'Brecht as Great Shakespearean: A Lifelong Connection', in Ruth Morse (ed.), *Great Shakespeareans*, vol. 14 (London: Bloomsbury, 2013), pp. 114–27.

[1] All dates attributed to the theoretical writings are taken from the apparatus that accompanies the BFA.
[2] Brecht, '[Welche Stoffe liefert die Gegenwart dem Dramatiker?]', BFA 21: 113.
[3] Wilhelm Hortmann, *Shakespeare on the German Stage: The Twentieth Century* (Cambridge: Cambridge University Press, 1998), 440.
[4] Brecht, '[Neue Dramatik]', BFA 21: 272.

One recognizes in the disjointedness of his acts the disjointedness of a human life [*Schicksals*]⁵ when it is narrated by someone who's not interested in ordering it in order to match an idea, which can only be an imposition, with an argument which isn't taken from life. There can be nothing more stupid than staging Shakespeare so that it's clear. He is naturally unclear. He is absolute material.⁶

The relationship that Brecht posits between the form of the plays and life is reminiscent of Peter Bürger's theses on the historical avant-garde's attempts to re-forge a relationship between art and everyday life.⁷ Such an impulse is reduced by the imposition of order in the form of an 'idea', something which makes art contrived and thus falsifies it. The adjective 'absolute' reinforces the ways in which readers or spectators may connect their various experiences of reality with the material associatively; the work is connotative rather than denotative. Brecht called the quality 'the great Shakespearean resource of suggestive transmission [*Wirkung*]'.⁸ This formulation describes the way in which Shakespeare's work can hover above singular meanings because it is less constrained by restrictive interpretations from within the plays themselves. This idea also chimed with Brecht because he sought to activate his audience by deliberately provoking their curiosity and inviting them to produce meaning together with the actors. Later, around 1945, the figure of the Philosopher⁹ in Brecht's *Messingkauf* calls Shakespeare 'a great realist' who 'always shovelled piles of raw material onto the stage, disorganized depictions of events'.¹⁰ The idea of realism here is central because it gives context to the praise of the apparently unprocessed dramatic material.

The prerequisite for Brecht's writing and directing practice was an idea of realism. This is defined in *Theaterarbeit*, the book which documents the first six productions of the Berliner Ensemble, in a quotation from Friedrich Engels as 'the reproduction [*Wiedergabe*] of typical people under typical circumstances'.¹¹ This postulate is placed in contradistinction to an unashamedly partisan definition of naturalism as 'an artistic direction which strives for the reproduction of natural appearances with embarrassing precision, which, however, often hides meaningful connections by pedantically accumulating random details'.¹² 'Realism' has a special meaning in Brecht's theatre because it includes a generalizing principle which goes beyond the superficial imitation of reality. Realism here is something which applies to society as a whole because it sets out the laws under which the dialectic works, regardless of apparent differences between individuals. The dialectical worldview sees individuals and society in a process of perpetual dialogue which, through contradiction, brings about change in perpetuity. A thesis and

---

⁵'Schicksal' is German for 'fate' or 'destiny', yet clearly in this quotation Brecht is talking about life in the raw, without teleology. As a Marxist, he had no time for such metaphysical speculation.
⁶Brecht, 'Vorrede zu *Macbeth*', BFA 24: 55.
⁷See Peter Bürger, *Theory of the Avant-Garde*, trans. by Michael Shaw (Minneapolis: University of Minnesota Press, 1984). Originally published in German in 1974.
⁸Brecht, '[Neue Dramatik]', BFA 21: 274.
⁹Brecht is clearly his own model for this figure, and in the *Messingkauf* fragments, the Philosopher is sometime referred to as 'the Augsburger' (BFA 22: 722 or 738, for example). Augsburg was Brecht's home town.
¹⁰Brecht, '[*Messingkauf*: Fragment B 141]', BFA 22, 807.
¹¹Ruth Berlau, Bertolt Brecht, Claus Hubalek, Peter Palitzsch and Käthe Rülicke, (eds), *Theaterarbeit: 6 Aufführungen des Berliner Ensembles* (Dresden: VVV Dresdner Verlag, 1952), 434. The Berliner Ensemble is the theatre company Brecht and his wife Helene Weigel founded in 1949.
¹²Ibid., 433.

an antithesis stand in contradiction, and only when the negation is itself negated does change occur in the form of a dialectical synthesis. This philosophy is political because it proposes that both human behaviour and society are unfixed; there is nothing to suggest that either need continue as it has been. Thus, put rather simply, if one changes society, one changes human beings, as the conditions under which people function will help to produce different behaviours. Brecht was exposed to Marxism in the mid-1920s and while he was beginning to articulate a relationship to what a dialectical dramaturgy might entail in the years that followed, his thoughts had reached a more developed state by the 1930s and 1940s. The quotation from the Philosopher, above, allows one to conclude that the mass of material found in Shakespeare suggested a dialectically materialist grasp of reality *avant la lettre*.

Brecht praised what he perceived to be Shakespeare's lack of education in connection with his ability to deliver unformed material: 'Just like the actor who, even if he's stupid, can play clever people by simply copying their *Gestus*, the dramatist can also, if unknowing, exhibit knowledge in his plays. He doesn't need to attain knowledge, he only needs to observe the knowledgeable [...].'[13] Here Brecht identified a category he found central to his own dramatic enterprise: the naïve. Naïvety is the ability to write or indeed to perform material without reducing it with prejudices or preconceptions, an idea which tallies with Schiller's famous distinction of 1795 between the naïve and the sentimental. To the writer, this is the ability to perceive reality without collapsing it to fit particular agendas. This did not mean, however, that there was something artless at work here. Brecht wrote disapprovingly that 'our narrow bourgeois [spectators] can't imagine naïvety and complexity living together'.[14] That is, naïvety about approaching the world does not equate with the world itself being in some way uncomplicated. The dramatist needs to be able to look at the complex world with wonder, thus leaving it open for the spectator to make connections between its tensions while at the same time understanding that those tensions contain the 'right' kind of material in the first place.

Brecht allied a dialectical depiction of reality with special devices which he developed first in the form of his epic theatre. Ilya Fradkin comments: 'all the virtues of Shakespeare's realism – the broad apprehension of life, the absence of rationalist construction etc – always bound Brecht to an especially valuable quality in his eyes: the epic'.[15] The epic was something of a catch-all term that Brecht used to describe the formal features of a political theatre in which the spectator was to be activated by being presented with dialectical material for his or her consideration. A major role was attributed to interruption or disturbing the flow of the material on offer. The fits and starts of the epic play were to prevent the unquestioned consumption of the performance. In this way, the material would not necessarily succumb to naturalization or universalization, two mechanisms common to the broad dissemination of dominant ideologies as ways to conceal their human origin.[16] The principle of *Verfremdung*[17] was established as a way of making the familiar strange, that is, disturbing the audience's inured faculties of perception by confronting them with

---

[13] Brecht, journal entry of 8 December 1940, BFA 26: 444.
[14] Brecht, journal entry of 11 December 1940, BFA 26: 447.
[15] I[lya] Fradkin, 'Brecht, die Bibel, die Aufklärung und Shakespeare', *Kunst und Literatur*, 13: 2 (1965), 156–75, here 171.
[16] See Terry Eagelton, *Ideology: An Introduction* (London: Verso, 1996), 56–60.
[17] This term is often translated into English as 'alienation' but this is misleading. 'De-familiarization' or 'distanciation' are closer and less loaded than 'alienation' but I prefer to retain the untranslatable German term.

people, objects or situations the spectators thought they understood and presenting them in a different light. (Again one notes a link with the naïve: the plenitude of the world is curtailed by the interests of capital, in Brecht's reading. What is required is a fresh, unencumbered view to allow new connections to be made, for the exploitative system to be criticized and, preferably, overcome.)

The question of genre also interested Brecht in his interpretation of Shakespeare, and this, too, was related to the rich textures of the plays. He noted late in his career, around 1954, that 'the comic aspect appears strongly in the tragic [...] or the tragic in the comic as a contrast. (The difference which is often made on this point disappears in the process.)'[18] What Brecht suggests here is that the opposition between tragedy and comedy can be deconstructed. At a purely formal level, the richness of the text allows for a critical reassessment which can offer a *Verfremdung* of the audience's expectations. The tragic is viewed with the cool gaze of those born later and can be reformulated away from individual 'tragic flaws' into contradictions between the individual and social structures. Consequently, Brecht suggested, for example, that Lear tear up the map of his kingdom in Act I Scene 1 on stage as a *Verfremdung*: 'thus it would not only direct the gaze onto the empire but, in that Lear is so clearly treating the empire as his own private property, he throws light onto the fundaments of feudal family ideology'.[19] Brecht's idea that the opening of *King Lear* distances the spectator from the tragic ending led Georg Seehase to see this strategy as 'the starting point for changing the specificity of genre in the old tragedy'.[20] The tragic, about which Brecht was at best ambivalent, as we shall see below in the discussion of *Coriolanus*, offered itself as the product of cultural orthodoxy rather than as immutable essence, and could hence be subjected to radical review. The important aspect for Brecht was that this review was not driven by an imposition from outside but found its rationale within the texts themselves.

Brecht was keen to uncover aspects of what he perceived to be Shakespeare's epic form within his texts which either tallied with Brecht's own or which he could appropriate. His favourite site was the Histories where he found 'the epic to be most in evidence'.[21] He considered the montage principle, which joined scenes of different locations and times, a productive means to disrupt the audience's sense of continuity. Spectators had to adjust their perspective and understand the ways in which the divergent elements connected to each other, thus foregrounding the productivity of the audience over that of the writer and the director, who are helpless to produce such connections. Although the Histories have often been viewed as the obvious place for Brecht to find traits of his epic theatre, Thomas Metscher argues that Shakespeare's later works provide perhaps even more fecund ground. Focusing on *The Tempest*, he suggests that Prospero offers himself as an epic narrator who continually interrupts the action with explanation and commentary; that the diverse styles of the scenes invite different modes of viewing; and that Caliban in particular draws attention to his own use of language, making it worthy of careful consideration from the audience.[22]

---

[18]Brecht, '[Vom epischen zum dialektischen Theater 2]', BFA 23: 300.
[19]Brecht, 'Kurze Beschreibung einer neuen Technik der Schauspielkunst, die einen Verfremdungseffekt hervorbringt', BFA 22: 653.
[20]Georg Seehase, 'Brecht, Shakespeare und König Lear', *Shakespeare Jahrbuch*, 115 (1979), 59–62, here 60.
[21]Brecht, '[Epische Züge bei Shakespeare]', BFA 22: 613.
[22]See Thomas Metscher, 'Shakespeares Spätstücke, als episches Theater betrachtet', *Shakespeare Jahrbuch*, 115 (1979), 35–50.

Brecht, through the Dramaturge of the *Messingkauf*, also considered the Renaissance stage to be one 'full of V-Effects'. He found, for example, that the empty stage itself compelled the audience to admit that they were in a theatre and not subject to an illusionism which would take hold in the nineteenth century, and noted that boys played women, thus interrupting an easy fit between actor and role.[23] R. B. Parker agrees that the Elizabethan actor, subjected to a repertoire in which the same play was never performed on successive days, played 'parts as *roles*', thus countering the uninterrupted flow of empathy between spectator and character.[24] John Rouse, however, carefully counsels: 'I am not trying to maintain that Shakespeare invented *Verfremdung*, but Brecht knew parallels when he saw them, and learned from what he saw.'[25] Consequently, one should note, as Rodney T. K. Symington does, that Brecht 'sought elements in Shakespeare's works for which he could find a place in his already conceptualized understanding of the epic theatre'.[26] Brecht undertook his exploration of Shakespearean form with an agenda which both included and excluded important aspects of the source material. The major problems that Brecht encountered when re-reading Shakespeare concerned the central subject matter of so many of the plays – their great individuals.

## THE CHALLENGES OF HISTORICIZING SUBJECT MATTER

A key element of what Brecht valued so highly in Shakespeare was that he was writing at the dawn of the modern period. On the one hand, Shakespeare was the perfect chronicler of the new individualism, as Brecht noted in 1927: 'Shakespearean dramas anticipated the 300 years in which the individual developed himself into a capitalist [...].'[27] On the other, he was able to contextualize these new formations by contrasting the modern with the feudal, as Brecht's Philosopher expressed around 1945: 'there are those precious points of fracture in his [Shakespeare's] works where the new of his time collide with the old'.[28] The two quotations offer further insights into Brecht's fascination with Shakespeare and suggest why he appealed so much to Brecht *qua* Marxist. However, Shakespeare's focus on great individuals posed a problem because of their perceived autonomy within the dramas. Brecht would solve that problem by historicizing such figures, but this required much care, thought and application.

If one lingers a little on the first quotation, one finds that the theme of individualism is something of a contradictory attraction to Brecht. On the positive side, Shakespeare provided the most important quality to a socialist reception: he was, according to Brecht, a great realist, which meant that he was a materialist and not an idealist. Such tenets were essential if reality was to be represented on stage, and here Brecht presented the reader with some rare, specific analysis, in this case, of *Othello*, around 1953. Writing about

---

[23] Brecht, '[*Messingkauf*: Fragment B 60]', BFA 22: 737.
[24] R. B. Parker, 'Dramaturgy in Shakespeare and Brecht', *University of Toronto Quarterly*, 32:3 (1963), 229–46, here 233.
[25] John Rouse, 'Shakespeare and Brecht: The Perils and Pleasures of Inheritance', *Comparative Drama*, 17 (1983), 266–80, here 273.
[26] Rodney T. K. Symington, *Brecht und Shakespeare* (Bonn: Bouvier, 1970), 118.
[27] Brecht, 'Sollten wir nicht die Ästhetik liquidieren?', BFA 21: 203.
[28] Brecht, '[*Messingkauf*: Fragment B 141]', BFA 22: 807.

Constantin Stanislavsky's theories of acting, Brecht was keen to demonstrate how an actor's psychological study of Shakespeare's protagonist missed important social details:

> Shakespeare specifically chooses a general who hasn't inherited his position and who, on the contrary, has had to fight for it through his own achievements and has presumably taken it by force from another. [...] In short, he lives in a world of struggle for property and position. [...] Thus his relationship to his beloved wife reveals itself to be a relationship to a chattel.[29]

Brecht's analysis sets out the material situation which gives rise to the tragedy and offers an historicization. *Othello* is not only an example of human passion run wild but also behaviour typical in certain sections of a commodity society. Paul Kussmaul argues, however, that the materialist reading is incomplete and thus does not encompass the reality of the historical situation: 'Indeed, Brecht makes every effort to read the play [*Othello*] historically but since he only has, so to speak, half the worldview in his sights, his interpretation is skewed and banal.'[30] Kussmaul considers the dialectical reading flattening and reductive, bringing everything down to a crude mechanism of economic cause and effect. But this observation in an early modern character does not equate with Brecht's practice for his own characters. W. E. Yuill warns against this tendency when he comments that the 'relative simplicity [of Brecht's theories of textual adaptation] does no justice to the complexity and diversity of Brecht's actual versions'.[31] That is, Brecht's own characters are not automata, and despite the emphasis on social relations in his plays, they are complex figures.

A way of illustrating this is to follow how Brecht countered the charge of reductionism in a dialogue from the *Messingkauf* in which the Philosopher is discussing the tragic in Shakespeare:

> PHILOSOPHER: The demise of the feudal is seen as tragic. [...] All [Shakespeare's tragic heroes] exist in a new world under which they are crushed.
> ACTOR: Many would say this explanation flattens the plays.
> PHILOSOPHER: But what could be richer, more important and more interesting than the demise of great ruling classes?[32]

Brecht suggests that the historicized interpretation of Shakespeare is the starting point for processes which affect the whole gamut of human experience. The cause will connect with a variety of possible effects which make their presence felt in the emotional, the moral *and* the political spheres. But what is emphasized is that that cause is material and historical.

---

[29] Brecht, 'Stanslavski-Studien [6]', BFA 23: 231.
[30] Paul Kussmaul, *Bertolt Brecht und das englische Drama der Renaissance* (Frankfurt/Main et al: Peter Lang, 1974), 28. Here he is referring to what he considers Brecht's overemphasis on the freedom of the individual and social mobility at the time (27).
[31] W. E. Yuill, *The Art of Vandalism: Bertolt Brecht and the English Drama* (London: University of London, 1977), 11.
[32] Brecht, '[*Messingkauf*: Fragment B 54]', BFA 22: 735.

Brecht's reading of Shakespeare's materialism brought with it the focus on the great individual, something with which Brecht had to grapple if he was to shift the emphasis from the personal to the social. Looking at the negative side,[33] Brecht stated in 1929:

> the great individuals were the subject matter and this subject matter produced the form of these dramas. [...] What was this dramatic form like? What was its purpose? We see this in Shakespeare very clearly. Shakespeare drives the great individual, Lear, Othello, Macbeth, through four acts out of all his human relations with the family, with the state, out onto the heath, into complete isolation where he shows greatness in his own demise. [...] Later times will call this a drama for cannibals.[34]

The link of greatness and suffering was, in Shakespeare's day, one which glorified the individual in a way that was nostalgic and unacceptable to the young Marxist. Over time, though, Brecht developed a series of strategies to make a Brechtian virtue out of a Shakespearean necessity. The key term here is historicization, which Brecht was to understand as a powerful means of 'making theatre politically'. Brecht was convinced that theatre could be produced in such a way that virtually everything performed on stage could be connected back to the dominant political, economic and social conditions of the particular time. Thus even a simple greeting between two people in a street could reveal something about their social differences or similarities. 'Making theatre politically' invokes a formal approach to staging all dramatic material whereas 'making political theatre' would concentrate on political themes or issues.

Historicization says that no point in history is ever the same and this provides hope for political change, because the human is continually being reconfigured by its dialogue with its environment and is thus capable of change. But as John J. White points out, 'processes of *Verfremdung* and *Historisierung* need to be shown to be ways of treating the present, rather than just the past'.[35] That is, it is not so much a question of recreating an accurate image of the past as demonstrating differences between the past and the present with the aim not only of showing that change is possible but also that historical conditions produce different behaviours and attitudes. Thus Brecht was able to muse around 1940 that if Antony lost an empire while dallying with Cleopatra, a contemporary English king would simply lose his job but remain happy under similar circumstances.[36] While the parallel of Antony and Edward VIII is hardly exact, and does not take into account what Cleopatra lost, Brecht's point is that consequences that follow socially prohibited relationships for 'great' men have changed markedly over the centuries.

Historicization is perhaps most clearly seen as a way of opening up productive contradictions if one turns to Brecht's thoughts on *Hamlet*. Brecht's relationship to this play underwent subtle changes over time, each pointing to the difficulties of interpreting the material historically. Brecht rated this as the great drama which confronted the old feudal order with the new individualistic one; therein lay its fascination for Brecht, away from the de-historicized portrait of Hamlet's character as timelessly vacillating between

---

[33]Helge Hultberg proposes that 'Shakespeare is [...] the synonym of that which is to be opposed and Brecht never really discarded this attitude in reality', in 'Bert Brecht und Shakespeare', *Orbis Litterarum*, 14: 1 (1959), 89–104, here 90. This rather unsustainable opinion is roundly refuted in my essay.
[34]Brecht, '[Neue Dramatik]', BFA 21: 272. These 'later times' are post-revolutionary, when a collective understanding of the individual will replace its bourgeois implications.
[35]John J. White, *Bertolt Brecht's Dramatic Theory* (Rochester, NY: Camden House, 2004), 96.
[36]See Brecht, '[Zeitenunterschiede]', BFA 22: 611.

inaction and revenge, offered by the theatre of the time. An early reading, written around 1928, proposed that Hamlet's task was to 'clean out the Augean stables', a metaphor for considering Hamlet the bringer of a new age by sweeping away the old.[37] His vacillation thus becomes historical, concerned with the introduction of new ways of thinking and behaving. Later, around 1940, Brecht contrasted vacillation as a sign of 'Hamlet's weakness' in the value system of the Middle Ages with a more modern interpretation of his failure to act as the positive application of reason. Hamlet does not rush headlong into murder as vengeance, but ponders the validity of the act. In the end, however, Brecht condemned Hamlet's giving in to old practices as a 'relapse'.[38] And this relapse had a pedagogical function: 'the scream for revenge, ennobled by Greek tragedy, then disqualified by Christianity, is still reproduced loudly enough, infectiously enough, in *Hamlet* to throw the new doubt, inquiry [*Testen*] and planning into relief'.[39] That is, the persistence of bad, ingrained practices of the past in the present requires vigilance and the strength to confine them to history.

In a scene written for actors (to which I shall return below), Brecht presented a dialogue between Hamlet and a boatman in which the former asks the latter about a new fort on the river bank.[40] The boatman explains that it is used for the export of salted fish to Norway, the former enemy. In this new time, trade trumps war, but the boatman notes that Claudius himself vacillated a full six months before signing the contract, an action which explicitly connects him to Hamlet. Consequently, both are seen as modern men, yet contradictory in their new-found society: both follow the path of reason (for Claudius, a more instrumentalized reason in the case of old Hamlet's murder) but are undone by the temptation to reason while retaining the old ways of thinking. Brecht's historicization thus reveals itself as producing opposing outcomes. It sees Hamlet as inevitably contradictory: he is simultaneously a progressive example of the new thinking (preferring trade to war) *and* a model of the modern bourgeois individual (pursuing his own, ultimately fatal ends). Historicizing Hamlet brings out the different sides of his historical personality as a way of offering the audience a complex set of qualities to assess critically. By extension, the figure of Othello, discussed above, is both the brave and murderous child of his time.

Brecht was troubled by the centrality of the individual as subject in Shakespeare's plays because the emphasis on a single character underplayed the role of the social. However, historicization offered the possibility of contrasting the present with the past as a way of dispelling the assumption of a universal human nature which Brecht, like any Marxist, disputed as dependent on historical circumstances and thus changeable. However, historicization admitted one trans-historical feature in Shakespeare: 'the fallibility of instinct (the indistinctness of the inner voice) [which] cannot be updated'.[41] This comment says something important about the apparent economic one-sidedness criticized by Kussmaul in the example of *Othello*. Human beings are neither mechanical nor mere products of their environment; they are in active dialogue with it and this is why the art of theatre is not a science. Brecht's model of the human subject is certainly

---

[37] Brecht, 'Jiu Jitsu (= die leichte, die fröhliche Kunst)', BFA 21: 243.
[38] Brecht, '[Hamlets Zögern als Vernunft]', BFA 22: 611.
[39] Brecht, journal entry for 25 November 1948, BFA 27: 284.
[40] Brecht, '*Hamlet*: Fährenszene', BFA 22: 840–2.
[41] Brecht, journal entry for 20 September 1945, BFA 27: 232.

always historical but inflected by an unbridgeable gap between the conscious and the unconscious. Brecht may be asking us to curb the power of instinct but it is a power that cannot be eliminated, merely held in check by raised awareness.

## SHAKESPEARE'S THEATRE AS PARADIGM

Much of Brecht's further theoretical speculation about Shakespeare does not focus on specific aspects but refers to the ways in which the implicitly great Shakespeare is so badly served by contemporary theatres themselves. In these references it becomes clear that Brecht was allying his own theatrical innovations with Shakespeare's: 'it's relatively easy to take our plays into the repertoire, but it's difficult to stage them. (If it's ever easy to stage Shakespeare again, it'll be difficult not to take our plays into the repertoire.)'[42] Earlier in the same essay Brecht maintained that the theatre as it existed in Germany in the 1920s 'would certainly have to change itself, and completely at that' if it were to stage Brecht's plays.[43] Brecht postulates that '[theatre] theatres everything into theatre'.[44] This critical insight signals a wariness with respect to the processes and ends of theatrical production in the commercial theatre. It suggests that theatre as institution turns challenging text into marketable performance, thus nullifying any possible effect it might have in activating the audience. While Brecht tried to solve this problem in 1949 with the founding of the Berliner Ensemble (BE), his thoughts up until then often used Shakespeare as an example of the kind of play that was ruined by the institution of theatre in a capitalist society.

One failure in Shakespeare production arose from the dominant tendency of emphasizing character over plot. Around 1951, Brecht dismissed as thoroughly inadequate 'the pathos in comportment and speech which was appropriate to Schiller and the Shakespeare played in his time'.[45] At the same time, he wrote that 'a false understanding of greatness is an obstacle to staging Shakespeare's plays'.[46] Both observations stress the misplaced focus on character rather than on circumstances or relationships with others. Greatness sees man as an island and pathos links the audience to the actor through overblown emotionality. In both cases, which mutually support each other, Brecht read the production of the a-historically human on the conventional stage as a realization of bourgeois ideology with its emphasis on the individual and its banishment of historical consciousness.

The solutions to such problems could not be cosmetic. Brecht criticized modern-dress productions as superficial 'costume dramas'[47] and railed against one of the most famous examples of Shakespeare in cinema history:

> When the English actor [Laurence] Olivier filmed *Henry V*, he began the film with a portrayal of the premiere at Shakespeare's Globe. The acting style was presented as full of pathos, stiff, primitive, practically silly. Then the acting style became 'modern'. The crude old times were overcome, the acting was differentiated, elegant, superior. Hardly any other film has annoyed me as much as this one. What a suggestion that Shakespeare's direction could be any more stupid or crude than that of Mr Olivier.

---

[42]Brecht, '[Gegen Ihering]', BFA 21: 297.
[43]Ibid.
[44]Brecht, 'Anmerkungen zur *Dreigroschenoper*', BFA 25: 58.
[45]Brecht, 'Kontrolle des "Bühnentemperaments" und Reinigung der Bühnensprache', BFA 23: 169.
[46]Brecht, '[Größe bei Shakespeare]', BFA 23: 190.
[47]Brecht, 'Über experimentelles Theater', BFA 22: 541.

[...] The old works have their own values, their own differentiation, their own scale of beauty and truth. Those are what need to be uncovered.[48]

Brecht's criticisms attack first superficiality, that merely updating the costumes does not update the theatre, then the hubris to suggest that the modern interpretation and practice is qualitatively better than that of Shakespeare's day. Without considering Olivier's motives for his decisions, Brecht accuses Olivier of false historicization as he paints the history of the theatre as a journey out of darkness into the light. Brecht's final comment is the key one here: only by properly understanding the older theatre can contemporary theatre-makers survey the distances between the two properly. In the last two decades of his life Brecht signalled a desire to learn as much as possible about Shakespeare and the Globe, although it is difficult to know quite what he knew or how he used it.[49] A recent survey of Brecht's library reveals only one specific volume concerned with Shakespeare in performance, Ronald Watkins' *On Producing Shakespeare* of 1950.[50]

This is perhaps the place for a short excursus into what Brecht thought he had learned about Shakespeare from consulting academic studies of his time. Sadly, we have very little knowledge of what sources informed such reading. At various junctures, Brecht reflected on Shakespeare's work and working methods, often in ways which linked the two men of the theatre intimately. While simple connections, such as reworking other people's source material into new dramas,[51] were easy to establish, more contentious extrapolations tell us more about Brecht than Shakespeare. In a journal entry, Brecht declared that he *believed* that Shakespeare's technique suggested he worked, like Brecht, as the leading member of a theatrical collective, as 'the head of dramaturgy'.[52] While Brecht certainly talks tentatively here, Kussmaul sees Brecht hopelessly mired in the scholarship of the 1920s and 1930s.[53] Elsewhere, Brecht's contention that Shakespeare's stage directions for *Coriolanus* were mostly added by editors[54] is disputed by Symington when he argues that that play is one of Shakespeare's best-preserved texts.[55] Here Brecht was hoping to justify the adaptation process, discussed more fully below, by challenging the apparent authority of the received document. In both cases of scholarly error it should be noted that Brecht was working at a time in which research was less reliable and rigorous. That he manipulated what he did find to serve his purposes is also evident.

To combat what he saw as lazy, reactionary and unproductive engagements with Shakespeare, Brecht hoped to stage Shakespeare's plays with the BE, although he died before he was able to realize his plans. From 1949 until 1954, the BE had no theatre building of its own and was the often unwelcome guest at the Deutsches Theater. Even

---

[48]Brecht, 'Bessons Inszenierung des *Don Juan* beim Berliner Ensemble', BFA 24: 414–15.
[49]See two of Brecht's letters in which he asks friends to send him books of Shakespeare and the Globe, in BFA 29: 162 and 30: 99. In another, he bemoans the fact that he knows too little about original staging practices (BFA 30: 230).
[50]See Bertolt-Brecht-Archiv (ed.), *Die Bibliothek Bertolt Brechts*, 282. He also had Edmond Malone's *Historical Account of the Rise and Progress of the English Stage and of the Economy and Uses of the Ancient Theatres in England* (ibid., 278) but this book, published around 1800, can hardly be described as being at the cutting edge of modern research.
[51]See Brecht, 'Über Plagiate', BFA 21: 175.
[52]Brecht, journal entry for 8 December 1940, BFA 26: 444.
[53]See Kussmaul, *Bertolt Brecht*, 25.
[54]See Brecht, 'Studium des ersten Auftritts in Shakespeares *Coriolan*', BFA 23: 394.
[55]See Symington, *Brecht und Shakespeare*, 182.

without a proper apparatus of its own, the BE was able to introduce Brecht's way of making theatre and of undermining traditional hierarchical structures so that the institution was in harmony with the proposed openness of its own productions. One of its early productions was taken from the Sturm und Drang period of the late eighteenth century, when plays were heavily influenced by Shakespeare's dramaturgy, something considered an antidote to the neoclassicism the German theatre had imported from France.[56] One of the great Stürmer und Dränger was J. M. R. Lenz, and, in 1950, together with a small team of assistants, Brecht chose to adapt and direct *The Tutor* (1774), a practically unknown play at the time. The play leaps between times and locations and a set of interwoven plotlines, much in the style of Shakespeare. It offered the BE the opportunity to experiment with a contemporary staging of a classic text. While I will not go into the details of the production itself, Brecht preferred to have the lovers Fritz and Gustchen recite the poet Klopstock rather than Lenz's own quotations from *Romeo and Juliet*.[57] Klopstock would have been familiar to the audience as the author quoted by Goethe's Werther and Lotte. The substitution of Klopstock for Shakespeare would thus have helped to locate the production in the Sturm und Drang period.

Brecht viewed the production of *The Tutor* as a dry run for the BE's own attempts at staging Shakespeare. He directed with attention to historical detail and emphasized the differences between contemporary and historical attitudes. His journal records how he considered the production 'a study of a new way of performing Shakespeare', something about which he was more specific in a later entry: '*The Tutor* seems well chosen as an exercise for the actors in the realistic and simultaneously the grand style. That is the path to Shakespeare, the way back [...].'[58] The language of this line suggests that Brecht did not consider himself to be radicalizing Shakespearean performance but excavating it. Whether this is true or not is impossible to judge, as we know so little about how Shakespeare was originally staged. However, the approach taken, mixing what Brecht termed realistic detail with a declamatory style, suggested the amalgamation of artifice and reality Brecht identified in both Shakespeare's and his own theatre.

Of Brecht's never-completed projects, one was an adaptation of *Troilus and Cressida* for the BE in the early 1950s. As Robert Weimann argues, the play lent itself to Brecht's dramaturgical interests: 'the hitherto tried and tested form of a harmony between being and appearance is broken open and a deep discrepancy between being and appearance is thematized dramatically'.[59] Consequently speech and meaning are in a constant state of mutual '*Verfremdung*'.[60] The editors of the BFA report that Käthe Rülicke was given the task of working on a sketch of the play's *Fabel* in December 1950: 'According to her, the production [...] was abandoned because Brecht couldn't find a playable *Fabel*.'[61] I retain

---

[56] See, for example, Simon Williams, *Shakespeare on the German Stage: 1586–1914* (Cambridge: Cambridge University Press, 2004), 1–24.
[57] See Brecht, *Der Hofmeister*, BFA 8: 323. It is likely that Brecht used Klopstock due to his association with the most famous Stürmer und Dränger, Goethe. Klopstock is recited by Werther in *The Sufferings of Young Werther* and provided an ironic, metadramatic nod to the period as opposed to a possibly more clichéd reference to the archetypal lovers, an a-historical idea which Brecht, in any case, was keen to undermine.
[58] Brecht, journal entries for 22 December 1949 and 5 March 1950, respectively: BFA 27: 309 for both quotations.
[59] Robert Weimann, 'Shakespeare, Brecht und die deutsche Klassik: *Troilus und Cressida* als wirkungsgeschichtliches Paradigma', *Shakespeare Jahrbuch*, 115 (1979), 25–34, here 26.
[60] Ibid., 27.
[61] The Editors, BFA 9: 342.

the German term because it is different from the more neutral 'plot' in an important way: the *Fabel* is the materialist, realistic control element which ensures that what one sees on stage corresponds to reality by clearly articulating the social relations and thus also the contradictions found in reality. The *Fabel*, consequently, is the dynamic driver of the action as opposed to the attributes of the characters. The *Fabel* is history, whose laws are created by human beings and which can therefore be altered by them, too.

As a dialectician, Brecht was more interested in human relationships than individual human beings because a relationship also tells the audience about the social conditions of any given time in terms of 'who is allowed to do what to whom', to paraphrase Lenin's definition of politics. If social conditions are contradictory, which they inevitably are, then they produce contradictory characteristics in human beings and demonstrate the potential for change. As a result, Brecht continually stressed the *Fabel*. Brecht insisted that every BE production be accompanied by a description of its *Fabel* as a means of organizing the company's approach to staging. Without this key analytical tool, work could not take place.

Brecht's 'playable' requires qualification because *Troilus and Cressida* is obviously eminently 'playable' as a text for the theatre. Referring to Brecht's adaptation of *Coriolanus*, Arrigo Subiotto nonetheless offers a useful definition: 'for Brecht and his collaborators, it ["playable"] connotes an interpretation meaningful, as they see it, in terms of a modern audience'.[62] That is, the text has to bend according to the dialectical intent of the production team. Brecht's own way of writing drama meant that the *Fabel* as an active transformational agent attained a centrality and a clarity which affected the characters. There is no specific information, however, on why *Troilus* failed this test. (Brecht did not completely drop the project, as reported in the BFA. In a letter of 1954, Rülicke wrote: 'Brecht thinks we'll be preparing *Troilus*, *Coriolanus* and *Lear* by Shakespeare.')[63]

Shakespeare offered Brecht an exemplary type of theatre, alive with complexity, contradiction, and historical realism, against which he could contrast the shortcomings of the institution of bourgeois theatre. He could also provisionally use it as a model for his own revolutionary theatre practice. In a letter, Brecht wrote that the actor Wolf Kaiser would make a good Shylock, 'however, the whole Ensemble first has to pass *Shakespeare*'s acid test [*Feuerprobe*]'.[64] Shakespeare thus represented the bar the BE had to clear to prove itself a first-class theatre company. It had to negotiate textual richness, measure historical distance, and bring out the exigencies of the *Fabel*. These were all issues with which Brecht grappled in his practical work with Shakespeare, too, and so I shall now turn my attention to the shorter projects he undertook before focusing on the two more major ones.

---

[62] Arrigo Subiotto, *Bertolt Brecht's Adaptations for the Berliner Ensemble* (London: MHRA, 1975), 187 fn.11.
[63] Käthe Rülicke to Peter Palitzsch, 5 May 1954, in Bertolt-Brecht-Archiv (henceforth BBA), 732/2.
[64] Brecht to Kaiser, 7 January 1956, BFA 30: 412.

# Capitalism

# CHAPTER TWENTY-ONE

# Tracing the Crimes of Capitalism: From Mahagonny to Nazi Germany

ASTRID OESMANN

Brecht, like many leftists of his time, saw fascism as an extreme form of capitalism, but unlike many of his contemporaries, he pursued this critique less through moral condemnation of the two systems – though of course he did condemn them – than by exploring the forms of representation that capitalist societies produce and showing that they share with fascist forms of representation a fundamental immunity to effective social intervention.[1] He explores this theme with regard to capitalism in his *Dreigroschenprozeß*, a text in which he uses the lawsuit that he brought against the Nero Film AG, holders of the rights to the 'Dreigroschenfilm', to demonstrate the role that fictional elements play in the supposedly factual arena of law, a role that makes capital all but omnipotent in the courts. In *Aufstieg und Fall der Stadt Mahagonny* Brecht shows the omnipotent law of money working outside of courts by presenting a society based on a radical form of consumption that works as effectively as capital's control of the courts to block progressive social action. In these two works Brecht extends the critique of representation that he famously applied to traditional forms of western theater into a devastating analysis of the capitalist public sphere.

With the rise of National Socialism in Germany Brecht moved from his critique of capitalism toward the construction of a genealogy of fascism. In the move from *Mahagonny* to *Furcht und Elend des Dritten Reiches* one can see Brecht tracing the passivity and inability to interfere with the crimes committed by the fascist state. In *Mahagonny* unlimited consumption effectively displaces the possibility of social action

---

Astrid Oesmann, 'Tracing the Crimes of Capitalism: From Mahagonny to Nazi Germany', *Brecht Yearbook*, 29 (2004), pp. 99–110.

[1] I am not referring to fascist tendencies in the brutalized atmosphere of Mahagonny, which Brecht also certainly implied. About this topic see Andreas Hauff, '*Aufstieg und Fall der Stadt Mahagonny* als Zeitstück. Historische Anmerkungen zu einer unterschätzen Repertoireoper', in Kathrin Eberl und Wolfgang Ruf, Hrsg., *Musikkonzepte – Konzepte der Musikwissenschaft* (Kassel und New York: Bärenreiter, 2000), 661–68.

built on the solidarity that had earlier been produced by collective hardship and labor, a displacement that cannot eliminate the feelings of solidarity but that successfully renders them either meaningless or dangerous. Proletarians are left atomized and isolated in their consumption, but this is not true for proprietors, for capital creates a *Neutralitätsgürtel* that protects them against social interference (10.1: 689).[2] In *Furcht und Elend* the denial of difference and the elimination of conflict out of which collective consciousness can grow is extended into the most intimate and private realms of life.

If *Mahagonny* and *Furcht und Elend* trace this denial of difference in daily life, the *Dreigroschenprozeß* does parallel work by providing what amounts to an ideological critique of supposedly timeless qualities like justice and injustice. Brecht presents the lawsuit as an experiment in tracing how abstract concepts manifest themselves in real life and in the capitalist state: 'Man muß sich hüten, die großen gedanklichen Dinge, wie Gerechtigkeit oder Persönlichkeit, nur zu suchen, wo man sie findet – in einigen mittelmäßigen Köpfen oder Mäulern – man muß ihnen nachgehen in der gemeinen Wirklichkeit …' (21: 448). By tracing character and justice as they occur and are modified by the 'gemeine Wirklichkeit', Brecht reveals that they are complicated products of processes of cause and effect that take place in the everyday interactions of people and institutions. In short, they are products constructed by public reality and only masquerade as ahistorical qualities.

In his *Buch der Wendungen* Brecht sums up his experience of the decline of the Weimar Republic and the resulting National-Socialist takeover in 1933 in one of Me-Ti's aphorisms: 'Das Einführen der Demokratie kann zur Einführung der Diktatur führen. Das Einführen der Diktatur kann zur Demokratie führen' (18: 88). The question raised by Me-Ti and by the other works discussed in this essay – how we can recognize our true political situation in the face of the powerful forces compelling passivity – find an answer in Brecht's theater, where he seeks to model the construction of a theatrical consciousness that can produce a counter public sphere. In the teaching plays and in *Furcht und Elend*, Brecht experimented in search of techniques through which we might unlearn the passivity taught by the consumerism in *Mahagonny* and by perversions of the language of justice and the courts. Brecht insists that this can only happen if people escape the social isolation fostered under capitalism and compelled by fascism.

> Wenn die Verbrechen sich häufen, werden sie unsichtbar. Wenn die Leiden unerträglich werden, hört man die Schreie nicht mehr … Wenn die Untat kommt, wie der Regen fällt, dann ruft niemand mehr Halt. … Gibt es kein Mittel, den Menschen zu hindern, sich abzuwenden von den Greueln? Warum wendet er sich ab? Er wendet sich ab, weil er keine Möglichkeit des Eingreifens sieht.
>
> (22.1:142)

In this remark of 1935 Brecht describes the terrors of fascism in terms of human perception and social conduct. Terror's continuity disguises its presence, rendering it more difficult to fight. Frequency and regularity (here of crimes and screams) create the illusion of naturalness: no one cries 'Halt' and no one sees possibilities of 'Eingreifen'. 'Halt' as the disruption of the continuous event and 'eingreifen' as intervention into

---

[2] All parenthetical citations of Bertolt Brecht appear as (vol.: page) and refer to Bertolt Brecht, *Werke*, Große kommentierte Berliner und Frankfurter Ausgabe, ed. Werner Hecht, Jan Knopf, Werner Mittenzwei and Klaus-Detlef Müller, 30 vols. (Berlin / Weimar and Frankfurt am Main: Aufbau and Suhrkamp, 1989–2000).

an event were to become defining elements of Brecht's theater and by extension of his concepts of subjectivity and politics. 'Wir können den andern nur begreifen, wenn wir in ihn eingreifen können. Auch uns selbst können wir nur begreifen, indem wir in uns eingreifen,' Brecht writes in his annotations to *Die Mutter* (24: 182). Only through direct encounter and mutual change can people recognize each other and by so doing alter social circumstances.

From this perspective, one might be able to understand Brecht's rather fearless examination of German fascism when he writes: 'Das Denken wird vom Faschismus als ein Verhalten behandelt. [...] Daran ist *nichts* Tadelnswertes. Bisher üblich: das Gedachte mit Gedachtem zu vergleichen, dahinter verschwindet der Denker' (21: 421). This Brechtian approach to reality is not to be mistaken for a reinvention of the subjective agency of the thinker. Instead Brecht attacks thinking as a purely intellectual activity, for he considers that to be a delusion of self-sufficiency. Reliable thought emerges not from the solitary thinker but 'in Form einer Antwort' (21: 404), a formulation requiring the thinker to respond to reality through other people and thus to remain in the field of social encounter. In the absence of other people and of social interaction no question can arise to stimulate an answer.

Valid thought not only requires a social setting to arise, its effects must also be manifest in the public realm where they can be examined by everyone involved: without others man is nothing, as Brecht states in his fragment 'Aus Nichts wird Nichts', and he blames capitalism for creating forms of representation that are immune to social intervention:

> Die kommunistische Forderung, der Einzelne möge seine Bedeutung von der Masse beziehen, kommt von der Beobachtung, daß in unserem (kapitalistischen) Wirtschaftssystem dies faktisch geschieht, indem der Einzelne die Masse ausbeutet und seine Bedeutung eben in der Beute liegt. Daß er seine Bedeutung lediglich an den Besitz der Produktionsmittel bindet und dadurch sich gewalttätig schützt, wieder nichts zu werden, ist ein Grund für die Revolution ...
>
> (10.1: 689)

For Brecht it is the 'Beute' as captured material rather than the simple act of exploitation that constitutes this capitalist contradiction. The capitalist subject excludes himself from the realm of social intervention, thereby rendering himself incomprehensible to others. Because they own the means of production, capitalists ensure their continuous validity in society, even as they absent themselves from the production process as such. In his *Dreigroschenprozeß* Brecht shows that freedom and justice as they occur in bourgeois culture are meaningful only in an ideological constellation that separates thought and expression from material and social life. He thus called the trial a 'soziologisches Experiment', designed to demonstrate the powerlessness of court systems to uphold democratic laws when capitalists have established an omnipotent law of their own. By writing the *Dreigroschenprozeß* Brecht undertakes what Burkhardt Lindner calls a 'Verwandlung einer Privatangelegenheit in eine öffentliche'.[3]

In *Mahagonny* Brecht stages a different sociological experiment by imagining a city of pure consumption. The city of Mahagonny differs from all other cities in that it is

---

[3] Burkhardt Lindner, 'Der Dreigroschenprozeß', in *Brecht Handbuch*, Bd. 4: *Schriften, Journale, Briefe*, hg. von Jan Knopf (Stuttgart und Weimar; Metzler, 2003), 153.

without the pains of production and labor: 'Eine Woche ist hier: sieben Tage ohne Arbeit' (2: 336). This city of leisure is entirely concerned with supply and consumption.

The opera begins when Paul Ackermann, having spent seven years engaged in backbreaking labor in Alaska, comes to Mahagonny to spend his hard-earned money on 'Ruhe, Eintracht, Whisky, Mädchen' (2: 353). Ultimately he loses all his money in a bet on a friend in a boxing match, and lacking money and the legal status as a consumer that it provides, he is sentenced to death.

The opera recalls Baal's perspective on consumption by portraying Paul and the other men drinking, fighting, and pursuing sex. But in *Mahagonny*, unlike *Baal*, these activities are unambiguously pleasurable, lacking any of the painful aspects of pleasure-seeking. The result is a conflict-free and boring realm, 'Weil hier nichts los ist ... / Weil zuviel Ruhe herrscht / Und zuviel Eintracht / Und weil's zu viel gibt / Woran man sich halten kann' (2: 354). Oversupply guarantees harmony, which leads to a loss of social contact. The capitalists who own Mahagonny can keep themselves free of the direct encounter with others because they only participate in supplying pleasure, while the buyer perceives his consumerism as liberation from social constraint. Such is the case when Paul orders Jenny to walk around without her underwear in order to be more readily available (2: 346). As the inventor of Mahagonny, Leokadja Begbick says, 'Denn es ist die Wollust der Männer / Nicht zu leiden und alles zu dürfen' (2: 336), a drive to be satisfied as long as the men can pay. Consumers need not take responsibility for their acts because their money does, but there is a price for this safety: they are excluded from the production of pleasure and thus they cannot influence what is offered to them. In *Mahagonny* consuming pleasure provides empty satisfaction, as Paul's refrain of 'Aber etwas fehlt' (2: 350) clearly shows.

Paul's frustration with Mahagonny and his eventual downfall are both rooted in his need for the one thing Mahagonny cannot provide – social connection. Paul reacts to this need by recalling a past friendship forged through shared labor in Alaska. The memory misleads him regarding his present situation, as shown in the famous argument in which Paul tells his friends that he wants to eat his hat. His friends react by brutally ensuring Paul of their physical presence:

> Treib es nicht zu dick!
> Paule, da ist ein Strick! ...
> Wir schlagen dich einfach nieder
> Ach, Paule, bis du wieder
> ein Mensch bist!
> Paul *ruhig*:
> Oh, Jungens, ich will doch gar kein Mensch sein.
>
> (10.1: 689)

Here Brecht invokes 'Strick' very much as he famously does in the *Fatzer* fragment. In both cases the 'Strick' or rope is used to bind someone who expects too much (Fatzer and Paul alike) to the ground of reality. Paul's quiet response, in which he states that he does not want to be a human being, further separates him from the social reality of Mahagonny. Just as in *Aus Nichts wird Nichts* isolation gives way to dictatorship, which is immediately followed by the final downfall.

Tying Paul down, grounding him, is but an empty threat, and Paul remains in Adorno's words 'ein Bündel von Regungen und Bedeutungen, die sich überschneiden, ein Mensch in der Zerstreutheit seiner Züge ... ein Fetzen Produktivkraft, der die Anarchie realisiert und aufdeckt und deshalb sterben muß; ein Wesen vielleicht, das überhaupt nicht in die sozialen Relationen eingeht ...'[4] Paul doesn't even enter a social relationship, nor can he, for nobody in Mahagonny does. His need to be productive leads only to a void and, when he proves unable to suppress it, ultimately to self-destruction. Here Adorno and Brecht find remarkable common ground in their diagnoses of failed subjectivity under capitalism.[5] According to Brecht, Paul must remain a productive force devoid of form and meaning in Mahagonny, because only through the social relations of production could he acquire significance. This becomes clear when Paul undermines the previously existing regulations created by the providers of sex and alcohol in Mahagonny. Showing no sign of fear during the hurricane, Paul acquires an invulnerability that allows him to dominate the one fearful situation in Mahagonny: 'Ja, denn ich, der ich lustig bin, zerschlage lieber deine Tafeln und deine Gesetze, und deine Mauern müssen hin sein. Wie der Hurrikan es auch macht, so mache ich es. Du bekommst Geld dafür. Hier ist es' (2: 359). By accepting the fearful moments caused by the Hurricane ('So, wie wenn's einen Hurrikan gibt / So wollen wir immer leben', 2: 359), Paul extends his agreement with the situation to his own subjectivity, which he perceives to be without limits – no laws, no walls – in terms of social and spatial restriction.

His triumph is marked when he sings the 'Du darfst' song while facing death during the hurricane. With his 'Du darfst' Paul discovers 'die Gesetze der menschlichen Glückseligkeit', and the legal system of the town changes accordingly; 'Du darfst' becomes the law of human happiness with Paul Ackermann as its creator. But Paul's dictatorship of the moment deludes him about the fundamental law of Mahagonny, which rests subjectivity upon the ability to spend money. From this perspective Paul's demand of 'Du darfst' is nothing but the preference of a paying consumer without any reference to universal rights. Paul's delusion of omnipotence, however, seduces him into a fatal act of solidarity in which he risks and loses everything on his friend Joe's boxing match, Paul's love for Joe developed during seven years of labor in Alaska, and Paul seeks to revitalize his love in Mahagonny by invoking it as a timeless possession that lasts 'von der Wiege bis zum Grabe' (2: 367). This recollection proves fatal to both friends in Mahagonny, for their commitment grew out of their shared battle for survival in Alaska, and this commitment lacks validity in Mahagonny. The signs carried around the stage at the end of the opera – including 'Für die Liebe' followed by 'Für die Käuflichkeit der Liebe' (2: 387) – re-enforce Brecht's decision to elide the contradiction between capitalist practice and bourgeois values by presenting a moral completely in tune with consumption, a moral in which love is neither an act nor a virtue, but a commodity. Therefore, Paul can show solidarity with Joe only by betting money on him. Each man pays with his life for this commitment: Joe dies during the fight, and Paul is executed for the crime of lacking money.

Paul's conflation of friendship and consumerism can best be described through Oskar Negt's and Alexander Kluge's treatment of the contradiction between the proletarian experience and commodification:

---

[4] Theodor W. Adorno, 'Mahagonny', *Gesammelte Schriften* 17, hg. v. Rolf Tiedemann (Frankfurt am Main; Suhrkamp, 1982), 114–122, here 117–18.
[5] In their critique of modern subjectivity Brecht and Adorno had more in common than conventionally believed. On the conflict between Adorno and Brecht see, for example, Theodor W. Adorno, 'Engagement', *Noten zur Literatur* (Frankfurt am Main Suhrkamp, 1981), 409–30.

> Erfahrungen werden in dem Maße zu Waren, in dem sie auf einen Generalnenner zu bringen sind. Alle Erfahrungen des Proletariats sind spezifisch ... Sie werden als qualitative Momente produziert. Die Aufarbeitung der proletarischen Erfahrung ist deshalb so schwer, weil sie nicht die Kommensurabilität der Warenbeziehungen hat. Sie verändert sich mit jeder Veränderung der Situation.[6]

In Mahagonny no production of the specific moment exists 'weil es nichts gibt, woran man sich halten', according to Leokadja, or according to Paul 'weil es zuviel gibt, woran man sich halten kann'. Both statements mean the same thing, as Adorno points out: where there is nothing, there is too much.[7] The capitalist law of consumption isolates people from each other, a separation that ends in self-consumption. Four short scenes in *Mahagonny* demonstrate how unlimited indulgence creates dissatisfaction that leads to self-destruction, 'Jakob der Vielfraß', for example, eats two calves and complains: 'Alles ist nur halb / Ich äße mich gerne selber' (2: 362). Jakob's isolation produces self-absorption that he expresses as exhibitionism when he asks others to watch him eat. Jakob, as 'ein Mann ohne Furcht' (2: 363), deludes himself that he is free because he can eat without limitations, a delusion that causes his premature if 'natural' death. Paul, on the other hand, receives a death sentence because of his lack of money. He becomes a criminal by importing a solidarity rooted in the realm of labor in Alaska into Mahagonny's realm of pure consumption. Production and commitment fuel Paul's ascent in Alaska, but they destroy him in Mahagonny – the 'Aufarbeitung der proletarischen Erfahrung' is impossible. The social dynamics of Mahagonny lack 'Verhalten' as the production of the specific moment, and Brecht diagnoses a fundamental lack of social conduct in capitalist societies in general, as his *Dreigroschenprozeß* shows.

Without possibilities of social intervention economic interests acquire the quality of natural forces that are immune to human laws and regulations, a condition that proved infinitely supportive of fascist ideologies during the rise of National Socialism in Germany. Separating prerogative power from the public realm – one goal shared by capitalism and fascism – makes it impossible to trace the diverse interests that motivate the various parts of the social body. According to Brecht, material interests should be presented openly: 'Das soziologische Experiment zeigt die gesellschaftlichen Antagonismen, ohne sie aufzulösen. Die Veranstalter müssen also im Kräftefeld der widersprechenden Interessen selber eine Interessenstellung einnehmen, einen durchaus subjektiven, absolut parteiischen Standpunkt' (21: 512f.). Brecht's *Dreigroschenprozeß* as sociological experiment performs conflict, revealing in the process the persistence of social antagonisms rather than offering solutions to them.

To turn the sociological experiment into a theatrical experience in terms of a 'Kräftefeld der widersprechenden Interessen', Brecht developed his most experimental form of theater, the *Lehrstücke* (teaching plays), designed to produce and examine social conduct as dependent on time and circumstance. Constraint improves the visibility of social conduct as the reduced patterns of the *Lehrstücke* show. For example, the *Badener Lehrstück vom Einverständnis* starts out with an interactive definition of space when the stage becomes a 'in seinen Abmessungen der Anzahl der Mitspielenden entsprechenden

---

[6]Oskar Negt and Alexander Kluge, *Öffentlichkeit und Erfahrung: Zur Organisationsanalyse von bürgerlicher und proletarischer Öffentlichkeit* (Frankfurt am Main: Suhrkamp, 1972), 44.
[7]Adorno, 'Mahagonny', 116.

Podium' (3: 27). Brecht later extends this approach to his concept of a dialectical theater when he writes about the stage: 'Der Raum ist gegeben durch die Stellungen, welche die Personen zueinander einnehmen, und die Bewegungen, welche sie vollführen' (22: 242). The stage is created out of the encounters among and activity of the participants. Political thought, then, is released into an experimental field in which it becomes a matter of social experience that grows out of the intellectual and physical activity of each participant.

These exercises in limitation can be considered Brecht's counter public sphere, which is in its practice entirely tied to the here and now. Because they remain in the eternal present, the teaching plays produce more of an ideological critique than an exercise in ideological commitment. They are in this way the counter model to the Mahagonny of unlimited satisfaction. This anticipates the critique that Negt and Kluge would later offer of bourgeois thought and moves the critique into the realm of experience. Negt and Kluge follow a similar trajectory by comparing bourgeois and proletarian concepts of freedom in their reading of Hobbes:

> Wenn Hobbes als Freiheit den tatsächlichen physischen Bewegungsspielraum eines Menschen bezeichnet, so trifft das genau die materielle Erfahrungsweise der Massen. Ein Mensch im Gefängnis hat so viel Freiheit, wie er sich bewegen kann. Seine Gedanken mögen ihn trösten, sie geben ihm keinen Schritt mehr Freiheit. Der Schillersche Satz 'Der Mensch ist frei geschaffen, ist frei, und wär' er in Ketten geboren' ist für die Massen absolut unverständlich, sobald sie sich auf ihre eigene Erfahrung stützen. Erdrückt lediglich die radikale Trennung von geistiger und körperlicher Arbeit aus.[8]

Instead of unlimited freedom, Brecht creates flexible concepts of the theater and the public, but these concepts are limited, as Brecht fully understood, as guides to social reality, because reality occurs in complicated historical contexts rather than in a simplified ethnographic present. People's interests vary from situation to situation, and an absolute opposition is rarely presented in the historical contingencies of the real world. In the teaching plays, however, the theatrical meets the sociological experiment that Brecht describes in his *Dreigroschenprozeß* as such: 'Das Begreifen des soziologischen Experiments ist ein "Griffe finden". Es kommt nicht auf Grund eines Anschauungsaktes zustande, es endet nicht mit dem Zustandekommen einer Anschauung. Hier soll Erfahrung die Grundlage der Handhabung abgeben' (21: 513). Comprehension as 'Griffe finden' is built on experience with a given situation, Brecht calls this concept of thought 'eingreifendes Denken', a particularly theatrical form of thought that is based on the observance of and response to the behavior of others.

The concept of 'eingreifendes Denken' gains particular significance in Brecht's analysis of fascism. In 1935, after the establishment of fascism in Germany, Brecht sought to develop techniques and methods to examine fascism and the mechanics of its persistence, or, as he calls it, 'Die Theatralisierung der Politik durch den Faschismus' (26: 443). Given that Brecht himself opted to stage politics in order to construct a public sphere and a political rationale, he sought to clarify the distinction between the theater of fascism and the theater of anti-fascism. *Furcht und Elend des Dritten Reiches*, which was originally intended to be performed by emigrant actors in exile, uses speech and corporeal gesture to

---

[8]Negt and Kluge, 43–44.

demonstrate political terror in reduced private settings.[9] One recognizes the tactics of the state through the everyday, commonplace gestures of its subjects. The play is a montage of twenty-seven scenes that come together as a 'Gestentafel', demonstrating 'Gesten des Verstummens, Sich-Umblickens, Erschreckens usw. Die Gestik unter der Diktatur' (26: 318). Each scene demonstrates in specific detail either the regime's violence and cruelty toward its victims or the day-to-day complicity of 'normal Germans' in the regime's survival.

Brecht's concept of the public sphere sheds light on his approach to fascism. The fear and misery he depicts in the play occur most often in private; in fact, the ascent of fascism is congruent with the fearful withdrawal of people into greater and greater privacy, seclusion, and isolation. Personal seclusion breeds public dishonesty. Walter Benjamin writes about *Furcht und Elend*. 'Jeder dieser kurzen Akte weist *eines* auf: wie unabwendbar die Schreckensherrschaft, die sich als Drittes Reich vor den Walter brüstet, alle Verhältnisse zwischen Menschen unter die Botmäßigkeit der Lüge zwingt.'[10] The characters cannot accurately perceive their relationships to others, nor can they evaluate the situations in which they find themselves in order to determine how to behave reasonably toward others. Attempting to comprehend what happens by relying solely on themselves, characters become vigilant spies. This regression causes disorientation as the scene 'Der Spitzel' shows. A husband and wife argue about rejecting a formerly befriended family, and the incident releases a chain of arguments fueled by fear and accusations ranging from 'Es ist unangenehm, daß wir uns gerade jetzt von ihnen zurückziehen, wo sich alles von ihnen zurückzieht' (4: 392) to a quarrel about their own son, 'Einen Judas hast du mir geboren! Der sitzt bei Tisch und horcht. ... und merkt sich alles, was seine Erzeuger sagen, der Spitzel!' (4: 399). The realistic fear of being spied upon combines with a general feeling of exclusion to fuel paranoia. This dynamic results from the family's regression into seclusion while further encouraging that very regression. Constant, secret observation renders social life private and destroys the public sphere.

The only scene that presents a way out of this dynamic is entitled 'Der Entlassene'. It presents a communist who, after being released from a concentration camp, visits a couple who were former comrades (a relationship built in the past, as was the case with Paul and Joe in *Mahagonny*). In order to find out if their former comrade has revealed any information under torture, the man and the woman decide to treat him as a spy and interrogate him. While the entire scene presents cautious distrust, the characters' behavior toward one another proves to be liberating precisely because the interrogation is performed openly. The three participants create a public sphere by refusing to withdraw into privacy: the husband asks his wife not to leave the room during the conversation with their visitor. The interrogation becomes a Brechtian experiment when the man states, 'Wir können es schon feststellen, wo er steht', and the woman warns, 'Das kann aber dauern' (4: 411). All three seek to reveal the political positions of the others and are acutely aware that these positions change with time and circumstance. They identify each other's political position (signified through their spatial position toward each other) through constant interrogation and observation.

---

[9] For an explicit treatment of 'Gestus' in *Furcht und Elend* see Robert Cohen, 'Brecht's *Furcht und Elend des Dritten Reiches* und der Status des Gestus'. *The Brecht Yearbook* 24 (2000), 193–208.
[10] Walter Benjamin, 'Das Land, in dem das Proletariat nicht genannt werden darf', *Gesammelte Schriften* II.2, hg. v. Rolf Tiedemann and Hermann Schweppenhäuser (Frankfurt am Main: Suhrkamp, 1980), 517–18.

The three comrades reveal their awareness of the mutability of individual political loyalty through their distrust of one another. The released prisoner, for example, chooses not to tell his hosts that Nazi torturers mutilated his hand because he fears that the couple will believe that he cracked in the face of such pain. Paradoxically, his lie communicates the more important truth that he is strong enough to resist interrogation. This presentation of the creation of a progressive public sphere through open confrontation, distrust, and self-interested dissimulation directly contradicts the Nazi ideology of 'Volksgemeinschaft'. The fascist regime sought to perpetuate prevailing power structures by pretending to unite everyone in a harmonious and homogeneous community. By presenting the rise of fascism in a variety of scenes, Brecht shows the way that a theater of unity drives social differences off the streets and into the private realm, thus contributing to the rise of fascism. The individual's decision to protect her or his personal integrity by withdrawing from fascism proves to be its most powerful promoter.

The surrender to fascism is thus rooted in the original desire to withdraw from it. Only the three comrades in 'Der Entlassene' avoid this, and they do so by constantly negotiating with one another their unavoidable involvement in the fascist state. By challenging each other, they confront each potential compromise with the state and thus retain the ability to distinguish between accommodating and subverting fascism. Each navigates a personal position toward the state through her or his position toward the other two as individuals and toward their collective. This allows them to detect and thus resist fascism's constantly shifting modes of attack.

Fascism's delusion to unite and capitalism's delusion to satisfy both hinder the production of the specific moments in which actual relations among people become visible and thus changeable. In *Mahagonny* Brecht presents a capitalist world in which 'Verhalten' as social conduct has become obsolete through unlimited supply that ends up in nothing. The opera concludes in 'zunehmender Verwirrung' in which 'die noch nicht Erledigten' move in a throng with placards declaring their political ideals while they sing about their complete passivity: 'Können uns und euch und niemand helfen' (2: 392)

Brecht's alternative is constraint for the purpose of social intervention: staying together and creating a public sphere makes an investigation of the moment possible. To comprehend a given situation, 'eingreifendes Denken' uses 'solche Definitionen, die die Handhabung eines definierten Feldes gestatten. Unter den determinierenden Faktoren tritt immer das Verhalten des Definierenden auf' (21: 422). In *Furcht und Elend* Brecht places fascist thought in specific contexts in order to examine a range of gestures and the ways those gestures change as the contexts producing them alter.[11] Fascism and anti-fascism result from the interaction among people in specific moments. What might be intended as an antifascist act by one individual can nevertheless become a fascist act, depending on circumstance. Political conviction, then, is not a matter of a subjective decision based on principles, but something to be deciphered and constructed from social reality. Brecht shows how the process of deciphering must inform the construction of progressive political perception and how that action is hindered under fascism through

---

[11] From this perspective the scenes in *Furcht und Elend* make use of Brecht's concept of 'Gestus' especially in the circular movement from 'Grundgestus' to fable to characters and their inter-subjectivity and back to 'Grundgestus', See Patrice Pavis, 'On Brecht's Notion of Gestus', in *Languages of the Stage: Essays on the Semiology of the Theatre* (Baltimore: The Johns Hopkins UP, 1982), 37–50.

the use of terror to deny difference, as well as under capitalism through the fetishism of consumption to efface the conflicts of production.

Brecht's teaching plays constitute the theatrical genre invented to create social action in a theatrical context. By perceiving ourselves and others as actors or demonstrators, we overcome the divide not just between thought and life, but also between production and consumption. In turn, the theater can break out of its traditional institutional context. Brecht transforms the public into a theater and the theater into a public, not as an institution, but as a playing field. This field as experimental space, Brecht's 'Kräftefeld der widersprechenden Interessen' (21: 512-13), proves to be essential for understanding the political situation that surrounds us. Once thought becomes living matter, it becomes historical because it is subject to historical contingency, and those who perceive it in this way and are able to act upon that perception become a public. From this perspective the teaching plays are designed to strengthen our perception of reality instead of instructing us in ideology: 'Die Form der Lehrstücke ist streng, jedoch nur, damit Teile eigener Erfindung und aktueller Art desto leichter eingefügt werden können' (22 1: 351). The teaching plays as a theater of situation certainly provided an experience on which a theater of emergency such as *Furcht und Elend des Dritten Reiches* could draw. To produce situations in which one can intervene is the function of the teaching play, and the absence of such situations in *Mahagonny* accounts for Paul Ackermann's overall weakness. In 1932 Brecht notes the following: 'In den Zeiten der Schwäche ist man engagiert und man engagiert sich nicht, … ist viel nötig und kann weniges geschehen; der Ausgeschaltete ist in Ruhe versetzt und hat keine Ruhe' (21: 585). It is no coincidence that Brecht began at this time to develop his concept of 'eingreifendes Denken', which would equally affect his approaches to theater and politics.

# The Natural Sciences

# CHAPTER TWENTY-TWO

# Brecht and Science – Science and Brecht?: A Dialectical View

KATHARINA BRINKERT
TRANSLATED BY ROMY FURSLAND

On a brief reading of the *Short Organon for the Theatre*, which Brecht described in his *Journal* in 1948 as a summary of *Buying Brass*, it soon becomes clear how much the new insights in the field of science, and their social consequences, shaped his thoughts and statements on a new, dialectical theatre – a 'theatre of the scientific age', as he described it in the preface. From his observation that the old theatre and its ideas about aesthetics are no longer 'fit for the times' in the wake of the social progress brought about by scientific and technological innovations, to his concrete criticism of society's engagement with scientific discoveries and the social responsibility of the scientist in *Life of Galileo*, Brecht's view of science and his understanding of scientific concepts such as the wave-particle duality in Heisenberg's uncertainty principle are not only essential to the development of his theory of epic theatre and its realization in the *Lehrstücke*, but also enable a reflexive view of the sciences from a different, much more social perspective.

This article will undertake a dialectical reflection with the title 'Brecht and Science – Science and Brecht?' In a dialogue addressing the question 'Who is learning from whom?', it will analyse not only the extent to which scientific methods of acquiring knowledge feature in Brecht's works but also the reciprocal relationships between Brecht's work and the sciences. I will attempt to make a connection between the theoretical and practical reflections in Brecht's theoretical work on theatre, on the one hand, and scientific approaches on the other. I will also try to identify how Brecht's concepts of epic theatre and his statements and thoughts on science and scientific discoveries actually influence science itself in a lasting way by calling for 'new thinking' and 'correct seeing'. On closer inspection, it seems that Brecht's answer to the question: 'But what does science have to do with art?' is as relevant today as it was then.

---

Katharina Brinkert, 'Brecht und die Naturwissenschaften – die Naturwissenschaften und Brecht?', in Christian Hippe and Volker Ißbrücker (eds), *Brecht und Naturwissenschaften* (Berlin: Verbrecher, 2017), pp. 251–63.

## SCIENTIFIC RESEARCH AND ITS RELATIONSHIP TO THE HUMANITIES

When Alfred Nobel wrote in his will on 27 November 1895 that his wealth was to be used to set up a fund, 'the interest on which is to be distributed annually as prizes to those who, during the preceding year, have conferred the greatest benefit to humankind',[1] he could never have guessed how important this prize would become over time, and the social significance that would one day be accorded to it. It seems almost as if there is no other prize where the sciences are more inclined to open their doors to the public and offer a momentary glimpse into a world which is trying to investigate fundamental principles and laws of nature, and use the discoveries it makes to promote our social development. But how is research into nature and its phenomena actually conducted? How do we design an experiment whereby researchers and explorers are granted an insight into the functioning of nature's highly complex mechanisms, which it has been consistently optimising over the course of millions of years? These are question whose answers enable and indeed almost require us to make connections with other disciplines – whose explanations make the sciences in their turn seem almost philosophical, even artistic. This proximity and affinity between the sciences and the humanities – which may seem antithetical at first glance, due to the different orientations, structures, philosophies and directions of the two faculties in their approaches to acquiring knowledge – will be examined in more detail below.

## THE PROBLEM OF OBJECTIVITY IN THE SCIENTIFIC EXPERIMENT

In the nineteenth century, the separation of the 'natural' and the 'human' sciences was defended by Wilhelm Dilthey, who argued that the phenomena to be investigated pose different problems which the two faculties investigate in different ways. The natural sciences, claimed Dilthey, examine a situation objectively and in line with established laws, whereas objective research is not possible in the humanities because 'the person studying history is the person making history'.[2] It follows from this that the object of study in the humanities is not straightforwardly pre-existing, as in the sciences, but is actually constituted and defined by the subject. This fact led, despite the emphasis on universalism in the nineteenth century, to a strict division between the sciences and the humanities, which was only revised in the first half of the twentieth century as a result of observations in scientific experiments. With the postulation of Heisenberg's uncertainty principle and the birth of quantum mechanics, the sciences – which had previously been capable of such precise and objective conclusions – encountered a new problem: the fact that, unlike on the macrocosmic level, processes on the microcosmic level cannot be observed without being altered. It is impossible to observe and describe an object without it being disrupted by the person observing it. The object under investigation is so tiny that it can only be properly observed

---

[1] Translation taken from the full text of Alfred Nobel's will, available online at https://www.nobelprize.org/alfred-nobel/full-text-of-alfred-nobels-will-2/ (accessed 31/05/19)
[2] Wilhelm Dilthey, 'Der Aufbau der geschichtlichen Welt in den Geisteswissenschaften', in *Gesammelte Schriften*, Vol. 7, ed. Bernhard Groethuysen (Stuttgart, 1958), 278.

using some kind of instrument. This in turn means that the object is deformed by the examination methods used, or that the object is in fact constituted by the perceiving subject. Thus an objective observation in the traditional scientific sense is no longer possible.[3] These newly emerging parallels with the research approaches of the humanities are summarised by Werner Heisenberg:

> When you try, based on the situation in modern science, to feel your way towards the foundations which have now been set in motion, you get the impression that it is probably not a gross simplification of the case to say that for the first time in history, human beings on this earth are confronted only with themselves, and have no other partners or adversaries. [...] In the sciences too, therefore, the object of study is no longer nature in and of itself, but nature subjected to human questioning, and in this sense humankind again comes face to face with itself.[4]

But direct intervention in the immediate surroundings of the studied object, and the object's response to this change, also represent an intrinsic property of the object: Brecht, who was demonstrably fascinated by the fact that there is no sharp distinction between the activity of the subject and the reaction of the object, and the fact that subject and object are so 'connected' to each other, noted that the observed uncertainty is a property of the object which forces the subject to rethink and revise his or her previous categories, logic and ways of thinking, and to submit to this property of the object if he or she wants to characterise and examine it in more detail.[5] This observation of Brecht's is summed up by Francis Bacon's axiom (which is also found in Brecht's notes and which Brecht recommends as a 'good motto for realists'): *'natura non nisi parendo vincitur* (if you want to command nature, you must obey it)'.[6]

So what does this mutual dependency of subject and object mean for research into the laws of the macro world? In an age of high-resolution technologies which ostensibly give us insights into the ongoing processes of nature and help us formulate models and laws – more broadly defined – is there any such thing as objectivity? The list of Nobel Prize winners shows that clearly there is. We seem to be able to observe natural phenomena in a subjective way and derive objective and universally valid laws from these observations. But how? By making sure, when we study nature, that we follow those of its laws that we are aware of and adapt our research methods as necessary. This will be illustrated by an example from research into photosynthesis.

---

[3] See also Jan Knopf, 'Bertolt Brecht und die Naturwissenschaften', in *Brecht-Jarhbuch* 1978, 13–38.
[4] Peter Krausser, *Kritik der endlichen Vernunft. Diltheys Revolution der allgemeinen Wissenschafts- und Handlungstheorie* (Frankfurt, 1968), 44.
[5] See Knopf, 'Bertolt Brecht und die Naturwissenschaften', 22.
[6] Bertolt Brecht, *Werke. Große kommentierte Berliner und Frankfurter Ausgabe*, ed. Werner Hecht, Jan Knopf, Werner Mittenzwei and Klaus-Detlef Müller (Berlin and Weimar and Frankfurt am Main, 1988ff.) BFA 22.2: 638. (Cited hereinafter as BFA with volume and page number). See also Francis Bacon, *The Works of Francis Bacon, Baron of Verulam, Viscount St. Alban, and Lord High Chancellor of England*, ed. James Spedding, Robert Leslie Ellis, Douglas Denon Heath (London, 1857ff.), Vol. 6 (Literary and professional works; Vol. 1), 157.

# UNDERSTANDING THE 'DYNAMO OF LIFE': THE DEVELOPMENT OF EXPERIMENTS IN PHOTOSYNTHESIS RESEARCH

With the development of oxygenic photosynthesis in the ancestors of cyanobacteria around 2.3 billion years ago, nature made a landmark achievement: it was now able to convert solar energy to chemical energy, a form it was able to use. Photosynthesis is the energy base for almost all living organisms, making it the most important biological process on earth.[7] Forty-five per cent of the solar energy that reaches us on a sunny day is converted into biomass, with an average efficiency rate of 4–6 per cent.[8] Every year, cyanobacteria alone – which only represent around 25 per cent of photosynthetically active species – convert some 450 TW of solar energy into chemical energy in the world's lakes and oceans.[9] So how does this unique process work and how do we study it? With oxygenic photosynthesis, we distinguish between two key reactions: in the light reaction, which uses light energy as the driver for the oxidation of water in order to reduce the iron-sulphur complex ferredoxin, a proton motive force is generated which provides the amount of energy needed to produce the chemical energy carrier ATP. In the dark reaction, or carbon fixation reaction, atmospheric carbon dioxide is converted into simple sugar using nicotinamide adenine dinucleotide phosphate hydrogen (NADPH), another energy carrier which is formed in the light reaction. The key reaction in the conversion of solar energy into chemical energy is the oxidation or 'splitting' of water. This fundamental reaction takes place in the reaction centre of photosystem II, which is located in the thylakoid membrane of the chloroplasts of higher plants and algae and oxidizes water using a catalyst, the so-called oxygen-evolving complex (also called OEC or $CaMn_4O_5$ cluster) according to the following reaction scheme (I):

$$2H_2O \rightarrow 4H^+ + O_2 + 4e^-$$

A fundamental discovery concerning photosystem II was made in 1969 by Pierre Joliot,[10] who carried out an experiment in which he fired a series of short flashes of light at a sample of dark-adapted thylakoid membranes of the chloroplasts of cyanobacteria, and recorded the production of oxygen depending on the number of flashes of light. In this experiment, he established that oxygen was first released after the third flash and then after every fourth flash. This result was interpreted a year later by Bessel Kok and his colleagues and led to the model of the so-called Kok cycle or S-cycle. In this cycle, the $S_1$-state represents a stable dark state of the catalyst, while the $S_4$-state converts spontaneously into the $S_0$-state and generates an oxygen molecule.[11] The S-cycle is controlled in four of the five stages by the photoexcitation of several chlorophyll pigments in close proximity

---

[7]Patrick Jordan, Petra Fromme, Horst Tobias Witt, Olaf Klukas, Wolfram Saenger, Norbert Krauß, 'Three-dimensional structure of cyanobacterial photosystem I at 2.5 Å resolution', in *Nature* 411 (2001), 909–917.
[8]Anastasios Melis, 'Solar energy conversion efficiencies in photosynthesis: Minimizing the chlorophyll antennae to maximize efficiency', in *Plant Science* 177 (2009), 272–280.
[9]John B. Waterbury, 'Widespread occurrence of a unicellular, marine, planktonic cyanobacterium' in *Nature* 277 (1979), 293–294.
[10]P. Joliot, G. Barbieri, R. Cjabaud, 'Un nouveau modèle des centres photochimiques du système II' in *Photochemistry and Photobiology* 10 (1969), 309–329.
[11]B. Kok, B. Forbush, M. McGloin, 'Cooperation of charges in photosynthetic $O_2$ evolution: I. A linear four-step mechanism' in *Photochemistry and Photobiology* 11 (1970), 457–475.

to each other (according to the wavelength of the light at which the system shows an absorption maximum, also called P680). The resulting excited P680* then transfers an electron to a neighbouring pheophytin, which then reduces a bound quinone QA and is thereby oxidized. This quinone also reduces a mobile quinone QB, which, when it has taken on two electrons, is transferred into a quinone pool in the membrane. The electron is now transported via the so-called cytochrome $b_6f$ complex and a plastocyanin to the reaction centre photosystem I (more precisely: P700), which is also able to emit electrons thanks to photoexcitation of the chlorophylls found there. These electrons are transferred to the enzyme ferredoxin-NADP+-oxidoreductase, which generates the energy carrier NADPH.[12] Depending on the status of the S-cycle, the oxidized P680$^+$ is reduced by a redox-active tyrosine unit within 20–40 nanoseconds. This in turn is reduced further by the oxygen evolving complex in the Kok cycle, as described above.[13]

## STUDYING BIOLOGICAL WATER-SPLITTING

Water oxidation in the OEC, consisting of a tetranuclear four-coordinate Manganese cluster in which four Manganese atoms are joined via five oxygen atoms and a calcium ion, is a complex reaction – and also one of the most important reactions to take place in the natural world. Despite many years of intensive research, we still do not know the finer details of how it really works. As mentioned above, the oxidation of water as a multi-stage process can be described using the S-cycle. We have known for some time that water is the oxygen supplier in the reaction; and we have also known for a while that molecular oxygen is released during the transition from the $S_{4-}$ into the $S_{0-}$ state. Despite comprehensive studies, which were conducted, for example, using EPR (electronic paramagnetic resonance) spectroscopy and showed that the two water molecules of the reaction in the $S_2$ state bond with the cluster, the exact mechanism of proton release is still not fully explained. Methods for the further study of this process of so-called 'natural water-splitting' – in order, for example, to be able to carry out 'artificial' photosynthesis and gain new insights in the field of solar energy research – include the selective exchange of calcium ions in the cluster for a strontium ion with the same charge.[14] Because strontium is about twice as heavy as calcium, it is possible to investigate, among other things, whether the catalytic process is affected by the ion exchange (i.e., whether it happens more quickly or more slowly). This in turn makes it possible to draw conclusions about the importance of the calcium ion to the bonding of water with the catalyst, for instance. Thus, through targeted interventions in the photosynthesis apparatus, we can establish step by step the importance and functioning of specific co-factors in the reaction centres, helping us to understand this highly complex biological apparatus. It is important when carrying out the experiment, however, that the studied object is examined under the right physiological conditions and thus remains stable for the duration of the experiment. This

---

[12] T. Cardona, A. Sedoud, N. Cox, A. W. Rutherford, 'Charge separation in Photosystem I: A comparative and evolutionary overview', in *BBA – Bioenergetics* 1817 (2012), 26–43.

[13] H. Dau, I. Zahariev, M. Haumann, 'Recent developments in research on water oxidation by Photosystem II', in: *Curr. Opin. Chem. Biol.* 16 (2012), 3–10; and Y. Umena, K. Kawakami, J. R. Shen, N. Kamiya, 'Crystal structure of oxygen-evolving Photosystem II at a resolution of 1.9 Å' in *Nature* 473 (2011), 55–60.

[14] Roehl M. Cinco, John H. Robblee, Annette Rompel, Carmen Fernandez, Vittal K. Yachandra, Kenneth Sauer, Melvin P. Klein, 'Strontium EXAFS Reveals the Proximity of Calcium to the Manganese Cluster of Oxygen-Evolving Photosystem II' in *J. Phys. Chem. B* 102 (1998), 8248–8256.

means that only certain buffers with a fixed pH can be used (the reaction centres, enzymes and light-harvesting complexes of the photosynthesis apparatus are dissolved in these buffers for the duration of the experiment). If we want to be privy to nature's well-kept secrets, then it is important that we researchers obey its rules and laws. Only then can we begin to actively intervene in nature, to change it and also subject it to *Verfremdung*, to study these changes and to develop laws and models relating to their functioning.

## THE EPIC PLAY AS A SCIENTIFIC EXPERIMENT

The scientist and experimenter thus becomes the director of a series of experiments similar to a stage play: he or she plans an experiment, a scene, which is subjected to *Verfremdung* in accordance with certain rules in order to illustrate and highlight the situation being observed. The *Verfremdung* applied to the experiment thus also becomes an investigative tool without which it would not be possible to observe and explain natural laws, processes and phenomena. The scientist's task is to (simultaneously) observe closely, maintain a critical attitude to the design of the experiment, continuously evaluate it and analyse the results carefully and objectively. Brecht has the student Andrea learn this skill of careful looking and observation from the famous scholar Galileo. It soon brings an entire world view to the point of collapse. The telescope, the measuring instrument which enables Galileo to see and observe things in detail, may not initially subject his view of the night sky to *Verfremdung*, but it ultimately leads – since direct observation of the celestial bodies from the earth is not possible without special tools – to the revolution of the Copernican world view and thus to a discovery which is also of great social relevance. If we take the design and execution of a scientific experiment, then, and compare it in its theoretical conception with the theory of epic theatre, surprising parallels emerge. Brecht designs the plays of his epic theatre like a series of experiments: each individual scene is considered and interpreted separately, and V-effects are used to facilitate a more precise, distanced observation, allowing the spectator – who also becomes the experimenter – to engage with the action in a critically reflective way, and calling on him or her to remain active throughout the play. Brecht even addresses the issue of the scientific experiment directly through Galileo, whose own experiment ultimately reveals the truth and thereby changes the way people view the world. This outcome is only achieved, however, because Galileo as the experimenter has the skill to design, carry out and interpret his experiments correctly and in a way that takes into account the laws of nature. The experiment itself thus becomes a *Lehrstück* about reality and truth and, as Brecht puts it in *The Decision*: 'Only when instructed by reality can we change reality.' (BFA 3: 125).

## SCIENTISTS AND THEIR SOCIAL RESPONSIBILITY

Many facets of the scientific experiment, then, are to be found in Brecht's theories on theatre. But Brecht goes one step further by not only describing the role of the experimenter in his theatre of learning but also by repeatedly emphasising the experimenter's social responsibility. Experimenters must take responsibility for their environment and society when carrying out experiments; one way in which Brecht illustrates this is to have Galileo, at the end of the play, call for a Hippocratic oath for scientists – influenced by the dropping of the atom bomb and the trial of Robert J. Oppenheimer in 1953. Brecht was also very interested in the 'Einstein material'. All that has survived of his last play project *Life of*

*Einstein* is a single monologue – eight lines of verse in which Einstein tries to explain his changed attitude toward the war – but Brecht did leave behind a substantial collection of material relating to the life and work of Albert Einstein (now held by the Brecht estate).[15] Brecht first became interested in Einstein as early as 1930, when he attended a lecture on causality which Einstein gave at the Marxist Workers' School in Berlin. After that, Brecht made many attempts to apply the concept to art; he saw Einstein's thinking as a touchstone of the scientific age. Einstein – like Henry Ford or Lenin – represented the progressive attitude which Brecht wanted to see in the spectators of his epic theatre. At the same time, however, Einstein also embodied the failure of modern science in Brecht's eyes. Brecht was stunned by the former pacifist's support for the development of the atomic bomb. Long before the publication of UNESCO's 'Recommendation on the Status of Scientific Researchers' in 1974,[16] Brecht lent Galileo his voice to stress the importance of ethics in science. Present-day debates in the field of genetic research, for example, show that these concerns have lost none of their relevance.

This dialectical deliberation on Brecht's reciprocal relationship with the sciences shows how many considerations and approaches Brecht borrowed from science and used in his statements about theatrical theory; it is clear, too, that scientists can also learn from Brecht's work and that his plays are still highly relevant to all of us, scientists included.

The close relationship between the sciences and the humanities which is found throughout Brecht's work can perhaps best be described using his own words:

> 'But what does science have to do with art? [...]' [...] I think that the great and complex things that go on in the world of human beings cannot be properly identified if people do not use all the tools at their disposal to understand them.
>
> (BFA 22.1: 113)

---

[15] Erdmut Wizisla, 'Vortreffliches für verbildete Zeitgenossen: Galileo Galilei: Albert Einsteins Brief an Bertolt Brecht', in *FAZ* (29.09.2004), available online at http://www.faz.net/aktuell/feuilleton/geisteswissenschaften/vortreffliches-fuer-verbildete-zeitgenossen-1178088.html (accessed on 14.10.2015).

[16] 'Empfehlung zur Stellung der wissenschaftlichen Forscher, verabschiedet von der 18. Generalkonferenz der UNESCO am 23. November 1974', available online at http://www.unesco.de/infothek/dokumente/unesco-empfehlung-stellung-forscher.html (accessed on 14.10.2015).

# Thought from the Far East

CHAPTER TWENTY-THREE

# Brecht's Materialist Ethics between Confucianism and Mohism

MARKUS WESSENDORF

Bertolt Brecht (1898–1956) is internationally known as one of the most influential dramatists, directors, and theater theorists of the twentieth century and also, within German culture, as one of its most innovative modern poets and prose stylists. Whereas Brecht's contributions to a Marxist aesthetics of drama, theater, poetry, and prose are widely acknowledged, he is less well known as a major thinker on ethical issues, mostly because of his materialist orientation, which conflicts with ethical traditions rooted in metaphysics. Against these traditions, Brecht envisioned an 'ethics for the satisfaction of needs'[1] and claimed that 'material needs as ethical, ethical ones as material, this is not grasped'.[2] This essay, though, will try to show that Brecht's examination of ethical questions from a materialist perspective is more complex than what is suggested by one of his most famous lines, from *The Threepenny Opera* (1928): 'Food is the first thing. Morals follow on.'[3] The admonition to be kind, for example, which recurs in different contexts throughout Brecht's writings,[4] indicates that ethical values are not always the result of specific conditions of production but may be purposefully employed to facilitate

---

Markus Wessendorf, 'Brecht's Materialist Ethics between Confucianism and Mohism', *Philosophy East and West*, 66: 1 (2016), pp. 122–45.

The following abbreviation appears in the Notes:

BFA    Bertolt Brecht. *Werke: Große Kommentierte Berliner und Frankfurter Ausgabe*. 30 vols. Edited by Werner Hecht, Jan Knopf, Werner Mittenzwei, and Klaus-Detlef Müller. Berlin and Weimar: Aufbau-Verlag; Frankfurt am Main: Suhrkamp Verlag, 1988–2000.

[1] Bertolt Brecht, '25 may 39', in *Journals 1934–1955*, ed. John Willett, trans. Hugh Rorrison (London: Methuen, 1993), p. 338.
[2] Ibid.
[3] Bertolt Brecht, *The Threepenny Opera*, trans. and ed. Ralph Manheim and John Willett (New York: Arcade Publishing, 1994), pp. 55, 56.
[4] For example, in Bertolt Brecht, 'Hilflosigkeit alter Menschen', in *BFA*, vol. 18, pp. 61–62: 'The helplessness of old people ... results from the fact that they can no longer rely on their powers of persuasion and therefore have to insist on their authority. ... They have to be treated with special kindness.' (This and all subsequent quotations from the *BFA* in English are my own translations.)

a process of political struggle. Even though Brecht could be said to aim for an 'ethical response [that] is in itself only relevant or made possible by the consideration of material or economic elements',[5] a remnant of value ethics persists in his work, even though its justification may be utilitarian rather than metaphysical.

Brecht was not a systematic thinker tied to one specific mode of reflection, but rather he developed and tested his ideas across various literary and non-literary genres. As a result, many of his key insights are reiterated in multiple forms, for example as dramatic dialogue, song text, journal entry, aphorism, prose fragment, and theoretical essay. Brecht often theatricalized these genres and turned them into stages, masks, or foils for the articulation and representation of his ideas. Some of the philosophical models that he drew upon, however, already perform their own type of *theatrum philosophicum* (Gilles Deleuze) by opening up a dialogic space between the supposed authorial voice of the text and the utterances of its *dramatis personae* – for example in Plato's Socratic dialogues, Nietzsche's philosophical novel *Thus Spoke Zarathustra* (which 'resonated deeply'[6] with the young Brecht), and the sage pronouncements of Confucius and Mo Zi, whose recorded conversations often start with 'The Master said … '.

If Brecht addresses ethical issues at numerous levels of his artistic and theoretical production, his theater concepts, by the same token, are applicable not just to questions of dramatic representation but also to questions of social performance at large. Since they will be of relevance for the discussion to follow, three of Brecht's key concepts identified with his Epic Theatre will be introduced here: estrangement (*Verfremdung*), historicization, and gestus as the embodiment of social attitudes. The estrangement or defamiliarization effect (*Verfremdungseffekt*) is a technique of distancing the audience from their psychological identification and empathy (*Einfühlung*) with the theatrical representation by interrupting the flow of the narrative to draw their attention to the signifying processes of the production itself, with the intention of turning them into critical and socially pro-active observers. Historicization is related to *Verfremdung* and can mean two things. On the one hand there is the foregrounding of 'the historical aspect of a specific social condition'[7] to make the audience realize that social reality is not a 'natural' given but the alterable result of socioeconomic processes. On the other hand there is the transplanting of familiar conflicts into different historical eras to invite audiences to confront them from unexplored angles. The social gestus embodies the 'domain of the attitudes adopted by the characters towards one another'[8] and determines '[p]osture, tone of voice and facial expression'.[9] Gestus implies an 'entire complex'[10] of attitudes and expressions that may be 'highly complicated and contradictory'[11] but allows for 'conclusions to be drawn about the social

---

[5]Sonia Arribas, 'The Subject Herr Keuner: Towards a Brechtian Ethics', in *The Brecht Yearbook 35: Brecht/Marxism/Ethics*, ed. Friedemann Weidauer and Dorothee Ostmeier (Madison: University of Wisconsin Press, 2010), p. 10.
[6]Stephen Parker, *Bertolt Brecht: A Literary Life* (London and New York: Bloomsbury Methuen Drama, 2014), p. 66.
[7]Bertolt Brecht, '*Verfremdung* Effects in Chinese Acting', in *Brecht on Theatre*, 3rd edition, ed. Marc Silberman, Steve Giles, and Tom Kuhn (London and New York: Bloomsbury Methuen Drama, 2015), p. 158.
[8]Bertolt Brecht, 'Short Organon for the Theatre', in *Brecht on Theatre*, p. 248.
[9]Ibid.
[10]Ibid.
[11]Ibid.

circumstances'.[12] Brecht the dramatist prefers to put his characters into social situations in which they are compelled to produce attitudes and gestures that reveal who they are as social beings, for example when standing trial, conducting a business transaction, reporting a traffic accident, going on strike, or teaching a lesson.

In the 1920s Brecht discovered not only the theories of Hegel, Marx, and Lenin but also the writings of the Chinese philosophers Confucius, Mencius, Mo Zi, Lao Zi, and Zhuang Zi, and he would critically engage with both the Marxist school of thought and classical Chinese philosophy until the end of his life. Since Brecht's notions of a materialist ethics were particularly shaped by the writings of Confucius and Mo Zi, two philosophers often perceived in diametrical opposition to each other, this essay primarily focuses on Brecht's dialogue with these two classical Chinese thinkers in two of his texts, which remained fragments and were only published after his death. They are his notes for a play, *Life of Confucius*,[13] and the extensive prose text that was first published under the title *Me-ti: Buch der Wendungen* (Mozi: Book of turns),[14] in 1965.

Brecht first discovered the writings of Confucius (551–479 B.C.) in the 1920s, through Richard Wilhelm's German translation of the *Analects*.[15] One of Brecht's earliest writings on Confucius from 1929/1930, titled 'Modest Success of Confucius', articulates the key contradiction that Brecht saw in Confucius' work. He points out that Confucius, despite his reputation as one of 'the most successful teachers of mankind',[16] achieved only limited results with his teachings on morality, music, and religion since he failed to realize that 'the form of government of his time',[17] which he tried to preserve 'through the general raising of moral standards',[18] was the primary reason for the decline of morality. Brecht early on attacked the lack of dialectical thinking in Confucius' notion that the feudalistic society of his era could not only be maintained but also be made more humane by a return to the value system of ancient times. Despite his critical perception of the philosopher, however, Brecht's early text also emphasizes one particular aspect of Confucius that he would continue to consider useful, namely his social attitude:

> [The people] could use so much of him, when they imitated his attitude! His judgments, relating to life forms from long ago, would have been unjust, had they been replicated, but his attitude was one of justice.[19]

Even though Confucius' moral teachings, as uncritically adapted from the past, are of questionable political value, his attitude of trying to act justly in any given situation is socially useful and worthy of imitation: 'The attitude of Confucius can be easily copied externally, and then turns out to be unusually useful.'[20] The notion that the imitation of certain 'model' attitudes and gestures might improve social behavior also informed Brecht's experimentation with his 'learning-plays' (*Lehrstücke*) in the late 1920s. The

---

[12]Bertolt Brecht, 'On Gestic Music', in *Brecht on Theatre*, p. 168.
[13]In what follows, Brecht's many translations of the philosopher's name (Konfutse, Confutse, Konfuzius, Confucius, Kung) will be consistently rendered as 'Confucius'.
[14]See note 103 below.
[15]Kung-futse, *Gespräche* (*Lun Yü*), trans. Richard Wilhelm (Jena: Eugen Diederichs, 1921).
[16]Brecht, 'Konfutse', BFA 21: 369.
[17]Ibid.
[18]Ibid.
[19]Brecht, 'Geringer Erfolg des Kung Futse', BFA 21: 369–370.
[20]Brecht, 'Konfutse', BFA 21: 369.

*Analects* themselves repeatedly emphasize Confucius' particular gestus: 'In his leisure hours the Master's manner was very free-and-easy, and his expression alert and cheerful' (7.4);[21] 'The Master's manner was affable yet firm, commanding but not harsh, polite but easy' (7.37).[22] Brecht clearly embraces Confucius' gestus as well as the practical wisdom that is usually associated with it in the *Analects*. (In a letter to his collaborator Ruth Berlau, for example, Brecht recommends to 'forget the good we ourselves have done and remember the good others have done',[23] which paraphrases *Analects* 12.16: 'The Master said, The gentleman calls attention to the good points in others; he does not call attention to their defects.'[24])

Since Brecht was trying to establish a materialist ethics, he very much appreciated 'C.'s antimetaphysical attitude, his emphasis on conduct',[25] particularly in contrast to the more familiar (since prevalent) ethics of the Kantian tradition: 'When one considers how little moralising and how little invocation of "higher ideals" that great moralist [i.e. Confucius] managed with, it gives you a clearer picture of our debased times.'[26]

Another aspect of Confucian thought relevant to Brecht is the philosopher's insistence that any well-ordered society depends on the precise usage of language ('If language is incorrect, then what is said does not concord with what was meant; and if what is said does not concord with what was meant, what is to be done cannot be effected'[27]). In an essay from 1935 on 'Five Difficulties in Writing the Truth', Brecht praises Confucius for falsifying and altering words in 'an old patriotic calendar of historical events'[28] (i.e., the *Spring and Autumn Annals* [*Chunqiu*] as the first chronological history of Confucius' home state of Lu) in order to reveal the truth about certain events that had been suppressed or concealed for ideological reasons. Brecht considers Confucius' method of replacing 'unjustified assessments of national events with justified ones'[29] as still valid for his own time, and he makes his own suggestions for substituting ideologically charged words: 'Anyone in our times who says *population instead of "Volk" and land ownership instead of "soil"* is already denying his support to many lies. He divests the words of their lazy mysticism.'[30]

Even though Brecht embraces Confucius' gestus, practical wisdom, and 'ethics of language', he disapproves of the philosopher's virtue ethics as well as his preservation of traditional values, rites, and social hierarchies (i.e., the five principal relationships of ruler to subject, father to son, elder brother to younger brother, husband to wife, and friend to friend). Brecht, for example, generally rejects the notion of *junzi* – an exemplary or

---

[21]*The Analects of Confucius*, trans. and annot. Arthur Waley (London: George Allen and Unwin, 1938), p. 123. There may be more critically informed and culturally attuned recent translations of the *Analects* (by Roger T. Ames, Raymond Dawson, and others), but since this was the only English translation that Brecht was familiar with, all the following quotations from Confucius will be from Waley's edition.
[22]Waley, *The Analects of Confucius*, p. 131.
[23]Bertolt Brecht, 'To Ruth Berlau [10 March 1950]', in *Letters 1913–1956*, trans. Ralph Manheim, ed. John Willett (New York: Routledge, 1990), p. 491.
[24]Waley, *The Analects of Confucius*, p. 167.
[25]Bertolt Brecht, 'To Fredrik Martner [25 July 1939]', in *Letters 1913–1956*, p. 315.
[26]Bertolt Brecht, 'To Fredrik Martner [beginning of January 1940]', *Letters 1913–1956*, p. 320.
[27]Waley, *The Analects of Confucius*, p. 171.
[28]Bertolt Brecht, 'Five Difficulties in Writing the Truth', in *Brecht on Art and Politics*, ed. Tom Kuhn and Steve Giles (London: Methuen, 2003), p. 149.
[29]Ibid., pp. 149–150.
[30]Ibid., p. 149.

superior person, but translated as 'gentleman' by Waley[31] – which Confucius articulates in *Analects* 4.11: 'Where gentlemen set their hearts upon moral force (*tê*), the commoners set theirs upon the soil. Where gentlemen think only of punishments, the commoners think only of exemptions.'[32] One recurring motif in Brecht's work is the notion that a well-organized society doesn't require particular virtues from its members but allows everyone to be ordinary.

In another early text from 1929/1930, titled 'Confucius', Brecht attacks the veneration of the Chinese philosopher as an exemplary person since the virtues represented by him are so useless to society that the gap between material reality and ethical ideal opened up by this veneration helps to facilitate unethical behavior rather than to curtail it:

> To portray him as a paragon facilitates the condemnation of entire lineages, if not entire eras. His idealized image is fully tied to a special and rare disposition, and while almost none of the human deeds generally considered great by mankind can be achieved by persons of this disposition, one could imagine a vast number of crimes that a person might perpetrate without repudiating certain virtues that have distinguished Confucius.[33]

Different from his close collaborator Margarete Steffin, though, who clearly rejected Confucius' philosophy as 'enormously reactionary' (because of his 'demand for *one* prince' and his 'attitude to the woman question'[34]), Brecht's own attitude toward the philosopher tended to oscillate between veneration and condemnation.

Already in 1937 the Russian playwright and journalist Sergei Tretyakov, a friend of Brecht, claimed that the German writer somehow identified with Confucius,[35] and Brecht seems to have perceived parallels between Confucius' career and his own life later on. While in Switzerland in December 1947, Brecht met the Sinologist Wilhelm M. Treichlinger, who showed him his translation of a collection of lyrics by Confucius. Brecht noted that 'the songs were the object of a book burning which they survived, and tradition has it that a new regime sent out officials to collect them from the lips of the people, as a means of discovering the mood in the county'.[36] Brecht, whose own books had been burned by the Nazis in 1933, and who had just returned from exile in the United States and was now trying to determine his next step, probably would have liked his own works, and the way people had remembered them, to serve as a political barometer in the way that Confucius' songs did. Brecht must also have seen a parallel between his and the philosopher's career in the years of wandering and the many fruitless attempts to get into a position that would have allowed either one of them to put their ideas into practice. Nevertheless, Brecht not only saw a mirror image but also an antithesis in Confucius.

---

[31] 'I'd just like to know whether [Waley] himself noticed and intended the criticism implied by his always substituting "The Gentleman" for "The Wise Man". ... A Wise Man can't very well lose his wisdom, but a "Gentleman" can, since he is the product of a class' (Brecht, 'To Fredrik Martner [25 July 1939]', *Letters 1913–1956*, p. 315).
[32] Waley, *The Analects of Confucius*, p. 104.
[33] Brecht, 'Konfutse', *BFA* 21: 369.
[34] Brecht, '14 jan 41', in *Journals 1934–1955*, p. 126.
[35] Sergei Tretiakov, 'Bert Brecht', in Peter Demetz, ed., *Brecht: A Collection of Critical Essays* (Englewood Cliffs: Prentice-Hall, 1962), p. 27 (quoted in Renata Berg-Pan, 'Brecht and Chinese Philosophy', *Philosophy and Literature* 1, no. 3 [Fall 1977]: 313).
[36] Brecht, '19 dec 47', in *Journals 1934–1955*, p. 377.

This is particularly evident in those passages in which Brecht disparagingly compares Confucius to Johann Wolfgang von Goethe, a comparison that Richard Wilhelm had already established (though favorably) in the introduction to his German translation of the *Analects*.[37]

The analogies between the careers of Confucius and Goethe, according to Brecht, include their elevated status within their respective cultures, their work as ministers in the service of the aristocracy, their attempts at implementing reforms that failed to bring any significant change, and their privileged status with regard to the acquisition of knowledge. In his short text on 'Confucius' Brecht discusses Goethe's 'incredible wealth of intellectual acquisitions' and 'the brutal and essentially servile manner' in which he accumulated it, and links him to Confucius when he concludes that this 'kind of self-education is only too reconcilable with what we cannot praise as virtue, as much as we would like to be paragons ourselves'.[38]

From November 1940 to February 1941, while in exile in Finland, Brecht developed ideas for a play with the title *Life of Confucius*, inspired by Arthur Waley's English translation of the *Analects*[39] and Carl Crow's biography of the philosopher.[40] Even though Brecht never completed the play, he finished one scene ('The Ginger Jar'), created several scene listings, and left behind various notes with dramaturgical ideas and fragments of dialog, which all allow for the hypothetical reconstruction of a basic outline of the play. The most complete of the three extent scene listings includes nine scene titles without any additional information:

1. The Ginger Jar
2. The Kings of Antiquity
3. The Good and the Bad Judge
4. The School
5. The Teacher as Student
6. Confucius and the Rebel
7. The Reforms of the Sage
8. Peace Negotiations
9. The Dismissal of the Sage.[41]

This sequence suggests an episodic play in Epic Theatre style, with scenes that depict significant events in Confucius' life closely following Crow's biography. A second scene listing[42] includes only the first six scenes of the larger first listing but provides supplementary information for scenes 2 to 4,[43] and several other notes by Brecht provide additional suggestions for how some of these scenes might have been fleshed out.

---

[37]See Kung-futse, *Gespräche (Lun Yü)*, pp. xii–xiv.
[38]Brecht, 'Konfutse', BFA 21: 369.
[39]See note 18 above.
[40]Carl Crow, *Master Kung: The Story of Confucius* (New York and London: Harper and Brothers, 1938).
[41]Bertolt Brecht, 'Leben des Konfutse', BFA, vol. 10, part 2, pp. 878, 879–880.
[42]Ibid., pp. 879–880.
[43]A third scene listing (BFA 10.2: 878) will be disregarded here: it lists ten numbered scenes but doesn't provide any information on scene 8; it also doesn't include 'The Ginger Jar' as the one scene that Brecht was able to complete.

'The Ginger Jar' draws on two pieces of information provided by Crow, namely that Confucius enjoyed eating ginger as a treat from childhood on[44] and that he liked to imitate ancient rites and ceremonies with his friends as a young boy.[45] The scene starts with a self-introduction of the protagonist:

> I am Kung, the son of Kung the soldier. My father died poor, and my mother raises me in a spirit of loathing against anything violent. ... She told me that there are no ghosts, no bogeymen and no dragons. Anyone here who believes in ghosts? Or dragons? I know all five reasons why there can't be such reasons.[46]

The young Confucius then talks his three friends into playing school, with today's lesson being 'about the proper etiquette for eating from a ginger jar'.[47] It is the promise of the treat that makes his friends agree to the proposal, despite their negative memories of Confucius' earlier lessons: 'Last time we had to practice greeting rituals, there's no point in that.'[48] To practice the correct table manners with his friends, Confucius asks them to pretend to be famous generals of Chinese history while he himself enacts the legendary King Yen. Each of the boys tries to snatch as many ginger pieces as possible from the jar while pretending to be interested in Confucius' game and his attempts at correcting their gestures and bearing. Confucius, on the other hand, is so invested in teaching the exact etiquette of receiving the 'royal jar' that he is completely oblivious to his friends' motivation:

> First I bow. Like this. Then I refuse the gift with both hands. Like this. Thereby I have indicated that I consider the gift too large. Since, however, King Yen offers me the jar for a second time, I do accept it now, after I have bowed again to demonstrate that I only take it to obey him.[49]

When he finally praises the selflessness of Li, the smallest of his friends, for having correctly performed the sequence of required gestures without picking a single piece of ginger for himself, he only belatedly realizes that his other friends had already emptied the jar. Confucius comes to the materialist realization that two things are necessary 'to retain a dignified restraint during the emptying of a ginger jar: first a fine sense of decorum, second a full jar.'[50]

As the major focus of the second scene, 'The Kings of Antiquity', Brecht seems to have intended the conflict between the exploitation of the peasants, in which Confucius is complicit, and his desire for a return to the primitive communism[51] of ancient times. The young Confucius, 'while collecting tithes'[52] from the peasant population for the

---

[44]Crow, *Master Kung*, chap. 3, p. 54.
[45]Ibid., pp. 57–58.
[46]Bertolt Brecht, 'Der Ingwertopf', in 'Leben des Konfutse', BFA 10.2: 888–889.
[47]Ibid., p. 889.
[48]Ibid.
[49]Ibid., p. 890.
[50]Ibid., p. 892.
[51]According to the 1930s Marxist historian Li Chi, this is the first of five stages in China's history, ending around 1400 B.C. (see Arif Dirlik, *Revolution and History: The Origins of Marxist Historiography in China, 1919–1937* (Berkeley, Los Angeles, and Oxford: University of California Press, 1989), p. 200).
[52]Brecht, 'Leben des Konfutse', BFA 10.2: 879.

powerful Chi (or Ji) family in his home state of Lu, studies Yao, Shun, and Yu,[53] the three semi-mythical rulers of exceptional virtue from the beginnings of Chinese civilization.[54] Brecht's note on how the grain tax introduced under the kings of antiquity has been doubled from one tenth to one fifth of the produce[55] refers to one of the dukes of Lu who decided upon this measure to pay for 'his own extravagances' and to satisfy 'the avaricious demands of the powerful barons'.[56] Crow writes that the experience as a tithe collector brought Confucius into touch with regular people and contributed to his later resolution to 'bring about a return to the "golden age" through a reform of the government and a restoration of the ancient virtues of the people'.[57] He also mentions that Confucius, while working as a tithe collector, 'spent his spare time in studying and giving instruction'[58] not only to the boys in his area, whom he had known for a long time, but also to the group of disciples that gradually began to assemble around him. The scene might also have included a student, or perhaps an old man, 'whose entire life's work consisted (clandestinely) in trying to prove that there were no actual kings during the "Era of the Kings"'.[59] Brecht's fascination with the primitive communism of ancient China and his uneasiness with the idea that three kings established this system are combined in a separate note in lyrical form with the title 'The Golden Age of the Kings Yao, Shun and Yu', which might have been written for inclusion in this scene:

> No police, as there is no crime
>
> Only a few laws
>
> No notion of property
>
> Voluntary donations to the community
>
> No thieves
>
> No taxes
>
> No soldiers, as there are no wars
>
> No poverty, as there is no wealth
>
> No kings?[60]

This poem lyrically paraphrases a key passage in Crow's biography[61] in which the author mentions that neither 'of the three rulers was of princely descent, for there had been no princes before them'.[62]

The title of the third scene, 'The Good and the Bad Judge', probably refers to that period in Confucius' career when he worked as the 'Minister of Crime'[63] for his home state of Lu, a position that combined the functions of 'investigator, prosecutor, judge and

---

[53] Ibid.
[54] Ibid.
[55] Ibid.
[56] Crow, *Master Kung*, chap. 4, p. 64.
[57] Ibid., p. 67.
[58] Ibid., p. 68.
[59] Brecht, 'Leben des Konfutse', *BFA* 10.2: 879.
[60] Brecht, 'Das goldene Zeitalter der Könige Yao, Shun und Yu', in 'Leben des Konfutse', *BFA* 10.2: 885.
[61] Crow, *Master Kung*, chap. 5, p. 80.
[62] Ibid.
[63] Crow, *Master Kung*, chap. 10, p. 161.

executioner'.⁶⁴ Brecht only provides two short notes for this scene: 'Better to instruct than to pass a sentence on someone!' and 'The bad judge chairs the trial. He is better for regular people.'⁶⁵ They both relate to a well-known anecdote that portrays Confucius as a 'bad' judge overriding traditional values. When a father sued his 'wicked and unruly son',⁶⁶ Confucius refused to sentence the son to death (as would have been expected) but felt that the situation was so 'contrary to the established usages of filial piety, of duty of son to father, father to son, that he had no rule to go by'.⁶⁷ So he imprisoned both father and son for three months, treating them with equal severity. Only when the father withdrew the charge did Confucius release them both. When pressed to justify his decision, Confucius argued that the father was as much to blame for the disobedience of his son because he failed to provide the necessary instruction.⁶⁸ Crow also quotes a comment by Confucius on his own judicial activities: 'I am like others in administering justice. I apply the law to each case as a separate problem.'⁶⁹ Even though Brecht never completed this scene, he later used this idea for the creation of the famous 'corrupt-but-just' people's judge Azdak in *The Caucasian Chalk Circle* (itself based on a Yuan drama).

For the fourth scene, 'The School', Brecht provides the note 'truth for truth's sake',⁷⁰ which is a response to *Analects* 15.31: 'The Master said, A gentleman, in his plans, thinks of the Way; he does not think how he is going to make a living.'⁷¹ It is likely that this scene would have dealt with Confucius' teachings and his relationships with his disciples. Brecht also drafted two speeches by Confucius that could have been included either in this scene or in scene 2. While working on his *Life of Confucius*, Brecht critically commented on Confucius in his journal: 'there is a difference between treading the golden mean and actually constructing it, and there is a difference between a code of behavior and a code of ceremonies'.⁷² In the speeches that he drafted for the play, though, Brecht lets his Confucius character present a materialist version of the philosopher's *Doctrine of the Mean* (Zhongyong – both a Confucian doctrine as well as the title of one of the 'Four Books' of Confucianism), which now emphasizes a case-by-case consideration of conditions, context, and means over strict adherence to predetermined notions of natural order, universal obligations, and worldly status. In the first fragment, Confucius states that 'justice is obtained both from compassion for the victim and compassion for the tormentor. ... The golden mean is not a comfortable path, but a path that leads to the goal.'⁷³ In the second fragment, Confucius praises the ancient kings because 'they spared no effort to eliminate effort from this world. They worked hard to minimize hard work. ... The golden mean is not the path that doesn't require sacrifices but the path for which one makes useful sacrifices.'⁷⁴ Another dialogue fragment that may have been intended

---

⁶⁴Ibid.
⁶⁵Ibid.
⁶⁶Ibid., p. 165.
⁶⁷Ibid.
⁶⁸See ibid. Richard Wilhelm reiterates the same anecdote in the introduction to his German translation of the *Analects* (Kung-futse, *Gespräche [Lun Yü]*, p. xvi).
⁶⁹Quoted in Crow, *Master Kung*, chap. 10, p. 166.
⁷⁰Brecht, 'Leben des Konfutse', BFA 10.2: 879.
⁷¹Waley, *The Analects of Confucius*, p. 199.
⁷²Brecht, '14 jan 41', in *Journals 1934–1955*, p. 126 (modified translation).
⁷³Brecht, 'Leben des Konfutse', BFA 10.2: 894.
⁷⁴Ibid.

for this or the second scene provides a variation on Brecht's notions of attitude and gestus. According to this fragment, it is important not only to adapt a socially useful attitude, but also to learn how to appreciate one:

THE STUDENT: Fang-hi is unlikable.
CONFUCIUS: Why?
THE STUDENT: I don't know.
CONFUCIUS: Why don't you describe his positive characteristics to me?

*Confucius realizes that the student considers a meritorious and helpful person unlikable, and warns him against the consequences of such fallacious instincts. It is necessary to find the good likeable, and this is an art that can be learned.*[75]

The fifth scene, 'The Teacher as Student', would probably have dealt with Confucius' famous excursion to the capital, Loyang, where 'he was not a teacher but a disciple',[76] and where he had frequent meetings with the octogenarian philosopher Lao Zi. Since Lao Zi was another key influence on Brecht, this scene likely would have focused on the conversations between the two philosophers as well as their ideological differences: as Crow points out, Lao Zi's 'doctrine of non-resistance was exactly counter to [Confucius'] while the other's thinly veiled contempt for established authority came dangerously near being revolutionary'.[77]

Scene title 6, 'Confucius and the Rebel', refers to the incident in the history of Lu when a well-known rebel, the Commander of Pi, seized power after the dictator Yang Hoo had been forced to leave the state and, to consolidate his influence, invited Confucius to be one of his advisors. Confucius seriously considered the invitation since he was so worried about the desperate situation of his home state that he felt obliged to do anything to help the new leadership steer Lu away from the brink of anarchy. His disciples were shocked that he did not reject the invitation of a rebel outright, but 'he pointed out to them that the great Chow dynasty itself had been founded by a rebellion against the preceding weak and corrupt Shang dynasty'.[78]

The title of the seventh scene, 'The Reforms of the Sage', suggests the episode in Confucius' life when he was appointed governor of a township and, for the first time in thirty years, finally had the opportunity to implement, among many other reforms, 'the introduction of an honest system in the collection of taxes'.[79] Brecht's scene would probably have focused on the 'honesty' of the tax reform: 'Confucius has reduced the tax burden (from a third) to a fourth, but is still handing over the same amount to the princes at the end of each year since he has abolished corruption. But later, upon his return, he hears that they are once more collecting a third, but now without corruption.'[80]

The eighth scene, 'Peace Negotiations', may have dramatized how Confucius, as the prime minister or chancellor of Lu, through foresight and diplomatic skill, not only prevented the political assassination of the duke of Lu and himself during a ceremonial ratification of a supposed peace treaty but managed to gain territorial concessions for Lu

---

[75] Ibid., p. 893.
[76] Crow, *Master Kung*, chap. 6, p. 100.
[77] Ibid., p. 104.
[78] Ibid., chapter 10, p. 153.
[79] Ibid., p. 156.
[80] Brecht, 'Leben des Konfutse', *BFA* 10.2: 882.

from the treacherous negotiating partner, the neighboring state of Tsi (or Qi), once he had revealed and sabotaged their plot.[81]

The title of the final scene, 'The Dismissal of the Sage', relates to another plot by the Tsi rulers to undermine the leadership of Lu. When the counselors of the Tsi court sent a delegation of eighty courtesans as well as one hundred beautiful horses to the court of the middle-aged and amorous Duke of Lu, the duke was so infatuated with his new pleasures that he no longer had any time to govern. When he finally failed to carry out the most important religious ceremony of the year, Confucius handed in his resignation.[82] Based on a journal entry in which he compares Confucius and Goethe, it seems likely that Brecht had this episode in mind for the final scene: 'from [Confucius'] one and only decent job, which resembles goethe's in weimar, he is supplanted by some horses and courtesans acquired by the prince. reminds you of the weimar dog'.[83] (In 1817 Goethe resigned from his position as director of the Weimar court theater after the Grand Duke had insisted on a performance of the French melodrama *The Dog of Aubry*, which featured a poodle on stage.)

The young protagonist of the first scene, 'The Ginger Jar', condenses many of the interests and endeavors that the historical Confucius only explored much later in life. Brecht generally intended *Life of Confucius* to be performed by child actors. He wanted the play to be performed as a comedy and advised 'to treat profound subjects in a cheerful spirit, and to greet authorities with friendly goodwill'.[84] Brecht intended to use the known inability of child performers to suggest a 'nuanced psychological inner life'[85] to estrange the highly articulate 'public figure who put any information he considered useful into words'.[86]

In his notes to *Life of Confucius* Brecht claims that the philosopher recognized as a key problem of his time the exploitation of the people by dukes and barons, but then misdiagnosed the major reason for this condition as the general decline of morals, as caused both by a disregard for the teachings of the ancients as well as a neglect of traditional rites. Since Confucius' reforms aimed at a change of conduct, not a change of conditions, they never tackled the root of the social malaise: 'He wants the agricultural reform and a change of conduct. The first one he is not allowed to implement. The second remains.'[87] The peasants remain poor, though now they nicely bow three times 'before they pay one-third instead of one-fourth'[88] in grain taxes. Confucius' misrecognition of what needs to be reformed, according to Brecht, leads to a kind of 'formalism':

> C. attributes the decline of morals to the conceptual confusion and decides to define the behavior of humans towards each other more closely. The refinement of manners refines exploitation. The renaissance of the 'classics' has succeeded, but their ideas have lost touch with their base (primitive communism).[89]

---

[81]Crow, *Master Kung*, chap. 11.
[82]Ibid., chap. 12, pp. 190–195.
[83]Brecht, '11 nov 40', in *Journals 1934–1955*, p. 377.
[84]Brecht, 'Anmerkungen zum Leben des Konfutse', in 'Leben des Konfutse', BFA 10.2: 881–882.
[85]Ibid., p. 881.
[86]Ibid.
[87]Brecht, 'Leben des Konfutse', BFA 10.2: 886.
[88]Ibid.
[89]Brecht, 'Konfutse', in 'Leben des Konfutse', BFA 10.2: 881.

If Brecht condemns the teachings and ideas of Confucius in this passage, he reverses this verdict four years later by reappraising the philosopher's endeavors from the perspective of his social attitude, now listing among the latter's achievements the 'unmasking of formalism, the conceptual revolution, [and] the establishment of patterns of behavior from the days of primitive communism'.[90]

This ambiguity also seems to have informed the project of *Life of Confucius* overall. Whereas the only completed scene, 'The Ginger Jar', appears to attack the traditionalism and rigid code of conduct of the philosopher, most of the other scene titles refer to episodes in Crow's biography in which Confucius had to make *ad hoc* decisions, often in situations in which the traditional framework of values no longer provided guidance (scene 3) or in states of emergency in which the rule of law was suspended (scenes 6 and 8). The figure of Confucius suggested by the overall plot outline is less the sage pronouncing, and acting upon, his own codified rules of conduct than a pragmatic individual trying to act ethically in unprecedented circumstances. It may be this particular tension that prevented Brecht from pursuing this project any further. In September 1944 Brecht writes in his journal that 'while talking to [charles] laughton I brought up my old plan to write a LIFE OF CONFUCIUS'.[91] But he never again resumed work on this project.

Another key influence on Brecht was the anti-Confucian philosopher Mo Zi (ca. 470–ca. 391 B.C.), the founder of the school of Mohism, whose thoughts and conversations were compiled by his disciples and later followers and published under the title *Mozi*.[92] Brecht was familiar with the first, almost complete German translation of this text, which Alfred Forke published in 1922 under a title that could be rendered as *The Philosophical Works of the Social Ethicist Mo Zi and His Disciples*.[93] Brecht cherished his copy of the book so much that he had it bound in leather[94] and also listed it as one of the key items that he owned while living in exile in Sweden in 1939.[95] Forke's historical contextualization and contemporary assessment of Mo Zi's philosophy in his extensive introductory chapters may have caught Brecht's attention and perhaps, to a certain extent, even steered his interpretation of the *Mozi*. Forke not only mentions that Mo Zi is considered 'the oldest socialist by the Chinese and Japanese'[96] but also emphasizes that the philosopher's all-encompassing principle of universal love, which undermines Confucius' five principal hierarchical relationships, not only represents an 'ethical socialism' but also a 'straightforward communist trait'.[97] Forke acknowledges socialist characteristics in Mo Zi's principle of universal love ('a general love of mankind ... is

---

[90]Brecht, '10 sept 44', in *Journals 1934–1955*, p. 327.
[91]Ibid.
[92]This essay adapts the distinction between the philosopher Mo Zi and the text compilation by his disciples, the *Mozi*, as established in *The Mozi: A Complete Translation*, trans. and annot. Ian Johnston (New York: Columbia University Press, 2010). Even though the German tradition knows the philosopher by the name Mê Ti (or Me-ti), all of the English references and quotations that follow refer to the philosopher as Mo Zi.
[93]*Mê Ti des Sozialethikers und seiner Schüler philosophische Werke*, trans., ed., and comment. Alfred Forke (Berlin: Kommissionsverlag der Vereinigung wissenschaftlicher Verleger, 1922). (All subsequent quotations from Forke's *Mê Ti* in English are my own translations.)
[94]See Brecht, 'To Helene Weigel', in *Letters 1913–1956*, p. 202 n. 597. According to the editors of *BFA* 28: 496, Brecht wrote this letter from Moscow in late March 1935.
[95]See Brecht, '8 dec 39', in *Journals 1934–1955*, p. 40.
[96]Forke, *Mê Ti*, p. viii.
[97]Ibid., p. 73.

also the foundation of international social democracy'[98]), his notion that appointment to the highest offices should depend on merit, not rank ('many of the most famous ministers of antiquity originated from the working class'[99]), his condemnation of aggressive war ('which leads to unspeakable misery and is of no use to anyone'[100]), and his abolition of luxury and art to secure a simple material and spiritual lifestyle for everyone (similar to the 'communist theories of Babeuf and Robert Owen'[101]).

Forke also points out that since Mo Zi bases his ethics not on a 'categorical imperative but, in a utilitarian manner, on considerations of usefulness and adequacy of purpose', he 'therefore always asks about the effects of moral rules on human society and the life of the state'.[102]

One of Brecht's largest prose works, the *Book of Turns*, resulted from his long-standing engagement with Mo Zi's philosophy.[103] Very different from his *Life of Confucius*, the *Book of Turns* is exclusively about Mo Zi's ideas and not at all about the philosopher's biography or ranking as a historical figure. The *Book of Turns* consists of 319 texts and was probably developed by Brecht during three periods of concentrated work: from late 1934 to spring 1935; in 1937; and from mid-1939 to the beginning of 1940 (a few additional texts were produced sporadically between 1941 and 1955).[104] The major goal of the *Book of Turns* was to use the *Mozi* as a device to estrange and historicize the political developments in Germany and Russia in the 1930s and to derive a materialist code of conduct from these reflections. This is alluded to in introductory remarks that Brecht wrote for the *Book of Turns*:

> The *Book of Turns* has been translated into German by using Charles Stephen's English translation from the Chinese. It doesn't belong to the classical books of Chinese antiquity, even though its core stems from Mo Zi. After their almost complete suppression by the Confucians during the last century, the teachings of Mo Zi have come to the fore again since some of their key elements are reminiscent of certain Western philosophical movements and almost seem modern. The chapters 'On Music' and 'On Manners' are genuine Mo Zi. Other chapters are not by Mo Zi, but also old. Others again are of more recent date, even though in the Chinese version they were written in the style of the classics. ... It is precisely the incorporation of modern

---

[98] Ibid., p. 74.
[99] Ibid.
[100] Ibid.
[101] Ibid.
[102] Ibid., p. 51.
[103] Uwe Johnson, the first editor of the prose fragment, published it under the title *Me-ti: Buch der Wendungen* (Mozi: Book of turns) in 1965. Since the editors of the most recent edition of Brecht's collected works, the *BFA*, just refer to the prose fragment as *Buch der Wendungen*, this title will also be used in the following. However, I have not followed the common practice of translating *Buch der Wendungen* as *Book of Changes* since Brecht's text is mostly an engagement with the philosophy of Mo Zi and includes very few references to Lao Zi's Daoist text, the *I Ching* or *Book of Changes* (in German: *I Ging: Das Buch der Wandlungen*, trans. Richard Wilhelm [Jena: Eugen Diederichs Verlag, 1924]). Even though Daoism was of profound importance to Brecht, it is of no major relevance to his *Buch der Wendungen*. Also, the semantic differences between *Wandlung* and *Wendung* are crucial to the understanding of Brecht's undertaking. *Wandlung* translates as 'transformation', 'transition', or 'conversion' and implies a gradual process of change. *Wendung*, on the other hand, can be translated as 'turn' or 'twist', implying surprising yet significant reversals, but it can also mean 'turn of phrase' (*Redewendung*).
[104] See Roland Jost, 'Buch der Wendungen', in *Brecht Handbuch*, Band 3, *Prosa, Filme, Drehbücher*, ed. Jan Knopf (Stuttgart and Weimer: J. B. Metzler, 2002), p. 236.

reasoning and the partially amusing substitution of comparisons from modern history for the basic ideas of an old Chinese philosopher that will please some readers.[105]

Even though the *Mozi* touches upon music and manners, it doesn't include any specific chapters with the indicated titles – nor does the *Book of Turns*. The 'amusing substitutions from modern history' mostly relate to contemporary political developments in Soviet Russia and Nazi Germany (e.g., Stalin's autocratic rule and show trials and Hitler's massive public-works programs as a preparation for war), and are not amusing for the most part. Brecht does not incorporate any 'genuine' or verbatim passages from the *Mozi*, but engages with Mo Zi's concepts in other ways. Many of the pronouncements attributed to Mo Zi in Brecht's text paraphrase the philosopher's sayings, while others represent the ideas either of Brecht himself or of other Marxist thinkers. Even though Mo Zi may be the most frequently recurring character in the *Book of Turns*, many other historical figures make their appearance in Brecht's text, but under invented Chinese names: their respective code names include 'Ka-meh' for Marx, 'Mi-en-Leh' for Lenin, 'Nien' for Stalin, 'Hu-ih' for Hitler, 'Lai-tu' for Brecht's collaborator Ruth Berlau, and 'Kin-jeh' for Brecht himself.

There are many correspondences between the *Book of Turns* and the *Mozi*, from an insistence on human agency that repudiates the notion of fate, to a condemnation of warmongering and wars of aggression, to a celebration of a utilitarian aesthetic that rejects the notion of art as luxury. There are also parallels in their respective ethical outlooks, for example regarding an ethics of language. Whereas Brecht shares with Confucius an insistence on the precision of language, he agrees with Mo Zi about the need for its purposefulness and applicability. Mo Zi states in 46 : 12: 'Words that are good enough to be put into practice, use frequently. [Words] that are not good enough to be put into practice, do not use frequently. Words that are not good enough to be put into practice, yet are frequently used, are a waste of breath.'[106] Brecht varies the idea in a short text titled 'Bad Habits' but renders it more poignant by making the major criterion not just practicability but the achievement of a goal: 'One must break the habit of walking towards destinations that cannot be reached by walking. One must break the habit of talking about matters that cannot be decided through talking. One must break the habit of thinking about problems that cannot be resolved through thinking.'[107] By establishing a parallel between walking, talking, and thinking Brecht stresses the fact that all of these three activities are actions in the material world. By contrasting three different kinds of activities, he indicates that different goals require different courses of action.

As far as language is concerned, Brecht's emphasis is not on the purposefulness of words but on the performative aspect of language in J. L. Austin's sense. In *How to Do Things with Words*, Austin defines as performative an utterance that doesn't just describe or constate something but actually consists in the 'performing of an action'[108] with consequences in the real world. For this kind of action to be efficacious, however, various conditions need to be fulfilled to guarantee the 'smooth or "happy" functioning of a performative',[109] including the existence of an accepted conventional procedure, the

---

[105]Brecht, 'Buch der Wendungen', *BFA* 18: 194.
[106]Johnston, *The Mozi*, p. 651.
[107]Brecht, 'Schlechte Gewohnheiten', in 'Buch der Wendungen', *BFA* 18: 130.
[108]J. L. Austin, *How to Do Things with Words* (Cambridge, MA: Harvard University Press, 1962), p. 6.
[109]Ibid., p. 14.

appropriateness of the particular participants and circumstances for the invocation of that procedure, and the correct execution of the procedure.[110] For Brecht, talking can be a performative – namely, one that decides matters – if the conditions under which it occurs are not 'infelicitous',[111] that is, if the matters that need to be decided can be decided through talking.

Interestingly, and against philosophical tradition, Brecht also treats thinking not merely as speculative but also as a performative that, given the right circumstances, solves problems, and not just those of an abstract, metaphysical, or mathematical nature. (The notion of 'thinking as intervention' – *eingreifendes Denken* – recurs repeatedly in the *Book of Turns*, for example in a short aphorism in which Karl Marx is referred to as 'the intervening thinker'.[112]) Even though the *Mozi* includes a passage in which the performative dimension of language is discussed – 'Words that are enough to change conduct (for the better) should be spoken frequently. Words that are not enough to change conduct (for the better) should not be spoken frequently'[113] – its notion of the performative remains largely linguistic. Brecht, on the other hand, refuses to limit himself to one particular type of performative but is more interested in identifying the right performative for the goal one tries to achieve: if words are not enough to change conduct, if matters cannot be decided through talking, and if problems cannot be resolved through thinking, one needs to come up with other courses of action to achieve one's goals.

Brecht's *Book of Turns* includes a subsection with shorter texts that is titled 'Condemnation of All Ethics'. The first aphorism in this section reads: 'Mo Zi said: Under moral behavior I can only understand productive behavior. The relations of production are the sources of all morality and immorality.'[114] Moral values, for Brecht, emerge in specific social formations under specific historical and economic conditions and reflect the attitudes as well as interests that are necessary to sustain those specific formations and conditions. Like social formations, moral values are subject to historical change. In one of his *Journal* entries, Brecht illustrates this point by examining 'ought-and-may sentences, which relate to social behavior, which derive from old ethical systems'.[115] Brecht distinguishes between 'you ass' and 'you swine' sentences: while 'you ass' sentences condemn behavior that interferes with the actual relationships of production in a given society, 'you swine' sentences relate to conditions where these relationships have disappeared 'so that the "matter" has now become ethics pure and simple',[116] – in other words, a normative ethics. As an example he discusses incest between mother and son, which, 'in an earlier organization of society … involved great confusion in the matter of property and production relationships. in this regard it is today no longer a "you ass" sentence, but just a "you swine" sentence',[117] and should therefore 'be dropped entirely'.[118]

---

[110]See ibid., pp. 14–15.
[111]Ibid., p. 16.
[112]Brecht, 'Ein Rest zu tun', in 'Buch der Wendungen', *BFA* 18: 110.
[113]*Mozi* 47: 5, in Johnston, *The Mozi*, p. 665.
[114]Brecht, 'Buch der Wendungen', *BFA* 18: 152.
[115]Brecht, '15 jan 40', *Journals 1934–1955*, p. 355.
[116]Ibid.
[117]Ibid.
[118]Ibid.

The major criterion for judging behavior as moral or immoral, according to this example, is the extent to which it facilitates or blocks the flow of production within a given formation. Brecht even makes the point that the incest taboo, despite its archaic origin, could be justified from the perspective of proletarian struggle: 'you ought not to sleep with your mother, you ass, because your partners in the struggle have their prejudices and thus you could put your struggle into jeopardy'.[119] As Brecht states in a different context: 'The judgements "good" and "bad" are transposed into the judgements "useful" and "not useful", and even so these judgements are applied more often to actions than to persons.'[120]

As these examples demonstrate, moral behavior is productive behavior, but what these terms mean changes not only with each society and its respective property relationships but also with the position of the person making these judgments within these relationships. Brecht argues that 'Exploiters constantly preach morality to their workers. But while their preachers coerce the workers to behave morally, the circumstances coerce them to behave immorally. In their struggle against their oppressors the workers sweat morality from every pore'.[121] Brecht rejects the idealistic notion that 'only those virtues should count which are pursued for their own sake'[122] and approvingly quotes Marx's recommendation to workers 'to only practice virtues which will be useful to them'.[123] The *Book of Turns* considers any virtues not tied to the elimination of social ills useless to the working class: 'if they remain long after these ills have been overcome, they often become the source of new social ills. This has often happened with courage, patience, veraciousness and altruism.'[124] A well-ordered society that meets all basic material needs, on the other hand, renders irrelevant the notion that people have to be particularly virtuous to act morally. This Brechtian idea is already prefigured in the *Mozi*: 'When, within, there is food for the hungry and rest for the weary, and there is support and care for their ten thousand people, then rulers and ministers, and superiors and inferiors, are kind and loyal, and fathers and sons, and older and younger brothers, are compassionate and filial.'[125]

In the short text 'Mo Zi and Ethics', Brecht makes the philosopher say: 'I haven't found that many "you shall" sentences that I would like to enunciate. I mean sentences of a general nature, sentences that could be addressed to the general public. Yet one such sentence would be: *You shall produce.*'[126] The prerequisite for the ability to be productive, however, is knowledge of the 'great method', or dialectics:

> The great method is a practical theory of alliances and the dissolution of alliances, the utilization of changes and the dependence on changes, the facilitation of change and the change of the facilitators, the separation and formation of units, the lack of independence of opposites if separated, the compatibility of mutually exclusive

---

[119]Ibid.
[120]Brecht, 'To Ruth Berlau [10 March 1950]', in *Letters 1913–1956*, p. 491.
[121]Brecht, 'Buch der Wendungen', BFA 18: 152.
[122]Ibid., p. 154.
[123]Ibid.
[124]Ibid., p. 153.
[125]*Mozi* 27: 3, in Johnston, *The Mozi*, p. 249.
[126]Brecht, 'Me-ti und die Ethik', in 'Buch der Wendungen', BFA 18: 179.

opposites. The great method allows to recognize processes in things and to use them. The great method teaches how to ask questions that enable action.[127]

Only the ability to recognize processes and to ask the right questions allows for action that helps to produce a new society. Brecht's materialist code of conduct follows from the knowledge of the great method: 'Not being one with oneself, to thrust oneself into crises, to turn small changes into large ones, and so on, all of this cannot only be studied but also be done. ... One can achieve or seek a consistent change of mind by changing one's social existence. One can help to make state institutions contradictory or developable.'[128] One of the key challenges, though (as Brecht suggests in another context), is 'to apprehend the true turning points'.[129] Also, Brecht develops his notion of non-identity further in a reflection on the statement 'One does not equal one', which, according to him, articulates the impossibility of finding either an object or a concept that will stay true to itself over an extended period of time.[130] This notion of 'slippage' is also prefigured in the *Mozi*: 'With respect to things, there is that by which they are the same yet not completely the same.'[131]

Brecht's materialist ethics starts with a frank assessment of one's egoistic needs: 'There is nothing objectionable about self-love, if it is not directed against others.'[132] Brecht admits that 'bad conditions are caused both by the self-love of some and the lack of self-love of others',[133] but, overall, society benefits from this trait. 'Those who don't love themselves enough, who don't secure the means by which to make themselves lovable, ... who don't acquire knowledge to educate themselves ... poison society with their misery.'[134] But a lack of self-love may also be a disadvantage for political struggle: 'If someone is incapable of getting furious about a private wrong committed against him, it will be very difficult for him to put up a fight.'[135]

The primary ethical relationship for Brecht is not between individuals but between an individual and society at large, an idea that is already anticipated in a passage in the *Mozi* in which Mo Zi quotes the ancient saying, '"Seeing with one eye is not like seeing with two eyes. Hearing with one ear is not like hearing with two ears. Grasping something with one hand is not like the strength of two hands"'[136] – and then concludes: 'it was only because they were able to put their trust in the people in conducting their affairs that they enjoyed benefits like this'.[137] Brecht is generally closer to Mo Zi's notion of universal love than to either a (Confucian or Kantian) categorical imperative based on an imagined reciprocal relationship between individuals or the Christian commandment to love your

---

[127]Brecht, 'Die große Methode', in 'Buch der Wendungen,' *BFA* 18: 104.
[128]Brecht, 'Leben nach der großen Methode', in 'Buch der Wendungen', *BFA* 18: 192–193.
[129]Brecht, 'Was Me-ti nicht liebte', in 'Buch der Wendungen', *BFA* 18: 148.
[130]Brecht, 'Der Ungleichheitssatz in der Großen Methode', in 'Buch der Wendungen', *BFA* 18: 98.
[131]*Mozi* 45.3, in Johnston, *The Mozi*, p. 625.
[132]Brecht, 'Über den Egoismus', in 'Buch der Wendungen', *BFA* 18: 72.
[133]Ibid.
[134]Ibid.
[135]Brecht, 'Der Zorn über das Unrecht', in 'Buch der Wendungen', *BFA* 18: 155.
[136]*Mozi* 13.10, in Johnston, *The Mozi*, p. 127.
[137]Ibid. A dramatization of this passage can be found in Brecht's 'learning play' *The Measures Taken*: 'THE CONTROL CHORUS: One single man may have two eyes / But the Party has a thousand. ...' (Bertolt Brecht, *The Measures Taken and Other Lehrstücke*, ed. John Willett and Ralph Manheim, trans. Carl R. Mueller [London: Methuen, 1977], p. 29).

neighbor as yourself (which Brecht rejects because of its foundation in self-denial[138]). Even so, Brecht's 'self love' is based not on narcissistic self-centeredness but on a de-centered not-being-one-with-oneself. It is a relationship toward oneself that implies that by 'taking care of oneself one takes care of the community at the same time'.[139]

Brecht's ethics are not based on reciprocity but on what he calls historicization in a theatrical context, namely the idea that one should always behave as if not the next person but 'history' (i.e., the history of class struggle) would be the judge: 'Mo Zi advised his students to note down their respective pursuits as if they were writing a biography aimed for those classes for which they intended to fight.'[140] (One of Brecht's estrangement techniques for actors was to transpose the lines of a character into the third person.[141]) In another short text Brecht's Mo Zi recommends 'to look at oneself, and at classes and multiplicities as well, as if from a historical perspective, and to behave according to that perspective. Life, if experienced consciously as the material of one's future biography, acquires a certain importance and may make history in its own right.'[142] This passage draws upon the historical Mo Zi, who, different from Confucius, already had a dialectical understanding of historical change: 'What is called ancient in speech and dress was all once upon a time new.'[143] Brecht extrapolates this statement and suggests that by regarding oneself as a player within larger historical developments and political struggles, one will probably be more astute and diligent about the decisions one is going to make: 'Mo Zi said: "If everyone would be their own historiographer, they would live more thoughtfully and discerningly."'[144] One reason why this ethical model may be more difficult to realize than one based on empathy and interpersonal reciprocity may have to do with the fact that it requires knowledge, learning, and interpretive skills: to perceive oneself as an agent of change within a broader historical panorama is only possible if one has an understanding not only of the socioeconomic forces that shape history but also of the 'great method' that allows one to insert oneself productively into these larger contexts.

Brecht links his non-reciprocal, historicizing ethics to what the calls the 'third cause' (which he identifies with Socialism):

> Mo Zi said that the relationship between two people would be good if there were a third thing that they would have a shared interest in. Mi-en-leh added that this would also apply to the relationships among groups of people of any size. By devoting themselves jointly to an external cause, all of their matters sort themselves out more easily, simply according to the requirements of this thing.[145]

In a letter to Ruth Berlau, Brecht indicates how a focus on reciprocal relationships between individuals is supplanted by a non-reciprocal and non-retributive relationship between individuals and the larger collective causes they are fighting for: 'In future there will no longer be tributes (which are owed) but gifts (which are gladly given). ... No one

---

[138] See Brecht, 'Buch der Wendungen', *BFA* 18: 152.
[139] Brecht, 'Schlechte Zeiten', in 'Buch der Wendungen', *BFA* 18: 68.
[140] Brecht, 'In der dritten Person leben', in 'Buch der Wendungen', *BFA* 18: 188.
[141] See Bertolt Brecht, 'Short Description of a New Technique of Acting That Produces a *Verfremdung* Effect' (*Brecht on Theatre*, p. 186).
[142] Brecht, 'Über die historische Selbstbetrachtung', in 'Buch der Wendungen', *BFA* 18: 188.
[143] *Mozi* 39.5, in Johnston, *The Mozi*, p. 355.
[144] Brecht, 'Auch der Einzelne hat seine Geschichte', in 'Buch der Wendungen', *BFA* 18: 131.
[145] Brecht, 'Die dritte Sache', in 'Buch der Wendungen', *BFA* 18: 173.

will owe anyone anything; everyone will owe everything to the *third thing*.'[146] Even love relationships to Brecht are not just about the interpersonal concerns of the two lovers but have a social and historical dimension. Brecht considers love a production, and lovers a special type of producers:

> The best succeed to bring their love into complete harmony with other productions: in that case their friendliness becomes a general one, their inventiveness becomes useful to many, and they support everything that is productive.[147]

Lovers, as described here, represent a best-case scenario of production in Brecht's envisioned society. But, as Brecht himself admits, 'love doesn't happen on command'[148] and is not a requirement for the productive members of society. Whereas Confucius insisted on the family as the main production unit, Brecht makes his Mo Zi say that the smallest production unit 'emerges where people work or ask for work'.[149] The members of these smallest units, however, don't have to love each other, 'they only need to love the common goal'.[150]

In his dramatic fragment *Life of Confucius* and his prose project *Book of Turns* Brecht conflates three conflicting positions regarding ethical behavior: the materialist-determinist notion that morality is shaped by the conditions of production; the mimetic-utilitarian idea that a social attitude or gestus of virtue can easily be copied ('The wise ones make wise, the benevolent ones make benevolent, the courageous ones make courageous'[151]) and is therefore useful for the facilitation of a more productive social climate; and the assumption that benevolence and kindness are expressions of human nature as opposed to aggressive and hostile behavior. This last position can be found in various of Brecht's works, including the play *The Good Person of Szechwan*:

> SHEN TEH:
> Why are you so unpleasant?
> To trample on one's fellows
> Is surely exhausting? Veins in your temples
> Stick out with the strenuousness of greed.
> Loosely held forth
> A hand gives and receives with the same suppleness. Yet
> Greedily snatching it has got to strain. Oh
> How tempting it is to be generous. How welcome
> Friendliness can somehow feel. A kindly word
> Escapes like a sigh of contentment.[152]

The idea that it is the natural tendency of humans to act morally is also addressed in a short text in the *Book of Turns*, which suggests that only a few occupations 'damage a person's morals as much as the preoccupation with morals':[153]

---

[146]Brecht, 'To Ruth Berlau [10 March 1950]', in *Letters 1913–1956*, p. 491.
[147]Brecht, 'Kin-jeh über die Liebe', in 'Buch der Wendungen', *BFA* 18: 175.
[148]Brecht, 'Über die kleinste Einheit', in 'Buch der Wendungen', *BFA* 18: 80.
[149]Ibid., p. 79.
[150]Ibid., p. 80.
[151]Brecht, 'Klug, gütig, tapfer', in 'Buch der Wendungen', *BFA* 18: 151.
[152]Bertolt Brecht, *The Good Person of Szechwan*, trans. John Willett (London: Penguin, 2008), p. 80.
[153]Brecht, 'Beschäftigung mit Moral', in 'Buch der Wendungen', *BFA* 18: 95.

I hear people say: You have to be veracious, you have to keep your promises, you have to fight for what is good. But the trees don't say: You have to be green, you have to drop your fruit to the ground vertically, you have to rustle with your leaves when the wind blows through.[154]

As mutually exclusive as these three positions may seem, they are actually aligned in Brecht's ethics: Even though social conditions largely determine moral behavior, they should not be accepted as fate; the insertion of a socially useful gestus may not only increase everyone's potential agency and productivity in the struggle for an egalitarian society but may also ease the constrictions that prevent everyone from acting morally by nature.

For Brecht, both Mo Zi and Confucius served as respected counterparts and foils that allowed him to develop and articulate his own materialist-ethical positions. Because of their cultural difference and historical remove from Brecht's own context they provided an echo chamber and testing ground that allowed him to estrange and historicize his own ideas as well as the Marxist discourse of his time, thereby rendering both developable. As Fredric Jameson has argued, Chinese philosophy in Brecht's work plays the role of a Lacanian 'place-keeper for the metaphysics that have become impossible',[155] thereby pointing to what a '"philosophy" of Marxism ... might turn out to be in a utopian future.'[156] It is exactly Brecht's affinity with key positions of both of these irreconcilable schools of thought that kept him actively engaged in an intellectual dialog with Confucius and Mo Zi for decades, thereby allowing him to put into practice the one single normative virtue of his own materialist ethics: 'You shall produce.'

---

[154]Ibid., pp. 95–96.
[155]Fredric Jameson, *Brecht and Method* (London and New York: Verso, 1998), p. 12.
[156]Ibid.

# Comedy/Humour

# CHAPTER TWENTY-FOUR

# The Poetic Anthropology of Comedy in Brecht's *Buying Brass*

RALF SIMON
TRANSLATED BY ROMY FURSLAND

## I. DISTANCING AND FICTIONALISATION AS A PREREQUISITE OF COMEDY

Imagine a scene, the kind of scene you might see in any slapstick comedy – to make things really simple let us take a scene in which a character slips on a banana skin and lands painfully on his behind. If we are to laugh at this scene we must *not* bring to bear the virtues recommended by the Aristotelians. Empathy, compassion and sympathetic identification with the character would not cause us to laugh; instead, our moral selves would be appalled at the unfortunate situation in which the film has placed this character and in which we as the audience are being placed by being expected to laugh at the misfortune, the pain and the suffering of the character we are observing. If we laugh, however, we have to rid ourselves of empathy – we have to redirect our interest in the situation into a detached observation. Laughter can only take the place of compassion once we have fundamentally distanced ourselves from what is going on. Incidentally: if catharsis relies on emotional investment in which compassion and identification are crucial elements, whereas laughter, as noted above, requires us to distance ourselves, then there can be no such thing as comic catharsis.[1] But let us return to our example.

---

Ralf Simon, 'Zur poetischen Anthropologie der Komödie in Brechts *Messingkauf*', *Brecht Yearbook*, 24 (1999), pp. 277–90.

[1] The question of whether comic catharsis can exist at all according to Aristotle's premise is a contentious one. Manfred Fuhrmann, *Einführung in die antike Dichtungstheorie* (Darmstadt, 1973), 65, writes: 'Aristotle would never have dreamt of describing enjoyment and laughter as states of heightened emotion (*pathemata*) of which the comedy must cleanse the spectator.' What this argument seems to be driving at is the idea that laughter itself already constitutes that moderate, even-tempered emotion which, in the case of tragedy, is allegedly only achievable through catharsis. If – as my thesis postulates – fictionalising and distancing are a prerequisite of laughter, whereas catharsis works mainly via strong identification, then the two concepts are not compatible. In spite of these very strong arguments, however, many comedy theorists still talk about 'comic catharsis'.

Let us assume we saw a man slip on a banana skin in real life – across the street, for example. We would have two options: we could be the better (i.e. more compassionate) person and hurry across the road to help our banana skin victim to his feet. But it is more likely that we would be reminded of similar scenes from slapstick comedy films, stay right where we were and find the whole thing highly comical. Instead of intervening compassionately we would look on with amusement, perhaps laughter. More precisely, we are not laughing at the mere fact that someone has fallen over; but seeing him fall over has made us observe our own observation that the incident resembles scenes from slapstick comedies. We therefore find ourselves in a form of Goffman's frame analysis. Our distancing of ourselves, and our observation of our observation of the communicative frame, lead to fictionalisation. The man who has fallen over is a comic archetype. If we were morally better people we would feel compassion, and since compassion does not serve to fictionalise but to concretise, we would feel obliged to help. When we laugh, however, we are fictionalising: the man falling over is an instance of a comic genre and we, by laughing, are observing our observation of having observed this and finding it comical. Here, then, comedy results from a decidedly aesthetic, both fictionalising and self-referential attitude. The physical effect of laughter – i.e. the body remaining present during the convulsive shock waves of laughter – points to the fundamental self-referentiality which, so the theory goes, is the key ingredient of all comedy. The bond of compassion and empathy between the incident and the spectator must be severed in order for comedy to be possible. The incident as such must become autonomous; it must be recognisable an example of a specific genre unencumbered by action or morals; and the spectator as such must self-referentialise, as it were, in order to swallow the impulse to act and then process this impulse internally, in convulsive laughter.

## II. OVERVIEW OF A THEORY OF COMEDY

I do not have the space here to set out a detailed theory of comedy: instead I will put forward three theses and attempt to justify them.

My *first thesis* is as follows: a poetics of comedy cannot be derived from the concept of the comic. Even comic situations in real life are, as I have attempted to describe, a different thing altogether: a consequence of prior distancing and fictionalisation. A theory of comedy would do better to draw on these moments than on established theories of laughter and comedy. With comedies, then, we cannot proceed in the same way as with tragedies: whereas tragedy as a text type can be derived from a concept of the tragic, comedy cannot be explained by the comic. The tragic exists in discourse; in real life there is no destiny, no fate. Concepts like these interpret life, they articulate it by developing a coherence of concepts and initiating a particular world view. Because the tragic is always of a linguistic nature, the step from this to the linguistic nature of tragedy as a literary genre remains within the same medium. The comic, on the other hand, is not linguistic *per se*. The step from the comic to comedy cannot take place on a linear continuum. Quite the opposite: comedy as a literary form starts afresh, beginning from a principle of self-observation and distancing into which the comic can (but does not have to) be integrated afterwards, as a second step.

But what does a theory of comedy look like when it takes precisely this distancing as its starting point? My *second thesis* is as follows: comedy raises the ability to distance ourselves from real-world events in the ways we observe them to a higher power and integrates this into an aesthetic form. In my banana example, we saw the observation of an observation: the spectator retreats to an aesthetic distance and observes his or her own observation, after which the slip on the banana skin becomes an example of a comic genre. It is precisely this real-life fictionalisation and doubling which is systematically incorporated into the medium of the comedy text and there reinforced. What happens in comedy at the various different levels of observation has its model in the basic distancing and fictionalising impulse of that onlooker on the other side of the street. In comedy, artistic devices like the play-within-a-play or theatre-within-the-theatre become a basic poetological pattern, because they convert distancing and fictionalisation into the plot structure of the comedy.

This brings me to my *third thesis*: comedy has a plot structure such that self-observation is made possible by the plot itself. It puts the agent of conflict in a position in which he can observe himself and consequently correct himself. For example: a pair of lovers want to marry, but first they must gain the approval of the groom's father, who is an avowed misogynist. In order to force this obstacle into a salutary self-observation, the bride disguises herself as a man and – thanks to her cleverness – gains the father's friendship. Eventually she lets her mask fall and manages to persuade the father to abandon all his prejudices about the stupidity of women, which have been roundly disproven. This plot – a summary of the plot of Lessing's *The Misogynist* – forces the father to observe his own world view in such a way that he realises how wrong it is. The strategy which is used to achieve this is the creation of a second reality, for the bride is playing a game – a game making communication asymmetrical. The thesis is that comedies, in one form or another, bring about such self-observations through self-referential plot twists. Their narrative praxis – i.e. their plot structure – is to a certain extent already theory, namely the contingency-generating relativization of hitherto entrenched opinions. The plot structure of comedies is inherently such that one level of the action is observed by another. For the purpose of differentiating between genres, then, we might argue that comedy is also the observation of the level on which tragedy is found. Comedies have happy endings because they can use metalevels of observation to transform conflict structures into relativizing contingency – the kind of conflict structures which go unquestioned in tragedies. In comedies, therefore, play-within-a-play structures are not merely an artistic device but a poetological cornerstone. Comedy is – to suggest a summary term for this plot structure – metafiction.[2] It plays a game of doublings and self-observations with the aim of defusing conflicts by repeatedly introducing new supervisor positions. Brecht's most comic text, *Mr Puntila and his Man Matti*, articulates in virtuoso fashion the grammar of observation

---

[2]The term 'metafiction' calls for a brief justification. A search through the Dissertation Abstracts showed that the term 'metafiction' is particularly well-established in the English-speaking world. In the last ten years alone, over 60 American dissertations include the term in their titles. It is part of the theoretical inventory of post-structuralist thought, along with terms like metahistory, mirror text and *mise en abyme*. Metafiction as a term does not primarily describe an increase in fictionality, but rather particular plot constructions in narrative texts (which, however, usually result in increased fictionality). Because the term is not widely used in German, however, I have taken the liberty of using it as a generic term for phenomena such as the play-within-a-play, among other things, and of linking it *expressis verbis* to a fictionality spiral. I have used the term metafiction as the umbrella term for artistic devices such as *mise-en-abyme*, fictional irony, illusion-shattering, frame duplication, mirror text, *métathéâtre*, various forms of commentary upon the text, asides, stepping out of role, various forms of intertextuality, exposing the workings of the plot, commentaries on eavesdropping scenes, etc. Fundamentally the plot of a comedy aims, through its structure, to initiate a salutary self-observation whereby a character is made to correct a conflict which he or she has caused. If this is achieved via the plot structure, through new levels of observation, I call such a plot construction 'metafiction'.

and at the same time identifies its far-reaching analogy with the dialectics of mastery and servitude. Here too it is not only language which is the medium of observation but also – and primarily – the plot structure. For the protagonists in a comedy have to experience its decentralising effects first-hand, within the actual plot, and this means that linguistic reflection, which is the preferred medium of tragedy, only serves to ratify, in retrospect, an already completed storyline.

## III. BRECHT'S *BUYING BRASS* AS A THEORY OF COMEDY

In relation to our example of the man slipping on the banana skin, Brecht would have no interest in a theory of laughter but he would be very interested in the distancing strategies. For his basic impulse, with which he sets his epic theatre against what he calls Aristotelian theatre, is to try to disrupt the empathy of the theatre of illusion, and to create distance using V-effects. Brecht, according to my thesis, adopts the entire inventory of the comic tradition[3] and uses basic distancing not to create comedy but to generate criticism. He is open to a theory of comedy if such a theory is based not on humour and laughter but on the structures underlying observation and reflection. Brecht, I would argue, wants comedy without its laughter. Laughter in and of itself is not cognitive enough for him, and the person doing the laughing is too oblivious to everything else that is going on: he or she gets lost, as it were, in the physical agitation of laughing, remains bound to his or her basic self-reference. This is better than getting lost in identifying with a character, but the best thing of all, in Brecht's eyes, would be for the distancing which is present in laughter *per se* to serve as a starting point for a process of reflection and criticism.

---

[3] The topic of Brecht and comedy has been addressed in various works. Peter Christian Giese, *Das 'Gesellschaftlich-Komische'. Zu Komik und Komödie am Beispiel der Stücke und Bearbeitungen Brechts* (Stuttgart, 1974), discusses the very specific concept of the 'socially comic' and provides several interpretations, although he confines himself to just a few plays and scenes (e.g. wedding scenes). He does not address rules relating to the structure of epic theatre more generally. Ulrich Weisstein, 'Die Komödie bei Brecht' in: *Die deutsche Komödie im zwanzigsten Jahrhundert*, ed. Wolfgang Paulsen (Heidelberg, 1976), 134–53, takes the concept of the socially comic as his starting point and then suggests that 'the dramatic category most ideally matched to Brecht [would have to be] the tragicomic' (140). Weisstein explicitly rejects the central plank of my thesis: the idea that it is possible to get to Brecht's plays at all via a generic concept of comedy (146, 153). Louise J. Bird, 'The comic world of Bertolt Brecht' in *Forum for Modern Language Studies* 4 (1968), generalises the notion of the comic into more of an ideological concept and thus loses the close relationship of comedy to literary tradition. Reinhold Grimm, 'Komik und Verfremdung' in *Wesen und Formen des Komischen im Drama*, ed. Reinhold Grimm and Klaus H. Berghahn (Darmstadt, 1975), 253–71, explores the extent to which V-effects give rise to comic effects. He only manages to give a series of examples of comical or funny situations, however, without using these examples to develop an idea of what a comedy actually is (in other words, comedy as a form is undoubtedly more than a series of jokes). Where Grimm does get around to talking about dramatic structure, his reflections lead him away from comedy and towards satire (270). Helmut Arntzen, 'Komödie und episches Theater', ibid. 441–55, separates the task of developing a theory of comedy from any direct link to the comic, and is thereby able to access Brecht's epic theatre as a form which is close to comedy. Although Arntzen's approach is the most productive one for my arguments, he does not offer a poetics of comedy in the sense that the plot structure of comedy is thematised. Eric Bentley's statement: 'Brecht's theory of theatre is, in my view, a theory of comedy' ('Die Theaterkunst Brechts' in *Sinn und Form*, 2nd Bertolt Brecht special edition [Berlin, 1957]: 159–77, here 174), is, unfortunately, not substantiated. Overall we can say that there is no attempt to move from a reasoned theory of comedy to Brecht's epic theatre. Arguments which make the concept of the comic, especially that of the socially comic, the be-all and end-all of their interpretation of Brecht, tend to remain abstract from the point of view of genre poetics.

The theory that Brecht adopts the structure of comedy without the intention of creating something comical[4] can be developed by looking at his most important theoretical work, the fragmentary *Buying Brass*.[5] In the first of the four nights, which build on one another in a dialectical way, the Dramaturg cites the well-known definition of tragedy from Aristotle's Poetics: 'He [Aristotle] says of tragedy that it is an imitative portrayal of a morally serious, self-contained action of a given duration, in elevated language whose different varieties are employed separately, divided up among different parts; that it is not narrated but performed by people acting; and that by evoking pity and fear it allows people to purge themselves of those same emotions.' (GW 15: 507).[6] Two sentences later the Dramaturg, commenting on the Aristotle quote, simply replaces the term 'tragedy' with 'theatre': 'Theatre has undergone many changes since Aristotle wrote those things, but not in this respect. We have to assume that if it changed in this respect, it would no longer be theatre' (GW 16: 508). At a stroke, Brecht turns a definition of the characteristics of tragedy into a speech about theatre more generally. This generalisation is not touched upon anywhere else in the whole of *Buying Brass*. Everything unfavourable that is said about the old kind of theatre (the kind Brecht calls Aristotelian) and against which epic theatre is defined, is left unspecified in relation to the genre differences between comedy and tragedy. Taken to its logical conclusion, one might argue that if Brecht's epic theatre is supposed to be the opposite of the old theatre, whilst in Aristotle the opposite of tragedy is comedy, then perhaps with his epic theatre Brecht is, de facto, thinking of the structure of comedy.

In fact, Brecht takes up the entire comic method as a conscious artistic device because he wants to build upon the distancing inherent in the structure of comedy for his own version of a didactic theatre of enlightenment. If characters in comedies turn situations on their heads in order to force a problem-causing character into an attitude of corrective self-reflection, then they must necessarily use Brechtian V-effects.[7] If they appear in disguise, or even just pretend to be different from who they actually are, then they are

---

[4] Fritz Martini, 'Einige Überlegungen zur Poetik des Lustspiels' in *Wesen und Formen des Komischen im Drama*, ed. Reinhold Grimm and Klaus H. Berghahn (Darmstadt, 1975), 342 and other places, and Helmut Arntzen (see above) are the only authors who deal with the relationship between the comic and comedy in such a way that they remove a prerequisite structure from the comic, meaning that only further work done by this prerequisite structure leads to the comic itself. Both use words to the effect that comedy is a structure which also intends to be comic. This wording does not oblige one to derive comedy directly from theories of laughter and the comic.

[5] The thing about this collection of texts is that it is not very easy to quote from. A conversation between a Marxist Philosopher who starts off as rather doctrinaire, an Actor who starts off as rather obsessed with success and craving recognition, and a Dramaturg who starts off as rather bourgeois, leads, over the course of four nights, to all three changing their positions and to a convergence of the initially stark antitheses. When we quote from the conversations, therefore, we must always be aware of the stage of insight from which the quoted passage is taken. A few pages later, the same speaker may already have moved on.

[6] See Aristotle, *Poetics*, Chapter 6, 1449b. I quote from Brecht's *Buying Brass* using the abbreviation GW, with the volume and page number, from the following edition: Bertolt Brecht, *Gesammelte Werke in 20 Bänden* (Frankfurt am Main: Suhrkamp, 1973). For each text I have checked the new edition and indicated in the footnotes when text appears in different places. The abbreviation BFA, followed by volume and page number, refers to: Bertolt Brecht, *Werke. Große kommentierte Berliner und Frankfurter Ausgabe*, ed. Werner Hecht, Jan Knopf, Werner Mittenzwei and Klaus-Detlef Müller. *Buying Brass* is found in Volume 2.2 (1993).

[7] See the list of V-effects in the *Brecht-Handbuch*, *Theater* by Jan Knopf (Stuttgart, 1996), 388–92; see also, in the same text, the references to the relevant locations in Brecht's work. The interpretations Knopf produces of individual Brecht plays focus particularly on play-within-a-play structures and are therefore a helpful source of material for my thesis that this comedy-specific plot structure is prevalent in Brecht's work generally (see also in Knopf, in the unfortunately incomplete index: 'Spiel'.)

already – within the play itself – *distanced from their role*. Brecht stipulated that actors must not identify with their roles, so that spectators would not get the idea they were watching anything other than a group of performers acting something out.[8] This is exactly what the structure of comedy does, too. Its basic disposition is metacommunicative: it relativizes, it breaks the fourth wall, it identifies the actor as somebody engaged in role-playing, whereas tragedy leads the actor to identify with his or her role.[9]

In order to achieve the distancing effect, according to Brecht, actors should speak their lines as *if they were quoting them* (BFA 16: 623, 655), and during rehearsals they should *speak first-person lines in the third person and replace the present tense with the past tense*.[10] In comedy, an attitude like this is necessary whenever a metafictional level of the play is introduced. A good example of this is the gender switching in Shakespeare's *As You Like It*, in which Rosalind (who in Shakespeare's day was played by a man) disguises herself as a shepherd boy, Ganymede, and gets Orlando to pretend Ganymede is a woman.[11] Wherever such plays-within-a-play occur in a comedy, the actors automatically have to speak their lines in the same way Brecht wants to see actors acting (based on V-effects) in his epic theatre. And since, as I have tried to illustrate, comedy *per se* is just as much metafiction as the observation of tragedy, the play-within-a-play and thus the practice of quoting oneself and putting oneself in the position of a third person is poetological standard practice in comedy.

If explicit plays-within-a-play are performed within such structures of meta-observation, then it is inevitable that the actors will *give each other stage directions*. Thus Brecht suggests as a V-effect that during rehearsals, *the actors should speak the stage directions out loud*. In the game of the comedy, agreements are constantly being made between the characters as to how they should dissimulate, which roles they should play and which postures they should strike in which situations, how to create a certain appearance using a certain behaviour. Comedy contains an inherent discourse of stage directions. This can be seen most clearly in Nestroy. If his comedies of situation and confusion seem to rush towards their climax, since almost every scene features new events that threaten to unmask the play-within-the-play, then the intriguers' communications are almost entirely confined to giving each other stage directions. To a much greater extent than tragedy, comedy integrates the choreography of blocking on the stage into the characters' speeches.

It is also clear that *establishing the Not/But* is directly related to the metafictional plot, since every new level of observation indicates new alternatives:[12] a given plot was *not* the only possible one, *but* one of multiple alternatives. If, according to Brecht, traditional theatre – tragedy, to be precise – portrays events as necessary and without alternative, then epic theatre is designed to make clear that plots generally do *not* represent the only option, but that there are several. This Not/But structure is also specific to comedy, in Brecht's view. Comedies draw their comedy and their tension from the fact that the metafictional counter-intrigues open up alternatives, reveal the multiple possibilities of a plot and thus, in contrast to tragedy, help to change the characters.

---

[8] See in *Buying Brass*: 'The Street Scene', see also GW 16: 610.
[9] See these definitions in Uri Rapp, *Handeln und Zuschauen* (Darmstadt und Neuwied, 1973), 77.
[10] See in *Buying Brass* the concept of historicization (GW 16: 610, 628, 656).
[11] See in *Buying Brass* the notion of performed gender-switching as the transformation of one first-person subject into another (GW 16: 611).
[12] See *Short Organon for the Theatre* (GW 16: 688).

Finally, Brecht argues that *the actor turning to the audience* is a V-effect. This has its origins in the parabasis of ancient comedy and also in the way Harlequin breaks the fourth wall in the commedia dell'arte. *Subtitles and summaries* – we might think of the typically Brechtian banners used to sum up a scene – and the *presence of a narrator on the stage* have a similar function. Every time the fourth wall is broken, the illusion is shattered. *Songs and music* also serve as levels of commentary on what is happening on stage, and exist outside of the continuum of the play. In the comedic tradition Nestroy's couplets are also located at the level of commentary, because the sung passages articulate insights which cannot be articulated within the plot itself.

## IV. ANTHROPOLOGY OF COMEDY IN BRECHT

Thus almost all Brecht's V-effects are named and characterised as basic processes familiar from the comedic tradition. In *Buying Brass* this technical identification, so to speak, of the structure of comedy with epic theatre is reflected on another level too. In the essay 'On the Theatricality of Fascism', which was to be integrated into *Buying Brass*,[13] Brecht makes the argument that Fascism uses Aristotelian dramaturgy politically as a propaganda tool to control the masses. A critical dramaturgy, therefore, cannot conform to the theatre of illusion and empathy. As an aside, the argument put forward by conservative theatre people – that theatre needs Aristotelian poetics to constitute its artistic value (GW 16: 508) – is refuted: Aristotelianism is not exclusively aesthetic at all, but just as political as the theatre theory put forward by the Marxist Philosopher.

The main argument in this line of thought is a cultural-anthropological one. Brecht states that it is our deep, atavistic and obscure emotions which the dramaturgy of identification appeals to. In Aristotelian theatre, as in the performances staged by Nazi Fascism, spectators are whipped up into a state of passionate excitement in which they identify narcissistically with great figures and thereby lose their critical abilities. If (based on what Brecht saw as the direct equivalence between Fascism and Aristotelian theatre in terms of their identification structure) it is vital to destroy Aristotelianism, then ultimately this destruction must begin where the need for narcissistic identification runs deep. The Philosopher in *Buying Brass* therefore proposes an alternative anthropology. We should no longer identify with the supposed hero, he says; we should no longer place any value on narcissistic emotional intensity. Instead we should pursue other passions. Curiosity, criticism, cheerfulness, cunning and levity are the emotions suggested as alternatives. Atavistic identification should be replaced by sentiments which are themselves already connected to the intellect and open to the passion of the thinker.

If, at the beginning of *Buying Brass*, art itself is called into question based on its complicity with Fascism, it soon transpires that the kind of art being renounced is the kind which demands empathy and a belief in illusions from its recipient. At the end of *Buying Brass* we find a defence of the kind of art which does not have these characteristics and which, on the contrary, enables critical distance. One might say that Brecht, with this concluding opposition, is again drawing on the difference between tragedy and comedy,

---

[13]The text is printed in GW 16: 558-68 in the context of *Buying Brass*. In BFA 22.2: 695 there is a note by Brecht listing the titles of works to be included in *Buying Brass*, and the theatricality essay is mentioned. BFA does not include the text, however, though it does refer in the commentary (BFA 22.2: 1075) to a statement by Brecht which places the essay very close to *Buying Brass*.

if we assume we are talking about the structure of comedy without comic intentions. In the so-called 'Street Scene'[14] in *Buying Brass*, it is clear that the difference between the genres of comedy and tragedy is also one of attitudes, habitus and gestus.[15] Comedy can be understood as a model for life if we contrast its fundamental characteristics – namely distancing, observation and consciousness of role-playing as a consequence of metafictional plot construction – with tragedy which, through identification, emotional investment and the suppression of role-consciousness, forms the anthropological model of a narcissistic hunger for fate.

If we look at Brecht's project through the lens of genre poetics, then, it is considerably diminished. The difference between tragedy and comedy is an idea rooted in European theatre. Brecht, who wanted to transcend European theatre altogether, is in fact still operating entirely within the rules arising from the difference between tragedy and comedy. His aversion to the old kind of theatre turns out to be an aversion to traditional tragedy and a preference for a modified interpretation of comedy. Viewed in this way, Brecht's theory of epic theatre serves as a justification for a change in the hierarchy of the genres.

Here he is in good company. For in the history of theatre in the twentieth century, comedy is tragedy's successor. The structural optimism which is still inherent in the tragic catastrophe's positing of metaphysical meaning is not found in comedy. Comedy can portray negativity free of metaphysics. Durrenmatt's view, that the worst possible turn a story can take is the turn into comedy, is a striking expression of the idea that only comedy is now capable of representing the absurdity of the state of the world.

## V. OVERVIEW OF A READING OF BRECHT PLAYS AS COMEDIES

The question which now needs to be asked, and answered through detailed interpretations, but which can only be briefly outlined and considered here, is to do with Brecht's stage plays. What does it mean, particularly for the avowedly Marxist plays, that they are in fact structural comedies? What does it mean for Brechtian Marxism that it is being argued for in plays which may not intend to be comical but which position their subjects the way they would have been positioned if the aim was for people to laugh at them? In the end, and especially in these post-socialist times, is it possible to read these plays as comedies we can laugh at, in which Marxism is not the subject of laughter but the object of derision?

What Brecht draws on in his plays is the idea of a reality which exists irrespective of any V-effects. He does not realise that this very referentiality is called into question by his own dramaturgical devices, namely the structural comedy, because comedy fictionalises (through distancing, see above): it deals with reality within the framework of its basic

---

[14] Here, too, BFA fails to print the text as part of the *Messingkauf*. In Brecht's lists of contents it appears twice as a text to be included in the *Messingkauf*: BFA 22.2: 695, 697. In the commentary, the 'Street Scene' is also explicitly assigned to the *Messingkauf* (BFA 22.2: 1021). In this case as in the case of the theatricality essay, I am working on the assumption that the text can be treated as part of the *Messingkauf*.

[15] In the long footnote 1 (GW 16: 550), it is explicitly stated that the 'basic model for epic theatre' (GW 16: 546) which Brecht selects here is, in most practical real-life situations, 'of a comic nature'. The natural epic theatre (GW 16: 557), is close to comedy in terms of its basic approach, whilst for a successful epic demonstration it is necessary to avoid any effects reminiscent of the modes of reception for tragedy.

poetological pattern, the 'play-within-a-play' or, as I have termed it, metafiction. Brecht's V-effects place us aesthetically in a position of keeping our distance, of standing on the other side of the street laughing at the man who has fallen over because we perceive him, through decontextualization, as an example of a comic genre. We fictionalise because we are directed by the whole of Brecht's methodological apparatus to perceive the structures of comedy. It may be that Brecht's shattering of the old nature of reception through his newly adopted comedy leads not to criticism but only to new postmodern confusion. We could see epic theatre as a series of video clips which unintentionally come across as comical because the seriousness of the didacticism calls for a continuity which, aesthetically, is always shattered into the discontinuous tiers of self-observation. If V-effects force us to stop empathising and the plot structure leads to the kind of distancing and fictionalisation that are typical of comedy, then Brecht's plays could culminate in a theatre which uses V-effects to enhance its postmodern appeal and uses the structure of comedy as a license to engage in entertaining aestheticization. *The Threepenny Opera* demonstrates this criticism of Brecht in a curious way: the play shows how the genuine misery of beggars becomes a staged misery, but does not try to get us to take seriously the position of those who are exploited – their misery as 'hard reality'. This is a good example of how Brecht's apparatus of *Verfremdung* makes reality seem less real. In *The Threepenny Opera*, a comedic principle triumphs over the assertion (crucial for a Marxist) of a non-simulated reality.

Ultimately it seems as though the comedy hidden in the structure of Brecht's epic plays may have come back to haunt them, by setting up Marxism itself to be laughed at. Brecht simply does not see that his analysis of the apparatus that he undertakes for the stage must also apply to those areas where he assumes an actual reality. Even Sternheim's snob Christian Maske knew that reality is to be found where it is best acted, and Max Frisch's Don Juan managed to outdo reality through the medium of theatre. This is the level at which a construction of reality must begin, in the twentieth century. Brecht acts as though he only has to look at those who are exploited in order to capture reality. At the same time, however, he adapts to the techniques of comedy and aesthetically negates this reality he has availed himself of. The fact that he still takes it as his starting point is ultimately only explicable from a position which, in a series of self-reflections, attempts to impose a unifying theory[16] on the aesthetic. But Brecht's didactic theatre, which has assimilated comedy wholesale, cannot eliminate the possibility that the comedy will assert itself against the author's intentions by causing people to laugh at things which Brecht intended as solutions and not as dilemmas. Because reality can always be packaged up by the simulacra generated by the media, an overly simple answer to an overly simplified reality is part and parcel of that process. If we read Brecht's plays as comedies, it is inevitable that Marxism will also be subject to comedy. If Brecht understands the transformation of Galy Gay into Jeraiah Jip in *Man Equals Man* as a heroic Marxist play,[17] and then a few

---

[16] I outline a process here which could be considered from two angles. Brecht tries to use theory and continual self-commentary to deal with plays that resist conceptualisation. But seen from the other side, theory is not spared by the furore of fictionalisation and ironizing self-observation. The theatrical dialogical scenes of *Buying Brass* demonstrate that theory is in turn intended as theatre and thus loses the clarity it wants to assert over plays. The figure will therefore have to be designed in such a way that theatre can be unified by a theory which in itself is theatrical and thus contains plurality within it.

[17] In 1927, in his preface to *Man Equals Man*, Brecht writes: 'I'm sure you will also say it's a shame for a man to be played with in this way and forced to give up his precious individual identity – the only thing he owns, so to

years later discovers parallels with Fascist brainwashing in the same play,[18] then perhaps we can allow ourselves to laugh at both forms: the problem, Fascism, and the solution, Marxism.

What remains is the comedy. And we might wonder whether his plays could *now* be read as deconstructive allegories – deconstructive allegories out of which the dead hand of comedy, which has hitherto been structurally hidden within them, breaks out and laughs at their serious elements, including Brechtian Marxism. Would *The Decision* be comprehensible as Karl Valentin-esque clowning in which deconstructed characters, through constant role-switching, performed an absurd ritual of violence? Or, to give another example: must not the inner plot of the *Caucasian Chalk Circle* be a source of amusement to the watching collective farmers – given their social condition, surely the circumstances of the play cannot strike them as anything but comical? In this way, is the recipient drawn into a play-within-a-play which he or she cannot help perceiving as comedy? Lastly: do the spectators not find themselves in an increasingly comedic situation, when watching *Mother Courage*, if they subscribe to Brecht's maxim that the important thing is not to make Courage capable of seeing, but that the spectator should learn how to see (GW 4: 1443)? Does this not make the events on stage into a kind of theatre of the absurd in which, from the recipient's point of view, any pedagogical effect is swallowed up in laughter at such an intention, because any outside observer can see through Courage's vanities straight away?

If Brecht's plays are indeed such corrupted and perhaps postmodern comedies, then their potential timeliness also represents a contradiction of all the intentions that were so important to their author.

---

speak – but it isn't. It's funny. Because this Galy Gay doesn't come to any harm – he benefits. And a man who adopts such an attitude will always benefit.' (GW 17: 978).

[18]Nine years later, in 1936, Brecht has completely changed his tune: 'The transformation of the petty-bourgeois Galy Gay into a "human fighting machine" can take place in Germany instead of India. The assembly of the army in Kilkoa can be replaced by the Nazi Party Rally in Nuremberg' (GW 17: 987). What was 'funny' and beneficial in 1927 is held up as an analysis of the Fascist mobilisation in 1936.

# CHAPTER TWENTY-FIVE

# On Humour

BERTOLT BRECHT
TRANSLATED BY ANTHONY TATLOW

Me-ti said: There are people who cannot laugh about serious things. You shouldn't hold it against them, but there's no need to be stopped from laughing at serious things.

You can talk humorously and seriously about serious things and humorously and seriously about humorous things.

Generally speaking, people without a sense of humour find it more difficult to understand the *Great Method*.

Brecht, 'On Humour', in Brecht, *Bertolt Brecht's Me-ti*, ed. and trans. Anthony Tatlow (London: Bloomsbury Methuen Drama, 2016), p. 81.

# Tragedy

# CHAPTER TWENTY-SIX

# Brecht and Tragedy

SEAN CARNEY

## MODERN TRAGEDY

The question then arises concerning the degree to which Brecht, in his politicized formalism, was self-consciously engaged in rewritings of dramatic genre. Here I should clarify my employment of the terms *genre* and *form*, since tragedy is certainly a *genre*, while *form* is a term I have used to describe the apprehension of more abstract, general shapes or structures within a work of art, outlines that necessarily lead us to grasp the material form of the art work, be it novel, poem or play. Yet the separation of genre from artistic form is constantly subject to a slippage: Jameson points out that Northrop Frye identifies 'narrative in general with the particular narrative genre of romance' (Jameson 1981: 105). At the same time, the study of genre is an ultimately futile exercise, much like trying to grasp smoke, since the recognition of genre at work within an aesthetic object is finally only phenomenologically verifiable: everyone knows it when they encounter it, but at the same time a genre seems ultimately defined by the work of art that explodes the genre by transgressing the generic law. This happens because genre does not 'exist' within any single work of art, but is rather the sedimented social life of art works. Genre is a positive construction out of differences. Thus, any single work of art may *be* tragic in its *form*, while the *genre* of tragedy transcends definition through any single work. Jameson comments that

> [t]he strategic value of generic concepts for Marxism clearly lies in the mediatory function of the notion of a genre, which allows the coordination of immanent formal analysis of the individual text with the twin diachronic perspective of the history of forms and the evolution of social life.
>
> (Jameson 1981: 105)

Thus if the study of genre is to have any use today, it will be in the consideration of how genre is always a mediation of social relations: 'Genres are essentially literary *institutions*, or social contracts between a writer and a specific public, whose function is to specify the proper use of a particular cultural artifact,' Jameson observes (106). As a result, genres always carry a certain sedimented ideological content at the level of abstract generic form. When Frye analyses genre as a 'mode', he studies it for its overarching worldview, the 'meaning' it confers on reality, while in a more Proppean, formal or structural analysis, genre will be studied as a model, for how it works. Separately, neither concept of genre seems to satisfy a generic analysis: both are necessary, but they are antithetical to one another.

Like any other recognizable genre, tragedy today is an ideologeme, bearing the accumulated content of the dominant class interests throughout the industrial revolution and carried forth into the moment of late capitalism. Combining a Frygian and structuralist analysis, Jameson suggests that romance is an ideologeme, the functions or structures of which operate by ordering human reality along binary oppositions of hero and villain, good and evil. Thus the 'meaning' of the romance ideologeme is now not a matter of content but of formal relations of opposition, positions without positive content but onto which content can be mapped. The genre of romance is thus 'a form without content which nonetheless ultimately confers signification on the various types of content (geographical, sexual, seasonal, social, perceptual, familial, zoological, physiological, and so on) which it organizes' (Jameson 1981: 113–14). The structural, ideological core of romance is ultimately ethical, and it is precisely the ethical oppositions of good and evil which, Jameson remarks, tragedy disrupts. In tragedy 'the triumph of an inhuman destiny or fate generates a perspective which radically transcends the purely individual categories of good and evil' (116). He confirms this with the observation that, when we encounter in a tragedy any moral and ethical judgements, we evaluate this drama as melodrama rather than tragedy. Yet Jameson also notes that readers today have a tendency to consider tragedy from just such a moral perspective, to evaluate figures from Shakespeare as 'villains' even though to do so ruins the aesthetic form's tragic force. This moralizing urge 'tells us much about the hold of ethical categories on our mental habits' (116). We read tragedy from an ideological perspective within which we are immersed, yet tragic form proper is a disruption of the structure of an ideologeme. We view it as myth, when in fact tragedy is the refusal of the closure of mythic thought.

Despite Brecht's categorical claims that the epic theatre was 'anti-Aristotelian', the elements of tragedy are often observed in Brecht's work, albeit in modified form. The assumption that his dramaturgy is utterly antithetical to the bourgeois theatre is a distortion, albeit one Brecht himself sometimes nurtured through his theoretical writings. Late in life Brecht clarified his position towards the extant theatre. Beginning from the eleventh thesis on Feuerbach, Brecht had suggested changes to the theatre:

> The changes, great or small, that ensued from this intention (which I myself only slowly came to admit) were all changes within the framework of the theatre, so that of course a whole mass of old rules remained wholly unaltered. It was in that little phrase 'of course' that my fault lay. I hardly ever got round to mentioning these still valid rules, and many who read my hints and explanations imagined that I worked to abolish them.
>
> (Brecht 1964: 248)

Thus we are in a position to see Brecht's theatre not so much as a rejection of tragedy, but as a dialectical rewriting of tragedy. Raymond Williams's unique insight into Brecht hinges on the early Brechtian idea of 'complex seeing' (a term that predates and echoes Jameson's 'dialectical stereoscopy'). For Williams, 'complex seeing', a term Brecht coined in relation to the *Threepenny Opera*, was not realized by Brecht before the group of major plays *c.* 1937–45; *The Caucasian Chalk Circle, Mother Courage and her Children, Life of Galileo* and *The Good Person of Szechwan*. Williams's study of Brecht's mature plays hinges upon the consideration of their tragic elements. As Williams points out, what Brecht calls 'Aristotelian' or 'dramatic' theatre in fact refers to 'the dominant naturalism of the European drama after Ibsen' (Williams 1968: 278). In *Modern Tragedy* (1966), Williams endeavours to redeem tragic form for the twentieth century, out of concern that under modernity, the loss of a sense of the tragic necessarily implies the loss of any sense of human agency. Williams's goals are, I think, particularly Brechtian, in that he wants to rewrite the meaning of tragedy under late capitalism to include a sense of dialectical freedom.

Williams asserts that in Attic tragedy, a sense of larger meaning or order, of 'the tragic', was not metaphysically distanced in the sense of the metaphysical that we employ today, because the spiritual and the material were inseparable in Greek beliefs. Moreover, necessity and human action are not separable in Greek tragedy, however they might be opposed within contemporary consciousness:

> It is commonplace, in the modern 'Greek' system, to abstract, for example, Necessity, and to place its laws above human wills. But the character of necessity, insofar as it can be generalised in this culture and these plays, is that its limits on human action are discovered in real actions, rather than known in advance or in general: the precise qualities that now characterise Necessity and are translated as determinism or fatalism.
>
> (Williams 1966: 17–18)

Tragedy proper, then, is not a drama of fate, or capitulation to destiny, although that is how it is received today. Instead it was the discovery of real freedom and human action within the very fabric of necessity itself, not in spite of it. We should be reminded here of Benjamin's Romantic observation that in tragedy, the silent acceptance by the protagonist of a blind and callous fate is in fact a judgement of this inhuman judgement, an assertion of humanity in the face of the inhuman, and a dialectical recreation of the human order out of disorder. Williams argues that under feudalism there came a significant shift, 'from a culture in which the metaphysical and social categories were indistinguishable, to a culture in which they were, by the changed nature of the metaphysical, quite sharply opposed' (23). Over time, the increasing alienation of the public from the private, the subjective from the objective, had consequences for tragic form: 'What had been a whole lived order, connecting man and state and world, became, finally, a purely abstract order. Tragic significance was made to depend on an event's relation to a supposed nature of things, yet without the specific connections which had once provided a particular relation and action of this kind,' Williams writes (50). Within bourgeois society the separation of the human from the social was totalized. Alienation gave rise to an ideology of 'nature', of a given, inert ahistorical reality, separate from humanity. Thus, 'increasingly, the idea of the permanent "nature of things" became separated from any action that could be felt as contemporary' (51). A sense of metaphysical loss of meaning, of the demise of metanarratives and the projection of them into an antique past, has been manufactured by an increasingly alienated modern world. As a result, 'significant suffering, and therefore tragedy, is pushed back in time to periods when fully connecting meanings were available, and contemporary tragedy is seen as impossible because there are now no such meanings' (51). Under this abstract sense of order, projected into the past as an inert backdrop for the present, real, enabling meanings and connections evaporated, as did any human freedom. Williams sees tragedy proper as a dialectic between human action and tragic order, but the possibility of dialectical thinking has been lost under a bourgeois ideology that abstracts order and renders it always antecedent to action. When order becomes nothing but abstract beliefs, tragedy is lost, because '[o]rder, in tragedy, is the *result* of the action [...]. It is not so much that the order is illustrated as that it is recreated' (52).

Williams gives a remarkable account of the effacement of dialectical thinking about human suffering. Like Brecht, Williams is dedicated to the exposure of human beings as changing and changeable. Tragedy today is appropriated by ideologues to demonstrate absolute and transcendent give as about human nature, such as 'Evil' (Williams 1966: 59). For Williams this is a distortion of the meaning of tragedy, since '[t]ragedy, as such, teaches nothing about evil, because it teaches many things about many kinds of action' (60). This ideological co-optation of the significance of tragedy has even affected the left. For Williams, tragedy arises in periods of profound social instability, when modes of production collide and overlap, such as in Elizabethan England, and thus tragedy may bear some relation to revolutionary social change. Yet much 'explicitly social thinking' by leftists rejects' 'tragedy as in itself defeatist. Against what they have known as the idea of tragedy, they have stressed man's powers to change his condition and to end a major part of the suffering which the tragic ideology seems to ratify. The idea of tragedy, that is to say, has been explicitly opposed by the idea of revolution' (63). For Williams, this leftist rejection of tragedy is in itself ideological thinking, a retrenchment of bourgeois ideology. It arose from how liberalism 'inherited this separation between ultimate human values and the social system' (68). Beginning from such a position of alienation, the growth of revolutionary ideas from liberalism was also a further reification of the idea of the tragic.

Williams, however, will insist that the tragic is essential to understanding the social significance of human suffering today. Most of all, he urges an acknowledgement of the intimate relationship between tragedy and revolution, because revolutionary social change, while essential to human liberation, necessarily involves human suffering. However, revolutionary change also tends towards the dehumanization of suffering:

> At the point of this recognition, however, where the received ideology of revolution, its simple quality as liberation, seems most to fail, there is waiting the received ideology of tragedy, in either of its common forms: the old tragic lesson, that man cannot change his condition, but can only drown his world in blood in the vain attempt; or the contemporary reflex, that the taking of rational control over our social destiny is defeated or at best deeply stained by our inevitable irrationality, and by the violence and cruelty that are so quickly released when habitual forms break down.
>
> (Williams 1966:74)

Williams rejects the ideology that claims that the suffering which takes place in revolution is caused by revolution; rather, revolution is 'the inevitable working through of a deep and tragic disorder' (75), just as is tragedy proper. They are both full actions, and must be apprehended dialectically, because revolution's violence, while liberating, is also obviously dehumanizing and alienating in new ways. A tragic perception of revolution would allow us 'to attend to the whole action, and to see actual liberation as part of the same process as the terror which appals us. I do not mean that the liberation cancels the terror; I mean only that they are connected, and that this connection is tragic' (82). Therefore the 'tragic action, in its deepest sense, is not the confirmation of disorder, but its experience, its comprehension and its resolution. In our own time, this action is general, and its common name is revolution' (83).

# BRECHTIAN TRAGEDY

Williams's terminology quite usefully separates for us tragedy from the tragic ideology, an ideology that Brecht clearly set himself against, and one that he clearly felt was reflected in the general contemporary reception of Attic and Elizabethan tragedy. Brecht ostensibly rejected tragedy altogether, yet his own late observations about how he worked from within the bourgeois theatre belie that sweeping distanciation. When Williams comes to position Brecht within the context of his argument in *Modern Tragedy*, he titles the chapter, 'A Rejection of Tragedy' (Williams 1966: 190), because Brecht clearly 'rejected the idea that suffering can ennoble us', and thus rejected 'sacrifice as a dramatic emotion' (197). Naturally, we need look no further than *Mother Courage and her Children* to see that in Brecht's most sustained examination of human suffering, the blows that Courage suffers are neither metaphysically inevitable, nor do they teach or transform her in any way. She learns nothing from her misery and is not elevated by the experience. Yet for Williams, this is not entirely a rejection of tragedy:

> In the end it is not only complex seeing. It is a very complex kind of feeling. Tragedy in some of its older senses is certainly rejected. There is nothing inevitable or ennobling about this kind of failure. It is a matter of human choice, and the choice is not once for all; it is a matter of continuing history. The major achievement of Brecht's mature work is this recovery of history as a dimension for tragedy.
>
> (Williams 1966:202)

At every stage in Courage's actions we see the decisions that, one by one, take her children from her. Yet the meaning of these crucial moments gains its significance not through a consideration of them in and of themselves, but rather through a consideration of what they are *not*. And what they are not emerges only when they are compared to the drama against which Brecht writes. From this perspective, then, the Brechtian maxim of fixing the 'not ... but' is a dialectical relating of the particular drama to drama in general. The idea that what the character 'doesn't do must be contained and conserved in what he does', and that '[i]n this way every sentence and every gesture signifies a decision' (Brecht 1964: 137), now means that what the character does *not* do is what characters in other plays *do* do. Thus *Mother Courage* is, and is not, a tragedy. It is 'not' a tragedy but, by virtue of its dramatic form, what the drama is not is contained and conserved in what it is.

It is most crucial to grasp how the meaning of *Mother Courage and her Children* does not reside in the drama alone, by which I mean that it is not locatable at the level of isolated content. Rather, the signification of *Mother Courage and her Children* is only apparent when one situates the play in the history of tragic form, as Williams does. The same can be said for *Life of Galileo*, the formal significations of which we considered in Chapter 4. It is in fact only through a consideration of the relationship between the form of *Mother Courage* and the form of tragedy in general that *Mother Courage* can be grasped for its dialectical elements. Its political meaning, then, resides not in the content but at the level of dramatic form, and even then, not in the form of the single play but in relation to the history of the form. It is only marginally as a comment upon contemporaneity that *Mother Courage* has political importance. Certainly, it is a comment upon war and dehumanization, and can be related to the breadth of the twentieth century on that count, but *Mother Courage's* ultimate importance is found in how it relates to the tragic ideologeme, for it is in estranging the tragic ideology through a dialectical representation of human events that it intervenes most directly into social life. Williams attempts to put the play's unique estrangement of the tragic ideologeme into words:

> In most modern drama, the best conclusion is: yes, this is how it was. Only an occasional play goes further, with the specific excitement of recognition: yes, this is how it is. Brecht, at his best, reaches out to and touches the necessary next stage: yes, this is how it is, for these reasons, but the action is continually being replayed, and it could be otherwise.
>
> (Williams 1966: 202)

Like Adorno, Williams knows that this dialectical thinking always risks a deceptive suggestion that it *is* otherwise: 'The trap, at this last moment, is the wrong kind of emphasis on the undoubted fact that it could indeed be otherwise. [...] We have to see not only that suffering is avoidable, but that it is not avoided' (202–3). Complex seeing, what Jameson calls the 'dialectical stereoscopy', entails an apprehension of a dramatic form that engages critically its own aesthetic 'social grounding', namely the entire history of dramatic form, in order to intervene in that form, change it and thus affect human thinking. Therefore it is entirely fair to say that Brecht's theatre is primarily about dramatic form, since Brecht's mature work is most fully grasped as a containment and modification of tragic form and content. Within the self-reflexive form of Brecht's theatre, a tragedy is nestled, in fact the entire history of tragic form is contained, and a dialectical theatre is an exercise in meta-theatrical commentary' upon the meaning of tragedy itself. This is not necessarily an insight that applies only to Brecht's late thought. If we look at the famous chart from the early essay, 'The Modern Theatre is the Epic Theatre', in which elements of the 'Dramatic Theatre' are apparently opposed by the elements of Brecht's new 'Epic Theatre', we immediately notice that Brecht footnotes this chart with the comment, 'This table does not show absolute antitheses but mere shifts of accent' (Brecht 1964: 37). The idea of 'man as a fixed point' is not, then, radically opposed by Brecht's idea of 'man as a process'. The space between these two visions of the human is a mere change 'of emphasis' (37), and they cannot be, in practice, distinguished radically from one another.[1] Following such surmises, I suggest that Brecht's theatre was, in general, intended as an experiment in form which would allow a containment and dialectical transformation of tragic form and content.

For Williams to suggest that *Mother Courage and her Children* is a play bearing a hopeful sign that things could be otherwise is problematic, in my estimation. While Brecht did not hesitate in public statements surrounding *Mother Courage* to assert that it was the proletariat that could bring an end to war, there is no sign of this positive prescription in the play. Moreover, Brecht repeatedly refused to present alternative possibilities in the drama Courage learns nothing, and the audience is forced to do its thinking for itself. In his later (1979) afterword to a revised edition of *Modern Tragedy*, Williams specifically criticizes the pessimism of modernistic theatre that refuses to envision future possibilities and thus lapses into surrender and capitulation. Williams valorizes the hopefulness of *Mother Courage* in *Modern Tragedy* yet is later critical of the universalizing of the 'forms of division and contradiction', in which 'what we want to become, rather than what we do not now want to be, remains a so largely unanswered question' (Williams 1979: 104–5). However, this may be less a criticism of the negativity of Adorno's dialectic than a rebuke of the apolitical valorization of stylistically nihilistic estrangement effects within the British academy. In his introduction to Williams's *The Politics of Modernism*, Tony

Pinkney notes that, throughout the late 1960s and the 1970s, Williams was concerned with how British critical discourse adopted Brechtian estrangement as an end in itself. Whereas Williams felt that Brecht's 'complex seeing' is not 'a mere set of presentational techniques of *Verfremdung* but [...] a dramatic "convention" embodied in the work's own deep structure' (Pinkney 1989: 20), the 'burgeoning British cult' of Brecht's work reduced Brechtian drama to '"a new method of staging" and "the enthronement of the critical spectator"' (20). Pinkney suggests that, for Williams, there is a problem when such 'formalist radicalism', which is really 'empty dynamism', is conflated with a real 'socialist radicalism' (22). Williams's intervention is compatible with our understanding of Brecht here: the *Verfremdungseffekt* is indeed depoliticized if it is reduced to nothing more than a 'distanced' style of acting or to special effects of the *mise en scēne*. Instead the *Verfremdungseffekt* is to be located deep within the form and content of the play itself. In Adorno's definition of the work of art as a 'critical mimesis' of our reified Western society we have an analogous definition of artistic estrangement, imitating the alienation of society in the deep structures of dramatic form and simultaneously rendering this alienation strange and visible.

Where, then, do we find this 'it could be otherwise but is not otherwise', the basic tragic intimation of loss and missed possibility, in Brecht's mature plays? My suggestion is that it is found in the unresolvable contradictions that tear the protagonists of these plays in two. Shen Te, Courage and Galileo, as protagonists, negotiate their way through a series of tragic deadlocks, which they can live through, but cannot resolve. Shen Te is a protagonist in a tragedy, the audience of which are the Gods, a trio of middle-class theatre-goers who feed off her suffering and her failure to resolve the contradictions of her situation. In this *The Good Person of Szechwan* resembles to a degree the meta-theatricality of *Waiting for Godot*, wherein Didi and Gogo serve as the reluctant audience to the liberal tragedy of Pozzo. Yet just as Beckett parodies the idea that suffering ennobles or elevates Pozzo in some way, so too does Brecht render strange for us the tragic ideologeme. At each point in her drama Shen Te is caught in contradictions between equally demanding forces, pushed by her circumstances to make impossible choices between equally legitimate goods. Like Antigone caught between the demands of kinship and the state, Shen Te is riven by contradictions she cannot reconcile, the poles of which are found in the various goods she tries to serve. Given money by the gods, she opens a shop so that she can be more broadly philanthropic. This long-term goodness is immediately contradicted by the need to be generous and giving in the immediate present. When she succumbs to the invention of Shui Ta, it is only in an attempt to be good both in the present and in the future. Shen Te's self-division is not the self-division of liberal conscience, exemplified by J. Pierpont Mauler in *Saint Joan of the Stockyards*, where inner suffering is in fact a form of pleasure. Shen Te's suffering is real, grounded in the concrete, but for the gods it does remain a form of theatre, to be enjoyed and used as confirmation of the inevitability of the existing order. Unlike the gods, we cannot judge Shen Te, for we can see that she is caught in a series of tragic deadlocks, impossible contradictions without correct solutions. When Shen Te falls in love, this irresistible force comes in conflict with those in the community who need her goodness for their survival. When she finds she is pregnant, this new priority cancels out her love for Yang and her desire to do good for the community. What keeps the action of *Good Person* from freezing in place each time Shen Te is caught in a new contradiction is the immediate presence of one pole of the contradiction: when Yang Sun is present, Shen Te succumbs to his demand, but when confronted a moment later by the aged couple who have lent her money, Shen Te is drawn to the need to be good. In each case her decision is a compromise that resolves nothing. While the play is somewhat light-hearted in its sense of humour, her conflict is not. In its resonance, her tragedy is no different than Antigone's struggle between civic duty and love of her dead brother. Why do the gods tolerate this? Wang asks. Why don't they intervene and change things? The answer: 'Suffering ennobles!' (Brecht 1970–2003, vol. 6i: 70). They find tragic resonance in her struggle. Therefore her struggle is justified as something good in and of itself. It is *good* to suffer. They are happy with her the way she is, even if she is in torment, Shen Te will not accept that she needs Shui Ta, but the gods accept it, in moderation. They can contain her contradictions within their ideology, comforted by the knowledge of her ongoing struggle. In Shen Te's final moments, she asserts the impossibility of her situation, crying for help, while the gods cheerfully depart, refreshed by her failure. The contradiction between Shen Te's real suffering and the pleasure drawn from it by the gods is the space between dialectical tragedy proper and the tragic ideology. From this perspective, the Epilogue, added later by Brecht, is a problematic weakness of the play, crippling the tragedy, and when it is performed, it risks masking Shen Te's suffering with a trite mask of altruistic voluntarism. In performance, the Epilogue is most effective when the player who speaks it pushes against the cheerful, absolving veneer of the speech, its rhetorical questioning, and instead emphasizes the heartfelt demand for help that is the actual action of these words. The player who speaks this speech must become Shen Te, giving voice to her suffering, to her demand that she be relieved of the unbearable burden of needs that have ripped her in two, but now instead of directing the demand for relief to the Gods, she is directing it as us, the audience, forcing us to acknowledge our enjoyment of her suffering, while also insisting that this suffering must end.

While *Mother Courage and her Children* does not suggest that war is inevitable, its central thesis is that, within the situation of war, the deaths of Courage's children *are* inevitable. It is a dialectical, not a metaphysical, tragedy, because the doom Courage disingenuously pronounces for her children in the play's opening scene is in fact the inevitable logical outcome of her own decision to bring them to the war. Courage profits from the war in order to nurture her children, but in order to protect her children from the war she must seek war profits. Each time Courage leaves a child alone in order to make money, she loses that child to the war, yet still she goes to the war in order to nurture the child she loses. Here is the play's tragic contradiction: Courage destroys her children through the activity of saving them. Even Kattrin's heroic act of self-sacrifice at the end of the play is deeply tragic in its contradictions. When Courage admonishes the peasants for having told Kattrin that there were children in the village, Courage knows that Kattrin has acted selflessly, against Courage's wishes. Yet Kattrin's sacrifice is, I believe, something she has learned from her own mother's example. While Courage espouses a philosophy of pragmatic self-interest, of dedication to the cart, and of sheer survival, in her actions, rather than her words, she teaches her daughter a praxis dedicated towards the survival of children. As a result, by trying to protect Kattrin and bring her through the war, Courage destroys her own daughter, since in protecting her she has taught her to do likewise and to care for and protect the children Kattrin wishes were her own. This tragic ambivalence, in its sheer dialectical power, resonates equally with Oedipus's attempt to escape his own destiny, an action that executes said destiny. It is this contradiction, unresolvable within the world represented in Brecht's play, which in the force of its tense vacuum of negativity, demands some resolution, while the play itself remains forcefully, necessarily, silent on the matter. It is a pure instance of the tragic, of 'the unity of salvation and annihilation' (Szondi 1961: 59).

Brecht's objections to the consideration of *Life of Galileo* as a tragedy are to be located once more in what the tragic ideology does to a tragic action proper. To have seen Galileo as ennobled by the failures of his life is to miss the point of what Galileo himself learns over the course of the play, and so Brecht amended the drama in order to eliminate aspects of Galileo's final scene which might allow one to see him as a man elevated by his suffering. Yet Galileo is also caught in a contradiction to which there is no solution, because it is a massive historical contradiction between the feudal aristocratic order and the emergent bourgeois order. By choosing the former over the latter, Galileo makes a decision, but does not resolve his problem. He cannot resolve this contradiction because it is not his, but all of Western civilization's. In the Court at Florence, he is given the freedom to pursue his research, but cannot publish it, while in the Venetian Republic, the progressive demands of commerce and the university at Padua hamper his freedom to research what he likes, while protecting him from censorship. Yet it is not so simple as to now say that Galileo had no choice, and was subject to the contradictions of history. We have only to attend to what Galileo himself announces at the end of the play: 'there is no scientific work that can only be written by one particular man' (Brecht 1970–2003, vol. 5i; 107). This is not a play about one man, but a play about Western civilization. Galileo here explains his fundamental misinterpretation of his own position in the drama: he took himself for the protagonist of the play, a tragic hero whose individual actions would have final consequences for society. It is with this misunderstanding in his mind that Galileo renounced his theories under threat of torture. His *hubris*, then, was in believing he could be guilty of *hubris*. When he retorts to Andrea Sarti, 'No. Unhappy the land where heroes are needed' (98), he is both right and wrong. He is right in thinking that this need for heroes renders a society 'unhappy'. He is wrong in thinking this is necessarily such a land. Galileo thinks a hero is needed. He refuses to be it, but in his very refusal he participates in the discourse of tragic heroism. Too late, he learns that he was much more powerful than he had imagined, because his importance was not as an individual 'hero' but as an element in the progressive historical force of the merchant class, the Venetian Republic of the Northern cities, who offer him their protection and which he foolishly scorns. Galileo's real power actually lies in his insignificance. As he tells Andrea in Scene 14, he was never in any real danger, but this is because he did not really matter, in the grand scheme of things. To have refused to recant would in fact merely have been to recant his own importance, to assert that he was a part of the progressive historical force of the Northern cities. Like his followers, Galileo took himself to be a significant individual, a tragic protagonist whose sacrifice would be a social force unto itself. In fact his insignificance was his true power. The hero of the play is, as Walter Benjamin first pointed out, the people, and it is just this that Galileo realizes belatedly. This is not to say, however, that the play is not a tragedy. It shows us a significant moment of counter-enlightenment, of the failure of progress that nevertheless contributes to enlightenment and progress. It is, I would suggest, a tragedy of history, and in this it realizes perfectly Raymond Williams's belief that the full, revolutionary movement of history is reflected through the prism of tragedy. *Life of Galileo* is a dramatic illustration of this thesis, that tragic failure and contradiction are the very engine out of which history emerges. This is Brecht's most substantial intervention into modernity. Through the estrangement of the tragic ideologeme he has taken alienation itself as his main subject matter and made it the site for a dialectical transformation. In his work, tragic loss becomes the raw material for production, not to be enjoyed for what it is, but transformed into something new.

Brecht's own inability to control these plays fully, the symptoms of which are found in his changes and paratextual materials, is the indication of their real dialectical strength. In each of them, he has thieved back from the social a key ideologeme, embodied in tragic form, the content of which is the sameness and repetition of ideology itself. The tragic ideology *is* reification. In appropriating reification, his art was forced to struggle with this ideological closure, and as a result, these plays engage in a dialectical stereoscopy: they are both ideological and dialectical, and these two aspects coexist uncomfortably, struggling against each other and cancelling each other's presence. With this in mind we may read them as we like: as dramas fulfilling the tragic ideology, or as tragedies which present a dialectical attitude towards human suffering through the staging of contradictions. The responsibility is ours. If we take up the challenge of complex seeing, then what yields to our perception is Brecht's rediscovery of the ongoing newness of an old dramatic form. What is always potentially new about tragedy is: that within its dramatic action of failure may be located the logic of contradiction, and in that struggle of contradictions lurks the intimation of the as-yet-unseen new.

# REFERENCES

Brecht, Bertolt (1964) *Brecht on Theatre: The Development of an Aesthetic*, John Willett (trans. and ed.), London: Methuen.

— (1970–2003) *Collected Plays*, John Willett and Ralph Manheim (eds), 8 vols, London: Methuen.

— (1981) *The Political Unconscious: Narrative as a Socially Symbolic Act*, Ithaca: Cornell University Press.

— (1961) *An Essay on the Tragic*, Paul Fleming (trans.), Stanford: Stanford University Press, 2002.

Williams, Raymond (1966) *Modern Tragedy*, London: Chatto and Windus.

— (1968) *Drama from Ibsen to Brecht*, London: Chatto and Windus.

— (1979) 'Afterword to *Modern Tragedy*', *The Politics of Modernism: Against the New Conformists*, Tony Pinkney (ed.), London: Verso, 1989, pp. 95–105.

# Gendered Performance/
Feminism

# CHAPTER TWENTY-SEVEN

# Brechtian Theory/Feminist Theory: Toward a Gestic Feminist Criticism

ELIN DIAMOND

This essay begins and ends with a short text on pointing.

> In the 1930s, Gertrude Stein and Alice Toklas, on their American lecture tour, were driving in the country in Western Massachusetts. Toklas pointed out a batch of clouds. Stein replied, 'Fresh eggs'. Toklas insisted that Stein look at the clouds. Stein replied again, 'Fresh eggs'. Then Toklas asked, 'Are you making symbolical language?' 'No', Stein answered, 'I'm reading the signs. I love to read the signs'.
>
> (Stimpson 1986:7)

One might devote an essay merely to unpacking this statement for its historical, discursive, and sexual resonances. Let me just say that Toklas's irritation seems justified. She is pointing to clouds; they have an ontological, referential status *as* clouds, but Stein playfully crosses ontology with textuality, object with symbol, referent with sign. Acting the self-conscious spectator, Stein produces a reading and says that *that* is more pleasurable than any Massachusetts clouds. I am concerned with how we point to and read signs in the theatre, and by 'we' I mean feminist critics and theorists and also students of Brecht's theatre theory – an unlikely group, but then this is part of my argument. I would suggest that feminist theory and Brechtian theory need to be read intertextually, for among the effects of such a reading are a recovery of the radical potential of the Brechtian critique and a discovery, for feminist theory, of the specificity of theatre.[1]

At the outset I should say that like Gertrude Stein's clouds, feminist theory and Brechtian theory are moving, changing discourses, open to multiple readings. The umbrella term 'feminist theory' covers feminist film theory, feminist literary theory, psychoanalytic feminist theory, socialist feminist theory, black feminist theory, lesbian feminist theory, cross-cultural feminist theory – many of which combine under different rubrics with

---

Elin Diamond, 'Brechtian Theory/Feminist Theory: Toward a Gestic Feminist Criticism', *TDR* 32: 1 (1988), pp. 82–94.

[1] An earlier version of this paper was presented at the American Theater in Higher Education (ATHE) Conference in Chicago, August 1987.

different topoi, different political inflections. Yet perhaps all theories that call themselves 'feminist' share a goal: the passionate analysis of gender in material social relations and in discursive and representational structures, especially theatre and film, which involve scopic pleasures and the body. Brecht's theatre theory, written over a 30-year period, constantly reformulates its concepts but it, too, has certain concerns: attention to the dialectical and contradictory forces within social relations, principally the agon of class conflict in its changing historical forms; commitment to alienation techniques and nonmimetic disunity in theatrical signification; 'literarization' of the theatre space to produce a spectator/reader who is not interpolated into ideology but is passionately and pleasurably engaged in observation and analysis.

Now feminists in film studies have been quick to appropriate elements of Brecht's critique of the theatre apparatus.[2] In Summer 1974, the British film journal *Screen* published a Brecht issue whose stated purpose was a consideration of Brecht's theoretical texts and the possibility of a revolutionary cinema. In Autumn 1975, Laura Mulvey published her influential essay 'Visual Pleasure and Narrative Cinema' in which, employing psychoanalysis 'as a political weapon', she argues that Hollywood film conventions construct a specifically male viewing position by aligning or suturing the male's gaze to that of the fictional hero, and by inviting him thereby both to identify narcissistically with that hero and to fetishize the female (turning her into an object of sexual stimulation) (1975:6). In rejecting this dominant cinematic tradition, Mulvey powerfully invokes Brechtian concepts:

> The first blow against the monolithic accumulation of traditional film conventions [...] is to free the look of the camera into its materiality in time and space and the look of the audience into dialectics, passionate detachment.
>
> (1975:18)

Demystifying representation, showing how and when the object of pleasure is made, releasing the spectator from imaginary and illusory identifications – these are crucial elements in Brecht's theoretical project. Yet we feminists in drama and theatre studies have attended more to the critique of the gaze than to the Brechtian intervention that signals a way of dismantling the gaze. Feminist film theorists, fellow-traveling with psychoanalysis and semiotics, have given us a lot to think about, but we, through Brechtian theory, have something to give them: a female body in representation that resists fetishization and a viable position for the female spectator.

In this essay, then, I have two purposes. One, an intertextual reading of key topoi of feminist theory: gender critique and sexual difference; questions of authority in women's writing and women's history; spectatorship and the body – with key topoi in Brechtian theory: *Verfremdungseffekt*, the 'not, but', historicization, and *Gestus*. Two, emerging from this intertexting, a proposal for a theatre-specific feminist criticism. I call it 'gestic criticism' and close the essay with a brief example (my second text on pointing).

Some quick qualifications and clarifications: I realize that feminists in drama studies might greet this coupling with some bemusement. Brecht exhibits a typical Marxian blindness toward gender relations, and except for some interesting excursions into male

---

[2] I am grateful to Barton Byg, whose excellent paper, 'Brecht on the Margins: Film and Feminist Theory' provided many useful insights.

erotic violence, he created conventionally gendered plays and too many saintly mothers (one is too many). Moreover, the postmodern critique of Brecht by Heiner Müllerites should not be ignored, particularly the rejection of the Brechtian 'fable' which Müller describes as a 'closed form' that the audience accepts as a 'package, a commodity' (Weber 1980:121). This essay brackets both Brecht's plays and their retrograde (and unBrechtian) stagings in the German Democratic Republic and the West over the last three decades. My interest lies in the potentiality of Brecht's theory for feminism, and, as I mentioned above, a possible re-radicalization of his theory through feminism. In current literary theory, especially from the English Left, Brecht's concepts have become weapons in campaigns against mimetic linearity (see Dollimore 1984), bourgeois naturalism (see Barker 1984), and, in a fine reading by Terry Eagleton (1986), on the side of deconstructive rhetoric. Even Toril Moi (Oxford-based Norwegian), in her notorious *Sexual/Textual Politics*, parses the feminisms by enlisting Brecht's debate with Lukacs on the question of socialist realism to challenge Anglo-American critics of Virginia Woolf (1985:17). Strange bedfellows perhaps, but the point I wish to make is that these critics have understood that Brechtian theory in all its gaps and inconsistencies is not literary criticism, but rather a theorizing of the workings of an apparatus of representation with enormous formal and political resonance. I think we should be long past the point of accepting Martin Esslin's view that Brecht's theories 'were merely rationalizations of intuition, taste, and imagination' (1971: 146), or Eric Bentley's view that the theory is a didactic distraction from Brecht's true art (1981:46ff). Herbert Blau has the best if not the last word on theory-versus-practice debates: 'Theater is theory, or a shadow of it. [...] In the act of seeing, there is already theory' (1982:1).

## GENDER, VERFREMDUNGSEFFEKT

The cornerstone of Brecht's theory is the Verfremdungseffekt, the technique of defamiliarizing a word, an idea, a gesture so as to enable the specator to see or hear it afresh: 'a representation that alienates is one which allows us to recognize its subject, but at the same time makes it seem unfamiliar' (Brecht 1964:192); 'the A-effect consists of turning an object from something ordinary and immediately accessible into something peculiar, striking, and unexpected' (1964:143). In performance the actor 'alienates' rather than impersonates her character; she 'quotes' or demonstrates the character's behavior instead of identifying with it. Brecht theorizes that if the performer remains outside the character's feelings, the audience may also, thereby remaining free to analyze and form opinions about the play's 'fable'. Verfremdungseffekt also challenges the mimetic property of acting that semioticians call iconicity, the fact that the performer's body conventionally resembles the object (or character) to which it refers. This is why gender critique in the theatre can be so powerful.

Gender refers to the words, gestures, appearances, ideas, and behavior that dominant culture understands as indices of feminine or masculine identity. When spectators 'see' gender they are seeing (and reproducing) the cultural signs of gender, and by implication, the gender ideology of a culture. Gender in fact provides a perfect illustration of ideology at work since 'feminine' or 'masculine' behavior usually appears to be a 'natural' – and thus fixed and unalterable – extension of biological sex. Feminist practice that seeks to expose or mock the strictures of gender usually uses some version of the Brechtian A-effect. That is, by alienating (not simply rejecting) iconicity, by foregrounding the expectation of resemblance, the ideology of gender is exposed and thrown back to the spectator.[3] In Caryl Churchill's play *Cloud 9*, cross-dressing, in which the male body can be seen in feminine clothes, provides A-effects for a gender critique of the familial and sexual roles in Victorian colonial society. In lesbian performances at New York's WOW Cafe – I'm thinking of Holly Hughes's *Lady Dick* and Split Britches' *Upwardly Mobile Home* – and in the broadly satirical monologs of Italy's Franca Rame, gender is exposed as a sexual costume, a sign of a role, not evidence of identity. Recalling such performances should remind us of the rigorous self-consciousness that goes into even the most playful gender-bending. A-effects are not easy to produce, but the payoffs can be stunning. When gender is 'alienated' or foregrounded, the spectator is enabled to see a sign system *as* a sign system – the appearance, words, gestures, ideas, attitudes, etc., that comprise the gender lexicon become so many illusionistic trappings to be put on or shed at will. Understanding gender as ideology – as a system of beliefs and behavior mapped across the bodies of females and males, which reinforces a social status quo – is to appreciate the continued timeliness of Verfremdungseffekt, the purpose of which is to denaturalize and defamiliarize what ideology makes seem normal, acceptable, inescapable.

## SEXUAL DIFFERENCE, THE 'NOT, BUT'

Gender critique in artistic and discursive practices is often and wrongly confused with another topos in feminist theory: sexual difference. I would propose that 'sexual difference' be understood not as a synonym for gender oppositions but as a possible reference to differences within sexuality. I take my cue here partly from the poststructuralist privileging of 'difference' across all representational systems, particularly language. Derridean deconstruction posits the disturbance of the signifier within the linguistic sign or word; the seemingly stable word is inhabited by a signifier that bears the trace of another signifier and another, so that contained within the meaning of any given word is the trace of the word it is not. Thus the word is always different from itself, or, as Barbara Johnson patiently teases out its connotations, 'difference' refers not to what distinguishes one identity from another – 'it is not a difference between [...] independent units [...] but a difference within' (1980:4). Texts, she argues, are not different from other texts but different from themselves. Deconstruction thus wreaks havoc on identity, with its connotations of wholeness and coherence: if an identity is always different from itself it can no longer *be* an identity. Sexual *difference*, then, might be seen to destabilize the bipolar oppositions that constitute gender identity.

Psychoanalysis offers other cues. Despite the normative tone of his gender distinctions, Freud also makes clear that the drives and desires that constitute sexuality do not add up to a stable identity:

> [W]e are accustomed to say that every human being displays both male and female instinctual impulses, needs and attributes; but though anatomy it is true, can point out the characteristic of maleness and femaleness, psychology cannot. For psychology the

---

[3] Without discussing gender per se, Brecht refers briefly to this phenomenon in the 'Short Organum', no. 59: '[...] it is also good for the actors when they see their characters copied or portrayed in another form. If the part is played by somebody of the opposite sex the sex of the character will be more clearly brought out [...]' (Brecht 1964:197).

contrast between the sexes fades away into one between activity and passivity, in which we far too readily identify activity with maleness and passivity with femaleness, a view which is by no means universally confirmed (in Watney 1986:16).

In fact the Freudian account of the diverse identifications and effects of childhood sexuality undermine the idea of a stable-gendered subject. To paraphrase Gayle Rubin, women and men are certainly different, but gender coercively translates the nuanced differences within sexuality into a structure of opposition: male vs. female, masculine vs. feminine, etc. (see 1978:179). In my reading of Rubin, the 'sex-gender system', the trace of the difference of sexuality is kept alive within the sterile opposition of gender. I am suggesting that sexual difference is where we imagine, where we theorize; gender is where we live, our social address, although most of us, with an effort, are trying to leave home. Let me put it another way: no feminist can ignore the social and political battlefield of gender, but no feminist can ignore the fact that the language of the battlefield is a system based on difference whose traces contain our most powerful desires.

Keeping differences in view instead of conforming to stable representations of identity, and *linking those differences to a practical politics* are key to Brecht's theory of the 'not, but', a feature of alienated acting that I read intertextually with the sex-gender system. 'When [an actor] appears on stage, besides what he actually is doing he will at all essential points discover, specify, imply what he is not doing; that is he will act in such a way that the alternative emerges as clearly as possible, that his acting allows the other possibilities to be inferred and only represents one of the possible variants. [...] Whatever he doesn't do must be contained and conserved in what he does' (Brecht 1964:137). Each action must contain the trace of the action it represses, thus the meaning of each action contains difference. The audience is invited to look beyond representation – beyond what is authoritatively put in view – to the possibilities of as yet unarticulated actions or judgments. Brecht's early plays, particularly *In the Jungle of Cities*, thematize the 'not, but': 'I'm never anything more than half', says Mary Garga, who doesn't have the pleasure of joining the men in what Brecht called 'the idealist dialectic' of the play or 'the pure joy of fighting'. Contemporary feminist plays by Michelene Wandor, Caryl Churchill, and Adrienne Kennedy also thematize the 'not, but' in their sex-gender referents, but it would be interesting to query sex-gender nuances in *Measure for Measure*, *The Master Builder*, and *No Man's Land* to name only three.

The Brechtian 'not, but' is the theatrical and theoretical analog to the subversiveness of sexual difference, because it allows us to imagine the deconstruction of gender – and all other – representations. Such deconstructions dramatize, at least at the level of theory, the infinite play of difference that Derrida calls *écriture* – the superfluity of signification that places meaning beyond capture within the covers of the play or the hours of performance. This is not to deny Brecht's wish for an instructive, analytical theatre; on the contrary, it invites the participatory play of the spectator, and the possibility for which Brecht most devoutly wished, that significance (the production of meaning) continue beyond play's end, congealing into choice and action after the spectator leaves the theatre.

## HISTORY, HISTORICIZATION

The sex-gender system requires contextualization. The understanding of women's material conditions in history and the problematics of uncovering 'women's history' are topoi in feminist theory that Brecht's theory of historicization greatly informs. Of course there must be limits to this discussion: Brecht was not writing history, but as a student devoted to the Marxist 'classics' Brecht understood social relations, particularly class relations, as part of a moving dialectic. The crux of 'historicization' is change: through A-effects spectators observe the potential movement in class relations, discover the limitations and strengths of their own perceptions, and begin to change their lives. There is a double movement in Brechtian historicization of preserving the 'distinguishing marks' of the past and acknowledging, even foregrounding, the audience's present perspective (Brecht 1964:190). When Brecht says that spectators should become historians, he refers both to the spectator's detachment, her 'critical' position, *and* to the fact that she is writing her own history even as she absorbs messages from the stage. Historicization is, then, *a way of seeing* and the enemy of recuperation and appropriation. One cannot historicize and colonize the Other or, as Luce Irigaray would have it, 'reduce all others to the economy of the same' (1985:76). Brecht considered bourgeois illusionism insidious because it is guilty of precisely that:

> When our theatres perform plays of other periods they like to annihilate distance, fill in the gap, gloss over the differences. But what comes in our delight in comparisons, in distance, in dissimilarity – which is at the same time a delight in what is close and proper to ourselves?.
>
> (Brecht 1964:276)

In historicized performance, gaps are not to be filled in, seams and contradictions show in all their roughness, and therein lies one aspect of spectatorial pleasure – when our differences *from* the past and *within* the present are palpable, graspable, applicable. Plays aspiring to realistically depict the present require the same historicization. Realism disgusted Brecht not only because it dissimulates its conventions but because it is hegemonic: by copying the surface details of the world it offers the illusion of lived experience, even as it marks off only one version of that experience.[4] This is perhaps why the most innovative women playwrights refuse the seamless narrative of conflicting egos in classic realism. Consider Adrienne Kennedy's *Funnyhouse of a Negro* or *The Owl Answers* which lurch and reach through memory/fantasy staking the real in obsessional repetition and in fragmented characters who embrace and speak from their difference. Kennedy rejects the Brechtian fable – narrative progress is meaningless in her worlds – and instead dramatizes gaps and contradictions as, precisely, the black woman's experience of history. Brechtian historicization challenges the presumed ideological neutrality of any historical reflection. Rather it assumes, and promotes, what historians are now claiming: that reader/spectators of 'facts' and 'events' will, like Gertrude Stein reading the clouds, translate what is inchoate into signs (and stories), a move that produces not 'truth', but mastery and pleasure.

---

[4]Brecht elaborates in various ways on this point: 'The individual whose innermost being is thus driven into the open then of course comes to stand for Man with a capital M. Everyone (including the spectator) is then carried away by the momentum of the events portrayed, so that in a performance of *Oedipus* one has for all practical purposes an auditorium full of little Oedipuses, an auditorium full of Emperor Joneses for a performance of *The Emperor Jones*' (in 'On the Use of Music in an Epic Theatre', Brecht 1964:87). Also: 'The bourgeois theatre emphasized the timelessness of its objects. Its representation of people is bound by the alleged "eternally human". Its story is arranged in such a way as to create "universal" situations that allow Man with a capital M to express himself: man of every period and every colour' (in 'Alienation Effects in Chinese Acting', Brecht 1964:97).

## SPECTATOR, BODY, HISTORICIZATION

Historicization in fact puts on the table the issue of spectatorship and the performer's body. According to Brecht, one way that the actor alienates or distances the audience from the character is to suggest the historicity of the character in contrast to the actor's own present-time self-awareness on stage. The actor must not lose herself in the character but rather *demonstrate* the character as a function of particular sociohistorical relations, a conduit of particular choices. As Timothy Wiles puts it, actor and audience, both in present time, 'look back on' the historical character as she fumbles through choices and judgments (1980:72). This does not, however, endow the actor with superiority, for as Wiles later points out this present-time actor is also fragmented: 'Brecht separates the historical man who acts from the aesthetic function of the actor' (1980:85). The historical subject *plays* an actor presumed to have superior knowledge in relation to an ignorant character from the past, but the subject herself remains as divided and uncertain as the spectators to whom the play is addressed. This performer-subject neither disappears into a representation of the character *nor* into a representation of the actor; each remains processual, historical, incomplete. And the spectator? Aware of three temporalities within a single stage figure the spectator cannot read one without the other; her/his gaze is constantly split; her/his *'vouloir-voir'* (Pavis 1982:88) – the wanting to see and know all without any obstacle – is deflected into the dialectic of which the divided performer is only a part. Moreover, in reading a complex ever-changing text, spectators are 'pulled out of [their] fixity' (Heath 1974:112); they become part of – indeed they produce – the dialectical comparisons and contributions that the text enacts.

The special characteristics of Brechtian reception emerge in relation to analogous processes in film theory. In psychoanalytic film theory, the film-text and the viewing-state are set in motion by unconscious fantasy.[5] In the darkened room, in immobile seats, the spectator enters what Jean-Louis Baudry calls a 'state of artificial regression' (1980:56), the womblike effects of film viewing which confuse boundaries and send the subject back to earlier stages of psychic development, particularly the Lacanian mirror phase in which the infant, lacking controlled motor development, sees its image in a mirror or in its caretaker's eyes as a coherent whole. Misrecognizing himself (the male infant is specifically at issue here) as a complete, autonomous other, he spends the rest of his life unconsciously seeking an imaginary ideal – and discovers him, so the theory goes, at the movies.

Now the differences between the Brechtian spectator and the cinematic spectator are obvious. The last thing Brecht wants is a spectator in a 'state of artificial regression', in thrall to his imaginary ideal. Brechtian theory formulates (and reformulates) a spectatorial state that breaks the suturing of imaginary identifications and keeps the spectator independent. Much influenced by Brecht, Patrice Pavis's semiotics of the mise-en-scene rests almost entirely on the spectator: '[...] the mise-en-scene is not entirely an indication of the intentionality of the director, but a structuring by the spectator of materials presented [...] whose linking is dependent on the perceiving subject' (Pavis 1982:138). In film theory the subject position is constructed ready-made for the spectator, only his capacity to regress is assumed. In Brechtian theory the subject's capacity to regress is

---

[5] I was very much helped by the extensive summary/analysis of psychoanalytic film theory in Sandy Flitterman-Lewis's 'Psychoanalysis in Film and Television' (1987) which I read in manuscript form.

suppressed. Film semiotics posits a spectator who is given the illusion that he creates the film; theatre semiotics posits a spectator whose active reception constantly revises the spectacle's meanings.

But Pavis is too much of a postmodernist to theorize a spectator with total authority. He deconstructs the spectatorial position by locating its difference within: 'What we need', he says, 'is a theory of "reception desire"' – a theory that, without positing a spectator 'in a state of artificial regression', accounts for the spectator's unconscious desire and thereby opens the door to pleasurable identification with stage figures (Pavis 1982:158).

What does Brecht contribute to 'reception desire'? Although he talks a lot about pleasure, it is the pleasure of cognition, of capturing meaning; Brecht does not apparently release the body, either on stage or in the audience. The actor's body is subsumed in the dialectical narrative of social relations; the spectator's body is given over to rational inquiry (unless there's pleasure to be had with the Brechtian cigar). And Brecht exhibits the blindness typical of all Marxist theorists regarding sex-gender configurations. Feminist theory, however, insists on the presence of the gendered body, on the sex-gender system, and on the problematics of desire.

It is at this point – at the point of conceptualizing an unfetishized female performer and a female spectator – that an intertextual reading of Brechtian and feminist theories works productively. If feminist theory sees the body as culturally mapped and gendered, Brechtian historicization insists that this body is not a fixed essence but a site of struggle and change. If feminist theory is concerned with the multiple and complex signs of a woman's life: her color, her age, her desires, her politics – what I want to call her *historicity*[6] – Brechtian theory gives us a way to put that historicity on view – in the theatre. In its conventional iconicity, theatre laminates body to character, but the body in historicization stands visibly and palpably separate from the 'role' of the actor as well as the role of the character; it is always insufficient and open. I want to be clear about this important point: The body, particularly the female body, by virtue of entering the stage space, enters representation – it is not just *there*, a live, unmediated presence, but rather (1) a signifying element in a dramatic fiction; (2) a part of a theatrical sign system whose conventions of gesturing, voicing, and impersonating are referents for both performer and audience; and (3) a sign in a system governed by a particular apparatus, usually owned and operated by men for the pleasure of a viewing public whose major wage earners are male.

Yet with all these qualifications, Brechtian theory imagines a polyvalence to the body's representation, for the performer's body is also *historicized*, loaded with its own history and that of the character, and these histories ruffle the smooth edges of the image, of representation. In my hybrid construction – based in feminist and Brechtian theory – the female performer, unlike her filmic counterpart, connotes not 'to-be-looked-at-ness' (Mulvey 1975:11) – the perfect fetish – but rather 'looking-at-being-looked-at-ness' or even just 'looking-ness'. This Brechtian-feminist body is paradoxically available for *both* analysis and identification, paradoxically within representation while refusing its fixity.

---

[6] I use 'historicity' not 'history' as the latter term suggests a narrative form which feminists have sought to problematize. In film studies see de Lauretis 1984; in fiction see Brewer 1984; in drama and theatre see Diamond 1985.

## SPECTATOR, AUTHOR, GESTUS

The explosive (and elusive) synthesis of alienation, historicization, and the 'not, but' is the Brechtian *Gestus*: a gesture, a word, an action, a tableau by which, separately or in series, the social attitudes encoded in the playtext become visible to the spectator. A gest becomes *social* when it 'allows conclusions to be drawn about social circumstances' (Brecht 1964:105). A famous social gest is Helene Weigel's snapping shut her leather money bag after each selling transaction in *Mother Courage*, thereby underscoring the contradictions between profiteering and survival – for Brecht the social reality of war. This gest has become something of a reification, but Brecht always emphasized complexity:

> [The] expressions of a gest are usually highly complicated and contradictory, so that they cannot be rendered by any single word and the actor must take care that in giving his image the necessary emphasis he does not lose anything, but emphasizes the entire complex.
>
> (1964:198)

The gestic moment in a sense explains the play, but it also exceeds the play, opening it to the social and discursive ideologies that inform its production. Brecht writes that the scene of the social gest 'should be played as a piece of history' (1964:86) and Pavis elaborates: Gestus makes visible (alienates) 'the class behind the individual, the critique behind the naive object, the commentary behind the affirmation. [...] [It] gives us the key to the relationship between the play being performed and the public. [...]' (1982:42). If we read feminist concerns back into this discussion, the social gest signifies a moment of theoretical insight into sex-gender complexities, not only in the play's 'fable', but in the culture which the play, at the moment of reception, is dialogically reflecting and shaping.

But this moment of visibility or insight is the very moment that complicates the viewing process. Because the Gestus is effected by a historical actor/subject, what the spectator sees is not a mere miming of social relationship, but a *reading* of it, an interpretation by a historical subject who supplements (rather than disappears into) the production of meaning. As noted earlier, the historical subject playing an actor, playing a character, splits the gaze of the spectator, who, as a reader of a complex sign system, cannot consume or reduce the object of her vision to a monolithic projection of the self. In fact, Gestus undermines the stability of the spectatorial 'self', for in the act of looking the spectator engages with her own temporality. She, too, becomes historicized – in motion and at risk, but also free to compare the actor/character's signs to 'what is close and proper to [herself]' – her material conditions, her politics, her skin, her desires. Sitting not in the dark, but in the Brechtian semi-lit smoker's theatre, the spectator still has the possibility of pleasurable identification. This is effected not through imaginary projection onto an ideal but through a triangular structure of actor/subject – character – spectator. Looking at the character, the spectator is constantly intercepted by the actor/subject, and the latter, heeding no fourth wall, is theoretically free to look back. The difference, then, between this triangle and the familiar oedipal one is that no one side signifies authority, knowledge, or the law. Brechtian theatre depends on a structure of representation, on exposing and making visible, but what appears even in the Gestus can only be provisional, indeterminate, nonauthoritative.[7]

---

[7]This is fully played out in Brecht's attitude toward textual authority. As is well known, he revised constantly and cared little about definitive or authoritative versions of his plays.

This feminist rereading of Gestus makes room, at least theoretically, for a viewing position for the female spectator. Because the semiosis of Gestus involves the gendered bodies of spectator, actor/subject, and character, all working together but *never harmoniously*, there can be no fetishization and no end to signification. In this Brechtian-feminist paradigm, the spectator's look is freed into 'dialectics, passionate detachment' (Mulvey 1975:18). She might borrow Gertrude Stein's line, and give equal emphasis to each word: 'I love to read the signs.'

If Gestus invites us to think about the performer and the spectator in their historical and sexual specificity, it also asks us to consider the author's inscription. 'The author's attitude to the public, that of the era represented and of the time in which the play is performed, the collective style of acting of the characters, etc., are a few of the parameters of the basic *Gestus*' (Pavis 1982:42). In the case of women writers and particularly of women dramatists, the erasure from history has been so nearly complete that the feminist critic feels compelled to make some attempt at recovery – and here Brechtian theory, fellow-traveling with feminist theory, suggests a critical practice – gestic feminist criticism – that would contextualize *and* reclaim the author.

A gestic feminist criticism would 'alienate' or foreground those moments in a playtext in which social attitudes about gender could be made visible. It would highlight sex-gender configurations as they conceal or disrupt a coercive or patriarchal ideology. It would refuse to appropriate and naturalize male or female dramatists, but rather focus on historical material constraints in the production of images. It would attempt to engage dialectically with, rather than master, the playtext. And in generating meanings, it would recover (specifically gestic) moments in which the historical actor, the character, the spectator, *and* the author enter representation, however provisionally.

## GESTIC FEMINIST CRITICISM, APHRA BEHN

In the brief space remaining, it is impossible to flesh out this critical schema, but I want to draw attention to a gestic moment that Aphra Behn has provided – in the prolog of her first play, produced in 1670. A middle-class woman with prestigious connections but no supporting family, a former spy and recent inmate in debtor's prison, Behn had her first play produced for the Duke's company, originally patented to William Davenant, and very much committed to the Davenant style of movable scenes, machines, spectacular tableaux, songs, and dances. The Restoration theatre was fully 'culinary' in its desire to lure and entertain the public exclusively for private profit. It was also, from the giver of the royal patent to the patentees and playwrights, upper class and male.[8]

The audience, historians are finally telling us, was more varied – and contradictory – than was previously believed. Professional men and respectable women and their maids went regularly to the theatre, as did noisy unattached rakes, prostitutes, and members of royal entourage. There had been women writers – the Duchess of Newcastle, Katherine Phillipps, and Frances Boothby each had a play produced. But when Behn's *The Forced*

---

[8]One of Behn's biographers, Maureen Duffy, provides this context: 'Of the fifteen living dramatists who had had two or more plays produced since the theatres reopened in 1660, two were earls, one a duke, one was to be a titular baron, four were knights. [...] In 1671 [most of the new writers] were of the gentry or nobility, and almost all had university or Inns of Court educations. Compared with such a company Aphra Behn's pretensions must have seemed even more extravagant' (1977:103–104).

*Marriage, or The Jealous Bridegroom* opened in December 1670, it was a novelty and no one knew whether she would have staying power. The female performer, having arrived on the professional stage only ten years earlier, though she was paid a lower salary than her male colleagues, had already proved her staying power; in décolletage, in breeches, in 'undress', the actress represented an important financial lure and provocation, especially to male spectators.

Conventionally, the Restoration prolog describes the state of literary production, complains about the lowly status of poetry, berates the audience for its stupidity, disparages the whores, condemns the factions of noisy fops, refers to any current political turmoil, introduces and/or playfully positions the author, and, in a vague way, describes the play.

In the prolog to her first play, Behn takes note of the factions in the audience and genders them. She writes lines for a performer (gender unclear, but I would guess male) who enjoins the males in the audience to be leery of 'spies' – by implication whores whom the author has planted 'to hold you in wanton Compliment/That so you may not censure what she'as writ,/ Which done, they face you down 'twas full of Wit' (Behn 1915:286).

I come now, at last, to my second short text on pointing.

Within moments the stage directions read '*Enter an Actress*', who '*pointing to the ladies*' asks, 'Can any see that glorious Sight and say/A Woman shall not Victor prove today?' In that pointing gesture, the actress sets up a triangular structure – between historical performer, the role she is destined to play, and the female spectators in the audience. She also mentions 'A Woman', a potential victor, and that seems to have a referent: the writer Aphra Behn (although it could be one of the females in the play). In that shared look, actor-subject, character, spectator, and author are momentarily joined, and for perhaps the first time on the English stage all four positions are filled by women. But not for long. In casting a closer eye at the female spectators, the actress soon differentiates, and in specifically sexual terms. Insisting, ironically perhaps, that 'There's not a Vizard in our whole Cabal' she condemns the lower-class whores, the Pickeroons, 'that scour for prey', but ends by promising total female 'sacrifice' to 'pleasure you' (Behn 1915:286).

Whom that 'you' now designates has become fully undecideable. In the sexual slang of the day, actress meant whore, authoress was soon to mean whore, and both were commodities in a pleasure market whose major consumers were male. Still, before conventional representation resumes, the signifying space is dominated by the interlocking look of women. I would call the actress's pointing, and the entire prolog, a Gestus, a moment when the sex-gender system, theatre politics, and social history cathect and become visible. For the feminist critic and theorist this Gestus marks a first step toward recovering a woman playwright in her sexual, historical, and theatrical specificity. It also marks a site, in the text, of indeterminacy, of multiple meanings – a pleasurable moment for reading the clouds.

# REFERENCES

Barker, Francis
1984    *The Tremulous Private Body*: *Essays on Subjection*. London: Methuen.

Byg, Barton
1986    'Brecht on the Margins: Film and Film Theory'. Paper presented at the annual convention of the Modern Language Association, New York, December.

Baudry, Jean-Louis
1980   'The Apparatus: Metapsychological Approaches to the Impression of Reality'. In *Apparatus*, edited by Theresa Hak Kyung, 41–62. New York: Tanam Press.

Behn, Aphra
1915   *The Forced Marriage, or The Jealous Bridegroom*. In *The Works of Aphra Behn*, vol. 3, edited by Montague Summers, 285–381. London: Wm Heinemann.

Bentley, Eric
1981   *The Brecht Commentaries*. London: Methuen.

Blau, Herbert
1982   *Take Up the Bodies: Theater at the Vanishing Point*. Urbana: University of Illinois Press.

Brecht, Bertolt
1964   *Brecht on Theatre*, edited by John Willet. New York: Hill and Wang.

Brewer, Maria Minich.
1984   'A Loosening of Tongues: From Narrative Economy to Women Writing'. *MLN* 9, no. 5 (December):1141–1161.

Diamond, Elin
1985   'Refusing the Romanticism of Identity: Narrative Interventions in Churchill, Benmussa, Duras'. *Theatre Journal* 37, no. 3 (October):273–286.

Dollimore, Jonathan
1984   *Radical Tragedy: Religion, Ideology and Power in the Drama of Shakespeare and His Contemporaries*. Chicago: University of Chicago Press.

Duffy, Maureen
1977   *The Passionate Shepardess: Aphra Behn (1640-89)*. London: Jonathan Cape.

Eagleton, Terry
1986   'Brecht and Rhetoric'. In *Against the Grain: Essays 1975-1985*, 167–172. London: Verso.

Esslin, Martin
1971   *Brecht: The Man and His Work*. New York: W.W. Norton.

Flitterman-Lewis, Sandy
1987   'Psychoanalysis in Film and Television'. In *Channels of Discourse: Television and Contemporary Criticism*, edited by Robert C. Allen, 170–210. Chapel Hill: University of North Carolina Press.

Heath, Stephen
1974   'Lessons from Brecht'. *Screen* 15, no. 2 (Summer): 103–127.

Irigaray, Luce
1985   'The Power of Discourse and the Subordination of the Feminine'. In *This Sex Which Is Not One*, translated by Catherine Porter with Carolyn Burke, 68–85. Ithaca, NY: Cornell University Press.

Johnson, Barbara
1980    *The Critical Difference: Essays in the Contemporary Rhetoric of Reading.* Baltimore, MD: Johns Hopkins University Press.

de Lauretis, Teresa
1984    *Alice Doesn't: Feminism, Semiotics, Cinema.* Bloomington: University of Indiana Press.

Moi, Toril
1985    *Sexual/Textual Politics: Feminist Literary Theory.* London: Methuen.

Mulvey, Laura
1975    'Visual Pleasure and Narrative Cinema'. *Screen* 16, no. 3 (Autumn):6–18.

Pavis, Patrice
1982    *Languages of the Stage: Essays in the Semiology of the Theatre.* New York: Performing Arts Journal Publications.

Rubin, Gayle
1978    'The Traffic in Women: Notes on the "Political Economy" of Sex'. In *Toward an Anthropology of Women*, edited by Rayna Reiter, 157–210. New York: Monthly Review Press.

Stimpson, Catherine R.
1986    'Stein and the Transposition of Gender'. In *The Poetics of Gender*, edited by Nancy K. Miller, 1–18. New York: Columbia University Press.

Watney, Simon
1986    'The Banality of Gender'. In *Sexual Difference*, edited by Robert Young, 13–21. London: The Oxford Literary Review.

Weber, Carl
1980    'Brecht in Eclipse?' *The Drama Review* 24, no. I (T85):114–124.

Wiles, Timothy J.
1980    *The Theater Event: Modern Theories of Performance.* Chicago: The University of Chicago Press.

# Postcolonial Brecht

# CHAPTER TWENTY-EIGHT

# A Postcolonial Brecht?

MARC SILBERMAN

Why the question mark in my title? The rise in intonation is not so much intended to express skepticism about whether there is such a thing as a postcolonial Brecht as to query the gains that another postal-theory can bring to those interested in Brechtian theater and thinking. I say 'another postal-theory' because I have engaged in a similar inquiry in a not dissimilar context. Almost two decades ago, at the 8th International Brecht Society Symposium held in December 1991 in Augsburg, Germany, my presentation was called: 'A Postmodernized Brecht?' There the paper title's final question mark was a response to the momentous changes and soaring expectations after the fall of the Berlin Wall and the implosion of communism: 'A new world order, a new Brecht', so I began my paper then and continued:

> If Marx was right that being determines consciousness (and granted, many today would deny him all credibility), then could we not expect with the end of the Cold War a different Brecht waiting to be discovered behind traditional scholarship and theatre practice? Does an other Brecht exist beyond the ideological encrustations of the past? Who needs this other Brecht in a postindustrial, postmodern epoch with new social relations unencumbered by class struggle and hegemony?[1]

Notwithstanding the tongue-in-cheek naiveté conveyed by these questions, I did proceed to consider how Brecht might fit into a postmodern theoretical framework, concluding that – as a strategy of reading (or rereading) – it opened up some new and challenging questions.

Here I will employ a similar approach, focusing not on Brecht's oeuvre, on his plays, novels, stories, poems, or even essays, but rather on our reading practices and how postcolonial theory might engage or clarify larger issues about Brechtian dramaturgy and thought in response to accelerating globalization. Thus, I will ask whether the postcolonial turn has rendered Brecht as just another 'dead, white, male European writer', whose very reputation as a major representative of high modernism is anchored in the epistemological interests of the binary divides between East and West or North and South that postcolonial studies interrogate. Furthermore, I will raise the question whether postcolonial theory reveals that Brecht's imagined displacements to China, Japan, and India, not to speak of his ethnically tinged fantasies of migration to Chicago, Alabama, Alaska, and Mahagonny, are

---

Marc Silberman, 'A Postcolonial Brecht?', *Brecht Yearbook*, 36 (2011), pp. 241–7.

[1] 'A Postmodernized Brecht?' *Theatre Journal* 45.1 (March 1993), pp. 1–19.

simply Eurocentric exoticism where the body of the Other offers a convenient projection screen for negotiating the diminished subject(ivities) of Western power? The short and emphatic answer to these questions is no, but the answer's seeming transparency conceals the way that postcolonial theory can shift perspectives and potentially open up new questions to complicate both critical and performance practices vis-à-vis Brecht. Since the 'postcolonial' signifies a position against imperialism and undoes Western hegemony by recognizing minority cultures as the global majority, it seems to overlap in important ways with issues of class and social violence that preoccupied Brecht. I will focus here on a 'postcolonial approach' with the goal of testing issues generated by its critical potential: where does Brecht fit into colonial discourse? Did his own exile experience generate a diasporic consciousness? Why have Brechtian techniques been adapted by some (post) colonial or subaltern writers for 'writing back?' And finally, can a Brechtian hermeneutics or dramaturgy serve the postcolonial goal of social and political change?

To begin with a few clarifications: postcolonial studies focus generally on the interactions between European nations and the societies they colonized in the modern period. The European empire is estimated to have controlled as much as 85 percent of the globe by the time of the First World War, having consolidated its control over several centuries.[2] Some have claimed that Germany's historically late entrance into colonial domination in the late nineteenth century and its quick exit after signing the Versailles Treaty in 1919 exempted it from the 'postcolonial condition', but there is ample evidence from historical chronicles as well as from sources in the realm of scientific exploration, travel literature, and philosophical speculation that Germany indeed participated in Europe's violent imperial reach.[3] Postcolonialism was a critical concept first employed in the 1960s and 1970s to designate a period of decolonizations following the Second World War, and thus seemingly exempting Germany, but in the meantime it has accrued a much wider meaning that references interdisciplinary political, theoretical, and historical investigations grounded in the context of colonialism as well as contemporary globalization. Because decolonization entailed more than just a political transfer of power, postcolonial studies have addressed it as a multilayered process, including political imagination, modernization, the formation of new elites, and cultural transformation. In short, a postcolonial approach aims to introduce a new perspective that shifts the focus in the twentieth century from the impact of two world wars to the process of global decolonization.

Brecht is rarely mentioned in the context of postcolonial writers, and one could legitimately ask why he should be? In its originary meaning postcolonial writers were identified as those who wrote out of resistance to colonial regimes or in the context of colonial discourses that continued to shape cultures where revolutions had overthrown formal ties to colonial rulers. Nonetheless, Brecht's works – poems, plays, and prose – are

---

[2]There is an enormous literature on postcolonial studies; a critical overview can be found in Ania Loomba, *Colonialism/Postcolonialism* (London and New York: Routledge, 1998); also Neil Lazarus, ed., *Cambridge Companion to Postcolonial Literary Studies* (New York: Cambridge University Press, 2004), offers diverse points of entry.

[3]On the German colonialist discourse, see Sara Friedrichsmeyer, Sara Lennox, and Susanne Zantop, eds., *The Imperialist Imagination: German Colonialism and Its Legacy* (Ann Arbor: University of Michigan Press, 1998), as well as the more recent and critical study by Monika Albrecht, *'Europa ist nicht die Welt': (Post)Kolonialismus in Literatur und Geschichte der westdeutschen Nachkriegszeit* (Bielefeld: Aisthesis, 2008), especially chapter 2 on '(Post-) Koloniale Amnesie? Zur deutschen Kolonialismusdiskussion', pp. 34–138.

saturated with references to East Asia, the Middle East, India, American expansionism, Niggers and Negroes, the yellow peril, the brown-skinned, etcetera. While scholars have traced these references to the colonial fantasies of Rudyard Kipling and Karl May or to the drastic portrayals of capitalist practices in novels by Upton Sinclair and Frank Norris, they belong as well to larger metaphors of modernity and the urban jungle in which the Other often stands in for the complexity of capitalist society. Here Brecht intersects with postcolonial writing that explores the dynamics of power and hegemony. He recognized early on how knowledge about the world is generated under specific relations between the powerful and the powerless and then circulated repetitively to legitimate imperial interests. Set in colonial India, his play *Mann ist Mann* (A Man's a Man), written in various stages between 1918 and 1931, deconstructs mechanisms of control and subjugation by creating characters with voices and faces that mimic cultural stereotypes, using techniques that postcolonial criticism has codified as ventriloquism, mimicry, and ethnic drag.[4] Similarly, the play *Puntila und sein Knecht Matti* (Puntila and His Man Matti) is a comic send-up of the Hegelian master-slave dialectic, presenting a parable of subjugation under capitalist conditions that shows how categories assumed to be natural and immutable are in fact reversible. The learning play *Die Ausnahme und die Regel* (The Exception and the Rule), which became a favored Brecht play in the 1950s in decolonizing countries, also thematizes the master-slave constellation but stages demonstrably the possible answers to the question: Whose side are you on? These are among the very issues and concepts that postcolonial studies analyze and contest.

While Edward Said's 1978 book *Orientalism*, a founding text in postcolonial studies, treated primarily fantasies about the Middle East, its major contribution lies in the more general argument that an archive of Western knowledges and languages acquired the capacity to shape external realities as well as the subjectivities of those subjected to colonial discourses and colonial rule.[5] It is relevant to ask, therefore, whether Brecht's use of the exotic Other contributes to the material-discursive construct that shapes real and imagined existences or whether his 'othering' – be it of race, class, or gender – engages and contests universalizing discourses, power structures, and social hierarchies. From the perspective of intellectual history Brecht emerged from the volatile context of the First World War and political revolution when modernization and secularization energized many European artists to seek alternatives to the mediocrity and social atomization they saw around them. The visions of renewal that characterized the historical avant-gardes found them turning to non-European sources for inspiration: to African 'primitivism', or Asian 'passivity', or Arab 'sensuality'. Yet Brecht distinguishes himself from German writers such as Hermann Hesse, Stefan Zweig, and Alfred Döblin, who also employ colonial tropes, by developing aesthetic forms and dramaturgical strategies that invoke a 'postcolonial potential'. Specifically he introduces figures like Galy Gay in *Mann ist Mann*, Kragler with his African trauma in *Trommeln in der Nacht* (Drums in the Night), Garga in *Dickicht der Städte* (The Jungle of the Cities), Shen Te in *Der gute Mensch von Sezuan* (The Good Person of Sezuan), Azdak in *Der kaukasische Kreidekreis* (The Caucasian Chalk Circle), just to mention the most obvious, all of them dramatic characters from the

---

[4] Katrin Sieg discusses oppositional strategies developed by Brecht that underpin postcolonial, feminist, anti-racist theater in Katrin Sieg, *Ethnic Drag: Performing Race, Nation, Sexuality in West Germany* (Ann Arbor: University of Michigan Press, 2002), pp. 14–15.
[5] Edward Said, *Orientalism* (New York: Vintage, 1978).

margins who sabotage hierarchies and complicate binaries. In this respect Brecht's plays offer a level of reflection about cultural difference and the reproduction of conventional discourse that is part and parcel of postcolonial critique. His overdrawn parodies aim at colonialism and capitalism as world systems; his irony undermines the widespread romantic images of the colonial Other; and it is no coincidence that Brecht's alter ego, Herr Keuner, who became a tool of self-reflection in anecdotes, stories, and journal notes throughout his life, has a subversive potential that Brecht considered to be the source of Asian wisdom.

Brecht was compelled to leave Germany by the rise of the Nazis: his journey began in 1933, taking him briefly to Prague, Vienna, Zurich, and Paris before he settled in Denmark to wait out the threat. But the Nazi threat came closer and lasted longer than he expected, forcing him to flee to Sweden for a year in 1939, and then Finland for another year, until he and his family were able to enter the United States via the Soviet Union, settling in Los Angeles for the next six years. Not until 1949 did he resettle in East Berlin after a hiatus in Switzerland for eighteen months. The anxiety of fleeing from the Nazis inflected Brecht's textual engagements with power structures and social hierarchies. The fifteen year migrancy put everything in his life into flux, providing an existential encounter that became his own personal 'alienation effect', so to speak, and bringing him into proximity with the diasporic writing of postcolonial subjects. Adaptation to changes and dislocations guided his productivity during these exile years. The shifting political, social, and personal conditions of survival confirmed and extended techniques of the Epic theater he had been developing prior to 1933 but also engendered new strategies to construct different forms of knowledge and ways of seeing the world. In the exile writings I pinpoint in particular a transformation in the relationship between the playwright and the audience, between the writer and the reader in his prose, between the speaker and the addressee of his poems. In the pre-exilic writings Brecht assumed an emphatically modernist position aimed against the preservation of tradition and cultural legacy. Both sides of the writer-recipient relationship were assumed to be quintessential anonymous city dwellers, wearing the mask of the alienated subject in the crowd who must learn to exist in a faceless collective. Brecht's irony and humor gave way to anger and injunctions in the diasporic experience of personal migrancy and political defeat. In other words, geographical distance and uncertainty changed the relation to the audience, reader, addressee, and the faceless collective became the affirming community of solidarity against his enemies.

As instructive as these contextual moments and biographical experiences may be, Brecht's most significant contribution to postcolonial studies is to be sought in his dramaturgy and hermeneutics, yet here the dynamics of mutual exchange should not be ignored. Brecht took global popular forms and transformed them not only into staging techniques but also into a *Weltanschauung* committed to undermining oppressive social structures. We find him borrowing the gestural quality of Chinese opera and the abstract structure of Japanese Nôh theater or adapting story-telling elements and forms of clownery from peasant cultures. No wonder, then, that from the perspective of audience spectatorship scholars and playwrights have identified common traits shared by Brecht's Epic theater and the popular theater of 'marginalized' or 'peripheral' societies in East Asia, South Asia, and Africa.[6] These traits include a presentational approach to acting,

---

[6]On Indian theater, see Virginie Magnat, 'Girish Karnad's *Hayavadana*: A Postcolonial Reading', *genre* 22 (2001): pp. 169–77 (discussing Karnad's rediscovery through a Brechtian lens of nonrealistic forms in traditional Indian

the presence of a narrator, the integration of song and music, the use of masks, and most striking, the interaction between stage and audience like that at a sports event. For some this compatibility with indigenous cultures has been considered Brechtianism *avant la lettre*, for others it offers a transformative model of 'talking back' or 'writing oneself into history', where colonial subjects and subalterns are integrated into the theatrical event as reasoning, thinking agents who can effect social change.

From another perspective Brecht's anti-Aristotelian, non-mimetic theater offers a counter model to hegemonic European forms of psychological realism and emotional identification. Especially his non-naturalistic plays with their elements of farce, satire, and agitprop can combine well with indigenous performance traditions or rituals, offering a more explicit engagement with the audience than conventional 'elite' European theater. Of course, Brecht is not the sole influence to be mentioned here; one thinks of Antonin Artaud and Jerzy Grotowski on the one hand, who experimented with different anti-illusionist techniques of engaging the audience through shock and emotional stress, or on the other hand of a mediator of Brecht like Augusto Boal who developed a theater of pedagogy for impoverished communities to rehearse social change. In any case it is important to keep in mind that the transfers back and forth have not been seamless. Brecht's borrowings occurred through his own contemporary lens and for his own needs, while his commitment to 'complex seeing' was a reaction to the historical context of European modernist theater and is not always adaptable to other vernacular or postcolonial modernisms. Moreover, the arena for postcolonial literatures and critiques is often situated ironically in urban theaters and universities, mediated by a class of well-educated people who themselves are implicated in the postcolonial structures of power. This is a conundrum that Brecht knew all too well at the end of his life.

Finally, postcolonial theory launched a vigorous epistemological critique of Western knowledge as Eurocentric and universalizing, that is, as a mode of rationalist thinking that excludes other traditions and ways of knowing. This is a reasonable position vis-à-vis the nineteenth-century tradition of hermeneutics that consistently conflates foreignness or otherness with error, uncertainty, or absence of understanding and thus regards it as a problem to be solved or a deviation to be disciplined. But while knowledge and reason may be forms of domination, they are not always complicit in Western hegemony; they can also critique and lead to changes in hegemonic relations by developing strategies of resistance and narratives of emancipation. Indeed Brecht was less interested in understanding or examining the Other than in transforming and measuring what it does to us as readers and spectators. This is the foundation of his interventionist aesthetics, which is both a collective experience and a cognitive *process*. His texts open up spaces to imagine self or group identity from a marginal perspective, that of the oppressed and the 'kleine Leute' fleeing their impossible circumstances. The empirical evidence for the global adaptation of Brecht's plays, theater practices, and model of thinking politically

---

Yakshagana), and Aparna Dharwadker, 'John Gay, Bertolt Brecht, and Postcolonial Antinationalisms', *Modern Drama* 38.1 (Spring 1995): pp. 4–21; on East Asian theater, see Antony Tatlow, *Shakespeare, Brecht, and the Intercultural Sign* (Durham: Duke University Press, 2001), especially chapter 2 on 'Intercultural Signs: Textual Anthropology', pp. 31–79, for a discussion of the construction of the subject and gestural acting; on African theater, see Amine Khalid and Marvin A. Carlson, 'Al-halqa in Arabic Theatre: An Emerging Site of Hybridity', *Theatre Journal* 60.1 (March 2008): pp. 71–85 (discussing Brecht as spiritual father for the story-telling techniques and epic structure in plays by several North African dramatists), and Brian Crow, 'African Brecht', *Research in African Literatures* 40.2 (Summer 2009): pp. 190–207.

about culture suggests that he continues to be a central player wherever new, postcolonial modernisms are forming.

Is this, then, the titular postcolonial Brecht, defining a space where epistemology, ethics, and politics come together in the service of emancipation? Maybe, but what have we gained from this brief excursion into postcolonial theory? First, decolonizing Brecht, or better, decolonizing scholarship on Brecht means analyzing anew from *our* contemporary time the historical context in which he generated his practices and critical thinking. He lived in the belly of the dragon but also developed modes of representing and performing the hierarchical power relations between the center and the periphery. Second, postcolonial studies recognize and hone in on the mutually constitutive process of 'othering' and its essentially binary structure, dovetailing with Brecht's dynamic, dialectical presentation of difference, insisting that relationships of inequality cannot be reduced to binary antagonisms. Third and finally, postcolonialism, like postmodernism, does not mark a temporal end but rather is the sign of an emancipatory project; that is, it announces a goal yet to be achieved, the dismantling of imperial and Eurocentric domination in a globalizing world. In fact, I myself am not convinced that we are advancing fast enough in this project. From my perch in the USA, it looks as if the show is largely still being run by the same old players. A postcolonial Brecht can sharpen our understanding of how knowledge was produced and disseminated in the past and thereby help focus attention on the emerging world where new (post) colonies are being formed with new forms of expression.

# PERMISSIONS ACKNOWLEDGEMENTS

Fredric Jameson, 'Episch, or, the Third Person', from *Brecht and Method*, pp. 51–8 and notes pp. 85–8. Copyright © Fredric Jameson, 1998. Reprinted with permission of VERSO.

David Barnett, 'Dialectics and the Brechtian Tradition', in *Performance Research*, volume 21, issue 3, pp. 6–15. Reprinted by permission of the publisher (Taylor & Francis Ltd, http://www.tandfonline.com).

Excerpt from Bertolt Brecht, 1918–1933. *Schriften zum Theater*. Band 2. © Suhrkamp Verlag Frankfurt am Main 1963. All rights reserved by and controlled through Suhrkamp Verlag Berlin.

Anthony Squiers, 'A Critical Response to Heidi M. Silcox's "What's Wrong with Alienation?"' in *Philosophy and Literature*, 39:1 (2015), 243–7. © 2015 Johns Hopkins University Press. Reprinted with permission of Johns Hopkins University Press.

Meg Mumford, 'Getting the Gist of Gestus', in *Showing the Gestus*, unpublished PhD thesis, pp. 1–22. Reprinted by permission of the author.

Excerpt from Bertolt Brecht, 1933–1947. *Schriften zum Theater*. Band 3. © Suhrkamp Verlag Frankfurt am Main 1963. All rights reserved by and controlled through Suhrkamp Verlag Berlin.

Craig Kinzer, 'Brecht, the "Fable" and the Teaching of Directing', from *The Brecht Yearbook*, 16 (1991), pp.24–37. Copyright 1991 by the International Brecht Society. All rights reserved.

Reprinted by permission from *Staging History: Brecht's Social Concepts of Ideology* by Astrid Oesmann, the State University of New York Press, copyright © 2005, State University of New York. All rights reserved.

Excerpt from Bertolt Brecht, 1918–1933. *Schriften zum Theater*. Band 2. © Suhrkamp Verlag Frankfurt am Main 1963. All rights reserved by and controlled through Suhrkamp Verlag Berlin.

Karl-Heinz Schoeps, 'From Distancing Alienation to Intuitive Naiveté: Bertolt Brecht's Establishment of a New Aesthetic Category', in *Monatshefte* 81.2 (1989): 186–98. Copyright © 1989 by the Board of Regents of the University of Wisconsin System. Reprinted by permission of the University of Wisconsin Press.

John J. White, 'On the Sociology of Opera,' and 'Scheming Brecht', in *Bertolt Brecht's Dramatic Theory*. Copyright © 2004 John J. White. Reprinted by permission of Boydell & Brewer Inc.

*The Drama of Ideas: Platonic Provocations in Theater and Philosophy*, by Martin Puchner (2010): Extracts totalling 15 pages (pp. 106–12 and 8 pages of notes at end of book). Reprinted by Permission of Oxford University Press, USA.

Antony Tatlow, 'Introduction' in *Bertolt Brecht's Me-ti: Book of Interventions in the Flow of Things*, Bertolt Brecht (London: Methuen Drama, 2016), pp. 1–39. Reprinted by permission of Bloomsbury Publishing, UK.

Detlev Schöttker, 'Brechts Theaterarbeit: Ein Grundlagenwerk und seine Ausgrenzungen', in *Weimarer Beiträge*, 53: 3 (2007). Reprinted by permission of publisher.

Patrick Primavesi, 'Apparat ohne Zuschauer? Zur Dekonstruktion des Mediums in Brechts Ozeanflug', from *The Brecht Yearbook*, 24 (1999), pp. 80–95. Copyright 1999 by the International Brecht Society. All rights reserved.

Angelos Koutsourakis, 'Utilizing the "Ideological Antiquity". Rethinking Brecht and Film Theory', in *Monatshefte* 107.2 (2015): 242–69. Copyright © 2015 by the Board of Regents of the University of Wisconsin System. Reprinted by permission of the University of Wisconsin Press.

Kim H. Kowalke, 'Brecht and Music: Theory and Practice,' in *The Cambridge Companion to Brecht*, eds. Peter Thomson and Glendyr Sacks. © Cambridge University Press 2006, reproduced with permission.

Dorothee Ostmeier, 'Bertolt Brecht and the Internet', from *The Brecht Yearbook*, 26 (2001), pp. 234–55. Copyright 2001 by the International Brecht Society. All rights reserved.

G. Ronald Murphy, *Brecht and the Bible: A Study of Religious Nihilism and Human Weakness in Brecht's Plays*. The University of North Carolina Studies in the Germanic Languages and Literatures. Copyright © 1980 by the University of North Carolina Press. Used by permission of the publisher.

David Barnett, 'Brecht as Great Shakespearean: A Lifelong Connection', in Ruth Morse (ed.), *Great Shakespeareans*, vol. 14 (London: Bloomsbury, 2013), pp. 114–27. Reprinted by permission of Bloomsbury Publishing.

Astrid Oesmann, 'Tracing the crimes of capitalism: from Mahagonny to Nazi Germany,' from *The Brecht Yearbook*, 29 (2004), pp. 99–110. Copyright 2004 by the International Brecht Society. All rights reserved.

Katharina Brinkert, 'Brecht und die Naturwissenschaften – die Naturwissenschaften und Brecht?' in Christian Hippe and Volker Ißbrucker (eds.), *Brecht und Naturwissenschaften*, pp. 251–63. Reprinted by permission of the author.

Markus Wessendorf, 'Brecht's Materialist Ethics between Confucianism and Mohism', in *Philosophy East and West*, 66: 1 (2016), pp. 122–45. Reprinted by permission of University of Hawai'i Press.

Ralf Simon, 'Zur poetisches Anthropologie der Komödie in Brechts Messingkauf', from *The Brecht Yearbook*, 24 (1999), 277–90. Copyright 1999 by the International Brecht Society. All rights reserved.

Brecht, 'On Humour', in Brecht, *Bertolt Brecht's Me-ti* (London: Bloomsbury, 2016), p.81. Reprinted by permission of Bloomsbury Publishing.

Sean Carney, 'Modern Tragedy' and 'Brechtian Tragedy', in *Brecht and Critical Theory*. Copyright © 2005 Sean Carney. Reprinted by permission of the author.

Elin Diamond, 'Brechtian Theory/Feminist Theory: Toward a Gestic Feminist Criticism', in *TDR/The Drama Review*, 32:1 (T117-Spring, 1988), pp. 82–94. © 1988 by New York University and the Massachusetts Institute of Technology. Reprinted by permission of MIT Press Journals.

Marc Silberman, 'A Postcolonial Brecht?' from *The Brecht Yearbook*, 36 (2011), pp. 241–7. Copyright 2011 by the International Brecht Society. All rights reserved.

Every effort has been made to trace copyright holders and to obtain their permission for the use of copyright material. The publisher apologizes for any errors or omissions in the above list and would be grateful if notified of any corrections that should be incorporated in future reprints or editions of this book.

# INDEX

'Abbild' theory   123
'Abstraction' (Hauser)   155
accidental gestures   45
acting   11, 39, 42, 47, 58, 115, 127, 128, 173, 260
actuality   19, 27
Adorno, Theodor W.   26, 69–71, 73–7, 183, 196, 272–4, 332–3
advertising   34, 180, 194, 235
A-effects   341–2, 344
aesthetics   39, 46, 72, 77, 90, 153, 180, 194, 209, 212, 281, 291, 328, 359
*Affairs of Mr. Julius Caesar, The* (Brecht)   128
'Against Formalism in Art and Literature'   152
Agamben, Giorgio   186
Albers, Jürgen   87
*Alcibiades Delivered* (Kaiser)   128
alienation (*Entfremdung*). See 'Verfremdung'
amateur music   171
A&M Records   221
*Analects* (Waley)   295–6, 299
*Analects* (Wilhelm)   293–4, 296
Angelopoulos, Theo   194–5, 199
anti-Aristotelian dramaturgy   182, 328, 359
anti-bourgeois art   222
*Antigonemodell 1948* (Brecht)   110 n.31, 116 n.36, 156
anti-illusionism   192–3, 197, 359
anti-realist film art   229 n.31
'Apparat'   229
'apparatus'   105–6, 165, 167–75, 181–92, 199, 228–32, 234, 265, 285–6, 321, 340–1, 346
Archer, Robyn   217
Aristotle   2, 129, 133, 183–4, 317
    Aristotelian dramaturgy   133, 182, 185, 198, 319
    Aristotelianism   133, 319
    Aristotelian theatre   316, 319, 329
Arntzen, Helmut   316 n.3, 317 n.4

Arslan, Thomas   199
art   159, 182–3, 227, 228, 236, 256, 287
    and history   70, 72
    works   72–3, 327
Artaud, Antonin   359
Association of Proletarian Revolutionary Authors   150
*As You Like It* (Shakespeare)   318
Auerbach, Erich   9
*Aufbau* magazine   157
Aufbau Verlag   154
Aufricht, Ernst-Josef   213
*Aufstieg und Fall der Stadt Mahagonny/ The Rise and Fall of the City of Mahagonny* (Brecht)   50, 97–100, 101 n.14, 102–4, 106–10, 108 n.25, 114–15, 117–21, 123, 208, 213–15, 228, 228 nn.24, 25, 251, 269–74, 277–8
Augsburg Puppet Theatre   174
Aumont, Jacques   186
Austin, J. L.   304
autonomous artwork   70–1, 73–4
avant garde   34, 103–6, 151, 222, 225, 227, 256, 357

*Baal* (Brecht)   251, 272
Bacon, Francis   283
*Baden-Baden Cantata of Acquiescence, The* (Brecht)   209
Baden-Baden Chamber Music Festival   168
*Baden-Baden Lesson on Consent, The* (Brecht)   165–6, 171, 173
Baden-Baden Spa Rooms   168
Balzac, Honoré de   78
Baroque   245
Barry, Hank   234
Barthes, Roland   12 n.3
Batorsky, Barry Joseph   51
*Battle in Winter* (Becher)   24
Baudry, Jean-Louis   192, 345
Bazin, André   191–2, 197
Beauvoir, Simone de   13

*Beaver Coat and Conflagration, The*
    (Hauptmann)  153
Behn, Aphra  348–9
Benjamin, Walter  69–70, 127–8, 132–3,
    158–9, 166, 168, 185, 187–8, 191,
    222 n.6, 225, 226 n.16, 227 n.21,
    276, 329, 335
Bentley, Eric  341
Berghaus, Ruth  26
Berlau, Ruth  142, 145, 156, 308
*Berliner Börsen-Courier*  98–9, 101, 103
Berliner Ensemble (BE)  3, 23–4, 26, 59–61,
    152, 152 n.14, 153–7, 165, 174,
    188, 256, 263–6
Berliner Rundfunk  154
Berlin Radio  174, 208
Bertelsmann  222, 236
Besson, Benno  84, 86, 88, 152 n.14
*Billiard um halb-zehn* (Böll)  11
Bitomsky, Hartmut  199
*Black Rider, The* (Wilson)  175
Blau, Herbert  341
Bloch, Ernst  33, 214
Boal, Augusto  359
Böll, Heinrich  11
Bonaparte, Louis-Napoléon  19
*Book of Changes (I Ching)*  143
Boothby, Frances  348
Bordwell, David  196, 196 n.9
bourgeois  275
    art  186, 223–4, 223 n.10, 229,
        229 n.31
    culture  233, 271
    drama  182–3
    ideology  263, 330
    theatre  47, 49, 53–4, 106 n.21,
        166, 227–8, 266, 328, 331,
        344 n.4
Bowie, David  217
Brandt, Thomas O.  248
Brecht, Bertolt
    anthropology of comedy  319–20
    and the Bible  159, 243–51
    and capitalism  269–78
    as dialectical theorist  20–3
    dialectics on stage  23–6
    dramatic Platonism  127–8
    estrangement effects  33–4, 303 (*see also*
        estrangement effects)
    and feminist theory  339–49
    film theory and  180, 182–8, 190–2,
        196, 199, 223, 345

and internet  221–37
and Lukács debate  150–1
Marxist theatre theory  39–45
materialist ethics  291–310
and music  205–17
plays as comedies  320–2
postcolonial  355–60
primacy of the apparatus  186, 190–1
productions  58–62, 127, 232–3, 292
relationship to Shakespeare  255–66
science and  281–7
specter of  198–9
and Stanislavsky  155–6
techniques  10–12, 32, 76–7, 275
theatre  3, 9, 76–7, 81, 85–6, 88, 91,
    256, 270–1, 286–7, 292, 332,
    339–40, 345–6, 348, 355
as theatre director  18–19, 61, 65
tradition  26–7
tragedy  331–6
and Weill's opera  103–4
works
    *Affairs of Mr. Julius Caesar, The*  128
    *Antigonemodell 1948*  110 n.31,
        116 n.36, 156
    *Aufstieg und Fall der Stadt Mahagonny
        (The Rise and Fall of the City
        of Mahagonny)*  50, 97–100,
        97n 228 nn.24, 25, 101 n.14,
        102–4, 106–10, 108 n.25, 114–15,
        117–21, 123, 208, 213–15, 228,
        251, 269–74, 277–8
    *Baal*  251, 272
    *Baden-Baden Cantata of Acquiescence,
        The*  209
    *Baden-Baden Lesson on Consent,
        The*  165–6, 171, 173
    *Berliner und Frankfurter Ausgabe
        (BFA)*  143–4, 156, 265
    *Buch der Wendungen (The Book of
        Twists and Turns)*  3, 14, 20–1, 23,
        25–7, 137–43, 137 n.1, 145, 270,
        293, 303–7, 303 n.103, 309
    'The Buddha's Parable of the Burning
        House'  138
    *Condemnation of Lucullus, The*  210
    *Constructing a Role: Laughton's
        Galileo*  156
    *Conversations of Refugees*  143
    *Couragemodell*  61
    *Das Badener Lehrstück vom
        Einverständnis*  232, 274

*Days of the Commune, The* 82, 89, 158, 209
*Decision, The* 150, 322
*Der Dreigroschenprozeß* 181, 183, 185, 190, 223, 228, 232, 234, 235, 269–71, 274–5
'Der Film ist eine Ware' (Film is a Commodity) 185
*Der gute Mensch von Sezuan (The Good Person of Sezuan)* 87, 120, 128, 210, 245, 251, 309, 328, 333–4, 357
*Der kaukasische Kreidekreis (The Caucasian Chalk Circle)* 24, 119–20, 128, 210, 245, 251, 299, 322, 328, 357
*Der Lindberghflug* 208
*Der Messingkauf (Buying Brass)* 49, 110, 117, 123, 128–9, 131–2, 150–1, 153, 197, 256, 259–60, 281, 316–19
'Der Nachschlag' ('The Trill Turn') 42
'Der soziologische Raum des bürgerlichen Theaters' 99
*Dialectics in the Theatre* 157–8
*Dickicht der Städte (The Jungle of the Cities)* 138, 343, 357
*Die Ausnahme und die Regel* 119, 357
*Die Beule: Ein Dreigroschenfilm* 191, 195
*Die Bibel* 244–5, 250–1
*Die Dreigroschenoper* 99, 107, 109, 111, 222n 228 n.24, 247
*Die Gesichte der Simone Machard (The Visions of Simone Machard)* 82, 86–91
*Die Maßnahme* 104, 119, 227
*Die Tage der Commune* 84
'Einschüchterung durch die Klassizität' 83
'An Example of Scenic Innovation' 158
*Exception and the Rule, The* 210
*Fear and Misery of the Third Reich* 151, 209
'Five Difficulties in Writing the Truth' 153, 294
'Fünf Schwierigkeiten beim Schreiben der Wahrheit' 199
*Furcht und Elend des Dritten Reiches* 269–70, 275–8

'The German Drama: Pre-Hitler' (Brecht) 114
'Gesticulation' 44–6
*Große kommentierte Berliner und Frankfurter Ausgabe* 149, 159, 224 n.10
*Happy End* 208
*He Who Said Yes* 208
*Herr Puntila und sein Knecht Matti (Mr Puntila and his Man Matti)* 153, 156, 158, 210, 315, 357
'Ist das Volk unfehlbar?' 225
*Kleines Organon* 108, 110, 116 n.36, 118, 120, 225
'Kräftefeld der widersprechenden Interessen' 274, 278
*Kriegsfibel* 195, 199
*Leben des Galilei (The Life of Galileo Galilo)* 58, 85 n.22, 128, 209, 251, 281, 328, 331, 335
*Leben Eduards des Zweiten von England (The Life of Edward the Second of England)* 74, 246
*Legend of the origin of the book Tao Te Ching* 138
*Life of Confucius, The* 138, 293, 296–301, 303
*Life of Einstein* 286–7
*Lindbergh's Flight/Ocean Flight* 165–9, 172, 174
*Macbeth* (lost adaptation) 255
*Mann ist Mann (A Man's a Man)* 98–9, 101 n.14, 115, 208, 210, 321, 357
*Measures Taken, The* 209
'Modelbooks of the Berliner Ensemble' 156
*Modellbücher* (model books) 59
'The Modern Theatre is the Epic Theatre' 332
'Modest Success of Confucius' 293
*Mother, The* 43, 153, 156, 158, 209, 213–14
*Mother Courage and her Children* 58, 61, 128, 138, 153, 156, 210, 244–6, 249, 251, 322, 328, 331–2, 334, 347
'Mo Zi and Ethics' 306
*Musik und Gesellschaft* 101, 110
*Nay-Sayer, The* 132
'On Gestic Music' 43–6, 48

'On the Folk Play' 158
'On the Theatricality of Fascism' 319
'On the Use of Music in an Epic Theatre' 42, 46, 51
'Reich und Reich gesellt sich gern' ('Rich birds flock together') 87–8
Resistible Rise of Arturo Ui, The 26–7
'The Retention of Gestures Through the Generations' 49
Roundheads and the Pointed Heads, The 87–8, 209
Saint Joan of the Stockyards 89–90, 333
Schweyk in the Second World War 87, 209
'Short Description of a New Technique of Acting which Produces a Defamiliarisation Effect' 43, 45
Short Organum for the Theatre, A 22, 45–6, 60, 81, 150, 153, 156–7, 281
Sinn und Form 149, 158
'Sollten wir nicht die Ästhetik liquidieren?' 98
Songspiel Mahagonny 208–9, 214
'Soziologische Betrachtungsweise' 99
'Street Scene' 320
Svendborg Poems 138
Theaterarbeit (Theatre Work) 149–50, 153–4, 153 n.14, 154 n.18, 156–9
'Theatre Chronicle of the Berliner Ensemble' 152
Threepenny Lawsuit, The 4, 25
Three-Penny Novel 10, 128
Threepenny Opera, The 49, 81, 87, 199, 206, 208, 214–15, 217, 291, 321, 328
Trial of Joan of Arc at Rouen, The 89–90
Trial of Lucullus, The 152
Trommeln in der Nacht (Drums in the Night) 357
Tutor, The 265
'Über Filmmusik' 191
'Über reimlose Lyrik mit unregelmäßigen Rhythmen'/On Rhymeless Verse with Irregular Rhythms 74
Urfaust 82–4

'Vergügnungstheater oder Lehrtheater?' 112, 116–17, 122
Versuche 120, 150, 166, 169, 171n 228 n.25
Yea-Sayer, The 132
Brechtianism 26, 180, 192, 359
Bredel, Willi 151
Bresson, Robert 195
Brezing, Sophie 244
'A Brief Editorial Intervention in the Debate' (Erpenbeck) 156
Brueghel, Pieter, the elder 91
Brüggemann, Heinz 115
Bruinier, Franz S. 208
Buch der Wendungen/The Book of Twists and Turns (Brecht) 3, 14, 20–1, 23, 25–7, 137–43, 137 n.1, 145, 270, 293, 303–7, 303 n.103, 309
Büchner, Georg 83
Buck-Morss, Susan 196
Buckwitz, Harry 89
'The Buddha's Parable of the Burning House' (Brecht) 138
Buddhism 138
Bund proletarisch-revolutionärer Schrifteteller (BPRS) 222, 222 n.6
Bürger, Peter 256
Burkhard, Paul 209
Busch, Ernst 213, 216
Busoni, Ferruccio 210

Caesar, Julius 14
Cahiers du Cinéma 186, 192
Capital in the Twenty-First Century (Piketty) 17
capitalism 3–4, 19, 70, 102, 107–8, 145, 183–5, 198, 224, 233, 236, 269–71, 273–4, 277–8, 328, 329, 357, 358
Capital (Marx) 179, 181
Carroll, Noël 197
Catastroica (2012) 199
censorship 222, 228–9, 335
Central Committee of the SED 152–3
Chaplin, Charlie 13
'character masks' 182
character traits 78
Chiang Kai Shek 140
Chinese culture 137–8, 143
Chinese philosophy 293, 310
Churchill, Caryl 342, 343
cinematic representation 185, 190

*Cinéthique* 192
*Cloud 9* (Churchill) 342
cognitive film theory 195–8
'collectivation' 224
collective
  concept 230–4
  dramaturgy 188
  imagination 190, 199
  process 168, 186
  progressive 230
  reactionary 230
  work 154
Cologne radio discussion 98, 106
colonialism 356, 358
comedy 258
  anthropology in Brecht 319–20
  Brecht plays as 320–2
  *Buying Brass* 316–19
  distancing and fictionalisation 313–15, 317–18, 321
  theory 314–16
commodification 97, 185, 228, 232–7, 273
communism 4, 138, 143, 145, 298, 355
*Communist Manifesto* (Engels and Marx) 139
Communist Party 13
Comolli, Jean-Louis 192
*Condemnation of Lucullus, The* (Brecht) 210
Confucius 292–3, 293–303, 308, 310
  Confucian Analects 138
  Confucianism 138–9, 143
*Constructing a Role: Laughton's Galileo* (Brecht) 156
consumerism 221, 270, 273
*Contribution to the Critique of Political Economy, A* (Marx) 155
*Conversations of Refugees* (Brecht) 143
copyright 221, 234, 236
Corbyn, Jeremy 17
*Coriolanus* (Shakespeare) 258, 264, 266
*Couragemodell* (Brecht) 61
'Courtney Love Does the Math' (Love) 234
Craig, Edward Gordon 131
Crow, Carl 296–8, 300, 302
culinary opera and drama 105–8

Dada 115
Daoism 138, 303 n.103
*Das Badener Lehrstück vom Einverständnis* (Brecht) 232, 274

*Das Berliner Requiem* (Weill) 208
*Das Kapital* (Marx) 98 n.4, 222
*Das Kunstblatt* 103
'Das moderne Theater ist das epische Theater' (Brecht) 97, 108
*Das Unbehagen in der Kultur* (Freud) 110
Dath, Dietmar 182
Davenant, William 348
Davis, George 212
*Days of the Commune, The* (Brecht) 82, 89, 158, 209
*Debtocracy* (2011) 199
*Decision, The* (Brecht) 150, 322
decolonization 356, 360
defamiliarization. *See 'Verfremdung'*
Deleuze, Gilles 11, 292
'Der Autor als Produzent' (Benjamin) 225
'Der Briefwechsel zwischen Schiller und Goethe' (Lukács) 116 n.36, 118–19
*Der Dreigroschenprozeß* (Brecht) 181, 183, 185, 190, 223, 228, 232, 234, 235, 269–71, 274–5
'Der Film ist eine Ware'/Film is a Commodity (Brecht) 185
*Der gute Mensch von Sezuan*/*The Good Person of Sezuan* (Brecht) 87, 120, 128, 210, 245, 251, 309, 328, 333–4, 357
*Der kaukasische Kreidekreis*/*The Caucasian Chalk Circle* (Brecht) 24, 119–20, 128, 210, 245, 251, 299, 322, 328, 357
*Der Lindberghflug* (Brecht) 208
*Der Messingkauf*/*Buying Brass* (Brecht) 49, 110, 117, 123, 128–9, 131–2, 150–1, 153, 197, 256, 259–60, 281, 316–19
'Der Nachschlag'/'The Trill Turn' 42
Derrida, Jacques 198, 343
'Der Schriftsteller und das sozialistische Dorf' (Tretiakov) 226
*Der Silbersee* (Weill) 216
'Der soziologische Raum des bürgerlichen Theaters' (Brecht) 99
De Sica, Vittorio 191
Dessau, Paul 152, 153, 209–10
Deutscher Demokratischer Rundfunk 174
*Deutsches Miserere* (Dessau) 210
Deutsches Theater 83, 264
*Deutschlandbilder* (1984) 199

Dialectical Materialism in Music  210
dialectics/dialectical  1–2, 4, 21–2, 27,
    78, 107, 140–1, 143, 165, 189,
    195, 216, 247, 251, 256–7,
    260, 293, 306, 308, 329–31,
    334, 336
  on Brechtian stage  23–6
  as form  180–2
  method  142, 179–82, 188, 192, 193
  process  18–19, 24, 61–2
  theatre  17, 59, 91, 157, 275, 281,
    332
  thinking  23, 293, 330, 332
*Dialectics in the Theatre* (Brecht)  157–8
*Dickicht der Städte*/The Jungle of the
    Cities (Brecht)  138, 343, 357
didacticism  115, 321
Diderot, Denis  131
*Die Ausnahme und die Regel* (Brecht)  119,
    357
*Die Beule: Ein Dreigroschenfilm*
    (Brecht)  191, 195
*Die Bibel* (Brecht)  244–5, 250–1
*Die Dreigroschenoper* (Brecht)  99, 107,
    109, 111, 222, 228 n.24, 247
*Die Gesichte der Simone Machard*/The
    Visions of Simone Machard
    (Brecht)  82, 86–91
*Die Maßnahme* (Brecht)  104, 119, 227
*Die Tage der Commune* (Brecht)  84–5,
    85 n.22
digital revolution  187
Dilthey, Wilhelm  282
directing  58–9, 61, 62–4, 256
directorial techniques  58
distanciation. See 'Verfremdung'
Döblin, Alfred  9, 357
*Dogville* (2003)  199
Dos Passos, John  12–13
Dostoevsky, Fyodor  175–6
dramatic art  157, 183–4, 229
dramatic opera  110–11, 113
dramatic theatre  108–9, 111, 116, 119,
    121, 329
dramaturgy  32, 34, 39, 128, 150, 153,
    155, 166, 182, 184, 188, 190–2,
    198, 212, 217, 257, 265, 319,
    328, 355
Drew, David  210
*Drums in the Night* (Ihering)  207
Dudow, Slatan  175, 223, 229 n.28
Durrenmatt, Friedrich  320

Eagleton, Terry  341
economics  43, 187, 213, 215, 222, 224,
    228–9, 233–4, 236, 260–2, 274,
    292, 305
  crisis  25, 198–9
  process  182
  system  233
economism  25
'1844 Manuscripts' (Marx)  19
*Eighteenth Brumaire of Louis Bonaparte, The*
    (Marx)  19
Einem, Gottfried von  209, 249
'Einschüchterung durch die Klassizität'
    (Brecht)  83
Einstein, Albert  287
Eisenstein, Sergei  179–80, 194
Eisler, Hanns  83, 207–8, 209–11, 214–15,
    222 n.6, 229 n.28
Elsaesser, Thomas  180
emotions/feelings  10, 120, 121–2, 127,
    130–1, 173, 184, 190–8, 359
  content  50
  engagement  32
  response  33, 52, 121, 196–7, 196–8
empathy  10, 12, 32–3, 90, 129, 197, 292,
    308, 313
Engels, Friedrich  97–8, 120, 222, 256
Enlightenment  69–70, 72, 159
ensemble  182, 214, 217
epic elements  86–7, 91, 122, 157
epic opera  103, 110 11, 113, 123
epic play as scientific experiment  286
'epic' principle  33, 108
epic theatre  2, 33, 34–5, 42, 53, 59, 76,
    81–2, 90, 91, 99, 101–4, 108–9,
    111, 113–17, 119–21, 123, 127–9,
    133, 150, 152, 153, 157, 158,
    166, 205, 209, 211, 214, 257–9,
    281, 286, 287, 292, 296, 316,
    317, 321, 328, 358
'Epic Theatre or Dramatic Art?'
    (Erpenbeck)  157
epistemology  22
Erpenbeck, Fritz  152, 154–7
Eschenbach, Wolfram von  245
Esslin, Martin  86–7, 341
estrangement effects  32–4, 85, 86,
    88–90, 91, 128, 129, 292,
    303, 310, 332–3. See also
    'Verfremdung'
ethics  12–13, 287, 291–2, 294–5, 303,
    305, 308–9, 328

INDEX

European art cinema  193
European theatre  320, 359
Ewen, Frederick  86
'An Example of Scenic Innovation' (Brecht)  158
*Exception and the Rule, The* (Brecht)  210
expressive gestures  46

*Fabel*  2, 57–62, 265–6
  in teaching of directing  62–4
  use by director  64–6
facial expression  45, 47–50, 52, 53, 292
Fargier, Jean-Paul  192, 194
Farocki, Harun  199
fascism  131, 151, 269–71, 275, 277, 319, 322
*Fascism Inc.* (2014)  199
*Faust* (Goethe)  83, 131, 245
*Fear and Misery of the Third Reich* (Brecht)  151, 209
feminism  339–40, 341, 342, 343, 346
Feuchtwanger, Lion  86–9, 151
Feuer, Jane  194
Feuerbach, Ludwig  33, 328
'Feuerbach-Thesis' (Marx)  100
film/cinema
  art  181–2, 187, 191, 232
  genre  228, 229 n.27
  technology  222, 229–30, 232, 234, 236
  theory  180, 185–6, 190–2, 194–9, 223, 345
  viewing process  185, 196, 345
Fischer-Dieskau, Dietrich  217
'Five Difficulties in Writing the Truth' (Brecht)  153, 294
*Forced Marriage, The* (Behn)  348–9
Ford, Henry  287
Forke, Alfred  137, 137 n.1, 139–41, 302–3
Fowler, Kenneth  39–41, 43, 45–7, 50–1
Fradkin, Ilya  257
Freud, Sigmund  9, 70, 110
Friedrich, Berthold  244
Frisch, Arno  193
Frisch, Max  321
Früh, Huldreich Georg  209
Frye, Northrop  327
Fuegi, John  18, 59, 85 n.22
functional music  168, 171
'Fünf Schwierigkeiten beim Schreiben der Wahrheit' (Brecht)  199

*Funny Games* (1997)  193
*Funnyhouse of a Negro* (Kennedy)  344
*Furcht und Elend des Dritten Reiches* (Brecht)  269–70, 275–8

Gaillard, Ottofritz  154
Galileo  286–7, 335
Gallas, Helga  222 n.6
Garner, Gary Neil  248
'Gefühl'/'Ratio' contrast  110 n.30, 114, 121–2
Gemünden, Gerd  180
gender  340–3
genre
  comic  314–15, 320–1
  didactic  211
  dramatic  327
  epic  2
  film  228
  and form  327
  of Greek theater  133
  hybrid  208
  literary  2, 128, 292, 314
  musical  206
  romance  327–8
  theatrical  278
  tragedy  320, 327
German classics  82–3
German culture  116, 291
German Democratic Republic (GDR)  23, 25–6, 82–3, 88–9, 141–2, 150, 188–9, 210, 341
'The German Drama: Pre-Hitler' (Brecht)  114
*Germania Tod in Berlin* (Müller)  188
*German Stanislavsky Book. A Handbook of Acting According to the Stanislavsky System, The* (Gaillard)  154
German Theatre Institute  154
Gerron, Kurt  216
Gersch, Wolfgang  188, 231
*Gesamtkunstwerk*  106, 118, 122, 211
*Geschichte und Klassenbewußtsein* (Lukács)  98, 106
'gestic'  50, 174, 191
  effects  195
  feminist criticism  348–9
  music  47, 212–13
'Gesticulation' (Brecht)  44–6
*Gestik*  41, 47–51, 54
'gestisches Sprechen'/gestic speaking  74–5

gestures 40–50, 52–3, 60, 120, 168, 181, 189, 275–7, 293, 297, 341
*gestus/geste* 2, 39–52, 44–7, 47 n.41, 51, 54, 60, 74–6, 167, 191–5, 212–13, 257, 292, 294, 300, 309, 320, 340, 347–8, 349
Giering, Frank 193
Giles, Steve 22–3, 185–6
globalization 26, 355–6
Godard, Jean-Luc 193
Goethe, Johann Wolfgang von 9, 82–3, 116, 116 n.36, 117–19, 131, 152, 245, 265, 296, 301
Goldhahn, Johannes 90–1
Goll, Iwan 210
Gorelik, Max 82
Gorky, Maxim 153–4, 213
'Great Method' (Brecht) 21–3, 143
Greek tragedy 329
Grimm, Reinhold 246–9, 251, 316 n.3
Grodal, Torben 196
Große, Wilhelm 87
Grotowski, Jerzy 12, 359
Gruman, H. L. 227, 227 n.23
Guo Morou 140

Habermas, Jürgen 9
*Haltung/Haltungen* (attitudes) 44–5, 51–4, 123, 191, 225 n.13, 293, 300
*Hamletmachine, The* (Müller) 166, 175
*Hamlet* (Shakespeare) 43, 60–1, 198, 261–2
Haneke, Michael 193–4, 198–9
*Hangmen Also Die* (1942) 209
Hansen, Miriam Bratu 183
*Happy End* (Brecht) 208
Hardt, Ernst 99
Harvey, David 25
Hatfield, Henry 248
Hauptmann, Elisabeth 87, 138, 154, 157, 208
Hauptmann, Gerhart 154
Hauser, Harald 155
Hay, Julius 151
Heath, Stephen 192, 194
Hebbel, Friedrich 244
Hecht, Werner 106, 111, 115, 120–1, 231
Heeg, Günther 21
Hegel, G. W. F. 2, 17–19, 21, 139, 181, 293

Heidegger, Martin 11
Heinze, Helmut 44, 50
Heise, Thomas 188–90, 199
Heisenberg, Werner 281, 282–3
Hellman, Lillian 63–4
*Henry V* (Olivier) 263
*Herr Puntila und sein Knecht Matti/ Mr Puntila and his Man Matti* (Brecht) 153, 156, 158, 210, 315, 357
Hesse, Hermann 245, 357
*He Who Said Yes* (Brecht) 208
Hill, Claude 86–7
Hindemith, Paul 171, 175, 208–9
historical materialism 22, 43, 132, 151
historicization 2, 259–64, 292, 303, 308, 310, 340, 343–6
*Historisierung* 261
history 69, 72–3, 76–7, 258, 343–4
Hitler, Adolf 26–7, 128, 131, 304
Hofmannsthal, Hugo von 123
Hölderlin, Friedrich 75–6
Hollywood films 193–4
Holtzhauer, Helmut 154
Homolka, Oskar 216
Hortmann, Wilhelm 255
*How to Do Things with Words* (Austin) 304
Hubalek, Claus 152
Hughes, Holly 342
Huillet, Danièle 11
Hultberg, Helge 111–12, 112 n.33, 113–14, 120
humanities 282–3, 287
humour 323, 334
Hurwicz, Angelika 154

*Ich will ein Kind haben* (Tretiakov) 225 n.15
idealism 132, 224, 231
Ihering, Herbert 99, 154, 207
imperialism 190, 356
individualism 259
individuum and dividuum 231–2
innovation 3, 49, 66, 102–6, 109, 119, 194, 263, 281
intellectual property 222, 229, 232–4, 236
*In the Penal Colony* (Kafka) 172
Irigaray, Luce 344
Irmer, Thomas 152 n.14
'Ist das Volk unfehlbar?' (Brecht) 225

Jameson, Fredric 18–19, 22, 184, 310, 327–8, 332
*Jealous Bridegroom, The* (Behn) 349
*Johann Faustus* (Eisler) 83
Jones, David 59
Joyce, James 179
*Judith* (Hebbel) 244
*Julius Caesar* (Shakespeare) 101 n.12
Jung, Jean-François 165, 174
*Juno and the Paycock* (O'Casey) 64

Kafka, Franz 172
Kaiser, Georg 128, 133, 210
Kaiser, Wolf 266
Kant, Immanuel 10
*Katzgraben* (Strittmatter) 25
Kennedy, Adrienne 343, 344
Kerr, Alfred 106
*King Lear* (Shakespeare) 258, 266
Kipling, Rudyard 357
*Kleines Organon* (Brecht) 104, 110, 116 n.36, 118, 120, 225
Kleist, Heinrich von 83, 166
Klopstock, Friedrich Gottlieb 265
Klotz, Volker 119
Kluge, Alexander 179–80, 193, 199, 273, 275
Knopf, Jan 87, 107, 123
Knust, Herbert 90
Kok, Bessel 284
Korsch, Karl 99, 101 n.14, 144
Krabiel, Klaus-Dieter 168 n.5
Kracauer, Siegfried 191, 223–4, 223 n.10
'Kräftefeld der widersprechenden Interessen' (Brecht) 274, 278
Krause, Dagmar 217
*Kriegsfibel* (Brecht) 195, 199
Kühl, Kate 216
*Kuhle Wampe* (Dudow) 175, 209, 223, 229 n.28, 231
'kulinarisch' 108
'Kulinarismus' 107–8
Kurz, Paul Konrad 246
Kussmaul, Paul 260, 262, 264

Labour Party (UK) 17
*Ladri di Biciclette* (1948) 191
*Lady Dick* (Hughes) 342
*Landscape with Argonauts* (Müller) 175
Lang, Otto 154
Lao Zi 293, 300

Lastra, James 186
*La Terra Trema* (1948) 191
'learning play' 172, 208, 232, 293, 357
*Leben des Galilei/Life of Galileo, The* (Brecht) 58, 85 n.22, 128, 209, 251, 281, 328, 331, 335
*Leben Eduards des Zweiten von England/ The Life of Edward the Second of England* (Brecht) 74, 246
*Legend of the origin of the book Tao Te Ching* (Brecht) 138
Lehar, Franz 209
*Lehrstücke* 132, 165–6, 168–70, 172–3, 173–6, 181, 209, 227, 270, 274–5, 278, 281, 286, 293
Leipzig Theatre School 154
Lenin, Vladimir Ilyich 21–2, 142, 145, 159, 266, 287, 293
Lenya, Lotte 212, 216
Lenz, J. M. R. 153, 265
Lessing, Gotthold Ephraim 245, 315
*Lied* 209, 214
*Life of Confucius, The* (Brecht) 138, 293, 296–301, 303, 309
*Life of Einstein* (Brecht) 286–7
*Lindbergh's Flight. Radiophonic Cantata* 174
*Lindbergh's Flight/Ocean Flight* (Brecht) 165–9, 172, 174
*Lindbergh's Flight/Ocean Flight* (film, 1992) 174
Lindner, Burkhardt 271
Lingen, Theo 213, 216
*Little Foxes, The* (Hellman) 63–5
Livingstone, Rodney 21
'Locating an Aesthetic Category' (Wekwerth) 158
Lorre, Peter 216
Lothar, Susanne 193
Love, Courtney 221, 234–5
Loyola, Ignatius 12
Lukács, Georg 70, 98, 106, 116 n.36, 118, 150–2, 154, 184
Lutz, Regine 154
Lyon, James K. 86

*Macbeth* (Brecht) 255
MacCabe, Colin 192, 194
'making the familiar strange'. *See* '*Verfremdung*'
male gaze 340
*Manderlay* (2005) 199

Mann, Thomas  229, 245
*Mann ist Mann*/A Man's a Man
    (Brecht)  98–9, 101 n.14, 115,
    208, 210, 321, 357
Man Ray  175
Mao Zedong  24, 157
marionette theatre  166
Marlowe, Christopher  74
Marquardt, Fritz  188–9
Marx, Karl  19, 21, 26, 98–9, 105, 114,
    120, 145, 155, 179, 181, 182,
    198, 222, 229, 233, 236, 293,
    305–6, 355
    Marxism/Marxist  1–2, 4, 17, 19–20,
    23, 25, 26, 39–46, 69–70, 106–8,
    120, 130, 155, 179, 182, 186,
    198, 209–11, 214, 249, 257, 259,
    261–2, 291, 293, 310, 320–2, 327,
    344
Marxist Workers' School  287
*Master Builder, The* (Ibsen)  343
*Material* (2009)  188, 190
materialist/materialism  22, 43, 114, 132,
    151, 157, 256–7, 260–1
May, Karl  357
Mayer, Hans  249
*Measure for Measure* (Shakespeare)  343
*Measures Taken, The* (Brecht)  209
Medek, Tilo  174
media communication  175
mediation  73, 182–3, 185–7, 190, 207,
    327
Mei Lanfang  137
Meisel, Edmund  208
Mencius (Mengzi)  139, 293
Mersmann, Hans  205
metafiction  315 n.2, 318, 321
*Me-ti*  14, 21–2, 25, 144, 270, 323
Metscher, Thomas  258
Meyer, Hans  154
Midgley, David  119
Mierau, Fritz  225 n.15, 226 n.16
*Millet for the Eighth Army* (Ding et al)
    158
*Mimesis* (Auerbach)  9
*Mimik* (mime)  47–50, 52–4
Minetti, Bernhard  175
'mini-fable'. *See* 'scene titles'
*Misogynist, The* (Lessing)  315
*Modellbücher*/model books (Brecht)  59
modern art  183, 193, 222 n.6
modern drama  58, 133

modernism  69, 133, 192, 193, 355, 359–60
modernity  190, 191, 357
modern science  287
'The Modern Theatre is the Epic Theatre'
    (Brecht)  332
*Modern Tragedy* (Williams)  329, 331–2
'Modest Success of Confucius' (Brecht)
    293
Mo Di  137 n.1, 138, 139–41, 144, 145
Moi, Toril  341
*Mong Dsi. Die Lehrgespräche des Meisters
    Meng K'o* (Wilhelm)  139
Monk, Egon  83
montage  21, 108, 108 n.25, 115–17, 151,
    166–7, 175, 190–8, 194 n.8, 211,
    216, 223, 231, 258, 276
*Moonlighting* (TV series)  193–4
moral behavior  34, 305–6, 310
*Mother, The* (Brecht)  43, 153, 156, 158,
    209, 213–14
*Mother Courage and her Children*
    (Brecht)  58, 61, 128, 138, 153,
    156, 210, 244–6, 249, 251, 322,
    328, 331–2, 334, 347
Mo Zi  292–3, 302–5, 302 n.92, 307–10
'Mo Zi and Ethics' (Brecht)  306
*Mr Bojangles' Memory* (Wilson)  175
Mühlenbrock, Heiner  199
Müller, Heiner  26, 166, 174–6, 188, 190
Müller, Klaus-Detlef  22, 341
Mulvey, Laura  340
Mumford, Meg  24
Murphet, Julian  185
music  53, 127, 128, 168, 205, 221–2,
    234–6
    and Brecht  205–17
    theatre  205, 208, 210–13, 215
*Musik und Gesellschaft* (Brecht)  101, 110
*My Life in Art* (Stanislavsky)  155

*Nachrichten aus der ideologischen Antike –
    Marx/Eisenstein/Das Kapital/News
    from ideological Antiquity: Marx/
    Eisenstein/Capital* (2008)  179
Nägele, Rainer  170
naiveté  2, 82, 84–6, 88–91, 159, 257
Napster  221–2, 234–6, 236 n.53
Narboni, Jean  192
Naremore, James  198
narrative/narration  9–12, 72, 77, 78, 119,
    120, 179–87, 190, 192, 194–6,
    216, 359

National Socialism   269–70, 274
natural history   75
naturalism   26, 130, 154, 155, 205, 256, 329
naturalist theatre   130, 155
natural sciences   282
*Nay-Sayer, The* (Brecht)   132
Nazism   24, 87, 199, 277, 295, 358
    Nazi Germany   304
*Negative Dialektik/Negative Dialectics*
    (Adorno)   26, 73
Negt, Oskar   273, 275
Neher, Carola   216
Neher, Caspar   213
neo-Nazism   18
neo-Romanticism   123
Nero film company   222–3, 225, 232, 269
New Berlin School   199
New German Cinema   199
New Life Movement   140
New Music Festival (1930)   209
New Testament   247–8, 250
*New Theatres for Old* (Gorelik)   82
'nicht-aristotelisches Theater'   110
*nicht/sondern* (not/but)   69, 74, 83–4, 89,
    122, 227, 318
*Nicht Versöhnt* (1965)   11
Nietzsche, Friedrich   11, 132, 245, 292
Nobel, Alfred   282
*No Man's Land* (Pinter)   343
non-Aristotelian drama   185, 207
non-Aristotelian theory   133
Norris, Frank   357
'Notes for a film of Capital'
    (Eisenstein)   179–80
*Notes from a Dead House*
    (Dostoevsky)   175

O'Casey, Sean   64
Old Testament   247–8, 250
Olivier, Laurence   263–4
*On Climbing High Mountains* (Lenin)   142
'On Contradiction' (Mao Zedong)   24–5, 157
'On Gestic Music' (Brecht)   43–6, 48
'On the Folk Play' (Brecht)   158
'On the Theatricality of Fascism'
    (Brecht)   319
'On the Use of Music in an Epic Theatre'
    (Brecht)   42, 46, 51
opera   97–8, 104, 105, 210, 228
Oppenheimer, Robert J.   286
Orff, Carl   209
*Orientalism* (Said)   357

*Othello* (Shakespeare)   259–60, 262
Ottwald, Ernst   223
*Owl Answers, The* (Kennedy)   344

Pabst, Hans   248
*Paisà* (Rossellini)   191
Palitzsch, Peter   86, 152, 152 n.14
*Pantomime*   53
parable   159
*Paradoxe* (Diderot)   131
'Parataxis' (Adorno)   75–6
Parker, R. B.   259
Parmet, Simon   209
Paulsen, Harald   216
Pavis, Patrice   47, 345–7
pedagogy   69, 76, 143, 153–4, 168–70,
    174–5, 181, 262, 322, 359
*Phaedo* (Plato)   127
Phillipps, Katherine   348
*Philosophical Works of the Social Ethicist
    Mo Zi and His Disciples, The*
    (Forke)   302
philosophy of history   69–70
photography/photographs   186–7,
    195, 230
Piketty, Thomas   17
Pinkney, Tony   332–3
Pirandello, Luigi   133
Piscator, Erwin   82, 101 n.12, 155, 208
Plato   127–8, 131–3, 292
    Platonic drama   127–8, 133
    Platonic theatre   132–3
    Platonism   128, 133
*Poetics* (Aristotle)   2
poetic theatre   205
poetry/poems   74, 76, 159, 206, 207, 211,
    212–13
'point of view'   19, 43, 51, 60–4, 180,
    249–50, 322
Polan, Dana   193
politics/political
    and aesthetics   194
    art   197, 227
    crisis   25
    discourse   17
    effect   143
    movements   19
    philosophy   180
    process   182, 195
    struggle   307–8
    theatre   257, 261, 319
    theory   138

*Politische Ökonomie* (Marx)   114
polysemy   40–1, 52
post-Brechtian theatre   26–7
postcolonial theory   355–60
post-Fordist economics   26
postmodernism   360
Prince   221
proletarianism   214, 222, 227, 270, 273, 275, 306
Proust, Marcel   70
psychoanalysis   9, 186, 340, 342
public sphere   269–70, 275–7

racial issue   87
radicalism   98
'radical monotony'   214
radical politics   17–26
radio   166–7, 168–9, 174, 223
'Radio Theory'   167
Rame, Franca   342
rationality/rational   33, 46, 60–1, 69, 71, 207, 257–8, 275, 330, 341, 346, 359
realism/reason/realistic   17, 19–20, 24–5, 34, 53–4, 61, 69, 108–9, 122, 123, 127, 132, 150–1, 153, 155, 165, 167, 172–3, 181, 190–8, 205, 224, 227, 231, 251, 256, 262, 266, 293–4, 297, 301, 304, 308, 316, 332, 344, 359
reality   1, 17, 19–20, 26, 27, 32, 61, 69, 70, 72–3, 76, 114, 151, 190–2, 225, 229, 231, 233, 256, 257, 266, 286, 295, 320–1
'Recommendation on the Status of Scientific Researchers'   287
Recording Industry Association of America (RIAA)   221
reduction and typification   151
Reformation literature   245
Reichel, Käthe   83
'*Reich und Reich gesellt sich gern*'/'Rich birds flock together' (Brecht)   87–8
Reinhardt, Max   118
reportage technique   150
*Republic* (Plato)   129
*Resistible Rise of Arturo Ui, The* (Brecht)   26–7
Restoration theatre   348–9
'The Retention of Gestures Through the Generations' (Brecht)   49
Rhodes, John David   196
Rilla, Paul   154
Ritter, Hans Martin   42, 47 n.41

*Robert Guiskard* (Kleist)   83
*Romeo and Juliet* (Shakespeare)   265
Rosenberg, Scott   234
Rossellini, Roberto   191
*Roundheads and the Pointed Heads, The* (Brecht)   87–8, 209
Rouse, John   259
Rubin, Gayle   343
Rülicke, Käthe   24–5, 152, 265

Said, Edward   357
*Saint Joan of the Stockyards* (Brecht)   89–90, 333
Sartre, Jean Paul   12–13
Schanelec, Angela   199
Scherchen, Hermann   168
Schiller, Friedrich   9, 82–3, 89, 116, 116 n.36, 117–19, 245, 257, 263
Schleef, Einar   26
Schoenberg, Arnold   209, 210
'Schriftsteller in die Kolchose!' (Tretiakov)   226
Schumacher, Ernst   153 n.14, 159
Schwarz, Roberto   34, 193
*Schweyk in the Second World War* (Brecht)   87, 209
science   281, 287
science fiction   166
scientific research and humanities   282
scientific theatre   130, 132
scientists and social responsibility   286–7
Seehase, Georg   258
Seghers, Anna   154
self-reflexivity   190–8
semiotics   10, 340, 346
Serreau, Jean-Marie   88
*Seven Deadly Sins, The* (Weill)   208
*Seventeen Contradictions and the End of Capitalism* (Harvey)   25
sex-gender system   343, 346–9
sexual difference   342–3
sexuality   342–3
Shakespeare, William   3, 74, 83, 90, 101 n.12, 198, 318, 328
  *As You Like It*   318
  Brecht's relationship to   255–63
  *Coriolanus*   258, 264, 266
  *Hamlet*   198, 261–2
  *Julius Caesar*   101 n.12
  *King Lear*   258, 266
  *Measure for Measure*   343
  *Othello*   259–60, 262
  *Romeo and Juliet*   265

*Tempest, The* 258
theatre as paradigm 263–6
*Troilus and Cressida* 265–6
Shakespeare's Globe 263
Shaw, George Bernard 90, 127, 133
Shepherd, Cybill 193
'Short Description of a New Technique of Acting which Produces a Defamiliarisation Effect' (Brecht) 43, 45
*Short Organum for the Theatre, A* (Brecht) 22, 45–6, 60, 81, 150, 156–7
Silberman, Marc 185, 187, 191
Silcox, Heidi M. 32–5
Sinclair, Upton 357
slapstick comedy 313–14
Smith, Murray 180, 197
social activism 222, 225, 225 n.13
social gestus. *See gestus/geste*
socialism 26, 42, 131, 143, 189, 308
socialist realism 25, 150, 152, 153
'socially comic', concept of 316 n.3
socially critical art 231
social process 181–2, 185, 187, 225, 227
social relationship 43–5, 183–4, 212, 273
Socrates 127–8, 129, 132, 140
'Sollten wir nicht die Ästhetik liquidieren?' (Brecht) 98
*Songspiel Mahagonny* (Brecht) 208–9, 214
Sophocles 245
*Soul of Man under Socialism, The* (Wilde) 142
sound cinema 195
Soviet Russia 304
'Soziologische Betrachtungsweise' (Brecht) 99
spectatorship 186, 196, 340, 345–8, 358
Split Britches 342
Staiger, Emil 119, 122 n.44
Stalin, Joseph 144–5, 304
Stanislavsky, Constantin 1, 10, 59, 120, 155–6, 260
State Commission for the Arts 155
*Stau Jetzt geht's los* (1993) 188
Steffin, Margarete 142, 213, 295
Stegemann, Bernd 18–19, 26
Stein, Gertrude 339, 344, 348
*Stella Dallas* (1937) 197
Stephen, Charles 142, 303
Sternberg, Fritz 98–101, 101 nn.11–14, 102, 104, 106

Sternheim, Carl 321
Sting 217
Stratas, Teresa 217
Straub, Jean-Marie 11
'Street Scene' (Brecht) 320
Strehler, Giorgio 81
Strindberg, August 33, 41
Strittmatter, Erwin 25
Sturm und Drang 265
Subiotto, Arrigo 266
Suhrkamp, Peter 86, 104, 214
Surrealism 115
Suvin, Darko 51–2
*Svendborg Poems* (Brecht) 138
Symington, Rodney T. K. 259, 264
*Symposium* (Plato) 128

Tatlow, Antony 21, 23
*Taube und Samurai/Dove and Samurai* (Wilson) 166
*Tempest, The* (Shakespeare) 258
text–music relationships 205, 209, 213, 215
*thaeter* 131–3
Theater am Kurfürstendamm 213
Theater am Schiffbauerdamm 131
*Theaterarbeit/Theatre Work* (Brecht) 149–50, 153–4, 153 n.14, 154 n.18, 156–9
'Theatre Chronicle of the Berliner Ensemble' (Brecht) 152
'Theatre is a Tribunal' (Gorelik) 82
theatrical genre 278
*There are Crimes and Crimes* (Strindberg) 41
third-person acting/narrative 10–11, 13
*Threepenny Lawsuit, The* (Brecht) 4, 25
*Three-Penny Novel* (Brecht) 10, 128
*Threepenny Opera, The* (Brecht) 49, 81, 87, 199, 206, 208, 214–15, 217, 291, 321, 328
*Thus Spoke Zarathustra* (Nietzsche) 292
Tiedemann, Rolf 73
Toklas, Alice 339
tragedy 127, 133, 183, 251, 258, 260, 262, 314–15, 317–20, 318
  Brechtian 331–6
  modern 327–30
*Travelling Players, The* (1975) 194
Treichlinger, Wilhelm M. 295
Tretyakov, Sergei 225, 225–6 nn.15, 18, 226–8, 227 n.21, 295
*Trial of Joan of Arc at Rouen, The* (Brecht) 89–90

*Trial of Lucullus, The* (Brecht) 152
*Troilus and Cressida* (Shakespeare) 265–6
*Trommeln in der Nacht*/Drums in the Night (Brecht) 357
Trotter, David 187
*Tutor, The* (Brecht) 265
*Tutor, The* (Lenz) 153

'Über den Film' (Mann) 229
'Über Filmmusik' (Brecht) 191
*Über naive und sentimentalische Dichtung* (Schiller) 89
'Über reimlose Lyrik mit unregelmäßigen Rhythmen'/On Rhymeless Verse with Irregular Rhythms (Brecht) 74
*Ulysses* (Joyce) 179
uncertainty principle 281–2
*Unholdes Frankreich*/*The Devil in France* (Feuchtwanger) 88
United States 81–2, 128, 150, 295, 358
*Upwardly Mobile* (Split Britches) 342
*Urfaust* (Brecht) 82–4
*Urfaust* (Goethe) 152 n.11

Valentin, Karl 85 n.22
Vallentin, Maxim 154
*Vassa Zheleznova* (Gorky) 153
V-effects 31, 48, 259, 286, 316, 317–19, 320–1
ventriloquism 212
verbal expression 49
'Verfremdung' 2, 11, 26, 31–4, 48, 52–4, 69, 73, 82, 91, 108 n.25, 109–10, 121, 127–8, 153, 180, 182, 185, 190, 193–4, 231, 247, 257–9, 261, 265, 286, 292, 329–31, 333, 341–2, 345
*Verfremdungseffekt* 59, 113, 180, 183, 292, 333, 340–2
'Vergügnungstheater oder Lehrtheater?' (Brecht) 112, 116–17, 122, 122 n.44
*Versuche* (Brecht) 120, 150, 157, 166, 169, 171, 228 n.25
Vertov, Dziga 199
Veth, Kurt 174
Viertel, Berthold 154
'A Virtue out of a Necessity' (Lukács) 150
Visconti, Luchino 191
'Visual Pleasure and Narrative Cinema' (Mulvey) 340
Voigts, Manfred 101

*Vom Tod im Wald* (Weill) 208
von Trier, Lars 199

Wagner, Klaus D. 23
Wagner, Richard 207
Wagner-Regeny, Rudolf 209
*Wahrheitsgehalt*/truth content 71–2
*Waiting for Godot* (Beckett) 333
Waits, Tom 217
Waley, Arthur 295–6
Wandor, Michelene 343
Watkins, Ronald 264
Weber, Carl 58–9
Weber, Max 44
Wedekind, Frank 206
Weigel, Helene 23, 137, 152, 155, 213, 216, 217, 347
Weill, Kurt 101, 103–4, 168, 175, 205, 208, 210–16
Weimann, Robert 265
Weimar Republic 97, 102, 106, 222, 270
Weisstein, Ulrich 316 n.3
Wekwerth, Manfred 84–6, 89, 152 n.14, 158
'What's Wrong with Alienation?' (Silcox) 32
White, John J. 261
Wilde, Oscar 131, 133, 142
Wiles, Timothy 345
Wilhelm, Richard 139, 143, 293, 296
Willett, John 1–2, 22, 41, 51–3, 104–5, 113–14, 119
Williams, Raymond 328–33, 335
Willis, Bruce 193
Wilson, Robert 165–6, 174–6
Wolf, Friedrich 154
Wollen, Peter 192
Woods, Barbara 248
Woolf, Virginia 341
'The World of Art in the Age of its Technological Reproducibility' (Benjamin) 185
*Woyzeck* (Büchner) 83
Wyatt, Justin 193

*Yea-Sayer, The* (Brecht) 132
Yuill, W. E. 260

Zhuang Zi 293
Žižek, Slavoj 18
Zuckmayer, Carl 206
Zweig, Stefan 357